2—

D1279528

America's Strategic Choices

REVISED EDITION

International Security Readers

Strategy and Nuclear Deterrence (1984)

Military Strategy and the Origins of the First World War (1985)

Conventional Forces and American Defense Policy (1986)

The Star Wars Controversy (1986)

Naval Strategy and National Security (1988)

Military Strategy and the Origins of the First World War,
revised and expanded edition (1991)

—published by Princeton University Press

Soviet Military Policy (1989)

Conventional Forces and American Defense Policy, revised edition (1989)

Nuclear Diplomacy and Crisis Management (1990)

The Cold War and After: Prospects for Peace (1991)

America's Strategy in a Changing World (1992)

The Cold War and After: Prospects for Peace, expanded edition (1993)

Global Dangers: Changing Dimensions of International Security (1995)

The Perils of Anarchy: Contemporary Realism and International Security (1995)

Debating the Democratic Peace (1996)

East Asian Security (1996)

Nationalism and Ethnic Conflict (1997)

America's Strategic Choices (1997)

Theories of War and Peace (1998)

America's Strategic Choices, revised edition (2000)

Rational Choice and Security Studies: Stephen Walt and His Critics (2000)

The Rise of China (2000)

—published by The MIT Press

America's Strategic Choices

AN *International Security* READER

REVISED EDITION

EDITED BY
Michael E. Brown
Owen R. Coté, Jr.
Sean M. Lynn-Jones
and Steven E. Miller

THE MIT PRESS
CAMBRIDGE, MASSACHUSETTS
LONDON, ENGLAND

Library of Congress Cataloging-in-Publication Data

America's strategic choices / edited by Michael E. Brown . . . [et al.]—Rev. ed.
   p. cm. — (An international security reader)
   Includes bibliographical references and index.
   ISBN 0-262-52274-8 (pb : alk. paper)
   1. United States—Military policy. 2. National security—United States. 3. Security, International.
   I. Brown, Michael E. II. International security readers

UA23.A663527 2000
355'.033573—dc21   99-058455

Contents

The Contributors

MICHAEL E. BROWN teaches in and is Director of Research for the National Security Studies Program, Edmund A. Walsh School of Foreign Service, Georgetown University, and is Editor of *International Security*.

OWEN R. COTÉ, JR., is Associate Director of the Security Studies Program at the Massachusetts Institute of Technology and Editor of *International Security*.

SEAN M. LYNN-JONES is Editor of *International Security* and a Research Associate at the Belfer Center for Science and International Affairs (BCSIA), John F. Kennedy School of Government, Harvard University.

STEVEN E. MILLER is the Editor-in-Chief of *International Security* and Director of the International Security Program at BCSIA.

ROBERT J. ART is Christian A. Herter Professor of International Relations at Brandeis University.

EUGENE GHOLZ is a Research Associate in the Security Studies Program at the Massachusetts Institute of Technology.

CHARLES A. KUPCHAN is Associate Professor of International Relations at Georgetown University and a Senior Fellow at the Council on Foreign Relations.

CLIFFORD A. KUPCHAN is a Professional Staff Member of the Committee on International Relations, U.S. House of Representatives.

CHRISTOPHER LAYNE is a Visiting Scholar at the Center for International Studies at the University of Southern California.

MICHAEL MASTANDUNO is Associate Professor of Government at Dartmouth College.

JANNE E. NOLAN is a Visiting Professor in the National Security Studies Program at Georgetown University.

BARRY R. POSEN is Professor of Political Science in the Security Studies Program at the Massachusetts Institute of Technology.

DARYL G. PRESS is Instructor in the Department of Government at Dartmouth College.

ANDREW L. ROSS is Professor of National Security Affairs at the Naval War College.

HARVEY M. SAPOLSKY is Professor of Public Policy and Organization in the Department of Political Science at Massachusetts Institute of Technology and Director of MIT's Security Studies Studies Program.

WILLIAM C. WOHLFORTH is Assistant Professor of Government in the Edmund A. Walsh School of Foreign Service at Georgetown University.

Acknowledgments

The editors gratefully acknowledge the assistance that has made this book possible. A deep debt is owed to all those at the Belfer Center for Science and International Affairs (BCSIA), Harvard University, who have played an editorial role at *International Security*. We are grateful for support from the Carnegie Corporation of New York. Special thanks go to Diane McCree and Meara Keegan Zaheer at BCSIA for their invaluable help in preparing this volume for publication. We also thank the Brookings Institution for granting permission to reprint the chapter by Janne Nolan, and Charles Kupchan and Clifford Kupchan for writing a new restrospective on their article that is included in this volume.

Preface | *Sean M. Lynn-Jones*

In the preface to the first edition of *America's Strategic Choices* I wrote that "the United States has not found a new set of guiding principles to replace containment. As the millennium approaches, the United States continues to debate its post-Cold War grand strategy and foreign policy." That debate has continued in the three years since the first edition of this book was published, but the United States seems no closer to a consensus on its role in the world. We hope that this revised edition can contribute to the ongoing debate by focusing analysis on the main strategic options that the United States faces.

When the Cold War ended and the Soviet Union disintegrated in 1991, the United States found itself in a new strategic situation. The demise of the Soviet threat left the United States unchallenged as the world's only superpower. Containment, the grand strategy that Washington had followed since the late 1940s, could no longer serve as a guide for American policy. The United States therefore began to consider its new strategic options in a radically different strategic environment.

The central strategic questions confronting the United States remain the same: What are the principal threats to American interests? How can those interests best be defended? What combination of economic, diplomatic, and military instruments should be used to protect and advance U.S. interests? These are the enduring questions of U.S. strategy, even if they are often obscured by political rhetoric and heated debate over particular military policies and weapons programs.

In the 1990s, America's strategy often seemed hesitant and uncertain. The Clinton administration struggled with the problem of how to manage U.S. relations with other major powers in the post-Cold War world. While attempting to build a new cooperative relationship with Russia, the United States worked to enlarge NATO, provoking Moscow's opposition. Washington oscillated between policies of engagement and containment toward Beijing, as U.S. policymakers debated the implications of China's growing power.[1] In addition, the criteria for when U.S. forces should intervene in internal and regional conflicts remained unclear. The United States sent troops to Somalia to end a famine and civil war, then withdrew them after suffering casualties. It eventually intervened in Bosnia to impose peace, but did not commit forces to prevent

---

1. For analyses of the implications of China's increasing power and changing international role, see Michael E. Brown, Owen R. Coté, Jr., Sean M. Lynn-Jones, and Steven E. Miller, eds., *The Rise of China* (Cambridge, Mass.: The MIT Press, 2000).

genocide and a refugee crisis in Rwanda. The United States and its NATO allies bombed Yugoslavia and committed ground forces to protect ethnic Albanians in Kosovo, but a few months later hesitated to provide peacekeeping forces to prevent violence in East Timor. These events have stimulated continuing debate over the purposes of U.S. power.

Since 1991, many commentators, experts, and policymakers have attempted to understand the changing security environment facing the United States. There has been no shortage of new visions and paradigms for understanding world politics. Some observers have argued that the world will soon see war become obsolete, while others claim that there will be an explosion of internal violence in many countries. Some have called for devoting more attention to problems of environmental degradation, while others say that the traditional issues of military strategy and statecraft deserve priority. Predictions of the future of international politics include visions of the end of history, a return to unstable multipolar politics, and clashes between competing civilizations.

Forecasts of the changing security environment do not agree on which specific threats to the United States and American interests are the most dangerous. Some have argued that the greatest threat to U.S. interests is chaos and instability throughout the world. The turmoil in the former Yugoslavia, internal conflicts in Africa and the former Soviet Union, and the disturbing return of genocide all exemplify this apparent pattern of upheaval. Others have argued that the next threat to U.S. interests will come from a more traditional source: the rise of a hostile great power. In the early 1990s, Japan appeared to be the most likely candidate to become America's leading rival. Several writers predicted war between the United States and Japan, whereas others emphasized the threat from Japan's dynamic economy.[2] When Japan's economy slowed in the mid–1990s, China loomed larger as the most likely future adversary for the United States.[3] The debate over U.S. grand strategy is unlikely to be resolved until there is more agreement on the threats facing the United States.

The essays collected in this volume consider America's strategic choices. This revised edition has been reorganized so that the essays focus on four prominent recommendations for U.S. grand strategy and military policy: restraint, selective engagement, cooperative security, and primacy. In addition to offering arguments for each of these four strategies, the contributors present analyses

2. See George Friedman and Meredith LeBard, *The Coming War with Japan* (New York: St. Martin's, 1990).
3. See Richard Bernstein and Ross H. Munro, *The Coming Conflict with China* (New York: Knopf, 1997).

of the contemporary security environment and the potential threats to U.S. interests. The revised edition also has been updated to include more recent essays that make the case for some of the proposed strategies.

In "Competing Visions for U.S. Grand Strategy," Barry Posen and Andrew Ross offer an overview and critical analysis of the strategic options that the United States faces. Posen and Ross explicate the four alternative grand strategies considered in this volume: (1) neo-isolationism (which we label "restraint"—see p. xv); (2) selective engagement; (3) cooperative security; and (4) primacy. They analyze the strengths and weaknesses of each.

Neo-isolationism argues that no country can threaten the sovereignty and territorial integrity of the United States. Proponents of this strategy contend that the United States is extraordinarily secure, because it is powerful, surrounded by oceans, and in possession of a nuclear force that could devastate any potential attacker. Potential competitors are much weaker than the United States and are likely to balance one another's power. Because it is so secure, the United States should stay out of foreign conflicts. It should not use its political and military power to impose world order, to spread democracy, or to advance U.S. economic interests. Neo-isolationism calls for an end to U.S. participation in NATO and other alliances and recommends a dramatic reduction in U.S. conventional military capabilities.

Posen and Ross argue that a neo-isolationist grand strategy would not serve U.S. interests. Disengagement from the world is likely to make the United States less secure, because without U.S. military protection other states would compete more aggressively for security. Potential regional hegemons would be emboldened. Former U.S. allies would acquire larger military arsenals, triggering arms competitions and possibly nuclear proliferation. The probability of war would increase, as would the likelihood that the United States would be forced to intervene militarily to respond to threats to its security. Although the United States would be able to cut its defense budget, these savings would come at the price of losing much of its international influence.

Selective engagement calls for using U.S. military power to prevent wars among the world's great powers, including Russia, China, Japan, and Germany. It also attempts to stop the spread of nuclear weapons to states that might threaten the United States: Iran, Iraq, and North Korea, in particular. Selective engagement would focus U.S. attention on Europe, East Asia, and the Middle East/Southwest Asia, because these are the regions where great powers may come into conflict and where the natural and industrial resources that might fuel a bid for hegemony are found. The United States should not rule out interventions in other regions for humanitarian or other purposes, but such operations should be undertaken only when they impose low U.S. costs and casualties.

Posen and Ross point out that selective engagement has several flaws. Lacking an idealistic vision, it may not win public support in the United States. It also would require the United States to ignore conflicts and humanitarian disasters that did not threaten its core interest in maintaining great—power peace. The strategy also is ambiguous on which conflicts require U.S. action and which do not; thus it might not be very selective in practice. Finally, it has difficulty answering the neo-isolationist claim that the best way for the United States to avoid wars is to stay out of international conflicts.

Cooperative security rests on classic liberal internationalist premises. It assumes that peace is indivisible, because wars are likely to spread, and that the United States as an overriding interest in preserving global peace. The strategy would be implemented though international institutions with the assistance of other democracies. Institutions would coordinate military actions against "rogue" aggressor states, create and maintain arms control and confidence—building regimes, and prevent nuclear proliferation.

Posen and Ross note that cooperative security has several shortcomings. It assumes that the world's major powers will stop acting in their narrow self-interest and instead uphold global, collective interests. Multilateral institutions might have to fight many wars to establish their credibility. Democracies, in particular, will have trouble convincing their citizens to risk their lives in distant battles. Finally, cooperative security places more faith in arms control than is warranted by the historical record.

Primacy argues that the United States should maintain a preponderance of world power. The strategy aims to prevent the rise of any great powers that could compete with the United States. Its proponents argue that the rest of the world will accept American leadership because most other countries know that U.S. hegemony will be benign. Under the strategy of primacy, the United States would maintain a large overseas military presence to prevent the rise of regional or global hegemons. In particular, U.S. political and military power would be ready to contain Russia, China, or both.

Primacy, according to Posen and Ross, is problematic, because it is unsustainable and ultimately self-defeating. Other countries will acquire the power to challenge American preponderance. U.S. attempts to achieve primacy will spur others to balance against it. If the United States relies on its own power and shuns multilateral policies, it may find itself isolated when it confronts challenges from rising powers.

Posen and Ross compare the apparent grand strategy of the Clinton administration to the four basic options and find that it contains elements of several. The Clinton administration appears to have hoped to follow a strategy of cooperative security, but the difficulties in pursuing such a strategy have led it to embrace elements of selective engagement and primacy. The administration's most complete exposition of its grand strategy, A National Security Strategy of Engagement and Enlargement,[4] proclaims the need for U.S. participation in multilateral peace operations, but also places limits on U.S. involvement. The document also calls for U.S. leadership and the strengthening of U.S. military capabilities. Posen and Ross thus characterize the Clinton administration's grand strategy as "Selective (but Cooperative) Primacy."

Looking forward, Posen and Ross argue that the United States may not be able to sustain a policy that now contains many elements of a strategy of primacy. Domestic budgetary pressures and insular public opinion may combine with an erosion of America's relative power to render such a strategy impossible. U.S. involvement in a bloody and unpopular war also might provoke the American public to embrace neo-isolationism.

Posen and Ross conclude that the United States ultimately will be forced to make an explicit choice between strategies, because each generates a different U.S. force structure and policy implications. Military forces configured for multilateral peacekeeping/cooperative security missions, for example, may not be effective instruments for maintaining U.S. primacy. It may take a crisis to force America's leaders to make such a choice.

The essay by Posen and Ross sets the stage for a more detailed analysis of each of America's four strategic choices. The remaining essays in this volume present arguments for these four choices: restraint, selective engagement, cooperative security, and primacy.

The next two essays in this volume offer alternative strategies of restraint. Because "isolationism" has become a politically charged word that many regard as an epithet, we prefer to use the term "restraint" to describe these proposed strategies. In "Come Home America: The Strategy of Restraint in the Face of Temptation," Eugene Gholz, Daryl Press, and Harvey Sapolsky make the case for strategic entrenchment. They argue for military withdrawal from most of America's overseas commitments, while calling for continued U.S. economic engagement with the rest of the world and rejecting the protection-

---

4. The Clinton administration has issued several versions of this document. The most recent available as this volume goes to press, *A National Security Strategy for a New Century*, is included in this book.

ism of earlier forms of isolationism. In their view, the end of the Cold War has made it possible for the United States to exercise restraint internationally and to focus its energies on domestic problems.

Gholz, Press, and Sapolsky argue that the United States faces no threats to its physical security. It is surrounded by oceans and friendly countries. Its military forces are the largest and most powerful in the world. No potential adversary has the power to conquer Eurasia and then use its industrial and natural resources against the United States. With the exception of a hostile military takeover of the Persian Gulf's oil reserves, other countries cannot threaten America's peace and prosperity.

In these circumstances, the principal threat to U.S. national interests is the danger that the United States will overspend on defense and intervene needlessly in international conflicts. The authors recommend that the United States devote no more than $120 billion to defense spending—approximately half the 1997 level. U.S. restraint would encourage America's allies to accept responsibility for providing their own security and managing their own problems. It would also force them to pay for their own defense, thereby releasing U.S. resources for domestic investments.

Gholz, Press, and Sapolsky recommend that the United States withdraw its forces from Europe and dismantle NATO, leaving the European powers to defend themselves against any threat from a resurgent Russia. The United States also should bring home and demobilize the 100,000 U.S. military personnel in East Asia, and end its military commitments in that region. Like the European members of NATO, U.S. allies in East Asia have the economic capabilities to defend themselves. South Korea, for example, has twice the population and twenty times the economic output of North Korea. In the Middle East, however, the United States should maintain some forces to protect the region's oil reserves, but not to defend Israel, which can look after itself.

Gholz, Press, and Sapolsky recognize that their proposals will provoke many objections, including claims that U.S. disengagement will increase the risk of war, deny America the advantages of primacy, accelerate nuclear proliferation, stop the spread of American values, end economic openness, and fail to prevent the inevitable U.S. involvement in major wars. They offer rebuttals of each of these counterarguments, emphasizing that no country threatens U.S. security, great power wars are unlikely, the costs of a large overseas military presence are high, and a more activist U.S. security posture would provoke other countries to resent and resist the United States.

Gholz, Press, and Sapolsky believe that a U.S. policy of restraint would have to be abandoned only if three conditions are met: the rise of a major regional power with offensive capabilities, the possibility that an aggressor state could consolidate much of the world's industrial might under its control, and the emergence of an aggressor that could somehow neutralize the nuclear capabilities of the existing major powers. The conditions are unlikely to emerge, so restraint is likely to be the best course for the United States for many years.

Christopher Layne's "From Preponderance to Offshore Balancing: America's Future" argues that the United States has yet to make the strategic changes required by the end of the Cold War. U.S. grand strategy continues to seek American preponderance, but this aspiration will not be tenable as new great powers rise. The strategy of preponderance will soon become too risky and too costly. Layne thus calls for a shift to a strategy of offshore balancing that would minimize the risks of U.S. involvement in war. This strategy would entail U.S. disengagement from alliance commitments in Europe and East Asia. It would avoid the risks of the strategy of preponderance, while preserving U.S power.

Layne regards offshore balancing as a balance of power strategy, not a form of what Posen and Ross call neo-isolationism. In their contribution to this volume (p. 8, notes 7 and 9), Posen and Ross concur that Layne's proposed strategy differs from neo-isolationism. The essence of the strategy of offshore balancing is, nevertheless, restraint and retrenchment.

Layne contends that the United States has pursued a strategy of preponderance since the late 1940s. This strategy has attempted to create and maintain a U.S.-led world order based on preeminent U.S. power and international economic interdependence, which U.S. leaders regarded as a condition for peace. Extended deterrence has been the principal instrument for responding to threats to instability. The United States sought preponderance even before the Soviet Union emerged as the leading threat. Since the end of the Cold War, the United States has continued to pursue preponderance by maintaining military protectorates in Europe and East Asia—security guarantees that prevent Germany and Japan from renationalizing their foreign and military policies and ensure that they will not challenge U.S. leadership. These policies are still justified by supporters of preponderance on the grounds that they preserve stability and economic interdependence.

Preponderance is supported by theoretical arguments made by offensive and defensive realists. Offensive realists argue that U.S. hegemony is the best way to preserve peace in a competitive and unstable international system. Defensive realists argue that U.S. hegemony does not threaten other states, and therefore will be welcomed by the rest of the world. Proponents of preponderance argue that only American hegemony can prevent the instability that might emerge in a bipolar or multipolar international system.

Layne argues that the strategy of preponderance is dangerous and wasteful. The strategy will lead to strategic overextension, because U.S. efforts to preserve stability through a policy of extended deterrence will require the United States to take on additional security commitments to preserve the credibility of its commitments to defend its allies and their interests. The initial U.S. involvement in Indochina between 1948 and 1954 and its 1990s intervention in Bosnia are just two examples of this creeping overextension.

The pursuit of preponderance also will cause the United States to exaggerate threats. Attempts to maintain global stability lead the United States to intervene in places without strategic value. These interventions then must be justified by inflating the threat to the United States.

Preponderance also relies too heavily on extended deterrence. Because proponents of the strategy believe that the spread of nuclear weapons threatens the United States, preponderance requires that the United States prevent nuclear proliferation by extending its deterrent umbrella over potential nuclear nations. But extended deterrence is likely to fail in a complex and conflict-ridden world that is no longer neatly demarcated the way the bipolar world of the Cold War was.

Layne argues that the strategy of preponderance has contributed to the relative decline of U.S. power and will continue to do so. The United States has paid a high price for its strategic policies: budget deficits, stagnant real incomes, and social decay. Domestic factors are partly responsible for some of these problems, but it would be easier to address all of them if the United States devoted more of its resources to domestic problems and spent less on its international commitments.

Layne calls for the United States to abandon preponderance and to adopt a strategy of offshore balancing instead. This strategy would define U.S. interests more narrowly: the United States would defend its territorial integrity and prevent the rise of a Eurasian hegemon. It would withdraw its forces from Europe, Japan, and South Korea. The United States also would cease exporting democracy and participating in peacekeeping operations and humanitarian interventions. This strategy would require defense budgets of 2–2.5 percent of U.S. GNP.

Offshore balancing is supported by elements of realist theories of international relations. The strategy assumes that states tend to balance against powerful states and that it is impossible for any one state to maintain a hegemonic position for long. It is therefore a realist, counterhegemonic strategy that aims to avoid anti-U.S. geopolitical backlash likely to result from America's pursuit of primacy. Offshore balancing also recognizes that economic interdependence is limited and that the United States can afford to pursue an insular grand strategy. The strategy is particularly appealing to the United States, because geography protects the country from attack; the United States can capitalize on its geographic advantages to maximize its relative power in the emerging multipolar post–Cold War international system. Even the rise of a Eurasian hegemon might not threaten the United States, but a strategy of offshore balancing would attempt to prevent this outcome because technological changes might make such a power shift threatening.

Layne responds to two potential criticisms of the strategy of offshore balancing. First, he argues that it is not true that the United States must remain in Europe because it inevitably will be drawn into European wars. The United States has fought in some European wars, but it has avoided many others. Second, Layne denies that the benefits of preponderance outweigh the costs. Although the United States and its allies ultimately won the Cold War, the economic and social costs were high. The United States will have to pay even higher costs in the future. It is far from self-evident that preponderance is profitable.

In "Geopolitics Updated: The Strategy of Selective Engagement," Robert Art presents a detailed case for selective engagement. The distinguishing features of selective engagement, according to Art, are that it steers a middle course between isolationism and global interventionism, pursues liberal goals such as democracy as well as realist ones such as security, accepts that military force is a useful instrument of statecraft, relies on preventive action, retains core U.S. alliances and troop deployments in Europe, the Middle East, and East Asia, and assumes that U.S. leadership is essential.

Art argues that the United States has six national interests: (1) preventing an attack—particularly one involving nuclear, biological, or chemical (NBC) weapons—on the U.S. homeland; (2) preventing wars and destructive security competitions among the major Eurasian powers; (3) maintaining secure oil supplies at stable prices; (4) preserving an open international economy; (5) promoting democracy and human rights; and (6) protecting the global environment from ozone depletion and global warming. The first three are vital interests that are central to U.S. physical security and prosperity. The second three are desirable interests; realizing them makes the international environment more congenial to the United States.

The strategy of selective engagement employs U.S. military power to help the United States to realize its three vital interests, in the following ways. First, U.S. military power can reduce the likelihood of NBC attacks on the United States by preventing or slowing the spread of such weapons. Any NBC attack on the United States is unlikely, but terrorists or rogue states are more likely to launch such an attack than are "normal" states. The key to reducing the danger of NBC attacks is to forestall the spread of NBC weapons and to maintain the global norm against proliferation. The U.S. nuclear umbrella over Japan and Germany and the presence of U.S. forces in each make it highly unlikely that those states—and their neighbors—will seek nuclear weapons. U.S. military forces should be prepared to take preventive or preemptive action against rogue states or terrorists who are attempting to acquire or develop NBC weapons. Finally, the United States should make a clear commitment to retaliate against any state that uses NBC weapons aggressively or against U.S. troops.

Second, U.S. military power can help to prevent wars and intense security competitions among the major powers of Eurasia. Such wars and competitions would threaten to involve the United States, reduce international trade, and might even make the spread or use of NBC weapons more likely. The American military presence in Europe and East Asia maintains the peace in each region by reassuring the countries in each region that they will not be threatened by Germany, Japan, or China.

Third, U.S. military power enables the United States to retain access to Persian Gulf oil by preventing any one state from dominating the region. The Persian Gulf has half or more of the world's oil reserves and the United States imports over half of its oil. Even though the United States imports relatively little oil from the Gulf, control over Gulf oil matters because oil is fungible and the world oil market is tightly integrated. If one or two states controlled the Gulf's oil reserves, oil prices would almost certainly go up. By ensuring that states like Kuwait and Saudi Arabia remain independent and that neither Iraq nor Iran becomes a regional hegemon, U.S. military power contributes to maintaining U.S. access to oil at stable prices.

Art also argues that the strategy of selective engagement assists the United States in realizing its desirable interests: promoting free trade, spreading democracy, and protecting the environment. Military power plays an indirect role in promoting these interests, except in the rare instances where military intervention can make the difference in restoring or creating democracy, or in cases where force can be used to stop genocide. The best way to achieve these desirable interests, according to Art, is for the United States to use its military power to protect its vital interests. If the United States can prevent or limit the spread of NBC weapons, maintain access to Gulf oil, and prevent great-power conflicts in Eurasia, the chances for keeping trade free, spreading democracy, and protecting the environment will go up.

Art considers the alternatives to selective engagement. Offering a slightly different list of choices than the four considered in this volume, he contends that the United States has six options: dominion, global collective security, regional collective security, cooperative security, containment, and isolationism. The first four are not feasible. Dominion—the "world policeman" role—is infeasible because the United States lacks the resources. Collective security, whether global or regional, and cooperative security also are infeasible, because states rarely agree to yield control over their armed forces and to make a commitment to punish all aggressors. Containment is feasible, but the only hostile powers that the United States might seek to contain are regional powers that the strategy of selective engagement would attempt to contain.

Art argues that isolationism is thus the only serious competitor to selective engagement. Isolationism would retain U.S. political and economic engagement in the world, but would eliminate U.S. commitments to use military power and would limit the use of force by the United States. Art contends that isolationism has four major shortcomings: (1) it would not serve all six U.S. interests; (2) it would react conflicts instead of preventing them; (3) it would deny the United States the advantage of basing some of its military forces overseas where they can train with allies and move rapidly to where they might be used; and (4) it fails to hedge against uncertainties because it assumes that the international environment will remain benign to U.S. interests.

Art recognizes that selective engagement has two pitfalls. First, U.S. commitments may grow, depriving the strategy of its selectivity and making it too costly. Second, the United States may provoke the rise of countervailing coalitions if it exercises its military power too frequently. But these problems can be avoided if the United States is disciplined in making and not inflating commitments and deft in avoiding provoking opposing coalitions.

The strategy of cooperative security was proposed in the early 1990s by several writers, some of whom subsequently held important positions in the Clinton administration. This volume includes two essays that explicate and analyze cooperative security and the related concept of collective security.

In "Cooperative Security in the United States," Janne Nolan considers whether the United States is prepared to pursue a strategy based on the principles of cooperative security, which include "preventive diplomacy, nonmilitary instruments for conflict prevention, mediation in place of war, and collective intervention only when other instruments fail." She argues that the essential premise of cooperative security is "selective engagement based on cooperative planning."

Nolan notes that there is no consensus in the United States on a new international strategy. Some American analysts have endorsed the idea of a "Pax Americana" based on the unilateral exercise of U.S. power, while isolationists call for global disengagement. These approaches emphasize unilateral U.S. action, but a growing number of U.S. analysts and officials accept the need for multilateral action when the United States uses military force. This growing appreciation of multilateralism may provide a foundation for policies based on cooperative security.

Nolan then examines how the principles of cooperative security could be applied to U.S. policy in five areas: (1) the use of force; (2) the conduct of regional relations; (3) the perceived role of nuclear weapons; (4) efforts to control the proliferation of weapons internationally; and (5) the overall characteristics of U.S. defense investment.

Since the end of the Cold War, the U.S. defense policy has been designed to use force to counter regional threats, such as a war in Korea, new and old nuclear threats, and domestic instability and humanitarian cases. U.S. military forces and defense spending have shrunk from their Cold War peak, but they remain large. Proponents of a Pax Americana have generally argued that the United States needs greater defense capabilities and should focus on unilateral, not multinational action. Advocates of global disengagement have said that the United States is spending too much on defense and should avoid most international military interventions.

Advocates of cooperative security would place more emphasis on conflict prevention, reduce reliance on nuclear weapons, configure U.S. forces for defensive missions instead of preemptive attacks, prepare to act in concert with other countries, and pursue cooperative approaches to limiting the spread of weapons of mass destruction. Nolan contends that the United States has yet to embrace these principles and to incorporate them into its defense policy.

When it comes to regional relations, a strategy based on cooperative security would build a "new European cooperative security structure" that would complement NATO. In Asia, the United States should maintain a military presence and rely less on threats to take punitive measures against China and Japan if they do not comply with U.S. preferences on human rights and trade. In the Middle East, a strategy of cooperative security would mean continued U.S. efforts to mediate the Arab-Israeli conflict, expanded multilateral efforts to control arms sales, and a reduction in U.S. forces and punitive military strikes.

Cooperative security calls for reducing U.S. reliance on nuclear weapons, cutting existing nuclear arsenals, taking some nuclear warheads off alert status, ending nuclear testing, and not threatening to use nuclear weapons against other states. These policies would reduce the danger of nuclear war and limit incentives for nuclear proliferation. Current U.S. nuclear policy, however, has not fully endorsed these principles.

A strategy of cooperative security would include multilateral controls on the diffusion of weapons and weapons-related technologies, but the United States has not moved far enough toward such a policy. U.S. policy promotes technology proliferation and arms sales when they are expedient. Washington's bureaucratic apparatus fails to control arms transfers, and international attempts to limit arms sales have fared little better. The increasing U.S. interest in "coercive arms control"—preemptive military strikes against military installations—violates the principles of cooperative security and may simply drive other states to pursue clandestine weapons programs.

When applied to U.S. defense investment, the principles of cooperative security call for limiting defense firms' dependence on exports. As the defense industry has contracted in the 1990s, firms have turned to arms exports to increase their profits. In some cases, firms may need to subsidize defense-related technological innovations by increasing their arms exports. Maintaining U.S. superiority in military technologies while preserving its defense industrial base without relying too heavily on military exports may require a decision to slow the pace of acquiring new military capabilities.

Nolan concludes that the United States is still reluctant to commit itself to multilateral policies. Washington has the opportunity to lead a global transition to cooperative security. Like other states, the United States faces the challenge of embracing an international security regime that requires it to sacrifice traditional military-based sovereignty.

Collective security resembles cooperative security in that it calls for states to act collectively to prevent or respond to aggression. In "Concerts, Collective Security, and the Future of Europe," Charles Kupchan and Clifford Kupchan propose that a collective security system be created to preserve peace in Europe. They argue that the level of agreement among Europe's major powers has created the conditions for a concert-based collective security system, which would avoid the pitfalls of earlier attempts at collective security such as the League of Nations. The Kupchans explain how collective security could overcome the uncertainties that plague attempts to balance power in an anarchic international system. The essence of collective security is universal agreement to oppose any aggressor. Different types of collective security systems exist, but the Kupchans argue that a concert-based system is most likely to be effective. By institutionalizing cooperative behavior to oppose aggressors and entrusting the responsibilities of leadership to a small group of powerful states, a concert-based collective security system can deter or counter aggression. A concert-based system in post-Cold War Europe would build upon the existing structures of the Conference on Security and Cooperation in Europe (CSCE). Like the nineteenth-century Concert of Europe, they argue, it would rely on coordination among the major powers to prevent wars.

In a retrospective written for this volume, the Kupchans consider how well their arguments have stood up since their original article was published in 1991. They argue that the case for collective security remains strong. In their opinion, NATO has remained an important European security institution precisely because it has embraced elements of collective security. During the Cold War, NATO was a traditional alliance designed to defend Western Europe against the Soviet Union. NATO continues to serve as a hedge against potential Russian expansionism, but it now focuses on preventing and ending wars in Europe—particularly in the Balkans. The alliance has embraced this mission in fits and starts, but its military actions in Bosnia and Kosovo were consistent with the spirit of collective security. NATO is becoming an organization devoted to preserving stability in Europe by taking collective action.

The Kupchans also contend that NATO's admission of Poland, Hungary, and the Czech Republic as new members, and its expanded cooperation with Russia and other former Soviet republics exemplify the practice of collective security. These initiatives are intended to turn former adversaries into partners in an enlarged zone of cooperation. Because NATO is in a hybrid state between collective defense and collective security, NATO enlargement and cooperation with Russia remain in tension. In the future, however, the conditions for concert-based collective security to operate are likely to be consolidated. If Russian reform continues, all of Europe's major states will be capitalist, democratic, status quo powers.

In hindsight, the Kupchans recognize that they need to amend their analysis in two ways. First, NATO, not the CSCE, has become Europe's central security institution. NATO's continued importance reflects the desire of the United States to preserve and strengthen an institution in which it plays the leading role. The Kupchans argue that NATO can and should continue to expand to include Russia and become a pan-European security institution.

Second, the Kupchans recognize that the European Union (EU) has come to play a larger security role than they had expected. In addition to consolidating a single European market and introducing the Euro, it has begun to develop military capabilities and a common defense policy. The EU will thus be a member of any eventual concert-based security structure for Europe.

The next two essays in this volume consider the implications of a unipolar world and the prospects for strategies based on U.S. primacy. In "The Stability of a Unipolar World," William Wohlforth argues that the United States enjoys an unprecedented margin of superiority over its potential great-power rivals and that the resulting unipolar world is peaceful and stable. He suggests that the United States has the capabilities to pursue a strategy of primacy.

Wohlforth contends that the current international system is "unambiguously unipolar." Although many commentators have argued that the United States lacks the power to shape world politics decisively, Wohlforth presents evidence that shows that the United States has extraordinary advantages over all other major states. No great power in the past two centuries has enjoyed such a wide advantage in every component of power—economic, military, technological, and geopolitical. The U.S. lead appears even wider when measured in terms of information-age indicators such as high-technology manufacturing and research and development. The "unipolar moment" that emerged at the end of the Cold War may well become a unipolar era.

Several scholars have argued that unipolarity is inherently unstable, conflict-ridden, and transitory, because other great powers will challenge the preponderant power.[5] Wohlforth, however, argues that unipolarity is peaceful and stable, for two reasons. First, because the United States has such a large advantage in raw power, no other state can hope to challenge it. Hegemonic rivalry will not emerge in the current international system; no major power can afford to incur U.S. enmity. In addition, the other major powers are unlikely to go to war or engage in intense security competitions because the United States has the capabilities to ease and prevent local security conflicts.

Second, unipolarity is peaceful because in a unipolar world states never miscalculate or misperceive the resolve of alliances or the distribution of power. In multipolar systems, the complexity and uncertainty of alliance systems and the importance of shifts in relative power often cause leaders to blunder into war. When one state is dominant, however, other states cannot form alliances against it, so there is no need to assess the resolve, power, and solidarity of rival alliances. In conflicts, the side that the dominant state takes is likely to prevail.

Wohlforth argues that unipolarity is likely to last. In addition to having an overwhelming advantage in raw power, the United States is in the favorable position of being the only actual or potential pole that is not in or around

---

5. See, for example, Christopher Layne, "The Unipolar Illusion: Why New Great Powers Will Rise," *International Security*, Vol. 17, No. 4 (Spring 1993), pp. 5–51.

Eurasia. This geographical fact means that other potential poles that seek to increase their power will provoke the countries near them to balance against them. If, for example, Germany, Japan, or Russia were to attempt to challenge U.S. preeminence, their geographical neighbors would resist this attempt—much as they have resisted earlier German, Japanese, and Russian bids for hegemony.

Some observers believe that other states are already balancing against what they see as the arrogance of U.S. power, but Wohlforth points out that most of this balancing remains rhetorical. States may complain about American preponderance, but most of them are reducing their military spending while they align themselves implicitly or explicitly with the United States.

U.S. preeminence will not last forever, but U.S. policymakers should focus on strategies for a unipolar world instead of making premature plans for a transition to a new international system. Wohlforth recommends that the United States should attempt to prolong unipolarity by playing a major role in providing regional security, thereby forestalling the emergence of great power struggles for power and security. Although some critics of U.S. foreign policy complain that the United States intervenes in too many overseas conflicts, Wohlforth argues that the United States should continue to use its capabilities to provide order and security. This strategy need not be too costly, because it does require limitless commitments. The United States should focus on "managing the central security regimes in Europe and Asia, and maintaining the expectation on the part of other states that any geopolitical challenge to the United States is futile."

In "Preserving the Unipolar Moment: Realist Theories and U.S. Grand Strategy After the Cold War," Michael Mastanduno examines whether realist theories can explain U.S. grand strategy after the Cold War. Unlike the other essays in this volume, Mastanduno's does not offer prescriptions for U.S. policy but instead seeks to account for it. He recognizes that there are several different, competing realist theories and chooses to focus on two: balance-of-power theory as elaborated by Kenneth Waltz, and the balance-of-threat theory developed by Stephen Walt.

Waltz's balance-of-power theory is the most prominent contemporary realist theory. It argues that states will tend to balance against powerful states in the anarchic international system. Changes in the distribution of power produce different patterns of alliances and military buildups. Although Waltz has denied that his theory can explain the foreign policies of particular states, Mastanduno notes that Waltz himself has used balance-of-power theory to explain foreign policy. Mastanduno therefore argues that the theory can be applied to U.S. foreign policy. He suggests that the end of the Cold War and the demise of the Soviet Union transformed the bipolar world into a unipolar one characterized by U.S. primacy. This change in the structure of the international system, according to balance-of-power theory, should have three implications for U.S. security strategy: (1) the United States will be able to act with much greater freedom, (2) other states will balance against the United States, and (3) the United States will be compelled to accept the inevitability of mulitpolarity and to disengage from its Cold War commitments.

Mastanduno argues that there is some evidence to support the first prediction of balance-of-power theory. The United States has had the latitude to intervene or not intervene in many regional crises. But there is less evidence for the other two predictions. U.S. allies in Europe and Asia want to maintain their ties to the United States instead of forming anti-U.S. alliances. And the United States has yet to disengage from its Cold War commitments.

In the realm of economic strategy, balance-of-power theory predicts that under unipolarity the United States will seek to maximize its relative power position in its economic competition with other major powers. This prediction flows from the theory's emphasis on the need to maintain economic power to provide a foundation for military capabilities. During the Cold War, the United States embraced cooperative economic policies to maintain its anti-Soviet alliances. Now that the United States is attempting to maintain its primacy and no longer needs to contain the Soviet Union, balance-of-power theory predicts that the United States will attempt to reduce the costs of its foreign policy commitments, increase its assistance to U.S. firms, and limit support for international economic policies that help U.S. economic competitors.

Mastanduno finds considerable evidence to support the economic predictions of balance-of-power theory. The United States has asked its allies to share defense burdens more fully, particularly in the 1990–1991 Gulf War. It has aggressively promoted U.S. exports. In trade policy, U.S. negotiators have demanded that other countries open their markets to American exports and abandoned the principle of free trade when it did not offer the United States unilateral advantages.

Walt's balance-of-threat theory argues that states balance against threats instead of against power. The most powerful state may not be the most threatening if it is distant, lacks offensive power, or has benign intentions. Balance-of-threat theory implies that the United States should want to preserve its primacy and will do so by signalling its restraint and reassuring potential adversaries. The United States can send such signals by emphasizing multilateral diplomacy and by following conciliatory policies toward status-quo states. These policies will prevent other states from balancing against the United States in a unipolar world.

Mastanduno finds that post–Cold War U.S. security strategy has conformed to the predictions of balance-of-threat theory. The United States has sought to maintain its dominant global position, but generally has pursued policies of conciliation and engagement, with an emphasis on multilateral institutions.

Balance-of-threat theory predicts that a cooperative post–Cold War U.S. economic strategy will complement conciliatory security policies. The United States should avoid aggressive financial and commercial policies because such policies would be perceived as threatening by other states, which might then balance against the United States. The evidence, however, suggests that the United States has aggressively sought to maximize its relative economic advantages, even in cases where this course has undermined U.S. security policy. Washington has adopted a hard line in its economic dealings with Japan, China, and Europe, although it has attempted to aid Russia's transition to a market economy.

Mastanduno finds that each realist theory explains part of U.S. post–Cold War strategy. Balance-of-threat theory accounts for U.S. policies that attempt to maintain U.S. primacy by engaging and reassuring other major powers. Balance-of-power theory explains why U.S. foreign economic policy has emphasized competition with other leading economic powers. These different policies amount to "security softball" and "economic hardball."

In Mastanduno's view, the divergent tendencies in post–Cold War U.S. security and economic strategies add up to a coherent overall strategy of primacy. Both sets of policies are intended to preserve America's preeminent global position. The Bush and Clinton administrations' grand strategies both have aimed to preserve U.S. primacy, despite the differences in their rhetoric.

Mastanduno concludes that it is not surprising that the United States is attempting to prolong the "unipolar moment." Primacy offers many benefits. In the near future, however, the United States will have to face the conflicting demands of its economic and security strategies. "Economic hardball" may induce other states to resent the United States and to balance against it. More generally, U.S. attempts to maintain primacy may have to end if the American public refuses to pay the costs of global engagement.

This volume also includes *A National Security Strategy for a New Century*, a White House document that presents the grand strategy of the Clinton administration.[6] This document emphasizes that American leadership and international engagement are essential to maintain U.S. and global security and to promote prosperity. It argues that U.S. strategy has three central goals: (1) to enhance its security; (2) to bolster America's economic prosperity; and (3) to promote democracy abroad.

Much of *A National Security Strategy for a New Century* is devoted to discussing threats to U.S. interests and how the United States can respond to them. The main threats include states such as Iraq, Iran, and North Korea that threaten their neighbors and international access to resources; transnational threats, including terrorism, international crime, drug trafficking, uncontrolled refugee flows, and environmental damage; the spread of weapons of mass destruction; foreign intelligence operations intended to obtain U.S. secrets; and failed states that generate internal conflict, humanitarian crises, and regional instability. The document enumerates the integrated diplomatic and military approaches that the United States has adopted to respond to these threats. Some of the new initiatives discussed are international and domestic efforts to prevent terrorism and to respond to terrorism involving weapons of mass destruction, as well as attempts to protect critical information infrastructures.

A National Security Strategy for a New Century also recognizes that U.S. power depends on the strength of the U.S. economy and enumerates the many steps the United States has taken to promote prosperity. These include strengthening macroeconomic coordination—particularly in response to the 1997 Asian financial crisis, enhancing American competitiveness, opening markets to free trade, and maintaining energy security. The document also briefly reviews U.S. policies intended to promote democracy. Finally, it provides an overview of policies toward each of the world's important regions.

Several recurring themes are evident in the debate over post–Cold War U.S. grand strategy. First, most observers agree that the United States enjoys an unusual—perhaps unprecedented—level of security against international threats. Although the contributors to this volume disagree over precisely how secure the United States is, they generally agree that the demise of the Soviet threat has made the United States more secure. The United States thus faces the challenge of devising a strategy in the absence of a clear threat or obvious enemy.

Second, the traditional divide between isolationism and internationalism is apparent in the contending perspectives on American strategy. Before the Cold

---

6. As this volume went to press, the Clinton Administration issued a new version of *A National Security Strategy for a New Century*. The new version is broadly similar to the one reprinted here.

War, the isolationist-internationalist debate pervaded discussions of U.S. foreign policy. During the Cold War, the consensus on Containment removed isolationist ideas from the mainstream of U.S. foreign-policy debates. Now that Containment has dissolved with the demise of the Soviet Union, isolationist proposals have re-emerged. The United States already has reduced the number of forces it deploys overseas. Many observers think the United States will (or should) further cut its military presence in Europe and the Asia-Pacific region.

Third, current discussions of U.S. grand strategy reflect the long-standing tension between realism and idealism (or liberalism-moralism) in American foreign policy.[7] Proposals for cooperative security and U.S. efforts to spread democracy reflect elements of the idealist strain in thinking about American strategy. Realist principles, which emphasize U.S. interests, are apparent in proposals for U.S primacy as well as in calls for U.S. disengagement.

Finally, the debate over America's strategic choices is implicitly (and sometimes explicitly) influenced by debates over theories of international relations. The logic of realist theories, which hold that countries tend to pursue power and/or security in international politics, is apparent in several competing proposals for U.S. grand strategy. The debate between different realist theories is mirrored in the debate between proponents of alternative grand strategies.[8] Those who argue for limited U.S. engagement in the world tend to be "defensive realists" who believe that states generally balance against powerful or threatening states. This theoretical perspective implies that the United States can rely on other major powers to form alliances against potential hegemonic states and that U.S. attempts to increase its power will provoke others to balance against the United States. On the other hand, proponents of a more assertive U.S. quest for global primacy tend to draw on "offensive realism" and hegemonic stability theory, which hold that states aspire to maximize their control over the international system and that international stability is achieved when one great power imposes order.

The essays collected in this volume do not cover every aspect of the current debate over U.S. grand strategy. Other authors have argued, for example, that the United States should adopt a "Bismarckian" strategy or that it should

---

7. See George F. Kennan, *American Diplomacy, 1900–1950* (Chicago: University of Chicago Press, 1951), and Robert Endicott Osgood, *Ideals and Self-Interest in America's Foreign Relations* (Chicago: University of Chicago Press, 1953).
8. For an overview of contending contemporary realist theories, see Michael E. Brown, Sean M. Lynn-Jones, and Steven E. Miller, eds., *The Perils of Anarchy: Contemporary Realism and International Security* (Cambridge, Mass.: The MIT Press, 1995).

encourage the emergence of regional hegemons in Europe, East Asia, and other regions.[9] The analyses presented here do, however, offer a comprehensive explication of many of the strategic choices that the United States faces at the turn of the millennium. Several authors make a strong case for the strategy that they prefer. We hope that this combination of explication and advocacy clarifies the trade-offs that the United States must make and stimulates further debate.

---

9. See Josef Joffe, "'Bismarck' or 'Britain'? Toward an American Grand Strategy after Bipolarity," *International Security*, Vol. 19, No. 4 (Spring 1995), pp. 94–117; and Charles A. Kupchan, "After Pax Americana: Benign Power, Regional Integration, and the Sources of a Stable Multipolarity," *International Security*, Vol. 23, No. 2 (Fall 1998), pp. 40–79.

Part I:
A Framework for Analyzing U.S.
Strategic Choices

Competing Visions for U.S. Grand Strategy

Barry R. Posen and Andrew L. Ross

The dramatic events that marked the end of the Cold War and the subsequent early end of the twentieth century require the United States to reconsider its national security policy. What are U.S. interests and objectives? What are the threats to those interests and objectives? What are the appropriate strategic responses to those threats? What principles should guide the development of U.S. policy and strategy? In short, what should be the new grand strategy of the United States?

Four grand strategies, relatively discrete and coherent arguments about the U.S. role in the world, now compete in our public discourse. They may be termed neo-isolationism; selective engagement; cooperative security; and primacy (see Table 1 for a summary presentation of the four alternative visions). Below, we describe each of these four strategies in its purest form; we borrow liberally from the academics, government officials, journalists, and policy analysts who have contributed to this debate, but on issues where others have kept silent, or been inconsistent, we impose consistency in the interest of clarity. Our purpose is not advocacy; it is transparency. We hope to sharpen the public debate, not settle it. We then offer our characterization and critique of the evolving grand strategy of the Clinton administration, an uneasy amalgam of selective engagement, cooperative security, and primacy. Finally, we speculate on what might cause the United States to make a clearer grand strategy choice.

The state of the U.S. economy, the national finances, and persistent social problems largely drove foreign and defense policy out of the 1992 presidential race. The 1996 campaign was little different. The first months of the first Clinton administration were characterized by indirection, and later by a nearly single-minded focus on economic issues. Security matters were dealt with sequentially and incrementally; no obvious grand scheme emerged until Assistant to the President for National Security Affairs Anthony Lake proposed in Septem-

Barry R. Posen is Professor of Political Science in the Defense and Arms Control Studies Program at MIT. Andrew Ross is Professor of National Security Affairs at the U.S. Naval War College.

The original version of this essay was submitted by Barry R. Posen as written testimony for the House Armed Services Committee on March 3, 1993. Earlier versions of this piece appeared in Strategy and Force Planning Faculty, eds., *Strategy and Force Planning* (Newport, R.I.: Naval War College Press, 1995), pp. 115–134; and in Robert J. Lieber, ed., *Eagle Adrift: American Foreign Policy At the End of the Century* (New York: Longman, 1997), pp. 100–134. The views expressed here are those of the authors and do not necessarily reflect the views of the Naval War College, the Department of the Navy, or any other U.S. government department or agency.

International Security, Vol. 21, No. 3 (Winter 1996/97), pp. 5–53
© 1996 by the President and Fellows of Harvard College and the Massachusetts Institute of Technology.

Table 1. Competing Grand Strategy Visions.

	Neo-Isolationism	Selective Engagement	Cooperative Security	Primacy
Analytical Anchor	Minimal, defensive realism	Traditional balance of power realism	Liberalism	Maximal realism/unilateralism
Major Problem of Int'l Politics	Avoiding entanglement in the affairs of others	Peace among the major powers	The indivisibility of peace	The rise of a peer competitor
Preferred World Order	Distant balance of power	Balance of power	Interdependence	Hegemonic
Nuclear Dynamics	Supports status quo	Supports status quo	Supports aggression	Supports aggression
Conception of National Interests	Narrow	Restricted	Transnational	Broad
Regional Priorities	North America	Industrial Eurasia	Global	Industrial Eurasia & the home of any potential peer competitor
Nuclear Proliferation	Not our problem	Discriminate prevention	Indiscriminate prevention	Indiscriminate prevention
NATO	Withdraw	Maintain	Transform & expand	Expand
Regional Conflict	Abstain	Contain; discriminate intervention	Intervene	Contain; discriminate intervention
Ethnic Conflict	Abstain	Contain	Nearly indiscriminate intervention	Contain
Humanitarian Intervention	Abstain	Discriminate intervention	Nearly indiscriminate intervention	Discriminate intervention
Use of Force	Self-defense	Discriminate	Frequent	At will
Force Posture	Minimal self-defense force	Two-MRC force	Reconnaissance strike complex for mutilateral action	A two-power-standard force

ber 1993 that U.S. policy shift "From Containment to Enlargement." Not until July 1994 were the ideas initially advanced by Lake codified in the administration's *National Security Strategy of Engagement and Enlargement*. Those ideas remain intact in the February 1996 version of that White House document.[1] Yet the Clinton administration, like the Bush administration before it, has failed to build a domestic political consensus in support of its strategic vision. Thus the post–Cold War grand strategy debate continues.

We distinguish the four alternative strategies in four ways. We ask, first, what are the major purposes or objectives each identifies for the United States in international politics? These range from a narrow commitment to the basic safety of the United States to an ambitious effort to secure permanent U.S. global preeminence.

Second, we ask: what are each strategy's basic premises about international politics? Though advocates are seldom explicit, underlying disagreements among the strategies on basic questions help to explain their other disagreements. In particular, the four strategies disagree on the "fragility" of international politics—the propensity for developments unfavorable to the United States to cascade rapidly in ever more unfavorable directions, and for developments favorable to the United States to move in ever more favorable directions. A fragile international political system both requires and responds to U.S. activism. Answers to three central questions of modern international relations theory affect each strategy's assessment of the fragility of international politics: (1) Do states tend to balance against, or bandwagon with, expansionists? That is, will most states, faced with a neighbor growing in power and ambition, take steps to improve their power through some combination of internal military preparation and external alignment? (2) Do nuclear weapons make conquest easier or harder? If secure retaliatory nuclear deterrent forces are easy to get, and the risks they impose for ambitious aggressors are easy for those aggressors to grasp, then they make it difficult for aspiring hegemons to improve their power position through intimidation or conquest. If, on the other hand, they cause hegemons to perceive themselves as invulnerable to attack, such states may be emboldened to act aggressively. (3) How much potential influence does the United States actually have in international politics? How do we measure relative power in international politics; is it reasonable to speak of a unipolar world? Here, there are two subsidiary issues. Measured globally,

---

1. Anthony Lake, "From Containment to Enlargement," *U.S. Department of State Dispatch*, Vol. 4, No. 39 (September 27, 1993), pp. 658–664; *A National Security Strategy of Engagement and Enlargement* (Washington, D.C.: U.S. Government Printing Office [U.S. GPO], July 1994); and *A National Security Strategy of Engagement and Enlargement* (Washington, D.C.: U.S. GPO, February 1996).

how much international political influence can the current U.S. "share" of gross world power resources—economic, technological, and military capabilities—buy? How much money, and how many lives, are the American people willing to pay for influence in international politics in the absence of a major threat? If the United States is relatively quite powerful in international politics, then it can think in terms of great objectives. If not, its objectives will need to be limited. If the United States is inherently much more powerful than is often believed, then the American people may not need to sacrifice much more than they already do for the United States to undertake ambitious policies successfully.[2]

We ask, third, what are the preferred political and military instruments of each strategy? Do advocates prefer to work multilaterally or unilaterally? Do they favor international organizations or prefer traditional alliances? How much military force does the United States require, and what kind? Our force structure analysis is indicative rather than comprehensive; as a heuristic device we rely substantially on the array of alternative force structures developed by the late Les Aspin during his tenure as Chairman of the House Armed Services Committee and then as Secretary of Defense early in the Clinton administration.[3] The force structures (see Table 2) were developed with an eye to the number and variety of contingencies they could support—the "business end" of grand strategy.[4]

---

2. Each grand strategy should have an economic component. Most of the literature, however, treats the economic component in a cursory way, if at all. As we began to consider the possible economic elements of each alternative we determined that a separate essay would be required to offer more than a superficial treatment. Therefore, this essay confines itself to the political and military aspects of alternative U.S. grand strategies.

3. We also rely on these options because they have the unusual attribute that five of them largely employ the same basic methodology to develop force structure and to estimate the costs of those force structures. Representative Les Aspin, "An Approach to Sizing American Conventional Forces for the Post-Soviet Era," February 25, 1992 (unpublished manuscript); Secretary of Defense Les Aspin, *Report on the Bottom-Up Review* (Washington, D.C.: Department of Defense, 1993); Congressional Budget Office (CBO), Staff Memorandum, "Fiscal Implications of the Administration's Proposed Base Force," December 1991 (unpublished manuscript); see also Andrew F. Krepinevich, *The Bottom-Up Review: An Assessment* (Washington, D.C.: Defense Budget Project, 1994); and Dov S. Zakheim and Jeffrey M. Ranney, "Matching Defense Strategies to Resources: Challenges for the Clinton Administration," *International Security*, Vol. 18, No. 1 (Summer 1993), pp. 51–78. The Bush-Cheney-Powell "Base Force" was probably generated by a somewhat different methodology. The individuals who made the budget estimates in every case had access to the best available cost information. Other analysts have developed force structures and estimated costs on the basis of their individual methodologies; we chose not to employ them because we could not be sure they were strictly comparable.

4. However, there are reasons why the cost estimates in Table 2 could be too high or too low. Most estimates, particularly those for the Base Force and Clinton Bottom-Up Review (BUR) force,

Fourth, to illustrate the real world implications of each grand strategy, we ask: what are their positions on a number of basic issues now on the U.S. agenda, including nuclear proliferation, NATO enlargement, and regional conflict?

After describing each strategy along these four dimensions, we offer a short critique, which reflects both our own specific concerns and what we believe are the most credible counter-arguments that the proponents of the other strategies might offer.

The essay closes with a brief review and analysis of the Clinton administration's grand strategy, which consists of a core of cooperative security principles and impulses, drawn toward primacy as it has faced a less tractable international environment than it expected, but constrained toward selectivity by a U.S. citizenry whose support for ambitious foreign projects seems shallow at best. We explain why this compromise has proven necessary, and offer some hypotheses about what could cause this grand strategy to change.

Neo-Isolationism

Neo-isolationism is the least ambitious, and, at least among foreign policy professionals, probably the least popular grand strategy option.[5] The new isolationists have embraced a constricted view of U.S. national interests that renders internationalism not only unnecessary but counterproductive. National

---

probably underestimate the cost of major procurement after the turn of the century. On the other hand, many estimates of the costs of smaller forces probably do not take credit for the savings that ought to accrue from proportional reductions in defense infrastructure that ought to accompany reductions in force structure. This tends to occur for two reasons. First, because U.S. defense politics focuses on the Future Years Defense Plan, or FYDP, most policy-oriented budget analysts focus primarily on the near-term budgetary consequences that would directly arise from incremental reductions in existing forces. Second, infrastructure, particularly bases and depots, are often politically protected. It is only slightly absurd to suggest, therefore, that nearly all the conventional combat power in the U.S. military could be eliminated, and still leave us with a defense budget of $100 billion a year, which is the implication of the trend of costs versus force structure in Options A–D.

5. The new isolationists seldom refer to themselves as isolationists. Indeed, they often vociferously deny isolationist tendencies. Earl Ravenal, "The Case for Adjustment," *Foreign Policy*, No. 81 (Winter 1990–91), pp. 3–19, prefers "disengagement." Patrick J. Buchanan, too, in "America First— and Second, and Third," *National Interest*, No. 19 (Spring 1990), pp. 77–82, uses "disengagement." Doug Bandow, "Keeping the Troops and the Money at Home," *Current History*, Vol. 93, No. 579 (January 1994), pp. 8–13, prefers "benign detachment." Eric A. Nordlinger, however, in the most sophisticated, and perhaps least conventional version of the new isolationism, *Isolationism Reconfigured: American Foreign Policy for a New Century* (Princeton, N.J.: Princeton University Press, 1995), embraces "isolationism."

Table 2. Comparison of Alternative Future Force Structures.

	Force A[1]	Force B[2]	Force C[3]	Force D[4]	Base Force[5]	Clinton-BUR[6]
ARMY						
Active divisions	8	8	9	10	12	10
Reserve divisions	2	2	6	6	6	8
MARINES[7]						
Active divisions	2	2	2	3	2⅓	3
Reserve divisions	1	1	1	1	1	1
AIR FORCE						
Active wings	6	8	10	11	15	13
Reserve wings	4	6	8	9	11	7
NAVY						
Total ships	220	290	340	430	450	346
Carriers	6	8	12	15	13	12
Attack subs	20	40	40	50	80	45–55
Amphibious assault ships[8]	50	50	50	82	50	44
PERSONNEL						
Active	1,247,000	1,312,000	1,409,000	1,575,000	1,626,000	1,450,000
Reserve	666,000	691,000	904,000	933,000	920,000	905,000
1997 BUDGET AUTHORITY, billions 97$ (DOD+DOE)[9]	231	246	270	295	291–301	253

NOTES:

1. Alternatives A,B,C, and D were devised by the House Armed Services Committee under the leadership of then Chairman Les Aspin. Force A: A "foundation" of nuclear, forward presence, special operations, and continental defense forces, and an industrial mobilization base, plus forces for one "major regional contingency" (MRC) such as the 1991 war against Iraq, and a modest humanitarian intervention capability.

2. Force B: Preceding plus sufficient airpower to support heavily an ally in a second major regional contingency.

3. Force C: Preceding plus sufficient forces in reserve to sustain comfortably a large new forward deployment for a major regional contingency, plus the capability to mount simultaneously a small invasion similar to the attack on Panama in 1989.

4. Force D: Preceding with "a more robust response," plus a second humanitarian intervention and naval "power projection" for the second MRC.

5. Base Force: Proposed by President Bush and Former Chairman of the Joint Chiefs of Staff Colin Powell. General Powell was attempting to develop a force structure that accommodated the widespread expectation of a "peace dividend," and at the same time clearly preserved the image and the fact of U.S. superpower status.

6. Clinton Bottom-Up Review: Two "near simultaneous regional contingencies" plus a moderate peace-keeping operation and substantial forward presence; objective for the year 2000; 1997 force structure is close but not identical. The "Bottom-Up Review" was developed by Secretary of Defense Les Aspin early in the Clinton administration. It relied substantially on the analysis that he had conducted as a Congressman to generate Options A–D. The BUR Force Structure is meant to be able to fight two Desert Storm–scale "Major Regional Contingencies" (MRCs) "nearly" simultaneously, and to sustain a high level of forward military presence in peacetime. The BUR force structure has the unusual attribute of being slightly larger, but costing somewhat less than Force C, Aspin's earlier preference.

7. Marine divisions and Navy Carriers each have associated air wings, respectively slightly larger and slightly smaller than their Air Force counterparts, which number 72 aircraft.

8. These transport Marine units to their attack positions; some of these ships (10–12 in the current force) are very large, roughly half the size of a standard Nimitz class carrier, and carry VSTOL aircraft, helicopters, and hovercraft.

9. Totals include roughly ten billion dollars of DOE funding to maintain the nuclear weapons complex. Among budget analysts, it is generally agreed that the available defense dollars that the Bush administration projected and the Clinton administration projects after the turn of the century would be inadequate to support their preferred force structures. By 2005, $20–65 billion more than the projected 1997 budget would be required to fund the Base Force; see Congressional Budget Office, "Fiscal Implications of the Base Force," p. 11. The CBO estimates that after the turn of the century the modernization of the smaller Bottom-Up Review Force Structure with new technology weapons currently in development or production would require between $7 billion and $31 billion more per year than the current budget plans for the year 1999, which is little different from the 1997 plan. See CBO, *An Analysis of the Administration's Future Years Defense Program for 1995–1999* (Washington, D.C.: Congressional Budget Office, January 1995), p. 50.

defense—the protection of "the security, liberty, and property of the American people"[6]—is the only vital U.S. interest.

The new isolationism subscribes to a fundamentally realist view of international politics and thus focuses on power.[7] Its advocates ask: who has the power to threaten the sovereignty of the United States, its territorial integrity, or its safety? They answer that nobody does.[8] The collapse of the Soviet Union has left a rough balance of power in Eurasia. If either Russia or China begins to build up its military power, there are plenty of wealthy and capable states at either end of Eurasia to contain them. Indeed, Russia and China help to contain one another. Thus no state has the capability to conquer the rest and so agglomerate enough economic capability and military mobilization potential to threaten the American way of life. Like traditional isolationism, this strategy observes that the oceans make such a threat improbable in any event. The United States controls about one quarter of the gross world product, twice as much as its nearest competitor, Japan, and while not totally self-sufficient, is better placed than most to "go it alone." U.S. neighbors to the north and south are militarily weak and destined to stay that way for quite some time. The United States is inherently a very secure country.[9] Indeed, the United States can be said to be strategically immune.[10]

The new isolationism is strongly motivated by a particular understanding of nuclear weapons. It concedes that nuclear weapons have increased the poten-

---

6. Bandow, "Keeping the Troops and the Money at Home," p. 10.
7. The version of realism that underlies the new isolationism is minimal. Its strategic imperatives are even more limited than those of the minimal realism outlined by Christopher Layne, "Less is More: Minimal Realism in East Asia," *National Interest*, No. 43 (Spring 1996), pp. 64–77. Layne distinguishes between maximal and minimal realism. He views a balance of power approach (which we call "selective engagement") as minimal realism. Layne links primacy with maximal realism. For an earlier version of minimal realism and neo-isolationism, see Robert W. Tucker, *A New Isolationism: Threat or Promise?* (New York: Universe Books, 1972). Nordlinger, *Isolationism Reconfigured*, is the most significant exception to the generalization that neo-isolationism is driven by a realist interpretation of international politics. His eclectic approach to developing a national strategy of isolationism and its concurrent foreign policy is, in the end, informed more by liberalism than realism.
8. Alan Tonelson, "Superpower Without a Sword," *Foreign Affairs*, Vol. 72, No. 3 (Summer 1993), p. 179, observes that "few international conflicts will directly threaten the nation's territorial integrity, political independence or material welfare."
9. Christopher Layne, "The Unipolar Illusion: Why New Great Powers Will Rise," *International Security*, Vol. 17, No. 4 (Spring 1993), p. 48, makes this point. He uses it to support an argument for a grand strategy that he calls "strategic independence." It bears some similarity to the selective engagement strategy outlined below, albeit a rather inactive version of it.
10. Nordlinger, *Isolationism Reconsidered*, pp. 6 and 63–91.

tial capacity of others to threaten the safety of the United States. But nuclear weapons make it very hard, indeed nearly inconceivable, for any power to win a traditional military victory over the United States. Nuclear weapons assure the political sovereignty and the territorial integrity of the United States. The collapse of the Soviet Union has so reduced the military resources available to its successor states that a counterforce attack on U.S. nuclear forces, an old and exaggerated fear, is out of the question. There can be no politically rational motive for any country large or small to explode a nuclear weapon on North America. U.S. retaliation would be devastating. Moreover, the fact that Britain, France, the People's Republic of China, and Russia have nuclear retaliatory forces makes it quite likely that these powers will deter each other, further reducing the risk that an ambitious hegemon could dominate and militarily exploit the economic resources of the Eurasian landmass.

ISSUES AND INSTRUMENTS

Given the absence of threats to the U.S. homeland, neo-isolationism holds that national defense will seldom justify intervention abroad. The United States is not responsible for, and cannot afford the costs of, maintaining world order. The pursuit of economic well-being is best left to the private sector. The promotion of values such as democracy and human rights inspires ill-advised crusades that serve only to generate resentment against the United States; consequently, it is a poor guide to policy and strategy.

The new isolationism would concede, however, that our great capabilities are a magnet for trouble so long as we are involved in any way in various political disputes around the world. Intervention in these disputes is thus a good way to attract attention to the United States. The strong try to deter the United States; the weak to seduce it; the dispossessed to blame it. Neo-isolationism would argue that those who fear terrorism, especially terrorism with nuclear, biological, or chemical weapons, can increase U.S. safety by keeping it out of foreign conflicts. Middle Eastern terrorists, for instance, whether sponsored by Syria, Iran, Iraq, or Libya, would find little reason to target the United States and its citizens, either abroad or at home, if the United States refrained from meddling in the Middle East.

Neo-isolationism advises the United States to preserve its freedom of action and strategic independence. Because neo-isolationism proposes that the United States stay out of political conflicts and wars abroad, it has no particular need for political instruments. Even traditional alliance relationships that obligate the United States in advance, such as NATO, ought to be dismantled. International organizations are a place to talk, perhaps to coordinate international efforts to improve the overall global quality of life, but not to make or keep peace. This would implicate the United States and draw it into conflicts.

Most of the foreign policy issues now facing the United States would disappear under the new isolationism. The future of NATO, for instance, would be left to Europe. Neo-isolationists would have the United States abandon that anachronistic alliance, not lead the way in its ill-conceived expansion. Bosnia, too, is a European problem in which the United States has no concrete, material stake. The United States would no longer be preoccupied with Russian political and economic reform, or the lack thereof. Arabs and Israelis would have to sort out their affairs (or not) without U.S. meddling. Islamists would be deprived of the Great Satan. The North Korean threat would be left to South Korea, the country whose interests are actually threatened. In Latin America and Africa, the United States would no longer rescue Haitis and Somalias. Humanitarian assistance, if and when provided, would be confined to disasters—famines, epidemics, earthquakes, and storms. The United States might be willing to help clean up the mess after foreign wars have sorted themselves out. But intervention of any kind during wars would be viewed as a mistake, since at least one side is likely to be disadvantaged by humanitarian assistance to the others and would thus come to view the United States as an enemy.

FORCE STRUCTURE. Neo-isolationism generates a rather small force structure. It is unlikely to cost more than two percent of GDP.[11] First and foremost, the United States would need to retain a secure nuclear second-strike capability to

---

11. Ravenal, "The Case for Adjustment," pp. 15–19, develops a force structure and defense budget within these parameters which is explicitly geared to support a grand strategy quite similar to what we label isolationism. He suggests an active force of 1.1 million people, with six Army and two Marine divisions, eleven tactical air wings, six carriers with five air wings, and a strategic dyad of submarines and bombers, which could be funded for about $150 billion in constant 1991 dollars, perhaps $175 billion in 1997 dollars, or roughly 2.5 percent of GDP. See Force A in Table 1, which is roughly the same size, but which then-Congressman Aspin estimated would cost considerably more, $231 billion in 1997 dollars, roughly 3 percent of GDP. See also Tonelson, "Superpower Without a Sword," pp. 179–180, who argues for a similar force structure, but who seems to subscribe to a conservative version of selective engagement. The Center for Defense Information has proposed that an even smaller force structure would be sufficient to support a strategy of disengagement. For $104 billion in constant 1993 dollars, CDI proposed to field a force of only 500,000 people, one Marine and three Army divisions, four Air Force tactical wings, two carriers and 221 other combat vessels, and a nuclear force of 16 submarines. See "Defending America: CDI Options for Military Spending," *Defense Monitor*, Vol. 21, No. 4 (1992). Nordlinger, *Isolationism Reconfigured*, p. 46, suggested that forces at half the levels sustained during the Cold War and early post–Cold War years would be sufficient.

deter nuclear attacks from any quarter. Modest air and missile defenses might be put in place to deal with low-grade threats. Second, the U.S. intelligence community would have the task of watching worldwide developments of weapons of mass destruction in order to forestall any terrorist threats against the United States. If such threats occurred, it would be their job to find an address against which retaliation could be directed. Third, the United States would probably wish to retain a capable navy (perhaps a third to a half the current size), and diverse special operations forces. The purpose would largely be to protect U.S. commerce abroad from criminal activity—piracy, kidnapping, and extortion. The remainder of U.S. forces would be structured to preserve skills at ground and tactical air warfare in the event that the balance of power on the Eurasian land mass eroded, perhaps requiring a return to a more activist U.S. policy. Since the burden of defending wealthy allies can be discarded in the aftermath of the Soviet Union's fortuitous collapse, those forces need not be forward-deployed in Europe and Asia. A major mission of the intelligence community would be to provide timely warning of strategic developments in Eurasia that would warrant a return to a more activist foreign and security policy. The U.S. force structure would no longer be driven either by demanding and costly forward presence requirements or by the need to prepare to engage in multiple foreign contingencies. American military forces would be used only to defend narrowly construed U.S. interests. Given these limited requirements, even "Force A" (see Table 2), the smallest of Aspin's notional force structures, is larger than necessary.

CRITIQUE

The United States can, more easily than most, go it alone. Yet we do not find the arguments of the neo-isolationists compelling. Their strategy serves U.S. interests only if they are narrowly construed. First, though the neo-isolationists have a strong case in their argument that the United States is currently quite secure, disengagement is unlikely to make the United States more secure, and would probably make it less secure. The disappearance of the United States from the world stage would likely precipitate a good deal of competition abroad for security. Without a U.S. presence, aspiring regional hegemons would see more opportunities. States formerly defended by the United States would have to look to their own military power; local arms competitions are to be expected. Proliferation of nuclear weapons would intensify if the U.S. nuclear guarantee were withdrawn. Some states would seek weapons of mass destruction because they were simply unable to compete conventionally with their neighbors. This new flurry of competitive behavior would probably energize many hypothesized immediate causes of war, including preemptive motives, preventive motives, economic motives, and the propensity for miscalculation. There would likely be more war. Weapons of mass destruction might be used in some of these wars, with unpleasant effects even for those not directly involved.

Second, if these predictions about the international environment are correct, as competition intensified U.S. decision-makers would continuously have to reassess whether their original assumptions about the workings of the balance of power in Eurasia and the deterrent power of nuclear weapons were still valid. Decision-makers require both good political intelligence and compelling cause-effect knowledge about international politics to determine that a policy shift is in order. More importantly, decision-makers would have to persuade the country that a policy reversal is necessary, but U.S. foreign policy is a tough thing to change. Given these problems, how much trouble would have to occur before the United States returned to a more active role? Would the United States return in time to exert its influence to help prevent a great power war? If the United States did decide that a more active role was necessary, how much influence would it have after years of inactivity? Would the United States return in time to prevent an aspiring hegemon from getting a jump ahead, as Nazi Germany did in World War II? If not, the costs of containment or rollback could prove substantial.

Third, though the United States would save a great deal of money in its defense budget, perhaps 1–1.5 percent of GDP, or $70–100 billion per year relative to the budgets planned by the Clinton administration, these annual savings do not seem commensurate with the international influence the strategy would forgo. Though this is a lot of money, which has many worthy alternative uses, the redirection of these resources from the military is unlikely to make the difference between a healthy and an unhealthy economy that is already some seven trillion dollars in size. Neo-isolationists seem willing to trade away considerable international influence for a relatively modest improvement in domestic welfare. Given the potential stakes in international politics, the trade-off is imprudent. Engagement in international politics imposes obvious burdens and risks. Shedding an active role in international politics, however, increases the risks of unintended consequences and reduces U.S. influence over the management of those consequences, and over issues that we can hardly anticipate.

Selective Engagement

Selective engagement endeavors to ensure peace among powers that have substantial industrial and military potential—the great powers.[12] By virtue of the great military capabilities that would be brought into play, great power conflicts are much more dangerous to the United States than conflicts elsewhere. Thus Russia, the wealthier states of the European Union, the People's Republic of China, and Japan matter most. The purpose of U.S. engagement should be to affect directly the propensity of these powers to go to war with one another. These wars have the greatest chance of producing large-scale resort to weapons of mass destruction, a global experiment that the United States ought to try to prevent. These are the areas of the world where the world wars have originated, wars that have managed to reach out and draw in the United States in spite of its strong inclination to stay out.

Like the new isolationism, selective engagement emerges from the realist tradition of international politics and its focus on large concentrations of power.[13] Like cooperative security, it is also interested in peace. Though some of its proponents agree with the neo-isolationist premise that U.S. geography and nuclear deterrence make the United States so secure that a Eurasian hegemon would not pose much of a security problem for the United States,[14] selective engagement holds that any great power war in Eurasia is a danger to the United States.[15] On the basis of both the increased destructive power of modern weaponry and the demonstrated inability of the United States to stay

---

12. Robert Art, "A Defensible Defense: America's Grand Strategy After the Cold War," *International Security*, Vol. 15, No. 4 (Spring 1991), pp. 5–53; and Stephen Van Evera, "Why Europe Matters, Why the Third World Doesn't: American Grand Strategy After the Cold War," *Journal of Strategic Studies*, Vol. 13, No. 2 (June 1990), pp. 1–51, are the two most complete expositions of selective engagement. See also Ronald Steel, *Temptations of a Superpower* (Cambridge, Mass.: Harvard University Press, 1995).

13. Selective engagement is informed neither by the minimal realism that underlies the new isolationism nor the maximal realism that drives primacy; it is instead based on the traditional mainstream balance-of-power realism evident in Hans J. Morgenthau, *Politics Among Nations: The Struggle for Power and Peace*, 5th ed., rev. (New York: Alfred A. Knopf, 1978).

14. Posen classifies himself as a "selective engagement" advocate. He does believe, however, that the United States should not only act to reduce the probability of great power war, it should also pursue the traditional policy of opposing the rise of a Eurasian hegemon who would conquer or even dominate the world's centers of industrial and economic power. The latter risk seems very low in the short term, but preserving the political division of industrial Eurasia remains a U.S. interest.

15. On this point see Van Evera, "Why Europe Matters," pp. 8–10; and Art, "Defensible Defense," pp. 45–50.

out of large European and Asian wars in the first half of this century, selective engagement argues that the United States has an interest in great power peace.

Selective engagement shares the neo-isolationist expectation that states balance, and that nuclear weapons favor the defender of the status quo. However, selective engagers also recognize that balancing may be tardy, statesmen may miscalculate, and nuclear deterrence could fail. Given the interest in great power peace, the United States should engage itself abroad in order to ensure against these possibilities in the places where the consequences could be the most serious. Balancing happens, but it happens earlier and more easily with a leader. Nuclear weapons deter, but why not place the weight of U.S. strategic nuclear forces behind the status quo powers, just to simplify the calculations of the ambitious? Selective engagement tries to ensure that the great powers understand that the United States does not wish to find out how a future Eurasian great power war might progress, and that it has sufficient military power to deny victory to the aggressor.

Advocates of selective engagement do start from the premise that U.S. resources are scarce: it is simply impossible to muster sufficient power and will to keep domestic and international peace worldwide, or to preserve the United States as the undisputed leader in a unipolar world.[16] The United States does have 22 percent of gross world product, at least half again as much as Japan, its closest economic competitor, but only 4.6 percent of the global population. Global economic development will gradually reduce the U.S. economic advantage, and demographics already limit U.S. capacity for intervention in labor intensive civil wars. Desert Storm does not suggest a permanent, overwhelming U.S. military superiority; other wars may not be so easy. Moreover, short of a compelling argument about an extant threat, the people of the United States are unlikely to want to invest much money or many lives either in global police duties—cooperative security—or in trying to cow others into accepting U.S. hegemony—primacy.

ISSUES AND INSTRUMENTS

Selective engagement advocates are worried about nuclear proliferation, but proliferation in some countries matters more than in others.[17] Countries seek-

---

16. Art, "Defensible Defense," p. 45. See also Jonathan Clarke, "Leaders and Followers," *Foreign Policy*, No. 101 (Winter 1995–96), pp. 37–51, arguing both that the U.S. share of global power is too small to support cooperative security or primacy, and that U.S. public support for such strategies is too weak.
17. See Art, "Defensible Defense," pp. 23–30.

ing nuclear weapons who have no conflict of interest with the United States or its friends are viewed more favorably than those who do. The Nuclear Non-Proliferation Treaty (NPT) is viewed as an instrument to permit countries who have neither the wealth to support nuclear forces, nor the political insecurity or ambition to need or want them, to find a refuge from a race that they would rather not run. Selective engagement advocates may be willing to try to cajole India, Israel, Pakistan, or Ukraine into surrendering their nuclear capabilities and joining the NPT, but they hold that it would be absurd to turn neutrals or friends into enemies on this issue alone.

Proliferation really matters in politically ambitious countries that have demonstrated a certain insensitivity to risks and costs. North Korea, Iraq, and Iran fall into this category. The most important response is to convince them that they are being watched, and that the United States intends to stand against any nuclear ambitions they might have. Depending on the pace of their weapons programs, and the extent of their bellicosity, stronger measures may be warranted. There is no consensus on the use of force, however. Advocates of selective engagement are always sensitive to costs; preventive attacks may not be feasible.

Regional competitions among small states matter to the extent that they could energize intense great power security competition. This risk preserves the Persian Gulf as a core U.S. security interest.[18] The problem is not so much U.S. dependence on Gulf oil but the far greater dependence on it by many other great powers. A struggle over the control of the Gulf could draw in great powers on opposing sides, or set off competition elsewhere to expropriate energy resources. Moreover, should most of the economic potential associated with this oil fall into the hands of one ambitious actor, it could provide the underpinnings for a substantial regional military challenge. If Iraq could achieve the military development it did on its own oil revenues, how much more might it have achieved with the revenues of Kuwait or Saudi Arabia? Even if such a power would not pose a direct threat to the United States, it would certainly be in a position to pose a threat to many of its neighbors. A great war in the Persian Gulf, with the risk of large-scale use of weapons of

---

18. Art, "Defensible Defense," p. 47. Stephen Van Evera, "The United States and the Third World: When to Intervene?" in Kenneth A. Oye, Robert J. Lieber, and Donald Rothchild, eds., *Eagle in a New World* (New York: Harper Collins, 1992), pp. 127–131, makes a comprehensive case for the U.S. intervention in the Persian Gulf in 1990, Operation Desert Shield, but expresses skepticism about the necessity for Operation Desert Storm.

mass destruction, is the kind of experiment that the United States probably ought not to wish to run.

For the advocates of selective engagement, then, the parts of the world that matter most are the two ends of Eurasia—Europe and East Asia—and the Middle East/Southwest Asia. Traditional alliances are the appropriate vehicle to pursue these interests. Selective engagement especially favors the preservation of NATO, though not its expansion. That is not to say that the rest of the world can be completely ignored. Some countries may matter more than others for particular reasons. For example, proximity alone makes Mexico an important U.S. foreign policy interest. Moreover, if selective engagement is to remain a viable strategy, it will need to adapt to the likely emergence of sizeable new powers, and the potential for conflict among them.[19]

Advocates of selective engagement are concerned with ethnic conflict where it runs the risk of producing a great power war. Fortunately, there are not many places where this seems likely. Arguably, there is only one dangerous potential conflict of this type in Eurasia today—the currently dormant rivalry between Russia and Ukraine. Conflicts elsewhere in Eurasia may tempt one or more great powers to intervene, and thus they merit a certain degree of judicious diplomatic management. Most of these conflicts do not engage the vital interests of any state; they are strategically uninteresting. The former Yugoslavia, for instance, contains no military or economic resources that would affect the security of any European great power.

Advocates of selective engagement view humanitarian intervention as a question to be settled by the normal processes of U.S. domestic politics. There is no clear strategic guide that tells which interventions are worth pursuing and which are not. Their perspective does suggest several critical considerations. The most important strategic question is the opportunity cost. Given one's best estimate of the plausible course of the humanitarian intervention, what will be its consequences for U.S. material and political ability to intervene in more strategically important areas if trouble should arise during or after the humanitarian intervention? An intervention to bring sufficient order to Somalia

---

19. Robert S. Chase, Emily B. Hill, and Paul Kennedy, "Pivotal States and U.S. Strategy," *Foreign Affairs*, Vol. 75, No. 1 (January/February 1996), p. 33, have singled out Mexico, Brazil, South Africa, Algeria, Egypt, Turkey, India, Pakistan, and Indonesia as pivotal states "whose future will profoundly affect their surrounding regions." The list is long, the adjective "pivotal" seems premature, and systematic attention to these states in addition to the great powers is hardly selective. Nevertheless, the list does highlight states that may pose special problems today, or which may become serious contenders for regional power in the future.

to permit the distribution of humanitarian assistance required the equivalent of a single division of ground forces and involved the risk of relatively modest U.S. casualties. But even the horror of what had transpired earlier in Somalia proved insufficient to preserve U.S. public support through the relatively modest U.S. casualties that ensued. To preserve by force the unitary, multi-ethnic, ethnically intermingled Bosnia-Herzegovina that existed at the moment of Yugoslavia's dissolution could have required three or more U.S. divisions for the indefinite future, plus European forces.[20] There would likely have been more than a few casualties. Intervention in Yugoslavia would have made it more difficult to intervene elsewhere. As the casualties mount in any intervention, and the bloodshed begins to make the U.S. position more morally ambiguous to the American public, the political will to act in more important regions could erode.

FORCE STRUCTURE. A selective engagement policy probably requires a force structure similar to those proposed by the late Secretary of Defense Les Aspin in 1992 as "Force B" or "Force C" (see Table 2). A strong nuclear deterrent is still needed to deter nuclear attack on the United States and to protect its freedom of action in a world of several nuclear powers. Since the United States has an interest in stability in three critical areas of the world (both ends of Eurasia and the Middle East), and since simultaneous trouble in two or more areas cannot be ruled out, it is reasonable to retain a "two regional wars" capability. Both force structures have sufficient air and ground forces for one major regional contingency ("MRC"), and sufficient air forces to support a regional ally in a second contingency. "Force C" places additional emphasis on sea and air lift and on aircraft carrier task forces, perhaps more than is truly necessary given that the United States ought to be able to identify in advance the location of the interests over which it might be willing to threaten or wage war. "Force C" also assumes that the United States must maintain sufficient reserve forces to sustain with ease a new major forward deployment of indeterminate duration, and at the same time conduct a small offensive operation such as the invasion of Panama. These additions seem an overly conservative interpretation of the forces necessary for selective engagement; "Force B" may be adequate.

---

20. Barry R. Posen, "A Balkan Vietnam Awaits 'Peacekeepers'," *Los Angeles Times*, February 4, 1993, p. B7. The article assesses the force requirements to police the "Vance-Owen Plan," which intended to preserve a unitary Bosnia-Herzegovina. The three principal ethnic and religious groups in Bosnia would have remained intermingled, as they were at the outset of the war. Thus the police problem would have been quite complex and demanding, similar to the British problem in Northern Ireland.

CRITIQUE

Selective engagement has its own problems. First, the strategy lacks a certain romance: will the cool and quiet, steady, long-term exercise of U.S. power in the service of stable great power relations win the political support of any major constituency in the United States? Compared to other strategies, there is relatively little idealism or commitment to principle behind the strategy. It lacks the exuberant U.S. nationalism of primacy, or the commitment to liberal principle of cooperative security. It focuses rather narrowly on interests defined in terms of power. Can such strategy sustain the support of a liberal democracy long addicted to viewing international relations as a struggle between good and evil?

Second, the strategy expects the United States to ignore much of the trouble that is likely to occur in the world. America's prestige and reputation might suffer from such apparent lethargy, however, which could limit its ability to persuade others on more important issues. Great power rivalries are currently muted, and if successful, the strategy will quietly keep them so. This would be an enormous contribution to the welfare of the entire world. However, it is an open question whether a regular tendency to avoid involvement in the issues that do arise will ultimately affect the ability of the United States to pursue its more important interests. Arguably, it was fear of such a result that provided one of the impulses for the ultimate U.S. involvement in trying to end the war in Bosnia.

Third, selective engagement does not provide clear guidance on which ostensibly "minor" issues have implications for great power relations, and thus merit U.S. involvement. It posits that most will not matter, but admits that some will. Some connections are more obvious than others, but all will be the subject of debate. Since trouble in peripheral areas is likely to be more common than trouble in core areas, the selective engagement strategy gives its least precise positive guidance on matters that will most commonly figure prominently in the media, and hence in the public debate on U.S. foreign policy. The responsible practice of selective engagement will thus require considerable case-by-case analysis and public debate.

Fourth, selective engagement is not as selective as its advocates would have us believe. Europe and Asia matter because that is where the major powers reside; and the Middle East matters because of its oil resources. Much of the world, therefore, matters. Developments on the periphery of this rather large expanse of the earth will invariably and regularly produce intense media coverage and committed partisans of intervention. The argument will often prove tempting that the frontiers of "what matters" need to be pacified to protect "what matters." NATO enlargement is a good example; advocates want to pacify eastern Europe "preventively" even though Russia is weak and there is no obvious simmering major power conflict there. Few advocates of selective engagement favor this policy, in part because they believe in balancing behavior, and fear that Russia will be catalyzed into reactions that will cause exactly the kind of trouble the United States hopes to avoid. It is likely that those who subscribe to selective engagement would be doomed to spend their careers arguing against grand strategy "mission creep," even if U.S. policymakers explicitly chose selective engagement as the national strategy.[21]

Finally, neo-isolationists would argue that there is one huge tension in the selective engagement argument. The United States must maintain substantial military forces, threaten war, and risk war largely for the purpose of preventing war. A traditional realist position accepts the risk of war, and the costs of waging war, to prevent aggressors from building sufficient power to challenge the United States directly. Neo-isolationists, however, argue that if you want to avoid war, you must stay out of the affairs of others. They remind us that it is quite unlikely that the results of even a great power war could decisively shift the balance of power against the United States. If the United States goes out into the world to prevent hypothetical wars, it will surely find some real ones. Advocates of selective engagement resist this deductive logic for two reasons: the United States was drawn against its intentions into two costly world wars that started in Eurasia; and the United States pursued an activist policy during the Cold War which both contained Soviet expansionism and avoided great power war.

Cooperative Security

The most important distinguishing feature of cooperative security is the proposition that peace is effectively indivisible.[22] Cooperative security, therefore, begins with an expansive conception of U.S. interests: the United States has a

---

21. Chase, Hill, and Kennedy, "Pivotal States and U.S. Strategy," provide an illustration of how the project grows. See also James A. Baker III, "Selective Engagement: Principles for American Foreign Policy in a New Era," *Vital Speeches of the Day*, Vol. 60, No. 10 (March 1, 1994), pp. 299–302. The former secretary of state argues for an expansive strategic agenda that looks more like primacy than selective engagement.
22. Inis L. Claude, *Swords into Plowshares: The Problems and Progress of International Organization*, 4th ed. (New York: Random House, 1971), p. 247; Arnold Wolfers, *Discord and Collaboration: Essays*

huge national interest in world peace. Cooperative security is the only one of the four strategic alternatives that is informed by liberalism rather than realism.[23] Advocates propose to act collectively, through international institutions as much as possible. They presume that democracies will find it easier to work together in cooperative security regimes than would states with less progressive domestic polities.

Cooperative security does not view the great powers as a generic security problem. Because most are democracies, or on the road to democracy, and democracies have historically tended not to fall into war with one another, little great power security competition is expected.[24] A transitional Russia and an oligarchical China remain troublesome, but the answer there is to help them toward democracy as in the Clinton administration formulation, "Engagement and Enlargement." The motives for great powers to collaborate are presumed to be greater than in the past, and the barriers to cooperation are presumed to be lower.

The cooperative security enterprise represents an effort to overcome the shortcomings of traditional collective security.[25] For both, aggression anywhere, and by anyone, cannot be allowed to stand. Both place a premium on international cooperation to deter and thwart aggression. It is to be "all for one and

on International Politics (Baltimore: Johns Hopkins University Press, 1962), pp. 183–184: "'any aggressor anywhere' is in fact the national enemy of every country because in violating the peace and law of the community of nations it endangers, if indirectly, the peace and security of every nation."

23. On the differences between realism and liberalism, see David A. Baldwin, ed., *Neorealism and Neoliberalism: The Contemporary Debate* (New York: Columbia University Press, 1993); Michael E. Brown, Sean M. Lynn-Jones, and Steven E. Miller, eds., *Debating the Democratic Peace* (Cambridge, Mass.: MIT Press, 1996); Michael E. Brown, Sean M. Lynn-Jones, and Steven E. Miller, eds., *The Perils of Anarchy: Contemporary Realism and International Security* (Cambridge, Mass.: MIT Press, 1995); Robert Gilpin, *The Political Economy of International Relations* (Princeton, N.J.: Princeton University Press, 1987); Charles W. Kegley, Jr., ed., *Controversies in International Relations Theory: Realism and the Neoliberal Challenge* (New York: St. Martin's Press, 1995); Robert O. Keohane, ed., *Neorealism and Its Critics* (New York: Columbia University Press, 1986); and Richard Ned Lebow and Thomas Risse-Kappen, eds., *International Relations Theory and the End of the Cold War* (New York: Columbia University Press, 1995).

24. Charles A. Kupchan and Clifford A. Kupchan, "Concerts, Collective Security, and the Future of Europe," *International Security*, Vol. 16, No. 1 (Summer 1991), pp. 149–150; and Richard Ullman, *Securing Europe* (Princeton, N.J.: Princeton University Press, 1991), p. 76.

25. For the core works, see Ashton B. Carter, William J. Perry, and John D. Steinbruner, *A New Concept of Cooperative Security*, Occasional Paper (Washington, D.C.: Brookings Institution, 1992); Janne E. Nolan, ed., *Global Engagement: Cooperation and Security in the 21st Century* (Washington, D.C.: Brookings Institution, 1994); Paul B. Stares and John D. Steinbruner, "Cooperative Security and the New Europe," in Stares, ed., *The New Germany and the New Europe* (Washington, D.C.: Brookings Institution, 1992), pp. 218–248. For a shorter exposition, see Randall Forsberg, "Creating a Cooperative Security System," in *After the Cold War: A Debate on Cooperative Security*, Institute for Defense and Disarmament Studies, Reprint, Cambridge, Mass., first published in *Boston Review*, Vol. 17, No. 6 (November/December 1992).

one for all." Cooperative security advocates do not rely on spontaneous power balancing because this is only likely when traditional vital interests are engaged. Instead, international institutions, particularly the United Nations, are to play a critical role in coordinating the deterrence and defeat of aggression. Regional institutions, particularly a transformed NATO, have an important role to play where international institutions are weak. Institutions respond to imminent threats, and deter all who would break the peace.

Previously, great powers could view small wars as unlikely threats to their national security. But the emergence of weapons of mass destruction means that any arms race or war can produce a world-class disaster.[26] The United States, and indeed the rest of the industrialized world, simply cannot live with these risks indefinitely. Nuclear weapons do not favor the status quo, except for the very small number of great powers who have them. Most states do not have the resources or organizational skills to deploy secure retaliatory forces. Most do not yet have, and many will not be able to acquire, nuclear weapons. The casualty-sensitivity of the democracies suggests that the risk of even a small nuclear attack might discourage them from coming to the assistance of a country in trouble. Aggressors are expected to be undemocratic, greedy, and casualty-insensitive; nuclear weapons favor them. Thus nuclear arms control, particularly non-proliferation, is at the heart of cooperative security.

Cooperative security subscribes to one premise that, for the most part, the other three strategies do not even consider. A high level of what one might term "strategic interdependence" is posited. Wars in one place are likely to spread; unsavory military practices employed in one war will be employed in other wars. The use of weapons of mass destruction will beget their use elsewhere; ethnic cleansing will beget more ethnic cleansing. Refugees fleeing the nationalist violence of one country will energize xenophobia in countries of refuge. The organization of a global information system helps to connect these events by providing strategic intelligence to good guys and bad guys alike; it connects them politically by providing images of one horror after another in the living rooms of the citizens of economically advanced democracies.[27] The result is a chain of logic that connects the security of the United

---

26. "Proliferation of destructive technology casts a shadow over future U.S. security in a way that cannot be directly addressed through superior force or readiness. Serious economic and environmental problems point to an inescapable interdependence of U.S. interests with the interests of other nations." Carter, Perry, and Steinbruner, *A New Concept of Cooperative Security*, p. 4.
27. Madeleine K. Albright, U.S. Permanent Representative to the United Nations, "Realism and Idealism in American Foreign Policy Today," *U.S. Department of State Dispatch*, Vol. 5, No. 26 (June 27, 1994), pp. 434–437, offers an explicit and comprehensive statement of these views.

States and its more traditional allies to a host of distant troubles. Thus, these distant troubles cannot be ignored.

ISSUES AND INSTRUMENTS

Cooperative security advocates believe that they now have more effective means to achieve their goals. The United States is presumed, based on the Desert Storm victory, to hold decisive military-technological superiority and thus to be able to wage speedy, low-casualty wars. In the past, advocates of collective security relied on world public opinion, and on economic sanctions. They understood that it is difficult to get self-interested states to support military intervention on the side of peace in distant places, so they stressed the impact of these less costly measures. Cooperative security advocates still like these mechanisms, but history has taught them to be skeptical that they will prove sufficient. Instead it is argued that real military action is cheaper than it once was.[28]

Advocates of cooperative security have added the arms control mechanisms developed in the last three decades to the traditional collective security repertoire. With enough arms control agreements, transparency, and confidence-and security-building measures (CSBMs), and enough intrusive verification, states around the world will be able to avoid conflicts arising from misperception or first-strike advantages. The offensive military capabilities that enable states to engage in aggression will thus be acquired by few countries. Peace-loving states will adopt defensive military postures and an international military division of labor that will provide only their combined forces with an offensive capability. The few "rogue states" left after all this arms control and institution-building can either be intimidated by the threat of high technology warfare or decisively defeated in short order.

A cooperative security strategy depends on international organizations to coordinate collective action. They are part of the complicated process of building sufficient credibility to convince all prospective aggressors that they will regularly be met with decisive countervailing power. The threat of great powers to intervene—even when they have no immediate interests at stake—must be made credible. A standing international organization with substantial domestic and international legitimacy is necessary to coordinate multilateral action and to create the expectation of regular, effective intervention for peace.

---

28. See Carter, Perry, and Steinbruner, *A New Concept of Cooperative Security*, pp. 24–30.

Its advocates stress that cooperative security is a work in progress.[29] Global cooperative security structures will not emerge fully developed. Indeed it is argued that they need not: existing "overlapping, mutually reinforcing arrangements" provide the foundation upon which cooperative security can be built. As three leading proponents have written, "military establishments around the world already are entangled in a large web of internationally sanctioned restraints on how they equip themselves and operate in peacetime. Cooperative security means making the effort to thicken and unify this web."[30] That, clearly, entails a long term project.

In at least one area of the world, the project is seen as already well under way. Europe has begun to practice cooperative security with a web of diplomatic, economic, and security arrangements, particularly the arms control, transparency, and CSBMs associated with the Organization for Security and Cooperation in Europe. The Clinton administration views NATO enlargement, in part, as an extension of the cooperative security project.[31] If Europe, even during the Cold War, could develop such arrangements, the proponents of cooperative security ask, can other regions not do the same now that the distractions of the Cold War are behind us?

Proliferation is a key issue for cooperative security advocates. They support very strong measures to prevent and reverse it.[32] They supported not only the indefinite extension of the Nuclear Non-Proliferation Treaty in 1995 but also the strengthening of its safeguards. The demonstration effect of any new proliferation is presumed to be great. It is therefore reasonable to oppose any new nuclear power beyond those declared nuclear weapons states in the original treaty. Moreover, the policy must be pursued equally versus friends, enemies, and neutrals. Israeli, Indian, and Ukrainian nuclear weapons are all

---

29. Ross, who is sympathetic to cooperative security, emphasizes this point.
30. Carter, Perry, and Steinbruner, *A New Concept of Cooperative Security,* pp. 8 and 9.
31. Strobe Talbott, "Why NATO Should Grow," *New York Review of Books,* Vol. 42, No. 13 (August 10, 1995), p. 28: "Enlargement of NATO would be a force for the rule of law both within Europe's new democracies and among them. . . . An expanded NATO is likely to extend the area in which conflicts like the one in the Balkans simply do not happen." The administration's case for expansion incorporates the logic of containment as well as that of cooperative security. As Talbot put it, "among the contingencies for which NATO must be prepared is that Russia will abandon democracy and return to the threatening patterns of international behavior that have sometimes characterized its history" (p. 29). See also Ronald Asmus, Richard Kugler, and Stephen Larrabee, "NATO Expansion: The Next Steps," *Survival,* Vol. 37, No. 1 (Spring 1995), p. 9; and the systematic critique offered by Michael E. Brown, "The Flawed Logic of NATO Expansion," *Survival,* Vol. 37, No. 1 (Spring 1995), pp. 38–39.
32. Commission on America and the New World, *Changing Our Ways: America and the New World* (Washington, D.C.: Carnegie Endowment for International Peace, 1992), pp. 73–75.

bad, regardless of the fact that the United States has no political conflict of interest with any of these countries. Proliferation must also be headed off for another reason: the more nuclear powers there are in the world, the more dangerous it will be for international organizations to act aggressively against miscreants, the less likely they will be to act, and the more likely it is that the entire cooperative security edifice will collapse.[33] War to prevent new nuclear powers from emerging would be reasonable in some circumstances.[34]

Regional conflicts among states are of critical interest to cooperative security advocates. Cross-border aggression has always been the most clear-cut problem; it is never acceptable. Conflicts within states emerge as a new, serious problem for a cooperative security strategy.[35] Historically, collective security tried to establish the conditions for peace among a small number of great powers and empires. Today we have many more states, and even more groups aspiring to statehood. Politically conscious groups often span the boundaries of several territorially defined states. Thus inter-group conflict may become inter-state conflict. Even when irredenta are not involved, civil wars may attract outside intervention by the greedy, and thus precipitate international wars. Finally, ethnic conflict tends to be ferocious. The brutal behavior portrayed on the television screens of the world creates a malign precedent.

Cooperative security advocates favor military action for humanitarian purposes.[36] But the connection between immediate humanitarian concerns and the task of building sufficient credibility to deter future aggressors is tenuous. Indeed, the goals may conflict, as often seemed the case in Bosnia-Herzegovina. In the first phase of that war, the United States and other democratic states could have supplied arms to the Bosnian Muslims with relative ease to help

---

33. Advocates seldom make this point explicitly, but a similar point is made by Carter, Perry, and Steinbruner in *A New Concept of Cooperative Security*, p. 51: "many countries that feel threatened by an intrusive reconnaissance strike capability they cannot match can aspire to chemical agents as a strategic counterweight."
34. "The Commission believes that the use of military force to prevent nuclear proliferation must be retained as an option of last resort." Commission on America and the New World, *Changing Our Ways*, p. 75.
35. See Gareth Evans, "Cooperative Security and Intrastate Conflict," *Foreign Policy*, No. 96 (Fall 1991), pp. 3–20. Comments by cooperative security advocates on the war in Yugoslavia reveal a strong desire for some cooperative security organization to intervene militarily. See Forsberg, "Creating a Cooperative Security System," p. 3; and Jonathan Dean, "Moving Toward a Less Violent World—Test Case, Europe," *Boston Review*, Vol. 17, No. 6 (November/December 1992), p. 7.
36. Commission on America and the New World, *Changing Our Ways*, p. 51: "The United States should be more actively engaged in strengthening the collective machinery to carry out humanitarian actions. In this way we can reduce the likelihood of having to choose between unilateral military intervention and standing idle in the face of human tragedy."

them fend off the military attacks of the Serbs. They might even have flown tactical air sorties to assist the Muslims. This would have made the point that aggression does not pay. But it is unlikely that UN humanitarian efforts would have survived such a policy. A large-scale intervention with several hundred thousand troops might have been necessary both to stop the Serbs and to sustain the UN humanitarian effort to care for those in need of the everyday necessities of life. Despite such difficulties, cooperative security advocates seem to want to pursue short-term humanitarianism and long-term political principle at the same time. This makes for demanding military operations.

FORCE STRUCTURE. What kind of U.S. force structure is required to support a cooperative security strategy? While cooperative security envisions the adoption of defensive military postures, "a small number of nations, including the United States, must maintain certain elements of their armed forces beyond that required for territorial defense and make those elements available to multinational forces when needed."[37] The U.S. contribution to this multinational force would emphasize the country's comparative advantage in aerospace power: the three elements of the reconnaissance strike complex—command, control, communications and intelligence; defense suppression; and precision-guided munitions—that were employed in Desert Storm.

Advocates have suggested that this force would be smaller than the "Bottom-Up Review" force advocated by the Clinton administration (see Table 2).[38] But their assessment focuses on means, while assuming that others will cooperate to the maximum extent of their ability—i.e., that they will maintain larger forces than they currently plan. Moreover, it ignores the necessity for a period

37. William J. Perry, "Military Action: When to Use It and How to Ensure Its Effectiveness," in Nolan, *Global Engagement*, p. 235.
38. See William W. Kaufmann and John Steinbruner, *Decisions for Defense* (Washington, D.C.: Brookings Institution, 1991), pp. 67–76, which offers a cooperative security force structure that would cost roughly $150 billion (1992 dollars, excluding Department of Energy expenses on nuclear weaponry) annually by the end of the century. Their recommended force structure is quite similar to Aspin's "Force A," Table 2. The authors seem to argue that the adequacy of such a force structure would depend on a series of prior diplomatic developments in the world that would, for all intents and purposes, put a functioning cooperative security regime in place. Jerome B. Wiesner, Philip Morrison, and Kosta Tsipis, "Ending Overkill," *Bulletin of the Atomic Scientists*, Vol. 49, No. 2 (March 1993), pp. 12–23, offer a force structure, costing $115 billion per year, which they seem to believe is consistent with a collective security strategy. Though small, the air and naval forces they recommend are quite capable; the Army they recommend, however, with a total active personnel strength of 180,000, would barely be adequate for a repetition of Operation Desert Shield/Desert Storm. It is difficult to see how it could support a collective security strategy. More recently, Michael O'Hanlon, *Defense Planning For the Late 1990s: Beyond the Desert Storm Framework* (Washington, D.C.: Brookings Institution, 1995), pp. 32–40, has proposed a force structure estimated to cost about $20 billion a year less than the Bottom-Up Review force.

of regular and consistent military action if there is to be any hope of building the international credibility necessary to affect the calculations of prospective aggressors everywhere.

A true cooperative security strategy could involve the United States in several simultaneous military actions. U.S. forces were recently engaged in Iraq and in Somalia simultaneously, while advocates clamored for a third U.S. military action in Bosnia. Haiti subsequently replaced Somalia on this list, even as the U.S. military role in Bosnia expanded. UN forces were deployed in several other places—arguably in insufficient numbers to accomplish their missions completely. The experiences in Desert Shield/Desert Storm and in the Somali relief operation suggest that U.S. leadership is often the key ingredient for substantial international cooperation.[39] It is not the subtle diplomacy of the United States that proves critical, but rather its military reputation, which depends on large, diverse, technologically sophisticated, and lushly supplied military forces capable of decisive operations. At least initially, the United States would have to provide disproportionate military power to launch a global cooperative security regime. A force structure in the range of the Clinton administration's "Bottom-Up Review" force and the "Base Force" (see Table 2) may be necessary to pursue a true cooperative security policy with a good chance of success.

CRITIQUE

Cooperative security is vulnerable to a range of criticisms. First, individual states are still expected to be able to rise above narrow conceptions of national interest in response to appeals for action on behalf of the collective good, and to engage in what will seem to them as armed altruism. In theory, some collective action problems associated with collective security[40] may be ameliorated by cooperative security. In particular, the combination of intensive arms control, military technological superiority, and U.S. leadership is meant to reduce substantially the costs of cooperation for any given member of the cooperative security regime. Nevertheless, there will still be defectors and free

---

39. Laying out the realist theoretical argument for why coalitions need leaders, and why leaders are defined by great power, is Josef Joffe, "Collective Security and the Future of Europe: Failed Dreams and Dead Ends," *Survival,* Vol. 34, No. 1 (Spring 1992), pp. 40–43.

40. See Richard K. Betts, "Systems for Peace or Causes of War? Collective Security, Arms Control, and the New Europe," *International Security,* Vol. 17, No. 1 (Summer 1992), pp. 5–43; Joffe, "Collective Security and the Future of Europe"; and John J. Mearsheimer, "The False Promise of International Institutions," *International Security,* Vol. 19, No. 3 (Winter 1994/95), pp. 5–49.

riders. Major power aggression would still be a problem for cooperative security, as it was for collective security, if some powers perceive the intrinsic stakes as small and the aggressor as far away and difficult to fight. It seems unlikely, for example, that the NATO allies would ever fight the People's Republic of China over Taiwan, even if the United States wanted to do so. States concerned about the possible competitions of the future will still ask if any given opportunity for current cooperation to achieve a common good, or oppose a common bad, changes their power position relative to all other potential challengers, including one another.

Second, the task of building sufficient general multilateral credibility to deter a series of new and different potential aggressors seems very difficult. Regular U.S. action to oppose the Soviet Union during the Cold War did not entirely dissuade that regime from new challenges. Since this was an iterative bipolar game, credibility should have accumulated, but that does not seem to have happened. Although U.S. credibility appears to have been quite high in Europe, where direct interests were great and deployed military power was strong, elsewhere Soviet behavior was often mischievous. It is quite likely, therefore, that a true cooperative security strategy would involve the UN, designated regional organizations, and effectively the United States, in a number of wars over many years if it is to have any hope of establishing the ability to deter the ambitious and reassure the fearful. This would, however, serve to further strain public support for a demanding strategy.

Third, democracies are problematical partners in a cooperative security project in a crucial respect: their publics must be persuaded to go to war. Since the publics in modern liberal democracies seem to be quite casualty-sensitive, the case for risking the lives of their troops in *distant* wars is inherently difficult to make. This is one reason why the decisive military superiority of a technologically dominant coalition of peace-loving states is a necessary condition for cooperative security to work. This in turn depends on the military power of the United States.

Fourth, cooperative security places a heavy burden on arms control. It is not clear that arms control can bear that burden. Nonproliferation efforts have met with mixed success. Verification and, especially, enforcement remain problematic. The open international economic system, which most cooperative security advocates strongly favor, inevitably accelerates the diffusion of the economic and technological underpinnings of military power. While arms control can increase the economic costs and political risks of engaging in proscribed activities, determined states will continue to acquire and employ military forces.

Thus the members of a cooperative security regime are likely to have to respond to aggression more often than the proponents of such a regime predict. Cooperative security must oversell the probability and magnitude of an international happy ending in order to elicit political support for an indeterminate initial period of high activism.

Primacy

Primacy, like selective engagement, is motivated by both power and peace. But the particular configuration of power is key: this strategy holds that only a preponderance of U.S. power ensures peace.[41] The pre–Cold War practice of aggregating power through coalitions and alliances, which underlies selective engagement, is viewed as insufficient. Peace is the result of an imbalance of power in which U.S. capabilities are sufficient, operating on their own, to cow all potential challengers and to comfort all coalition partners. It is not enough, consequently, to be *primus inter pares,* a comfortable position for selective engagement. Even the most clever Bismarckian orchestrator of the balance of power will ultimately fall short. One must be *primus solus.* Therefore, both world order and national security require that the United States maintain the primacy with which it emerged from the Cold War. The collapse of bipolarity cannot be permitted to allow the emergence of multipolarity; unipolarity is best. Primacy would have been the strategy of a Dole administration.

Primacy is most concerned with the trajectories of present and possible future great powers. As with selective engagement, Russia, China, Japan, and the most significant members of the European Union (essentially Germany, France, and Britain), matter most. War among the great powers poses the greatest threat to U.S. security for advocates of primacy as well as those of selective engagement. But primacy goes beyond the logic of selective engagement and its focus on managing relations among present and potential future great powers. Advocates of primacy view the rise of a peer competitor from the midst of the great powers to offer the greatest threat to international order and thus the greatest risk of war. The objective for primacy, therefore, is not merely to preserve peace among the great powers, but to preserve U.S. supremacy by politically, economically, and militarily outdistancing any global challenger.

---

41. This is the maximal realism of hegemonic stability theory. See Robert Gilpin, *War and Change in World Politics* (Cambridge, U.K.: Cambridge University Press, 1981).

The Bush administration's draft Defense Planning Guidance (DPG), leaked to the press in March of 1992, provides the most fully developed blueprint for precluding the rise of such a peer competitor. The DPG is the high-level strategic statement that launches, and in theory governs, the Pentagon's annual internal defense budget preparation process. Subsequent published commentary by former Secretary of Defense Richard Cheney suggests that the Bush administration broadly subscribed to the principles suggested by the leaked passages.[42] The authors of the draft DPG were unyielding in their insistence that the United States maintain its status as the world's sole superpower:

Our first objective is to prevent the reemergence of a new rival, either on the territory of the former Soviet Union or elsewhere, that poses a threat on the order of that posed formerly by the Soviet Union. This is a dominant consideration . . . and requires that we endeavor to prevent any hostile power from dominating a region whose resources would, under consolidated control, be sufficient to generate global power. . . . Our strategy must now refocus on precluding the emergence of any potential future global competitor.[43]

Those parts of the world identified as most likely to harbor potential peer competitors were Western Europe, East Asia, the territories of the former Soviet Union, and Southwest Asia.

Strategic planners in the Department of Defense and more recent advocates argue that others already believe, or can be led to believe, that the United States is a benign hegemon. Thus the project is expected to meet with global support rather than opposition.[44] Other states will not balance against the United States. Thus:

the U.S. must show the leadership necessary to establish and protect a new order that holds the promise of convincing potential competitors that they need not aspire to a greater role or pursue a more aggressive posture to protect their legitimate interests. . . . In the non-defense areas, we must account sufficiently for the interests of the advanced industrial nations to discourage them from

---

42. See Dick Cheney, "Active Leadership? You Better Believe It," *New York Times,* March 15, 1992, Section 4, p. 17. The draft DPG is placed in the larger contexts of the Bush administration's national security policy and strategy, and a discussion of primacy in U.S. policy and strategy by David Callahan, *Between Two Worlds: Realism, Idealism, and American Foreign Policy After the Cold War* (New York: HarperCollins, 1994).
43. "Excerpts from Pentagon's Plan: 'Prevent the Emergence of a New Rival'," *New York Times,* March 8, 1992, p. 14.
44. The notion that U.S. hegemony is benevolent and perceived as such by others is evident also in William Kristol and Robert Kagan, "Toward a Neo-Reaganite Foreign Policy," *Foreign Affairs,* Vol. 75, No. 4 (July/August 1996), pp. 18–32; and Joshua Muravchik, *The Imperative of American Leadership: A Challenge to Neo-Isolationism* (Washington, D.C.: AEI Press, 1996).

challenging our leadership or seeking to overturn the established political and economic order. . . . We will retain the pre-eminent responsibility for addressing selectively those wrongs which threaten not only our interests, but those of our allies or friends, or which could seriously unsettle international relations.[45]

Present and aspiring major powers are to be persuaded, it seems, that they can rest easy, and need not bother investing in the political, economic, and military means they might otherwise require to safeguard their interests. Indeed, any assertion of strategic independence by the likes of Germany and Japan would only erode the global and regional stability sought by all.[46]

In addition to maintaining U.S. primacy by reassuring others of the purity of its intentions, the draft DPG envisioned the United States seeking to prevent the rise of challengers by promoting international law, democracy, and free-market economies, and precluding the emergence of regional hegemons. It is important to note that though primacy focuses on the maintenance of overwhelming U.S. power and influence, it remains strongly committed to liberal principles. It is simply more judicious about the commitment of U.S. military power to particular liberal projects than is the cooperative security strategy. Support for political and economic transformation are seen as the best way to ensure that Russia will not revert to the authoritarian, expansionist habits of old, though the United States should hedge against the failure of such reform. In Europe, the United States would work against any erosion of NATO's preeminent role in European security and the development of any security arrangements that would undermine the role of NATO, and therefore the role of the United States, in European security affairs. The countries of East and Central Europe would be integrated into the political, economic, and even security institutions of Western Europe. In East Asia, the United States would maintain a military presence sufficient to ensure regional stability and prevent the emergence of a power vacuum or a regional hegemon. The same approach applied to the Middle East and Southwest Asia, where the United States intended to remain the preeminent extraregional power. The United States would also endeavor to discourage India's hegemonic ambitions in South Asia. The regional dimension of the strategy outlined in the draft DPG is thus

---

45. "Excerpts from Pentagon's Plan: 'Prevent the Emergence of a New Rival'."
46. The Assistant Under Secretary of Defense for Policy Planning when the draft DPG was prepared, Zalmay Khalilzad, has suggested that "the United States would not want Germany and Japan to be able to conduct expeditionary wars." Khalilzad, "Losing the Moment? The United States and the World After the Cold War," *Washington Quarterly*, Vol. 18, No. 2 (Spring 1995), p. 105.

consistent with the global dimension: the aspirations of regional as well as global hegemons are to be thwarted.

Proponents of primacy are more than a little upbeat about the post–Cold War international position of the United States. Even though all too few Americans recognize their good fortune, "they have never had it so good."[47] In this best of all possible worlds, the United States today is the only world superpower. It "enjoys strategic and ideological predominance" and exercises hegemonic influence and authority.[48] The U.S share of gross world product is considered to be more than sufficient to sustain primacy. According to primacy advocates, this is in line with its share at the outset of World War II, in which the United States led a global war and simultaneously enjoyed the highest standard of living in the world.[49] Moreover, looking only at GDP masks the extent of U.S. dominance. The United States has more hard-to-measure "soft power"—domination of the news media, mass culture, computers, and international communications—than any other nation.[50] And the United States is the master of the most advanced military technologies, especially intelligence and command and control capabilities and precision-guided munitions. This technological advantage renders traditional military organizations vastly less capable against the United States than traditional military analysis would suggest. (Primacy and cooperative security share this premise.) Advocates of primacy, like those of selective engagement, do recognize that U.S. resources are limited, but they contend that the United States is a wealthy country that all too often acts as if it were poor.[51] The problem is not a lack of resources, but a lack of political will. Advocates of primacy are quite optimistic, however, that the U.S. public can be induced to sacrifice for this project.[52]

---

47. Kristol and Kagan, "Toward a Neo-Reaganite Foreign Policy," p. 22.
48. Ibid., p. 20.
49. Muravchik, *The Imperative of American Leadership*, pp. 32–33.
50. Kristol and Kagan, "Toward a Neo-Reaganite Foreign Policy," p. 21. The term "soft power" is associated with Joseph Nye, Dean of the Kennedy School of Government and former Assistant Secretary of Defense for International Security Affairs. He and former Vice Chairman of the Joint Chiefs of Staff William A. Owens develop the notion of U.S. dominance in these new tools of power in Nye and Owens, "America's Information Edge," *Foreign Affairs*, Vol. 75, No. 2 (March/April 1996), pp. 20–36.
51. According to Muravchik, *The Imperative of American Leadership*, p. 36: "We can afford whatever foreign policy we need or choose. We are the richest country in the world, the richest country the world has ever known. And we are richer today than we have ever been before. We command not fewer but more resources than ever." He calls for spending 5 percent of GDP on what he calls foreign policy ("defense, foreign aid, and everything else"); p. 44.
52. Kristol and Kagan, "Toward a Neo-Reaganite Foreign Policy," pp. 26–27, 30–32; and Muravchik, *The Imperative of American Leadership*, pp. 36–50. Muravchik argues both that the United States allocates too few resources to the military and to foreign aid to support a strategy of primacy

ISSUES AND INSTRUMENTS

Certainly the most serious threat to U.S. primacy would be an across-the-board political, economic, and military challenger. Yet even a power that rivaled the United States in only one or two of these three dimensions of national power could erode U.S. preponderance. That the Soviet Union during the Cold War was unable to issue a credible challenge in the economic realm, as well as the political and military, did little to allay U.S. fears. It is generally the one-dimensional challenge that is seen as providing the near-term threat to continued U.S. primacy.[53] Some fear a resurgence of a militarily capable Russia. Others argue that the United States is most vulnerable in the economic realm. For a time, Japan was viewed as the main contender. Others worry about the rise of China, fearing an imminent, mutually reinforcing growth of its economic and military power.

The debate on NATO enlargement has shown that some still view Russia as strong and dangerous. Though smaller and weaker than its Soviet predecessor, it is presumed to be on the move again.[54] The remedy is a revived policy of containment. This "new containment," however, is little more than a stalking horse for primacy. Whether targeted at Russia or China, the new containment, like the old containment, identifies a threat that provides the rationale for remaining heavily involved in Eurasia and for maintaining the political, economic, and especially military capabilities needed to pursue an intense global strategic competition. One advocate of primacy who wants the United States "to be the global hegemon of the regional hegemons, the boss of all the bosses" has explicitly called for the "potential" or "latent" containment of both Russia and China, while others prefer a more active version.[55]

---

and that it requires a balanced budget. He suggests that to remedy these deficiencies the U.S. should solve the problem of rising medical costs and social security solvency, and add revenues, and in just two pages, he explains how (pp. 42–43).

53. As the Cold War drew to a close, some saw an economic challenge from Japan as the principal threat to U.S. primacy. See, e.g., Samuel P. Huntington, "America's Changing Strategic Interests," *Survival*, Vol. 33, No. 1 (January/February 1991), p. 10; Huntington, "The Economic Renewal of America," *National Interest*, No. 27, Spring 1992, p. 15; and Huntington, "Why International Primacy Matters," *International Security*, Vol. 17, No. 4 (Spring 1993), pp. 71–81. Huntington's concern about U.S. economic strength and how it might be preserved and strengthened are echoed in Zalmay Khalilzad, "Losing the Moment?" pp. 103–104.

54. Zbigniew Brzezinski, "The Premature Partnership," *Foreign Affairs*, Vol. 73, No. 2 (March/April 1994), p. 76. Oddly, though he presents many of the same arguments for NATO expansion in a subsequent article, he is somewhat less alarmist there about the extent of the current danger emanating from Russia. See Zbigniew Brzezinski, "A Plan for Europe," *Foreign Affairs*, Vol. 74, No. 1 (January/February 1995), p. 34.

55. James Kurth, "America's Grand Strategy: A Pattern of History," *National Interest*, No. 43 (Spring 1996), pp. 3–19; the quotation is from p. 19.

Calls for containing Russia are most prominently identified with Zbigniew Brzezinski and Henry Kissinger, and have surfaced with the greatest clarity in the debate on whether NATO should formally expand and offer membership and protection to former Eastern European members of the Warsaw Pact. Both fear the seductive effect of a "security vacuum" in Eastern (newly re-christened "Central") Europe. "A Russia facing a divided Europe would find the temptation to fill the vacuum irresistible."[56] Observers should not be lulled by the relative decline in capability precipitated by the dissolution of the Soviet Union, the collapse of the Soviet economy, and the deterioration of the Soviet (now Russian) military. Containment advocates cite a new Russian assertiveness, demonstrated in diplomatic, military, and economic interventions large and small around its periphery.[57] Russia brings three dangerous qualities to the table: it possesses tremendous inherent strategic reach, considerable material reserves; and the largest single homogeneous ethnic-cultural population in Europe. Brzezinski asserts that Russian culture somehow contains within it the seeds of expansion.[58] (One notes here echoes of Cold War logic, which viewed Communism as inherently aggressive.)

Because the new containment is so closely tied to NATO expansion, advocates say little about other regions of the world. It seems, however, that NATO expansion is part of a much more ambitious policy. Brzezinski adds a more forward U.S. policy around the Russian periphery.[59] In some recent work, he describes an "oblong of maximum danger," which extends from the Adriatic to the border of the Chinese province of Sinkiang and from the Persian Gulf to the Russian-Kazahk frontier.[60] Here he expects a stew of ethnic and nationalist conflict and proliferation of weapons of mass destruction—a "whirlpool of violence"—although the precise nature of U.S. interests here is not well developed. Similarly, Kissinger alludes to the role of a revived NATO in the resolution of the crises that will surely attend the adjustment of Russia, China,

56. Henry Kissinger, "Expand NATO Now," *Washington Post,* December 19, 1994.
57. See Brzezinski, "The Premature Partnership," pp. 72–73. A disturbing account of Russian actions is found in Fiona Hill and Pamela Jewett, *Back in the USSR: Russia's Intervention in the Internal Affairs of the Former Soviet Republics and the Implications of United States Policy Toward Russia,* Strengthening Democratic Institutions Project (Cambridge, Mass.: John F. Kennedy School of Government, Harvard University, January 1994).
58. Brzezinski, "The Premature Partnership," pp. 71–75, calls this "the imperial impulse." See also Brzezinski, *Out of Control: Global Turmoil on the Eve of the Twenty-First Century* (New York: Collier, 1993), pp. 173–181.
59. Brzezinski, "The Premature Partnership," pp. 79–82. He urges "political assurances for Ukraine's independence and territorial integrity"; "a more visible American show of interest in the independence of the Central Asian states, as well as of the three states in the Caucasus"; and "some quiet American-Chinese political consultations regarding the area."
60. Brzezinski, *Out of Control,* pp. 163–166.

and Japan to the changed circumstances of the post–Cold War world; Kissinger has also alluded to a NATO role in Korea, Indonesia, Brazil, and India.[61]

Two elements in the case for NATO expansion suggest that its advocates perceive the Russian threat as less imminent than they often imply. First, they think that Russia's fears of an expanded NATO can be rather easily assuaged. Second, they see the Russian military threat as quite manageable. Advocates of NATO expansion usually advocate a simultaneous diplomatic approach to Russia in the form of some sort of "security treaty."[62] They concede that NATO should not move large forces forward onto the territory of new members.[63] The combination of a formal diplomatic act of reassurance and military restraint is expected to ameliorate the possibility that the eastward march of a mighty and formerly adversarial military coalition could be perceived by Russia to pose a threat. These expectations seem inconsistent with the image of a looming Russian threat.

Similarly, advocates of NATO expansion are relaxed about its costs because they are relaxed about the current Russian military threat. As of late 1996, NATO had yet to release a public estimate of the costs of expansion.[64] One general statement of the threat has been offered by a team of political and military analysts from the Rand Corporation:

One should avoid assuming worst-case scenarios. Even a re-armed Russia would not be the military Leviathan the Soviet Union once was. It would have an imposing military force, but probably not a great deal more than that of Iran, Iraq, or North Korea—in short, a major regional contingency–sized threat. Defending against such a threat would be very different than against the theater-wide challenge posed by the Warsaw Pact during the Cold War.[65]

Thus, there is no imminent or even remote military threat to these Eastern European countries that NATO cannot deal with rather comfortably with its current capabilities.

Given the politically and militarily relaxed image of the Russian threat expressed by NATO expansion advocates, one wonders what is actually driv-

---

61. Kissinger, "Expand NATO Now."
62. Brzezinski, "Premature Partnership," pp. 81–82; Kissinger, "Expand NATO Now."
63. Ibid.; and Zbigniew Brzezinski, "A Bigger—and Safer—Europe," *New York Times*, December 1, 1993, p. A23.
64. The Congressional Budget Office has estimated that NATO expansion would cost from $61 billion to $125 billion over the years 1996–2010. See Congressional Budget Office, CBO Papers, "The Costs of Expanding the NATO Alliance" (Washington, D.C.: Congressional Budget Office, March 1996).
65. Asmus, Kugler, and Larrabee, "NATO Expansion," p. 32.

ing them. In our judgment, it is first the desire to anchor the United States in a diplomatic enterprise that will preserve and widen its involvement in European and international affairs, simply because this is viewed as an unalloyed good in its own right. Second, it is to forestall even a hint of an independent German foreign policy in the east.[66] A revived containment policy in Europe may be nothing more than the adaptation of a politically familiar vehicle to the task of preserving U.S. primacy.

Another candidate for future peer competitor, and therefore long-term threat, is China.[67] Current economic trends in that country suggest that it could become a formidable economic competitor in the first quarter of the next century. Its new economic capability could easily be translated into not only regional but also perhaps global military might.[68] The admission of Vietnam into ASEAN (the Association of Southeast Asian Nations) can be read in part as reflecting regional concerns about China's intentions. China's rapid economic growth, improving military capabilities, stridency on Taiwan, and interest in the South China Sea have led to the suggestion that it would be prudent to hedge against the failure of engagement with China by means of a strategy of "hidden containment." Such a strategy would include maintaining U.S. military presence in the region, establishing a robust diplomatic relationship with Vietnam, and perhaps even reviving something along the lines of SEATO.[69] According to *The Economist*, containment "should mean recognizing that China is a destabilizing force and impressing upon it the need to forswear force in trying to settle its grievances."[70]

Advocates of primacy share with the new isolationists and selective engagers a healthy skepticism of international organizations.[71] International organizations have little if any power and therefore can do little to maintain or, particu-

---

66. Ronald Asmus, Richard Kugler, and Stephen Larrabee, "Building a New NATO," *Foreign Affairs*, Vol. 72, No. 4 (September/October 1993), p. 34: "While Germany remains pre-occupied with the staggering challenge of the political and economic reconstruction of its Eastern half, the need to stabilize its eastern flank is Bonn's number one security concern." See also Brzezinski, "A Plan for Europe," p. 42: "Most important, a united and powerful Germany can be more firmly anchored within this larger Europe if the European security system fully coincides with America's."
67. Khalilzad, an ardent proponent of primacy, has written that China "is the most likely candidate for global rival." Zalmay Khalilzad, *From Containment to Global Leadership? America and the World After the Cold War* (Santa Monica, Calif.: RAND, 1995), p. 30.
68. Karen Elliott House, "The Second Cold War," *Wall Street Journal*, February 17, 1994. She alludes to "the looming threat of a militarizing, autocratic China" and observes that "a resurgent China flexes its muscles at increasingly fearful neighbors."
69. Thomas L. Friedman, "Dust Off the SEATO Charter," *New York Times*, June 28, 1995, p. A19.
70. "Containing China," *Economist*, July 29, 1995, pp. 11 and 12.
71. See, for instance, Muravchik, *The Imperative of American Leadership*, pp. 71–82.

larly, restore peace. Yet international organizations should not be entirely rejected because of fears that they may draw the United States into conflicts or concerns that they cannot credibly deter aggression. Even a hegemonic power will, from time to time, find it useful to exploit the diplomatic cover provided by international organizations. If the facade of multilateralism renders the rule of an extraordinary power more palatable to ordinary powers, as it did during the Gulf War, international organizations are a strategic asset.

Proliferation is as much a concern for primacy as it is for cooperative security.[72] The threat to U.S. interests posed by the proliferation of nuclear and other weapons of mass destruction and their means of delivery was highlighted in the draft DPG. Proliferation is a problem because it undermines U.S. freedom of action by increasing the costs and risks of U.S. military interventions around the world. Because they serve to perpetuate a U.S. military advantage, current nonproliferation efforts should be continued. But while prevention is a useful first line of defense in combating proliferation, by itself it is inadequate to the task. The United States must also be able to deter and defend against the use of nuclear, biological, or chemical weapons by present and future powers which might develop such capabilities.

Proponents of primacy view regional conflict, ethnic conflict, and humanitarian intervention in much the same light as do the advocates of selective engagement. Regional conflict matters most when it impinges on major power relations and the rise of potential peer competitors and regional hegemons. Outside of the Persian Gulf, most conflicts in what was once referred to as the Third World will be of little concern. Much the same can be said for ethnic conflict, however reprehensible it may be, and the need for U.S. humanitarian intervention.[73] There is no obvious security rationale, under primacy, for humanitarian military operations, though some operations (such as Bosnia) may offer opportunities to demonstrate and assert U.S. power and leadership.

FORCE STRUCTURE. The forces needed to support a grand strategy of primacy should inspire a sense of *déjà vu*. A nearly Cold War–size force, in particular the Bush administration's "Base Force," would do just fine (see Table 2). The draft DPG was intended to provide the classified rationale for a 1.62 million

---

72. Charles Krauthammer, "The Unipolar Moment," *Foreign Affairs*, Vol. 70, No. 1 (1991), pp. 31–32. In previous versions of this essay we classified Krauthammer as a "cooperative security" advocate, but his emphasis on the dominant role of the U.S. warrants his inclusion here.

73. At least one advocate of primacy, however, sees the United States as having been, from the start, insufficiently active in Bosnia. See Muravchik, *The Imperative of American Leadership*, pp. 85–131.

person Base Force. General Colin Powell apparently saw this force as essential if U.S. primacy was to be preserved.[74] Two advocates of primacy recently called for increasing defense spending by as much as $80 billion above current levels, to roughly the level required to support the "Base Force." They propose that the adequacy of U.S. military forces be measured against a "two- (or three-, or four-) power standard," analogous to Britain's two-power standard of old, in which the Royal Navy was meant to be superior to the two next strongest navies in the world combined. This would serve to perpetuate the current disparity in military capabilities between the United States and other powers.[75] Presumably, the disparity to be maintained is qualitative rather than quantitative.

Military modernization is a high priority for the advocates of primacy. Indeed, if the objective is actually to deter any state from considering a challenge to U.S. preeminence, then it is logical for the United States military to pursue a level of qualitative superiority over potential challengers that would discourage them from entering the competition. That requires higher levels of research and development and procurement funding. The force must also be capable of what the Bush administration termed reconstitution: the ability to expand U.S. military capabilities in order to deter, and if necessary respond to, the rise of a global challenger. Thus the level of defense spending required to support a grand strategy of primacy would likely be greater in the future than it would be now, as a consequence of both modernization and expansion.

American military preeminence should ensure that U.S. forces could be used at will, but would seldom have to be, since threats to U.S. interests would be deterred by overwhelming military capabilities. Advocates of primacy, perhaps in an effort to reassure the rest of the world, have counseled that the United States use force sparingly. They advise against the use of military force on behalf of purely economic interests, or to promote American values, reverse setbacks to democracy, support the United Nations, or resolve civil wars. Protracted military involvement in non-critical regions is to be avoided. Because world order and stability are to be maintained, however, the United

---

74. Callahan, *Between Two Worlds*, p. 135.

75. Kristol and Kagan, "Toward a Neo-Reaganite Foreign Policy," p. 26. Similarly, Muravchik, *The Imperative of American Leadership*, p. 138, calls for defense spending that would be "somewhere around 4 percent of GDP." Khalilzad, "Losing the Moment," p. 102, offers a less ambiguous, and less demanding, multipower standard than do Kristol and Kagan. He proposes that U.S. forces be able to defeat simultaneously "the *two* next most powerful military forces in the world that are not allied with the United States."

States is to look favorably on the use of force to resist aggression.[76] Despite the lip service given to restraint, this self-appointed mission could involve a lot of fighting.

CRITIQUE

One of the foremost advocates of primacy has argued that "it matters which state exercises the most power in the international system"; that U.S. primacy is to be preferred to that of another power and is superior to a world in which no one is able to exercise primacy (the balance-of-power world implicitly embraced by selective engagement); and that primacy enables a state to achieve its objectives without resorting to war.[77] However, although primacy may offer many benefits for the United States and even for the world, the quest for primacy is likely to prove futile for five reasons.

First, the diffusion of economic and technological capabilities—precipitated in part by the open international economic system that the United States supports, in part by the spread of literacy, and in part by the embrace of market economics—suggests that other countries will develop the foundations to compete in international politics. New great powers will rise in the future. Indeed, though there is no recognized rule of thumb that specifies the share of gross world product a state must command in order to bid for hegemony, it seems peculiar to suggest that the situation today is not much different from the end of World War II, when an unbombed United States produced 40 percent of gross world product.[78]

Second, contrary to the expectations of primacy advocates, it is likely that some states will balance against the United States. They will not wish to remain in a permanent position of military inferiority, just as the United States would struggle to reverse the position if it were imposed even by a benevolent state. Primacy underestimates the power of nationalism. Some states, simply out of

---

76. On these issues see Khalilzad, "Losing the Moment?" pp. 104–105; and Muravchik, *The Imperative of American Leadership*, pp. 152–170.

77. Huntington, "Why International Primacy Matters," p. 70. Huntington more specifically argues that "power enables an actor to shape his environment so as to reflect his interests. In particular it enables a state to protect its security and prevent, deflect, or defeat threats to that security. It also enables a state to promote its values among other peoples and to shape the international environment so as to reflect its values"; pp. 69–70.

78. Muravchik, *The Imperative of American Leadership*, p. 32: "America is even more powerful today than it was in the immediate aftermath of World War II, although that moment is cited by many heralds of American decline as the apogee of American power."

national pride, may not accept U.S. leadership. States coalesce against hegemons rather than rally around them. Primacy is therefore a virtual invitation to struggle.

Third, American insistence on hegemonic leadership can engender resistance that may undermine the long-term effectiveness of any multilateral mechanisms that the United States may wish to exploit should challengers actually emerge. If a rising power such as China cannot be accommodated, as Britain accommodated the rise of the United States, the collective defense mechanisms of selective engagement or the collective security component of cooperative security would ensure that the United States need not alone bear the burden of taking on those who would undermine international order and stability: primacy may make this remedy unavailable.

Fourth, primacy carries the logical implication that the United States should be willing to wage preventive war. For now, such discussions focus on depriving "rogue" states of their nascent capabilities to assemble weapons of mass destruction. However difficult this may be, it is easy compared to the problem of restraining larger states. Will U.S. domestic politics permit a preventive war to forestall the rise of a challenger if other measures have proven insufficient? How will other major powers react to preventive war?

Fifth, the pursuit of primacy poses the constant risk of imperial overstretch. Primacy is inherently open-ended. A little bit more power will always seem better. Selective engagement is vulnerable to this temptation; primacy is even more so. Attempting to sustain an image of such overwhelming power that others will not even think of making the effort to match U.S. capabilities, or challenge U.S. leadership, seems a good recipe for draining the national treasury. Primacy may be affordable today, but it is less likely to be had on the cheap in the future. Ultimately, primacy is probably unsustainable and self-defeating. Primacy is little more than a rationale for the continued pursuit of Cold War policy and strategy in the absence of an enemy.[79]

---

79. See Christopher Layne and Benjamin Schwarz, "American Hegemony—Without an Enemy," *Foreign Policy,* No. 92 (Fall 1993), pp. 5–23; and Benjamin Schwarz, "Why America Thinks It Has to Run the World," *Atlantic Monthly,* June 1996, pp. 92–102. Layne and Schwarz draw heavily on Melvyn P. Leffler, *A Preponderance of Power: National Security, the Truman Administration, and the Cold War* (Stanford, Calif.: Stanford University Press, 1992). More extended critiques of primacy are provided by Callahan, *Between Two Worlds;* Robert Jervis, "International Primacy: Is the Game Worth the Candle?" *International Security,* Vol. 17, No. 4 (Spring 1993), pp. 52–67; Layne, "The Unipolar Illusion"; and Nordlinger, *Isolationism Reconfigured,* pp. 134–141.

The Clinton Administration's Grand Strategy: Selective (but Cooperative) Primacy

The Clinton administration came to office strongly inclined to pursue a cooperative security policy. Several of its senior national security officials were identified with the development of cooperative security ideas before the 1992 election.[80] The international and domestic constraints that the administration has encountered in its efforts to execute the strategy have forced both real and rhetorical compromises.

A National Security Strategy of Engagement and Enlargement (February 1996), the most complete statement of the administration's grand strategy vision, prominently contains within it the language of cooperative security and selective engagement, plus a dash of primacy.[81] The document reveals a curiously dialectical quality, alternating between cooperative security rhetoric and selective engagement rhetoric. The administration has adopted an avowedly internationalist posture founded on a broad conception of national interests. The phrase "engagement and enlargement" conveys both the mode and the purpose, or vision, of the strategy: the United States must be engaged in the world to enlarge the community of democratic free-market countries. Neo-isolationism is explicitly rejected. The repeated calls for U.S. leadership may be interpreted as a bow in the direction of primacy, as is the stress on U.S. unilateral military capabilities.[82]

The document promotes, on the one hand, "cooperative security measures." On the other hand, it acknowledges "limits to America's involvement in the world—limits imposed by careful evaluation of our fundamental interests and frank assessment of the costs and benefits of possible actions," and notes that

---

80. Prominent members of the administration who were associated with the theoretical development of cooperative security ideas include Ashton Carter, Morton Halperin, Catherine Kelleher, and William Perry; see works cited in footnote 25. John Deutsch participated in the development of a similar approach to U.S. foreign policy; Commission on America and the New World, *Changing Our Ways*.

81. *A National Security Strategy of Engagement and Enlargement*. Since the adminstration's presentation of its strategy has been more consistent than its actions, we focus here solely on the third version of this Clinton White House document (February 1996).

82. U.S. leadership appears to be necessary in every class of international problem; the word "leadership" appears four times on p. 2 alone. See *A National Security Strategy of Engagement and Enlargement*, p. 2. Military requirements are discussed on p. 14, where the language of primacy also emerges: "A strategy for deterring and defeating aggression in more than one theater ensures we maintain the flexibility to meet unknown future threats, while our continued engagement represented by that strategy helps *preclude* such threats from developing in the first place" (emphasis added).

"we cannot become involved in every problem." The array of transnational threats and challenges confronting the post–Cold War world "demand cooperative, multilateral solutions." Arms control is unequivocally embraced as "an integral part of our national security strategy" and seen as becoming increasingly multilateral. But the country's force structure must enable the United States to deal with threats not just multilaterally but unilaterally. "Our leadership must stress preventive diplomacy . . . in order to help resolve problems, reduce tensions and defuse conflicts before they become crises," yet "our engagement must be selective, focusing on the challenges that are most important [to] our own interests and focusing our resources where we can make the most difference."[83]

While the document issues calls for strengthening the United Nations, and for the United States to be prepared to participate in a wide variety of multilateral peace operations, that participation is nevertheless subject to a restrictive set of conditions that, if taken at face value, would ensure that the United States is seldom actually engaged in such operations. Economic multilateralism too is championed, but a self-regarding emphasis on "enhancing American competitiveness," which might be expected of selective engagement or primacy, is present as well.[84] Democracy must be promoted, but a selective approach prevails: some parts of the world and some countries, particularly the states of the former Soviet Union and Eastern and Central Europe, matter more than others. The United States will intervene in the morass of ethnic and other intra-state conflicts only if there is an exit strategy. Humanitarian interventions too will occur under the strategy, but only under "certain conditions."[85] More generally, decisions on whether, when, and how to use military force are subject to stringent guidelines that, if consistently adhered to, ensure that it will be used quite selectively. The administration's highest-priority regions—the two ends of Eurasia—are the same as those of selective engagement and primacy.

The Clinton administration has been forced to water down a commitment to cooperative security because its purposes proved too grand and its premises faulty; the U.S. power necessary to pursue the strategy proved greater than expected. The liberal internationalist rhetoric that accompanies cooperative security generates a long agenda and great expectations for action. But to succeed without the commitment of substantial U.S. power, both international

---

83. Ibid., pp. 3, 9–12, 21.
84. Ibid., p. 27.
85. Ibid., p. 18.

and multilateral institutions need to be strong and cohesive. And, more generally, very extensive international cooperation would be required. Both assumptions were flawed.

The UN remains a weak institution. Though it has been remarkably busy at peacekeeping over the last five or six years, it has proven ineffectual wherever the local parties have been even moderately resistant. Regional institutions did not do much better: the European Union and to a lesser extent the Organization for Security and Cooperation in Europe made attempts to help manage the dissolution of Yugoslavia, but they were unable to produce any results. The UN was able to organize some humanitarian relief in Yugoslavia, but was unable to bring about a settlement, or even to ameliorate the brutality of the fighting. Moreover, all three of these institutions contained ample numbers of democratic, peace-loving states. The EU is made up entirely of such states. Democracies may not fight one another, but this does not mean that they will always cooperate to settle disputes at the margins of traditional national interests.

The Clinton administration discovered that although international institutions are weak, the forces of U.S. domestic politics are not particularly supportive of strengthening them. The rhetoric of U.S. "leadership" that both the Democrats and the Republicans have adopted in their foreign policy statements is as much an expression of what the U.S. public seems to be against in international affairs as what it is for. It is against giving up much U.S. autonomy. As several observers have noted, the freshmen Republicans elected in 1994 are not so much isolationist as "unilateralist."[86] This means that the United States is in no position to strengthen weak international institutions. The only multilateral organization that is loved across the U.S. political spectrum seems to be NATO, which is why it is carrying so much U.S. foreign policy weight.

The Clinton administration also discovered that international cooperation is not so easy to arrange. Even the good guys can conceptualize their national interests in opposition to one another. Three conflicts with liberal democratic allies have surfaced during the Clinton administration. While all of these conflicts cannot be attributed to cooperative security projects, they nevertheless illustrate the broader problem: democracies can be "uncooperative." First, the

---

86. Dick Kirschten, "Mixed Signals," *National Journal,* May 27, 1995, pp. 1274–1277; see also Robert Greenberger, "Dateline Capitol Hill: The New Majority's Foreign Policy," *Foreign Policy,* No. 101 (Winter 1995–96), pp. 159–169.

Clinton administration itself pursued a strangely "non-cooperative" economic policy with the Japanese for most of 1993–96. This caused many in Asia to wonder if the United States was abandoning its commitment to a multilateral trading system.[87] Second, the United States vehemently disagreed with the policy pursued in Bosnia by Britain and France. U.S. policymakers believed that there was some way to produce a unified, pluralist, democratic Bosnia-Herzegovina. The British and French believed that once the war got going, some variant of a partition solution was the right answer. Privately, both British and U.S. officials admit that differences over Bosnia brought U.S.-British relations to their lowest point since the 1956 Suez crisis. In the end, the United States and the allies compromised on a Bosnia settlement: the United States agreed to commit troops to support an effort to achieve a Bosnia settlement more to its liking, while the allies agreed to support such a settlement so long as it included a very high level of autonomy for the three communities of Bosnia. Finally, in August 1996 the United States initiated a dispute with its allies and trading partners over their economic relations with countries that the United States intended to sanction economically. The U.S. proposed unilaterally to punish the citizens of countries who do business with Cuba, Iran, and Libya. While in the latter two cases the allies may broadly agree with the anti-terrorism principles that motivate U.S. actions, they do not consider these actions to be commensurate with their own national interests. More importantly, they recoil from what they perceive as the arrogance of U.S. policy.

If friends and allies have their own interpretations of U.S. actions, "rivals" are even more likely to be suspicious, and less likely to prove cooperative. Though the Clinton administration has gone to great lengths to portray NATO expansion in cooperative security terms, Russian political figures and policymakers do not seem to accept the notion that NATO expansion is good for their country. Clinton administration officials remain optimistic that the Russians will accommodate themselves to NATO expansion. This is probably true in the sense that since there is nothing they can do about it, at some point they have nothing to gain by opposition. This does not mean, however, that a positive Russian consensus will develop around the project. Indeed, it seems equally

---

87. Jeffrey Garten, "Is America Abandoning Multilateral Trade?" *Foreign Affairs*, Vol. 74, No. 6 (November/December 1995), pp. 50–62. For the most part, economic tensions did not directly affect the security relationship, but former Ambassador to Japan Michael H. Armacost suggests that "trade frictions generated mistrust and resentment that threatened to contaminate our security relations." Armacost, *Friends or Rivals? The Insider's Account of U.S.-Japan Relations* (New York: Columbia University Press, 1996), p. 194.

plausible that the fact of NATO expansion will be a continuing sore point in Russian domestic politics. Similarly, the United States initially pursued a very energetic policy of "engagement" with the People's Republic of China, "engaging" the Chinese simultaneously on their domestic politics, their economic policies, and several aspects of their foreign policy. Engagement usually took the form of the United States explaining to Chinese officials how they should change their behavior, and ignoring Chinese sensitivities about interference in their internal affairs, and the status of Taiwan. The result was a generally non-cooperative China.

Because international and regional security institutions are weak, more U.S. leadership is required to make things happen than cooperative security advocates had hoped. Resources are necessary to supply this leadership, and resources for international affairs have become more scarce than they were during the Cold War. In particular, foreign aid and the State Department budget have been cut in half since 1984, largely at the instigation of the Congress, and are destined to fall another 20 per cent by 2002.[88] The defense budget remains large, even by Cold War standards; real defense spending nearly equals the outlays of the 1970s, and is roughly 80 percent of what it was in the early 1960s. It is also very large relative to the rest of the world, equaling the total defense spending of the next five major military powers in 1994 (Russia, China, Japan, France, and Germany).[89] Yet these resources, which would be more than adequate to support a policy of selective engagement, seem to produce a military that is not quite capable of the range of projects that it now faces.

The Clinton administration's defense program faces persistent tensions among force size, activity, readiness, and modernization. Most observers believe that the force structure cannot be funded for the level of resources planned after the turn of the century. The "Bottom-Up Review" avowedly sized the military for two nearly simultaneous Major Regional Contingencies (MRCs), and then added extra capabilities to support a vigorous forward presence. The quest for permanent military-technological dominance has proven expensive. In contrast to many doubters, it does seem to us that the force structure may well be able to deal with two simultaneous MRC's today, but it appears that both "Major" and "Minor" Regional Contingencies (MaRCs and MiRCs?) are difficult to end definitively. This high level of activity seems to have imposed

---

88. Casimir Yost and Mary Locke, "The Raid on Aid," *Washington Post,* July 28, 1996, p. C1.
89. See Congressional Budget Office, *Reducing the Deficit: Spending and Revenue Options* (Washington, D.C.: CBO, August 1996), Figure 3-1, p. 98; U.S. Arms Control and Disarmament Agency, *World Military Expenditures and Arms Transfers, 1995* (Washington, D.C.: U.S. GPO, 1996), Figure 4, p. 4.

stresses and strains on the organization that may require additional resources to resolve. The United States today deals with two simultaneous MiRCs on a daily basis: the military containment of Iraq, including protection of the Kurds, and the combined ground, naval, and air operation in Bosnia. For a brief period, the U.S. military was also simultaneously involved in Haiti. Calls are occasionally heard for forcible intervention in Rwanda and Burundi; humanitarian military assistance was provided in Rwanda; and logistical military support has been offered for multilateral military interventions in both places. The U.S. military presence in the Republic of Korea has an edgy quality to it that makes the mission anything but garrison duty, arguably a "MiRC" that could quickly turn into a "MaRC." The U.S. military is busy, and new missions are suggested daily. Finally, resources that were expected from the "downsizing" of the U.S. military have not materialized. Cuts in the infrastructure that supported the Cold War effort have not been proportional to the cuts in the divisions, wings, and warships that are the "business end" of the force. Neither the Congress nor the executive have shown much discipline in this matter. Thus, though the financial resources to remedy many problems may be present within the defense budget, they are fenced off politically. In sum, pursuit of the objectives of cooperative security, with weak or non-existent cooperative security institutions, probably requires more U.S. resources than advocates projected.

The Clinton administration's grand strategy is the result, therefore, of four conflicting sets of pressures. Its own ambitious purposes impel considerable activism. The constraints presented by the current realities of international politics make these purposes difficult to achieve without the exercise of U.S. leadership and power. A substantial portion of the U.S. political elite, in particular congressional Republicans, displays an erratic impulse toward unilateral U.S. actions on selected issues, particularly those that have to do with perceived unfinished Cold War business, such as national ballistic missile defense, Cuba, and Taiwan's independence. The general public is far from isolationist, but is nevertheless not particularly interested in foreign affairs. The Clinton administration has moved toward a grand strategy that tries to address these conflicting pressures. The accommodations that the Clinton administration strategy has made with the obstacles it has encountered have been incremental, rhetorical , disjointed, and incomplete. In theory, the incoherence of the current strategy could produce a series of new difficulties for the administration, and conceivably a disaster. In practice, the Clinton administration may succeed in avoiding a disaster through its well-known skills at "triangulation."

At the first sign of serious resistance on the domestic or international front, it adapts or backs away in order to keep costs under control. The second Clinton administration may muddle through.

LONG TERM PROSPECTS FOR CHANGE

What is the longer-term prognosis for U.S. grand strategy? What could cause this strategy to change and in what direction might it change? The answer depends upon a number of contingencies.

Ironically, the Clinton administration grand strategy has already evolved to a point where it has many of the trappings of primacy. Indeed, Clinton's foreign and defense policy team has discovered that considerable U.S. leadership and major commitments of U.S. power are necessary for the pursuit of the transformed world order they seek. The Republicans would probably follow a somewhat purer version of primacy, and move even further away from cooperative security than the Clinton administration already has, if they could take back the presidency.[90] What might cause U.S. foreign policy makers in both parties to abandon primacy?

One likely source of a major change in U.S. grand strategy is change in U.S. domestic politics. The aging of the "baby boomers" will put substantial pressure on the federal budget after the turn of the century. An increasing portion of the politically active adult population will have dim memories of the Cold War. Even the Persian Gulf War is beginning to fade into the past. The combination of these developments could produce decreasing budgetary and political support for an activist U.S. foreign policy. U.S. leaders will have to husband these scarce resources; selective engagement may become the U.S. grand strategy by default.

Primacy could die the death of a thousand cuts. The overall U.S. share of global power will decline a little. Scientific, technological, and productive capacities will spread across the world. Niche players will develop in economics, warfare, and even ideology. Close allies will grow tired of incessant U.S. demands. Traditional adversaries will balk as the United States tries to set the criteria for responsible membership in the "international community." A series of not very costly but ultimately indecisive interventions could exhaust the

---

90. See Bob Dole, "Shaping America's Global Future," *Foreign Policy*, No. 98 (Spring 1995), pp. 29–43. One quotation reveals much: "From Bosnia to China, from North Korea to Poland, our allies and our adversaries doubt our resolve and question our commitment"; p. 31. See also "Remarks by Senate Majority Leader Dole, March 1, 1995," *Foreign Policy Bulletin*, Vol. 5, No. 6 (May/June 1995), pp. 33–35; and Baker, "Selective Engagement."

patience of the U.S. public. Selective engagement again could be the default strategy, but retreat to isolationism is also possible.

Alternatively, the U.S. share of gross world power could decline significantly. Though some skepticism is in order on this score, the prospect ought not to be ruled out entirely. Russia may recover economically and politically; the Japanese economy could improve, the Chinese economy might continue to enjoy very high growth rates. Global statistical comparisons may increasingly conform to the description "multipolar world." In such a world the United States would be constrained by other powers. Selective engagement, again, seems a plausible fall-back position.

The temptations of U.S. power could prove too strong in the short term. Many Democrats and many Republicans believe that democratic principles and liberal values are universal, or should be, and that this country should act to spread them. Moreover, the end of the Cold War left a lot of foreign policy and security specialists without much to do; they will find new dragons to slay. Thus, it is plausible that the United States will get itself into a major war over these values and principles. The United States is quite powerful militarily, and it is possible that the war would be another Desert Storm. On the other hand, it is just as likely, given the kind of world we face and beliefs we carry, that the war will be a Vietnam, or Boer War, or Algeria, or "the troubles" of Northern Ireland. Such a war could easily produce a retreat to neo-isolationism. This is no great insight, and responsible foreign policy professionals will try to avoid this war, because they understand its risks. But blunders are possible.

Finally, a change in a more ambitious direction would result if an aspiring peer competitor jumped the gun, like Saddam Hussein did, challenging the United States before its power was adequate. The behavior of such a state could create threats to many while the United States is still strong and active, and the challenger is still too weak. Such a threat could permit primacy to evolve into "containment." The fearful would once again be eager to embrace U.S. leadership. The people of the United States would allocate plenty to military preparedness and to foreign aid. In a host of small and large ways, medium and great powers would encourage and subsidize U.S. leadership.

Conclusions

This brief overview cannot do justice to the full range of argumentation about which the advocates of neo-isolationism, selective engagement, cooperative security, primacy, and engagement and enlargement disagree. But it is a start. By way of conclusion we offer three general points.

First, it should be clear that these strategic alternatives produce different advice about when the United States should use force abroad, and the advice is not equally explicit. The new isolationism suggests "almost never." Cooperative security could imply "frequently." Selective engagement advises "it all depends," but suggests some rough criteria for judgment. Primacy implies the employment of force whenever it is necessary to secure or improve the U.S. relative power position, but permits it whenever the United States is moved to do so. An understandable desire for clear decision rules on when to use force should not, however, outweigh the more fundamental concerns that ought to drive the U.S. choice of strategy.

Second, these alternative strategies generate different force structures, two of which may prove attractive because of the money they save. But leaders should understand that these force structures constrain future political leaders—or ought to constrain them. A neo-isolationist force structure cannot quickly be recast for cooperative security or humanitarian intervention. A force structure designed for selective engagement may prove inadequate for the full range of cooperative security missions. A true cooperative security force structure may include more intervention capabilities than needed for strategic weight in great power wars, perhaps at some cost to the ability of the United States to wage high intensity warfare, unless the defense budget grows accordingly. A force structure tailored for primacy permits most kinds of military operations but may be so imposing that it causes some states to compete more rather than less with the United States.

Finally, although the alternatives are not entirely mutually exclusive, for the most part one cannot indiscriminately mix and match across strategies (as both post–Cold War administrations have attempted to do) without running into trouble. They contain fundamental disagreements about strategic objectives and priorities, the extent to which the United States should be engaged in international affairs, the form that engagement should assume, the means that should be employed, the degree of autonomy that must be maintained, and when and under what conditions military force should be employed. Some combinations just do not go together. One cannot expect to reap the rewards of isolationism if one still intends to engage on behalf of friends such as Israel. One cannot wage war in the name of cooperative security in Bosnia-Herzegovina, fail to do the same if Russia helps destabilize the Georgian Republic, and still expect to establish a well-founded fear of international reaction on the part of aggressors everywhere. Selective engagement may ultimately draw the United States into strategically unimportant conflicts if its leaders consistently try to wrap their actions in the rhetoric and institutions of cooperative security. Those who dream of cooperative security, but practice primacy, must understand that they may gradually erode the international institutions upon which their dream depends, postponing it to an ever more distant future. And the rhetoric and diplomacy of a new containment strategy, even if it is only a convenient vehicle for the pursuit of primacy, probably does not permit, as the advocates would claim, particularly friendly relations with the objects of the policy. The Clinton administration has found it expedient to draw opportunistically from three grand strategies. It seems plausible that a future Republican administration would succumb to the same temptations, and for similar reasons. Though primacy figures prominently in the strategic inclinations of both parties, elements of other strategies pop up as needed. Given the realities of U.S. politics, such an *ad hoc* approach is probably inevitable until a crisis impels a choice. And the failure to develop a clearer consensus on grand strategy may hasten the arrival of that crisis. Perhaps the best we can do now is to lay out those choices.

Part II:
Restraint

Come Home, America

The Strategy of Restraint in the Face of Temptation

Eugene Gholz,
Daryl G. Press, and
Harvey M. Sapolsky

The Cold War lasted so long and grew to be such a comfortable part of everyday life that it is now very difficult to chart a new foreign policy course for the nation. U.S. national strategy is a confusing mix of grand rhetoric, false starts, and well-advised caution. U.S. troops remain forward deployed, but in smaller numbers than they were during the Cold War. The United States intervenes often in the conflicts of others, but without a consistent rationale, without a clear sense of how to advance U.S. interests, and sometimes with unintended and expensive consequences. It is time to choose a new course. Here we advocate a foreign policy of restraint—the disengagement of America's military forces from the rest of the world. Restraint is a modern form of isolationism: we adopt its military policy of withdrawal, but reject its traditional economic protectionism.

The Cold War was worth fighting and winning. Soviet expansionism threatened vital U.S. interests; it seemed ready to swallow America's allies in Europe and Asia, who were exhausted by World War II and racked by national self-doubt. After victory over the monumental insanity of Nazism and Japanese militarism, the United States sought the prosperity interrupted by depression and a long war. But full enjoyment of its national wealth was postponed by the need to ward off the Soviet Union.

Despite the collapse of the Soviet threat, American interests have not changed. The United States still seeks peace and prosperity. But now this preferred state is best obtained by restraining America's great power, a power unmatched by any rival and unchallenged in any important dimension. Rather than lead a new crusade, America should absorb itself in the somewhat delayed task of addressing imperfections in its own society.

The restraint we propose should not be misdescribed as a total withdrawal from the world. On the contrary, we believe in a vigorous trade with other

Eugene Gholz and Daryl G. Press are doctoral candidates in the Department of Political Science at the Massachusetts Institute of Technology. Harvey M. Sapolsky is Professor of Public Policy and Organization in the Department of Political Science at M.I.T. and Director of the M.I.T. Defense and Arms Control Studies (DACS) Program. This paper began as a project for the DACS Working Group on Defense Politics.

The authors would like to thank Robert Art, Dan Byman, Carl Kaysen, Barry Posen, Richard Samuels, Jeremy Shapiro, Chris Twomey, and an anonymous reviewer for insightful comments on previous drafts.

International Security, Vol. 21, No. 4 (Spring 1997), pp. 5–48
© 1997 by the President and Fellows of Harvard College and the Massachusetts Institute of Technology.

nations and the thriving commerce of ideas. Military restraint need not, and will not, bring economic protectionism.[1]

In fact, restraint does not even require unconditional military isolation. Terrorism should still elicit a strong response, and if America's vital interests are challenged, there should be hell to pay. We advocate a strong military, just not a large or busy one. Isolationism in the 1920s was inappropriate, because conquest on a continental scale was then possible. Now, nuclear weapons assure great power sovereignty—and certainly America's defense.

Americans want to enjoy the freedom and opportunity that their forefathers sought and for which many of them fought and died. They can achieve this, if only they restrain the urge to claim interconnectivity in all human conflict. U.S. power may be massive, but it is still limited. To quote a famous, although premature, expression of the policy we advocate: it is time to come home, America. Now that the Cold War is over, George McGovern is right.

This paper has four sections. In the first we present our core argument in favor of restraint. We argue that the highest priorities of American foreign policy are to protect U.S. national security and to promote America's prosperity. A policy of restraint is the best way to satisfy these objectives. In the second section we discuss the details of restraint. We describe how restraint should be implemented around the world, how the United States should extricate itself from its current commitments, and where America should remain engaged. In the third section we rebut six of the primary counterarguments against our position. In the fourth we describe the circumstances that would invalidate our prescriptions. Restraint is not a universally good policy; in fact it has not been an appropriate American strategy until now. It is, however, America's best option today because of the paucity of international threats. In this section we detail the circumstances that would require reengagement—which are very unlikely to be fulfilled anytime soon.

The Core Argument for Restraint

To develop the case for a new American foreign policy, we begin with a discussion of America's foreign policy goals. Those national interests are then considered in light of the post–Cold War security environment.

---

1. Daryl G. Press and Eugene Gholz, "Searching for that Vision Thing," *Breakthroughs*, Vol. 5, No. 1 (Spring 1996), pp. 4–10.

MATCHING MILITARY MEANS TO FOREIGN POLICY ENDS

America has many foreign policy goals and two tools with which to achieve them: economic and military power. Some goals are well suited to military means, but for others, military force will be ineffective, too costly, or even counterproductive. In this paper we ask, "when should the United States use, or threaten to use, *military* power to secure its national interests?" This analysis finds that America is in an extremely rare historical position. The United States can achieve its most critical goals without sending its children to fight and without spending great amounts of national wealth on defense.

Most Americans share a global vision in which America has many national interests: ensuring U.S. physical security, facilitating American prosperity, protecting human rights, spreading democracy and market-based economic systems, ending the drug trade, safeguarding the environment, etc. Americans assign various priorities to these interests, but two of them stand out—security and prosperity.[2] Advocates of policies to address the other interests on the list, e.g., protecting the environment, routinely couch their appeals in terms of national security to make their concerns seem urgent to a wider audience.[3] Ultimately, however, the environment is important because Americans value the environment. Deforestation in South America may make the world less pleasant for everyone, and policy should address that problem, but deforestation would not undermine America's national security.[4] Once we separate

---

2. Some analysts suggest that spreading American values is of equal importance in America's national interest. Most of these analysts, however, are actually arguing that engaging in moral crusades is necessary to mobilize Americans to prepare to defend their security. At heart, therefore, these arguments recognize security as the first priority. See, for example, Terry L. Deibel, "Strategies before Containment: Patterns for the Future," *International Security*, Vol. 16, No. 4 (Spring 1992), pp. 79–108. See also James Kurth, "America's Grand Strategy," *The National Interest*, No. 43 (Spring 1996), p. 15.

3. Marc A. Levy, "Is the Environment a National Security Issue?" *International Security*, Vol. 20, No. 2 (Fall 1995), pp. 35–62, and especially p. 53, suggests—and soundly criticizes—this motivation. For examples of advocates of a general link between environmental degradation and national security, see Jessica Tuchman Mathews, "Redefining Security," *Foreign Affairs*, Vol. 68, No. 2 (Spring 1989), pp. 162–177; and Norman Myers, *Ultimate Security: The Environmental Basis of Political Stability* (New York: W.W. Norton & Company, 1993), especially pp. 12, 31–34. Better-specified work links the environment to national security by reference to the potential collapse of particular states in the developing world that might be important to U.S. security. See, for example, Norman Myers, *Not Far Afield: U.S. Interests and the Global Environment* (Washington, D.C.: World Resources Institute, 1987), p. 13. Below, we argue that there are no such pivotal states to protect.

4. Kenneth Keller, "Environmentalism and Security," presentation in the MIT Defense and Arms Control Studies Program Seminar Series, September 11, 1996. See also Thomas F. Homer-Dixon, "Environmental Scarcities and Violent Conflict," *International Security*, Vol. 19, No. 1 (Summer 1994), pp. 18–31, 36–37, for a careful distinction between the effects of environmental collapse on intrastate violence in the developing world and on interstate violence that might affect the United States.

Figure 1. 1995 Defense Spending in Billions of U.S. Dollars.

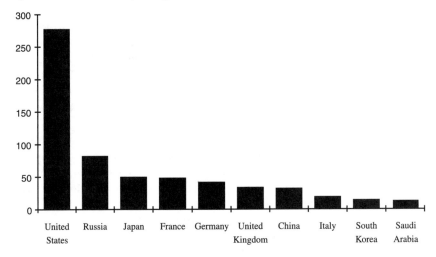

SOURCE: International Institute for Strategic Studies, *The Military Balance 1996–1997* (London: Oxford University Press, 1996), Table 1, pp. 306–308.

America's goals into distinct categories (e.g., security, prosperity, democracy abroad, environmental management), we can assess the critical issue: which of these national goals should be pursued with military power?

Of America's goals, the highest priority is the physical security of the United States—the protection of territory and the ability to make domestic political decisions as free as possible from foreign coercion. The great news is that America faces almost no discernible security threats. To the north and south are weak, friendly neighbors; to the east and west are fish. Nobody can cross the oceans to threaten America at home.[5]

The United States towers over other nations in terms of its current and potential military power. Its defense budget, measuring more than a quarter of a trillion dollars, accounts for about 35 percent of the world's total annual military expenditures. Figure 1 shows the military spending of the ten countries that spend the most on defense. The United States not only leads the pack but out-distances its closest rival by more than a factor of three. Seven of the nine other countries in the top ten are U.S. allies.

---

5. Terrorists are an exception and are discussed below.

The result of America's profligate defense spending is that the United States has by far the largest and most capable of the world's air forces and navies; an army that can defeat any other; and a marine corps that has personnel and equipment comparable to the entire armed forces of the United Kingdom, one of America's leading "competitors." The United States can project and sustain military strength further and longer than anyone else.

In the past, the United States feared that a hostile adversary might unite the rest of the world's industrial capacity through conquest, generating enough military and economic power to threaten U.S. security. But unlike the situation during the Cold War, no hostile country now has a chance of conquering Europe or East Asia. Each of the Eurasian great powers (with the exception of Russia) spends about the same amount on its military as the others, which suggests that none could easily overpower the rest. There is a rough balance of power on the continent. Furthermore, France, the United Kingdom, Russia, and China all have nuclear weapons, which provide the ultimate guarantee against conquest. Great power conflict may continue, but Eurasia's industrial resources will stay divided. America's primary national interest, physical security, does not demand much in the way of defense spending or overseas deployment.

The second most fundamental American interest is continued prosperity. Prosperity is both a "means" and an "end." As a means, economic strength is the foundation for long-term security, because wealth can be converted into military power; as an end, prosperity provides a high standard of living. Fortunately, America's prosperity is almost as insulated from hostile foreign actions as its security is. The bulk of America's economic interactions with the world are decentralized, market-based trade and investment decisions that are affected only indirectly by government policy. The exception would be a scenario in which a hostile country in the Persian Gulf gained leverage to hurt America's economy by consolidating the world's major oil reserves. The small populations of the oil-rich Gulf states do not suggest a natural balance of power, and none of the oil-rich states is shielded by nuclear weapons. Consequently, the United States should maintain sufficient military forces in the region to prevent regional conquest.

But the oil scenario aside, other countries have little power over the U.S. economy. Even Japan, America's biggest creditor, would have difficulty exercising leverage against American prosperity. Sophisticated international capital markets adjust rapidly to changes in supply and demand. If Japanese lenders shifted their money to other borrowers, alternate sources would emerge to satisfy American demand, and the equilibrium world interest rate would not be changed much. The American cost of capital, specifically including the rate of interest on the national debt, would not increase, and American prosperity would not be harmed.[6]

The key to America's economic future lies in maintaining a well-educated workforce and addressing its problems at home, not in stationing troops overseas. America's prospects are quite bright. The greatest foreign policy threat to U.S. prosperity is that America will spend too much on the military.

Unlike security and prosperity, however, America's other foreign policy goals are unlikely to be achieved effortlessly. The questions to address are whether military force is the best means to pursue these goals and whether the costs of these operations are justified by the likely results. We conclude that the answer to each question is "no." First, military organizations are not well suited to spreading democracy, protecting human rights, or stemming drug abuse in America. Militaries' hierarchical design and sophisticated command and control capabilities make them extremely capable in response to intense, short-term problems such as those found on the battlefield. But spreading values, monitoring human rights, or reducing drug abuse require different types of skills than militaries supply. It is no coincidence that military organizations have a very different structure and ethos than aid organizations and humanitarian groups.[7]

Second, the costs of campaigning for democracy or human rights with military force would be staggering. These missions could require tens of billions of dollars each year just to outfit enough troops, in addition to significant financial costs and casualties every time America deployed.[8] Using the military to spread democratic values would likely be costly and bloody and could endanger America's paramount concerns: the physical security and economic strength of the nation.

For the first time in five decades, America's core national interests are easily within reach. Small wars will likely continue to be frequent, but those wars cannot spread easily to U.S. shores, and their results will not shift the global

6. Even if Japan reacted to American restraint by increasing defense expenditures (increasing Japanese consumption and diverting capital from investment), the effect would be balanced by America's tremendous reduction in defense spending. This is discussed in greater detail below.
7. Morris Janowitz, *The Professional Soldier: A Social and Political Portrait* (New York: Free Press, 1971), p. 15, 33–34, 46–47.
8. On the enormous size of military forces required for stability operations, see James T. Quinlivan, "Force Requirements in Stability Operations," *Parameters*, Vol. 25, No. 4 (Winter 1995–96), pp. 59–69.

power balance. Similarly, military threats to America's prosperity are quite low. In fact, the only way the United States could jeopardize its favorable position is to meddle in other nations' affairs, join their wars, and overspend on defense.

BALANCING SECURITY AND PROSPERITY

The United States is a very wealthy country and, as Joshua Muravchik argues, America's high per capita gross domestic product (GDP) allows the United States to spend more on defense than its competitors.[9] The right question to ask, however, is, what are Americans getting for that extra investment? The money spent on defense could be used for education, entitlements, private consumption (through tax reductions), or other opportunities. Even during the Cold War, defense spending was constrained by the high value Americans place on freedom from too onerous a military burden.[10] America's interest in prosperity commands attention to "right-sizing" the defense budget.

The marginal increment of security that the United States gains from high levels of defense spending is vanishingly small. Security, like most investments, is subject to diminishing returns, even for a country that has as much comparative advantage in defense production as the United States. Capitalizing on the learning effects of the Cold War, the advantages of scale economies, America's wonderful natural resource endowments, and important geographic advantages, the United States is far more capable than any of its competitors of squeezing security from a marginal defense dollar. But once Americans are already quite secure, there is a tremendous cost to incremental additions to their safety.

The rate at which cost and security trade off depends on the technologies available to the offense and the defense, on the geographic relationship between a country and its adversaries, on the type of terrain on which battles might be fought, and on the opportunity cost of devoting resources to defense that could otherwise be employed productively in other ways. The absolute level of security that is purchased for each dollar of investment in the defense budget, however, is largely dependent on the harshness of the threat environment: facing many severe threats, a small defense budget will not buy much security; that same expenditure will buy a great deal of security if most other countries are weak or are supporters of the territorial status quo.

---

9. Joshua Muravchik, "Affording Foreign Policy: The Problem Is Not Wallet, But Will," *Foreign Affairs*, Vol. 75, No. 2 (March/April 1996), pp. 8–13.
10. Aaron Friedberg, "Why Didn't the United States Become a Garrison State?" *International Security*, Vol. 16, No. 4 (Spring 1992), pp. 109–142.

Figure 2. U.S. Defense Outlays, 1951 to 1995 (billions of FY95 dollars).

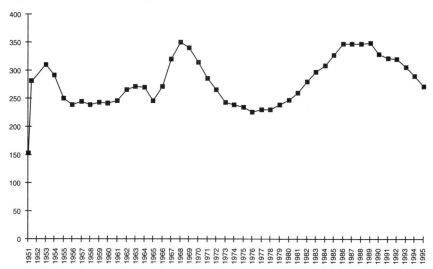

SOURCE: Carl W. Borklund, *U.S. Defense and Military Fact Book* (Santa Barbara, Calif.: ABC-CLIO, 1991), pp. 58–61; and U.S. Office of Management and Budget (OMB), *Historical Tables,* annual. The 1995 point is an OMB estimate.

Given its geographical advantages and nuclear arsenal, the United States would be very secure even if Japan, China, and Russia matched its defense expenditures. The fact is that, since the collapse of the Soviet Union, no one else comes close. It is not at all clear what, if anything, Americans are getting for their extra defense dollars. The United States can spend much less than it does today and still be much more secure than it was during the Cold War.

U.S. defense spending has dropped from its Cold War peak, but the budget is still within its Cold War range (see Figure 2). In fact, defense outlays in 1995 were very close to those of an average peaceful year of the Cold War. America has not cashed in a "peace dividend," but has traded it for a "security dividend," even as the external threat has disappeared.[11] The United States can cut defense greatly and still enjoy the security that geography and the end of the Cold War provide.

---

11. Thomas L. McNaugher, "Planning Future Defense: Time to Confront the Cold War Mindset," *Brookings Review,* Vol. 14, No. 3 (Summer 1996), p. 27.

Advocates of a larger defense budget often point out that America's defense spending as a share of GDP has dropped to pre–Cold War levels, largely because of the steady growth of the U.S. economy. This statistic indicates a reduction in the defense budget's drain on the economy, but the fact remains that America is buying as much military capability as it bought during typical Cold War years. Unless this military capability is needed, America is wasting valuable resources.

Even for the United States, the cost of keeping armed and involved beyond security needs is large. The United States could pay for a robust defense, fully capable of protecting its security and economic interests anywhere in the world, with a budget of $120 billion—half the current size but still significantly higher than the world's second biggest defense budget.[12] Spending twice that, as the United States currently does, deprives taxpayers of the fruit of their labor and society of the resources to engage domestic problems.

Advocates of continued military activism argue that their policy is a form of insurance. Insurance is intended to mitigate the costs of unlikely events, but military engagement abroad accomplishes the reverse: it magnifies the costs and risks of faraway wars by involving Americans directly in them. Its hefty premiums sap U.S. prosperity.

THE FOUNDATIONS OF RESTRAINT

The case for restraint rests on three theoretical foundations. First, the offense-defense balance influences both the likelihood of war and the mechanisms by which wars start. War begins either when status quo powers fail to deter aggressor states (the "deterrence model") or when a status quo state's defense policies undermine the security of one of its status quo neighbors, precipitating an action-reaction cycle (the "spiral model").[13] Second, when faced with external threats to their security, states tend to balance against the emerging threat, either internally by converting latent military power into deployed forces, or externally by searching for allies.[14] As threats become more intense, govern-

---

12. Even $120 billion would still be generous. If the United States succeeded in reducing the defense budget to that level, it would be in a position to reassess the strategic environment and perhaps pare down the budget further.
13. Robert Jervis, "Cooperation Under the Security Dilemma," *World Politics*, Vol. 30, No. 2 (January 1978), pp. 167–214; and Robert Jervis, *Perception and Misperception in International Politics* (Princeton, N.J.: Princeton University Press, 1976), chap. 3.
14. Stephen M. Walt, *The Origins of Alliances* (Ithaca, N.Y.: Cornell University Press, 1987), pp. 32–33, 263–266.

ments think more seriously about their security and are more likely to use "realist" analysis in designing their defense policy.[15]

Third, nuclear weapons do not make war obsolete, but they make it impossible to conquer a nuclear-armed adversary.[16] Because nuclear weapons explode with far more destructive force than conventional munitions, a devastating strike can be delivered with a handful of ballistic missiles or other delivery vehicles not subject to interception. Even the loser of a war—a country that has completely lost control of its airspace, sea lanes, and strategic, elevated territory—can now fire off a last-ditch punitive strike, devastating the "winner." No conquest would justify the costs of a large nuclear exchange, so no aggressor can conquer a nuclear-armed great power. Wars may still happen; risk-tolerant leaders might still engage in limited wars against nuclear powers.[17] But because of the risk of nuclear escalation, even conventional battles between nuclear powers should be rare.[18] The bottom line on nuclear weapons is that they make the conquest of great powers unthinkable.

IS RESTRAINT A BREAK FROM THE PAST?

The policy of restraint advocated here means specifically two things: a significant reduction in the number of active-duty forces and a significant reduction in America's overseas military presence. Spending $120 billion a year, the United States would still spend more than the second biggest military power, even if that power's budget were to increase in response to America's retrenchment. A $120 billion budget would buy the capability to deal with one major regional contingency (MRC)—needed to respond to, e.g., a Persian Gulf oil grab.[19]

---

15. Barry R. Posen, *The Sources of Military Doctrine: France, Britain, and Germany Between the Wars* (Ithaca, N.Y.: Cornell University Press, 1984), pp. 40, 239–241.
16. By "nuclear armed adversary" we mean an adversary with a secure second-strike force. See Robert Jervis, *The Meaning of the Nuclear Revolution* (Ithaca, N.Y.: Cornell University Press, 1989), pp. 5–6, 28; Stephen Van Evera, "Why Europe Matters, Why the Third World Doesn't: American Grand Strategy after the Cold War," *Journal of Strategic Studies*, Vol. 13, No. 2 (June 1990), pp. 4–5.
17. One example of this is the 1973 Middle East War.
18. Kenneth N. Waltz, *The Spread of Nuclear Weapons: More May Be Better*, Adelphi Paper No. 171 (London: International Institute of Strategic Studies [IISS], 1981); John J. Mearsheimer, "The Case for a Ukrainian Nuclear Deterrent," *Foreign Affairs*, Vol. 72, No. 3 (Summer 1993), pp. 50–66.
19. It seems quite conservative to assume that the U.S. could maintain a one-MRC force for $120 billion. The Clinton Bottom-Up Review (BUR) force, designed to conduct two nearly simultaneous MRCs, was estimated to cost approximately $250 billion (FY97 dollars). See Les Aspin, *The Bottom-Up Review: Forces For A New Era* (Washington, D.C.: U.S. Government Printing Office [U.S. GPO], 1993). It appears that the United States could get one MRC for less than half of this total.
  In the BUR "building block" method, force packages were simply added to an unchanging

Proposing to cut the defense budget by 50 percent and to withdraw from long-standing alliances in Europe and Asia may seem radical, but restraint would bring more continuity than change. During the Cold War the United States sought to ensure its security and prosperity by maintaining the division of Eurasia's industrial might, preserving freedom of the seas, and, since at least the 1970s, preventing the consolidation of Persian Gulf oil. These goals should still be the guiding principles of U.S. foreign policy today and into the future, and a strategy of restraint is explicitly designed to achieve them. Advocates of continued American engagement, however, have created new, revolutionary principles to guide U.S. foreign policy.[20] They propose to take on new overseas tasks like ensuring global "stability." Restraint is the best strategy for achieving America's traditional national interests; it is not a "break from the past" but a continuation of classical goals in a new strategic setting.

OTHER BENEFITS OF RESTRAINT

Military restraint has other benefits. First, and perhaps most important, an American withdrawal would force U.S. allies to accept political responsibility for managing their own affairs. Starting in the early days of the Cold War, the United States discouraged initiative on the part of its allies. The British and French concentrated on their economic recovery; America promised to defend them until they got back on their feet. The vanquished World War II enemies were held back for a different reason: they were on probation. But now, fifty years later, America's allies still depend on the United States to solve problems they could tackle themselves. They lack the incentive to act responsibly.

America's NATO allies are among the most powerful countries in the world. But not only did they fail to stop the war in Yugoslavia, they dithered for four years, not even deciding whether to try. President Bill Clinton sent U.S. troops to Bosnia as the next step in the history of America's twentieth-century leadership, but why do 300 million wealthy West Europeans need the United States

---

"foundation," which alone costs $110 billion. But the $110 billion foundation, according to the Department of Defense analysis, is capable of supporting a two-and-a-half MRC "Base Force." Clearly the United States does not need a Base Force–sized foundation to support a one-MRC force. If America cuts one third out of the defense foundation then it would be left with $45 billion to buy a single MRC force package. This, incidentally, is twice as much money as it costs, in the BUR metric, to move from a single MRC to a two-MRC force. See Barry R. Posen and Andrew L. Ross, "Competing Visions for U.S. Grand Strategy," *International Security*, Vol. 21, No. 3 (Winter 1996/97), Table 2 and notes.

20. Robert W. Tucker, "The Future of a Contradiction," *The National Interest*, No. 43 (Spring 1996), p. 24.

to shake them into action? When will they take these responsibilities upon themselves? America's willingness to provide assistance surely dampens any leadership urges among U.S. allies.

America's alliances reduce the strategic risks that its allies face and, therefore, eliminate their need to engage in internal balancing.[21] In a low-threat environment, bureaucratic politics and domestic political coalitions can replace rational calculation in security policy institutions.[22] On the rare occasions that America's allies do act alone, they act with less caution than they ought to, an example of the classic problem of "moral hazard." When someone else is going to pay the price for an ill-advised action—that is, when the United States is going to come "fix" any predicament that its allies get into—there is little incentive to avoid trouble. It is easy to gamble with someone else's money.[23]

Many foreign policy analysts believe that the Bosnian crisis was exacerbated by German irresponsibility; the German government recognized the secession of parts of the Yugoslav Republic, despite the risk of inciting civil war.[24] A Germany without the United States to guard its interests would be likely to think harder about the effects of such actions. Japan, too, has ducked its responsibilities under the guardianship of the United States. It has not come to terms with its neighbors for its conduct during World War II. A Japan without U.S. protection would likely discover that reconciliation is cheaper and more effective than confrontation.[25] In a multipolar world, it is often easier for states to try to make themselves alliance-worthy than to balance through purely internal means.[26]

It may be that America's allies, left to their own devices, will not choose policies that would have been preferred by an engaged United States. Accepting that reality is the key to the strategy of restraint; the United States need not

21. Stephen M. Walt, "Alliances, Threats and U.S. Grand Strategy: A Reply to Kaufman and Labs," *Security Studies*, Vol. 1, No. 3 (Spring 1992), p. 458; see also Mancur Olson, Jr., and Richard Zeckhauser, "An Economic Theory of Alliances," *Review of Economics and Statistics*, Vol. 48, No. 3 (August 1966), pp. 175–198; John R. Oneal, "The Theory of Collective Action and Burden Sharing in NATO," *International Organization*, Vol. 44, No. 3 (Summer 1990), pp. 379–402.

22. See Posen, *The Sources of Military Doctrine*, pp. 130–135, 164–167.

23. Steven Shavell, "On Moral Hazard and Insurance," *Quarterly Journal of Economics*, Vol. 93, No. 4 (November 1979), pp. 541–562. We owe the idea of applying the concept of moral hazard to alliances to Kenneth Oye.

24. Beverly Crawford, "Explaining Defection from International Cooperation: Germany's Unilateral Recognition of Croatia," *World Politics*, Vol. 48, No. 4 (July 1996), pp. 482–521, is a good, detailed summary of the diplomatic and German domestic political history; John Zametica, *The Yugoslav Conflict*, Adelphi Paper No. 270 (London: IISS, Summer 1992), pp. 64, 69–70.

25. Robert A. Manning, "Future Shock or Renewed Partnership? The U.S.-Japan Alliance Facing the Millennium," *Washington Quarterly*, Vol. 18, No. 4 (Autumn 1995), p. 88.

26. Kenneth N. Waltz, *Theory of International Politics* (New York: McGraw-Hill, 1979), pp. 165, 168–170; Posen, *The Sources of Military Doctrine*, p. 65.

manage every crisis in the world. America's preferences should not dictate its allies' affairs. As long as no outcome can threaten the core American interests of security and prosperity, the United States can afford to accept the solutions of powers whose interests are directly engaged.

A second subsidiary benefit to restraint comes on the economic front. For fifty years, America encouraged its allies to concentrate on economic development while it carried most of the defense burden. Today, the United States subsidizes Japan's defense,[27] which allows Japanese industry to compete "unfairly": Japanese firms pay lower taxes than they otherwise would. The Cold War did not bankrupt America, but it did have economic and social costs. The allies, now in the same economic league as America, should discover the full cost of their defense while the United States turns to long-avoided problems with its infrastructure, education system, budget deficit, and race relations.

Implementing a Policy of Restraint

Shifting to a restrained military policy will require major changes to America's alliance commitments, regional crisis planning, and force structure. This section reviews the steps required to withdraw from strategic commitments. It is organized geographically to cover the world's key regions: Europe, the Pacific Rim, and the Middle East.

PULLING OUT OF EUROPE

Since the collapse of the Berlin Wall, the United States has expanded its security commitments, sending troops into the Balkans and pledging to admit Eastern Europe's newly democratized countries into NATO. NATO has been trying to make it appear that its European members are now less dependent on America, but its reforms have not changed America's role as the heavyweight military backstop to the alliance. Due to America's near monopoly in logistics and mobility resources, the United States will be centrally involved in any future NATO operation.[28]

---

27. Proponents of U.S. engagement in Asia argue that the Japanese pay "Host Nation Support," which covers the costs of America's forward deployment. Their calculations, however, neglect the $60 billion that the United States spends each year to equip and train the forces to fight an Asian MRC.

28. Charles Barry, "NATO's Combined Joint Task Forces in Theory and Practice," *Survival*, Vol. 38, No. 1 (Spring 1996), pp. 81–97. Also, Rick Atkinson and Bradley Graham, "As Europe Seeks Wider NATO Role, Its Armies Shrink," *Washington Post*, July 29, 1996, p. 1.

To implement a policy of restraint, the United States should reverse course on NATO policy. The threat that NATO was created to deter disappeared when the Soviet Union collapsed. Consequently, NATO should be dismantled. In an orderly fashion, America should withdraw the 100,000 soldiers currently stationed in Europe, demobilize most of them, and bring home the equipment currently strewn around Europe as POMCUS sets;[29] this would be a clear signal that America would not return U.S. forces to the continent at the drop of a hat. It would take time, perhaps a year or two, for the U.S. military to pack up its units and for America's allies to acquire equipment to replace that currently provided by the United States. If the allies decide to purchase new equipment, America should eagerly sell it to them; if they insist on supporting their own domestic defense industries, America should license its designs to get their production capability up to speed.[30] In the interim, the United States should honor its commitments to provide the conventional capabilities that the European powers lack.[31] The key to the transition to a restrained national security policy is quick reduction of the exposure of American forces to overseas conflicts without opening "windows of vulnerability" for current allies.

NATO's European members are wealthy, and they will be able to provide for their own conventional defense without American help. In an extreme scenario, if Russia were to elect a hyper-nationalist leader, he could not magically restore the power of the Warsaw Pact. Germany's economy is nearly twice the size of Russia's.[32] Even if Russia's GDP were to double in the next ten years, Germany *alone* should be able to match Russian military spending. Furthermore, unified Germany's eastern border is far shorter than the Inter-German Border that NATO patrolled during the Cold War. It is hard to believe that prosperous, technologically sophisticated Germany—let alone the combined

---

29. POMCUS sets are "prepositioned overseas materiel, configured in unit sets," storehouses of military equipment in regions to which the United States may want to quickly deploy. In times of crisis, units can travel without carrying their equipment, "marrying up" with the weapons waiting at the POMCUS site.

30. Faced with the need to provide for their own defense for the first time in decades, the European allies are likely to realize that they have an immediate need for first-rate weapons that cannot currently be produced by their own industries. They may import American designs, at least until their industries catch up. Eugene Gholz, "Defense Industry Export Opportunities," Presentation at the DACS/Women in International Security Conference on the Arms Trade, Washington, D.C., October 1996.

31. For example, the United States should fulfill its promise to help if the French need logistics and mobility assets to evacuate their citizens from Algeria but should not provide ground troops for that mission, because the French have plenty of ground troops of their own.

32. IISS estimates Germany's GDP is 1.7 times that of Russia. International Institute for Strategic Studies, *The Military Balance 1996–97* (London: Oxford University Press, 1996), pp. 56, 113.

European force that would likely evolve if there were a serious threat of Russian hegemony—would be unable to stop a resurgent Russian invasion.[33]

Potentially the most complicated transition issue resulting from America's withdrawal from NATO would be the closure of America's nuclear umbrella over Germany. The other major European powers—France, the United Kingdom, and Russia—have their own nuclear arsenals, but Germany would be left exposed by an American withdrawal. For many years Germany has had the capability to build nuclear weapons almost instantly, but has chosen not to, because the United States provided nuclear cover; if America were to withdraw, Germany would be unlikely to deny itself the protection that nuclear weapons afford.

The primary danger associated with German nuclear proliferation is transition instability. Russia or another current nuclear power might have an interest in preventive war or at least in applying nuclear coercion to keep Germany non-nuclear. Facing such a threat, the most dangerous time for Germany to go nuclear would be during a crisis, but that is a danger that the United States can address directly by helping Germany develop a secure nuclear deterrent now, in a time of relatively low tension. If the United States maintains its current nuclear guarantee during the German weaponization program, Germany can develop nuclear weapons without opening a window of vulnerability.[34]

MILITARY WITHDRAWAL FROM ASIA

American foreign policy in Asia, too, has been captured by Cold War alliances, although in this region the formal institutions are less developed than the European NATO structure. The United States has already pulled out of its largest overseas bases, the facilities at Clark Air Force Base and Subic Bay Naval Base in the Philippines, but has reinvigorated the Japan-U.S. Security Treaty and reaffirmed the "tripwire" deployment in Korea.[35] Indeed, one of the principal architects of the Clinton administration's Asia strategy, Joseph S. Nye, Jr.,

---

33. This picture of German strength need not worry Americans. The Russian defense against an invasion from the West retains its traditional bastions of strength: strategic depth, cold winters, and, ultimately, nuclear weapons.

34. Peter D. Feaver and Emerson M.S. Niou, "Managing Nuclear Proliferation: Condemn, Strike, or Assault?" *International Studies Quarterly*, Vol. 40, No. 2 (June 1996), pp. 212–214 and 218–222; Steven E. Miller, "Assistance to Newly Proliferating Nations," in Robert D. Blackwill and Albert Carnesale, eds., *The New Nuclear Nations: Consequences for U.S. Policy* (New York: Council on Foreign Relations, 1993), pp. 103–105.

35. Chalmers Johnson and E.B. Keehn, "The Pentagon's Ossified Strategy," *Foreign Affairs,* Vol. 74, No. 4 (July/August 1995), pp. 103–114.

has suggested that the United States remain engaged in the Pacific Rim with the specific intent of slowly developing formal institutions of regional integration.[36] We argue, however, that this forward presence in Asia has lost its Cold War security rationale, exposes American soldiers to risk, costs Americans money, and artificially reduces the defense burden on America's leading economic competitors, helping them compete against U.S. companies.

As in Europe, the United States currently has about 100,000 military personnel stationed in Asia, all of whom should be brought home and demobilized. The United States should end its commitments to Japan and South Korea, cease military cooperation with the Association of Southeast Asian Nations (ASEAN), withdraw from the Australia, New Zealand, United States Pact (ANZUS), and terminate the implicit guarantee to Taiwan, giving those nations new incentives to take care of themselves.

No Asian ally of the United States faces an overwhelming conventional threat. It requires astounding assumptions about the relative fighting strength of North and South Korean soldiers to develop a military balance requirement for U.S. troops on the Korean peninsula.[37] South Korea may want to improve its defenses further to replace capabilities that the United States is expected to supply—e.g., build a larger air force—but it is difficult to understand how a country with twice the population and twenty times the economic power of its primary competitor, not to mention a substantial technological lead, cannot find the resources to defend itself.[38]

Current U.S. strategy implicitly assumes that America must remain engaged because of the Asian countries' failure to balance against Chinese strength.[39] But Japan and Taiwan, the two plausible targets for Chinese aggression, are more than capable of defending themselves from conventional attack. Both enjoy the geographic advantage of being islands. The surrounding oceans ensure a defense dominance that could only be overcome with enormous material or technological advantages.

36. Joseph S. Nye, Jr., "The Case for Deep Engagement," *Foreign Affairs*, Vol. 74, No. 4 (July/August 1995), pp. 90–102.

37. Nick Beldecos and Eric Heginbotham, "The Conventional Military Balance in Korea," *Breakthroughs*, Vol. 4, No. 1 (Spring 1995), pp. 1–8. The analysis focuses on the ability of a joint U.S.–South Korean force to stop an attack, but in sensitivity analyses they confirm that the current South Korean force could provide a robust defense without American assistance.

38. North Korean GDP is approximately $21 billion, compared with $422 billion for South Korea. IISS, *Military Balance*, pp. 186–188.

39. Gerald Segal, "East Asia and the 'Constrainment' of China," *International Security*, Vol. 20, No. 4 (Spring 1996), p. 124.

The amphibious operations required for a Chinese invasion of Taiwan or Japan would be extremely difficult and at a minimum would require substantial investment in amphibious warfare capability.[40] Taiwan could extract a withering toll on invading forces. Its air force is large, sophisticated, and growing; its navy has deadly missile boats; and it produces anti-ship cruise missiles. The same Taiwanese forces would make a Chinese blockade of Taiwan even harder. China would find it difficult to harass Taiwanese ports on the eastern side of the island with ground-launched anti-ship cruise missiles.[41] Chinese attacks on shipping would be blocked by Taiwan's air superiority and sea control, and Chinese blockading forces would find it difficult to cover the wide swath of ocean around Taiwan. China could use its ballistic missile force to conduct terror attacks against Taiwanese targets, but terror attacks have negligible military or long-run political effects—witness the failures of the German Blitz and of the sustained IRA bombing campaign against the United Kingdom.[42] As long as Taiwan has access to advanced Western weapons, it will be able to defend itself.

Japan's threat environment is even more benign. Its "moat" is wider than the Taiwan Strait. Japan's large, sophisticated air and naval forces give it great defensive capabilities, and air and naval warfare play directly to Japan's technological advantage.[43] The side with the best sensors can target the enemy first, gaining an enormous advantage; empirical evidence suggests that a better-trained or technologically superior air force can achieve favorable exchange ratios of 10:1 or greater.[44] Japan's east-coast ports would make a blockade with

---

40. Gary Klintworth, *New Taiwan, New China: Taiwan's Changing Role in the Asia-Pacific Region* (New York: St. Martin's Press, 1995), pp. 206–207.

41. One of Taiwan's largest ports, Keelung, is on the northeastern tip of the island. It is shielded from the Chinese mainland by a twenty-mile long peninsula that juts out to the north. Keelung handles a full range of port cargo, including petroleum. Taiwan has two other major ports on the eastern side of the island, one of which handles petroleum. See *Lloyd's Maritime Atlas of World Ports and Shipping Places* (London: Lloyd's Publishing Company, 1995); and *Guide to Port Entry, 1995/6* (London: Shipping Guides Limited, 1995), pp. 1899–1907.

42. For an excellent analysis of the history of strategic coercion, see Robert A. Pape, *Bombing to Win: Air Power and Coercion in War* (Ithaca, N.Y.: Cornell University Press, 1996). See especially pp. 343–346 on the Blitz and pp. 314–316 on the difficulty of strategic coercion in general.

43. Eric Heginbotham and Richard J. Samuels, "Mercantile Realism and Japanese Foreign Policy," MIT Japan Program Working Paper No. 96–22, pp. 30–31, 36, suggest that Japanese economic policy is aimed at maintaining just such an advantage. Also, Mark Z. Taylor, "Dominance Through Technology," *Foreign Affairs*, Vol. 74, No. 6 (November/December 1995), pp. 14–20; and Eiichi Katahara, "Japan's Concept of Comprehensive Security in the Post–Cold War World," in Susan L. Shirk and Christopher P. Twomey, eds., *Power and Prosperity: Economics and Security Linkages in Asia-Pacific* (New Brunswick, N.J.: Transaction Publishers, 1996), pp. 213–232.

44. In the 1973 Middle East War, Israel achieved a 14:1 air exchange ratio against the Arab air forces; in 1982, Israel did even better, shooting down 87 Syrian planes and losing no aircraft in

ground-launched anti-ship cruise missiles technically impossible and would increase the area of coverage for blockading forces beyond the reasonable limits of any non-American navy's sustainment capability. Finally, anti-submarine warfare capability is a particular strength of the Japanese armed forces because of the Cold War mission for which they were designed.

This sanguine analysis of the Asian military balances has not yet considered a last defensive advantage: the ability of defenders to seek balancing alliances. In a 1994 article, Gerald Segal argues that continued American military engagement in Asia is necessary because Asian nations have failed to balance Chinese power. Segal's conclusions, however, are inconsistent with the details he recounts of balancing by Asian countries whenever American military protection is absent. He reports that Vietnam has made enough progress at internal balancing to restrict the Chinese military actions in the South China Sea, and that Australia and Indonesia have made new commitments, jointly and separately, to oppose Chinese expansionism.[45] If China sought to acquire significant power projection assets, U.S. allies could no longer afford to voice their minor disputes with each other; they would work together to contain Chinese threats.

Despite the favorable Asian conventional balances, some Asian powers might feel pressure at the nuclear level from an American withdrawal. Japan and South Korea currently enjoy the security of the American nuclear umbrella, and some of their neighbors, with whom they share a history of conflict, already have nuclear arsenals.[46] It would not be surprising if South Korea and Japan wished to replace the American nuclear commitment with their own deterrent forces. On the other hand, they might be restrained by the chance that proliferation would scare their neighbors; the Japanese are at least officially sensitive to the "fallacy of the last move."[47] Fortunately, if they do decide to develop nuclear weapons, Japan and South Korea are good candidates for safe

---

air-air duels and only one airplane and two helicopters to ground fire. In the 1990–91 Gulf War, the U.S.-led Coalition shot down 36 Iraqi aircraft against only one probable Coalition loss from aerial combat. See Trevor N. Dupuy and Paul Martell, *The Arab-Israeli Conflict and the 1982 War in Lebanon* (Fairfax, Va.: Hero Books, 1986), pp. 144–145; Dupuy, *Elusive Victory: The Arab-Israeli Wars, 1947–1974* (Fairfax, Va.: Hero Books, 1984), p. 609, Table E on the 1973 air war; and James A. Winnefeld et al., *A League of Airmen: U.S. Airpower in the Gulf War* (Santa Monica, Calif.: RAND Corporation, 1994), Table A-13, on the war against Iraq.

45. Segal, "East Asia and the 'Constrainment' of China," pp. 123, 127, 131. For a consideration of the South China Sea military balance, see Michael G. Gallagher, "China's Illusory Threat to the South China Sea," *International Security*, Vol. 19, No. 1 (Summer 1994), pp. 169–194.

46. China, of course, has nuclear weapons. North Korea is also rumored to have a small nuclear capability.

47. Christopher W. Hughes, "The North Korean Nuclear Crisis and Japanese Security," *Survival*, Vol. 38, No. 2 (Summer 1996), p. 82.

proliferation.[48] Both countries have the military power to protect their nuclear forces from conventional attack, mitigating fears of inadvertent escalation,[49] and both possess the technological prowess to develop secure, second-strike arsenals. The only proliferation danger lies in transition. The United States, therefore, should maintain its current nuclear commitments while it pulls out of Asia. During that time America should offer assistance on nuclear technology issues to the South Koreans and Japanese if they decide to pursue their own deterrent forces.

Taiwan is a less likely candidate for nuclear proliferation. America's withdrawal from Asia would not deprive Taiwan of an American nuclear commitment, because Taiwan never had one. Even with the United States engaged in Asia, Taiwan is vulnerable to a nuclear first strike from China; restraint will do nothing to change this. Taiwan seems to have concluded that the risks of a Chinese nuclear strike do not require a nuclear deterrent. Many analysts have long doubted the utility of nuclear weapons in civil wars, and if China really believes it "owns" Taiwan, then a nuclear attack would be like an attack on itself.[50] The bottom line for American defense policy is that, while the issue of Taiwan's nuclear vulnerability is tricky, America's current military posture in Asia does little to relieve any nuclear tension there. With or without American power in the region, Taiwan will do what it has to do to defend itself.

The final issue to be considered regarding America's withdrawal from Asia is the possibility of economic retaliation by U.S. allies. Japan might retaliate for an American withdrawal from the U.S.-Japan Security Treaty by escalating its export competition with American industry or by raising the interest rates at which it is willing to loan money to the United States.[51] Although neither of these alternatives would threaten American security, both could attack the other core American goal: prosperity.

These concerns are unfounded. First, a significant fraction of Japanese politicians favor a transition to a "normal" international role, including expanded attention to self-defense. The political ramifications of the rape of a twelve-year-old Japanese girl by U.S. Marines on Okinawa revealed considerable

---

48. Christopher Layne, "Less Is More: Minimal Realism in East Asia," *The National Interest*, No. 43 (Spring 1996), p. 73.

49. Barry R. Posen, *Inadvertent Escalation: Conventional War and Nuclear Risks* (Ithaca, N.Y.: Cornell University Press, 1991), pp. 12–23.

50. Thomas Christensen, "Chinese Realpolitik," *Foreign Affairs*, Vol. 75, No. 5 (September/October 1996), pp. 37–52.

51. Hans Binnendijk, "U.S. Strategic Objectives in East Asia," *National Defense University Strategic Forum*, No. 68 (March 1996), pp. 2–3.

popular support for American disengagement.[52] If American military withdrawal were greeted with a favorable response from the electorate, even leaders who favor America's presence might not retaliate.

Second, the Japanese have few levers to inflict additional economic pain on America. In the trade case, it is hard to imagine how the Japanese could compete more intensively than they already do or how they could more decisively stonewall American market-opening initiatives. In fact, one of the benefits of a policy of restraint might come in the realm of international trade, if the reduction in American resources spent on the military resulted in better American industrial competitiveness, or if the reduction in U.S. defense spending led to a higher domestic savings rate. Restraint could promote a macroeconomic environment better suited to reducing America's trade deficit.[53]

These sanguine observations aside, it is possible to envision new Japanese financial regulations or nationalist choices by Japanese banks to discourage lending to the United States. Many have observed that America has imported massive sums of Japanese capital each year for more than a decade, implying that the United States would be vulnerable to a reduction or cutoff in that flow. But that vulnerability is exaggerated, because international capital flows freely and non-Japanese sources could readily substitute for restricted Japanese investment in the United States.[54] The only route whereby Japanese reactions to U.S. withdrawal might hurt U.S. prosperity is if Japanese defense expenditures increased substantially, consuming Japanese investment dollars that would otherwise have gone to international capital markets. But the reduction in the supply of global capital would be compensated by a reduction in worldwide demand for borrowing, because the U.S. defense budget burden would be substantially lightened. Furthermore, if investors fear international instability in the wake of U.S. military retrenchment, it is likely that more money would flow to the United States seeking a "safe haven," potentially reduc-

---

52. Mike Mochizuki and Michael O'Hanlon, "The Marines Should Come Home: Adapting the U.S.-Japan Alliance to a New Security Era," *Brookings Review*, Vol. 14, No. 2 (Spring 1996), pp. 10–13, and Chalmers Johnson, "Go-banken-sama, go home!" *Bulletin of the Atomic Scientists*, Vol. 52, No. 4 (July/August 1996), pp. 22–29.

53. Robert Gilpin, *The Political Economy of International Relations* (Princeton, N.J.: Princeton University Press, 1987), pp. 370–371.

54. Michael C. Webb, "International Economic Structure, Government Interests, and International Coordination of Macroeconomic Adjustment Policies," *International Organization*, Vol. 45, No. 3 (Summer 1991), pp. 309–342; and Jeffry A. Frieden, "Invested Interests: Politics of National Economic Policies in a World of Global Finance," *International Organization*, Vol. 45, No. 4 (Autumn 1991), pp. 425–452.

ing American interest rates further and faster than those of the rest of the world.[55]

For many years now America's allies in Asia have been getting a cheap ride in the security realm. In the past, facing the Soviet threat, the United States had good reason to provide the public good of Pacific defense; now, however, America's allies are wealthy and its interests are less threatened, so the United States should come home. Former Assistant Secretary of Defense Nye has explained the political difficulties faced by the Japanese faction that advocates an expanded military and diplomatic role for Japan as a result of the substantial cost involved in building up the required capabilities, inadvertently confirming that the Japanese government and people understand the economic benefit that U.S.-supplied security has conferred on them.[56] But the U.S. government is not in the business of providing for Japanese security and prosperity; instead, America's core foreign policy interests are its own security and prosperity, which can best be served in the Pacific by a policy of restraint.

A LIMITED PULLBACK FROM THE MIDDLE EAST

The strategic environment in the Middle East is significantly different than in either Asia or Europe. America's allies elsewhere are more than capable of defending themselves, guaranteeing the continued division of global industrial might. But many countries in the Middle East, particularly in the Persian Gulf, are incapable of developing a robust defense capability. Without American military power to defend them, a regional aggressor could consolidate Persian Gulf oil, threatening one of America's core interests, prosperity. The strategic realities of the Middle East, therefore, require a different policy than is appropriate for Asia or Europe. The United States should maintain sufficient forces in the Persian Gulf to prevent any country from monopolizing control over significant amounts of the region's oil.

Several thousand American soldiers are stationed in Saudi Arabia and Kuwait. An additional 3,000 marines and 1,300 air force personnel have been stationed in Jordan on "temporary" duty. Still more troops service American aircraft in Qatar and Bahrain, where the U.S. presence is augmented by the headquarters of the Navy's Fifth Fleet. The Navy's forward deployment is completed by the nearly year-round patrol of an aircraft carrier battle group in

---

55. Jeffrey A. Frankel, "Still the Lingua Franca: The Exaggerated Death of the Dollar," *Foreign Affairs*, Vol. 74, No. 4 (July/August 1995), pp. 9–16.
56. Nye, "The Case for Deep Engagement," p. 96.

Persian Gulf waters, whose aircraft supplement the Air Force's land-based planes in the Southern Watch "no-fly zone" over Iraq. None of these deployments is required by a formal treaty, and in fact the United States goes to great lengths to move its forces around regularly, supposedly reducing the visibility of the American military to the populace of each Middle Eastern country.

Defending American interests in the Gulf requires the United States to balance two conflicting concerns. The United States needs to maintain sufficient forces to prevent cross-border attacks that could conquer significant oil fields. At the same time, the U.S. military presence must be minimized to avoid heightening religious or nationalist pressures that destabilize the regimes of friendly Gulf countries. Balancing the "external" and "internal" threats to U.S. allies should be the principal concern of American military policy in the Gulf.

Specifically, the United States should withdraw its ground forces from the Persian Gulf, leaving behind POMCUS serviced by civilian contractors. Maintaining approximately 100 air superiority aircraft and 100 attack aircraft at remote Saudi air bases would ensure a robust ability to protect U.S. allies from external attack.[57] The no-fly zone over Iraq would be terminated, but if Iraq moved ground forces toward the borders of America's allies, the United States should strike first, not allowing Iraq to pull back and repeat the process later.[58]

The reason that the United States needs to prevent the consolidation of Persian Gulf oil has changed since the end of the Cold War, but preventing consolidation is still critical. During the Cold War, the United States feared Soviet conquest of the region, which would have strengthened the Soviet military machine and offered new political leverage against America's European and Asian allies.[59] Now that the Soviet threat is gone, the threat of future changes to the territorial status quo in the Gulf would come from a regional hegemon, who would not add the oil reserves to nearly as formidable a base as the Soviets would have. Even if the GDPs of all of the Gulf oil states were combined, the total would pale in comparison to the GDP of the United States.[60] Consolidation of Gulf oil would no longer create a security threat.

---

57. For an earlier consideration of the effects of tactical air power against a hegemonic bid in the Gulf, see Daryl G. Press, "What If Saddam Hadn't Stopped?" *Breakthroughs*, Vol. 3, No. 1 (Spring 1994), pp. 5–11.
58. This "no-drive" zone is already in effect.
59. Robert H. Johnson, "The Persian Gulf in U.S. Strategy: A Skeptical View," *International Security*, Vol. 14, No. 1 (Summer 1989), pp. 126–160, raises some well-reasoned objections to this logic, both with respect to Soviet capabilities and with respect to the political ramifications of a Soviet move.
60. According to IISS figures, the U.S. GDP is roughly $7.5 trillion. If Iran conquered all of Iraq, Kuwait, Saudi Arabia, and the United Arab Emirates and consolidated these economies into its

However, allowing a regional hegemon to seize significant quantities of Gulf oil would constitute a threat to America's prosperity. Some analysts disagree. Even if all of the oil reserves were united under a hostile leader, they argue, oil would still be available because its value comes from its sale, not from keeping it in the ground. Past price shocks have come from overreactions rather than from real supply-demand imbalances, suggesting that the ideal oil policy is to improve market efficiency rather than to use the military to prevent attempts at price hikes. Furthermore, these analysts observe, Western Europe and Japan import more oil from the Gulf than the United States does, hence they should bear the cost of preserving its free flow.[61] Each of these arguments is unfortunately wrong.

The risk to U.S. prosperity in the Gulf is that a regional hegemon could manipulate supply as a method of economic coercion. In the past, the Saudis have adjusted their production levels to preserve price stability in the face of accelerations and cutbacks by other Gulf states.[62] When Iranian production ceased after the overthrow of the shah, Saudi Arabia made up for most of the production shortfall. When 4 million barrels per day of Iraqi and Kuwaiti output suddenly disappeared from the world market in August 1990, the Saudis rapidly expanded their production to make up the difference, minimizing the effects of the Gulf War on the world price of oil.[63] But if Saudi production capacity were conquered, damaged, or politically neutralized (in the case of a hostile Saudi Arabia), the global economy would be vulnerable to manipulations in supply. American military policy in the Gulf must be designed to ensure that significant amounts of Saudi, Kuwaiti, Iraqi, and other Middle Eastern oil are not monopolized by a regional hegemon.

Even a Middle Eastern oil monopoly might not raise oil prices, some would argue, because to do so would not increase the regional hegemon's long-run

---

own without any loss, its new GDP would still be only approximately 4 percent of the American GDP. See *The Military Balance 1996–97*, pp. 22, 131, 133, 137, 145, and 148.

61. David Henderson, "Sorry Saddam, Oil Embargoes Don't Hurt the U.S.," *Wall Street Journal*, August 29, 1990, p. A10, argues that the price of a barrel of oil would only rise to $30 if all Middle Eastern production were consolidated and the output quantity were reduced to the monopoly level, for a loss of only $20.5 billion to the U.S. economy. Henderson claims to be making extremely unfavorable estimates of the price elasticity and demand response to the price shock. Earl C. Ravenall, *Designing Defense for a New World Order: The Military Budget in 1992 and Beyond* (Washington, D.C.: CATO Institute, 1991), pp. 43–59, suggests that the cost of committing troops to the Gulf is quite high in terms of peacetime yearly funding and the risk-adjusted cost of wars—higher than the cost to the United States of foregoing Middle Eastern oil.
62. Michael Sterner, "Navigating the Gulf," *Foreign Policy*, No. 81 (Winter 1990–91), pp. 39–52.
63. Robert J. Lieber, "Oil and Power after the Gulf War," *International Security*, Vol. 17, No. 1 (Summer 1992), pp. 155–175.

GDP. Higher oil prices just encourage more exploration in other parts of the world and a shift to other sources of fuel. Furthermore, Middle Eastern countries remain trade-interdependent and vulnerable to embargo.[64] But these arguments are unconvincing: a fresh regional hegemon, anxious to enjoy the fruits of conquest, might seek high short-run profits from oil price manipulation rather than long-term returns.[65] Furthermore, a new hegemonic leader might just be vindictive or anti-Western. Saddam Hussein has been insensitive to the harsh economic sanctions imposed on Iraq since the Gulf War; he or another Gulf dictator could be indifferent to the economic effects of Western retaliation for an oil shock.

Finally, contrary to conventional wisdom, the American economy is *more* vulnerable to shocks in oil prices than are the industrialized countries of Europe and Asia. At present the United States imports very little Middle Eastern oil, and the Europeans and Japanese import a considerably greater portion of their consumption from the Gulf. But oil is a fungible resource, meaning that all oil of equivalent quality sells for a single world price. If the price of Middle Eastern oil rises, so will the price of oil consumed in the United States from non-Gulf sources. And U.S. energy demand is a higher share of GDP than comparable European or Japanese consumption.[66] So in reality, the U.S. economy would pay a greater prosperity price in a future oil shock.

All of the usual arguments about adopting an American economic policy to limit the effects of a future surge in the price of oil remain true under a policy of restraint. Use of alternate sources of energy, renewed conservation efforts, and more responsive operation of the Strategic Petroleum Reserve would help insulate the American economy from oil shocks and reduce the need for American engagement in the Persian Gulf. But all of these responses have costs, and at the current price of oil it has not been worthwhile to invest a great deal in reducing short-term dependence on oil. An American military policy of restraint would highlight the defense budget costs of its lone remaining overseas military engagement, help Americans recognize the true costs of "cheap" oil, and spur the United States to find ways to reduce this vulnerability.

---

64. Eric A. Nordlinger, *Isolationism Reconfigured* (Princeton, N.J.: Princeton University Press, 1995), pp. 83–88.
65. See M.A. Adelman, "Oil Fallacies," *Foreign Policy*, No. 82 (Spring 1991), pp. 3–16. Adelman notes that unstable political regimes, dominated by minority elites, might rationally emphasize short-term interests in their oil pricing strategies.
66. Sterner, "Navigating the Gulf," p. 41.

In the meantime, America must be prepared to defend its Middle Eastern oil interests. Luckily, this is not a very demanding job. To conquer the majority of territory containing Gulf oil, an aggressor's army would have to cover a vast area. Even modern, mechanized armies do not move very fast, and two hundred American aircraft stationed in Saudi Arabia should take the steam out of a ground advance. The aircraft would harass enemy forces and drop air-deployed minefields along their route of advance. American reinforcements would begin to flow into the theater in less than 48 hours.[67] Within a week, ground units could begin to marry up with POMCUS equipment, blocking the aggressor's advance entirely.

The security environment with respect to America's other Middle Eastern ally is quite different. Israel, like U.S. allies in Europe and Asia, is quite capable of defending itself. No American forces need to be earmarked for its defense. Analysis of the military capabilities of the Arab ring states (Lebanon, Syria, Jordan, and Egypt) suggests that Israel's conventional defenses are in little danger.[68] Israel continues to field the best conventional military in the region. As a last resort, Israel's territorial integrity is guaranteed by a nuclear arsenal.

For decades America has been a close friend of Israel, and a policy of restraint would not change this. The United States is better off when its friends are safe and secure, even if their safety has no effect on American security or prosperity. Surrounded by enemies, Israel has always fought its own battles, never requiring American troops to protect its borders. Israel's determination to defend itself without American troops should embarrass America's allies in Europe and Asia. As long as Americans feel strongly about Israel's well-being, loan guarantees, direct economic aid, and military sales will continue. But Israeli security makes no demands on American force structure and in no way justifies American military engagement.

---

67. In both the 1990 and 1994 American deployments to the Persian Gulf, the first squadron of American combat aircraft (approximately 24 planes) arrived in the theater in 48 hours; for the next two weeks, U.S. ground attack planes arrived at roughly ten per day. See Press, "What If Saddam Hadn't Stopped," pp. 5–11.

68. Anthony H. Cordesman, *Perilous Prospects: The Peace Process and the Arab-Israeli Military Balance*, (Boulder, Colo.: Westview Press, 1996). Cordesman concludes that Israel can defend itself conventionally from attack by any of its neighbors. A combined Egyptian-Jordanian-Syrian attack would push Israel to its limits, but the timing of this attack would be difficult to work out because Egyptian forces would need many weeks to cross the Sinai and establish logistics depots for an attack on Israel. This would give Israel the chance to fight its adversaries piecemeal. For an analysis of the military balance on the Golan Heights, see Aryeh Shalev, *Israel and Syria: Peace and Security on the Golan* (Boulder, Colo.: Westview Press, 1994). For an excellent analysis of the military effectiveness of Arab countries over the past fifty years, see Kenneth M. Pollack, "The Influence of Arab Culture on Arab Military Effectiveness," Ph.D. dissertation, MIT, June, 1996.

THE LIMITS OF RESTRAINT: CONTINUED ENGAGEMENT IN WORLD AFFAIRS
American military restraint does not imply a total withdrawal from the world. The U.S. economy will remain open, and the United States will participate in international economic, environmental, and humanitarian agreements. America will help allies in need with financial support and will use its great economic might to sanction aggressive countries.

The United States should continue its efforts to prevent and respond to terrorism. Restraint should reduce the incentive of terrorists to attack the United States, and it will minimize the vulnerability of American forces to overseas bombings, but it will not stop all attacks against U.S. targets. The United States should redouble its intelligence efforts against terrorists, and their sponsors should feel America's wrath. Restraint should not be confused with pacifism; America will no longer meddle in other countries' disputes, but it should respond with force when its citizens are attacked.

Finally, the United States should continue in its traditional role of cooperating with allies to maintain freedom of the seas. Stopping interference with seaborne trade has always been a mission of the world's navies, and continuing that mission would enhance America's wealth. Some of America's allies have sizable navies and will see cooperation with the United States against pirates to be in their interest.[69]

Counterarguments and Rebuttal

Six main arguments are raised against proposals for American military disengagement. In the following six subsections, they are addressed in turn.

THE INCREASED CHANCE OF GREAT POWER WAR
Several prominent analysts favor a policy of selective engagement.[70] These analysts fear that American military retrenchment would increase the risk of

---

69. "Stalking Modern Pirates," *Boston Globe*, May 10, 1993, p. A14.
70. See Robert J. Art, "A Defensible Defense: America's Grand Strategy After the Cold War," *International Security*, Vol. 15, No. 4 (Spring 1991), pp. 5–53; Art, "Why Western Europe Needs the United States and NATO," *Political Science Quarterly*, Vol. 111, No. 1 (Spring 1996), pp. 1–39; Stephen Van Evera, "Primed for Peace: Europe After the Cold War," and John J. Mearsheimer, "Back to the Future: Instability in Europe After the Cold War," which can both be found in Sean M. Lynn-Jones, ed., *The Cold War and After: Prospects For Peace* (Cambridge, Mass.: MIT Press, 1991). Van Evera and Art believe that great power war is relatively unlikely today, and would be even less likely with continued American military presence overseas. They advocate continued engagement as a form of insurance. See Art, "Defensible Defense," pp. 10, 46–47 and Van Evera, "Primed for Peace," pp. 195–218. Mearsheimer, on the other hand, is less optimistic and suggests that without American engagement the likelihood of future great power war is quite significant.

great power war. A great power war today would be a calamity, even for those countries that manage to stay out of the fighting. The best way to prevent great power war, according to these analysts, is to remain engaged in Europe and East Asia. Twice in this century the United States has pulled out of Europe, and both times great power war followed. Then America chose to stay engaged, and the longest period of European great power peace ensued. In sum, selective engagers point to the costs of others' great power wars and the relative ease of preventing them.

The selective engagers' strategy is wrong for two reasons. First, selective engagers overstate the effect of U.S. military presence as a positive force for great power peace. In today's world, disengagement will not cause great power war, and continued engagement will not reliably prevent it. In some circumstances, engagement may actually increase the likelihood of conflict. Second, selective engagers overstate the costs of distant wars and seriously understate the costs and risks of their strategies. Overseas deployments require a large force structure. Even worse, selective engagement will ensure that when a future great power war erupts, the United States will be in the thick of things. Although distant great power wars are bad for America, the only sure path to ruin is to step in the middle of a faraway fight.

Selective engagers overstate America's effect on the likelihood of future great power wars. There is little reason to believe that withdrawal from Europe or Asia would lead to deterrence failures. With or without a forward U.S. presence, America's major allies have sufficient military strength to deter any potential aggressors. Conflict is far more likely to erupt from a sequence described in the spiral model.

The danger of spirals leading to war in East Asia is remote. Spirals happen when states, seeking security, frighten their neighbors. The risk of spirals is great when offense is easier than defense, because any country's attempt to achieve security will give it an offensive capability against its neighbors. The neighbors' attempts to eliminate the vulnerability give them fleeting offensive capabilities and tempt them to launch preventive war.[71] But Asia, as discussed earlier, is blessed with inherent defensive advantages. Japan and Taiwan are islands, which makes them very difficult to invade. China has a long land border with Russia, but enjoys the protection of the East China Sea, which stands between it and Japan. The expanse of Siberia gives Russia, its ever-trusted ally, strategic depth. South Korea benefits from mountainous terrain

---

71. Stephen Van Evera, *Causes of War*, Volume I: *The Structure of Power and the Roots of War* (Ithaca, N.Y.: Cornell University Press, forthcoming), chap. 5.

which would channel an attacking force from the north. Offense is difficult in East Asia, so spirals should not be acute. In fact, no other region in which great powers interact offers more defensive advantage than East Asia.

The prospect for spirals is greater in Europe, but continued U.S. engagement does not reduce that danger; rather, it exacerbates the risk. A West European military union, controlling more than 21 percent of the world's GDP, may worry Russia. But NATO, with 44 percent of the world's GDP, is far more threatening, especially if it expands eastward. The more NATO frightens Russia, the more likely it is that Russia will turn dangerously nationalist, redirect its economy toward the military, and try to re-absorb its old buffer states.[72] But if the U.S. military were to withdraw from Europe, even Germany, Europe's strongest advocate for NATO expansion, might become less enthusiastic, because it would be German rather than American troops standing guard on the new borders.

Some advocates of selective engagement point to the past fifty years as evidence that America's forward military presence reduces the chance of war. The Cold War's great power peace, however, was overdetermined. Nuclear weapons brought a powerful restraining influence.[73] Furthermore, throughout the Cold War, European and Asian powers had a common foe which encouraged them to cooperate. After an American withdrawal, the Japanese, Koreans, and Russians would still have to worry about China; the Europeans would still need to keep an eye on Russia. These threats can be managed without U.S. assistance, and the challenge will encourage European and Asian regional cooperation.

In fact, some evidence suggests that America's overseas presence was not the principal cause of great power peace during the Cold War; nuclear weapons and the presence of a unifying threat played a greater role. The Sino-Soviet dispute has been one of the bitterest in the world since the 1960s. The Soviets and Chinese have had all the ingredients for a great power war—border disputes, hostile ideologies, and occasional military clashes along their frontier—yet they managed to keep things from getting out of hand. Maybe the presence of nuclear weapons damped the conflict; maybe having a common foe (the United States) tempered their hostility toward each other. But it is clear

---

72. Michael Mandelbaum, "Foreign Policy as Social Work," *Foreign Affairs*, Vol. 75, No. 1 (January/February 1996), pp. 31–32.
73. Most of the members of the "selective engagement" camp agree that nuclear weapons are a significant cause of peace. See, for example, Mearsheimer, "Back to the Future," pp. 155–156; Van Evera, "Primed for Peace," pp. 198–200.

that U.S. engagement was not necessary for peaceful great power relations during the Cold War.

Some analysts agree that the probability of great power wars stemming from American withdrawal is very low, but they still advocate engagement because they fear low-probability, high-cost events. A war would be a human tragedy, the environment would suffer, and international trade would be disrupted. But the costs of distant great power wars must be compared to the costs of the strategy intended to prevent them.

Advocates of selective engagement argue that their policy's costs are small.[74] We disagree with this assessment. Two costs are associated with selective engagement and both are high: the cost of maintaining forces in Europe and Asia and the risk that, with engagement, the United States will have to fight a war. Maintaining substantial military power in Europe and Asia and the capability to surge forces to the Persian Gulf will require most of America's current military assets, a two-MRC force. Any savings from force cuts will be marginal.[75]

The larger long-term cost of selective engagement is the risk of involvement in faraway great power wars. Great power conflicts will continue to be a rare occurrence, but when they happen, the United States is much better off staying as far away from the combatants as possible. World War II resulted in the deaths of 400,000 Americans, many times that number wounded, and nearly 40 percent of GDP devoted to defense (compared to 4 percent today).[76] A new great power conflict, with the possibility of nuclear use, might exact even higher costs from the participants. World War II was fought to prevent the consolidation of Europe and Asia by hostile, fanatical adversaries, but a new great power war would not raise that specter. The biggest cost of selective

---

74. Art, "Defensible Defense," p. 51.
75. Posen and Ross estimate that a force structure adequate for selective engagement might cost between $246 and $270 billion in FY97 dollars, or roughly comparable to what the United States spends today. See Posen and Ross, "Competing Visions for U.S. Grand Strategy," p. 21 and Table 2. Suggestions that America could save by shifting to small, "tripwire" forces are exaggerated (e.g., Art, "Defensible Defense," pp. 39–42, 51–53, and footnote 94). Tripwires are unlikely to deter aggressors or reassure allies. First, potential aggressors may not be deterred. Recent adversaries appear to believe that early American casualties will force a withdrawal, but unless aggressors believe that causing American casualties will bring dramatic escalation, token forces will not reliably strengthen deterrence. Second, allies will be unlikely to depend on tripwires for their defense; they will not be comforted by America's pledge to reconquer them after the tripwire is brushed aside. Instead they will build up their own defenses, and potentially trigger the spirals that the tripwire was supposed to prevent.
76. See Harvey M. Sapolsky, "War Without Killing," in S. Sarkesian and J. Flanagin, eds., *U.S. Domestic and National Security Agendas* (Westport, Conn.: Greenwood Press, 1994), p. 34 and Table 2.2. In World War II, 292,000 American military personnel died in combat; another 114,000 were non-combat fatalities.

engagement is the risk of being drawn into someone else's faraway great power war.

The global economy may be disrupted by war, depending on who is involved, but even in the worst case, the costs would be manageable. Trade accounts for roughly 20 percent of the American economy,[77] and sudden, forced autarky would be devastating for American prosperity. But no great power war could come close to forcing American autarky: essentially all goods have substitute sources of supply at varying marginal increases in cost. Furthermore, wars never isolate the fighting countries completely from external trade. Some dislocation is a real possibility, but these short-term costs would not justify the risks of fighting a great power war.

The risk of nuclear escalation is a reason to worry about great power war, but it is a highly suspect reason to favor a military policy that puts U.S. forces between feuding great powers. Nuclear weapons may not be used in a future great power war; the fear of retaliation should breed great caution on the part of the belligerents.[78] But the larger point is that the *possibility* of a faraway nuclear exchange is precisely the reason that America should keep its military forces out of other country's disputes.[79] An Indo-Pakistani nuclear war would be a terrible thing, but it makes no sense to get in the middle. Distant wars would be costly, but not nearly as costly as the solution that selective engagers propose.

Five decades ago, America's leaders asked the people to defend the world from Soviet military power. Admirably, Americans rose to the occasion. But now they are being asked to shoulder a dangerous new burden: to protect the great powers from themselves. Before undertaking this costly and dangerous "social science experiment," Americans should look closely at the costs of engagement, the prospects for success, and the risks if things go awry. Careful comparison shows restraint to be the better strategy.

---

77. Paul Krugman, "Competitiveness: A Dangerous Obsession," *Foreign Affairs*, Vol. 73, No. 2 (March/April 1994), p. 34.
78. There have been many wars involving nuclear armed countries since World War II, and none has resulted in nuclear use. Note also that Nazi Germany, a country obviously willing to take risks, never used its arsenal of chemical weapons against the Allies during World War II because it feared retaliation. See Stockholm International Peace Research Institute [SIPRI], *The Problem of Chemical and Biological Warfare*, Volume I: *The Rise of CB Weapons* (New York: Humanities Press, 1971), pp. 314, 324–328.
79. Layne, "Less Is More," pp. 71–72.

THE VALUE OF AMERICAN PRIMACY

A second argument against restraint says that the United States should exploit its huge advantages as the world's sole superpower to prevent any country from becoming a new rival. Advocates of primacy feel that the United States should lock in America's current hegemonic position by keeping down any prospective "number two."[80] They do not simply want the United States to maintain the world's biggest armed forces; this could be accomplished with half the current defense budget. Rather, they want to ensure that no country is even in the same league.[81] The United States should have the military power to go anywhere in the world and beat any army quickly and decisively. America should be so strong that neither its allies nor its adversaries even try to compete.[82] And it should exercise political leadership to enhance its current global hegemony and prevent the emergence of any challenger.[83]

We raise four major objections to primacy. First, America should try to avoid a new bipolar confrontation, but the simplest and surest way to do this is to come home. No aggressor can conquer America's allies and consolidate global industrial might, so the United States does not need to balance emerging

---

80. See, for example, Samuel P. Huntington, "America's Changing Strategic Interests," *Survival*, Vol. 33, No. 1 (January/February 1991), pp. 3–17; Zalmay Khalilzad, "Losing the Moment? The United States and the World After the Cold War," *Washington Quarterly*, Vol. 18, No. 2 (Spring 1995), pp. 87–107; Joshua Muravchik, *The Imperative of American Leadership: A Challenge to Neo-isolationism* (Washington, D.C.: American Enterprise Institute, 1996); William Kristol and Robert Kagan, "Toward a Neo-Reaganite Foreign Policy," *Foreign Affairs*, Vol. 75, No. 4 (July/August 1996), pp. 18–32; Charles Lane, "Habsburgism," *New Republic*, No. 4229 (February 5, 1996), p. 10. A draft of the Pentagon's Defense Planning Guidance for Fiscal Years 1994–99 echoed these views. See "Excerpts from Pentagon's Plan: Prevent Re-Emergence of a New Rival," *New York Times*, March 8, 1992, p. 14.
81. One advocate even implies that the United States should annex Europe in order to deter or win a new Cold War with an Asian superpower. See Michael Lind, "Pax Atlantica: The Case for Euramerica," *World Policy Journal*, Vol. 13, No. 1 (Spring 1996), pp. 1–7.
82. Khalilzad, "Losing the Moment," pp. 101–103; Kristol and Kagan, "Neo-Reaganite Foreign Policy," p. 26.
83. This paper is about American military policy, so the group of primacy advocates to whom we respond are those who advocate military policies to counter the emergence of a new rival. On the other hand, Samuel Huntington proposes an economic strategy to maintain American primacy by spurring domestic savings and investment. We favor these policies because they would increase America's long-term prosperity, but we do not fear the security consequences of a united Europe or a richer Japan. Furthermore, we argue that the best way to implement Huntington's plan for economic growth would be to adopt a military policy of restraint. See Huntington, "America's Changing Strategic Interests"; and Huntington, "Why Primacy Matters," *International Security*, Vol. 17, No. 4 (Spring 1993), pp. 68–83. For a lucid analysis of the exaggerated concerns of "primacists," see Robert Jervis, "International Primacy: Is the Game Worth the Candle?" *International Security*, Vol. 17, No. 4 (Spring 1993), pp. 52–67.

powers. America should "just say no" to future bipolar confrontations by adopting a policy of restraint.

Second, the general prescriptions of primacy are likely to cause the problems they are supposed to avoid. Primacy is designed to prevent the costs of a future bipolar confrontation, but primacy's prescription is to pay those costs today.[84] America spends more today on defense than it did during most peacetime years of the Cold War, yet many advocates of primacy want to increase defense spending toward its Cold War peak.[85] Primacy advocates remember the military casualties of the Cold War's confrontations, but their strategy would immediately involve the United States in disputes in the South China Sea, Eastern Ukraine, and Chechnya. It makes no sense to pay the costs of a new Cold War today—and into the indefinite future—to avoid the possibility of incurring these costs later.

Furthermore, primacy increases the chances of a full-fledged confrontation with a new rival. As things stand now, all of America's potential competitors have other countries to worry about; they all live near one another and far from the United States. Number two, no matter who it is, has plenty of problems without American engagement. But by adopting a policy of confrontation, attempting to limit the economic and military power of Russia, China, Japan, and perhaps a united Europe, the United States would make itself these countries' biggest problem—more powerful and threatening than their natural, geographic adversaries. Primacy is the surest recipe for starting bipolar military confrontation.

Our third objection to primacy has to do with the unspecified details of the policy. How, exactly, do advocates of primacy plan to use the military to prevent the growth of Chinese, Japanese, or European power? Recent changes in relative power have not resulted from military conquest but from domestic economic development. It is China's high economic growth rate that suggests its potential as a twenty-first century superpower.[86] How will redoubled American defense spending prevent Chinese ascendance? Do advocates of

---

84. Ronald Steel, "The Hard Questions: We're Number One," *New Republic*, No. 4260 (September 9, 1996), p. 35.
85. William Kristol and Robert Kagan assert that "no serious analyst of American military capabilities today doubts that the defense budget has been cut much too far," but this overstates the case. Is it really self-evident that spending more than twice as much on defense as the Russians and the Chinese combined is inadequate? Kristol and Kagan, "Neo-Reaganite Foreign Policy," pp. 23–24.
86. James Shinn, "Introduction," in James Shinn, ed., *Weaving the Net: Conditional Engagement with China* (New York: Council on Foreign Relations, 1996), pp. 7–8.

primacy intend to launch a preventive war against China, Japan, or Europe? If this is the plan, would the moral, human, and financial costs be justified by the desire to be number one? If this is not the plan, advocates of primacy should be more specific about which steps the United States should take to keep down number two.

Fourth, a policy of primacy, even without a preventive war, will breed anger and resentment around the world. It will turn allies into neutrals and neutrals into enemies. American culture, prominently represented by movies and television programs, is already eating away at traditional cultures around the world. English has become the universal language of business, science, entertainment, and diplomacy. American consumer products have become a part of daily life around the world, and high product standards, regulations, civil liberties, and political styles beckon all.[87] Even without a foreign policy of hegemony, the United States threatens those who hold power in much of the world.[88]

It is quite surprising that no coalition has banded together to balance against America's overwhelming power—a testimony to the trust that its defense-oriented foreign policy engendered among its Cold War allies.[89] A decision to consolidate American hegemony would undo that good will. Americans wonder today who the next threat to great power security may be. To the rest of the world, it may be becoming clear: the only country capable of threatening them is the United States.

THE DANGERS OF NUCLEAR PROLIFERATION

Some advocates of continued engagement argue that America should use its military to prevent hostile countries (e.g., Iran, Syria, and Libya) from developing nuclear weapons. These critics of restraint argue that, due to the nuclear revolution, the oceans grant less security than ever before; even poor faraway countries can do serious harm.[90] Counterproliferators conclude that today more than ever America needs to discourage proliferation by allies and adversaries.[91]

---

87. David Vogel, *Trading Up: Consumer and Environmental Regulation in a Global Economy* (Cambridge, Mass.: Harvard University Press, 1995).
88. Ronald Steel, "When Worlds Collide," *New York Times*, July 21, 1996, Sec. 4, p. 15.
89. Christopher Layne describes what he sees as the beginning of coalitions to balance American military preponderance. See Christopher Layne, "The Unipolar Illusion: Why New Great Powers Will Rise," *International Security*, Vol. 17, No. 4 (Spring 1993), pp. 33–39.
90. Adam Garfinkle, "Road Hogs," *The National Interest*, No. 44 (Summer 1996), p. 103.
91. U.S. Office of the Secretary of Defense, *Proliferation: Threat and Response* (Washington, D.C.: U.S. GPO, April, 1996), pp. 48–50, 52–54.

The spread of nuclear weapons to hostile countries is not good news. Certain countries may use nuclear weapons in irrational attacks on Americans or their friends. Accidental nuclear wars are not likely but are possible, especially if new nuclear states lack technical safeguards for their weapons. Continued military engagement, however, will not help stop proliferation to America's enemies.

In 1981 Israel attacked the Iraqi nuclear facilities near the city of Osirak, setting back the Iraqi nuclear program by at least a decade. The raid taught Iraq and other countries with nuclear ambitions an important lesson: nuclear weapons facilities must be hidden and dispersed. In the decade following the Israeli attack, Iraq rebuilt its nuclear weapons program, and efforts to hide its size and progress were very effective. In 1990, as American military planners designed the Gulf War air campaign, they knew of only two major Iraqi nuclear weapons facilities. In the months following the war, UN inspectors on the ground discovered sixteen additional major sites.[92] Until troops and inspectors were on the ground and searching warehouses, factories, and military installations for clandestine nuclear facilities, the world was almost completely in the dark about Iraq's weapons program.[93]

A military counterproliferation operation against a regional power with a dispersed, concealed weapons program would require weeks or months of ground operations. Stopping an Iranian weapons program, for example, would not be a precision strike. Iran's armed forces would have to be neutralized and its major military and industrial areas occupied. In other words, Iran would have to be conquered.

Counterproliferation operations would be long, complex, and costly, but more to the point, these operations would multiply, not reduce, the risk that America will be the target of nuclear attacks. The reason to attack an Iranian nuclear program is that Iran might, in some fit of irrationality, use nuclear weapons against the United States. But during an attack, Iran would be forced to defend itself. It would not face the difficulty of delivering a warhead against a distant U.S. homeland, because American troops would be on its shore. Even worse, the Iranian government might believe it had little to lose.

Nuclear proliferation among hostile states would not be a pleasant development, but an activist security policy does not reduce the danger. To the contrary,

---

92. Thomas A. Keaney and Eliot A. Cohen, *Gulf War Air Power Survey: Summary Report* (Washington, D.C.: U.S. GPO, 1993), p. 79.
93. David A. Kay, "Denial and Deception Practices of WMD Proliferators: Iraq and Beyond," *Washington Quarterly*, Vol. 18, No. 1 (Winter 1995), pp. 85–106.

the best the United States may be able to do is to stay out of hostile countries' disputes and maintain a powerful nuclear deterrent. Fortunately, that is probably good enough. Military restraint would not increase the danger of rogue states developing nuclear weapons, because even an activist policy could not halt their efforts.

THE CHANCE TO SPREAD AMERICA'S VALUES

Another set of criticisms emphasizes less the problems restraint would create than the opportunities it would miss. Advocates of a "Wilsonian" foreign policy argue that the United States has a historic opportunity to make the world a better place.[94] Never before has the international environment been more conducive to an American foreign policy to promote democracy, end war, and reduce human suffering. The end of the Cold War has freed America of the constraints which, for fifty years, forced the choice of security over morality. Now, finally, the United States can refashion a better world.[95]

We agree with the premise of this argument: we would like democracy to flourish overseas, we prefer peace abroad to war, and we support human rights. Furthermore, we agree that U.S. foreign policy should promote these values. But we diverge from advocates of a Wilsonian foreign policy on the role of military force in achieving these objectives. The United States should reward liberal democracies with trade opportunities and sanction countries

---

94. Tony Smith, "A Wilsonian World," *World Policy Journal*, Vol. 12, No. 2 (Summer 1995), pp. 62–66.
95. According to Secretary of Defense William Perry, one of the foundations of U.S. national security strategy is to spread and consolidate democracy abroad. See William Perry, *Annual Report of the Secretary of Defense* (Washington, D.C.: U.S. GPO, 1996), p. 2. For other supporters of spreading democracy, see Strobe Talbott, "Democracy and the National Interest," *Foreign Affairs*, Vol. 75, No. 6 (November/December 1996); Chester A. Crocker, "All Aid Is Political," *New York Times*, November 21, 1996, p. 29; J. Brian Atwood, "On the Right Path in Haiti," *Washington Post*, October 14, 1994, p. A27. For advocates of collective security, see Charles A. Kupchan and Clifford A. Kupchan, "Concerts, Collective Security, and the Future of Europe," *International Security*, Vol. 16, No. 1 (Summer 1991), pp. 114–161; Kupchan and Kupchan, "The Promise of Collective Security," *International Security*, Vol. 20, No. 1 (Summer 1995), pp. 52–61; Carl Kaysen and George Rathjens, *Peace Operations by the United Nations: The Case for a Volunteer U.N. Military Force*, (Cambridge, Mass.: American Academy of Arts and Sciences, 1995); Morton H. Halperin and David J. Scheffer, *Self-Determination in the New World Order* (Washington, D.C.: Carnegie Endowment for International Peace, 1992), pp. 105–111. For advocates of interventions for humanitarian reasons, see James Turner Johnson, "Just War I: The Broken Tradition," *The National Interest*, No. 45 (Fall 1996), pp. 35–36; J. Bryan Hehir, "World of Fault Lines: Sovereignty, Self-Determination, Intervention," *Commonweal*, Vol. 119 (September 25, 1992), pp. 8–9; Fouad Ajami, "Beyond Words: History Rewards the Aggressors," *New Republic*, No. 4203 (August 7, 1995), pp. 15–17; Charles A. Kupchan, "Reclaiming the Moral High Ground: What Does the West Stand for If It Does Nothing?" *Los Angeles Times*, July 23, 1995, p. M1; James A. Barry, "President Who 'Feels Others' Pain' Should Take Steps to Help Burundi," *Christian Science Monitor*, September 27, 1996, p. 19.

that attack their neighbors or brutalize their citizens. But fighting overseas in the name of democracy, peace, and an end to human suffering would be dangerous and counterproductive.

Spreading liberal values abroad is an interest that many Americans share, but it is not a national security interest. We insist on maintaining the distinction between America's security at home and its values abroad for the same reason that advocates try to link them: genuine security concerns justify the sacrifice of many lives and much money. However, America's freedom from physical attack or coercion does not depend on peace in Africa, democracy in Latin America, or human rights in Cambodia. Advocates of "enlargement" who want to spread democracy connect their policy with security by noting that democracies tend not to fight each other.[96] More democracies means fewer potential adversaries. Supporters of collective security point out that an indivisible peace, by definition, leaves everyone safe. But while democracies are unlikely to fight the United States, even non-democracies tend not to be crazy enough to attack it. And while global peace would, by definition, mean peace for America, wars on distant continents will only threaten U.S. security if the United States travels overseas to join in. America's interest in democracy and peace is real, but it is unrelated to national security.

Even if democracy, peace, and human rights are not security interests of the United States, America should still use military force to achieve them if the costs were low, the gains were significant, and the alternatives were unsatisfying. However, none of these conditions is met. Spreading democracy will undermine local elites.[97] They will impugn America's global political ideals by attributing old imperialist motives. When they choose to fight back, the cost of combat may be horrendous.[98] Even very low levels of resistance might require

---

96. For example, see Talbott, "Democracy and the National Interest," pp. 48–49.
97. Edward D. Mansfield and Jack Snyder, "Democratization and the Danger of War," *International Security*, Vol. 20, No. 1 (Summer 1995), pp. 7, 28–30; Anna Simons, "Shades of Somalia," *Washington Post*, November 17, 1996, p. C7. In Somalia, America's decision to impose democracy threatened the local warlords and encouraged them to resist.
98. See Michael T. Klare and Peter Kornbluh, eds., *Low Intensity Warfare: Counterinsurgency, Proinsurgency, and Antiterrorism in the Eighties* (New York: Pantheon Books, 1988), especially chaps. 2, 5, 8, and 9, for a description of the difficulties of counterinsurgency operations. The case of Vietnam might overstate the damage that a weak country could inflict on the United States if America tried to force its social system on them, because the PRC and the Soviet Union played roles in the Vietnam War. But the point is that small countries do have the power to resist, and this resistance can be fierce and costly. See Alistair Horne, *Savage War of Peace: Algeria 1954–1962* (New York: Viking Press, 1978), p. 538, for the costs of the Algerian civil war.

large peacekeeping forces and surprising financial expense.[99] Spreading democracy by military force would be very costly.

Even worse, there are good reasons to believe that a military crusade for democracy would fail. American wars in Southeast Asia turned out badly, and the United States could not bring democracy to the Somalis. Over the next few years we will know whether the operation in Haiti stabilized its electoral system, but the prospects are not bright.[100] Where democracy was successfully created—in Germany, Japan, and Italy—the United States had to conquer and occupy foreign territory, grant generous economic assistance, and defend the new governments from external threats.[101] Even American democracy took time to form, required a civil war to confirm, has involved much learning, and after two hundred years is still not perfect. The 10th Mountain Division could not have rewritten that American history, nor can it force the pace of other countries' evolution.

A minimalist version of enlargement does not seek to *expand* the reach of democracy forcibly but instead would defend those democracies that emerged on their own. This is the Brezhnev Doctrine in reverse: states that are authoritarian may become democratic, but democracies will not be allowed to go back. There are two problems with this doctrine. First, the distinction between creating democracies and defending them is more subtle than it might appear. Young democracies often face authoritarian coups.[102] Distinguishing between internal opposition and foreign subversion is not easy. Second, U.S. security guarantees might embolden new democracies to provoke their non-democratic neighbors. Liberalization in the Baltic states has not caused them to be cautious in their treatment of ethnic Russian nationals; a defense commitment from NATO, which some "enlargers" suggest, might further embolden them. The Bosnian Muslims hardened their demands toward their enemies as the United

---

99. Quinlivan, "Force Requirements for Stability Operations." See Barry R. Posen, "A Balkan Vietnam Awaits 'Peacekeepers,'" *Los Angeles Times*, February 4, 1993, p. B7, for an application of Quinlivan's force sizing methods to Bosnia. The cost of operations, even ones in which there is almost no resistance, can be substantial. Keeping twenty thousand troops in Bosnia for the past year had a price tag of more than $3.5 billion. John Hillen, "Having It Both Ways on Defense," *Investors' Business Daily*, September 25, 1996, p. A2. Had there been resistance, the costs would have gone up substantially.

100. Mandelbaum, "Foreign Policy as Social Work," p. 21.

101. Stephen Van Evera, presentation at the Joint MIT Defense and Arms Control Studies-Harvard Olin Institute for Strategic Studies Conference on Force Projection and Sustainment, March 23–24, 1995, summarized by Richard Wilcox, *Force Projection and Sustainment*, MIT DACS Working Paper, pp. 19–20.

102. Mansfield and Snyder, "Democratization and the Danger of War," pp. 18–19, 34–35.

States became more committed to their side.[103] Pledging to support nascent democracies will not diffuse local tensions, but it may embroil the United States in guerrilla war.

Promoting global peace, like encouraging democracy, is a worthy goal for American foreign policy; unfortunately, a military policy to prevent wars, usually called collective security, would be too costly and too ineffective. A force structure that can back up a threat to oppose any aggression would have to be very large. The United States would need to prepare to fight many enemies at once, all around the world. Advocates of this policy might argue that prospective aggressors will soon abandon any expansive intentions, but no one knows how long this would take, how long it would last, and how many wars the United States would have to fight to establish and maintain its credibility. Committing the United States to oppose all aggression would require a force structure significantly bigger than the current one. The cost of this force has been estimated to be $250–300 billion (in 1997 dollars), approximately $150 billion higher per year than the cost of restraint.[104] That extra money simply equips U.S. forces and does not include the cost of operations.

The potential achievements of such a tremendous undertaking are easy to exaggerate. One benefit of collective security is that it would, if successful, reduce the number of wars in the third world where weak states are easy marks for their larger neighbors. Preventing these wars is simply a means toward achieving America's humanitarian goals and, as we argue below, is not worth the cost. The establishment of collective security arrangements to prevent wars in the first world might be more dependable than simply relying on balance of power,[105] but it does not require that the United States be part of those arrangements. As we argued above, no one can consolidate Eurasia, and America's allies can defend themselves. If they believe that the best way to protect themselves is to band together in a concert, then they should do so. But there is no reason that the United States should be involved in their collective security agreements, any more than it needs to be part of their balancing alliances.

---

103. Walter Russell Mead, "On Bosnia—Don't Let Lloyd George Be a Guide," *Los Angeles Times*, July 30, 1995, p. M2; Ian Traynor, "Muslims Proffer Olive Branch to Avert Bloodshed in Serb Bastion," *The Guardian*, September 19, 1995, p. 2; Elaine Sciolino, Roger Cohen, and Stephen Engelberg, "In U.S. Eyes, 'Good' Muslims and 'Bad' Serbs Did a Switch," *New York Times*, November 23, 1995, p. A1.
104. Posen and Ross, "Competing Visions for U.S. Grand Strategy," p. 30 and Table 2.
105. See Charles A. Kupchan and Clifford A. Kupchan, "The Promise of Collective Security," pp. 52–61.

Finally, fighting to alleviate human suffering is a worthy but misguided goal. America should use some of its considerable power to make people around the world better off. But money spent for humanitarian missions will do far less good if it is spent on the military than if it is used for food, medicine, and disaster relief. Natural disasters do not fight back or interdict U.S. aid. Directing U.S. humanitarian aid efforts away from civil wars and toward combating disease and malnutrition will help people without challenging the power of foreign elites. Sometimes, the local elites will block even this type of aid,[106] but the United States will not soon run out of places in which aid would be welcomed.

In sum, there is no surer way to turn millions of America's admirers into America's opponents than to force an unfamiliar social system on them. The United States would be blamed if things went badly and resented even if they did not. Fighting against war everywhere makes no sense in the third world, and is unnecessary in the advanced industrial world where the other great powers are strong enough to defend themselves. Relieving human suffering with military interventions wastes dollars and lives; more good can be done with vaccines than bullets.

THE END OF ECONOMIC OPENNESS

A fifth notable argument against restraint is raised by those who believe that a military withdrawal from Europe and Asia would threaten American prosperity more than its security. Even if great power wars are unlikely, without a stabilizing American military presence other great powers may eye each other suspiciously, concern themselves with relative economic gains, and close off the free international flow of goods and capital.[107] This argument draws its roots from the literature on hegemonic stability, in which the reigning hegemon (i.e., the United States) must provide international collective goods in order to maintain an open international economic environment.[108] If the United States

---

106. For example, in Bosnia the combatants blocked aid supplies to facilitate ethnic cleansing.
107. Art, "Defensible Defense," pp. 30–42. Richard Rosecrance, "Post–Cold War U.S. National Interests and Priorities," in L. Benjamin Ederington and Michael J. Mazarr, eds., *Turning Point: The Gulf War and U.S. Military Strategy* (Boulder, Colo.: Westview Press, 1994), pp. 23–37, combines the argument linking American engagement and global economic growth with advocacy of American leadership of a collective security regime.
108. A classic statement is in Charles Kindleberger, *The World in Depression, 1929–1939*, revised and enlarged edition (Berkeley: University of California Press, 1986). Of course, many hegemonic stability theories have a declinist undertone—the hegemon suffers over time under the burden of providing the collective goods; however, others believe that the selective benefits that the hegemon derives from the open international economic environment are quite large. For example, Webb, "International Economic Structure," p. 342.

ceases to provide those collective goods, huge prosperity benefits might be at risk.

This line of argument is wrong for two reasons: multipolar security competition does not require a focus on relative gains in purely economic affairs, and international economic openness has not historically been maintained by the actions of hegemons. First, among powers of approximately equal strength (as would be the case in Europe after an American withdrawal), the size of the relative economic gains from trade tends to be small compared to the size of the great power economies in question. Consequently, it would take a long time of static trade and alliance relationships for the relative economic gains to translate into a dangerous strategic imbalance. Meanwhile, there is no reason to believe that the trade and alliance relationships would remain static.[109] In fact, balance-of-threat theory suggests that, if an imbalance were to emerge, alliance relationships would change in response to the danger.

Furthermore, if great powers became concerned by their neighbors' military strength, they could not afford to waste national resources by distorting their pattern of trade. Protectionism costs money, and high levels of international threat tend to highlight wasteful policies whose reversal might lead to a greater power-generation capability.[110] Even if threatened states felt the need for economic closure with respect to a particular, threatening adversary for relative gains reasons, none would feel the need for protectionism *vis-à-vis* the United States. America would be likely to benefit from other countries' heightened desire to trade with the United States.

Finally, history does not confirm the hegemonic stability interpretation of the international economy. Most of the benefits of international openness are selective goods which the United States can capture through bilateral economic policies. For example, the spillover benefits of bilateral trade relationships helped reverse the worldwide economic decline of the 1930s—which the hegemonic stability theorists tend to cite as a crucial case for their theory.[111] The bottom line is that it is not American troops deployed overseas that make American products and services attractive to foreign consumers; it is the quality of American goods, the image of America's prosperity, and the productivity

---

109. Peter Liberman, "Trading with the Enemy: Security and Relative Economic Gains," *International Security*, Vol. 21, No. 1 (Summer 1996), pp. 147–175.
110. For example, Joanne Gowa, *Closing the Gold Window* (Ithaca, N.Y.: Cornell University Press, 1983), pp. 172 and 192, argues that Europeans' monetary policy in the 1960s was influenced by the Soviet threat, and the American decision to end the gold standard in the early 1970s was an effort to generate power.
111. Kenneth Oye, *Economic Discrimination and Political Exchange* (Princeton, N.J.: Princeton University Press, 1992).

of American workers. None of those factors would be affected by a policy of military restraint.

THE FUTILITY OF DISENGAGEMENT

The last major criticism of American military restraint denies that restraint is possible. According to this argument, big wars suck in powerful nations.[112] Twice in this century the United States tried to stay out of great power war in Europe, and both times it was pulled in. Trying to tie policymakers' hands by weakening U.S. military capabilities will only put America's eventual involvement on less favorable military terms.[113] The United States fielded small, unprepared armed forces in 1916, 1940, and 1950, but its weakness did not prevent its entrance into two world wars and the Korean conflict. History suggests that withdrawing from alliances and cutting forces will not keep the United States out of war; it will make these wars more likely and keep America ill prepared to fight.

This argument, however, relies on a selective view of history. Great power wars do not always suck in powerful countries. Neither the British nor the French were dragged into the Russo-Japanese War. The British stayed out of the Franco-Prussian War, and both the British and French stayed out of the Austro-Prussian war. The United States is not doomed by the laws of nature to go overseas and fight. In fact, the United States probably has more choice about the wars it fights than any other nation, because it does not share borders with other great powers.

Furthermore, it will be much easier to stay out of distant great power wars than it was in the past. First, the fact that no country can possibly unite the industrial resources of Eurasia eliminates America's traditional concern about the outcome of foreign wars.[114] Second, the potential costs of American intervention in an ongoing great power war have never been higher. Great power war has always been extremely costly, but nuclear weapons raise the potential costs of intervention immeasurably. A new war between Russia and Germany would be a tragedy, but the possibility of nuclear escalation would cool the enthusiasm of even the most committed American interventionists. Critics say that the United States is unable to stay out of big wars, but a thought experiment may shed a different light on this assertion. Would President Wilson have brought America into World War I if Germany had possessed a large nuclear

---

112. See, for example, Van Evera, "Why Europe Matters, Why the Third World Doesn't," p. 9.
113. Mark Helprin, "Mr. Clinton's Foreign Policy," *Wall Street Journal*, August 12, 1996, p. A10.
114. Van Evera, "Why Europe Matters, Why the Third World Doesn't," p. 9.

arsenal? Recall how hard it was to get America involved in World War II. The American people have a sense of the risks.

In sum, the United States is not inevitably drawn into foreign wars. If a future great power war erupts, there will be many powerful reasons to stay out. Rather than accept today's internationalist worldview as an unchangeable fact of life, Americans should reeducate themselves to the new strategic reality. In the late 1940s, America's leaders struggled to turn the American people away from their isolationist predispositions and contain Soviet expansionism. Today the challenge is to demonstrate that the world is safe for restraint.

When to Reengage

Adopting a foreign policy of restraint should not commit the United States to isolation for all time. Just as it was right for America to defend its allies during the Cold War, it may eventually be right for the United States to seek new overseas alliances. Although the conditions are not likely to be realized any time soon, it is important to consider when the United States should reengage militarily.

Before America's core national interests can be threatened, three stringent conditions must be satisfied. First, an aggressive state must develop the conventional capabilities for rapid conquest of its neighbors. A slow conquest, even if successful, would tend to destroy many of the conquered states' economic assets[115] and impose high costs on the aggressor, ending its hegemonic aspirations.[116] Second, the aggressor state must threaten to bring together enough power after its conquests to either mount an attack across the oceans or threaten U.S. prosperity by denying America access to the global economy. At present, only Western Europe or East Asia united with Russia's resource wealth constitutes a sufficiently dangerous union to satisfy this condition.[117] That these are the same regions that George Kennan identified fifty years ago as the key to global power speaks volumes about the real pace of change in the international threat environment.

---

115. Peter Liberman, "The Spoils of Conquest," *International Security*, Vol. 18, No. 2 (Fall 1993), pp. 125–153.
116. John J. Mearsheimer, *Conventional Deterrence* (Ithaca, N.Y.: Cornell University Press, 1983), pp. 63–66, 203, 208–212.
117. Although it is difficult to imagine the mechanics, an empire or alliance linking Western Europe and East Asia but excluding Russia would also consolidate dangerous quantities of industrial might.

Finally, any potential aggressor must solve the "nuclear problem." In order to agglomerate the world's power under one empire, a challenger would have to overcome the nuclear capabilities of other great powers: Russia would have to neutralize the British and French nuclear arsenals, if not a German arsenal as well; the Western European countries would face the overwhelming Russian nuclear force in addition to each other's second-strike capabilities. If China were to develop power-projection forces, it would drive its powerful neighbors to nuclearize. The regions of the world that boast significant industrial potential are inhabited by nuclear and potentially nuclear regional powers. In the unlikely event that a potential hegemon solved the nuclear problem and returned the world to pre–World War II conditions in which hostile states could accumulate significant power through rapid conquest, the United States should not stand idly by. Then, it would be time to reengage.

An astute observer might notice that the stringent conditions we set for American engagement were not satisfied in the later years of the Cold War. Eric Nordlinger's recent work, *Isolationism Reconfigured,* advances the classical isolationist view that America should not have engaged during the Cold War and did not even need to fight the Nazis in World War II.[118] Robert Art observes that by the 1970s, Western Europe had developed a secure nuclear second-strike capability in the form of French and British ballistic missile submarines; therefore, the "geostrategic logic" of accumulating power by conventional conquest no longer applied.[119] Why, then, was American engagement critical during the Cold War? It is here that our advocacy of "restraint" explicitly differs from the old isolationist logic.

First, we believe that had the United States left its NATO allies to defend themselves, the Soviet Union could have driven them into bankruptcy. The Soviets bankrupted themselves by trading long-run economic strength for short-run military power. Post–World War II Soviet military policy could only be sustained, it turned out, for about fifty years, after which time the resource allocation imbalance brought the economic system crashing down, destabilizing the political structure. In the meantime, however, even though the Western Europeans and Japanese were wealthier than the Soviets, they may not have been capable of generating enough short-term military power without exhausting themselves. U.S. withdrawal would have forced Western Europe and Japan

---

118. Nordlinger does allow that there may have been a brief period just after World War II when limited aid to Western Europe was appropriate, but that window closed during the 1950s with European economic reconstruction.
119. See Art, "Defensible Defense." We responded to Art's specific security and non-security arguments for engagement in earlier sections.

to choose between accepting a dangerous military imbalance or matching the Soviets' reckless levels of defense spending and bankrupting themselves.

Second, we believe that a transition out of NATO during the Cold War would have been dangerous. Although now it makes sense to help Germany acquire nuclear weapons as the United States pulls out of NATO, such a move during the Cold War would have run the risks associated with proliferation during crisis.

Restraint is a robust policy. China can rise and fall; Russia can create and break alliances; Europe could unite or the EU could disintegrate—and still restraint would be best. Until three unlikely conditions are met—the growth of a regional power capable of quickly overwhelming its adversaries, the possibility that an aggressor could consolidate a large fraction of the world's industrial might, and the discovery of a solution to the nuclear problem—the United States need not re-engage.

Conclusion

During the height of the Cold War, an admiral briefed the Army's War Plans Directorate on the strategic value of a big, powerful navy. After viewing slides depicting new Soviet warships, and hearing grave descriptions of the threats that the Soviet Navy posed to America's global interests, the admiral asked if there were any comments on the presentation. "Very interesting," one general told the Navy briefer, "but what you've just said is that if the Soviet navy sank tomorrow, we could do away with the U.S. Navy." The admiral disagreed. "If the Soviet navy sank tomorrow, I'd get me a new set of slides."[120]

Well, soon after this discussion the entire Soviet Union sank, and for the past six years the U.S. Armed Forces and the American foreign policy establishment have been scrambling to put together a new set of slides. The admiral was correct—if he is to justify America's continued role of global engagement, and argue for a defense budget three times as big as America's closest competitor, he will need a new threat or a fresh mission. Americans will have to be sold on some new, ambitious strategy—to prevent war everywhere, to make everyone democratic, or to keep everyone else down. But if Americans simply want to be free, enjoy peace, and concentrate more on the problems closer to home, the choice is clear: it is time to come home, America.

---

120. Colonel Harry G. Summers, Jr., "A Bankrupt Military Strategy," *Atlantic Monthly*, Vol. 263 (June 1989), p. 34.

From Preponderance to Offshore Balancing

America's Future Grand Strategy

Christopher Layne

The Soviet Union's collapse transformed the international system dramatically, but there has been no corresponding change in U.S. grand strategy. In terms of ambitions, interests, and alliances, the United States is following the same grand strategy it pursued from 1945 until 1991: that of preponderance.[1] Whether this strategy will serve U.S. interests in the early twenty-first century is problematic. Hence, in this article my purpose is to stimulate a more searching debate about future U.S. grand strategic options.[2] To accomplish this, I compare the strategy of preponderance to a proposed alternative grand strategy: offshore balancing.

Christopher Layne is Visiting Associate Professor at the Naval Postgraduate School in Monterey, California. The views expressed in this article are his own.

I wish to thank Robert J. Art, Sean Lynn-Jones, and Bradley A. Thayer for going above and beyond the call of friendship and collegiality and reviewing successive iterations of this article and providing insightful comments and advice. Ted Galen Carpenter and John Mearsheimer commented on the final draft. The following commented helpfully on an earlier draft, which I presented at a February 1996 seminar at Harvard University's Belfer Center for Science and International Affairs: Rachel Bronson, Owen Coté, Jr., Michael C. Desch, Colin Elman, Miriam Fendius Elman, Shai Feldman, Dan Lindley, Thomas Mahnken, John Matthews, and Steven E. Miller. Finally, the Earhart Foundation's generous research support—and the encouragement of the foundation's secretary and director of program, Tony Sullivan—is gratefully acknowledged.

1. I have borrowed Melvyn P. Leffler's description of post–World War II grand strategy as a strategy of preponderance to reflect what I demonstrate is the underlying continuity between America's postwar and post–Cold War strategies. See Melvyn P. Leffler, *A Preponderance of Power: National Security, the Truman Administration, and the Cold War* (Stanford, Calif.: Stanford University Press, 1992).
2. The post-1989 literature on U.S. grand strategy includes Robert J. Art, "A Defensible Defense: America's Grand Strategy After the Cold War," *International Security*, Vol. 15, No. 4 (Spring 1991), pp. 5–53; Samuel P. Huntington, "America's Changing Strategic Interests," *Survival*, Vol. 33, No. 4 (January/February 1991), pp. 3–17; Joseph Joffe, "'Bismarck' or 'Britain'? Toward an American Grand Strategy after Bipolarity," *International Security*, Vol. 19, No. 4 (Spring 1995), pp. 94–117; Zalmay Khalilzad, "U.S. Grand Strategies: Implications for the World, " in Zalmay Khalilzad, ed., *Strategic Appraisal 1996* (Santa Monica, Calif.: RAND, 1996), pp. 11–38; and Stephen Van Evera, "Why Europe Matters and the Third World Doesn't: American Grand Strategy After the Cold War, *Journal of Strategic Studies*, Vol. 13, No. 2 (June 1990), pp. 1–51. Also see John J. Kohut III, Steven J. Lambakis, Keith B. Payne, Robert S. Rudney, Willis A. Stanley, Bernard C. Victory, and Linda H. Vlahos, "Alternative Grand Strategy Options for the United States," *Comparative Strategy*, Vol. 14, No. 4 (October–December 1995), pp. 361–420, which usefully describes what the authors see as the current U.S. grand strategy and three alternative grand strategies, but does not examine the theoretical premises underlying these four grand strategies. Also, the relative advantages and disadvantages of the four grand strategies are not compared.

International Security, Vol. 22, No. 1 (Summer 1997), pp. 86–124

My argument for adopting an alternative grand strategy is prospective: although sustainable for perhaps another decade, the strategy of preponderance cannot be maintained much beyond that period. The changing distribution of power in the international system—specifically, the relative decline of U.S. power and the corresponding rise of new great powers—will render the strategy untenable. The strategy also is being undermined because the robustness of America's extended deterrence strategy is eroding rapidly. Over time, the costs and risks of the strategy of preponderance will rise to unacceptably high levels. The time to think about alternative grand strategies is now—before the United States is overtaken by events.

An offshore balancing strategy would have two crucial objectives: minimizing the risk of U.S. involvement in a future great power (possibly nuclear) war, and enhancing America's relative power in the international system. Capitalizing on its geopolitically insular position, the United States would disengage from its current alliance commitments in East Asia and Europe. By sharply circumscribing its overseas engagement, the United States would be more secure and more powerful as an offshore balancer in the early twenty-first century than it would be if it continues to follow the strategy of preponderance.

In advocating this strategy, I do not deprecate those who believe that bad things (e.g., increased geopolitical instability) could happen if the United States abandons its strategy of preponderance. Indeed, they may; however, that is only half of the argument. The other half, seldom acknowledged by champions of preponderance, is that bad things—perhaps far worse things—could happen if the United States stays on its present grand strategic course. Grand strategies must be judged by the amount of security they provide; whether, given international systemic constraints, they are sustainable; their cost; the degree of risk they entail; and their tangible and intangible domestic effects. Any serious debate about U.S. grand strategy must use these criteria to assess the comparative merits of both the current grand strategy and its competitors. I hope to foster an awareness that fairly soon the strategy of preponderance will be unable to pass these tests.

This article is structured as follows. First, I analyze the strategy of preponderance, paying particular attention to its theoretical underpinnings, causal logic, and policy components. Second, I demonstrate the strategy's weaknesses. Third, I outline the elements of an alternative grand strategy, offshore balancing, and show why it would be a better strategy for the United States to follow in the twenty-first century.

Theory and Grand Strategy: The Strategy of Preponderance

Grand strategy is a three-step process: determining a state's vital security interests; identifying the threats to those interests; and deciding how best to employ the state's political, military, and economic resources to protect those interests.[3] The outcome of the process, however, is indeterminate: the specific grand strategy that emerges will reflect policymakers' views of how the world works. Hence debates about grand strategy also are debates about international relations theory. Because theories are not monolithic, competing grand strategies can emanate not only from rival theories but also from the same theoretical approach. Thus both competing strategies I consider in this article—preponderance and offshore balancing—are rooted in the realist tradition notwithstanding their sharply different policy implications. In this section, I analyze the strategy of preponderance to clarify the realist premises upon which the strategy is based and demonstrate how its policy prescriptions are deduced from these premises.

U.S. Grand Strategy: A Pattern of Continuity

The United States has pursued the same grand strategy, preponderance, since the late 1940s. The key elements of this strategy are creation and maintenance of a U.S.-led world order based on preeminent U.S. political, military, and economic power, and on American values; maximization of U.S. control over the international system by preventing the emergence of rival great powers in Europe and East Asia; and maintenance of economic interdependence as a vital U.S. security interest. The logic of the strategy is that interdependence is the paramount interest the strategy promotes; instability is the threat to interdependence; and extended deterrence is the means by which the strategy deals with this threat.

The quest for world order has been integral to U.S. grand strategy since at least 1945. The grand strategic equation of world order with U.S. security reflects a historically rooted belief that to be secure, the United States must extend abroad both its power and its political and economic institutions and values.[4] Thus, even in the mid to late 1940s, the driving force behind U.S.

---

3. This definition is similar to Leffler's and Barry Posen's. Leffler, *A Preponderance of Power*, p. ix, and Barry R. Posen, *The Sources of Military Doctrine: France, Britain, and Germany Between the World Wars* (Ithaca, N.Y.: Cornell University Press, 1984), p. 13.
4. Driving U.S. strategy is the belief that "America must have a favorable climate for its institutions to thrive, and perhaps even for them to survive." Lloyd C. Gardner, *A Covenant with Power: America*

policy was more basic than the mere containment of the Soviet Union,[5] which explains why, despite the Cold War's end, the United States remains committed to the strategy of preponderance.

Since the end of World War II, the United States has attempted to prevent the emergence of new geopolitical rivals. In the 1940s, of course, it accepted the reality of Soviet power. Short of preventive war (a thought entertained by some U.S. policymakers), the United States could not prevent the Soviet Union's ascendance to superpower status.[6] From 1945 on, however, the United States was the sole great power in its own sphere of influence, the non-Soviet world. As the historian Melvyn P. Leffler points out, U.S. policymakers believed that "neither an integrated Europe nor a united Germany nor an independent Japan must be permitted to emerge as third force or a neutral bloc."[7]

Leffler's argument is not idiosyncratic. Observing that the United States "expected to lead the new world order" after 1945, the diplomatic historian John Lewis Gaddis states: "Few historians would deny, today, that the United States did expect to dominate the international scene after World War II, and that it did so well before the Soviet Union emerged as a clear and present antagonist."[8] It could be argued, of course, that far from suppressing the reemergence of competing power centers within its sphere, the United States encouraged their emergence by facilitating the postwar economic recoveries of Western Europe and Japan. While helping its allies rebuild economically, however, the United States maintained tight political control over them. Washington wanted Western Europe and Japan to be strong enough to help contain the Soviet Union; it did not want them to become strong enough to challenge its

---

and World Order from Wilson to Reagan (New York: Oxford University Press, 1984), p. 27. The belief that the United States is alone in a hostile world leads it to alleviate this chronic insecurity by seeking complete immunity from external threat. William Appleman Williams, *Empire as a Way of Life: An Essay on the Causes and Character of America's Present Predicament along with a Few Thoughts About an Alternative* (New York: Oxford University Press, 1980), p. 53. Also see James Chace and Caleb Carr, *America Invulnerable: The Quest for Absolute Security from 1812 to Star Wars* (New York: Summit Books, 1988), p. 12.

5. The link between America's security, its preponderance, and an American-led world order was articulated in NSC-68, which states that the purpose of American power is "to foster a world environment in which the American system can survive and flourish" and the strategy of preponderance is "a policy which [the United States] would probably pursue even if there were no Soviet Union." NSC-68 in Thomas Etzold and John Lewis Gaddis, eds., *Containment: Documents on American Policy and Strategy, 1945–1950* (New York: Columbia University Press, 1978), p. 401.

6. See Russell D. Buhite and Wm. Christopher Hamel, "War for Peace: The Question of American Preventive War against the Soviet Union, 1945–1955," *Diplomatic History*, Vol. 14, No. 3 (Summer 1990), pp. 367–385.

7. Leffler, *A Preponderance of Power*, p. 17.

8. John Lewis Gaddis, "The Tragedy of Cold War History," *Diplomatic History*, Vol. 17, No. 1 (Winter 1993), pp. 3–4.

leadership. The United States was especially concerned with circumscribing the resurgent power of (West) Germany and Japan. Thus, as the political scientist Wolfram Hanreider observed, America's post–World War II strategy was *double* containment (containment of the Soviet Union *and* of Germany and Japan).[9] Although the postwar American empire was an "empire by invitation," it was an empire nonetheless, and the United States sought to maintain its geopolitically privileged position vis-à-vis Western Europe and Japan.[10]

Economic interdependence has played a central role in U.S. grand strategy since 1945.[11] Indeed, the strategy of preponderance's hallmark is the interplay of security and economic factors.[12] Even before the Cold War's onset, the United States "deliberately fostered the economic interdependence of the major powers in order to ensure U.S. security and prosperity."[13] The centrality of interdependence in post-1945 foreign policy is explained in part by economic considerations. U.S. policymakers have come to believe that America's prosperity depends on its access to overseas markets and raw materials.[14] Even more important, however, are the perceived positive political and security externalities that flow from interdependence.

As World War II drew to a close, U.S. decision makers subscribed to three beliefs about interdependence's positive externalities. First, they embraced the

---

9. The term "double containment" is from Wolfram Hanreider, *Germany, Europe, and America* (New Haven, Conn.: Yale University Press, 1989).

10. See Geir Lundestad, *The American "Empire" and Other Studies of U.S. Foreign Policy in a Comparative Perspective* (New York: Oxford University Press, 1990).

11. Diplomatic historians agree that economic factors played an important role in postwar American foreign policy but disagree about whether geostrategic or economic considerations were accorded priority in U.S. strategy. Compare Leffler, *A Preponderance of Power* with Bruce Cumings, "The Poverty of Theory in Diplomatic History," in Michael J. Hogan, ed., *America in the World: The Historiography of American Foreign Relations Since 1941* (Cambridge, U.K.: Cambridge University Press, 1995). The crucial point, sometimes lost in the debate, is the seamless interconnection of strategy and economics.

12. As Robert A. Pollard and Samuel F. Wells, Jr. observe: "The global and comprehensive nature of American foreign economic policies and ideas makes it difficult to distinguish among the political, strategic, and economic sources of American conduct in the postwar years." Robert A. Pollard and Samuel F. Wells, Jr., "1945–1960: The Era of American Economic Hegemony," in William Becker and Samuel F. Wells, Jr., eds., *Economics and World Power* (New York: Columbia University Press, 1984), p. 387.

13. Robert A. Pollard, *Economic Security and the Origins of the Cold War* (New York: Columbia University Press, 1985), p. 2.

14. Brent Scowcroft argues that American prosperity depends on the global economy, and therefore the "U.S. cannot prosper amid chaos and conflict." Brent Scowcroft, "Who Can Harness History?" *New York Times*, July 2, 1993, p. A15. Then-Secretary of Defense Dick Cheney stated: "We are a trading nation, and our prosperity is directly linked to peace and stability in the world. . . . Simply stated, the worldwide market that we're part of cannot thrive where regional violence, instability and aggression put it in peril." Dick Cheney, "The Military We Need in the Future," *Vital Speeches of the Day*, Vol. 59, No. 1 (October 15, 1992), p. 13.

traditional perspective of commercial liberalism that by increasing prosperity, an open international trading system decreases the risk of war by raising its costs. Second, they believed a key "lesson" of the 1930s was that economic nationalism (autarky, rival trade blocs) led to totalitarianism and militarism in Germany and Japan, and thus was an important cause of geopolitical instability. An open postwar international trading system would prevent a replay of the 1930s by strengthening the domestic political position of elites who would be predisposed by economic interest and ideology to pursue pacific foreign policies. Third, they believed that World War II's origins were rooted in economic causes (i.e., competition for territorial control of markets and raw materials). An open international trading system would eliminate the need to capture resources and markets by providing nondiscriminatory access to all states. The Cold War added a fourth reason to regard economic interdependence as a vital American interest: an open international trading system would contribute to peace and international stability in the non-Soviet world, and hence reduce its vulnerability to communism.

Although the Cold War has ended, the United States remains wedded to the strategy of preponderance. The Bush administration's "new world order" and the Clinton administration's strategy of "engagement and enlargement" reflect Washington's continuing aspiration to maintain an international system shaped by America's power and values. The U.S. foreign policy community understands that little can be done to prevent the emergence of a new great power challenger (China) outside the U.S. sphere of influence. Within its own sphere, however, the United States remains determined to suppress the rise of rival powers: Germany and Japan are to be contained by embedding them firmly in U.S.-dominated security and economic frameworks.[15] Now, as during the Cold War, the U.S. military protectorate's purpose in Europe and East Asia is to facilitate interdependence by removing the security dilemma and relative

---

15. Arguments that the post–Cold War purpose of American security commitments in Europe and East Asia is to contain Germany and Japan, respectively, and thus prevent the "renationalization" of their foreign and security policies, are legion. On Germany, see, for example, Robert J. Art, "Why Western Europe Needs the United States and NATO," *Political Science Quarterly*, Vol. 111, No. 1 (Spring 1996), pp. 1–40, and Charles L. Glaser, "Why NATO is Still Best: Future Security Arrangements for Europe," *International Security*, Vol. 18, No. 1 (Summer 1993), pp. 5–50. On Japan, see Richard K. Betts, "Wealth, Power and Instability: East Asia and the United States after the Cold War," *International Security*, Vol. 18, No. 3 (Winter 1993/94), pp. 56–64, and Aaron L. Friedberg, "Ripe for Rivalry: Prospects for Peace in a Multipolar Asia," *International Security*, Vol. 18, No. 3 (Winter 1993/94), pp. 31–32. In 1990 the then commander of U.S. Marine Corps bases in Japan, Maj. Gen. Henry C. Stackpole III, bluntly explained the reason for the American military presence in East Asia: "No one wants a rearmed, resurgent Japan. So we are the cap in the bottle, if you will." Quoted in Sam Jameson, "A Reluctant Superpower Agonizes Over Military," *Los Angeles Times*, August 1, 1995, p. H4.

gains issue from relations among the states in Washington's orbit. U.S. security commitments continue to be extended beyond the European and East Asian core into the periphery. Preponderance's strategic imperatives are the same as they were during the post–World War II era: pacification and reassurance in Europe and East Asia, and protection of these regions from the contagion of instability in the periphery.

Interests, Threats, and Means

Preponderance is a realist strategy that subsumes two distinct approaches: offensive realism and defensive realism.[16] Offensive and defensive realists define U.S. interests identically and agree broadly about the threats to them. Offensive and defensive realists disagree, however, about the relative salience of "hard" versus "soft" power in the strategy of preponderance, and consequently, they have disparate views of the means required to sustain the strategy.[17]

---

16. John J. Mearsheimer is the leading academic proponent of offensive realism. See John J. Mearsheimer, "The False Promise of Liberal Institutions," *International Security*, Vol. 19, No. 3 (Winter 1993/94), pp. 9–14. For applications of offensive realism to U.S. grand strategy, see Patrick E. Tyler, "U.S. Strategy Plan Calls for Ensuring No Rivals Develop, *New York Times*, March 8, 1992, p. A1 [draft FY 1994–1999 *Defense Planning Guidance*]; *Regional Defense Strategy* (Washington, D.C.: Department of Defense, Office of the Undersecretary of Defense for Policy, 1992); and *1991 Summer Study* (Organized by the director, Net Assessment, held at the U.S. Naval War College, Newport R.I., August 5–13, 1991). Also see Robert Kagan, "The Case for Global Activism," *Commentary*, Vol. 98, No. 3 (September 1994); Robert Kagan, "A Retreat from Power?" *Commentary*, Vol. 100, No. 1 (July 1995); Charles Krauthammer, "The Unipolar Moment," *Foreign Affairs: America and the World*, Vol. 70, No. 1 (1990–91); William Kristol and Robert Kagan, "Toward a Neo-Reaganite Foreign Policy," *Foreign Affairs*, Vol. 75, No. 4 (July/August 1996), pp. 18–32; Zalmay Khalilzad, "Losing the Moment? The United States and the World After the Cold War," *Washington Quarterly*, Vol. 18, No. 2 (Spring 1995), pp. 87–107; and Khalilzad, "U.S. Grand Strategies."

Leading academic proponents of defensive realism include Barry Posen, Jack Snyder, Stephen Van Evera, and Stephen M. Walt. For scholarly works embodying defensive realism, see Fareed Zakaria, "Realism and Domestic Politics," *International Security*, Vol. 17, No. 1 (Summer 1992), p. 191, fn. 34. Another important defensive realist work, reviewed in Zakaria's article, is Jack Snyder, *Myths of Empire: Domestic Politics and International Ambition* (Ithaca, N.Y.: Cornell University Press, 1991). For applications of defensive realism to U.S. grand strategy, see *A National Security Strategy of Engagements and Enlargement* (Washington, D.C.: The White House, 1995); *United States Security Strategy for the East Asia-Pacific Region* (Washington, D.C.: Department of Defense, Office of International Security Affairs, 1995); Anthony Lake, "Laying the Foundations for a New American Century" (The White House: Office of the Press Secretary, April 25, 1996); Anthony Lake, "Defining Missions, Setting Deadlines: Meeting New Security Challenges in the Post–Cold War World" (The White House: Office of the Press Secretary, March 6, 1996); Joseph S. Nye, Jr., *Bound to Lead: The Changing Nature of American Power* (New York: Basic Books, 1990); Joseph S. Nye, Jr., "The Case for Deep Engagement," *Foreign Affairs*, Vol. 74, No. 4 (July/August 1995), pp. 90–102; and Joseph S. Nye, Jr., "Conflicts After the Cold War," *Washington Quarterly*, Vol. 19, No. 1 (Winter 1996), pp. 5–24.

17. On the distinction between hard and soft power, see Nye, *Bound to Lead*.

Offensive and defensive realists concur that continued American hegemony is desirable; however, they employ different theoretical assumptions to support this shared conclusion. Offensive realists believe that states should attempt to maximize their relative power to gain security. They believe that in a harsh, competitive world, security rests on hard power (military power and its economic underpinnings) and it is best to be number one. For them, systemic stability (the absence of war, security competitions, and proliferation) is a function of U.S. military power. They contend that the chances of future great power war will remain low if U.S. hegemony is preserved but will be high if the international system becomes multipolar. Offensive realists claim that others will accept U.S. hegemony because they must do so, and they derive important security and economic benefits from U.S. hegemony, and further, because they have no choice. While not deprecating the importance of American liberal democratic values, offensive realists do not believe these values contribute to peace and stability independently of the military power that is the foundation of U.S. hegemony.

Defensive realists view international politics more optimistically. As Fareed Zakaria says, defensive realism "assumes that the international system provides incentives only for moderate, reasonable behavior."[18] Defensive realists argue that states seek to maximize their security, not their power, and that security is actually plentiful in the international system. From these assumptions they conclude that power-maximizing behavior by states (overexpansion) results from cognitive factors (misperception) or domestic political pathologies rather than from international systemic constraints. Hence aggression can be cured by rooting out the unit-level deformations that purportedly cause it. The spread of democracy, economic interdependence, and the development of international institutions can help accomplish this task. Thus in its diagnosis of, and prescription for, "irrational" state behavior, defensive realism converges with liberal international relations theory.

An apparent tension exists between defensive realism's theoretical assumptions and its professed grand strategic goal of maintaining U.S. preponderance. Defensive realists reconcile strategy with theory by invoking three arguments. First, "balance-of-threat" theory is used to support the proposition that others will not balance against a hegemonic United States.[19] Second, defensive realists

---

18. Zakaria, "Realism and Domestic Politics," p. 190.
19. On balance-of-threat theory, see Stephen M. Walt, *The Origins of Alliances* (Ithaca, N.Y.: Cornell University Press, 1987). For a critique of balance-of-threat theory's applicability in a unipolar world, see Christopher Layne, "The Unipolar Illusion: Why New Great Powers Will Rise," *International Security*, Vol. 17, No. 4 (Spring 1993), pp. 11–15.

argue that precisely because the United States does manifest concern for their interests, other states will want to bandwagon with it. Third, by using its soft power—the appeal of American values and culture—the United States can reduce the risk that others will regard it as a threat. For defensive realists, a hegemon's power rests not only on its military and economic power, but also on others' acceptance of its norms and principles.[20] Defensive realist advocates of preponderance invoke these arguments to support the claim that *American hegemony does not threaten other states' security; is essential to maintaining a stable international system from which all states benefit; and will be willingly accepted by all except "rogue" states* (nondemocratic states that do not accept the norms that the United States has imposed on the international system).

The strategy of preponderance assumes that the United States has a vital "milieu" interest in maintaining stability in the international system.[21] Underlying the strategy is fear of what *might* happen in a world no longer shaped by predominant U.S. power. Continued American hegemony is important because it is seen as the prerequisite for systemic stability (primacy *is* world order). Instability is dangerous because it threatens the link that connects U.S. security to the strategic and economic interests furthered by interdependence. Interdependence is an overriding U.S. interest for economic reasons and, more important, for politico-military reasons: it is viewed as both a cause and a consequence of peace and stability in the international system. Indeed, the role of interdependence in the strategy of preponderance is tautological: Interdependence is a vital interest because it leads to peace and stability (and prosperity); however, peace and stability must preexist in the international system order for interdependence to take root.

Geographically, the strategy of preponderance identifies Europe, East Asia, and the Persian Gulf as regions in which the United States has vital security interests. Europe and East Asia (the zone of peace and prosperity) are important because they are the regions from which new great powers could emerge and where future great power war could occur; central to the functioning of an interdependent international economic system; and vital to U.S. prosperity. The Persian Gulf is important because of oil. Geographically, these three regions constitute America's vital interests; however, its security interests are

---

20. See John G. Ikenberry and Charles A. Kupchan, "The Legitimation of Hegemonic Power," in David P. Rapkin, ed., *World Leadership and Hegemony* (Boulder, Colo.: Lynne Rienner, 1990), p. 52.
21. For the definition of "milieu goals," see Arnold Wolfers, *Discord and Collaboration: Essays in International Politics* (Baltimore, Md.: Johns Hopkins University Press, 1962), pp. 73–77.

not confined to these regions. The United States must also be concerned with the peripheries because turmoil there could affect the core.

The strategy of preponderance identifies the rise of new great powers and the spillover of instability from strategically peripheral areas to regions of core strategic interest as the two main threats to U.S. interests in stability and interdependence. The emergence of new great powers would have two deleterious consequences for the United States. First, new great powers could become aspiring hegemons and, if successful, would seriously threaten U.S. security.[22] Offensive and defensive realists concur that China is the state most likely to emerge as a hegemonic challenger in the early twenty-first century. Offensive realists believe that the United States should respond to the prospect of emerging Chinese power by moving now to contain Beijing.[23] While holding the containment option in reserve, defensive realists prefer to engage China now in the hope that democratization and interdependence will have meliorating effects on Beijing's foreign policy.[24]

Second, the emergence of new great powers is always a destabilizing geopolitical phenomenon. Although the United States may have to acquiesce in China's rise to great power status, the strategy of preponderance clearly aims to prevent the great power emergence of Germany and Japan. U.S. policymakers fear that a "renationalized" Japan or Germany could trigger an adverse geopolitical chain reaction. For their neighbors, resurgent German and Japanese power would revive the security dilemma (dormant during the Cold War). At best, the ensuing security competitions that could occur in Europe and East Asia would make cooperation more difficult. At worst, renationalization could fuel a cycle of rising tensions and arms racing (possibly including nuclear proliferation) that would undermine regional stability and perhaps lead to war. Either way, however, U.S. strategic and economic interests in interdependence would be imperiled.

---

22. See Khalilzad, "U.S. Grand Strategies," p. 18.
23. See Jacob Heilbrunn, "The Next Cold War," *The New Republic*, November 20, 1995, pp. 27–30; Gideon Rachman, "Containing China," *Washington Quarterly*, Vol. 19, No. 1 (Winter 1996), pp. 129–139; and Arthur Waldron, "Deterring China," *Commentary*, Vol. 100, No. 4 (October 1995), pp. 17–21.
24. See, for example, Audry Kurth Cronin and Patrick Cronin, "The Realistic Engagement of China," *Washington Quarterly*, Vol. 19, No. 1 (Winter 1996), pp. 141–169; Kenneth Lieberthal, "The China Challenge," *Foreign Affairs*, Vol. 74, No. 6 (November/December 1995), pp. 35–49; James L. Richardson, "Asia-Pacific: The Case for Geopolitical Optimism," *The National Interest*, No. 38 (Winter 1994/1995), pp. 28–39; and Jeffrey E. Garten, "Power Couple," *New York Times*, January 15, 1996, p. All. Joseph S. Nye, Jr. also is an advocate of engagement.

The strategy's aversion to the emergence of new great powers reflects the belief that multipolar international systems are unstable and war prone.[25] As former Pentagon official Zalmay Khalilzad argues, "U.S. leadership [i.e., continued U.S. hegemony] would be more conducive to global stability than a bipolar or a multipolar balance of power system."[26] Advocates of preponderance regard multipolarity with trepidation because they embrace the realist assumptions that in multipolar systems balancing may fail (leading to war) because of coordination and collective action problems, and difficulties in calculating relative power relationships accurately.[27]

Instability in the peripheries (caused by failed states or by internal conflict triggered by ethnic, religious, or national strife) can also jeopardize America's interest in international stability. Turmoil in the periphery could prompt America's allies to act independently to maintain order (again raising the specter of renationalization), or could ripple back into the core and undercut prosperity by disrupting the economic links that bind the United States to Europe and East Asia.

U.S. security guarantees to Europe and East Asia—implemented by extended deterrence—are the means by which the strategy of preponderance maintains a benign international political order conducive to interdependence. Through extended deterrence, the United States retains the primary responsibility for defending German and Japanese security interests both in the core and in the periphery. The United States thereby negates German and Japanese incentives to renationalize their foreign and security policies. Thus, to implement the strategy of preponderance successfully, the United States "must account sufficiently for the interests of the large industrial nations *to discourage them from challenging our leadership* or seeking to overturn the established political or economic order."[28]

The strategy of preponderance is expensive. Offensive realists (who regard hard power as the basis of U.S. hegemony) believe the United States is not spending enough on defense. Their recommended annual defense spending

---

25. The most compelling articulation of the view that multipolar systems are fundamentally unstable is Mearsheimer, "Back to the Future."
26. Khalilzad, "Losing the Moment?" p. 94.
27. On why balancing sometimes fails, see Kenneth N. Waltz, *Theory of International Politics* (Reading, Mass.: Addison-Wesley, 1979), pp. 164–165; Mearsheimer, "Back to the Future," pp. 15–16; Stephen M. Walt, *The Origins of Alliances* (Ithaca, N.Y.: Cornell University Press, 1987), pp. 123–128; and Mancur Olson and Richard Zeckhauser, "An Economic Theory of Alliances," *Review of Economics and Statistics*, Vol. 48, No. 3 (August 1966), pp. 266–279.
28. Tyler, "U.S. Strategy Plan" (emphasis added).

increases vary from William Kristol and Robert Kagan's proposed $60–80 billion (an increase of plus 1 percent of gross national product [GNP] above current spending) to the $140 billion recommended in the *Agenda for America* (which would amount to a defense hike of just under 2 percent of GNP).[29] Defensive realists (who assign a greater role to soft power in maintaining U.S. preponderance) want to keep defense spending at approximately its current level. (At present, the Clinton administration projects that U.S. defense spending in fiscal year 1997 will amount to about 3.8 percent of GNP.)

Preponderance in the Post–Cold War World: A Critique

In this section I critique the strategy of preponderance, focusing on interdependence's central geopolitical role in American grand strategy. Interdependence leads to strategic overextension, encourages threat inflation, and forces the United States to rely on an increasingly problematic extended deterrence strategy.

The strategy's fixation with international stability stems from its concern with ensuring that conditions exist in which interdependence can survive and flourish. The causal logic of commercial liberalism holds that economic interdependence leads to peace. The causal logic of preponderance, however, reflects a different view of the relationship between peace and interdependence: it is peace—specifically the international security framework the United States has maintained from 1945 to the present—that makes economic interdependence possible. As former Assistant Secretary of Defense Joseph S. Nye, Jr. puts it:

Political order is not sufficient to explain economic prosperity, but it is necessary. Analysts who ignore the importance of this political order are like people who forget the importance of the oxygen they breathe. Security is like oxygen—you tend not to notice it until you begin to lose it, but once that occurs there is nothing else that you will think about.[30]

---

29. Kristol and Kagan, "Toward a Neo-Reaganite Foreign Policy," p. 25, and Haley Barbour, *Agenda for America: A Republican Direction for the Future* (Washington, D.C.: Regenery Press, 1996). For a discussion of the *Agenda for America* and other recent Republican foreign and defense policy proposals, see Jonathan Clarke, "Gone to the Lake: Republicans and Foreign Policy," *The National Interest*, No. 44 (Summer 1996), pp. 34–45.
30. Nye, "The Case for Deep Engagement," p. 91. Art makes a similar argument for post–Cold War American military engagement in Europe. Art, "Why Western Europe Needs the United States," p. 36. Because interdependence requires the United States to maintain an extensive overseas military presence (and occasionally to use force to maintain the security environment that interdependence requires), it could be said that interdependence is like carbon monoxide: it is not noticeable until it kills.

Interdependence and Security: An Overlooked Connection

There is a tight linkage—too often neglected by many international relations theorists—between security and economic interdependence. I call this the "security/interdependence nexus." To preserve an international environment conducive to economic interdependence, the United States must engage in an extended deterrence strategy that undertakes to defend its allies' vital interests by protecting them from hostile powers, threats emanating in the periphery, and each other. The need to rely on extended deterrence to maintain the conditions in which interdependence can take root leads inexorably to strategic overextension: the United States must extend deterrence to secure interdependence against threats emanating in both the core and the periphery, and the synergy between credibility concerns and threat inflation causes the United States to expand the scope of its security commitments. Economic interdependence therefore brings with it an increased risk of war and a decrease in America's relative power.

INTERDEPENDENCE AND STRATEGIC OVEREXTENSION
The strategy of preponderance assumes that the international system will be relatively orderly and stable if the United States defends others' vital interests, but would become disorderly and unstable if others acquired the means to defend their own vital interests. Thus, to ensure a post–Cold War geopolitical setting conductive to interdependence, the United States "will retain the pre-eminent responsibility for selectively addressing those wrongs which threaten *not only our interests but those of our allies or friends*, which could seriously unsettle international relations."[31] The corollary is that the United States must defend its allies' interests in both the core *and* in the periphery. Two cases illustrate how the security/interdependence nexus invariably leads to U.S. strategic overextension: the United States' role in Indochina from 1948 to 1954 and its current intervention in Bosnia.

In the late 1940s and early 1950s, America's Cold War strategic imperatives required Japan's economic recovery, which U.S. policymakers believed depended on Japan's access to both export markets and raw materials in Southeast Asia.[32] The Truman and Eisenhower administrations understood that, for

---

31. "Excerpts from Pentagon's Plan" (emphasis added).
32. This discussion is based on William S. Borden, *The Pacific Alliance: United States Foreign Economic Policy and Japanese Trade Recovery, 1947–1955* (Madison: University of Wisconsin Press, 1984); Lloyd C. Gardner, *Approaching Vietnam: From World War II Through Dienbienphu* (New York: W.W. Norton,

America's Asian strategy to succeed, the United States had to guarantee Japan's military *and* economic security. This security/interdependence nexus—specifically, the U.S. strategic interest in defending Japan's economic access to Southeast Asia—propelled America's deepening involvement in Indochina.

Notwithstanding its lack of intrinsic economic and strategic importance, Indochina became the focal point of U.S. policy because of "domino theory" concerns.[33] The United States regarded Indochina as a fire wall needed to prevent the more economically vital parts of the region—especially Malaya and Indonesia—from falling under communist control. Washington's concern was that the economic repercussions of toppling dominoes would have geopolitical consequences: if Japan were cut off from Southeast Asia, the resulting economic hardship might cause domestic instability in Japan and result in Tokyo drifting out of the U.S. orbit. The connection between Japan's geopolitical orientation, its economic recovery, and its access to Southeast Asia—that is, the belief that core and periphery are economically *and* strategically interdependent—catalyzed Washington's support of France during the First Indochina War and, after 1954, its support of a noncommunist state in South Vietnam. In retrospect, the United States crossed the most crucial threshold on the road to the Vietnam War in the early 1950s, when Washington concluded that interdependence's strategic requirements (specifically, Japan's security and prosperity) necessitated that containment be extended to Southeast Asia.

The United States' 1995 military intervention in Bosnia also illustrates how the security/interdependence nexus leads to strategic overextension. The parallels between Indochina and Bosnia are striking even though, unlike the perceived interdependence between Japan and Southeast Asia in the late 1940s and early 1950s, the Balkans' economic importance to Western Europe is nil

---

1988); Steven Hugh Lee, *Outposts of Empire: Korea, Vietnam, and the Origins of the Cold War in Asia, 1949–1954* (Montreal: McGill-Queen's University Press, 1995); Leffler, *A Preponderance of Power;* Ronald L. McGlothen, *Controlling the Waves: Dean Acheson and U.S. Foreign Policy* (New York: W.W. Norton, 1993); Andrew J. Rotter, *The Path to Vietnam: Origins of the American Commitment to Southeast Asia* (Ithaca, N.Y.: Cornell University Press, 1987); Michael Schaller, *The American Occupation of Japan: The Origins of the Cold War in Asia* (New York: Oxford University Press, 1985); Pollard and Wells, "American Economic Hegemony"; Michael Schaller, "Securing the Great Crescent: Occupied Japan and the Origins of Containment in Southeast Asia," *Journal of American History,* Vol. 69, No. 2 (Summer 1982), pp. 392–414; Howard B. Schonberger, "The Cold War and the American Empire in Asia," *Radical History Review,* Vol. 33 (September 1985), pp. 139–154; Akio Watanabe, "Southeast Asia in U.S.-Japan Relations," in Akira Iriye and Warren I. Cohen, eds., *The United States and Japan in the Postwar World* (Lexington: University Press of Kentucky, 1989), pp. 36–60.
33. On the domino theory, see Robert Jervis, "Domino Beliefs and Strategic Behavior," in Robert Jervis and Jack Snyder, eds., *Dominoes and Bandwagons: Strategic Beliefs and Great Power Competition in the Eurasian Rimland* (New York: Oxford University Press, 1991), pp. 20–50.

and there is no geopolitical threat in the Balkans that corresponds to Washington's (mistaken) belief that the Vietminh were the agents of a monolithic, Kremlin-directed communist bloc. Given these differences the case for intervention was even less compelling strategically in Bosnia than in Indochina. Nevertheless, the rationale for intervention has been the same. U.S. Bosnia policy has been justified by invoking arguments—based on domino imagery and the perceived need to protect economic interdependence—similar to those used to justify U.S. involvement in Indochina in the early 1950s.

Although a few commentators have contended that U.S. intervention in Bosnia was animated by humanitarian concerns, this is not the case. U.S. policymakers, including President Bill Clinton, made clear that their overriding concerns were to ensure European stability by preventing the Balkan conflict from spreading, and to reestablish NATO's credibility. Indeed, some of preponderance's proponents believe that U.S. intervention in Bosnia alone is insufficient to prevent peripheral instability from spreading to Western Europe. To forestall a geopolitical snowball, they contend, it is necessary to enlarge NATO by incorporating the states of East Central Europe.[34]

These expressed fears about the spillover of instability from Bosnia (or East Central Europe) into Europe are, without explication, vague. A number of U.S. policymakers and analysts have detailed their concerns, however: they fear that spreading instability could affect the United States economically given its interdependence with Europe. Thus Senator Richard Lugar (R.-Ind.) urged U.S. intervention in Bosnia because "there will be devastating economic effects in Europe of a spread of war and, thus, the loss of jobs in this country as we try to base a recovery upon our export potential."[35] William E. Odom, former Director of the National Security Agency, explicates the perceived significance of the link between U.S. interests in interdependence and its concerns for European stability and NATO credibility:

Only a strong NATO with the U.S. centrally involved can prevent Western Europe from drifting into national parochialism and eventual regression from its present level of economic and political cooperation. Failure to act effectively in Yugoslavia will not only affect U.S. security interests but also U.S. economic interests. Our economic interdependency with Western Europe creates large numbers of American jobs.[36]

---

34. William E. Odom, "NATO's Expansion: Why the Critics Are Wrong," *The National Interest*, No. 39 (Spring 1995), p. 44.
35. *MacNeil-Lehrer News Hour*, May 6, 1993, Transcript No. 4622.
36. William E. Odom, "Yugoslavia: Quagmire or Strategic Challenge?" Hudson Briefing Paper, No. 146 (Indianapolis: Hudson Institute, November 1992), p. 2.

With respect to U.S. commitments, the strategy of preponderance is open-ended. Even the strategy's proponents who acknowledge that there are limits to U.S. security interests are hard-pressed to practice restraint in actual cases. Robert Art's writings are illustrative. In 1991 he argued the only U.S. security concern in Europe and the Far East is to ensure that great power war does not occur because only conflicts of that magnitude could negatively affect economic interdependence. "In contrast," he wrote, "wars among the lesser powers in either region (for example, a war between Hungary and Romania over Transylvania) would not require American involvement."[37] Yet in 1996 Art suggested that U.S. intervention in Bosnia (by any standard, a "war among lesser powers") was necessary because the Balkan war had implicated NATO's cohesion and viability and raised doubts about America's leadership and its willingness to remain engaged in Europe.[38] Absent continued U.S. involvement in European security matters, he argued, NATO would be unable to perform its post–Cold War tasks of maintaining a benign security order conducive to Western Europe's continuing politico-economic integration, containing resurgent German power, and preventing the West European states from renationalizing their security policies.

Indochina and Bosnia demonstrate how the strategy of preponderance expands America's frontiers of insecurity. The security/interdependence nexus requires the United States to impose order on, and control over, the international system. To do so, it must continually enlarge the geographic scope of its strategic responsibilities to maintain the security of its established interests. As Robert H. Johnson observes, this process becomes self-sustaining because each time the United States pushes its security interests outward, threats to the new security frontier will be apprehended: "uncertainty leads to self-extension, which leads in turn to new uncertainty and further self-extension."[39] Core and periphery are interdependent strategically; however, while the core remains constant, the turbulent frontier in the periphery is constantly expanding. There is a suggestive parallel between late-Victorian Britain and the United States today. The late-nineteenth-century British statesman Lord Rosebery clearly recognized that economic interdependence could lead to strategic overextension:

Our commerce is so universal and so penetrating that scarcely any question can arise in any part of the world without involving British interests. This consideration, instead of widening rather circumscribes the field of our actions.

---

37. Art, "A Defensible Defense," p. 45.
38. Art, "Why Western Europe Needs the United States and NATO."
39. Robert H. Johnson, *Improbable Dangers: U.S. Conceptions of Threat in the Cold War and After* (New York: St. Martin's Press, 1994), p. 206.

For did we not strictly limit the principle of intervention we should always be simultaneously engaged in some forty wars.[40]

Of course, it is an exaggeration to suggest that the strategy of preponderance will involve the United States in forty wars simultaneously. It is not, however, an exaggeration to note that the need to defend America's perceived interest in maintaining a security framework in which economic interdependence can flourish has become the primary rationale for expanding its security commitments in East Asia and in Europe. To preserve a security framework favorable to interdependence, the United States does not, in fact, intervene everywhere; however, the logic underlying the strategy of preponderance can be used to justify U.S. intervention anywhere.

Threat Inflation, Credibility, and Interdependence

The security/interdependence nexus results in the exaggeration of threats to American strategic interests because it requires the United States to defend its core interests by intervening in the peripheries. There are three reasons for this. First, as Johnson points out, order-maintenance strategies are biased inherently toward threat exaggeration. Threats to order generate an anxiety "that has at its center the fear of the unknown. It is not just security, but the pattern of order upon which the sense of security depends that is threatened."[41] Second, because the strategy of preponderance requires U.S. intervention in places that concededly have no intrinsic strategic value, U.S. policymakers are compelled to overstate the dangers to American interests to mobilize domestic support for their policies.[42] Third, the tendency to exaggerate threats is tightly linked to the strategy of preponderance's concern with maintaining U.S. credibility.

The diplomatic historian Robert J. McMahon has observed that since 1945 U.S. policymakers consistently have asserted that American credibility is "among the most critical of all foreign policy objectives."[43] As Khalilzad makes clear, they still are obsessed with the need to preserve America's reputation for honoring its security commitments: "The credibility of U.S. alliances can be

---

40. Quoted in Paul Kennedy, *The Realities Behind Diplomacy: Background Influences on British External Policy, 1865–1980* (London: George Allen and Unwin, 1981), p. 105.
41. Johnson, *Improbable Dangers*, p. 12.
42. Ibid., pp. 131–132; Jervis in *Dominoes and Bandwagons*; and John A. Thompson "The Exaggeration of American Vulnerability: The Anatomy of a Tradition," *Diplomatic History*, Vol. 16, No. 1 (Winter 1992), pp. 23–43.
43. Robert J. McMahon, "Credibility and World Power: Exploring the Psychological Dimension in Postwar American Diplomacy," *Diplomatic History*, Vol. 15, No. 4 (Fall 1991), p. 455.

undermined if key allies, such as Germany and Japan, believe that the current arrangements do not deal adequately with threats to their security. It could also be undermined if, over an extended period, the United States is perceived as lacking the will or capability to lead in protecting their interests."[44] Credibility is believed to be crucial if the extended deterrence guarantees on which the strategy of preponderance rests are to remain robust.

Preponderance's concern with credibility leads to the belief that U.S. commitments are interdependent. As Thomas C. Schelling has put it: "Few parts of the world are intrinsically worth the risk of serious war by themselves . . . but defending them or running risks to protect them may preserve one's commitments to action in other parts of the world at later times."[45] If others perceive that the United States has acted irresolutely in a specific crisis, they will conclude that it will not honor its commitments in future crises. Hence, as happened repeatedly in the Cold War, the United States has taken military action in peripheral areas to demonstrate—both to allies and potential adversaries—that it will uphold its security obligations in core areas.

Interdependence and Extended Deterrence in the Twenty-first Century

Views about U.S. grand strategy are linked inextricably to attitudes about nuclear proliferation and deterrence. In their recent debate Scott Sagan and Kenneth Waltz crystallized the percolating argument between "deterrence optimists" and "proliferation pessimists."[46] The strategy of preponderance reflects "proliferation pessimism," the belief that the spread of nuclear weapons will have negative consequences: specifically, renationalization and an increased risk of nuclear conflict. The strategy rests on the assumption that the United States can prevent these consequences by bringing potential proliferators within the shelter of its security umbrella. Thus the strategy is based not only on proliferation pessimism but on *extended* deterrence optimism: a belief (or faith) in the continuing robustness of the U.S. security umbrella.

Extended deterrence optimism is quite problematic, however. As Bradley A. Thayer points out, states that obtain nuclear weapons are driven to do so by

---

44. Khalilzad, "U.S. Grand Strategies," p. 24.
45. Thomas C. Schelling, *Arms and Influence* (New Haven, Conn.: Yale University Press, 1966), p. 124.
46. Scott D. Sagan and Kenneth N. Waltz, *The Spread of Nuclear Weapons: A Debate* (New York: W.W. Norton, 1995). This terminology is borrowed from Peter Lavoy, "The Strategic Consequences of Nuclear Proliferation," *Security Studies*, Vol. 4, No. 4 (Summer 1995), pp. 695–753.

security imperatives. Proliferation is a demand-driven problem: "If states feel that nuclear weapons are not needed for their security, then they will not seek to acquire them."[47] The strategy of preponderance attempts to solve this demand-driven cause of proliferation by assuaging the protected states' security fears. Whether the strategy can work is a function of two interrelated factors. First, is extended deterrence credible? That is, will it actually dissuade an adversary from attacking the target state? Second, will U.S. guarantees reassure the protected state?

Why Extended Deterrence Will Fail in the Post–Cold War World

In its current iteration, the strategy of preponderance is a reprise of America's Cold War extended deterrence strategy. Extended deterrence is a difficult strategy to implement successfully: "One of the perpetual problems of deterrence on behalf of third parties is that the costs a state is willing to bear are usually much less than if its own territory is at stake, and it is very difficult to pretend otherwise."[48] For extended deterrence to work, a potential challenger must be convinced that the defender's commitment is credible.[49]

During the Cold War, extending deterrence to Western Europe was thought to be especially problematic after the Soviet Union attained strategic nuclear parity with the United States because, in the course of defending Europe, the United States would have exposed itself to Soviet nuclear retaliation. Concern was expressed on both sides of the Atlantic that the U.S. pledge to use nuclear weapons to deter a Soviet conventional attack on Western Europe was irrational and incredible (in both senses of the latter term). Indeed, extended deterrence was a contentious issue that seriously corroded NATO's unity. During the Cold War, many U.S. strategists suggested that to solve the "credibility of commitment" problem, the United States needed to acquire strategic damage limitation capabilities (counterforce, ballistic missile defenses) and firmly establish its reputation for upholding its commitments (by defending

47. Bradley A. Thayer, "The Causes of Nuclear Proliferation and the Utility of the Nuclear Non-Proliferation Regime," *Security Studies*, Vol. 4, No. 3 (Spring 1995), p. 503.

48. Patrick Morgan, *Deterrence: A Conceptual Analysis* (Beverly Hills, Calif.: Sage, 1983), p. 86.

49. Thomas C. Schelling has explained why extended deterrence raises such important concerns about credibility: "To *fight* abroad is a military act, but to *persuade* enemies or allies that would fight abroad, under circumstances of great cost and risk, requires more than a military capability. It requires projecting intentions. It requires *having* those intentions, even deliberately acquiring them, and communicating them persuasively to make other countries behave," Schelling, *Arms and Influence*, p. 36 (emphasis in original).

intrinsically unimportant areas in the periphery, deliberately circumscribing its ability to back away from commitments, and demonstrating that it could act "irrationally").[50]

Despite its perceived complexities, it appears that extended deterrence "worked" in Europe during the Cold War and was easier to execute successfully than generally was thought.[51] One should not assume, however, that extended deterrence will work similarly well in the early twenty-first century, because the unique coincidence of contextual variables is unlikely to be replicated in the future; they include: bipolarity; a clearly defined, and accepted, geopolitical status quo; the intrinsic value to the defender of the protected region; and the permanent forward deployment by the defender of sizeable military forces in the protected region.

The international system's polarity affects extended deterrence's efficacy. During the Cold War, the bipolar nature of the U.S.-Soviet rivalry in Europe stabilized the superpower relationship by demarcating the continent into U.S. and Soviet spheres of influence that delineated the vital interests of both superpowers.[52] Each knew it courted disaster if it challenged the other's sphere. Also, the superpowers were able to exercise control over their major allies to minimize the risk of being chain-ganged into a conflict.[53] In the early twenty-first century, however, the international system will be multipolar and, argu-

---

50. See Colin S. Gray, "Nuclear Strategy: A Case for a Theory of Victory," *International Security*, Vol. 4, No. 1 (Summer 1979), pp. 54–87; Colin S. Gray and Keith Payne, "Victory Is Possible," *Foreign Policy*, No. 39 (Summer 1980), pp. 14–27; and Earl Ravenal, "Alliance and Counterforce," *International Security*, Vol. 6, No. 4 (Spring 1982), pp. 26–43. Unlike Gray and Payne, Ravenal concluded that it was impossible for the United States to attain the strategic prerequisites for credible extended deterrence. For the argument that extended deterrence is credible even under the condition of mutual assured destruction, see Robert Jervis, *Illogic of American Nuclear Strategy* (Ithaca, N.Y.: Cornell University Press, 1984), and Charles L. Glaser, *Analyzing Strategic Nuclear Policy* (Princeton, N.J.: Princeton University Press, 1990). On the "rationality of the irrational," see Stephen Maxwell, *Rationality in Deterrence*, Adelphi Paper No. 50 (London: International Institute for Strategic Studies, 1968).

51. Deterrence "success" often poses a non-barking dog problem—the difficulty of explaining why an event did not happen. What appears to be a successful instance of deterrence may, in fact, be attributable to other factors. For instance, the putative attacker may not, in fact, have intended to forcibly challenge the defender's deterrence commitment. See Morgan, *Deterrence*, p. 25.

52. See Kenneth N. Waltz, "The Stability of a Bipolar World," *Daedalus*, Vol. 93, No. 3 (Summer 1964), pp. 881–909, and Mearsheimer, "Back to the Future." For the argument that the international system's stability during the Cold War era was attributable to nuclear deterrence and that bipolarity was an irrelevant factor, see Ted Hopf, "Polarity, the Offense-Defense Balance, and War," *American Political Science Review*, Vol. 81, No. 3 (June 1991), pp. 475–494.

53. On "chain-ganging," see Jack Snyder and Thomas J. Christensen, "Chain Gangs and Passed Bucks: Predicting Alliance Patterns in Multipolarity," *International Organization*, Vol. 44, No. 2 (Spring 1990), pp. 137–168.

ably, less stable and more conflict prone than a bipolar international system.[54] Spheres of influence will not be delineated clearly. In addition, because other states will have more latitude to pursue their own foreign and security policy agendas than they did during the Cold War, the risk will be much greater that the United States could be chain-ganged into a conflict because of a protected state's irresponsible behavior.

Extended deterrence is bolstered by a clearly delineated geopolitical status quo and undermined by the absence of clearly defined spheres of influence. The resolution of the 1948–49 Berlin crisis formalized Europe's de facto postwar partition. After 1949 the very existence of a clear status quo in Europe itself bolstered deterrence. As Robert Jervis points out, in geopolitical rivalries the defender enjoys two advantages: the potential attacker must bear the onus (and risk) of moving first, and the defender's interests generally outweigh the challenger's (hence the defender is usually willing to run greater risks to defend the status quo than the challenger is to change it).[55] In the post–Cold War world, however, the number of political and territorial flashpoints where the status quo is hotly contested is on the rise, including: the Senkaku Islands,[56] the Spratly Islands, Taiwan, Tokdo/Takeshima, and a host of potential disputes in East Central and Eastern Europe. One could argue of course that the United States would not have to deter these potential conflicts because they are peripheral to its security interests. This, however, overlooks the fact that U.S. policymakers believe the strategy of preponderance requires the United States to stand firm in the peripheries. For example, many of the strategy's proponents believe that to prevent European renationalization and preserve its credibility, the United States could not remain indifferent to Russian aggression against the Baltics or Ukraine (notwithstanding that current policy would exclude these states from the security sphere of even an expanded NATO).

---

54. For the argument that bipolar systems are more stable than multipolar ones, see Waltz, "The Stability of a Bipolar World"; Waltz, *Theory of International Politics*, pp. 161–176; and Mearsheimer, "Back to the Future." For the counterargument, see Stephen Van Evera, "Primed for Peace: Europe After the Cold War," *International Security*, Vol. 15, No. 3 (Winter 1990/91), pp. 7–57.

55. Jervis, *The Meaning of the Nuclear Revolution: Statecraft and the Prospect of Peace* (Ithaca, N.Y.: Cornell University Press, 1989), pp. 30–31. Also see Schelling, *Arms and Influence*, p. 44.

56. China's claims to the islands have been supported by Taiwan and Hong Kong. Concerned that China may forcibly seize the islands, Tokyo has indicated that it might use Japan's naval forces to resist. The Japanese government believes the U.S.-Japan Mutual Security Treaty obligates the United States to defend the Senkakus. See Nicholas D. Kristof, "Would *You* Fight for These Islands?" *New York Times*, October 20, 1996, p. E3, and Nicholas D. Kristof, "A Mini Asian Tempest Over Mini Island Group," *New York Times*, September 16, 1996, p. A7.

Indeed, some evidence suggests that the United States is contemplating further NATO expansion into the peripheries.[57]

A crucial factor in weighing the credibility of a defender's extended deterrence commitments is the extent of its interest in the protected area.[58] Had the Soviets contemplated seriously an attack on Western Europe, the risk calculus probably would have dissuaded them. In a bipolar setting Western Europe's security was a matter of supreme importance to the United States for both strategic and reputational reasons. In the early twenty-first century, however, the intrinsic value of many of the regions where the United States may wish to extend deterrence will be doubtful. Indeed, in the post–Cold War world "few imaginable disputes will engage vital U.S. interests."[59] It thus will be difficult to convince a potential attacker that U.S. deterrence commitments are credible. Moreover, the attenuated nature of U.S. interests will result in motivational asymmetries favoring potential challengers. That is, the "balance of resolve" will lie with the challenger, not with the United States, because the challenger will have more at stake.[60]

It is doubtful that the United States could deter a Russian invasion of the Baltics or Ukraine, or, several decades hence, a Chinese assault on Taiwan. To engage in such actions, Moscow or Beijing would have to be highly motivated; conversely, the objects of possible attack are unimportant strategically to the

---

57. See Steven Erlanger, "U.S. Pushes Bigger NATO Despite Qualms on Russia," *New York Times,* October 10, 1996, p. A4.

58. Paul Huth, *Extended Deterrence and the Prevention of War* (New Haven, Conn.: Yale University Press, 1988), p. 43.

59. Robert Jervis, "What Do We Want to Deter and How Do We Deter It?" in L. Benjamin Ederington and Michael J. Mazar, eds., *Turning Point: The Gulf War and U.S. Military Strategy* (Boulder, Colo.: Westview Press, 1994), p. 130.

60. Nuclear deterrence is effective when the defender's own survival is at stake but much less so in other situations. In the case of "limited" or "specific" challenges, the outcome is "determined by the parties' relative determination regarding the issue in dispute." Shai Feldman, "Middle East Nuclear Stability: The State of the Region and the State of the Debate," *Journal of International Affairs,* Vol. 49, No. 1 (Summer 1995), p. 215. Also see T.V. Paul, *Asymmetric Conflicts: War Initiation by Weaker Powers* (Cambridge, U.K.: Cambridge University Press, 1994). Recently, some scholars have employed "prospect theory" to explain why a state could be motivated to choose war even though victory is doubtful. See John Arquilla and Paul K. Davis, *Extended Deterrence, Compellence and the "Old World Order"* (Santa Monica, Calif.: RAND, 1992); Paul K. Davis and John Arquilla, *Thinking About Opponent Behavior in Crisis and Conflict: A Generic Model for Analysis and Group Discussion,* N-3322-JS (Santa Monica, Calif.: RAND, 1991); and Barbara Farnham, ed., *Avoiding Loses/Taking Risks: Prospect Theory and International Conflict* (Ann Arbor: University of Michigan Press, 1995). For a balanced assessment prospect theory as applied to international relations, see Jack S. Levy, "Prospect Theory and International Relations: Theoretical Applications and Analytical Problems," *Political Psychology,* Vol. 13, No. 2 (1992), pp. 283–310.

United States, which would cause the challenger to discount U.S. credibility. The spring 1996 crisis between China and Taiwan suggests the difficulties that U.S. extended deterrence strategy will face in coming decades. (China provoked the crisis by conducting intimidating military exercises in an attempt to influence Taiwan's presidential elections.) During the crisis a Chinese official said that China could use force against Taiwan without fear of U.S. intervention because American decision makers "care more about Los Angeles than they do about Taiwan."[61] Although an empty threat today, as China becomes more powerful militarily and economically in coming decades, threats of this nature from Beijing will be more potent.

Deterrence theory holds that extended deterrence is strengthened when the guarantor deploys its own military forces on the protected state's territory. Thus during the Cold War, the presence of large numbers of U.S. combat forces and tactical nuclear weapons in Europe underscored its importance to the United States and bolstered extended deterrence's credibility. The defender's deployment of forces is one of the most powerful factors in ensuring extended deterrence success, because it is a visible signal that the defender "means business."[62] In contrast, in the early twenty-first century in many places where the United States may seek to implement extended deterrence, the strategy's effectiveness will be undercut because the United States will not have a permanent, sizeable military presence in the target state (Korea is a notable exception).

For example, it is unlikely that the United States would ever bolster the credibility of security guarantees (should they, in fact, be given) to states like Ukraine, the Baltics, or even Taiwan—each of which is threatened potentially by a nuclear rival—by deploying ground forces as tokens of its resolve. Indeed, assuming NATO expansion goes forward, Washington has taken an ambivalent stance with respect to whether the United States will deploy troops or tactical nuclear weapons or both in Poland (which, because of its proximity to Russia, would be an expanded NATO's most vulnerable member state). At currently projected force levels, moreover, the American presence in Europe

---

61. Quoted in Patrick E. Tyler, "As China Threatens Taiwan, It Makes Sure U.S. Listens," *New York Times*, January 24, 1996, p. A3. I stress that this analysis is *prospective*. Today, China lacks the military capabilities to invade Taiwan successfully; however, the balance of forces probably will shift decisively in China's favor in the next decade or two, and the deterrent effect of any American commitment to Taiwan would be vitiated. Conventional deterrence no longer would be robust and any U.S. intervention would carry with it the risk of escalation to nuclear war.
62. Snyder, *Deterrence and Defense*, p. 254, and McGeorge Bundy, *Danger and Survival: Choices About the Bomb in the First Fifty Years* (New York: Random House, 1988), p. 599.

and East Asia probably will be too small to make extended deterrence credible in the early twenty-first century; a challenger, with good reason, may question whether the United States has either the capability or the intent to honor its deterrent commitments. U.S. forward-deployed forces could constitute the worst kind of trip wire—one that invites challenges rather than deterring them.

The United States of course could attempt to enhance the robustness of extended deterrence by increasing the size of its conventional deployments in key regions; however, it is doubtful that this would be either feasible or effective. Significantly increasing the number of U.S. forward-deployed forces in Europe and East Asia would be expensive.[63] And even then, the effect on the credibility of U.S. extended deterrence guarantees would be uncertain. After all, during the Cold War even the presence of over 300,000 U.S. troops in Europe was insufficient to reassure policymakers in the United States and Western Europe that extended deterrence was robust.

Economic Interdependence and Declining Relative Power

The strategy of preponderance incorporates contradictory assumptions about the importance of relative power. On the one hand, the strategy seeks to maximize America's military power by perpetuating its role as the predominant great power in the international system. Yet the strategy's economic dimension is curiously indifferent to the security implications of the redistribution of relative power in the international political system resulting from economic interdependence. Nor does it resolve the following conundrum: given that economic power is the foundation of military strength, how will the United States be able to retain its hegemonic position in the international political system if its relative economic power continues to decline?

Contrary to the strategy of preponderance, the security/interdependence nexus posits that economic openness has adverse strategic consequences: it contributes to, and accelerates, a redistribution of relative power among states in the international system (allowing rising competitors to catch up to the United States more quickly than they otherwise would). This leads to the emergence of new great powers. The resulting power transition, which occurs

---

63. Indeed, America's ability to sustain even its current level of forward-deployed forces is uncertain. It has been reported that because of fiscal constraints, the Pentagon is considering reducing U.S. forces in the Pacific below the heretofore sacrosanct deployment of 100,000 U.S. personnel. Paul Richter, "U.S. Pacific Troop Strength May Be Cut, Admiral Says," *Los Angeles Times*, February 4, 1997, p. A14.

as a formerly dominant power declines and new challengers arise, usually climaxes in great power war.[64] Because great power emergence is driven by uneven growth rates, there is little—short of preventive war—that the United States can do to prevent the rise of new great powers. But, to some extent, U.S. grand strategy can affect both the pace and the magnitude of America's relative power decline.

A crucial relationship exists between America's relative power and its strategic commitments. Paul Kennedy and Robert Gilpin explain how strategic overcommitment leads first to "imperial overstretch" and then to relative decline.[65] Ultimately, the decline in its relative power leaves a waning hegemon less well placed to fend off challenges to its systemwide strategic interests. Preponderance's key strategic commitments were undertaken in the late 1940s, when the United States was near the zenith of its relative power. Yet, during the 1980s and 1990s, although its relative economic power has declined, U.S. commitments have continued to expand. It is not inappropriate to infer that the attempt to sustain expanding commitments on a shrinking relative power base is harmful to America's economic performance.

Is the strategy of preponderance directly responsible for America's relative economic decline (or for making it worse than it otherwise might have been)? This is a complex question. Defense spending does not invariably lead to economic decline; indeed, under certain conditions it can stimulate economic growth.[66] It could be argued in fact that America's sustained postwar economic growth would have been impossible without "military Keynesianism."[67] Nevertheless, the cumulative effect of the high levels of national security–related spending required to support preponderance is that the United States is less well off economically than it otherwise would have been.

---

64. This might be called the "hegemonic instability theory." See A.F.K Organski, *World Politics,* 2nd ed. (New York: Knopf, 1968); A.F.K. Organski and Jacek Kugler, *The War Ledger* (Chicago: University of Chicago Press, 1980); and Robert Gilpin, "Theory of Hegemonic War," in Robert I. Rotberg and Theodore K. Rabb, eds., *The Origin and Prevention of Major Wars* (Cambridge, U.K.: Cambridge University Press, 1989). pp. 15–37.

65. Paul Kennedy, *The Rise and Fall of Great Powers: Economic Change and Military Conflict from 1500 to 2000* (New York: Random House, 1987), and Robert Gilpin, *War and Change in World Politics* (Cambridge, U.K.: Cambridge University Press, 1981).

66. On this issue, see Charles A. Kupchan, "Empire, Military Power, and Economic Decline," *International Security,* Vol. 13, No. 4 (Spring 1989), pp. 36–53.

67. For a critique of military Keynesianism, see Seymour Melman, *The Permanent War Economy: American Capitalism in Decline* (New York: Simon and Schuster, 1974). For an implicit defense of military Keynesianism, see Diane B. Kunz, *Butter and Guns: America's Cold War Economic Diplomacy* (New York: Free Press, 1997).

Gilpin has outlined the causal logic supporting this conclusion. As he points out, the overhead costs of empire are high: "In order to maintain its dominant position, a state must expend its resources on military forces, the financing of allies, foreign aid, and the costs associated with maintaining the international economy. These protection and related costs are not productive investments; they constitute an economic drain on the economy of the dominant state."[68] Although not conclusive, some evidence suggests that, directly and indirectly, the strategy of preponderance has contributed significantly to the relative decline of U.S. economic power. David Calleo has shown that the inflationary spiral ignited by the Vietnam War, coupled with the dollar outflows required to sustain America's preeminent military and economic position, were factors in undermining U.S. economic competitiveness and relative economic power (reflected in the chronic balance-of-payments and trade deficits the United States has incurred since 1971).[69] The high levels of defense spending the strategy requires also have significant opportunity costs, and affect long-term economic performance by diverting scarce resources from the civilian economy.[70] Even though it constitutes a relatively small share of U.S. GNP, the adverse economic impact of defense spending, as the economist Lloyd L. Dumas observes, can "be dramatically out of proportion to its relative size" because it diverts from productive uses "substantial amounts of critical economic resources."[71]

It is difficult to quantify the strategy of preponderance's economic costs; Jim Hanson's 1993 analysis suggests, however, that the strategy's costs include: loss of domestic savings, trade deficits, overseas investment and loan losses, employment loss and welfare costs (attributable to the export of jobs), a swelling federal budget deficit, ballooning interest on the federal debt, foreign economic and military aid, and one-half of U.S. defense spending (attributable to "imperial" security responsibilities).[72] According to Hanson's study, as of 1990 the

---

68. Gilpin, *War and Change*, pp. 156–157.
69. David Calleo, *The Imperious Economy* (Cambridge, Mass.: Harvard University Press, 1982).
70. On the opportunity cost and resource diversion arguments, see Robert W. DeGrasse, *Military Expansion, Economic Decline: The Impact of Military Spending on U.S. Economic Performance* (Armonk, N.Y.: M.E. Sharpe 1983); Lloyd J. Dumas, *The Overburdened Economy: Uncovering the Causes of Chronic Unemployment, Inflation, and National Decline* (Berkeley: University of California Press, 1986); Robert Kuttner, *End of Laissez Faire: National Purpose and the Global Economy After the Cold War* (New York: Random House, 1991); Seymour Melman, *The Permanent War Economy;* and Seymour Melman "The Limits of Military Power: Economic and Other," *International Security*, Vol. 11, No. 1 (Summer 1986), pp. 72–87.
71. Dumas, *Overburdened Economy*, p. 208.
72. Jim Hanson, *The Decline of the American Empire* (Westport, Conn.: Praeger, 1993).

cost of maintaining the American empire was $970 trillion, nearly 20 percent of GNP. Although the specifics of the study's accounting methodology can be questioned, the basic point remains: There is a strong prima facie case that for the United States the strategy of preponderance is expensive, and over the long term the strategy will retard its economic performance; decrease its relative economic power; and weaken its geopolitical standing in the emerging twenty-first century–multipolar system.

Offshore Balancing: An Alternative Grand Strategy

An alternative to the strategy of preponderance is offshore balancing. In this section I describe a U.S. grand strategy of offshore balancing, delineate the realist premises on which the strategy rests, and demonstrate how the strategy is deduced from these premises.

Offshore balancing is a strategy for the multipolar world that already is emerging. Its underlying premise is that it will become increasingly more difficult, dangerous, and costly for the United States to maintain order in, and control over, the international political system as called for by the strategy of preponderance. Offshore balancing would define U.S. interests narrowly in terms of defending the United States' territorial integrity and preventing the rise of a Eurasian hegemon. As an offshore balancer, the United States would disengage from its military commitments in Europe, Japan, and South Korea. The overriding objectives of an offshore balancing strategy would be to insulate the United States from future great power wars and maximize its relative power position in the international system. Offshore balancing would reject the strategy of preponderance's commitment to economic interdependence because interdependence has negative strategic consequences. Offshore balancing also would eschew any ambition of perpetuating U.S. hegemony and would abandon the ideological pretensions embedded in the strategy of preponderance. As an offshore balancer, the United States would not assertively export democracy, engage directly in peace enforcement operations, attempt to save "failed states" (like Somalia and Haiti), or use military power for the purpose of humanitarian intervention.

An offshore balancing strategy would be considerably less expensive than the strategy of preponderance. It would require defense budgets in the range of 2–2.5 percent of GNP. American military strategy for possible interventions would be based on the principle of limited liability. In contrast to the force structure currently underpinning the strategy of preponderance, offshore balancing would sharply reduce the size and role of U.S. ground forces. The strategy's backbone would be robust nuclear deterrence, air power, and—most important—overwhelming naval power. In the latter respect, an offshore balancing strategy would stress sea-based ballistic missile defense (crucial in the event the United States has to wage coalitional warfare in the early twenty-first century) and sea-based precision, standoff weapons systems (enabling the United States to bring its military power to bear without committing ground forces to combat). The United States also could use naval power as a lever against others' economic interests to achieve its political objectives. As an offshore balancer, the United States would seek simultaneously to maximize its comparative military-technological advantages and its strategic flexibility.

Theoretical Assumptions

Offshore balancing is a grand strategy deduced from realist international relations theory. Specifically, the strategy is based on the following assumptions: balance-of-power strategies are superior to hegemonic ones; for a great power like the United States, interdependence is an illusion, not a reality; the robustness of U.S. extended deterrence commitments will be significantly degraded in coming years; U.S. strategy need not be burdened by excessive concern with credibility, resolve, and reputation; geography has important grand strategic implications; the risk of a rival Eurasian hegemon emerging is small; U.S. grand strategy can confidently assume that other states would balance against a potential hegemon; the dynamics of alliance relationships favor an offshore balancing strategy; and relative power concerns remain the bedrock of a prudent grand strategy.

Offshore balancing is a balance-of-power strategy, not a hegemonic one. It assumes that the United States would be more secure in a multipolar system than it would be by attempting to perpetuate its current preeminence. It is, up to a point, an offensive realist strategy. Unlike the offensive realist variant of the strategy of preponderance, however, this strategy would be predicated on the assumption that attempting to maintain U.S. hegemony is self-defeating because it will provoke other states to balance against the United States, and result in the depletion of America's relative power—thereby leaving it worse off than it would have been by accommodating multipolarity. An offshore balancing strategy also would reject the balance-of-threat argument advanced by preponderance's defensive realist proponents: it is the very fact of the hegemon's unbalanced power that threatens others (and spurs the emergence of new great powers). An offshore balancing strategy would accept that the United States cannot prevent the rise of new great powers either within or outside its sphere of influence.[73]

It is logically inconsistent for preponderance's proponents to claim simultaneously that the United States is preeminent and that it is interdependent. In fact, unlike states with smaller economies, very large and powerful states have relatively little interaction with the international economy.[74] Offshore balancing would recognize that the United States, in fact, is not economically interdependent with the international economy. The United States is well placed to adopt an insular grand strategy because it can diversify its export markets; it can minimize its reliance on overseas raw materials (including petroleum) by stockpiling, diversification, and substitution; and external trade is a relatively small component of its gross domestic product (GDP). Merchandise exports account for only about 6 percent of U.S. GDP (the average for industrialized states is about 24 percent).[75] To be sure, such aggregate figures may fail to capture the true extent of economic interdependence (because a large part of international trade now is attributable to cross-national trade within individual firms). Hence it could be claimed that turmoil in the international system would have a greater impact on U.S. prosperity than the above figure suggests. This argument should not be dismissed; however, if the United States adopts an offshore balancing strategy, markets would adjust to a changing political and strategic context, and over time investment and trade flows would be altered. More geopolitically secure regions—especially the United States—would be the beneficiaries of these alterations.

An offshore balancing strategy would recognize explicitly that the credibility of U.S. extended deterrence guarantees will be vitiated in coming years. The United States would be more secure if it withdraws its deterrent umbrella and allows other states to defend themselves. As an offshore balancer, the United States would accept that some (preferably managed) nuclear proliferation is inevitable. Extended deterrence's eroding credibility is an important reason why U.S. hegemony will be unsustainable in the twenty-first century. As

---

73. The arguments made in this paragraph are elaborated on in Layne, "The Unipolar Illusion."
74. Waltz, *Theory of International Politics*, pp. 145–146. On the dependence of small states on the international economy, see Peter Katzenstein, *Small States and World Markets* (Ithaca, N.Y.: Cornell University Press, 1985).
75. Helen V. Milner and Robert O. Keohane, "Internationalization and Domestic Politics: An Introduction," in Helen V. Milner and Robert O. Keohane, eds., *Internationalization and Domestic Politics* (New York: Cambridge University Press, 1996), pp. 12–13.

potential great powers come to doubt the reliability of the U.S. security umbrella (which will occur even if the United States sticks with the strategy of preponderance), they inevitably will seek strategic self-sufficiency (including nuclear weapons). It is unlikely, however, that an offshore balancing strategy would touch off a proliferation chain reaction. Middle and small powers, given their limited resources, might well decide that they would be more secure by enhancing their conventional forces than by acquiring nuclear weapons.[76]

Offshore balancing is not an extended deterrence strategy. Hence if it adopts this strategy, the United States would not need to be overly preoccupied with reputational concerns. Indeed, in this respect, the strategy of preponderance is based on incorrect premises about reputation. Jonathan Mercer has shown, for example, that whether a state stands firm in a crisis seldom affects its reputation for resoluteness with others (either adversaries or rivals) because others rarely predict the state's future behavior from that crisis's outcome.[77] That is, others' perceptions of a defender's resolve are context specific: resolve is a function of the magnitude of the defender's interests in a particular situation, not by its behavior in previous crises. Using recent empirical research, offshore balancing proponents reject the notion that America must fight in the peripheries to establish its commitment to defend its core interests.[78] The strategy would be based on the belief that concrete vital interests should determine U.S. commitments (rather than credibility determining commitments and commitments, in turn, determining interests).[79] When America's intrinsic stakes in a specific crisis are high (and its capabilities robust), neither adversaries nor others will question its resolve. Conversely, when the United States fails to intervene in peripheral areas, others will not draw adverse inferences about its willingness to defend vital, core interests.

The strategy of preponderance assumes that multipolar systems are unstable. As a generalization this may be true, but instability does not affect all states equally. Preponderance's advocates fail to consider geography's differential

---

76. See Steven E. Miller, "Fateful Choices: Nuclear Weapons, Ukrainian Security, and International Stability," in Scott D. Sagan, ed., *Civil-Military Relations and Nuclear Weapons* (Stanford, Calif.: Stanford University Press, 1994), pp. 139–163.
77. Jonathan Mercer, *Reputation and International Politics* (Ithaca, N.Y.: Cornell University Press, 1996).
78. During the Cold War the Soviet Union did not conclude that American defeats in the periphery undermined the credibility of U.S. commitments to areas of high intrinsic strategic value. See Ted Hopf, *Peripheral Visions: Deterrence Theory and American Foreign Policy in the Third World, 1965–1990* (Ann Arbor: University of Michigan Press, 1994).
79. This formulation is borrowed from Johnson, *Improbable Dangers*, p. 144.

effects. An offshore balancing strategy, however, would account explicitly for geography's impact on grand strategy. Insular great powers are substantially less likely to be affected by instability than are states that face geographically proximate rivals. Hence the United States could effectively insulate itself from the future great power wars likely to be caused by power transition effects. Because of the interlocking effects of geography, nuclear weapons (which enhance insularity's strategic advantages), and formidable military and economic capabilities, the United States is virtually impregnable against direct attack. The risk of conflict, and the possible exposure of the American homeland to attack, derive directly from the overseas commitments mandated by preponderance's expansive definition of U.S. interests.

In multipolar systems, insular great powers have a much broader range of strategic choices than less fortunately placed powers. Because their strategic interdependence with others is low, they can avoid being entrapped by alliance commitments and need worry little about being abandoned by actual or potential allies.[80] Offshore great powers also have the choice of staying out of great power wars altogether or of limiting their involvement—a choice unavailable to states that live in dangerous neighborhoods in which rivals lurk nearby. As an insular great power in a multipolar world, the United States would retain a free hand strategically: although it might need to enter into temporary coalitions, the United States would disengage from permanent alliance relationships. Because of its insularity and capabilities, the United States would seldom need to engage in external balancing. Internal balancing is always preferable to external balancing because alliance commitments are constraining strategically.[81] An insular great power like the United States seldom needs to subject itself to strategic constraints of this kind.

In the early-twenty-first-century multipolar system the risk that a Eurasian hegemon will emerge is slight. Even if a Eurasian hegemon were to appear, America's core security probably would be unthreatened. The fear that a future Eurasian hegemon would command sufficient resources to imperil the United

---

80. On entrapment, see Glenn H. Snyder, "The Security Dilemma in Alliance Politics," *World Politics*, Vol. 36, No. 4 (July 1984), pp. 466–468. For historical studies supporting the argument that insular great powers can afford to take a relaxed attitude about their allies' fates without endangering their own security, see Colin S. Gray, *The Leverage of Seapower: The Strategic Advantage of Navies in War* (New York: Free Press, 1992), and Daniel A. Baugh, "British Strategy During the First World War in the Context of Four Centuries: Blue-Water versus Continental Commitment," in Daniel M. Masterson, ed., *Naval History: The Sixth Symposium of the U.S. Naval Academy* (Wilmington, Del.: Scholarly Resources, 1987).
81. Waltz, *Theory of International Politics*, pp. 165–168.

States is a strategic artifact of the prenuclear era.[82] A good strategy, however, hedges against unknown (and unknowable) future contingencies. Hence an offshore balancing strategy would not rule out the possibility that, as the balancer of last resort, the United States might need to intervene to thwart the emergence of a hegemonic challenger. Three reasons explain why the possibility of intervention cannot be foreclosed completely. First, the military-technological backdrop to international politics may change in the future because of the Revolution in Military Affairs (RMA). Some analysts predict that the RMA will result in greatly enhanced conventional war-fighting capabilities. If so, deterrence could be weakened and the nuclear revolution (which bolsters insularity) could be partially offset. In that case, traditional concerns about the military effects of capability and resource distributions among states again could become salient. Second, a Eurasian hegemon might be able to use its power diplomatically to coerce the United States. Third, it might be too uncomfortable psychologically for the United States to live in a world dominated by another power.

The strategy of preponderance is based in part on the assumption that the United States must prevent the rise of a hegemonic challenger because other states either will not or will not do so effectively.[83] In contrast, an offshore balancing strategy would be based on the assumptions that in a multipolar world other states will balance against potential hegemons, and it is to America's advantage to shift this responsibility to others. In a multipolar world the United States could be confident that effective balancing ultimately would occur because to ensure their survival, other states have the incentive to balance against geographically proximate rivals, and great powers do not bandwagon.[84] Because of its insularity, the United States can stand aloof from others' security competitions and engage in "bystanding" and "buck-passing" behavior, thereby forcing others to assume the risks and costs of antihegemonic

---

82. See Robert W. Tucker, *The New Isolationism: Threat or Promise?* (New York: Universe Books, 1972), pp. 40–51.

83. See Khalilzad, "U.S. Grand Strategies," p. 22.

84. Offshore balancing is similar to what Samuel P. Huntington calls "secondary" balancing. He is skeptical that America is suited to the role of a secondary balancer. Samuel P. Huntington, *The Clash of Civilizations and the Remaking of World Order* (New York: Simon and Schuster, 1996), p. 233. I disagree with Huntington's argument because I do not believe that offshore balancing requires the United States to "play off" other great powers against each other, or to constantly shift its strategic alignment. Great powers balance against each other because structural constraints impel them to do so. In a nuclear multipolar world the United States would not need to engage in micromanagement of the geopolitical balance. Washington would only need to ensure against the unlikely failure of others to check the emergence of a rising potential hegemon.

balancing.[85] When an offshore balancer shifts to others the dangers entailed by "going first," it can reasonably hope that it may never have to become involved.

The strategy of preponderance commits the United States to alliance relationships that run counter to geostrategic logic: it imposes the greatest burden (in terms of danger and cost) on the alliance partner (the United States) whose security is least at risk. An offshore balancing strategy would reverse this pattern of alliance relations. There is no inherent reason that the United States should be compelled to bear the high costs of providing security for other states. Japan and Western Europe, for example, long have possessed the economic and technological capabilities to defend themselves. The strategy of preponderance, however (notwithstanding U.S. complaints about burden-sharing inequities), has actively discouraged them from doing so because American policymakers fear any diminution of U.S. control over the international system—including control over U.S. allies—would have adverse geopolitical consequences. Washington has decided that it is preferable strategically for the United States to defend Germany and Japan rather than for Germany and Japan to defend themselves. In contrast, offshore balancing would rest on the assumption that America's overall strategic position would be enhanced by devolving to others the responsibility for their own defense.

An offshore balancing strategy would be grounded on the assumption that relative economic power matters. Domestic economic revitalization and a neomercantilist international economic policy would be integral components of the strategy. The strategy, however, also would seek to maximize U.S. relative power by capitalizing on its geostrategically privileged position. If the United States adopted an offshore balancing strategy, security competitions almost certainly would occur in East Asia and Europe.[86] The United States would be the primary beneficiary of these rivalries between (among) the other great powers in the emerging multipolar system. Noninsular states' constant worry about possible threats from nearby neighbors is a factor that historically has increased the relative power position of insular states.[87] Offshore balancing

---

85. On the relationship between geography and buck-passing in multipolar systems, see Snyder and Christensen, "Chain Gangs and Passed Bucks." The arguments in favor of an offshore strategy were clearly articulated in the eighteenth century by the Tory proponents of an English "blue water" grand strategy. See Richard Pares, "American versus Continental Warfare, 1739–63," *English Historical Review*, Vol. 51, No. 203 (July 1936), pp. 436–437.
86. For a precise definition of "security competition," see Art, "Why Western Europe Still Needs the U.S. and NATO," pp. 6–9.
87. After 1815 Britain's interests were not challenged by an overwhelming antihegemonic coalition because of "the preoccupation of virtually all European statesman with continental power politics."

thus would be a more sophisticated power-maximizing strategy than preponderance: the United States would be able to enhance its relative power without having to confront rivals directly. Great powers that stand on the sidelines while their peers engage in security competitions and conflict invariably gain in relative power.[88]

Multipolarity challenges strategists because a state can be threatened by more than a single adversary. It is often unclear which of potential multiple rivals poses the most salient threat, whether measured in terms of capabilities, intentions, or time. In East Asia, where China and Japan are emerging great powers, the United States confronts this dilemma of multiple rivals. Offshore balancing is the classic grand strategic response of an insular great power facing two (or more) potential peer competitors in the same region. As an offshore balancer, the United States would increase its relative power against both China and Japan by letting them compete and balance against, and contain, each other.[89]

Offshore Balancing versus Preponderance: Defining the Debate

Two critical objections could be lodged against an offshore balancing grand strategy: an offshore balancing strategy would increase—not lower—the risk of U.S. involvement in a major war, and the strategy of preponderance should not be abandoned because its benefits exceed its costs. Advocates of preponderance believe it is illusory to think that the United States can disengage from international commitments, because it inevitably would be drawn into major wars even if initially it tried to remain aloof. The example of Europe is frequently invoked: whenever a major European war breaks out, it is said, the United States invariably is compelled to intervene. Preponderance's advocates also claim that U.S. security commitments in Europe and East Asia are a form

---

It "was the moves of their neighbors, not the usually discreet workings of British sea power, which interested them." Paul Kennedy, *The Rise and Fall of British Naval Mastery*, rev. ed. (London: Ashfield Press, 1983), pp. 162–163.

88. For example, the United States gained enormously in relative economic power and financial strength while standing on the sidelines during most of World War I. See Kathleen Burk, *Britain, America, and the Sinews of War, 1914–1918* (Boston: Allen and Unwin, 1985).

89. For a more detailed discussion of multipolarity's implications for U.S. grand strategy in East Asia, see Christopher Layne, "Less Is More: Minimal Realism in East Asia," *The National Interest*, No. 43 (Spring 1996), pp. 64–77. For the argument that civilizational and cultural imperatives probably will cause Japan to bandwagon with China rather than balance against it, see Huntington, *The Clash of Civilizations*, pp. 236–238. Huntington and I disagree on the issue of whether civilizational and cultural factors override the international system's structural constraints on state behavior.

of insurance: it is cheaper and safer for the United States to retain its security commitments and thereby deter wars from happening than to stand on the sidelines only to be compelled to intervene later under what presumably would be more dangerous conditions. Yet this argument is unsupported by the historical record, and it is not evident that the strategy of preponderance will in fact minimize the risk of U.S. involvement in future wars.

The argument that the United States invariably is drawn into major overseas conflicts is faulty. Since the United States achieved independence, great power wars have been waged in Europe in 1792–1802, 1804–15, 1853–55, 1859–60, 1866, 1870, 1877–78, 1912–13, 1914–18, and 1939–45. The United States has been involved in three of these wars, but it safely could have remained out of at least two of the wars in which it fought. In 1812, hoping to conquer Canada while the British were preoccupied with the Napoleonic Wars, the United States *initiated* war with Britain. And as Robert E. Osgood has demonstrated, the United States' intervention in World War I was not driven by any tangible threat to its security interests.[90] The United States was not compelled to enter the Great War; it chose to do so, arguably with disastrous consequences.

U.S. intervention in the Great War was driven by snowball/domino concerns similar to those embedded in today's strategy of preponderance. Woodrow Wilson was perhaps the first U.S. policymaker to worry that toppling dominoes could endanger the United States.[91] He feared that events in seemingly peripheral regions like the Balkans could trigger an uncontrollable chain reaction that would leave the United States isolated ideologically and confronting a hostile European hegemon that could use its military and economic power to "cut off the oxygen without which American society, and liberal institutions generally, would asphyxiate."[92]

An interesting counterfactual study awaits on what would have happened had the United States not intervened in 1917.[93] The argument can be made that the war would have ended in a compromise peace. Peace, indeed, might have come before the revolutions that destroyed the German, Austro-

---

90. Robert E. Osgood, *Ideals and Self-Interest in American Foreign Relations: The Great Transformation of the Twentieth Century* (Chicago: University of Chicago Press, 1953).
91. See Frank Ninkovich, *Modernity and Power: A History of the Domino Theory in the Twentieth Century* (Chicago: University of Chicago Press, 1994).
92. Ibid., pp. 52–53.
93. On the use of counterfactuals, see James D. Fearon, "Counterfactuals and Hypothesis Testing in Political Science," *World Politics*, Vol. 43, No. 2 (January 1991), pp. 169–195.

Hungarian, and Russian empires. A compromise peace might not have sown the seeds of social and economic unrest that facilitated Hitler's rise to power. Had such a peace occurred, would a second great war have been waged in Europe? Possibly. But, if so, it would have been a much different war than World War II; and it might have been a war the U.S. could have avoided.

A related argument is that U.S. isolationism in the 1920s and 1930s had disastrous consequences and would have a similar effect in the future. Recent work by diplomatic historians, however, has debunked the notion that the United States followed an isolationist policy during the 1930s.[94] Furthermore, the United States became involved in the Pacific War with Japan not because it followed an isolationist policy, but rather because it assertively defended its perceived East Asian interests (especially in China) from Japanese encroachment. It should also be noted that U.S. strategy toward Europe in 1939–41 was not isolationist, but rather a shrewd example of offshore balancing. In 1939–40 the United States stood on the sidelines in the reasonable expectation that Britain and France could successfully hold Germany at bay. When France was defeated stunningly in the brief May–June 1940 campaign, the United States was able to continue following an offshore balancing strategy based on providing military equipment and economic assistance to Britain and (after June 1941) the Soviet Union, and fighting a limited liability naval war against German U-boats in the Atlantic. Had Germany not declared war on the United States, Washington might have persisted in that strategy indefinitely. In short, the historical record does not support the claim that European and Asian wars invariably compel the United States to intervene. Wars are not a force of nature that magnetically draws states into conflict. States—that is, policymakers—have volition: they decide whether to go to war.

The insurance argument advanced by the strategy of preponderance's advocates is also problematic. Great power war is rare because it is always an uncertain undertaking: war is to some extent its own deterrent. It is, however,

---

94. Melvyn P. Leffler, *The Elusive Quest: America's Pursuit of European Stability and French Security, 1919–1933* (Chapel Hill: University of North Carolina Press, 1979); Michael J. Hogan, *Informal Entente: The Private Structure of Cooperation in Anglo-American Economic Diplomacy, 1918–1928* (Columbia: University of Missouri Press, 1977); and Akirye Iryie, *The Globalization of America 1913–1914*, Vol. 13, in Warren I. Cohen, ed., *Cambridge History of American Foreign Relations* (Cambridge, U.K.: Cambridge University Press, 1993). Indeed, as the historian Walter A. McDougall observes, isolationism is simply "a dirty word that interventionists, especially since Pearl Harbor, hurl at anyone who questions their policies." Walter A. McDougall, *Promised Land, Crusader State: The American Encounter with the World Since 1776* (Boston: Houghton Mifflin, 1997), p. 40.

an imperfect deterrent: great power wars do happen, and they will happen in the future. In a world where nuclear weapons exist the consequences of U.S. involvement could be enormous. The strategy of preponderance purports to insure the United States against the risk of war. If extended deterrence fails, however, the strategy actually ensures that America will be involved in war at its onset. As Californians know, there are some risks (earthquakes, for example) for which insurance is either prohibitively expensive or not available at any price because, although the probability of the event may be small, if it occurred the cost to the insurer would be catastrophic. Offshore balancing has the considerable advantage of giving the United States a high degree of strategic choice and, unlike the strategy of preponderance, a substantial measure of control over its fate.

Preponderance's advocates claim that from 1945 to 1990 the strategy was highly successful: the Soviet Union was defeated; Germany and Japan were transformed into democratic allies; and the open international trading system brought unprecedented prosperity to the United States and its allies. Although the strategy's economic costs were not inconsiderable, it could be argued that these gains were more than worth the price America paid to secure them. Nevertheless, the United States did not emerge from the Cold War unscathed. The litany of costs is familiar: ballooning trade and budget deficits; stagnant real incomes; and social decay (reflected in crime rates, drug use, pornography, illegitimate births, and illegal immigration).

I do not claim that the United States cannot "afford" the strategy of preponderance; the strategy is the sole cause of its domestic economic and social problems; or cutting defense spending alone will solve these problems. Nevertheless, the strategy's cumulative costs may be very high over the long term, and the United States is not compelled to pay these costs. The United States spends more on defense than it needs to spend (and thus less for domestic purposes) because of the manner in which the strategy conceives of U.S. security. Both proponents and critics of the strategy of preponderance must address the question of whether the strategy's *net* benefits outweigh its costs. At this point, neither the critics nor proponents of the strategy have proven their case. The critics have, however, come forward with both a causal explanation and sufficient empirical evidence to suggest that indeed their case can be made.

The American security studies community needs to take a close look at the cost-benefit trade-offs of the strategy of preponderance and alternative grand strategies. It is not enough for preponderance's proponents simply to assert that the "American empire is a profitable venture."[95] Given that East Asia and Europe are likely to be geopolitically volatile regions in the early twenty-first century, it is not self-evident that the strategy of preponderance will be profitable. Further empirical research is needed to confirm or challenge this assertion of profitability. Such research has been undertaken to ascertain the cost-benefit trade-off of the British and Soviet empires. In both instances empire was found not to be a paying proposition.[96] No a priori reason exists to suggest that a study of the American empire would reach a different conclusion.[97]

Conclusion: Strategies, Interests, and Values

It is unsurprising that having fulfilled their hegemonic ambitions following the Soviet Union's collapse, preponderance's advocates want to keep the world the way it is. U.S. grand strategists view the prospect of change in international politics in much the same way that British Prime Minister Lord Salisbury did toward the end of the nineteenth century. "What ever happens will be for the worse," Salisbury said, "and therefore it is in our interest that as little should happen as possible."[98] International politics, however, is dynamic, not static. U.S. hegemony cannot last indefinitely. As Paul Kennedy has observed, "it simply has not been given to any one society to remain *permanently* ahead of all the others . . ."[99] Thus the strategy of preponderance must be reassessed. I have attempted to demonstrate that, in fact, the United States can pursue an alternative grand strategy without sacrificing its security. The debate between

---

95. Odom, "NATO's Expansion," p. 44.
96. Charles Wolf, K.C. Yeh, Edmund D. Brunner, A. Gurwitz, and M.F. Lawrence, *The Costs of the Soviet Empire* (Santa Monica, Calif.: RAND, 1984), and Lance E. Davis and Robert A. Huttenback, *Mammon and the Pursuit of Empire: The Political Economy of British Imperialism, 1860–1912* (Cambridge, U.K.: Cambridge University Press, 1986).
97. To analyze the importance of maintaining undisturbed access to markets in Europe and East Asia, the following factors would need to be considered: the harm to the United States if access to these markets is disrupted, the likelihood of such disruption, and the availability of alternatives to reliance on these markets—such as increasing domestic demand to make up for lost exports and/or shifting to overseas markets in regions less vulnerable to political turmoil. Any economic benefits generated by interdependence would have to be offset against the ongoing costs of maintaining military forces dedicated to the task of pacifying Europe and East Asia and the potential dangers and costs the United States would incur if war broke out. Also, in weighing the overall impact of interdependence, it would be necessary as well to consider the opportunity costs of investing resources in military capabilities versus freeing up those resources for other economic and social purposes.
98. Quoted in Kennedy, *Realities Behind Diplomacy*, p. 97.
99. Kennedy, *The Rise and Fall of Great Powers*, p. 533 (emphasis in original).

advocates of preponderance and offshore balancing, however, is about more than strategy; it is also about values. The United States is secure enough from external threat that, should it wish to do so, it could choose restraint over intervention, nation over empire, and an emphasis on domestic needs over external ambitions. And it *should* do so. In this sense, offshore balancing—an *innenpolitik* grand strategy that posits the primacy of domestic over foreign policy—is ethically driven: America's mission lies at home, not abroad. As George F. Kennan says, there is nothing wrong with taking advantage of the Cold War's end to focus on economic and social challenges at home: "What we should want, in these circumstances, is the minimum, not the maximum, of external involvement."[100] No doubt, some would maintain that offshore balancing is both selfish and immoral. In fact, such a policy is indeed self-interested and most assuredly moral. America First is an imperative, not a pejorative: Offshore balancing is a twenty-first–century grand strategy consistent with America's interests *and* its values.

---

100. George F. Kennan, *Around the Cragged Hill: A Personal and Political Philosophy* (New York: W.W. Norton, 1993), p. 183.

Part III:
Selective Engagement

Geopolitics Updated | *Robert J. Art*

The Strategy of Selective Engagement

In the current era, what grand strategy best serves the United States? There are seven to choose from: dominion, global collective security, regional collective security, cooperative security, containment, isolationism, and selective engagement. I argue that selective engagement is the best strategy, and the purpose of this article is to show why.

Formulating an American grand strategy requires making two big choices: selecting basic goals (what are America's national interests?) and choosing appropriate means (how can America's military power best protect these interests?). Selective engagement is the superior strategy because it correctly understands America's interests and because it most effectively uses the nation's military power to protect them. It is also the most balanced of all the grand strategies because it is a hybrid, taking the good elements from its six competitors but avoiding their pitfalls. To make the case for selective engagement, I proceed as follows. First, I lay out the essential features of the strategy. Second, I explain the importance of the six national interests that selective engagement prescribes for the United States. Third, I compare selective engagement to its competitors and show why it is superior to them. Fourth, I analyze the two pitfalls of selective engagement; and fifth, I suggest how to avoid them.

The Strategy of Selective Engagement

As I conceive it, selective engagement has eight main features. The first three deal with the nature of America's national interests; the next five, with how to use America's military power to protect them.

Robert J. Art is Herter Professor of International Relations at Brandeis University, Research Associate at the John M. Olin Institute for Strategic Studies at Harvard University, and Senior Fellow at the Massachusetts Institute of Technology's Security Studies Program.

This article draws from my forthcoming *Selective Engagement: An American Grand Strategy,* a project supported by the Century Foundation. An abridged version appears in Pelham G. Boyer and Robert S. Wood, eds., *Strategic Transformation and Naval Power in the Twenty-first Century* (Newport, R.I.: Naval War College Press, 1998), pp. 167–195. For their penetrating comments, I thank Seyom Brown, Joseph Grieco, Glenn Snyder, Stephen Van Evera (who graciously read two drafts), Stephen Walt, and an anonymous reviewer for *International Security.* For his indefatigable research assistance, I am indebted to Loren Cass. Finally, I thank the Olin Institute for the opportunity to test out my ideas before a lively audience.

International Security, Vol. 23, No. 3 (Winter 1998/99), pp. 79–113

BASIC GOALS

Selective engagement prescribes six national interests (described more fully in the next section). They are (1) preventing an attack on the American homeland, primarily by keeping out of the wrong hands nuclear, biological, and chemical (NBC) weapons, which are also referred to as weapons of mass destruction (WMD); (2) preventing great power wars and destructive security competitions among the Eurasian great powers; (3) maintaining secure oil supplies at stable prices, in large part by keeping Persian Gulf reserves divided among the oil-rich Gulf states; (4) preserving an open international economic order; (5) fostering the spread of democracy and respect for human rights, and preventing mass murder and genocide; and (6) protecting the global environment from the adverse effects of global warming and ozone depletion.

SELECTIVE ACTION

Selective engagement is, by definition, selective. It steers the middle course between an isolationist, unilateralist course, on the one hand, and a world policeman, highly interventionist role, on the other. It avoids both an overly restrictive and an overly expansive definition of America's interests, and it strikes a balance between doing too much and too little militarily to support them. It allocates political attention and material resources to the vital interests first, but holds out hope that the desirable interests can be partially realized. Selective engagement continues, but with important modifications, the internationalist path the United States has followed since 1945.

REALISM CUM LIBERALISM

Selective engagement seeks both realist and liberal goals and can therefore be termed a "realpolitik plus" strategy. It aims to keep the United States secure and prosperous, but goes beyond those classical realist goals to attain liberal goals as well: to nudge the world toward the values the nation holds dear— democracy, free markets, human rights, and international openness. Selective engagement aims to do well not only for the United States, but for others too, in the belief that if others benefit in the ways just described, so too does the United States.

UTILITY OF FORCE

Selective engagement holds that military power remains a useful and fungible instrument of statecraft. This means that military power is useful for producing not only military but also nonmilitary results, and therefore that the United States can use its military forces to help shape the international environment so as to make it more congenial to America's political and economic interests.[1]

EARLY ACTION

Selective engagement is a precautionary strategy. Where possible, it seeks to prevent circumstances adverse to the United States from arising, rather than simply reacting to them once they have occurred. It argues that forestalling bad things is more effective and ultimately cheaper than having to pick up the pieces after they have happened.

FORWARD DEFENSE

Selective engagement is a forward-defense strategy. It therefore prescribes retention of America's core alliances—the North Atlantic Treaty Organization (NATO), the U.S.-Japan alliance, the U.S.-South Korea alliance, and those with Saudi Arabia and Kuwait—and the basing of American troops overseas in eastern and western Eurasia and the Persian Gulf to keep these alliances strong.

Selective engagement contends that America's core alliances and forward-deployed troops serve several useful functions. First, they help keep the peace and dampen security competitions among the great powers in western and eastern Eurasia and to a lesser degree among the states in the Persian Gulf by providing both military deterrence and political reassurance. Second, to the extent that they help maintain peace and dampen security competitions, these alliances and troops help retard NBC spread, preserve openness, and foster the spread of democracy. Third, these alliances facilitate war waging, peacekeeping, and peacemaking when the United States decides to undertake any of those tasks, because standing alliances permit more rapid and more effective action than assembling ad hoc coalitions. Fourth, America's alliances serve as institutional forums where important political-military issues can be managed by maintaining close political-military links with four of the world's six other great powers—Britain, France, Germany, and Japan. (To the extent that the Founding Act between Russia and NATO establishes a useful institutional link with Russia, a fifth great power may also come into America's

---

1. See Robert J. Art, "American Foreign Policy and the Fungibility of Force," *Security Studies*, Vol. 5, No. 4 (Summer 1996), pp. 7–43.

political-military institutional orbit.)[2] For these reasons, America's core alliances remain valuable instruments of its statecraft.

PRIMACY OF STATES

Selective engagement assumes that states continue to be the primary actors in world politics, that differences in national interests provide ever-present sources of conflict among states, and therefore that nationalism and national self-interest remain the most potent forces in international affairs today, overriding ethnic, religious, and cultural cleavages.[3] Consequently, selective engagement takes account of national differences and rivalries and uses them to serve American interests.

NECESSITY FOR AMERICAN LEADERSHIP

Selective engagement holds that America's leadership is both essential and advantaged. It is essential because effective coalitions of the willing to handle key international issues will not materialize unless the world's most powerful state throws its weight behind them. It is advantaged because none of the other great powers possesses America's military-economic might or its political acceptability. Other great powers often resent America's leadership, but their preference is for the United States to lead because they trust the United States more than they trust each other. In sum, America's indispensable role is based on both its power and its purpose, and no other state is yet able to compete with it on either ground, much less both at once.

---

2. For a good historical overview of alliances as tools of management, see Paul W. Schroeder, "Alliances, 1815–1945: Weapons of Power and Tools of Management," in Klaus Knorr, ed., *Historical Dimensions of National Security Problems* (Lawrence: University Press of Kansas, 1976), pp. 227–262. For the difficulties in managing alliances, see Glenn H. Snyder, *Alliance Politics* (Ithaca, N.Y.: Cornell University Press, 1997), chaps. 6, 9. For analyses of the institutional effects of alliances on state behavior, see Celeste A. Wallander and Robert O. Keohane, "When Threats Decline, Why Do Alliances Persist? An Institutional Approach," paper presented at the second Conference on Security Institutions, jointly sponsored by the Institute for International Politics and Regional Studies, the Free University of Berlin, and the Center for International Studies at Harvard University, Cambridge, Massachusetts, March 16–19, 1997; and Wallander, *Balancing Acts: Security, Institutions, and German-Russian Relations after the Cold War* (Ithaca, N.Y.: Cornell University Press, 1999), chap. 2.
3. Because of its stress on the continuing power of nationalism, selective engagement rejects two other popular contemporary models of the future: the triumph of liberalism and the end of history proposed by Francis Fukuyama and, equally, the coming clash of civilizations proposed by Samuel Huntington. See Fukuyama, "The End of History?" *National Interest*, No. 16 (Summer 1989), pp. 3–18; and Samuel P. Huntington, *The Clash of Civilizations and the Remaking of World Order* (New York: Simon and Schuster, 1996).

America's National Interests

Determining a nation's interests is the central task of grand strategy. How a nation defines its interests both sets its fundamental course in world affairs and significantly shapes the means chosen to get there. Selective engagement posits six American national interests. The first three—preventing NBC weapons from falling into the wrong hands, maintaining a deep Eurasian great power peace, and keeping Persian Gulf oil reserves divided—are vital and generally accord with what are termed realist goals. The last three—preserving an open international economy, fostering the spread of democracy and the observance of human rights, and averting severe climate change and ozone depletion—are desirable and generally accord with what are termed liberal goals.

Vital interests are those whose costs to the nation are somewhere between severe to catastrophic if not protected and whose benefits are large when protected. Homeland defense is the most important: upon it everything else depends, and failure here could bring catastrophe. Eurasian peace and access to oil bring large benefits to the United States, respectively, by keeping it out of great power wars and by helping fuel its economy. By the same token, embroilment in a major Eurasian war would threaten U.S. security, while a serious disruption in oil supplies risks either severe inflation or a steep economic decline. Thus vital interests are the ones most central to America's physical security and economic well-being.

Desirable interests are those whose realization contributes an additional amount to America's prosperity or makes its external environment more congenial to the values it espouses, and whose nonrealization imposes a cost, but not a severe one, to its well-being or to a congenial international environment. Participation in an open international economy, for example, benefits the United States, but 90 percent of America's gross domestic product (GDP) is produced at home. A retreat from openness would not cause a cessation of all imports, only more expensive ones. This would result in some decline in America's standard of living through higher prices, but not a catastrophic one. Similarly, the spread of democracy and the widespread protection of human rights would make the international environment more congenial to America's interests, but if neither materialized, the results would not be catastrophic. Thus desirable interests do not carry the same magnitude of potential costs and benefits to the nation as the vital ones.

VITAL INTERESTS

Most analysts would agree that retarding NBC spread, maintaining Eurasian great power peace, and preserving access to secure and stable oil supplies are important interests for the United States. Not all would agree, however, that they are vital interests. I explain why they are.

HOMELAND SECURITY. Homeland security is the prevention of attack, invasion, conquest, or destruction of a state's territory, and it is the prime directive of any grand strategy. For selective engagers, the threat to worry about today is rogue states or fanatical terrorists (or both) armed with NBC weapons, not conventional attacks from strong states or nuclear threats from "normal" states.[4]

Conventional attacks and "normal" nuclear threats pose little risk to the American homeland. First, the only realistic attack that could cause great destruction conventionally would have to come either by air- or sea-launched cruise missiles in the thousands or by massive bomber attacks. No state today, except the United States, can mount such attacks across the Atlantic and Pacific Oceans. Should either threat ever materialize, the United States could take effective countermeasures. Second, the United States need not worry much about nuclear attacks from "normal" nuclear-armed states, because they are governed by leaders committed to the traditional rules of great power politics—the prime one being the survival of the state. Such leaders do not attempt the deliberate destruction of other states that they know can swiftly destroy them in return. Deterrence—the threat of retaliation in kind against a nuclear attack—is the means by which the United States will protect itself against future nuclear threats from states that calculate according to the traditional rules. Deterrence worked during the Cold War; it will work after the Cold War.

---

4. The differences between rogue and normal states are as follows. Rogue states are usually dictatorships of one sort or another that share three attributes. First, they are opposed to the territorial status quo, committed to expanding their borders at the expense of another state or states. Second, they are prepared to use force, or already have a track record of having used force, to do so. Third, they sponsor terrorists to expand their territory or to achieve other foreign policy objectives. By these criteria, rogue states are committed expansionists, and Iran, Iraq, Libya, Syria, and North Korea fulfill the criteria. But China, for example, does not. It has not resorted to terrorism. The territories it now claims are either accepted as part of China (Taiwan) or are the subject of contestation and are claimed by many states (the Spratlys in the South China Sea, for example). Finally, China has agreed to settle the Spratly issue diplomatically. By contrast, normal states harbor little or no expansionist designs, are committed to the peaceful resolution of their border and other disputes, and eschew resort to terrorism for political gain. For a useful survey of America's policy toward the present-day rogues, see Raymond Tanter, *Rogue Regimes: Terrorism and Proliferation* (New York: St. Martin's Press, 1998).

It is the third type of threat—fanatical terrorists or rogue states armed with NBC weapons—that the United States should worry about most. Such groups and states possess three attributes that could make them harder to deter than normal actors.[5] First, they are highly motivated to gain their aims, making them more prepared than normal actors to use force to achieve their objectives. Second, they are indifferent to the suffering of their citizens or supporters, making them more willing to take greater losses. Third, they are poor calculators, making them more likely to misperceive a defender's threats or to ignore such threats. If governments or terrorist groups possess such traits, they will be hard to deter and more willing to use NBC weapons if they have them to achieve their political objectives.

Has this third threat fully materialized? "No, not yet." Will it definitely materialize? "No." Is it certain that rogues and terrorists are harder to deter and more likely to attack the United States if and when they become NBC-armed? "No." Is this threat therefore something we should ignore? "Only at our potential peril."[6]

Some analysts downplay the threat. Brian Jenkins has long argued that "terrorists want a lot of people watching, not a lot of people dead."[7] Following Jenkins's logic, Kenneth Waltz asserts that terrorists are rational political actors with long-term goals, and as a consequence they would not use nuclear weapons (or anything else that would achieve the same mass killing results), because terrorists cannot hope to achieve their aims "by issuing unsustainable threats to wreck great destruction, threats they would not want to execute anyway." In this view NBC terrorism is counterproductive: either it undermines the political support terrorists hope to obtain, or it makes the targeted state more determined than ever not to give in. Moreover, Waltz argues: "Nobody but an idiot can fail to comprehend their [nuclear weapons'] destructive force. How can leaders miscalculate? For a country to strike first without

---

5. I have borrowed these traits from Stephen Van Evera, *The Causes of War: Power and the Roots of War* (Ithaca, N.Y.: Cornell University Press, forthcoming 1999), chap. 8.

6. Excellent sources on the NBC rogue-regime and fanatical-terrorist threats are Richard A. Falkenrath, Robert D. Newman, and Bradley A. Thayer, *America's Achilles' Heel: Nuclear, Biological, and Chemical Terrorism and Covert Attack* (Cambridge, Mass.: MIT Press, 1998); Bruce Hoffman, "Terrorism and WMD: Some Preliminary Hypotheses," *Nonproliferation Review*, Vol. 4, No. 3 (Spring–Summer 1997), pp. 45–53; Hoffman, *Responding to Terrorism across the Technological Spectrum* (Santa Monica, Calif.: RAND, 1994), P-7874; Hoffman, *Inside Terrorism* (London: Macmillan, 1998); and Jessica Stern, *The Ultimate Terrorists* (Cambridge, Mass.: Harvard University Press, forthcoming, 1999). For an official analysis, see Office of the Secretary of Defense, U.S. Department of Defense, *Proliferation: Threat and Response*, November 1997.

7. Quoted in Falkenrath, Newman, and Thayer, *America's Achilles' Heel*, pp. 49–50.

certainty of success, most of those who control a nation's nuclear weapons would have to go mad at the same time."[8] By this logic, normal nuclear-armed states have nothing to fear from rogue nuclear-armed states. According to the Jenkins-Waltz logic, then, neither rogues nor terrorists that are NBC-armed should worry the United States. Finally, the evidence favors their case because it shows that (1) NBC terrorism has been practically nonexistent; (2) state use of NBC weapons has been rare; and (3) only non-NBC-armed states should worry about NBC attacks.[9]

In light of the Jenkins-Waltz logic and the supporting evidence, should we not accept the view that the United States has little or nothing to fear from NBC-armed rogues and terrorists? I believe not. It is folly to calculate that the past is prologue. This has never been the case in national security affairs; why should it be so now?

Three reasons should make us take the NBC-armed rogue-terrorist threat seriously. First, sadly, NBC weapons are coming increasingly within the reach of nonstate terrorist groups, largely as a consequence of more education about, and greater availability of, the basic scientific and engineering knowledge to produce these weapons, as well as the greater ease of acquiring the means to produce them.[10]

Second, terrorist motivations are changing. For starters, there is a disturbing tendency among some terrorist groups toward pure revenge, not political gain. For example, the ad hoc group of terrorists that bombed the New York World

---

8. The first Waltz quotation is from Kenneth N. Waltz and Scott D. Sagan, *The Spread of Nuclear Weapons: A Debate* (New York: W.W. Norton, 1995), p. 96; the second, from Waltz, "Peace, Stability, and Nuclear Weapons," unpublished ms., January 1997, p. 19.

9. First, there appear to be only two recorded instances of a terrorist group resorting to NBC weapons: the June 1995 sarin (nerve gas) attack on the Japanese city of Matsumoto, which killed 7 people and wounded more than 150; and the March 1995 sarin attack on the Tokyo subway, which killed 12 people and injured thousands of others; both of which were carried out by the Japanese cult group Aum Shinrikiyo. Second, apart from the unrestrained use of chemical weapons during World War I, there have been only twelve other known instances of NBC use by states—only one of which was nuclear (the United States against Japan in 1945); only one biological (Japan against China and the Soviet Union from 1937 to 1945); and the rest chemical, with only three since 1945 that count as rogue-state attacks, two of which involved Iraq. Third, in every one of these twelve cases, the NBC attacks were made on a state or group that could not retaliate in kind. See William J. Broad, "How Japan Germ Terror Alerted World," *New York Times*, May 26, 1998, p. A1, on the first point; and Falkenrath, Newman, and Thayer, *America's Achilles' Heel*, p. 91, on the second. For in-depth analyses of the Tokyo sarin attack, see Jessica Stern, "Terrorist Motivations and WMD," unpublished ms., pp. 5–13; and Falkenrath, Newman, and Thayer, *America's Achilles' Heel*, Box 1, pp. 19–26.

10. Falkenrath and his coauthors describe in chilling detail the growing ease with which nonstate actors can acquire NBC weapons. See Falkenrath, Newman, and Thayer, *America's Achilles' Heel*; and Stern, *Risk and Dread*, chap. 4.

Trade Center in 1996 simply wanted to kill 250,000 Americans. They were not trying to influence policy, only to exact retribution.[11] Deterring terrorists becomes nearly impossible if they are hell-bent only on revenge. In that case they have no need to identify themselves, and if there is no return address, there is no chance for retaliation. Deterrence, after all, is the threat to retaliate. Another disturbing trend is the growth of groups that are motivated by religious and millenarian imperatives.[12] Their terrorist acts have become more lethal than those inflicted by the more "traditional" ideological groups. (Aum Shinrikiyo is one such group.) These groups believe in martyrdom and the hereafter, or they believe themselves the agents of change for a new global order. They do not share the same rational objectives of the traditional politically motivated terrorist. Their motives are more ones of retribution and destruction, and they often view their adversaries as subhuman. As a consequence of such beliefs, these groups have become less restrained in their use of force.

Third, although overt and covert rogue-state NBC attacks against the United States appear unlikely, we cannot wholly discount them.[13] Hitler-like leaders who are willing to take their countries down with them when their plans do not succeed may be exceedingly rare, but they cannot be forever ruled out. It happened once in this century (Hitler); it could happen again in the next. We do not want such a leader to be NBC-armed, should one come to power.

None of this means that NBC attacks by rogues or terrorists are a foregone conclusion, but neither does it mean they are impossible. We have here a class of events whose probability of occurrence is low, but whose consequences if they occur are high, even catastrophic. In such cases, it is prudent to make expected value calculations: a small number (low likelihood of occurrence) multiplied by a very large number (adverse consequences of the event) still yields an unacceptably large number. This is, after all, how the United States treated the chance of nuclear war with the Soviet Union throughout most of the Cold War—as a low-probability but high-cost event—and took the necessary steps to make certain it would not happen. Similarly, selective engagers

---

11. Stern, "Terrorists Motivations and WMD," pp. 4–5. There is circumstantial evidence that Ramzi Yousef, the mastermind of the attack, also intended this to be a chemical weapons attack, because sodium cyanide was found. Had it vaporized instead of burned, it would have gone into the North Tower and killed the people there. See Falkenrath, Newman, and Thayer, *America's Achilles' Heel*, p. 32, n. 7.
12. For greater detail on these groups, see Hoffman, *Inside Terrorism*, chaps. 4, 7; Stern, *Risk and Dread*, chap. 5; and Falkenrath, Newman, and Thayer, *America's Achilles' Heel*, pp. 179–202.
13. For the reasons why, see the discussion in Falkenrath, Newman, and Thayer, *America's Achilles' Heel*, chap. 4.

make expected value calculations about what would happen if rogues and terrorists were to become NBC-armed, and they treat the threat as real, not fanciful.

Selective engagers also posit that the best way to forestall the threat is to take a strong stance against NBC spread in general. The logic for this stance rests on three propositions. None can be empirically validated, but none can be ruled out either. First, as more states acquire NBC weapons, the likelihood increases that rogue states and fanatical terrorists could obtain them. Wider ownership increases the chances of undesirable ownership, through theft, sale, or outright transfer. Second, weapons that can destroy cities or states in one fell swoop, or that can kill huge numbers of civilians easily and swiftly, should not be readily available to whoever wants them. Deterrence may not hold forever, and we should not tempt fate by allowing NBC weapons to spread widely. Third, rogue-state leaders will markedly increase their power to do evil and harm American interests through conventional means if they acquire NBC weapons. They may well become more emboldened to undertake aggression against their neighbors and in areas where the United States has important interests, seemingly secure in the belief that possession of NBC weapons makes them immune to U.S. retribution.

What, then, is the best way to prevent rogue states, fanatical groups, and other undesirables from acquiring NBC weapons? The first answer is to maintain a vigorous global political commitment against NBC spread. As the world's leader of this effort, the United States has little choice but to take a clear-cut, no-exceptions policy. It cannot publicly make exceptions because that would undermine the norm—and hence the cooperation of other states—against spread. Of necessity, however, if or when spread occurs, a no-exceptions public stance will have to be combined with a graded punishment regime that distinguishes between normal states, on the one hand, and rogue states and terrorists, on the other. None should get off scot-free, but because normal states are less dangerous than rogues and terrorists, the sanctions imposed on them should be less severe. The second way to retard or stop NBC spread is a grab bag of measures: strengthen institutions like the International Atomic Energy Agency, invest more in intelligence to discover covert nuclear and biological weapons programs, develop effective covert capabilities to sabotage terrorist and rogue-state NBC programs, sign treaties that publicly commit states to forgo acquisition, offer enticing carrots to states that abandon nuclear and biological weapons, and threaten adverse political-economic results for states that become NBC-armed. The third way is to use American military power in a fashion that supports the anti-NBC-spread regime.

To selective engagers, this means using American military power in three ways. First, it means the continued provision of reassurance—the maintenance of America's nuclear umbrella over Japan and Germany. These are America's two key allies in Eurasia today. Were they to go nuclear, it would signify the end of their confidence in the American nuclear umbrella. That might risk the end of America's major alliances and its stabilizing military presence in Eurasia, and might bring greater NBC spread to other Eurasian states and the consequent weakening of the global norm against NBC spread. Second, supporting the anti-NBC-spread regime may require the preventive use of force to disrupt or destroy a nascent rogue or terrorist NBC force if all other means, including covert sabotage attempts, have failed to prevent rogues or fanatics in their drive to acquire these weapons. Such use, either before an NBC force is operational or when it remains quite small, is by no means easy, but should not be ruled out in all circumstances. Third, American military power should be used to support a strong declaratory posture against NBC use for aggression. Any state or group that actually uses NBC weapons for aggression against unarmed NBC states or U.S. troops should fear beforehand severe military punishment. (If such use is not punishable, then the penalties against use go down, and the incentives to acquire these weapons go up.) The declaratory posture here is akin to what the United States said to the Soviet Union during the Cold War: "Attack us with nuclear weapons and we will devastate you in return." Whether the United States would have executed its threat, or whether it would have instead pulled its punches to avoid the inevitable Soviet retaliation, was left unclear. The stance should be the same for rogue or terrorist NBC use: an unqualified U.S. declaratory posture of punishment but a tacit understanding that the particular circumstances will determine what military action, if any, shall be taken.

In sum, a world with fewer NBC weapons, and with fewer states possessing them, is better for America's security than its opposite. An American military presence at both ends of Eurasia and in the Persian Gulf is a bulwark—not the only one but an important one—against their spread. Eurasia without an American military presence is likely to be a more heavily armed and dangerous place than with it.

EURASIAN GREAT POWER PEACE. America's second vital interest is to maintain a deep peace among the Eurasian great powers. This requires that there be neither major wars (ones that involve at least two great powers) nor intense, sustained security competitions (severe political conflicts that manifest themselves in the form of competitive military efforts short of war and that increase the chances of intense crises and war). The United States has three reasons to prevent these from happening.[14]

First, major wars or intense security competitions will reduce America's ability to hold the line against NBC spread. Like previous great power wars, a future one would not come out of the blue, but would be preceded by a series of intense crises, a prolonged period of arms racing, and arms buildups. These are bound to spur the acquisition and perhaps even the threatened use of NBC weapons, thereby making NBC limitation harder, not easier.

Second, great power wars or intense security competitions carry great risk of dragging in the United States. There are two possible scenarios: one where the United States has retained its Eurasian alliances; the other, where it has not. In the first, if a war or an intense security competition involved one of America's key Eurasian allies, the United States would be sucked in, certainly diplomatically and likely even militarily in order to meet its alliance commitments. In the second, unless it were strictly a Russian-Chinese affair, the United States would find it hard to stand aside. The reason: the lessons of the past. In the four major Eurasian great power wars since 1789, the United States was dragged in, in each case to defend its future security and in addition for at least one of the following reasons: to protect its trade, to support historical and cultural bonds, to oppose aggression, or to resist the imposition of odious forms of government on nations with which it identified. No great power has ever lived solely by the dictates of balance of power; the United States is no exception to this rule. We cannot predict the exact paths by which the United States would become entangled in a major Eurasian war, but the probability is better than even that it would.

Third, major wars and intense security competitions are not good for trade, and would be disruptive to America's considerable economic stakes in western and eastern Eurasia, as well as in the Gulf. Over the long term, trade and especially investment do better under stable, not unstable, political conditions.

---

14. Notice I have not argued that the United States has an interest in preventing all wars in Eurasia. Non–great power wars—those between a great and a smaller power or among smaller powers—affect American interests only to the extent that they dramatically enhance the risk of a great power war, stimulate WMD spread, lead to mass murder, or threaten U.S. alliances.

Peace is more stability-producing than intense security competitions and war; it is therefore more conducive to long-term trade and investment.[15] The protection of U.S. economic interests in Eurasia is not a vital interest, but certainly an important one, especially for a nation whose stake in international economic activity has doubled from its historic levels in the last twenty-five years. (Exports plus imports as a percentage of America's GDP held at the 6–10 percent range throughout most of America's history; beginning in the middle 1970s, it increased dramatically, reaching the 18–22 percent range by 1980 and remaining there ever since.)

The Eurasian great powers are presently at peace because of at least two factors: great power democracies and nuclear deterrence. First is the fact that four of the great powers (Germany, France, Britain, and Japan) are solid democracies. The fifth (Russia) has begun a rocky road to democratization, and the sixth (China) remains poised between the incompatible worlds of command politics and free markets. War is less likely among democracies than it is among nondemocracies or between democracies and nondemocracies. Second is the fact that four of the great powers (Britain, France, Russia, and China) are nuclear-armed, and the other two (Germany and Japan) are protected by the United States. It is hard to get a large war going between nuclear-armed or nuclear-protected states.

We should not be complacent, however, about the pacifying effects of either factor. The peace-among-democracies effect may be a strong force, but it is not an ironclad law of history. It has not overpowered, nor will it invariably overpower, all the other forces at work in world politics.[16] Moreover, although hard, it is not impossible to have a war between nuclear powers. Recall that the Soviet Union and China, both nuclear-armed at the time, did fight a minor border war in 1969. It has also been relatively easy to have intense crises among

---

15. The dampening effects of security competitions on trade is not an ironclad law because the former do not invariably reduce the latter. Peter Liberman has done the best published research to date on the relation between security competitions and trade and concludes that it had little effect in the cases he looked at. I have done research on some of his cases as well as on others, and found that security competitions did significantly reduce trade. See Liberman, "Trading with the Enemy: Security and Relative Economic Gains," *International Security*, Vol. 21, No. 1 (Summer 1996), pp. 147–176; and Robert J. Art, "Security Competitions and Trade in Historical Perspective," unpublished ms., Brandeis University, July 1998.

16. For a good review of the arguments, pro and con, on the democratic peace, see the preface by Sean Lynn-Jones in Michael E. Brown, Sean M. Lynn-Jones, and Steven E. Miller, eds., *Debating the Democratic Peace* (Cambridge, Mass.: MIT Press, 1996), pp. ix–xxxiii; and Miriam Fendius Elman, ed., *Paths to Peace: Is Democracy the Answer?* (Cambridge, Mass.: MIT Press, 1997), pp. 1–59.

nuclear-armed states, and they always carry great risk of war. Recall the intense crises between the United States and the Soviet Union during the first half of the Cold War.

To these two factors, therefore, we should add extra insurance: America's military presence at either end of Eurasia. In Western Europe that presence assures Germany's neighbors that it will not return to its ugly past; in East Asia it reassures Japan's neighbors about Japan, and China's neighbors about China.[17] At both ends of Eurasia, therefore, America's military presence makes interstate relations more stable and peacelike than they would otherwise be. In sum, many elements contribute to peace among the Eurasian great powers today. American policy should be to keep it that way.

DIVISION OF GULF RESERVES. America's third vital national interest is to have a secure supply of oil at stable prices.[18] Security in supply and stability in price are important in order to avoid severe disruptions to the U.S. and the world economies. Interruptions in oil supplies that result in severe cutbacks can wreak havoc by lowering economic activity; so, too, can wild and severe swings in the price of oil, because they disrupt economic calculations, subject economies to the price manipulations of oil suppliers, and make it difficult for oil-consuming states to begin weaning themselves from their heavy dependence on oil. One of the most important ways to keep oil supplies available at stable and reasonable prices is secure access to Persian Gulf oil. This, in turn, is facilitated by preventing a regional hegemon from controlling the Persian Gulf's oil reserves, either directly by military conquest or indirectly by the threat of conquest. Hence America's third vital national interest is well served by keeping the Gulf's oil reserves divided among several, preferably at least four, of the regional states.

The logic for this position rests on five propositions. First, the United States and most of the other industrialized and industrializing states remain heavily reliant on oil and oil imports to fuel their economies for at least the next several

---

17. For an analysis of the effects of the American military presence in Western Europe during the critical 1990–96 years, see Robert J. Art, "Why Western Europe Needs the United States and NATO," *Political Science Quarterly*, Vol. 111, No. 1 (Spring 1996), pp. 1–39. For analyses of its neighbors' worries about China and the role that the United States plays in lessening those worries, see the various essays in Alastair Iain Johnston and Robert S. Ross, eds., *Engaging China: The Management of a Rising Power* (London: Routledge, forthcoming); and Steve Glain, "New Arms Race: Fearing China's Plans and a U.S. Departure, Asians Rebuild Forces," *Wall Street Journal*, November 13, 1997, p. A1.

18. I favor oil prices that are high enough to encourage conservation and that make alternative sources of energy competitive. For the United States, this requires a higher tax on oil and especially on gasoline because almost two-thirds of America's daily oil consumption goes for transportation.

decades. America's dependence on imported oil was 25 percent of daily consumption in 1973, is about 53 percent now, and is projected to rise to 70 percent early in the twenty-first century.[19] At some point in the future, America's heavy dependence on oil will diminish as it continues the switch from oil to natural gas for electricity generation and as it gets serious about limiting fossil fuel burning in order to reduce global warming (see below). Until that day arrives, the United States remains vulnerable either to sustained disruptions in oil supplies, or to swift and steep swings in oil prices.

Second, in spite of discoveries elsewhere, the Gulf still contains the lion's share of the world's proven oil reserves and a significant percentage of its natural gas reserves. In 1949 Saudi Arabia, Iraq, the United Arab Emirates, Kuwait, Iran, Oman, and Qatar had 44 percent of the world's proven oil reserves; in 1975, 54 percent; and in 1993, 65 percent of the world's oil reserves and one-third of the world's proven natural gas reserves. Recent finds, mostly in the Caspian Sea, have changed the picture somewhat, dropping Gulf reserves as a percentage of proven world oil reserves in 1996 to somewhere between 46 percent and 63 percent, depending on whether the high end (200 billion barrels) or low end (70 billion barrels) estimates are used for Caspian Sea reserves.[20] Even if Caspian reserves prove to be at the higher end of the estimated range, Gulf reserves will remain central to global oil usage because the most current forecasts of the Energy Information Agency show world oil demand rising from 73.4 million barrels a day (mbd) in 1997 to 104.6 mbd in 2015, with the Gulf's share of world oil production capacity rising from its 1995 level of 28.6 percent to somewhere between 38 percent and 47 percent, depending on whether oil prices are high or low, respectively. Therefore, whatever the exact figure, the Gulf's oil and natural gas reserves will continue to constitute a large percentage of the world's proven hydrocarbon reserves for the next several decades.[21] Finally, possession of large reserves brings market power,

19. See Energy Information Agency, U.S. Department of Energy, *Annual Energy Review*, May 1991, p. 117; and Rick Wartzman and Anne Reifenberg, "Big Energy Imports Are Less of a Threat Than They Appear," *Wall Street Journal*, August 17, 1995, p. A6.

20. American Petroleum Institute, *Basic Petroleum Data Book*, Vol. 14, No. 2 (Washington, D.C.: American Petroleum Institute, May 1994), Section 2, Table 4; and Geoffrey Kemp and Robert E. Harkavy, *Strategic Geography and the Changing Middle East* (Washington, D.C.: Brookings Institution, 1997), p. 111. According to Charles Clover and Robert Corzine, they are somewhere between 25 and 70 billion barrels. See Clover and Corzine, "Treasure under the Sea," *Financial Times*, May 1, 1997, p. 11, but the most recent estimates by the U.S. Department of Energy put them at 200 billion barrels. See http://www.usia.gov/products/washfile.htm.

21. World oil production capacity refers to the total possible daily world production in millions of barrels per day. See Energy Information Agency, U.S. Department of Energy, http://www.

because states with large reserves, such as Saudi Arabia, have the capacity and the interest to act as swing producers, thereby affecting supply and prices.

Third, even though the United States imports little of its oil supplies from the Gulf, it is still dependent on what happens there. The United States today imports more petroleum products (crude oil and refined products) from Venezuela (1,657 mbd) and Canada (1,415 mbd) than it does from Saudi Arabia (1,363 mbd). Mexico ranks fourth at 1,240 mbd. The fact that a huge percentage of America's crude oil and petroleum product imports comes from the Western Hemisphere does not lessen the importance of the Gulf. The world oil market is highly competitive and integrated. What happens in the Gulf will affect the world price and supply should a major disruption occur there. It is therefore fallacious to argue that Gulf production and reserves are of little concern to the United States because it imports little from the region.[22]

Fourth, access to Gulf oil is made safer if proven reserves are divided among a larger rather than a smaller number of states—at least four or more rather than one or two. Consolidation of Gulf reserves among one or two states facilitates collusion; division of its reserves among four states or more makes collusion more difficult. To allow one or two states to control Gulf oil reserves is to put one or both in a powerful position to hold up the world. Oil is the one natural resource for which the demand is highly inelastic in the short to medium term. Oil prices, moreover, have never been determined solely by market factors, but have also been heavily influenced by political and military considerations. The Gulf's oil reserves are too important to be left to the market alone and too valuable to allow one or two regional hegemons to control.[23]

Fifth, an American military presence in the Gulf helps secure access to a stable oil supply by ensuring that neither Iraq nor Iran consolidates control over the Persian Gulf sheikdoms' considerable reserves. Since the late 1970s, the United States has followed a balance-of-power strategy in the Gulf, first leaning toward Iran when Iraq looked stronger, then tilting toward Iraq when Iran looked stronger, all the while acting to protect the Kuwaiti and Saudi oil

---

eia.doe.gov/emeu/aer/contents.html, Tables 5.12A and B; and http://www.eia.doe.gov/oiaf/ieo97/appa7.html, Table A40. For a useful survey of the hydrocarbon alternatives to Gulf and Caspian Sea reserves, see Kemp and Harkavy, *Strategic Geography and the Changing Middle East*, Appendix 1.

22. Daily American import figures come from the Energy Information Agency, U.S. Department of Energy, at http://www.eia.doe.gov/emeu/ aer/contents.html, Table 5.4.

23. For an exchange on the pros and cons of this point, see Joseph S. Nye, Jr., "Why the Gulf War Served the National Interest," and Christopher Layne, "Why the Gulf War Was Not in the National Interest," both in *The Atlantic*, July 1991, pp. 54–81.

fields from dominion by either one. This has been and remains a sensible policy, and under current circumstances requires an American military presence in the Gulf. "Divide but not conquer" must be America's dictum toward the Gulf.

DESIRABLE INTERESTS

America's next three interests are its desirable ones: preserve an open international economic order, foster the spread of democracy and respect for human rights, and protect the global environment. The fact that they are desirable does not make them unimportant, only of lesser importance when trade-offs between them and the vital ones must be made. Moreover, unlike the vital interests, the desirable ones are served less directly and tangibly by America's military power. That does not make military power useless to attain them, only that it is better used in a more indirect fashion.

INTERNATIONAL ECONOMIC OPENNESS. Openness means low or nonexistent barriers to the exchange of goods and services among states. Openness per se does not create wealth, but it does facilitate the most efficient allocation of the world's factors of production if markets are operating efficiently. This benefits the United States in three ways.[24]

First, international openness makes the United States richer than it would otherwise be because of the gains it reaps from trade. These gains are of two types: static gains—the onetime increase in productivity that occurs with the shift of resources from less to more efficient uses when a state switches from protectionism to freer trade; and dynamic gains—the continuing increases in productivity that more open and larger markets, fiercer competition, and

---

24. There are those who argue that openness hurts the United States because the United States cannot compete with states that pay lower wages. Openness, these critics assert, is the primary cause of America's loss of manufacturing capacity and lower wages for its unskilled labor. The evidence does not support either proposition. The United States remains the world's most competitive economy (because it maintains greater openness to international competition), and trade plays only a small role (about 20 percent) in the decline in wages for unskilled labor. For evidence on America's competitiveness, see the three studies by the McKinsey Global Institute (Washington, D.C.: McKinsey and Company): *Manufacturing Productivity* (October 1993), *Service Sector Productivity* (October 1992), and *Capital Productivity* (June 1996). For a review of the evidence on the effects of competition on American wages, see Richard B. Freeman, "Are Your Wages Set in Beijing?" and J. David Richardson, "Income Inequality and Trade: How to Think, What to Conclude," both in *Journal of Economic Perspectives*, Vol. 9, No. 3 (Summer 1995), pp. 15–32, 33–55, respectively; Lester B. Thurow, *The Future of Capitalism* (New York: William Morrow and Company, 1996), chap. 6; Dani Rodrik, *Has Globalization Gone Too Far?* (Washington, D.C.: Institute for International Economics [IIE], 1997), chap. 2; and William R. Cline, *Trade and Income Distribution* (Washington, D.C.: IIE, 1997), chaps. 2, 5.

economies of scale produce. Static gains, measured in terms of the costs of protection, are smaller for the United States than for most other states because the United States is the world's most open economy. These gains run at about 0.75 percent of America's gross national product, or $56 billion, a small sum for any given year, but a nontrivial loss in forgone output and wealth when cumulated over many years.[25] Dynamic gains are notoriously difficult to quantify, but most economists deem them to be considerable because they are the ones that lead to the continual increases in productivity, and hence real income, that global competition produces.

Second, openness makes other states richer than they would otherwise be, and this is good for the United States. All states can gain from trade and economic openness, although they will gain unequally because their national efficiencies differ. Each, however, will grow richer and more efficient if market, not political, considerations determine the allocation of resources. If states grow richer, they become better customers for American exports, because rich customers buy more than poor ones.

Third, as other states grow richer, their pacific tendencies should strengthen and so should their prospects for becoming democratic or more solidly democratic. The strengthening of a state's pacific and democratic proclivities is to America's benefit. Although we cannot assume that the economic interdependence that results from sustained openness by itself produces peace, surely it is a contributing factor. Rich states are likely to be more contented and therefore less aggressive than poor states when they believe that they can become rich through industrialization and trade. In addition, high levels of economic interdependence are peace-conducing because states have a strong self-interest in others doing well economically (they do better with trade if others are prospering).[26] Similarly, the single most important factor historically in the creation of stable democracies has been the creation of large stable middle

---

25. The static gains estimate comes from Paul Krugman, *The Age of Diminished Expectations: U.S. Economic Policy in the 1990s* (Cambridge, Mass.: MIT Press, 1990), p. 104. It represents Krugman's estimate of the cost to the United States of its protectionist measures in force around 1990. It should also be noted that large economies like the United States reap smaller static gains from free trade because they have already reaped considerable economies of scale from their large internal markets. See Krugman and Maurice Obstfeld, *International Economics: Theory and Practice*, 3d ed. (New York: HarperCollins, 1994), pp. 228–229, for a discussion of static and dynamic gains from trade.

26. For a review of the arguments on both sides of this issue, see Dale C. Copeland, "Economic Interdependence and War: A Theory of Trade Expectations," *International Security*, Vol. 20, No. 4 (Spring 1996), pp. 5–42.

classes.[27] In turn, since 1945 economic growth has been the single most important factor in the creation of large and stable middle classes. Economic growth, aided in part by an open international economic order, is therefore a democracy-producing engine.

DEMOCRATIC SPREAD AND HUMAN RIGHTS PROTECTION. The spread of democracy, the protection of human rights, and the prevention of mass murder are values Americans hold dear. All three are morally desirable in themselves and have greater global appeal than many analysts care to admit. They also tangibly benefit the United States in at least three ways.

First, the spread of democracy is likely to make states more pacific in their foreign policies when democracies confront other democracies. Therefore, if democracy spreads within regions, it will increase the number of peaceful zones, and this benefits the United States for the simple reason that a more pacific world is a less dangerous world.

Second, democratic spread is also the best insurance that human rights will be protected and mass murders avoided. By definition, stable democracies rarely incarcerate their citizens at will or slaughter huge numbers of them indiscriminately.[28] If the spread of democracy protects human lives and human rights, then the need for the international community to intervene in the internal affairs of states will be lessened. This will reduce the pressures and burdens on the United States, which is the state usually looked to by the world community to organize and lead such efforts.

Third, the spread of democracy is good for global economic growth. Command economies do poorly over the long term; market economies do much better. Command political systems are not entirely incompatible with market economies (witness Chile under Augusto Pinochet or China under Deng Xiaoping), but they are not sustainable over the long term, if the change of regime in Chile and the present tensions in China are reliable guides. Thus more peace zones, lessened need for intervention, and greater prosperity—these are the likely benefits of the global spread of democracy.

---

27. For evidence that economic growth facilitates the emergence of democracy, see John B. Londregan and Keith T. Poole, "Does High Income Promote Democracy?" *World Politics*, Vol. 49, No. 1 (October 1996), pp. 1–31; and Larry Diamond, "Economic Development and Democracy Reconsidered," *American Behavioral Scientist*, Vol. 35, Nos. 4/5 (March/June 1992), pp. 450–499.

28. R. J. Rummel has documented this assertion and quantified the relation between the nature of a regime and the degree to which it mass murders its citizenry. See Rummel, *Power Kills: Democracy as a Method of Nonviolence* (New Brunswick, N.J.: Transaction Publishers, 1997), chap. 6.

THE GLOBAL ENVIRONMENT. The last desirable interest is to prevent depletion of the earth's ozone layer and to avert a huge rise in the earth's average global temperature. Both present serious problems—the former, because of the destructive effects on all forms of life wrought by the increase in ultraviolet radiation reaching the earth; the latter, because of the climate change induced by global warming. Neither respects national boundaries, and both therefore threaten the quality of American life.

The threat of ozone depletion has been "solved," but not in the sense that the depletion has stopped. It has not; furthermore, it will continue for several decades, and it will take the ozone layer another fifty years to fully recover once the chemicals that destroy it are no longer released into the atmosphere. Instead, ozone depletion has been "solved" in the sense that an international treaty has been negotiated and signed to severely restrict and then phase out these dangerous chemicals. The task for international action now is to see that the treaty is fully implemented.

Global warming presents the United States with its greatest environmental threat. Although the country is better placed than most others to deal with its myriad adverse effects because of America's wealth and technology, nonetheless, the United States will not be exempt from them. These include more extreme weather, crop and species loss, coastal erosion caused by thermal expansion, stress on water supplies, increase in urban pollution, loss of up to 40 percent of America's forests, and so on.[29] Reliable and precise estimates of the damage to the United States are hard to come by, but William Cline provides one of the best, estimating that annual damage to the United States from global warming will run between $61.6 and $335.7 billion (in 1990 dollars), or between 1.1 percent and 6 percent of GDP, respectively.[30] These costs could be sustained indefinitely, if abatement costs (the costs to the United States of measures to avert global warming) are larger than damage costs.[31] If

29. The definitive scientific assessments of climate change can be found in two volumes published by the Intergovernmental Panel on Climate Change (IPCC), a body created by the World Meteorological Organization and the United Nations Environment Program. The first volume is *Climate Change: The IPCC Scientific Assessment* (Cambridge: Cambridge University Press, 1990); the second is *Climate Change 1995: The Science of Climate Change* (Cambridge: Cambridge University Press, 1996). For the most up-to-date analysis of the regional effects of climate change, see IPCC, "Summary for Policymakers," *The Regional Impacts of Climate Change: An Assessment of Vulnerability,* at http://www.IPCC.ch/.
30. See William R. Cline, *The Economics of Global Warming* (Washington, D.C.: IIE, 1992), p. 131.
31. Abatement cost estimates are hard to come by, but an intragovernmental working panel set up by the Clinton administration estimates that raising the price of a ton of carbon by $100 would produce in the short term losses of between 0.2 percent and 1.0 percent of GDP. This estimate

abatement costs run well below damage costs, however, then averting climate change represents a good bargain and a desirable interest for the United States.

There is, however, a catch. If global warming continues unabated, it could induce (trigger) a highly adverse, changed state in the earth's climate, with potentially catastrophic consequences. This possibility cannot be discounted, even though its likelihood cannot be estimated. What climatologists do know is this: the magnitude of predicted warming (2–9 degrees centigrade), unless countersteps are quickly taken, will by the end of the twenty-first century approach the range of temperature changes (5–10 degrees centigrade) that accompanied Ice Age transitions; and those transitions occurred in a matter of decades, not centuries.[32] If global warming threatens discontinuous climate change, then averting it becomes a vital, not a desirable, interest for the United States. It therefore makes sense to avert catastrophic climate change by making the investments necessary to retard and ultimately stop human-induced global warming.

WHY INDIRECT? Finally, America's military power is best used indirectly to support the achievement of its three desirable interests. The commitment of American military power to Eurasia and the Gulf plays a clear and direct role in retarding the spread of weapons of mass destruction, helping to maintain a deep peace among the great powers, and keeping Persian Gulf oil reserves divided. The link between America's military power and its desirable interests is more diffuse.

In general, the United States should not wage war to make states democratic, nor intervene militarily in their internal affairs to protect human rights. Military intervention for either purpose is a risky and costly proposition: one that usually requires a long-term presence to create the basis for success, as America's experiences with Germany and Japan have illustrated. A better path to democratization and, consequently, to the protection of human rights, is to increase the size of a state's middle class by increasing the state's wealth, which is best achieved through creating a market economy and then having it participate in the global economy. This is the path that South Korea and Taiwan

may well be too low. It is from Executive Summary, *Economic Effects of Global Climate Change Policies, Results of the Research Efforts of the Interagency Analytical Team,* June 1997, p. 1, http://www.weathervane.rff.org/features/features/007.html#report.

32. For the most recent evidence about climate triggers and the swiftness of past climate changes, see Jeffrey P. Severinghous et al., "Timing of Abrupt Climate Change at the End of the Younger Dryas Interval from Thermally Fractionated Gases in Polar Ice," *Nature,* January 8, 1998, pp. 141–146.

followed, for example. It is a longer lasting and certainly cheaper path than the imposition of democracy by military conquest and long occupation.

There are two clear exceptions to the injunction that the United States should refrain from forceful intervention to create democracy or to protect human rights. The first is the rare occasion when a military intervention by the United States can make the difference in restoring or creating democracy. Such occasions will generally involve small states with weak militaries, an ongoing political crisis, a suitable political base upon which to build democratic institutions, and a willingness on the part of a large segment of the population to welcome an American military presence. There is a further requirement to justify intervention: it must also serve other important American interests. The second exception is to prevent genocidal-like mass murders in those states where outside military intervention is feasible and can be effective. Humanity requires that the international community intervene to prevent or to stop them. Again, such instances are more likely to involve small states with weak militaries, not medium-sized or large states with strong militaries. Even in this instance, however, the United States must eschew going it alone and instead organize international coalitions of the willing, which should also include important actors in the region concerned if possible. Neither type of intervention will be short-term, in-and-out affairs, but will require both a long-term military presence and considerable economic assistance.

Finally, the United States cannot profitably coerce states to engage in free trade at the point of a gun, nor order them under threat of attack to cut back their generation of greenhouse gases. The coercive use of American military power for both these purposes is a losing proposition and beyond America's military might. Instead, a more indirect approach is called for.

America's best hope for achieving its desirable interests is to protect its vital interests. If the line against the spread of weapons of mass destruction can be held, if the world's access to Gulf oil is assured, and if the deep peace among the great powers can be maintained, then what results is an international system more peaceful, more prosperous, and more benign than would otherwise be the case. A more peacelike world is an important means for preserving international openness, and openness, in turn, helps generate the wealth that facilitates democratic transitions and that will be necessary to deal with what is likely to prove to be humankind's biggest challenge yet: averting global climatic disaster. A more warlike world, to the contrary, is likely to be less prosperous, more contentious, and less cooperative, and none of these things benefits the United States. In sum, by advancing its vital interests through its military power, the United States can indirectly contribute to realizing its desirable interests and in the process do some good for others.

The Alternatives to Selective Engagement

Showing that selective engagement has virtues is not equivalent to demonstrating that it is the best grand strategy. That requires a comparison with the six alternatives to it—dominion, global collective security, regional collective security, cooperative security, containment, and isolationism. I argue that the first four are not feasible; the fifth is feasible, but can be readily folded into selective engagement; the sixth is feasible but not desirable.[33]

THE ALTERNATIVES

Dominion is a strategy by which the United States literally rules the world. It represents the "Roman option": the United States uses its military power to impose order among all states and to make all of them conform internally to its values. Under the American dominion, world peace and 190-odd American look-alikes would be the results. Dominion is the world policeman role, and for that reason is financially and militarily beyond America's resources. Thus dominion is infeasible.

Next to dominion, collective security is the most demanding grand strategy. Its goal is to stop interstate war, and hence bring interstate peace to all areas where it is imposed. Whether implemented globally or regionally, all states that join a collective security organization take the collective security pledge: all agree to protect one another from aggression—from any and all aggressors. If this system is to work, however, it requires about a 100 percent success rate. Collective security cannot be a sometimes affair: sometimes it works, sometimes it does not. No state will entrust its protection to an organization that purports to protect it from all aggression, but that chooses to do so only selectively.

In the past, moreover, states have not been willing to yield national control over the use of force and give to an international organization a blank check upon which to draw in order to resist or punish aggression. Nor will they do

---

33. Space limitations do not permit a thorough review of these six alternatives. They are covered fully in Robert J. Art, "Selective Engagement: An American Grand Strategy," unpublished ms., chaps. 4, 5. For a good short assessment of America's available grand strategies, consult Barry R. Posen and Andrew L. Ross, "Competing Visions for U.S. Grand Strategy," *International Security*, Vol. 21, No. 3 (Winter 1996/97), pp. 5–54.

so in the future. Rather, states have retained national control, reserving for themselves the right to decide whether to empower the international organizations they have constructed to punish aggressors. Consequently, the world's two best institutional attempts to prevent aggression on a global scale—the League of Nations and the United Nations—were never genuine collective security organizations, but rather informal concerts of the great powers clothed in collective security rhetoric. For that reason, their combined, punish-the-aggressor record is weak.[34]

Finally, there have been no instances in recorded history of an effective regional collective security organization. The closest approximations in modern times occurred during the Cold War: the Rio Treaty for the Western Hemisphere and the NATO alliance for Western Europe. Neither, however, was a regional collective security organization; rather, both were regional imperiums run and operated by the United States. For all these reasons, then, collective security, too, is politically infeasible and therefore a bad grand strategy for the United States.

The last of the infeasible strategies is cooperative security, the 1990s update of collective security.[35] It consists of two elements: first, a rigorous arms control approach that aims to make aggression difficult by banning possession of NBC weapons, reducing armaments, emphasizing transparency in military matters, and most important, constructing only defensive weapons; and second, a residual collective security system to protect the victims of aggression in case the arms control measures fail to prevent it. With these two measures cooperative security seeks to reduce significantly, if not wholly eliminate, aggressive wars.

---

34. There were thirty-two interstate wars between 1922 and 1991. The League and the United Nations attempted collective security enforcement (punishment of interstate aggression) only three times. The first (League action against Italy in 1936) was a fiasco and effectively destroyed the League. The second (assistance to South Korea to repel a North Korean attack in 1950) was a United Nations operation in name, but in fact an American affair, and took place only because the Soviet Union happened to boycott the Security Council meeting on the day that the action was voted. The third (the 1991 Gulf War to evict Iraq from Kuwait) was another American-run affair and was blessed by the UN. The thirty-two interstate wars for these seventy years can be found in "Correlates of War Project: International and Civil War Data, 1816–1992" (ICPR 9905), Inter-University Consortium for Political and Social Research, Ann Arbor, Michigan, April 1994.

35. The concept of cooperative security was first proposed in Ashton B. Carter, William J. Perry, and John D. Steinbruner, *A New Concept of Cooperative Security* (Washington, D.C.: Brookings Institution, 1992); and further elaborated in Janne E. Nolan, ed., *Global Engagement: Cooperation and Security in the Twenty-first Century* (Washington, D.C.: Brookings Institution, 1994), esp. chaps. 1, 2.

This strategy has three problems. First, because cooperative security incorporates a residual collective security system, it depends on a fail-safe procedure that has proven impossible to implement. Second, defensive military systems are incompatible with the requirement for punishing aggressors, because punishment demands that some entity have the offensive military power to punish. Third, cooperative security lodges the punishment power in an entity—the United States and some of its great power allies—that is politically unacceptable. Cooperative security is in fact a guise for the lesser states of the world to accept a great power military condominium to impose peace on them. The overwhelming majority of the world's states, however, are not going to accept this and will not practically disarm themselves while the great powers do not. For these reasons, cooperative security is infeasible.

The last two strategies—containment and isolationism—are feasible. Containment is a strategy that seeks to cut down hostile candidate states that aspire to regional or global hegemony before they emerge, or if they do, that prevents them from either expanding territorially or exerting overweening influence over the political and economic affairs of states that come within the aspiring hegemon's orbit. Containment requires military power to prevent territorial expansion, and oftentimes economic and political aid to states on the front line to sustain them in maintaining their independence. For now, there is no state placed to strive for global hegemony; therefore, if the United States applies containment, it will be done regionally. For that reason, it can be easily folded into the strategy of selective engagement in those areas deemed of importance to the United States.

Thus, by a process of elimination, the only serious competitor to selective engagement is isolationism. A grand strategy of isolationism does not call for economic autarky, political noninvolvement with the rest of the world, or abstention from the use of force to protect American interests. Indeed, isolationism is compatible with extensive economic interaction with other nations, vigorous political interactions, and the occasional use of force, often in conjunction with other states, to defend American interests. Rather, the defining characteristics of strategic isolationism are (1) insistence that the United States make no binding commitments in peacetime to use American military power to aid another state or states, and (2) the most minimal use of force and military involvement abroad. Understood in this sense, isolationism is a unilateralist strategy that retains complete freedom for the United States to determine when, where, how, for what purpose, against whom, and with whom it will use its military power, combined with a determination to do as little militarily as possible abroad. Isolationism, in short, is the policy of the "free hand" and the lightest military touch.[36]

SELECTIVE ENGAGEMENT VERSUS ISOLATIONISM

An America gone isolationist would cancel all its military alliances because they are peacetime pledges to use American military power to protect other states; would bring all its military forces home, save for its powerful navy periodically sailing the seas and making occasional port stops; and last, would eschew most military involvement overseas. Is this a better option than selective engagement for the United States?

I believe not and think selective engagement preferable to isolationism on four grounds. First, today's isolationists do not embrace all six national interests prescribed above, whereas selective engagers embrace them all.[37] For example, isolationists maintain relative indifference to nuclear spread, and some of them even believe that it may be beneficial because it reduces the probability of war. They assert that America's overseas economic interests no longer require the projection of American military power, and see no great stake in keeping Persian Gulf reserves divided among several powers. To the extent that they believe a deep peace among the Eurasian great powers is important to the United States, they hold that offshore balancing (keeping all American troops in the United States) is as effective as onshore balancing (keeping American forces deployed forward in Eurasia at selected points) and safer. Indeed, most isolationists are prepared to use American military power to defend only two vital American interests: repelling an attack on the Ameri-

---

36. The best recent statements favoring isolationism are Eric Nordlinger, *Isolationism Reconfigured: American Foreign Policy for a New Century* (Princeton, N.J.: Princeton University Press, 1995); Eugene Gholz, Daryl G. Press, and Harvey M. Sapolsky, "Come Home America: The Strategy of Restraint in the Face of Temptation," *International Security*, Vol. 21, No. 4 (Spring 1997), pp. 1–43; and Christopher Layne, "From Preponderance to Offshore Balancing: America's Future Grand Strategy," *International Security*, Vol. 22, No. 1 (Summer 1997), pp. 86–125. Nordlinger advocates outright isolationism; Layne does not view himself as an isolationist, but because he advocates the end of America's military alliances and minimal involvement overseas, I consider him to fall within my definition of isolationist. Gholz, Press, and Sapolsky are nearly isolationists in both senses defined above, but do favor the use of American military power to secure access to Persian Gulf oil. The best older statement for isolationism is Robert W. Tucker, *A New Isolationism: Threat or Promise* (Washington, D.C.: Universe Books, 1972).

37. I realize that not every one of today's isolationists holds to every one of the propositions portrayed by the sketch in this paragraph. All of today's isolationists, however, do adhere to most of them. Therefore, although this picture distorts to a degree, as all composites do, still it is a rough approximation of the outlook of today's isolationists.

can homeland and preventing a great power hegemon from dominating Eurasia.[38] As a consequence, they can justifiably be called the most selective of selective engagers.

Second, isolationism forgoes the opportunity to exploit the full peacetime political utility of America's alliances and forward-deployed forces to shape events to its advantage. Isolationism's general approach is to cope with events after they have turned adverse rather than to prevent matters from turning adverse in the first place. Thus, even though it does not eschew the use of force, isolationism remains at heart a watching and reactive strategy, not, like selective engagement, a precautionary and proactive one.

Third, isolationism makes more difficult the warlike use of America's military power, when that is required, because it forgoes peacetime forward deployment. This provides the United States with valuable bases, staging areas, intelligence-gathering facilities, in-theater training facilities, and most important, close allies with whom it continuously trains and exercises. These are militarily significant advantages and constitute valuable assets if war needs to be waged. Should the United States have to go to war with an isolationist strategy in force, however, these assets would need to be put together under conditions ranging from less than auspicious to emergency-like. Isolationism thus makes war waging more difficult than need be.

Fourth, isolationism is not as balanced and diversified a strategy as is selective engagement and not as good a hedge against risk and uncertainty. Selective engagement achieves balance and diversity from its hybrid nature: it borrows the good features from its six competitors but endeavors to avoid their pitfalls and excesses. Like isolationism, selective engagement is wary of the risks of military entanglement overseas, but unlike isolationism, it believes that some entanglements either lower the chances of war or are necessary to protect important American interests even at the risk of war. Unlike collective security, selective engagement does not assume that peace is indivisible, but like collective security, it believes in operating multilaterally in military operations wherever possible to spread the burdens and risks, and asserts that standing alliances make such operations easier to organize and more successful when undertaken. Unlike global containment, selective engagement does not believe

---

38. Gholz, Press, and Sapolsky do add a third goal for which they are prepared to commit American military power—the defense of access to Persian Gulf oil. In this case they favor a minimal American air force, but not a ground force, presence. See Gholz, Press, and Sapolsky, "Come Home America," pp. 25–30.

current conditions require a full-court press against any great power, but like regional containment, it knows that balancing against an aspiring regional hegemon requires the sustained cooperation of the other powers in the area and that such cooperation is not sustainable without a visible American military presence. Unlike dominion, selective engagement does not seek to dominate others, but like dominion, it understands the power and influence that America's military primacy brings. Finally, like cooperative security, selective engagement seeks transparency in military relations, reductions in armaments, and the control of NBC spread, but unlike cooperative security, it does not put full faith in the reliability of collective security or defensive defense should these laudable aims fail.

Compared to selective engagement, isolationism is less balanced because it is less diversified. It allows standing military coalitions to crumble, forsakes forward deployment, and generally eschews attempts to control the armaments of the other great and not-so-great powers. Isolationism's outstanding virtue is that it achieves complete freedom for the United States to act or not to act whenever it sees fit, but the freedom comes at a cost: the loss of a diversified approach. Most isolationists, of course, are prepared to trade balance and diversity for complete freedom of action, because they see little worth fighting for (save for the two interests enumerated above), because they judge that prior military commitments are not necessary to protect them, and because they calculate that alliances will only put the United States in harm's way.

In sum, selective engagement is a hedging strategy; isolationism is not. To hedge is to make counterbalancing investments in order to avoid or lessen loss. Selective engagement makes hedging bets (primarily through alliances and overseas basing), because it does not believe that the international environment, absent America's precommitted stance and forward presence, will remain benign to America's interests, as apparently does isolationism. An isolationist America in the sense defined above would help produce a more dangerous and less prosperous world; an internationalist America, a more peaceful and prosperous one. As a consequence, engagement rejects the free hand for the selectively committed hand. Thus, for these four reasons—the goals it posits, its proactive stance, its warfighting advantages, and its hedging approach—selective engagement beats isolationism.

The Pitfalls of Selective Engagement

Desirable though it is, selective engagement is not risk free. Indeed, it has two serious dangers: loss of selectivity and provocation of powerful countervailing coalitions. If either danger were to materialize, selective engagement would become too expensive to implement and thereby be rendered infeasible.[39]

LOSS OF SELECTIVITY

The first danger—loss of selectivity—should not be underplayed. As critics of this strategy rightly point out, commitments can become open-ended unless proper care is taken.[40] To understand how to limit commitments, we must first understand why they expand.

Commitments can grow in four different ways. First, success in fulfilling one task can create the ambition to do more. In this case, hubris causes a commitment to expand. Second, the need to defend or salvage a commitment can cause additional resources to be allocated to the task. This usually happens because decisionmakers have underestimated the difficulty of the initial task, which is itself a product of bad planning or legitimate miscalculation (not all things can be foreseen). Third, domestic political calculations can cause leaders to undertake additional obligations. They decide to do more either because

---

39. Isolationists might argue that there are two other serious pitfalls to selective engagement: a weakening of America's economic resulting from larger-than-needed military expenditures, and an increased risk that the United States will become embroiled in unnecessary wars. I do not consider the first to be serious. The difference in resources consumed by an isolationist defense budget versus a selective engagement defense budget is not great: the former would consume roughly 1.5–2.5 percent of America's GNP; the latter, 2.5–3.5 percent. At America's current GNP, this represents about an $80 billion a year difference, clearly not a sum sufficient to break America's economic might, even when sustained over decades. (For those concerned about America's economic health, finding ways to boost its savings rate is the single most important thing on which to focus.) A far greater danger to the weakening of America's economic health would come from defense budgets grossly inflated by the need to meet the demands of expanding commitments and/or powerful hostile countercoalitions. These are the two hazards that all those who care about the effects of defense budgets on America's economic health should worry about, which is why I focus on them.

The second alleged danger—a greater likelihood of war embroilment—is not so readily dismissed. Two points are in order. First, selective engagement takes the position that its approach is more likely than isolationism's to prevent wars in those regions where the United States has important interests that could be harmed by the outbreak of hostilities. Some of those wars might even be ones that isolationists would favor fighting. Second, selective engagement takes the position that should its approach fail to prevent war, then war will have to be waged because America's interests require it. Justification for the second position depends of course on how America's interests and the threats to them are defined. On this score, selective engagers have a broader definition of interests and threats than do isolationists. The difference between the two strategies, therefore, is not just one of war avoidance per se, but also of what interests the United States should be prepared to defend with force when necessary. Thus, in the end, selective engagement holds greater likelihood than does isolationism of preventing wars, but is more willing to fight them, if they cannot be averted, in order to defend American interests. Whether the net result of this position is greater risk of war embroilment is not easy to say, but the answer is probably "yes." How much greater, however, is not clear.

40. For the view that commitments inevitably become open-ended, see Layne, "From Preponderance to Offshore Balancing," pp. 98–102.

they believe a foreign policy success will consolidate their grip at home, or because they reason they face irresistible domestic forces. Fourth, alliance considerations can cause commitments to expand. This factor operates either when allies demand more, or when the alliance leader believes its credibility and that of the alliance is at stake and action is required. Each of these factors alone, if powerful enough, can cause commitments to grow larger, but usually two or more are required for this to happen.

America's experience with Bosnia from 1991 to 1995 is illustrative here.[41] The Bush administration decided in 1991 to stay out of the Yugoslav imbroglio and delegate it to the Europeans. By mid-1995, however, the Clinton administration seized the issue from the Europeans, pushed NATO to powerful air strikes against the Serbs, brokered the Dayton peace accords, and then sent a large contingent of American troops to Bosnia as part of a NATO peace enforcement mission. What accounts for this reversal in policy?

Two key factors were at work. First was American electoral politics. Clinton worried about Republican criticism of his Bosnian policy and was determined to remove it from the 1996 elections. The more important factor, however, was the second: the Clinton administration's concern about NATO's credibility.[42] By the spring of 1995, NATO was rapidly becoming a casualty of the Bosnian war, largely because the allies had used its airpower in only pinprick fashion to try to stop Serbian ethnic cleansing. These strikes had little effect on Serbian policy, and NATO was looking increasingly ineffective. NATO's prestige was harmed because the West had wavered for three years between the two goals it had set for itself at the outset of the Bosnian war—staying out of the war and protecting innocent civilians from mass murder. It had wavered because it soon realized that these two goals were contradictory when the Serbs took advantage of Western restraint to slaughter Muslims in the name of ethnic cleansing. After three years of wavering, the United States finally found itself forced to choose in mid-1995 between staying out of the war or going in to

---

41. A good short overview of U.S. and Western policy toward the breakup of Yugoslavia is found in Ivo H. Daalder, "Fear and Loathing in the Former Yugoslavia," in Michael E. Brown, ed., *The International Dimensions of Internal Conflict* (Cambridge, Mass.: MIT Press, 1996), pp. 35–69. Detailed histories can be found in Susan L. Woodward, *Balkan Tragedy: Chaos and Dissolution after the Cold War* (Washington, D.C.: Brookings Institution, 1995), esp. chaps. 6, 9, 11; Wayne Bert, *The Reluctant Superpower: United States Policy in Bosnia, 1991–1995* (New York: St. Martin's Press, 1996); James Gow, *Triumph of the Lack of Will: International Diplomacy and the Yugoslav War* (New York: Columbia University Press, 1997); Warren Zimmermann, *Origins of a Catastrophe* (New York: Times Books, 1996); and Richard Holbrooke, *To End a War* (New York: Random House, 1998).
42. See Holbrooke, *To End a War*, pp. 65–75, 359–360.

stop the killing. What tipped the scales for going in was the threat to NATO's credibility.[43]

The Bosnian case provides three lessons. First, do not make commitments that are clearly self-contradictory because they will eventually come back to haunt you. Second, do not stake out positions that you are not prepared to back up with force when force is likely to be required. Third, do not use force in a haphazard and ineffective manner when it has to be used, especially when such use tars and feathers your most important military alliance.

PROVOCATION OF COUNTERVAILING COALITIONS

The second equally serious danger is that selective engagement will provoke powerful countervailing coalitions. By wielding its military power, so the argument goes, the United States will inevitably provoke opposition from powerful regional actors, and they will take countermeasures to thwart American actions, including increasing their armaments, entering into blocking coalitions, or both. The danger is not that one or a few states will oppose the United States; clearly, at least one of them always will—the one that is the target of America's deterrent or compellent actions. Rather, the danger is that several of the region's most powerful actors will ally against the United States. Should this happen in several regions at once, selective engagement would most likely impose such a heavy burden that it would become too expensive for the United States to sustain. The risk, in short, is that America's exercise of its military power will quickly beget its own check. The danger is real. Can it be averted?

The answer hangs heavily on how the United States wields its power: for what purposes, in what fashion, under what circumstances, and with what effects. In this list the single most important element is the first—the purposes of power. Will America's exercise of power serve only its interests, or will it serve the interests of many, if not most, of the significant regional actors as well? If the interests served are broadly shared, American power will be accepted, even if it is not rapturously embraced. If they are perceived to be

---

43. On this score, America's ultimate military intervention was in accord with the stipulations I set forth earlier for these types of cases. First, the United States intervened forcefully with other important regional actors—Britain and France. Second, the intervention served other American interests—salvaging NATO's credibility and preserving America's role as an important European actor. Third, the United States and its allies faced a military force (the Bosnian Serbs) that was no match for Western military power when properly used.

exclusively and selfishly American, America's exercise of power will be widely resisted, if not immediately, then eventually.

Can the United States serve the interests of others while still serving its own? In general, the answer is "yes." In East Asia, Europe, and even the Persian Gulf, enough of the key regional actors embrace, first and foremost, the interests that the United States deems vital for itself. In comparative terms, the overlap between America's interests and those of the regional influentials is greatest in Europe, smallest in the Persian Gulf, and somewhere in-between in East Asia. The Eurasian great powers favor combating the spread of weapons of mass destruction, preserving peace among themselves, and preserving unimpeded access to Persian Gulf (and Caspian Sea) oil. These three goals are not as widely shared in the Persian Gulf, but enough of the powerful actors embrace them such that America's goals remain acceptable, although admittedly more difficult to implement than in Eurasia. Even the American interests that I deem desirable—preserving an open international economic order, promoting the spread of democracy and the protection of human rights, and combating the dangers of global warming—have significant international appeal, even if not as wide and deep as the vital interests and even if more popular among peoples than governments. For the reasons given earlier in this article, however, the vital interests are key and the ones on which the United States must concentrate when wielding its military power. Their broad acceptability means that the United States can serve some of the important interests of others while at the same time serving many of its own.[44]

This proposition holds even when one or a few of a region's influentials have significant conflicts of interest with the United States. The example of China illustrates the point.[45] Two opposing dynamics are at work in China's views about America's military presence in East Asia. On the one hand, China's standard public position is that no state should have foreign bases and troops abroad and that the United States seeks to dominate East Asia. The logic of this position is that the United States should withdraw its forces and bases

---

44. For a perceptive elaboration of this point, see Josef Joffe, "How America Does It," *Foreign Affairs*, Vol. 76, No. 5 (September/October 1997), pp. 1–28.
45. The observations in this paragraph are based on a set of thirty interviews I conducted in the summer of 1992 in Beijing with military leaders and civilian analysts close to official thinking in seven separate governmental or quasi-governmental think tanks, including China's National War College. At that time, at least, governmental officials would not talk openly about such matters, but analysts who worked in these think tanks would. Recent reconfirmation of China's preference for an American military presence in East Asia is to be found in Thomas Christensen, "Chinese Realpolitik," *Foreign Affairs*, Vol. 75, No. 5 (September/October 1996), pp. 37–53.

from the region. On the other hand, China's privately stated position and clear preference is for the United States to remain in the region in order to prevent Japan from acquiring nuclear weapons and to protect the region, including itself, from a potential revival of Japanese militarism. China opposes America's interposing itself militarily with the Seventh Fleet between it and Taiwan, but it also wants the United States in the region to sit on Japan. It puts up with the former partly because it has no choice, but also partly because it desires the latter. Thus, publicly, China bewails America's hegemony; privately, it supports its military presence in East Asia—at least for the time being.[46]

In each of the three regions where the United States maintains a significant military presence, the number of states that oppose its forces is astonishingly small. This fact, however, is no reason for complacency. The wrongful exercise of American power can quickly dissipate its regional acceptability. Therefore the task for American statecraft is clear: keep a large enough number of the regional influentials convinced that there is a significant overlap between America's interests and theirs. What makes the job of persuasion possible is the reality that there is, in fact, an underlying coincidence of interests: what is vital for the United States is, at the least, important for the bulk of the regional influentials.

Policy Implications

For the preceding reasons, I believe selective engagement to be the best grand strategy for the United States at this time. It chooses the most appropriate goals for the nation, and it best employs America's military prowess to sustain them. It represents a calculated but reasoned gamble that the costs of overseas commitments, and their attendant risks, are less than the costs and risks of isolationism or of any other grand strategy. Superior though it may be, selec-

---

46. The China case is not an exception. Malaysia, for example, may wail against America's economic might and Singapore may severely discipline young Americans living there, but both, as all the other states of Southeast Asia, want an American military presence as a counter to China. (Singapore has given the U.S. Navy some basing rights to compensate for the loss of Subic Bay in the Philippines.) In the Persian Gulf, only Iraq unequivocally opposes an American presence, but Iran quietly favors it as a check on Iraq, although not as a check on its own claims to regional hegemony. Kuwait and Bahrain welcome the United States with open arms, and Saudi Arabia wants American forces to be based on its territory but as unobstrusively as possible. (Hence the American air base is in the middle of the Saudi desert, far removed from any town, and American soldiers are largely confined to it.) Europe may be the only region where no real opposition to an American military presence exists, although the French periodically complain about American hegemony.

tive engagement is not an easy but a demanding strategy to implement. To be successful, it must be disciplined so as to avoid inflating commitments and deft so as to avoid provoking opposing coalitions. I offer three policy prescriptions to help the United States muster a disciplined and deft statecraft.

First, the best way to guard against commitment creep in the use of force is to apply four tests. The most basic is to determine whether the commitment being considered is essential to advance or protect any of America's six national interests. Second, if additional commitments are subsequently proposed to support the one initially undertaken, are they truly required to salvage it? Third, if the original commitment requires additional ones, then it should be reexamined to determine whether it still remains of sufficient importance to invest even more to protect it. Fourth, are the policies being implemented mutually supportive or contradictory? If the latter, either change the policy or scuttle the commitment. Thus, maintaining a disciplined diplomacy is akin to keeping physically fit: both require hard work and continual effort to sustain. Discipline, like physical fitness, is a never-ending affair.

Second, never rely on a coincidence of interests alone to produce concerted action. The overlap in interests between the United States and the regional influentials that selective engagement requires makes concerted action only possible, not inevitable. Were shared interests alone sufficient to induce cooperation among states, diplomacy itself could be dispensed with. Because matters do not work this way, America's diplomatic task must be to convince other states that what it finds in its interest is in theirs, too, once they clearly understand where their interests lie. Among other things, deft diplomacy requires detailed elaboration about what policies are necessary to support their shared interests, clear leadership in organizing coalitions to protect these interests, constant consultation about the best ways to attain them, concerting action to the extent feasible, and protection of the consensus in those rare occasions when unilateral American action is required. A clumsy, heavy-handed diplomacy is likely to provoke strong counters to America's overseas military presence. On the other hand, deft diplomacy, although it cannot guarantee that countercoalitions will always be averted, nevertheless does enhance the chances that they can. Diplomatic deftness is an essential ingredient of selective engagement.

Third, for a nation as militarily powerful as the United States, the temptation to do too much is more serious than the temptation to do too little. The greatest nemesis of an imperial power—and the United States is an imperial power—is overreach. The United States today has no peers and stands alone as the world's preeminent military and economic power. For that very reason, the temptation of imperial overstretch, to become the Athens of the twenty-first century and embark on self-defeating Sicilian expeditions, is ever-present and powerful.[47] American leaders must be vigilant against succumbing to this temptation, which is born of the arrogance of power. Making certain that America's interests also serve the interests of others is the best means to avoid this well-worn path to imperial ruin.

Our world remains one of independent states. In such a world, the interests of states will continue to clash as much as they overlap, and therefore the centrifugal forces of national self-interest will continue to vie with the centripetal forces of democracy, economic interdependence, and the pressing necessity to coordinate state action in order to cope with global problems like climate change. The key to managing the tensions between national interests and collective goods is what it has always been: enlightened leadership by the great powers. In this era, the task of marshaling the great powers into regional and global concerts falls on the United States because it is the greatest great power, and selective engagement is the grand strategy best suited to marshaling these concerts. It is not a strategy for all times, but selective engagement is the best strategy for these times.

---

47. In 415 B.C., Athens sent a fleet and an army of 40,000 to defeat Syracuse and conquer Sicily. The expedition, reported by Thucydides to be the largest force ever assembled by the Greeks, proved a disaster: Athens lost both the fleet and the army and never recovered from the resource drain of this folly, which was the single most important factor in its ultimate defeat at Sparta's hands in 404 B.C. See Thucydides, *History of the Peloponnesian War*, trans. Rex Warner (New York: Penguin Books, 1972), Books 6 and 7, for the gripping account of the Sicilian campaign.

Part IV:
Cooperative Security

Cooperative Security in the United States

Janne E. Nolan

$\mathbf{A}$ COOPERATIVE se-
curity regime stands little chance of success if the advanced countries do
not adapt their national and foreign policies to align with its core principles
and precepts. The United States, in particular, would have difficulty championing security cooperation if it engaged in policies that were seen as
contributing to global confrontation, unwarranted technical diffusion, or regional tensions. This is not simply a matter of non-native or diplomatic
sensitivity, but a practical reality. A regime that applies laws and norms
selectively, exempting some states according to their relative status or for
reasons of expedience, is destined to fall. The only alternative to legitimacy
is coercion, hardly a realistic basis for fostering cooperation in a highly
diffused world order.

A number of the guiding principles that continue to inform U.S. security
policy are the product of an international system whose underpinnings no
longer exist. These principles emerged in a world in which state relations were
dominated by the military rivalry between the two superpowers and the
technological preeminence of the United States went largely unquestioned, and
at a time when there was little serious interference in the prerogatives of large
powers by less-developed countries. The massive transformations of the international order in recent years are obviously forcing a reevaluation of emerging
security conditions and U.S. policy responses.

Comfort in U.S. military superiority, which has served to build support for
U.S. defense spending and strategy for decades, is now tempered by the
growing realization that its use may be heavily circumscribed and as a practical
reality may prove transitory. Because of political and resource constraints, the
United States is unlikely to initiate any significant military action in the future
without some form of broad international approval. However reluctant some
may be to come to the conclusion, there nonetheless is a growing awareness
that U.S. military power cannot be used without an internationally supported
framework that accords it legitimacy. How this framework will be defined is
still a matter of debate and controversy. It is yet to be fully recognized that
delays in coming to grips with the demand for an articulated, multinational
concept of force projection-one that is widely perceived as legitimate-may
undercut U.S. leadership and exacerbate suspicions among smaller powers
about long-term U.S. security objectives.

Over time, the global diffusion of advanced technology may preclude an
enduring U.S. military superiority unless that superiority is accepted as serving
the general international interest. Superior U.S. conventional power projection
is derived primarily from the application of dramatic advances in the collec-

tion, processing, and transmission of information. The core technologies that support these decisive military functions are being developed in commercial markets, and access to them cannot be denied. Nor can access be denied to the knowledge and materials required to make weapons of mass destruction, which, because of their destructiveness and the fear they engender, could come to be seen by a larger number of states as a way to offset U.S. conventional military power. As such, the ability of the United States to prevent or manage international crises effectively will be affected by decisions made by regional powers, which in turn will be influenced by their perceptions of U.S. intent.

This chapter examines the elements of current U.S. security thinking that may be consonant with a concept of cooperative security and those that may require political or institutional reorientation to support such a regime. The analysis covers the potential influence of several alternative approaches to security on policies guiding military engagement, technical diffusion, and force planning.

The Current Political Climate

Lacking a clear framework within which to define the role of the United States in the world after the cold war, the domestic foreign policy debate in the early 1990s revealed a public mood of partisan divisiveness and general disillusionment. The absence of a foreign policy consensus was evident in the controversies generated in the latter part of the Bush administration by its first draft 1992 defense planning guidance document, in the round of divisive debates set off by the Clinton administration's first defense budget and initial policy statements in early 1993, in the controversies and recriminations surrounding the quest for credible options for intervention in Bosnia, Somalia, and Haiti, and in the isolationist sentiments within Congress and the public, which sought scapegoats to explain declining U.S. competitiveness. The country's perception of its global responsibilities and destiny seemed, in short, conceptually adrift.

In response to the transformation of the strategic landscape, a restructuring of the U.S. defense posture is under way. The adjustments are extensive, affecting nuclear and conventional forces, and the defense industry. Some of this restructuring is prompted by arms control agreements, but much of it is a nearly spontaneous reaction to budget reductions that are themselves the political consequence of a lessened perception of security threats. Most attempts to guide this restructuring have consisted of scenarios under which the United States is called upon to react to redefinitions of a past threat: a reconstituted superpower Russia, for nuclear forces; or one or several implicit re-plays of the Gulf War, for conventional forces. That U.S. security policy might instead be primarily directed at preventing such threats from arising in the first place is an idea that has not yet fully taken hold. Thus the desirable size of U.S. conventional and nuclear forces, the appropriate rate of modernization, and the degree of combat readiness to be maintained have not been assessed from this perspective.[1]

If the ongoing American security debates could be reduced to three disparate sets of principles, they would include an implicit yearning for American military superiority embodied in a Pax Americana, a strong push to isolationism or disengagement, and a growing trend toward explicit acceptance of multilateralism in the conduct of economic, political, and military affairs. In reality, there are overlapping elements of each of these views in current thinking, but their respective influences are more obvious in some aspects of policy than others.

Competing Definitions of the U.S. Role in the World

The notion of America as the "sole remaining superpower" emerged in the public debate after the demise of the Soviet Union and the success of U.S. forces in the defeat of Iraq. This modem version of a Pax Americana is based on the conviction that the United States can be strong only if it can project decisive power and use force unilaterally as necessary. Sovereign status and military superiority are virtually synonymous in this regard, and multilateralism is seen largely as a needless intrusion on or diversion from the goal of American preeminence. A draft version of the Bush administration's annual defense planning guidance document, leaked to the press in March 1992, reflected some aspects of this line of thinking. The document argued for an American military posture of sufficient capability to prevent any competitors from challenging America's global dominance. Potential competitors included both allies and enemies in a world inexorably destined to face multipolar competition and conflict. U.S. military capabilities and superior technology were depicted as the only reliable guarantors of global stability, to be used to intervene in many kinds of contingencies throughout the world.[2]

---

1. The secretary of defense's 1993 report is revealing in this regard. See Les Aspin, *Report on the Bottom-Up Review* (Office of the Secretary of Defense, 1993).
2. See Patrick E. Tyler, "Lone Superpower Plan: Ammunition for Critics," *New York Times*, March 10, 1992, p. A12; and Patrick E. Tyler, "U.S. Strategy Plan Calls for Insuring No Rivals to Develop," *New York Times*, March 8, 1992, p. A1.

Defense officials quickly disavowed the document in the face of public and media criticism, but the incident helped reinforce the view that there may be a substantial body of official opinion that supports such notions. Quite apart from bolstering the case for a large military establishment, a Pax Americana tends to characterize dependence on multilateral institutions, such as the UN, as especially naive and likely to undermine sovereign decisions to bolster the national resources and capabilities needed to defend U.S. interests. International partnerships of this kind cannot help but impose "intolerable limitations on American initiative," as one commentator put it.[3]

At the opposite end of the spectrum, advocates of U.S. global disengagement emerged as a more vocal force in the U.S. political debate in the late 1980s and early 1990s. Evidence of this sentiment was seen in public and congressional opposition to U.S. intervention in the crisis in Bosnia, to the provision of economic assistance to the countries in the former Soviet bloc, and to new trading arrangements, such as the North American Free Trade Agreement, which engendered deep suspicions about its perceived concessions to foreign countries at the expense of American jobs and prosperity.[4] Recessionary domestic economic trends always tend to encourage the perception of foreign policy as an intrusion on the nation's welfare. In both the postwar and current eras, the idea that the United States has an obligation to restore order and to provide for human welfare overseas is pure folly to a member of Congress who cannot secure sufficient funds to extend basic services to constituents.[5] This sentiment has intensified in the current fiscally constrained domestic environment.

Isolationism has strong historical roots in American political culture. It originates with the profound skepticism about foreign entanglements expressed by

---

3. Former presidential candidate Patrick Buchanan and Senator Joseph Biden (Democrat of Delaware) were among the more prominent critics of the Pentagon planning document, in a rare coincidence of views between people from opposite poles of the political spectrum. Both decried the notion that the United States should bear the price of being the "world's policeman" in a time of declining resources and an urgent domestic agenda. As Buchanan put it, the strategy is "a formula for endless American intervention in quarrels and war," in which the United States simply extends a "blank check" to other countries in an open-ended pledge to protect their interests. For further discussion see, for instance, Stephen S. Rosenfeld, "The Trouble with Going It Alone," *Washington Post*, March 20, 1992, p. A25.

4. For additional discussion, see David Rosenbaum, "The Nation: Good Economics Meet Protective Politics," *New York Times*, September 19, 1993, p. D5; Paul Krugman, "The Uncomfortable Truth about NAFTA," *Foreign Affairs*, vol. 72 (November-December 1993), pp. 13–19; and William A. Orme, Jr., "NAFTA: Myths verus Facts," ibid., pp. 2–12.

5. See Stephen A. Holmes, "Finding Strong Allies for Foreign Aid," *New York Times*, June 23, 1993, p. A19.

the founding fathers, perhaps best embodied in George Washington's farewell address warning of the dangers of American involvement in the controversies of European politics. Immediately after World War 11, isolationists were unified in their opposition to the Atlanticist view of the world embraced by conservatives, statesmen such as Dean Acheson, George Kennan, and John J. McCloy, Jr. At issue were policies that sought to advance America's sphere of influence by helping to rebuild Europe and forging international partnerships on behalf of containment. The split between Atlanticists and isolationists was about commitments and resources, however, not about the legitimacy of American military intervention.

Only the liberal theory of isolationism advocates true disengagement, at least with regard to the use of military or intelligence operations to coerce foreign governments. Even here its proponents often make exceptions for nonmilitary intervention, such as extending humanitarian assistance to countries in need or on behalf of transnational causes, such as environmental protection. But isolationism has rarely meant the renunciation of American military preeminence. On the contrary, at least conservative isolationists have always believed in the innately superior ability of the United States to influence if necessary.

Advocates of a Pax Americana are certainly distinct in their more overt embrace of America's global role, but conservative isolationists have not usually been opposed to military engagements in the less-developed world, whether in China in the 1950s, Vietnam in the 1960s, or Iraq in the 1990s. The underlying criteria for approving military ventures in both cases are that they be quick and decisive, and require minimal American sacrifice. As expressed by politicians such as conservative commentator Patrick Buchanan, for example, "America First" means opposition to alliances or other forms of international partnerships that imply equality, reciprocity, and obligations to others.[6] Alliances are synonymous with encumbrance. They are bound to impinge on the right of the United States to be self-sufficient and also to act unilaterally should it see fit to do so, especially militarily. A Pax Americana shares the isolationist spirit in its rejection of multilateralism as a credible basis for security. "Going it alone" is the dominant sentiment in both sets of beliefs.

---

6. As Buchanan put it in early 1992, "With a $4 trillion debt, with a U.S. budget chronically out of balance, should the United States be required to carry indefinitely the full burden of defending rich and prosperous allies who take American's generosity for granted as they invade our markets?" Quoted in William Greider, "Buchanan Rethinks the American Empire," *Rolling Stone,* February 6, 1992, p. 39.

A Pax Americana and conservative isolationism also converge in their belief in the importance of American technological prowess as the ultimate guarantor of U.S. security. The quest for the technological fix to security challenges was perhaps best encapsulated in the notion of a perfect defensive "shield" put forward in the original Strategic Defense Initiative (SDI) in 1983. The SDI, designed to permit the United States to engage globally without the risk of nuclear attack on its own territory, was also intended to unburden the United States from diplomatic obligations to negotiate nuclear agreements with its principal adversary, the Soviet Union. President Ronald Reagan's vision of the SDI was a perfect synthesis of isolationism and a Pax Americana, as such, arguing for American self- sufficiency as the core foundation for unchallenged American global superiority.

Strategic defenses have now been given a barely residual role in U.S. defense planning, but strains of the SDI's philosophical underpinnings still abound in the current discussions of U.S. defense spending and force objectives. U.S. military superiority, manifested in the most advanced weapons deployed for rapid global mobilization, remains the creed justifying many planning decisions. Consistent with this view, the mainstay of U.S. forces is now to be long-range and highly precise weapons that can destroy even distant targets "with little if any loss of U.S. lives and with a minimum of collateral damage and loss of civilian lives on the other side."[7] In other words, the United States can remain the sole superpower by being prepared to engage in decisive, short military engagements that incur minimal risks to Americans and, by implication, pose no risk of vulnerability to the U.S. homeland-a concept that, whatever its merits, is solidly rooted in isolationist philosophy.[8]

The third obvious trend in the current U.S. foreign policy debate is the reemergence of internationalism and multilateralism, manifested in the ascen-

---

7. The quotation is from a speech given by Representative Les Aspin, September 1992. Cited in *Congressional Quarterly*, January, 9, 1993, p. 82. See also Barton Gellman, "Pentagon May Seek $20 Billion More; Aspin Oulines Cost of Restructuring," *Washington Post*, August 13, 1993, p. A1.
8. Although obviously not was quixiotic as the SDI, some expert analyses of future force contingencies conducted in he early 1990s emphasized the role that air power could play in according the United States clear technological—and thus political and military—superiority in all conceivable conflicts at a minimum cost. As a RAND report argued in June 1993, for example, "By the turn of the century, if provided with available technology, U.S. airpower will be capable of stopping an attachk force of over 8,000 armored vehicles and 1,000 aircraft in little more than a week," and, with some assistance from land and sea forces, could allow the U.S. to manage concurrent crises in the Persian Gulf and Korea. Charles W. Corddry, "Air Power Must Be First in Future, Study Says," *Baltimore Sun*, June 23, 1993, p. 9. The public release version of this study in Christopher Bowie and others, *The New Calculus: Analyzing Airpower's Changing Role in Joint Theater Campaigns*, report prepared for the United States Air Force by the RAND Institution (Santa Monica, Calif., 1993).

dance of institutions such as the UN and in the growing level of collaboration among countries to deal with crises in Somalia, Bosnia, and elsewhere. At its most extreme, multilateralism reinvokes the spirit of world federalism or the views of other "one-world" advocates that would favor eliminating U.S. capabilities to act alone and subsuming all nations under international authority. As a practical matter, however, multilateralism is currently being pursued for pragmatic, not visionary, ends. Faced with limited resources and waning public support for foreign engagements, the Bush and Clinton administrations have had to seek multilateral backing for many objectives, not least to force Saddam Hussein out of Kuwait or, thus far unsuccessfully, to help bring about a resolution to the conflict over Bosnia.

In its initial phases, the Clinton administration sought to recast the emphasis of U.S. defense planning to include a more open acceptance of multilateralism and explicit limits on the projection of unilateral force. Driven by the momentum to cut U.S. defense spending by more than 20 percent, the administration advanced notions of "limited intervention" and a formulation of U.S. strategy to be tailored explicitly to recognize constraints on U.S. defense resources and according capabilities. This strategy included a shift away from the traditional U.S. commitment to have the capability to fight two significant regional conflicts simultaneously. Popularized in the press as the "win-hold-win" strategy, the new conception of intervention suggested that the United States should be able to mobilize air and sea power to defeat one aggressor while blunting aggression in another part of the world with air power until sufficient forces could be brought to bear to terminate the second conflict.[9]

Conservative critics were quick to blast the Clinton administration for this alleged sign of retrenchment, some referring to the strategy as "lose-hold-lose," while moderates and liberals expressed disappointment that the administration was still clinging to what they perceived as an unrealistic declaratory posture. The debate had a nostalgic quality in which proponents of the necessity of a "two-war" strategy tended to overlook budgetary and political realities in favor of nationalist ideology, while proponents of the new policy tried to depict it as no less of a commitment to American force projection than that of any previous administration's.

Whatever its substantive significance, the controversy highlighted the fact that the attachment to unilateral action is a powerful political undercurrent, prompting the Clinton administration early on to revise its rhetoric accordingly.

---

9. Barton Gellman and John Lancaster, "U.S. May Drop 2-War Capability," *Washington Post,* June 17, 1993, p. A.1.

Within weeks, administration officials reemphasized that the United States had to "be able to fight and win two major regional conflicts, and nearly simultaneously," an objective to be met, despite budget constraints, using advanced technology and the right mix of forces.[10] Similarly, when Undersecretary of State Peter Tarnoff in May 1993 depicted a constrained U.S. global role in a world in which "there will have to be genuine power sharing and responsibility sharing [among allies]," he was promptly and publicly criticized by fellow officials for misrepresenting U.S. policy.[11] After the June 1993 U.S. attack on an Iraqi intelligence facility in retaliation for an Iraqi-sponsored plot to assassinate former president George Bush, unilateralism enjoyed a brief renaissance in the public mind, albeit without affecting force plans in any discernible manner.

No debate has been as contentious as that provoked by the expanding conflict in Bosnia. The failed U.S. effort in early 1993 to elicit European support for various strategies of intervention was among the first stumbling blocks of the new administration, largely seen as a diplomatic catastrophe and a demonstration of the limits of U.S. influence. If nothing else, the experience helped to underscore the inescapable reality that multilateralism was not an option but a necessity, however elusive it has remained in the search for a common and effective policy. In arguing for new criteria for U.S. involvement in peacekeeping operations in June 1993, for example, the U.S. ambassador to the UN called for U.S. commitment to a strategy of "assertive multilateralism," a distinct shift in the rhetoric, if not yet the substance, of U.S. policy.[12]

Obvious limits remain to U.S. willingness to fully embrace multilateralism as an integral principle to guide force planning. Instead, elements of several of the belief systems discussed in this chapter are informing the current security policy framework, if not always consciously. The primary division can be reduced to the tension between a confrontational framework based on the primacy of unilateral uses of force (or international only to the degree that they involve alliances of convenience) and a more multilateral and cooperative approach to security that emphasizes preventive diplomacy, nonmilitary instruments for conflict prevention, mediation in place of war, and collective intervention only when other instruments fail. Despite the success of the coalition war against Iraq and the dismal experience of the lack of any such

---

10. Speech by Secretary of Defense Les Aspin at Andrews Air Force Base, cited in John Lancaster, "Aspin Opts for Winning Two Wars—Not $1^1/_2$— at Once," *Washington Post*, June 25, 1993, p. A6. For further discussion, see, for instance Bruce B. Auster, "A High-Tech Calvalry," *U.S. News and World Report*, June 28, 1993, p. 29.
11. See Michael Mandelbaum, "Like It or Not, We Must Lead," *Washington Post*, June 9, p. A21.
12. R. Jeffrey Smith and Julia Preston, "U.S. Plans Wider Role in U.N. Peace Keeping," *Wahington Post*, June 18, 1993, p. A1.

cooperation in Bosnia, however, joint actions are still unfamiliar instruments in the core of U.S. security planning. The idea of cooperation for preventive actions that could preclude the need for future intervention is even more remote, although it is embodied implicitly in efforts toward the denuclearization of the former Soviet Union and the dismantling of Iraq's arsenal of nonconventional weapons.

What has already occurred on both a national and an international scale, however, is at least an underlying recognition that multilateral security initiatives are likely to enhance rather than constrain legitimate and effective uses of political and military power. In the end, the reality of a re source-constrained and fragmented international system argues persuasively for a policy of selective engagement based on cooperative planning.

With this latter principle as its main premise, cooperative security is obviously distinct from both of the extremes, "one-world" multilateralism and lone superpower unilateralism. The concept of cooperative security does not attempt to reinvent power relations in an effort to assume away conflict in international affairs. Nor does it harken back to a distant past to imagine a world in which the United States can act alone. It is based instead on the recognition that conflicts and military threats are likely to persist, but that the effective use of American power will require political art to sustain support for U.S. international engagements. Eliciting multinational legitimacy for international ventures is not a politically or economically dispensable impulse. Notwithstanding the apparent popularity in the West of limited demonstrations of U.S. power, such as the June 1993 retaliation against Iraq, the choice is increasingly legitimacy or paralysis.

Effects of Alternative Frameworks on Policy

This section examines the potential influence of the three alternative policy frameworks on five areas. The areas are (1) the use of force, (2) the conduct of regional relations, (3) the perceived role of nuclear weapons, (4) efforts to control the proliferation of weapons internationally, and (5) the overall character of U.S. defense investment.

Principles Guiding the Use of Force

With the waning of the Soviet threat, regional aggression had already begun in the Bush administration to be viewed as the most important and demanding threat to U.S. interests, especially by nations armed with nonconventional munitions and long-range delivery systems.[13] The Clinton administration, building on this premise, introduced four new areas of security priorities for the post-cold war environment:

- "Regional threats," the basis for judging the requisite size and character of forces for future military intervention;
- "'New' nuclear threats," including nations in the former Soviet bloc as well as terrorist groups and lawless nations (which, it is believed, cannot be deterred by traditional means);
- The failure of democracy in countries where military coups or the ascendance of authoritarian regimes is thought to be more likely to prompt destabilizing actions and where peacekeeping and humanitarian intervention may be necessary;
- "Economic security," including national and international efforts to convert excess defense production capabilities and resources to civilian uses and to revitalize the U.S. defense technology base.[14]

The current administration's defense policy, like its predecessor's, asserts that "uncertainty" about who future adversaries may be requires a permanently high level of military preparedness for global application. In response to arguments that the United States faces a drastically diminished set of security risks, the former chairman of the Joint Chiefs of Staff, General Colin Powell, for example, argued that the world is far more turbulent than ever before. In presenting the U.S. defense program to Congress in 1992, he stated that "the real threat [to our security] is the unknown, the uncertain. In a very real sense the primary threat to our security is instability.[15] That statement summarizes

---

13. Congression Budget Office, Structuring U.S. Forces after the Cold War: Costs and Effects of Increased Reliance on the Reserves (September 1992).

14. Office of Assistant Secretary of Defense (Public Affairs), "FY 1994 Budget Begins New Era," New Release, March 27, 1993. In the Bush Administration, defense priorities were expressed in more traditional, confrontational terms, including the position that the United States would rely on four major elements to protect its overseas interests: "strategic deterrence and defense," based on a modified nuclear triad on a lower level of alert, along with missile defenses; "forward presence," including long-range bombers, carriers, and new overseas bases, if necessary; "crisis response," based on the ability to project power instantaneously "in diverse areas of the world," which means globally; and "reconstitution," an ability to provide for "a global warfighting capability" should the need arise. Technological superiority, robust nuclear forces, a more pronounced overseas military presence in the Gulf, and military options for countering proliferation were key elements of this strategy, with research and development and force deployments directed accordingly. See *Department of Defense Annual Report to the President and the Congress, Fiscal Year 1992*. It it too early to predict if the differences with suceeding administration will be significant in substance as well as in rhetoric.

15. "Statement of General Colin L. Powell, chairman of the Joint Chiefs of Staff, before the Senate Committee on Armed Services," January 31, 1992.

the prevailing security posture of the United States. The United States is planning for military confrontation against an enemy it does not think it can predict under circumstances whose uncertainty it does not think it can manage.

Countering threats and deterrence through readiness are the traditional bases for defense planning. Yet in both the conventional and the nuclear realms, today's defense policy problems are not anchored in immediate threats. That the world appears to have become more complex to policymakers long preoccupied with a "simpler" paradigm defined by the U.S.-Soviet rivalry is undeniable. But even under Secretary of Defense Les Aspin's initiative to conduct a so-called bottom-up review of budgetary and military needs in mid-1993, wherein new force requirements are supposed to be calibrated with the scale and character of regional threats, uncertainty has come to replace deterrence as the new open-ended rationale for justifying major U.S. military programs. Constraints are being imposed because of budgetary imperatives far more than because of any deliberate reconceptualization of America's future security role.

For advocates of a Pax Americana, the Clinton administration's plan is disappointing not only for its excessively multinational rhetoric but also for its failure to provide adequate forces or a concrete vision for ensuring superior U.S. military power in the future. Specific elements of the proposed force posture, such as cuts in the number of aircraft carriers, the failure to maintain a larger force of B-2 bombers, and the downscaling or outright cancellation plans to develop and deploy space-based strategic defenses are particularly contentious examples. New elements of the Clinton plan, such as larger allocations for peacekeeping, are also seen as an intrusion on more vital security priorities.[16]

For opponents of military intervention, by contrast, the administration's plan represents a security perspective that is excessively "globalist," out of date, and too expensive. According to both conservative and liberal critics, the administration simply set out to find new rationales for maintaining a military establishment that contains elements which should have become relics of the cold war or which suggest that the United States is recklessly becoming "the world's policeman."[17] Any veneer of multinationalism and calls for collective security is belied by the gross disparities in material and financial burdens being borne by allies and their continued reluctance to rectify this situation with commensurately larger allocations.

---

16. Art Pine, "Defense Budget Lists Funds for Peacekeeping," *Los Angeles Times,* March 26, 1993, p. A5.
17. See, for instance, Christopher Layne and Ted Galen Carpenter, "Arabian Nightmares: Washington's Persian Gulf Entanglement," *Policy Analysis* (Cato Institute), no. 142 (November 9, 1990).

The principles that would guide a cooperative approach to security would take issue with elements of the new administration's strategy for different reasons. Cooperative security foresees a security system in which military force is used as a last resort, after other instruments of dissuasion or coercion have been exhausted. The use of force for significant engagement would be unavoidably multinational. In either case, instruments for preventive diplomacy-well before a requirement for conflict mediation, peacekeeping, or intervention emerged-would serve as integral and far more prominent elements of an overall defense strategy. Despite their current salience for eastern Europe, the Middle East, and Africa, new conceptions of conflict prevention are barely mentioned in current Defense Department statements and remain now a vague diplomatic objective.

A cooperative security regime would also differ by moving far more expeditiously to renounce offensive force configurations and to reduce reliance on nuclear weapons, which would be replaced by an effective conventional deterrent. Residual nuclear forces would be taken off alert and disassembled, and nuclear-based deterrence would be drastically deemphasized (as discussed later in this chapter). This approach is distinct from the current administration's apparent reluctance to explicitly devalue the role and potential utility of nuclear forces in U.S. strategy or to impose significantly higher standards of operational safety, even at the lower levels established in recent agreements.

U.S. conventional forces, in turn, would be subject to restrictions guiding the types of forces developed, the patterns of their deployment, and declaratory and operational doctrines. An explicit objective would be to establish defensive standards for technological development and force deployment, reversing a growing trend toward the acquisition of capabilities for prompt, preemptive operations. Such forces could potentially be placed under multinational control, as William Perry argues in chapter 6, in an institutional arrangement that would adjudicate procedures and criteria for force configurations and judge when just cause exists for launching a major military initiative. The effect of these changes on policies guiding the acquisition and use of force would obviously be profound.

Although everyone agrees that the United States should remain prepared for ongoing instability throughout the world, the means by which threats would be identified and interests defended would be significantly different in a cooperative regime. Assessments of security needs under a cooperative security would have to be guided by criteria that are far more empirically rooted than the notion of hedging against the unknown. The U.S. preference for unilateralism would have to yield to a more realistic appreciation of the necessity for both military and nonmilitary intervention organized around politically legitimate coalitions, shared intelligence, and commonly agreed-upon guidelines intervention.

The ability to act in concert with others, in turn, would require the kind of military investment that gives the United States maximum flexibility and mobility, more than is currently envisioned. As was made clear during Operation Desert Storm, even the NATO allies were not fully prepared for joint military action. Each nation sent its forces to the region individually and then tried to assemble them into a military coalition after the fact. The logistical and command inadequacies were obvious ones, to which the United States contributed by its lack of adequate familiarity with the operational practices of European and other countries' militaries.

As a political message, the character of U.S. force objectives needs to be aligned with new security realities that focus seriously on regional instability as the key risk to U.S. interests. U.S. defense planning priorities are linked to decisions made by other countries to acquire particular military capabilities in several important ways. U.S. force decisions can abet proliferation indirectly, by helping to reify certain military capabilities as key currencies of state power or by suggesting that the technically advanced powers may collude to wield force against lesser powers for self-serving ends. American rhetoric may also inadvertently encourage states to acquire nuclear, chemical, or missile technologies by hyping the current capabilities of and risks posed by third world arsenals. More realistic assessments would avoid actions which suggest that possession of proscribed weapons automatically enhances a country's international status.

Of particular concern are discussions of plans for the conduct of preemptive military operations against countries seen to be violating international nonproliferation standards. There was considerable debate in the United States beginning in 1991 about the possibility of using military measures to stop North Korean nuclear developments, for example. American opinion was divided about the wisdom of this course, with only a few, though vocal, advocates in Congress and the executive branch urging prompt military destruction of suspect nuclear sites. Other U.S. officials, as well as key U.S. allies such as Japan, South Korea, and the members of the Association of South East Asian Nations, stressed the potentially self-defeating nature of military measures at a time when Pyongyang seemed to be moving gradually toward international accommodation or could retaliate with devastating effect against the

South.[18] The latter view has prevailed to date, although perhaps more because of operational military constraints than of political convictions.

It is not widely appreciated that a stated intent to manage proliferation largely by coercive means may prove as self-destructive as it is elusive. Coercion need not be only military. Disinterested or simply untutored in the domestic complexities of such a country as Ukraine, for example, the United States initially believed it could use its economic leverage to dictate the terms of Ukraine's denuclearization, demanding instant surrender of nuclear war heads to Russian control and obedience to treaty obligations that the Ukrainian government had had no part in negotiating. What began as a positive interaction with a country eager to join the international community and to rid itself of nuclear risk evolved into a confrontation over injured sovereignty and unheeded security concerns. The fate of Ukraine's nuclear weapons was thrown into doubt, and the weapons themselves transformed from military albatrosses into expensive diplomatic bargaining chips. Despite their obvious disutility for current security, the nuclear weapons on Ukrainian territory became a political vehicle for extracting concessions from the West and heightening Ukraine's political stature internationally.

The inadequacy of the American strategy was only slowly recognized by its architects, but it eventually prompted a reevaluation of policy and tactics. The need to accommodate Ukrainian historic sensitivities about Russian imperialism, to understand the recalcitrance prompted by American heavy—handedness in pressuring the Ukrainian government to accede to its demands, and to try to defuse domestic opposition in a newly activated democracy was more fully appreciated. The United States advanced proposals in June 1993 for dismantling and storing nuclear weapons under multinational safeguards on Ukrainian soil pending ratification of agreements for further constraints, along with discussions of extending security guarantees and additional economic inducements to facilitate Ukrainian accession.

An even more glaring policy deficiency is the continued lack of preparation for and effective response to the violence and political disorder sweeping across former Soviet bloc countries, as well as in other areas, such as Somalia. Traditional security approaches have little to contribute to the question of how to restore or protect stability in states that are fragmenting, where territorial

---

18. See, for instance, "DOD Revamps North Korea Contingency Plan to Focus on USAF Preemptive Strikes," *Inside the Air Force*, vol. 2 (November 29, 1991), p. 1; Gwen Ifill, "In Korea, Chilling Reminders of Cold War," *New York Times*, July 18, 1993, p. D1; and David E. Sanger, "Clinton, in Seoul, Tells North Korea to Drop Arms Plan," *New York Times*, July 11, 1993, p. A1.

boundaries are not recognized or honored and where massive influxes of displaced persons are becoming a common occurrence.[19]

For now, the UN has assumed responsibility for many crises that exceed the ability or interest of the United States to manage, but it has been forced to do so far out of proportion to its ability to conduct operations effectively. Controversies abound over whether existing peacekeeping mechanisms can or should take on larger security commitments, perhaps to the point of deploying multilateral forces in actual conflicts in the effort to establish cease-fires, a debate that intensified in 1993. The bitter domestic disputes over proposals for intervention in the former Yugoslavia made it clear not only that the U.S. public was not ready to contemplate sending Americans into combat situations in the interest of stability in the former Soviet bloc, but also that institutional arrangements for implementing such actions were wholly inadequate.

Proposals to develop well-equipped, specialized forces to help restore or protect political order under UN authority have foundered on governments' reluctance to commit resources commensurate to these challenges.[20] Nations, including the United States, still look upon investment in preventive actions as a subordinate objective that should not impinge on national plans for military preparedness. Before his resignation even Secretary of Defense Aspin had stressed that funding peacekeeping operations from the operating Pentagon budget could impede military readiness and lead to a "hollow force."[21]

Financial obligations could be redirected under a cooperative security regime to redress many resource and political constraints impinging on such preventive measures. If U.S. forces were organized and equipped so that they could actually be deployed in international coalitions anywhere in the world on short notice, resources could be allocated more equitably and efficiently among allies. The need for overseas basing and troop deployments-and their attendant costs—could also be reduced significantly. Remaining forces forward deployed

---

19. Other regional threats that are not likely to be responsive to enhanced U.S. power projection capabilities include, among others, the increasing concerns in Europe about further emigration from North Africa; the emergence of five new central Asian replublics and three new nations in the Caucasus that may not be cohesive and could become the objects of rivalry among regional powers; the continued expansion of intra-Middle East and intra-third world consortiums for the development and production of and trade in armaments, including ballistic missiles and unconventional munitions; and the reemergence of Iran as a major political power in the Gulf.

20. As is analyzed in detail in chapter 7 in this volume, the main donor countries in the UN are in serious arrears just in their payments for existing obligations. In mid-1993, for example, the United States owed an estimated $310 million for peacekeeping operations. See also Richard Bernstein, "Sniping Is Growing at U.N.'s Weakness as a Peacekeeper," *New York Times*, June 21, 1993, p. A1.

21. Pine, "Defense Budget Lists Funds for Peacekeeping."

could and should evolve from national to more fully international obligations in any case, helping to dampen the image that the United States upholds an outmoded, confrontational security order, reducing controversies over burden-sharing, and helping to mitigate potential frictions that can arise in regions where domestic tensions could be exacerbated by an exclusively U.S. military presence.

In the final analysis, the underpinning of a cooperative security regime is transparency and info-nation, maximizing the need for high-quality intelligence and analyses of politicomilitary developments to help anticipate, identify, and prevent conflicts before they occur. The Clinton administration is trying to move in this direction, certainly as compared with its predecessor. In his testimony before Congress in March 1993, for example, the current director of the Central Intelligence Agency, R. James Woolsey, pledged that the intelligence community would redirect its resources and talents to new forms of intelligence and analysis focused on global political and economic developments. In the previous administration, proposals from the Senate and House Select Committees on Intelligence to refocus Defense Intelligence and National Security Agency efforts in this manner encountered outright opposition from Secretary of Defense Richard Cheney, among others. Cheney argued that these agencies were compelled to be "combat support agencies" that must be "especially responsive to the needs of war-fighting commanders."[22] Even today, the latter view has yet to be dispelled among career and some appointed intelligence officials, for whom security may always remain a purely military concept.

Regional Relations

The previous administration's approach to security planning in Europe reflected the traditional U.S. distrust of new security partnerships and a dogged effort to maintain the status quo in the midst of overwhelming change. The belief that NATO was the only credible Western alliance organization overshadowed any serious support for a Europe-wide organization that might better reflect current political realities. Even as European security institutions have multiplied and begun to overwhelm NATO's relevance in key areas, elements of the current policymaking apparatus still try to cling to a NATO-centric

---

22. George Lardner, Jr., "Cheney Assails Intelligence Revision Plan," *Washington Post*, March 24, 1992, p. A5.

approach as the basis for European engagement, though less dogmatically than their predecessors.

Political rigidity toward institution building and the management of relations in Europe could prove especially damaging to U.S. leadership and continue to hinder effective preparation for collective approaches to future crises. Contrary to the beliefs of either isolationists or advocates of a Pax Americana, American participation in European security affairs will be necessary to ensure continued American influence and to secure the victory won in the cold war. Even if the forces of anarchy and civic violence do not spill over into the rest of Europe, these conditions just in the former Soviet bloc hardly signify a triumph for the West. A strong U.S. role is needed to help deter the escalation of regional instabilities, to help NATO countries forge enduring relationships with new democracies, to assist in the demobilization and conversion of the military sectors of former adversaries, and to help express the sense of common purpose between East and West.

A new European cooperative security structure could complement rather than undercut NATO and need not be damaging to American interests. Given the political diversity of Europe, no single institution can carry the weight of providing for European security in any case. American engagement does not mean an extensive American troop presence; the burden of European defense and collective security appropriately rests with the Europeans. But however the Europeans choose to organize themselves, the United States has to be involved as a partner if it intends to maintain a role in determining the region's future.

The United States has long believed itself to be the principal guarantor of stability in other regions, especially in Asia. Recently, however, domestic pressures for U.S. disengagement in this region have intensified. The opposition to U.S. involvement in Asia has focused largely on questions of trade with economic competitors, U.S. troop deployments in Korea and elsewhere, the future military role of Japan, and the desirability of continued U.S.-China ties.

The major regional powers, conversely, have made it clear that they want the United States to maintain some level of military presence to prevent dramatic changes in the regional balance, and are typically more concerned about U.S. protectionism or retrenchment than about other potential sources of instability.

The costs of either an isolationist or a Pax Americana approach to security in Asia are fairly easy to discern. Protectionist trade measures and pressures on Japan to dramatically alter its military policies could undermine regional stability and the foundations for a cooperative U.S.-Japanese approach to security. Urging Japan to augment its force posture and to discard the idea of its military as existing only for self-defense would be seen as provocative by other states. A widening divergence between the United States and Japan could even prompt the only major nonnuclear power in Northeast Asia to conclude that it could no longer rely on the American security commitment, and thus to reassess its own military policies. It is much more in the United States' interest to see Japan's security policies evolve in the context of a cooperative relationship, helping thereby to foster adherence to international norms guiding military behavior, defense-related technology exports, and free trade.

Current U.S. policy toward China has been the subject of protracted domestic controversy for several years, recently over the issues of China's human rights violations and its arms and technology export policies. The original rationale for forging a strategic relationship with China to provide a military counterweight to the Soviet Union-is no longer relevant. The United States is left with a complicated relationship with a recalcitrant government that it often seems not to understand. The perception of China as a rogue state bent on flouting international norms has also grown steadily in the public and in Congress in the last few years. As a metaphor for U.S.-China relations, U.S. failure to persuade China to abide by international human rights and defense technology trade standards reinforces the view among critics that the bilateral relationship is a one-way street, little more than a strategic expedience for the Chinese in which the United States is an unwitting or decidedly inept pawn.

Congressional initiatives calling for punitive measures against Japan, China, or other Asian countries that seem to be violating international standards are perhaps understandable, but for many reasons this strategy is not likely to be effective. Wholesale threats of embargoes or other punitive trade sanctions seem to have little positive impact on the behavior of sovereign powers. For China, fronta assaults seem simply to remind it of its separateness in the international order, or to drive proscribed activities underground. Unaccompanied by incentives and various other face-saving devices, efforts to effect reforms through punitive measures are usually counterproductive, especially if they are not fully supported by the international community as a whole.

It may be obvious that U.S. policy will never be effective as long as it is based on an inadequate appreciation of regional and domestic politics in Asia. But explaining the forces that impel unpopular policies in certain countries, while stressing the need for continued ties with those states, is a hard sell to Congress and to the American public. Controversies over trade or human rights policies are microcosms of the larger challenge of trying to persuade Americans that severing relations or imposing sanctions in response to infractions may not be the best way to promote democratization, military restraint, and overall U.S. interests.

This is a classic foreign policy dilemma in U.S. relations with countries whose governments differ from Western democracies. The question is how far one can stretch international norms to accommodate the domestic imperatives of intransigent states before appearing to be weak willed. Conversely, one has to gauge how stringently to pressure states to abide by norms before antagonizing them and thereby losing all leverage.

In emphasizing a cooperative over a confrontational approach, the United States may be able to gain critical leverage by appealing to the growing interest of China and other regional powers in becoming more equal partners in the international order, on the one hand, while being able to marshal strong international reaction if recalcitrance continues. Integration into the economic system is a potentially powerful form of self-interest to which the United States can appeal in promoting other objectives, especially with industrializing countries such as China or even North Korea. The United States already uses access to technology as an instrument of dissuasion, but a policy that trades critical technology for concessions on the nonproliferation front, for example, could be far more effectively exploited if undertaken in an internationally cooperative manner.

Similarly, decisions to reduce the U.S. force presence in Asia have always prompted controversy because they were seen as a sign of U.S. retrenchment. Even as forces are being drawn down in the current environment, the United States will still rely on maritime power in the western Pacific, some U.S. armed forces in Japan, and a combat-ready presence in South Korea until a peaceful resolution of Korean relations is worked out. Whatever the configuration of U.S. forces, however, the world community's stake in the world's most economically dynamic region has long been and will remain vital. Of all of the regions in the world, it is most obvious in Asia that international interests need not be defined either as unilaterally American or as largely military. A cooperative approach to security in this region, as such, is already unavoidable if the United States is to preserve its own interests and manage controversies arising from desirable or unavoidable alterations in its own commitments.

In mid-1993 the nuclear ambitions of North Korea helped to highlight the profound stakes of the international community in developments on the Korean peninsula. North Korea's refusal to allow adequate inspections of its suspect nuclear facilities and its threat in 1992 to leave the Nuclear Non-Proliferation Treaty (NPT) regime sent a clear message that North Korean intentions had international implications, with especially adverse consequences for the global effort to stop the spread of nuclear weapons. The United States took the lead in helping to dissuade North Korea from terminating its membership in the NPT (a decision reached in June 1993), but any enduring arrangement for North Korean adherence to international agreements clearly will require broader international involvement, including involvement by China, Japan, and Russia. Leaving an issue as sensitive as North Korea's nuclear program to the United States to rectify threatens to narrow the debate to a bilateral or quasi-regional dispute, in which the United States is forced to assume responsibility for unilateral-and potentially controversial and less than decisive-retaliation if the effort fails.

In the Middle East, the proliferation of weapons of mass destruction, especially in Syria, Iran, and Iraq, has been identified by the Clinton administration as the most serious threat to U.S. and allied interests. At the same time, the disappearance of a Soviet threat, the progressive disarmament of Iraq, and the agreement between Israel and the PLO signed in September 1993 have opened new diplomatic opportunities for mediating and reducing Israel and its Arab antagonists. The administration has sustained its predecessor's ambitious initiatives to promote peace in the region, including brokering peace talks and pressing for serious concessions from both sides. For the United States to take full advantage of the potential promises for accommodation in the region, diplomatic skill may prove far more important than the substance of U.S. force plans. A preoccupation with force projection, overseas basing, and other traditional indicators of military preparedness may not be relevant to many of the potential catalysts for instabilities in the region. The issue of arms and technology sales, currently being driven in large measure by economic competition among the major industrial suppliers, is especially sensitive. Only a multilateral approach to arms proliferation can redress the potentially adverse security effects of uncontrolled weapon sales pursued for short-term nationalistic interests.

U.S. plans in the early 1990s to sell more than $20 billion in major combat equipment to the region might be construed as inconsistent with an overall policy preaching military restraint and arms limitations.[23] The Bush and Clin-

---

23. See, for example, Natalie J. Goldring, "Transfer of Advanced Technology and Sophisticated Weapons," paper prepared for the United Nations Conference on Disarmament Issues, entitled "Disarmament and National Security in the Interdependent World," Kyoto, Japan, April 13–16, 1993.

ton administrations have correctly argued that there is a trade-off between arms sales and the U.S. ability to minimize the size of ground forces deployed in the Gulf, although the tendency is more often to stress the importance of these contracts for U.S. industry. Whatever the wisdom of these arms deals, however, they certainly will not reduce the economic strains in the region, nor will they encourage a political transition away from high levels of military control over government expenditures and economic planning in key states.[24] These latter problems are still relegated to a lower level of importance than force augmentation and modernization.

A more prominent U.S. military presence in certain countries, as is currently envisioned, may also not necessarily improve the prospects for successful management of regional problems. On the contrary, the deployment of troops in countries such as Saudi Arabia may exacerbate local opposition to what is seen as excessive Western influence, as occurred in Iran in the 1970s. To this end, even selective and seemingly justified unilateral punitive attacks on adversarial states such as Iraq may prove to be counterproductive in the long run if U.S. actions are seen by friendly Arab governments and populations as an illegitimate exercise of U.S. power.

In the rest of the world, the United States has exhibited a strong trend toward disengagement or at least indifference in large segments of Africa and even in Central America. Except for Somalia, these regions currently receive relatively little official U.S. attention, a far cry from the days when the Soviet airlift to Ethiopia in the late 1970s or the civil war in Nicaragua in the 1980s dominated the U.S. foreign policy agenda. No longer useful as surrogates in the superpowers' struggle for ascendancy, they loom instead as unwanted burdens on dwindling foreign assistance budgets.

Current U.S. policy in the third world is still predominantly driven by a perception that the future of U.S. security is imperiled by anarchic and aggressive states bent on disrupting global stability. This concept is not new in U.S. relations with the third world. In the 1970s U.S. concerns focused on the threat of economic blackmail from embittered former colonial states that felt disenfranchised from the international economic and political system.[25] Unlike during the 1970s, however, when it was largely conceded that these countries had legitimate grievances, the current view tends to dismiss the importance of root

---

24. For a detailed discussion of the political economy of the region and the link to military expenditures, see Yahya Sadowski, *Scuds or Butter? The Political Economy of Arms Control in the Middle East* (Brookings, 1992).

25. This focus is discussed eloquently in Robert W. Tucker and David C. Hendrickson, *The Imperial Temptation: The New World Order and America's Purpose* (New York: Council on Foreign Relations Press, 1992), pp. 37–39.

causes of third world aggression and simply seeks to contain or punish its perpetrators. As a basis for eliciting third world participation in a U.S.-led security regime, this notion is not exactly visionary and may not help enfranchise a large number of states on behalf of common goals.

Role and Utility of Nuclear Weapons

The agreement reached in June 1992 by Presidents George Bush and Boris to reduce the two states' nuclear inventories, signed by the two sides in the last days of the Bush administration, was unprecedented in both the scope of its provisions and its potential for further stabilizing actions in the future. Once implemented, the agreement would reduce the two nations' strategic inventories by about 70 percent from the levels established by the 1991 Strategic Arms Reduction Talks. More important, the new agreement calls for the complete elimination of both sides' most destabilizing weapons, land-based missiles with multiple independently targetable warheads.

The new limits on nuclear arsenals have overshadowed the more modest debate about the continued importance ascribed to nuclear weapons in U.S. strategy, or the criteria guiding the size, character, safety, or targeting of remaining nuclear forces. The perceived utility of nuclear weapons in defending U.S. interests is a subject of considerable confusion. The domestic debate about the role of nuclear weapons has never been particularly coherent, but it has now run logically amok. The competing strands of thinking are reflected in proposals as disparate as developing low-yield weapons or arming expeditionary forces with nuclear capabilities for intervention in third world contingencies, retaining a permanently robust nuclear deterrent that must always exceed the collective arsenals of other nuclear powers, encouraging allies to acquire nuclear weapons through a system of "managed proliferation," or proposing that nuclear weapons and warfare be outlawed as a "crime against humanity and the environment."[26]

Current strategy is to retain a triad of nuclear weapons sufficient to counter the Russian strategic force and to provide a secure retaliatory capability to deter

---

26. For discussion of these various points of view, see Thomas C. Reed and Michael O. Wheeler, "The Role of Nuclear Weapons in the New World Order," prepared for the director of the Joint Strategic Targeting and Planning Staff by the Study Group on the Future of Nuclear Weapons, July 1991; John J. Mearsheimer, "Back to the Future: Instability in Europe after the Cold War," in Sean M. Lynn-Jones, ed., *The Cold War and After: Prospects for Peace* (MIT Press, 1991), pp. 141–92; the statement issued by the Preparatory Committee for the UN Conference on Environment and Development Group, cited in *Chemical Weapons Convention Bulletin*, no. 16 (June 1992), p. 13; and Mark Thompson, "A Push for Mini-Nukes Research," *Philadelphia Inquirer*, June 17, 1993, p. 2.

the use of nuclear weapons by "hostile and irresponsible countries," as Secretary of Defense Cheney put it in 1992 in a statement that was reiterated in similar terms by Clinton officials.[27] The reasons for retaining a triad, a product of very conservative estimates of what would be required to cope with a disarming Soviet first strike, are not discussed officially. Current force levels and reductions, which have been driven largely by political events of the recent past, are also not necessarily tied to prior assessments of military requirements or efficiency. The assumption is that a floor exists beneath which U.S. force cannot be allowed to fall, but this minimum level is not necessarily determined by targeting doctrine or by the political goals that the doctrine is meant to uphold.

The question of which countries the United States will target with nuclear weapons in the future and under what circumstances is simply not articulated and certainly not clearly understood, even among planners. According to some officials, this question does not require an a priori answer. The preponderance of U.S. strategic forces remain targeted at the former Soviet nuclear arsenal, considered an immutable imperative. The targeting review conducted during the Bush administration in 1991, moreover, purportedly generated plans that provided for flexible options for global application, including the ability to retarget weapons in "real time" to meet any contingency. This plan is a modern version of a *tout azimuth* nuclear strategy. More recently, plans have been discussed among defense officials to target third world countries with highly accurate conventional forces as well.[28]

The vanishing nuclear order was the product of a need to deter aggression against NATO by superior Warsaw Pact conventional forces. NATO members were unwilling or unable to dedicate sufficient resources or to take the steps necessary to restructure their defense sectors to rectify the disparities in conventional capabilities. Nuclear weapons were thus a cheap way of maintaining a military balance. Outside NATO, nuclear guarantees were extended very selectively to close U.S. allies that confronted proximate enemies allied with or part of the Soviet bloc. Insofar as these arrangements were considered legitimate, it was as part of a bipolar system in which the United States, Europe, and a few other allies were united in a defensive alliance, while the Soviet Union was seen as an expansionist power bent on global hegemony.

---

27. See *Department of Defense Annual Report, Fiscal Year 1992*, p. 5. See also the transcript of the second presidential debate, in Washington Post, October 16, 1992, p. A36; and Aspin, *Report on the Bottom-Up Review.*
28. Eric Schmitt, "Head of Nuclear Forces Plans for a New World," *New York Times*, February 25, 1993.

With the exception of Russia and China, the current nuclear threat, to the extent that it can be reliably defined, consists of a handful of states with small or fledgling programs or sometimes just immodest ambitions. This definition is not meant to belittle the dangers such states may pose to international or regional stability in the future. But the sudden elevation of third world powers to the status of ruthless enemies on a par with the Soviet Union bears further examination, especially since it is now becoming a principal rationale for retaining a U.S. nuclear deterrent. According to former secretary of defense Aspin, the only remaining nuclear threat to the United States, except for the loss of control over Soviet nuclear assets, will come from a few nuclear-armed rogue states bent on aggression or terrorism. This unspecified group of nuclear thugs, which are untutored in and therefore undaunted by the refined logic of deterrence, may be able to "equalize" U.S. conventional superiority with just a few crude nuclear devices. Had Saddam Hussein had just six nuclear weapons capable of reaching Riyadh or Tel Aviv, according to this view, there is serious doubt that the United States would have succeeded in assembling a political coalition for Operation Desert Storm.

It is obviously not possible to prove or disprove such a premise. But if this argument is correct, it seems to pose immense implications for both the future utility of U.S. nuclear forces and the way in which the legacy of nuclear weapons is judged. NATO was prepared for more than three decades to risk nuclear confrontation with an equal or (according to some in more recent years) superior nuclear adversary. NATO doctrine included the intent to initiate nuclear conflict if necessary, regardless of the certainty that this act could prompt retaliation sufficient to annihilate Western society. That aside, the West today would be paralyzed in the face of a few weapons in the hands of "irrational" and "undeterrable" enemies such as Iraq, according to Aspin and others.

Part of the logic of this argument hinges on the notion that the Soviet Union was rational, valued its survival, and could be targeted effectively, whereas the nuclear powers of the future probably will not share these traits. As Aspin argued in a speech in June 1992, "Will our nuclear adversaries always be rational, or at least operate with the same logic as we do? We can't be sure. Will we always be able to put our adversaries at risk to make deterrence work? Not necessarily, particularly with terrorists whom we may not even be able to find.[29] But if one is going to make the argument that U.S. strategy falls apart in the

---

29. Representative Les Aspin, "Three Propositions for a New Era Nuclear Policy," speech given at the Massachusetts Institute of Technology, Cambridge, Mass., June 1, 1992.

face of a third world atomic adversary, one has the intellectual responsibility to explain the reasons. What is the basis for the vast differences in U.S. and Western resolve against enemies that are nuclear dwarfs compared to the Soviet Union? What do these differences say for the legacy of flexible response? Was the nuclear competition over Europe between the United States and the Soviet Union merely an abstraction, whereas the Iraqi scenario is serious?

The retroactive depiction of the Soviet Union as an essentially benign adversary that could be counted on to play by the rules certainly runs counter to the volumes written by erudite scholars about the Soviet proclivity for war or the lower value Soviet citizens placed on human life. Without even a decent interval, the Soviets have been strangely redeemed, and emerging or aspiring third world nuclear powers have inherited the Soviets' mantle. They are now the warmongers that have a higher tolerance for death and are driven by causes that supersede rational calculation. It hardly needs mention that this caricature of the third world is rather racist; one also can discern that it is often meant to depict the Islamic world. The notion that there are undeterrable states seems to suggest that the architecture of nuclear-based deterrence has little utility in the modern world. Deterrence has always relied on the demonstrated ability and willingness to use nuclear weapons if necessary and to communicate this intent to potential adversaries. However, officials have proved remarkably squeamish when asked to articulate the way in which targeting and nuclear forces will occur in the new world order. The political hazards of discussing such contingencies are obvious, and no agreed-upon procedures exist to even begin discussions about the future role of nuclear forces operating in the third world.

In the haste to define new threats, there has been no opportunity for an adequate evaluation of the legacy of nuclear weapons for American security, let alone time to think about their future. Did nuclear weapons prevent war? What are the lessons to be derived from the history of nuclear deterrence, different operational practices, or the use of nuclear threats? Which among these lessons would the United States want other states to emulate? Unless the nuclear powers are willing to confront the security benefits or dangers of their own policies, it is not possible to craft coherent policy for others. What is decided about the nuclear legacy, in short, has important ram for future force planning and, most important, for designing credible nonproliferation policies.

In contrast to the principles guiding cooperative security discussed in preceding chapters, current nuclear plans do not focus adequately on the most critical risk to U.S. security: the possible failure of operational control over nuclear weapons. For now, discussion has been limited about ways to make nuclear weapons less usable (such as the renunciation of prompt launch of nuclear forces, improvements in command and control, significant reductions in alert status, and other restraints on the ability to conduct a surprise attack) or about negative controls (such as permissive action links). Indeed, the rationales driving nuclear planning often seem more intent on preserving at least the edifice of the nuclear status quo, in anticipation of the return of a Soviet-type nuclear adversary.

The traditional objective of deterrence against the Soviet Union required the ability to initiate a large nuclear attack within a few minutes and to complete it within a few hours. The danger of a prior attack on U.S. deterrent forces required in turn that in a crisis it be possible to disperse this capability to a relatively large number of widely separated operational commanders. The commitments to rapid response, dispersed control, and detailed programming for large-scale attack, as such, made operational readiness rather than safety necessarily the preeminent goal of U.S. strategy. As long as the threat of sudden attack was considered the primary security problem, the safe management of weapons was accepted as a subordinate, though certainly vital, consideration. Extensive provisions were developed to protect against the accidental or unauthorized explosion of any nuclear weapon as well as against any compromise of physical custody. Still, these provisions were all designed to preserve a large inventory of weapons in an extremely responsive state of deployment. As best as it can be determined, despite the inherent tensions between operational readiness and control, the record has been a success. No unintended nuclear detonations occurred, and the only known compromises of physical custody have been the result of operational accidents whose frequency seems to have diminished with accumulating experience.[30]

The current risks, however, are different. The internal pressures on the strategic command system of the former Soviet Union are so extensive and of such uncertain consequence that its ability to maintain standards of safety while preserving a highly reactive operational posture cannot prudently be assumed. Moreover, the possibility that the two strategic forces could accidentally trigger each other because of their highly reactive postures is an enduring problem that simply cannot be measured on the basis of past experience.[31]

---

30. For a detailed study on nuclear false alarms and nuclear safety, see Scott D. Sagan, *The Limts of Safety: Organizations, Accidents, and Nuclear Weapons* (Princeton University Press, 1992).
31. In particular, the warning systems that mediate the critical judgment about whether a nuclear attack is or is not in progress have never encountered the unique flows of information and

The various initiatives that have been recently undertaken to reduce nuclear weapons deployments and to relax routine alert procedures will alleviate but not eliminate the internal pressures on the strategic command system in the former Soviet Union. And they will have very little material effect on the underlying problem of crisis interaction. The commitment to rapid reaction has not been altered, and traditional crisis alert procedures remain in effect on both sides, as does the pattern of dispersed control. Even the sharply reduced forces and reconfigured weapons deployments that are to result from the June 1992 framework agreement are capable of inflicting enormous damage on any industrial society. In fact, even at these lower force levels, an inadvertent trigger--ing of the strategic attack plans that are being continued as the basis for deterrence would still be the largest man-made catastrophe in history. Given the inherent inability to determine the probability of such an event, there is strong reason to seek higher standards of safety by removing the commitment to rapid reaction and dispersed control.

Aside from reducing the risk of strategic interaction, reductions in the alert status of U.S., Russian, and other states' nuclear weapons would be an important demonstration of the devaluation of nuclear weapons as instruments of state power. This could be a critical, if not sufficient, foundation for efforts to delegitimize nuclear weapons globally. Although such alterations may not be sufficient to dissuade some regional powers from their own agendas, the diminution of the global status of nuclear forces is an important first step toward the devaluation, reduction, and perhaps eventual elimination of all weapons of mass destruction.

Many officials and establishment experts, however, seem to believe that limits on U.S. nuclear capabilities that go much further than current constraints would weaken the ability of the United States to influence other countries. Rather than promote nuclear restraint, they argue, deeper cuts and operational changes could actually encourage hostile nations to acquire nuclear capabilities to threaten or to actually use such weapons against U.S. forces in a crisis. The United States might even lose the ability to offset superior conventional capabilities of future adversaries. The ultimately ironic argument, advanced by

---

problems of interpretation that a full process of alerting forces would create. It cannot be presumed that the probability of a catastrophic misjudgment would remain as low in crisis as it certainly has been under the peacetime and mild crisis circumstances encountered to date. The system has not yet been tested under severe stress. For a detailed discussion of the problems, see Bruce G. Blair, *The Logic of Accidental Nuclear War* (Brookings, 1993).

"centurists," is that the United States needs nuclear weapons to retaliate against countries that breach a nonproliferation regime.

Realistically, contradictions in nuclear beliefs and practices are not likely to be resolved soon. In the near term, however, the possibility of further constraints on the development of nuclear weapons has become a more acceptable topic within establishment circles. Long considered the domain of fringe disarmament advocates, a move toward a ban on testing nuclear weapons, for example, has finally won qualified support in the Clinton administration, beginning with a policy to extend the current moratorium on U.S. testing as long as no other nation conducts tests first.[32]

Perhaps for the first time, practical reality coincides with political objectives. The United States ceased production of special nuclear materials and new nuclear warheads in 1991 and announced an initiative for an international fissile material effect on the material production cut-off for weapons use in 1993. The administration's defense program for fiscal 1993–97 is slated to cancel all major modernization programs for nuclear forces except the Trident I II submarine-launched ballistic missile. As early as 1992, the Bush administration announced that in the future any nuclear tests would be limited and conducted strictly for safety or reliability, a position widely supported in Congress and by the Clinton administration.

An agreement to halt nuclear testing would not be the decisive element of a U.S. commitment to denuclearization, nor sufficient incentive for other nuclear powers to renounce their own ambitions. But if develop new types of nuclear weapons and it is agreed that the preparation to fight nuclear wars is an unnecessary and counterproductive precaution, clinging to the prerogative to test imposes costs with no discernible benefit. As George Perkovich has argued, "The central requirement of nonproliferation is to convince other countries that nuclear weapons are not usable and therefore not worth trying to acquire.

---

32. For more information on the U.S. decision not to test, see Ann Devroy and R. Jeffrey Smith, "U.S. Drops Nuclear Test Plans; Policy Now Would Be to Resume Blasts Only If Another Nation Does," *Washington Post*, June 30, 1993, p. A1. The former Soviet Union has not tested a nuclear weapon for nearly two years, and Rusian production of nuclear forces and materials have been cut back substantially. China, France, and the United Kingdom continue to modernize their much smaller nuclear forces with a small number of tests annually, although France recently imposed a moratorium on its testing program and the U.K.'s tests are performed as part of the U.S. program. That China resumed its nuclear testing program in late 1993 was not seen as sufficient reason for the United States to alter its policy. See the "Statement by the Press Secretary," The White House, Washington, October 5, 1993. For more information on China's most recent nuclear test, see Steven A. Holmes, "World Moratorium on Nuclear Tests Is Broken by China," *New York Times*, October 6, 1993, p. A1.

Continued nuclear testing sends just the opposite message. By ceaselessly refining and testing these weapons, we suggest they *are* usable."[33]

Obviously the concern about North-South asymmetries and the belief that a comprehensive test ban might enhance U.S. stature in championing the NPT are not views shared by all defense analysts. For some, testing is needed not just as a way to ensure warhead and stockpile reliability but also to maintain cadres of expert designers, engineers, and other specialists as a hedge against new threats or the return of the strategic threat. The United States may again find it desirable to develop new warhead designs, according to this view. As one commentator summarized the situation, "They must explore every possible technical option that renegade nations might exploit in developing their own versions of atomic bombs . . . and only testing can do that job . . . [The nuclear laboratories] must design, develop and test advanced warhead prototypes for the future to prove out new weapons systems that the United States might eventually need in an uncertain and unstable world."[34]

The rejection of testing limits serves as a useful microcosm of many of the arguments of isolationists, Pax Americana advocates, and those who feel nostalgic about the passing of the cold war. As a statement of isolationist sentiment, the position embraces the idea that the United States has little to gain from trying to influence other countries, and certainly not if this influence imposes undue self-restraint on American security options. For those who tend toward the views of Pax Americana, a continued commitment to nuclear weapon testing and innovation is a vital element of U.S. military and technological superiority, an objective whose benefits far surpass those of any tertiary diplomatic objective such as strengthening the NPT. For aging cold warriors, continued testing, like nuclear targeting, demonstrates in a concrete way that the United States will always be prepared for the enemy, whoever and wherever it may be.

Controlling Technology Proliferation

The majority of controls on weapons and weapons technologies that have evolved over the past four decades consist of initiatives undertaken by the larger powers to restrict access to proscribed technologies by smaller states, usually while preserving the right to retain these weapons in their own arse-

---

33. George Perkovich, "Proliferation by Example," *Washington Post*, May 5, 1993, p. A21.
34. David Perlman, "Lab's Weapons Experts Revise Rationale for Tests," *San Francisco Chronicle*, May 26, 1992, p. 4.

nals. That is certainly true for nuclear weapons but also for various conventional armaments and until recently chemical weapons.[35] Although invoking the interests of global security, nonproliferation arrangements ratify the right of the technologically powerful to impinge on the technical sovereignty of lesser states. The various control regimes range from arms embargoes, supplier cartels, safeguard agreements on sensitive technologies, to threats of attack. They rely on trade barriers, punitive sanctions, and high-minded principle to dissuade or prevent states from attempting to emulate some aspects of the military capabilities of the large powers. The NPT, the Coordinating Committee on Multilateral Export Controls (COCOM), and the Missile Technology Control Regime (MTCR) were unabashedly designed to protect a hierarchical international system in which the United States and some allies would retain certain advantages while encouraging restraint on the part of others.

The United States and other industrial states also reserve the right to promote technology proliferation when it is expedient. They have often abetted proliferation directly, by treating the defense trade at least in the conventional area as almost a standard form of commerce for all but the most sensitive technologies. It is not unusual for officials to discuss the burgeoning threat of third world militarization in one part of a statement and then turn to the importance of U.S. competitiveness in the global arms market. There was no intended irony in Secretary of Defense Cheney's statement to Congress in February 1992, for example, in which he championed the importance of arms sales to partners in the Middle East and shortly after warned of the dangers of a global diffusion of military and dual-use technologies: "[These technologies] will enable a growing number of countries to field highly capable weapons systems, such as ballistic missiles, stealthy cruise missile, integrated air defenses, submarines, modern command and control systems, and even space-based assets. *Unfortunately, there are both governments and individuals willing to supply proliferating countries with both systems and technical expertise.*"[36]

The few periodic attempts to control conventional arms proliferation over the last three decades have essentially failed.[37] Most industrial states believe it

---

35. Until 1991, the United States insisted it had to retain a chemical weapon stockpile until all states had ratified the Chemical Weapon Convention banning the production and use of these weapons.
36. *Department of Defense Annual Report, Fiscal Year 1992*, p. 5. Emphasis added.
37. One example was the Tripartite Agreement of 1950, in which the United Kingdom, France, and the United States agreed to refrain from transferring arms to the Middle East. This pact broke down when the Soviet Union and Czechoslovakia agreed to transfer armaments to Egypt in 1955. Similarly, the Conventional Arms Transfer talks between the United States and the Soviet Union

is to their advantage to be fairly permissive in the export of conventional arms, thought with some restraints on highly advanced weapon systems or technologies.[38] Arms transfers have been a key instrument of efforts by the large powers to gain influence in the third world, and more recently to defray the costs of their own arms industries with export revenues. In the aftermath of the Iraqi war, the five permanent members of the UN Security Council began to discuss broad guidelines to coordinate their respective exports of advanced conventional weaponry, but such guidelines have yet to affect national decisions to export arms in any demonstrable manner.[39]

Not incidentally the apparatus for managing defense technology trade in the U.S. bureaucracy is responsible for both promoting and controlling U.S. exports. U.S. technology transfer policy is fragmented institutionally and intellectually. It cuts across traditional demarcations of economic, military, and diplomatic interests and impinges on such disparate elements of policy as commercial investments and export promotion, management of the domestic defense industrial base, strategic trade controls, development and security assistance, and international trade cartels for controlling particularly sensitive technologies, such as those used in nuclear and chemical weapons. Weaknesses in the U.S. policy apparatus for technology transfers have been accentuated by the rapid changes and growing complexity of the international technology market. Commercially available components of military significance, including

in the 1970s failed in the face of tension between the two superpowers and lagging support from other industrial countries. See, for instance, Janne E. Nolan, "The U.S.-Soviet Conventional Arms Transfer Negotiations," in Alexander L. George, Philip J. Farley, and Alexander Dallin, *U.S.-Soviet Security Cooperation* (Oxford University Press, 1988), pp. 510–24.

38. Aside from COCOM, the only organized regime for controlling conventional weapon and dual-use technology to have endured for more than a few years is the MTCR agreement among industrial companies to restrict trade in ballistic and cruise missile technologies. Announced in April 1987, the regime now has twenty-three members. This voluntary supplier cartel controls ballistic and cruise missiles capable of carrying nuclear, chemical, or biological materials with a range of 300 kilometers, regardless of the payload. The MTCR is not reinforced by an accompanying international treaty to support its goals. It is simply a set of export guidelines that a group of industrial countries agreed to incorporate into national export laws or use in judging the approximateness of transfers of missiles or dual-use technologies. The original MTCR members chose explicitly not to involve potential recipient states at the offset, fearing that negotiation of an expanded agreement would be time consuming and ultimately not fruitful.

39. In a series of meetings beginning in July 1991, representatives of the United States, the United Kingdom, France, China, and Russia agreed to refrain from transfers that would "increase regional instability" and to notify the group when transferring certain types of conventional weaponry. The five also agreed to create an international arms trade registry to be administered by the UN. The reluctance of the permanent five members of the Security Council to seek more serious controls on the arms trade reflects the centrality of this instrument to the foreign policy of those nations. China, moreover, refused to continue participating in the talks in mid-1992 after the United States approved the sale of F-16 fighters to Taiwan.

guidance and telemetry equipment, satellites, and computer technology, have contributed to developing countries' capacity for independent or quasi-independent weapon production programs. Many countries have proceeded with military production programs with the assistance of an expanding international system of commercial entrepreneurs, in an elaborate pattern of military trade that operates largely outside U.S. control.

The evolution of the international technology market has not been accompanied by commensurate changes in the bureaucratic apparatus. The complex jurisdictional structures established for promoting or restraining technology transactions have evolved into a highly stratified bureaucratic regime, rife with discontinuities and contradictions. To illustrate, a decision in 1986 to sell advanced computers to India through commercial channels, heralded as "a major opportunity to increase American influence in that nation at the expense of the Soviet Union," led in 1989 to serious concerns about India's potential use of supercomputers in its missile and nuclear development programs, which the United States is actively trying to discourage. Similarly, the imposition of congressionally mandated U.S. sanctions on companies that violate the MTCR resulted in serious frictions between the United States and the Indian and Russian governments over a space technology contract at just the time when the United States had embarked on a major effort to expand trade and political relations with both countries.

The disparities in objectives and practices among agencies that oversee different types of technology transfer impede the implementation of coherent export guidelines. A common feature in COCOM discussions of the past, internecine controversies among the Commerce, State, and Defense departments and between Congress and the executive branch have plagued the effort to implement coherent export controls for decades.

In practice, the sheer volume of arms sales requests means that the preponderance of U.S. military licenses granted each year are approved or denied with a minimum of scrutiny or debate. Of the approximately 55,000 license requests or agreements processed annually through the State Department's Office of Defense Trade, for example, less than 20 percent are likely to be referred to other agencies for review, and less than 1 percent to Congress. In turn, most arms sales decisions are approved or denied on the basis of routine recommendations by midlevel officials and are only rarely examined by more senior officials.

In controversial cases, the factors weighed in the review process are a diffuse amalgam of technical, political, and military judgments, deriving as much from transitory political interests and different agencies' interpretations of policy as from any formal statutes or precedents. Although some export guidelines are enduring and clear-cut, such as the prohibitions on the transfer of nuclear weapons, interagency deliberations about significant arms transactions are rarely driven by objective assessments of long-term national security interests.

The recurring patterns of bureaucratic disputes, reflecting long-standing institutional biases, determine policy much more than formal criteria do. Although in theory all agencies are supposed to operate with a coherent and consistent concept of "the national interest," this ideal is far from reality. Insofar as biases can be summarized across cabinet agencies, the State Department will typically be concerned about the adverse political and diplomatic effects of turning down requests for arms, whereas the Department of Defense and its constituent agencies tend to focus on the potential effects on military capabilities of recipients an the costs or benefits of arms exports for U.S. military planning. The Commerce Department, which has played a more salient policy role as the content of trade has shifted toward a greater emphasis on commercial technologies, tends to protect American economic competitiveness and often opposes export controls on those grounds.

The outcome of deliberations over arms sales is often influenced by such factors as the relative clout of the agencies involved, the perceived importance of the recipient in domestic political terms, and even the expertise or endurance of individual participants involved in evaluating cases. Bureaucratic warfare, rather than analysis, tends to be the modus operandi in what is often a protracted process of plea bargaining and political compromise, which may or may not reflect long-term national objectives. Such a situation is particularly common when there is no unanimity about U.S. objectives at the highest levels of policymaking, as is now true in U.S. conventional arms transfer policy.

The spread of advanced chemical, biological, and conventional weapon manufacturing capabilities exemplifies the inherent weaknesses of supply-side controls for weapons readily produced with dual-use technologies. The maturation of developing countries' economies, coupled with the growing commercialization and internationalization of the technology market, virtually guarantees that countries determined to acquire these capabilities will do so. This certainly argues for a control system that begins to shift the focus away from controls only on the supply of technology to controls on the actual application of technologies. Such arrangements would require far greater levels of transparency in the international trading system and a system of cooperative enforcement among like-minded states to verify compliance and to isolate and penalize violators. Currently governments place blanket prohibitions on technologies that have legitimate uses, such as space launch vehicles, but when forced for political reasons to make exceptions lack the means to monitor the disposition of that technology after sales take place. This situation is the worst of all possible worlds: unenforceable export controls with no ability to monitor the destination or uses of transferred technologies.

Supplier restrictions still have a critical role to play in identifying and targeting a few of the technologies pertinent to weapons development. Many vital inputs for nuclear or missile development, such as advanced guidance needed for missile accuracy, remain in the hands of just a few suppliers. Future proliferation of such items therefore depends in part on policies devised by industrial guiding technological cooperation with other countries. Given current trends, however, the pace of international technical diffusion may eventually render controls on supply ineffectual for all but the most highly specialized or advanced products.

Emerging defense technologies may make the difficulty of differentiating among military and civilian exports even more pronounced. New technologies that are at the cutting edge of Western military modernization (including, for example, advanced information processing, composite materials, directed energy systems, and biotechnologies) are to varying degrees equally vital to civilian modernization. Advances in biotechnology enabling the production of superlethal pathogens usable in biological warfare, for instance, could also be used to develop more cost-effective and efficient agricultural techniques and medicines. Although certain biotechnologies could be highly destablizing in a military sense, they could also have positive effects on political stability in countries where poverty and disease are important catalysts for social unrest.

More recent additions to the instruments for managing proliferation are not diplomatic or trade related but technological. These include the idea of so-called coercive arms control, destroying military installations in countries whose objectives have been deemed problematic. The notion of unilateral military preemption, even on behalf of nonproliferation objectives, is unlikely to be consonant with the politics or operational assumptions of cooperative security. However desirable in theory, a danger exists that countermilitary options could distract attention from the real challenges of nonproliferation. The legitimacy of this instrument aside, the notion that the West can arm itself to remove unwanted military facilities when necessary is probably naïve.

As a political message, the notion of coercive arms control is also not consonant with a policy seeking to promote global military restraint. The idea that few states have the right to eliminate military capabilities in states of which they disapprove will not help Western credibility in its quest for international acceptance of nonproliferation objectives. Although military options will remain one of several instruments that could be used to punish those states that violate treaties, they are not likely to be a long-term or widely applicable solution.

One legacy of the successful Israeli strike on the Osiraq nuclear reactor in Iraq was to drive Iraqi military programs into clandestine, underground installations that could resist destruction. As was discovered after Operation Desert Storm in the effort to implement UN Resolution 687, it is not easy to destroy a military infrastructure of this kind, however superior one's forces. Indeed, the executive chairman of the UN special commission has repeatedly emphasized, inspections teams, not military strikes, have succeeded in destroying most of Iraq's nonconventional arsenal.[40] The core of Iraq's and other third world countries' military potential in entrenched in a growing industrial capability, human capital, and ability to attract suppliers. These factors are not readily susceptible to change by air strikes.

In turn, the sale of defensive systems and technology to states that have or are trying to develop missile production capabilities could inadvertently contribute to proliferation by granting those countries access to technologies useful for developing offensive systems. These range from guidance and rocket components to testing equipment and expertise about the phenomenology of missiles. Knowledge gained about the operation of antimissile systems is inherently applicable to other kinds of missile activities. South Korea, for example, succeeded in modifying the U.S. Nike-Hercules air defense system into a ballistic missile, a program that is pursued despite strenuous U.S. objections. This potential dilemma is another reason for developing effective safeguards on the end uses of sensitive technology.

A less obvious cost associated with the pursuit of technological fixes and countermilitary responses is that it typically occurs at the expense of effective diplomacy. Nonproliferation has never commanded the attention it deserved from policymakers, usually in the mistaken belief that the third world would never pose a serious military risk that the West could not counter. The effort to develop military solutions to proliferation tends to reinforce such a belief —

---

40. As Rolf Ekeus put it, "What has been destroyed [in Iraq] is through the peaceful means of inspection. I would like to say that arms control has demonstrated that it is that way to destroy weapons, and not through bombings and attacks." Quoted in Seth Faison, "Tracker of Iraqi Arms," *New York Times*, July 28, 1992, p. A8.

that diplomacy is not as urgent a priority as the development of new technologies to counter any new threat, even one to which the United States may have contributed. The quest for perpetual innovations to overwhelm potential adversaries, moreover, adds to pressures to develop technologies whose proliferation would be extremely dangerous, including antisatellite capabilities, biotechnologies, and highly accurate conventional weapons.

This threat argues for a new system of regional security consultation arrangements aimed at helping states to develop stable security postures without contributing to proliferation. Supplier policies to constrain the spread of weapons will have to be bolstered with efforts to lessen demand for proscribed military acquisitions. It is in this context that regional confidence- and security-building measures are vitally important. The developed world cannot control demand for weapons technology without simultaneously working to enhance developing states' security perceptions. Regional agreements have played too small a role in the promotion of nonproliferation and conflict resolution regimes in the past. Building on such agreements as the 1968 Treaty of Tlatelolco and 1986 Treaty of Rarotonga establishing nuclear weapon-free zones in Latin America and the South Pacific, initiatives that originate among the governments in the regions are likely to be much more readily supported and enforced.

U.S. Defense Investment

The overarching goal of U.S. defense investment is to preserve an American technological edge. The premise is that the United States will always be able to maintain superior status in a technologically stratified international system. This notion may be tested more severely in coming years, however. If current trends continue, the pace of technological diffusion may eventually vitiate the U.S. reliance on technological superiority to influence international events. By reducing the time between generations of weapons and between the creation of weapons and the development of countermeasures, the rapid passing of state-of-the-art technology into obsolescence may make the quest for technological advantage ever more elusive.

Moreover, the significance of this qualitative edge may be progressively undercut if equipment widely available internationally begins to approximate the capabilities of recent innovations or at least can interfere with the latter's performance. There may be a point of technical exhaustion, in other words, at which the quest for an increment of technological superiority hits unmistakably diminishing military returns. The notion that the industrial world can continue to subsidize its own military preparedness by helping smaller states to prepare for war may hasten the point at which technological superiority ceases to be a decisive determinant of national influence. The sale of weapons and weapons technology cannot be equated with the sale of other commodities, with the developed world simply unburdening its excess products for profit. As developing countries' military capabilities continue to improve, the redistribution of military capability may begin to alter the contours of any remaining international hierarchy.

As defense allocations continue to decline, the Pentagon and defense industries have taken to promoting overseas arms sales more explicitly as a way to preserve the U.S. defense industrial base. Efforts to get Export-Import Bank subsidies for arms export promotion, to use government funds to allow American companies to participate in international weapons trade shows, or to garner congressional votes for controversial arms sales on behalf of American workers are all elements of this new emphasis. Apart from being at odds with official policy statements that proliferation is the current main problem for U.S. national security, these actions are promoting the myth that export markets can significantly forestall recession and contraction in U.S. or other national defense industries.[41]

The current administration seems to be grappling with, and seeking opportunities to help guide American industry through this difficult transition. The defense market is in free fall, with downsizing of industry occurring randomly and apparently without benefit for a long-term vision. It is only logical that industry would be pressing for fewer restrictions on defense trade, such as lessening restrictions on third country sales, and using unions to lobby for arms exports in a desperate effort to keep jobs. The challenge now is for the government to actively encourage economic adjustment strategies that could promote the twin goals of economic stability and nonproliferation.

A vital security dilemma for the United States is finding the means to preserve superior military technologies and a healthy industrial base without a chronic dependency on exports of the kind that accelerate technical diffusion beyond what is prudent. In many respects proliferation is an economic and industrial issue. The extent to which defense-related technological innovations may require arms exports to defray their cost and the associate risks that highly

---

41. For a further discussion of the Clinton administration's arms sales practices, see "Meet Bill Clinton, Arms Merchant," *Business Week*, June 28, 1993, p. 32.

lethal technologies could proliferate suggest that nonproliferation policy must be crafted before decisions guiding defense investment. The cost of innovations and the dangers of the latter's proliferation need to be integrated into decisions about whether to acquire new capabilities and, if so, the pace at which they should be procured.

Conclusion

The United States is increasingly finding itself mired in multinational endeavors, from the Conference on Security and Cooperation in Europe to the Rio Summit to assistance programs for the former Soviet bloc. It is not largely by choice that this involvement has occurred. The United States still seems reluctant to commit fully to strengthening the international mechanisms on which it currently relies. U.S. payments to the UN are seriously in arrears. Elements in Congress oppose aid to the former Soviet Union to help consolidate its economy or even to dismantle its nuclear forces. Many officials question the wisdom of giving greater resources and authority to the International Atomic Energy Agency, an institution that in the last few years has been given tasks that greatly exceed its current budget. Although the United States is by no means solely responsible, the failure to support the UN has led to chronic underfunding of peacekeeping operations, the UN Special Commission, and other vital activities. Regional conflicts are in competition for resources that are already too scarce, pitting Bosnia against Somalia in a zero-sum game.[42]

The domestic debate about the future of U.S. security is obviously in turmoil, and competing trends both impel and constrain a move to a genuinely cooperative security system. There are now agreements of unprecedented scope for nuclear limitations, but their future is in some doubt. The United States triumphs in the victory over the cold war but is incapable of responding decisively as the fruits of that victory threaten to crumble into chaos and despair. Prevailing domestic skepticism about multilateral involvement has been particularly damaging to U.S. global interests. Much of the U.S. official rhetoric invites suspicions among states that think that any notion of cooperation in

---

42. In July 1992 the UN secretary-general revealed the gravity of the UN's position in a dispute with British officials over the European Community's effort to use UN forces to impose a cease-fire in Bosnia and Herzegovina. Boutrous-Gali accused Lord Carrington, the current head of the EC's peace efforsts in the region, of trying to deplete UN resources for a "war of the rich" at the expense of Somalia, whose situation was even more dire. See Seth Faison, "UN Chief Mired in Dispute with Security Council," *New York Times*, July 24, 1991, p. A3.

security may simply be a new cosmetic invented by the industrial powers to dress up old patterns of state behavior.

In the end, failure to recognize and to adapt successfully to new international imperatives may result from a stubborn reluctance to consider the interests of regional powers as a compelling determinant of U.S. policy and a new international order. Credible international norms cannot be designed by those who are not persuaded that other countries are worthy of equality or that their amity is important in crafting new rules for the international system. In the United States, in particular, this intellectual impediment is especially difficult to dislodge. It is the product of years of studied indifference to all but a narrow set of technical security issues and a proud embrace of ignorance about and rejection of politics, culture, and regional dynamics as legitimate influences on national policy.

Finally, the question is whether the United States will be forced into half-hearted cooperation by domestic constraints and international realities or will seize the opportunities presented to it, taking the lead in crafting a global transition. The core challenge is the degree to which the United States and other countries that are in a position to promote a new security regime will be willing to sacrifice traditional notions of military-based sovereignty on its behalf. Put differently, at what point does the potential cooperative regime infringe on traditional conceptions of national prerogatives to the point that old habits compete and make it no longer possible for states to support the regime? That is the measure of commitment and ultimately of success.

Concerts, Collective Security, and the Future of Europe

Charles A. Kupchan
and
Clifford A. Kupchan

Europe's strategic landscape has been transformed. Whether we like it or not, the architecture of the postwar order is outmoded. The Warsaw Pact has been disbanded. NATO is struggling to define a role for itself; the threat it was built to resist may soon be nonexistent. Profound and probably irreversible change in the Soviet Union and Eastern Europe means that we must confront the difficult task of erecting new security structures for a new era.

A debate rages over how to respond to these changes in Europe's landscape. Two broad schools of thought have emerged. The pessimists, pointing to the waning of the Cold War and the end of bipolarity, fear a return to a more fractious multipolar Europe.[1] The optimists, on the other hand, welcome the end of the East-West struggle and do not fear a return to multipolarity. They argue that many of the causes of war that produced conflict during the first half of the twentieth century have either been eliminated or substantially moderated. While these optimists recognize that the political and economic future of the Soviet Union and Eastern Europe remains uncertain, many argue that some form of collective security—a pan-European

---

Charles A. Kupchan is Assistant Professor of Politics at Princeton University. Clifford A. Kupchan is a Ph.D. candidate in Political Science at Columbia University.

The authors would like to than the following individuals for their assistance: Robert Art, Henry Bienen, James Chace, Cherrie Daniels, Joanne Gowa, Robert Jervis, Thomas Risse-Kappen, Nicholas Rizopoulos, Jack Snyder, Patricia Weitsman, and the participants of the International Relations Study Group at Princeton University, the Olin National Security Seminar at Harvard's Center for International Affairs, and the Foreign Policy Roundtable at the Council on Foreign Relations. Research support was provided by the Center of International Studies, Princeton University, and a German Marshall Fund grant to the Dulles Program on Leadership in International Affairs.

---

1. The most prominent proponent of this view is John Mearsheimer, "Back to the Future: Instability in Europe After the Cold War," *International Security*, Vol. 15, No. 1 (Summer 1990), pp. 1–56. Mearsheimer's main concerns stem from his assertion that multipolar worlds are inherently more unstable than bipolar ones.
   Other analysts, some of whom fall into the optimist camp, voice different concerns about the end of the Cold War: that Germany might again seek to dominate Europe; that failed attempts at political and economic reform in the Soviet Union and Eastern Europe might produce aggressive autocratic regimes; that ethnic hatreds might trigger border conflicts. For a review of these arguments and documentation, see Stephen Van Evera, "Primed for Peace: Europe After the Cold War," *International Security*, Vol. 15, No. 3 (Winter 1990/91), pp. 7–9.

International Security, Summer 1991 (Vol. 16, No. 1)
© 1991 by the President and Fellows of Harvard College and of the Massachusetts Institute of Technology.

order predicated on the notion of all against one—can best preserve peace in the post–Cold War era.[2]

Whether collective security can work in the new Europe is thus a critical issue underlying much contemporary debate over how to respond to the waning of the Cold War. A thorough analysis of collective security is also needed because, even though the concept has been invoked with increasing frequency by scholars and politicians alike, the debate has been muddied by differing interpretations of what collective security is and how it would operate to preserve peace in Europe. In addition, skeptics of collective security derive considerable ammunition from the apparent failure of the League of Nations to prevent aggression during the 1930s and the marginal significance of the United Nations during the Cold War. Unless this historical legacy can be proved inaccurate, collective security is not likely to win widespread acceptance.

This article will clarify what collective security is, and make the case that erecting a collective security structure in Europe is both viable and desirable. The conditions necessary for a collective security structure to form and function successfully are now present. Such a transition is not only possible, but also desirable; it would provide a more stable—that is, less war-prone—international environment. In designing a new collective security structure for Europe, we draw on the nineteenth-century Concert of Europe. The Concert kept the peace for forty years in the absence of bipolarity and nuclear weapons, the two factors that conventional wisdom credits with preserving stability since 1945.[3] We propose that a new concert-based collective security

---

2. See Malcolm Chalmers, "Beyond the Alliance System: The Case for a European Security Organization," *World Policy Journal*, Vol. 7, No. 2 (Spring 1990), pp. 215–250; Gregory Flynn and David Scheffer, "Limited Collective Security," *Foreign Policy*, No. 80 (Fall 1990), pp. 77–101; James Goodby, "A New European Concert: Settling Disputes in CSCE," *Arms Control Today*, Vol. 21, No. 1 (January/February 1991), pp. 3–6; Clifford Kupchan and Charles Kupchan, "After NATO: Concert of Europe" (Op-Ed), *New York Times*, July 6, 1990; Harald Mueller, "A United Nations of Europe and North America," *Arms Control Today*, Vol. 21, No. 1 (January/February 1991), pp. 3–8; John Mueller, "A New Concert of Europe," *Foreign Policy*, No. 77 (Winter 1989–90), pp. 3–16; Alice Rivlin, David Jones, and Edward Myer, "Beyond Alliances: Global Security Through Focused Partnerships," October 2, 1990, available from the Brookings Institution, Washington, D.C.; Jack Snyder, "Averting Anarchy in the New Europe," *International Security*, Vol. 14, No. 4 (Spring 1990), pp. 5–41; Richard Ullman, "Enlarging the Zone of Peace," *Foreign Policy*, No. 80 (Fall 1990), pp. 102–120; and Van Evera, "Primed for Peace."
3. See Kenneth Waltz, *Theory of International Politics* (Reading, Mass.: Addison-Wesley, 1979); John Lewis Gaddis, "The Long Peace: Elements of Stability in the Postwar International System," *International Security*, Vol. 10, No. 4 (Spring 1986), pp. 99–142; and Mearsheimer, "Back to the Future," pp. 6–7. For arguments challenging the notion that bipolarity is more stable than multipolarity, see Van Evera, "Primed for Peace," pp. 33–40.

organization for Europe be erected. Concert-based collective security relies on a small group of major powers to guide the operation of a region-wide security structure. This design reflects power realities—an essential condition for a workable structure—while capturing the advantages offered by collective security.

We present our design for a new European security order in the following manner. The first section makes the argument that collective security provides an alternative to the Realist, Hobbesian view of international relations in which self-help and the competitive pursuit of power are the only means through which nation-states can cope with an anarchic and conflict-prone system. We then define collective security, discuss the different types of structures that fall within the collective security family, and identify the conditions that allow such structures to take shape and preserve peace. Next, we explain why collective security is desirable, and how it would promote stability. We argue that adequate and timely balancing against aggressors is more likely to emerge under collective security than in a world in which each state is left to fend for itself; balancing under collective security more effectively deters and resists aggression than balancing under anarchy. Collective security also enhances stability by institutionalizing, and thereby promoting, cooperative behavior, and by ameliorating the security dilemma. In the section that follows, we argue that a concert-based structure provides the most practicable and effective form of collective security under current international conditions. We show that a concert is attainable today by demonstrating that the underlying features of the nineteenth-century international system that gave rise to the Concert of Europe are once again present. Moreover, we contend that the current international setting is even more suited than that of 1815 to a concert-based security structure. The concluding section describes how a new concert of Europe would work today. We argue that the Conference on Security and Cooperation in Europe (CSCE) should be recast to function as a concert-based collective security organization. A security group of Europe's major powers would guide the operation of a pan-European security structure. We spell out the essential architecture of such a system and point to new mechanisms that could be introduced to enhance the ability of a collective security organization to preserve peace in Europe.

Defining Collective Security

Realism has deeply influenced both the study and practice of international relations during the postwar era. Realism provides a stark vision of an anarchic, competitive international system in which states, in order to ensure survival, must be preoccupied with augmenting their economic and military power.[4] Cooperation is very difficult to achieve and sustain because states do not trust each other and because a competitive setting makes them concerned with relative as opposed to absolute gains.[5] States therefore rely on their own resources to provide security, unless forced to do otherwise. When unable to marshal sufficient resources to resist an external threat, states seek alliances to aggregate military capability. According to Realists, states therefore have two principal means of providing security in an anarchic setting— balancing against others through domestic mobilization (self-help) or, when necessary, balancing through the formation of temporary alliances. Even though states cannot escape from the Hobbesian world, balancing behavior, at least in theory, allows states to keep pace with each other, thereby maintaining a balance of power that deters aggression. Deterrence operates because states confront each other with relatively equal military capability.[6] Stability is thus the product of antagonism and confrontation.

In practice, however, balancing behavior in an anarchic world often fails to prevent wars. In some cases, deterrence fails because states balance belatedly or not at all; aggression meets little resistance and conquest augments the aggressor's power capabilities.[7] In other cases, states engage in excessive military preparations, setting off a spiral of reciprocal threats that may contribute to mounting hostility and quicken the onset of war.[8] Even if balancing

---

4. For classical statements of the Realist position see Hans Morgenthau, *Politics Among Nations: The Struggle for Power and Peace,* 5th ed. (New York: Knopf, 1973); Waltz, *Theory of International Politics;* and Stanley Hoffmann, *The State of War: Essays in the Theory and Practice of International Politics* (New York: Praeger, 1965). For a more recent and concise statement of the Realist vision see Mearsheimer, "Back to the Future."
5. See Joseph Grieco, "Anarchy and the Limits of Cooperation: A Realist Critique of the Newest Liberal Institutionalism," *International Organization,* Vol. 42, No. 3 (Summer 1988), pp. 485–508.
6. Many analysts of balance-of-power theory contend that balancing under anarchy, when it works properly, produces a roughly equal distribution of power. The underlying logic of this proposition is that states turn to internal mobilization and alliance formation to respond in kind to each other's actions, thereby producing a rough equilibrium of power. See, for example, Inis Claude, *Power and International Relations* (New York: Random House, 1962), p. 42.
7. The events of the 1930s represent a case in point. France, Britain, and the United States did little to stop Japan's initial bouts of aggression in the Far East or Germany's growing predominance in central Europe. French and British rearmament proceeded at a far slower pace than that of Germany. The United States remained relatively isolationist. As argued below, the absence of more timely and adequate balancing should not be blamed on the League of Nations, but was a product of political and economic conditions in France, Britain, and the United States.
8. Prior to World War I, the Anglo-German naval race and the competition for ground superiority between the Triple Alliance and the Triple Entente pushed the two blocs toward war. For a general discussion of spirals and deterrence failures see Robert Jervis, *Perception and Misperception in International Politics* (Princeton, N.J.: Princeton University Press, 1976), pp. 58–113.

works in accordance with the Realist vision, it tends to produce relatively equal balances, which lack the deterrent effect and the robust defensive capability of preponderant opposing force.[9]

Students of international politics have long pointed to two ways of mitigating the anarchy, competitiveness, and war-proneness of the Hobbesian world: world government and collective security. World government involves centralized management of international politics. States devolve control over their foreign policy to a central authority. Because it compromises national sovereignty, however, world government enjoys few proponents.[10]

Collective security rests on the notion of all against one. While states retain considerable autonomy over the conduct of their foreign policy, participation in a collective security organization entails a commitment by each member to join a coalition to confront any aggressor with opposing preponderant strength. The underlying logic of collective security is two-fold. First, the balancing mechanisms that operate under collective security should prevent war and stop aggression far more effectively than the balancing mechanisms that operate in an anarchic setting: At least in theory, collective security makes for more robust deterrence by ensuring that aggressors will be met with an opposing coalition that has preponderant rather than merely equivalent power. Second, a collective security organization, by institutionalizing the notion of all against one, contributes to the creation of an international setting in which stability emerges through cooperation rather than through competition. Because states believe that they will be met with overwhelming force if they aggress, and because they believe that other states will cooperate with them in resisting aggression, collective security mitigates the rivalry and hostility of a self-help world.[11]

---

9. Prior to the outbreak of hostilities in World War I, the Germans believed that the military balance between the Triple Alliance and the Triple Entente was roughly equal. The Germans believed they had a chance of attaining victory, but were by no means confident that they would prevail. Had the Germans faced an opposing force of overwhelming capability, they might well have been deterred. On German assessments of the balance, see Volker Berghahn, *Germany and the Approach of War in 1914* (New York: St. Martin's Press, 1973), pp. 167, 173; Fritz Fischer, *World Power or Decline: The Controversy over Germany's Aims in the First World War*, trans. Lancelot Farrar, et al. (New York: W.W. Norton, 1974), p. 26; Jack Snyder, *The Ideology of the Offensive: Military Decision Making and the Disasters of 1914* (Ithaca: Cornell University Press, 1984), pp. 112, 115, 148.

10. Works on world government include Grenville Clark and Louis Sohn, *World Peace through World Law*, 2nd ed. (Cambridge: Harvard University Press, 1960); Robert Hutchins, et al., *Preliminary Draft of a World Constitution* (Chicago: University of Chicago Press, 1947); and Wesley Wooley, *Alternatives to Anarchy: American Supranationalism since World War II* (Bloomington: Indiana University Press, 1988).

11. A considerable body of literature exists on collective security, much of it written during the

Collective security organizations can take many different institutional forms along a continuum ranging from ideal collective security to concerts.[12] These organizations vary as to number of members, geographic scope, and the nature of the commitment to collective action. What Inis Claude calls ideal collective security entails participation of all states of the world, covers all regions of the world, and involves a legally binding and codified commitment on the part of all members to respond to aggression whenever and wherever it might occur:

The scheme is collective in the fullest sense; it purports to provide security *for* all states, *by* the action of all states, *against* all states which might challenge the existing order by the arbitrary unleashing of their power. . . . Ideal collective security . . . offer[s] the certainty, backed by legal obligation, that any aggressor would be confronted with collective sanctions.[13]

---

first fifteen years of the post–World War II era. It falls into three broad categories. First, analysts sought to provide a historical account of the League of Nations and the United Nations. Research focused both on the formation of these bodies and on how they dealt—or failed to deal—with international aggression. See Richard Current, "The United States and Collective Security— Notes on the History of an Idea," in Alexander DeConde, ed., *Isolation and Security* (Durham, N.C.: Duke University Press, 1957); Gilbert Murray, *From the League to the UN* (London: Oxford University Press, 1948); F.S. Northedge, *The League of Nations: Its Life and Times, 1920–1946* (New York: Holmes and Meier, 1986); Charles Webster, *The League of Nations in Theory and Practice* (Boston: Houghton Mifflin, 1933); and Roland Stromberg, *Collective Security and American Foreign Policy: From the League of Nations to NATO* (New York: Praeger, 1963). Second, scholars attempted to address some of the underlying theoretical issues concerning how collective security operates, its relationship to the notion of balance of power, and the conditions under which it can preserve peace. See E.H. Carr, *The Twenty Years' Crisis, 1919–1939* (New York: Harper and Row, 1964); Inis Claude, *Power and International Relations*; Claude, *Swords into Plowshares* (New York: Random House, 1956); Morgenthau, *Politics Among Nations*; Roland Stromberg, "The Idea of Collective Security," *Journal of the History of Ideas*, Vol. 17 (April 1956), pp. 250–263; Kenneth Thompson, "Collective Security Re-examined," *American Political Science Review*, Vol. 47, No. 3 (September 1953), pp. 753–772; Arnold Wolfers, "Collective Defense versus Collective Security," in Arnold Wolfers, ed., *Discord and Collaboration* (Baltimore: Johns Hopkins Press, 1962); and Quincy Wright, *The Study of International Relations* (New York: Appleton-Century-Crofts, 1955). Third, research focused on evaluating collective security, and determining whether it should be pursued as a means of preserving peace or abandoned as a fundamentally flawed concept. See John Herz, *International Politics in the Atomic Age* (New York: Columbia University Press, 1959); Morgenthau, *Politics Among Nations*; Robert Osgood, "Woodrow Wilson, Collective Security, and the Lessons of History," *Confluence*, Vol. 5, No. 4 (Winter 1957), pp. 341–354; and Roland Stromberg, "The Riddle of Collective Security," in George Anderson, ed., *Issues and Conflicts: Studies in 20th Century American Diplomacy* (Lawrence: University of Kansas Press, 1959), pp. 147–167. An excellent anthology containing excerpts from many of these works is Marina Finkelstein and Lawrence Finkelstein, eds., *Collective Security* (San Francisco: Chandler Publishing Co., 1966).

12. Because a concert operates on the notion of all against one and relies on collective action to resist aggression, it falls into the collective security family. Robert Jervis refers to a concert as a "nascent collective security system." Jervis, "From Balance to Concert: A Study of International Security Cooperation," *World Politics*, Vol. 38, No. 1 (October 1985), pp. 58–59, 78.

13. Claude, *Power and International Relations*, pp. 110, 168.

An ideal collective security organization assumes a very high degree of congruent interest among its members. Inter-state rivalry and power politics are effectively eliminated. Balancing behavior occurs only in response to aggression.

A concert lies at the other end of the continuum; it represents the most attenuated form of collective security. Though predicated on the notion of all against one, membership in a concert is restricted to the great powers of the day. A small group of major powers agrees to work together to resist aggression; they meet on a regular basis to monitor events and, if necessary, to orchestrate collective initiatives. A concert's geographic scope is flexible. Members can choose to focus on a specific region or regions, or to combat aggression on a global basis. Finally, a concert entails no binding or codified commitments to collective action. Rather, decisions are taken through informal negotiations, through the emergence of a consensus. The flexibility and informality of a concert allow the structure to retain an ongoing undercurrent of balancing behavior among the major powers. Though a concert is predicated upon the assumption that its members share compatible views of a stable international order, it allows for subtle jockeying and competition to take place among them. Power politics is not completely eliminated; members may turn to internal mobilization and coalition formation to pursue divergent interests. But the cooperative framework of a concert, and its members' concern about preserving peace, prevent such balancing from escalating to overt hostility and conflict.

THE LEAGUE OF NATIONS, THE UNITED NATIONS, AND THE CONCERT OF EUROPE
In theory, the family of collective security organizations runs from those that are universal in membership, global in scope, and legally binding in terms of commitment to collective action, to those that are limited in membership, regional in scope, and non-binding as to the nature of commitments to collection action. In practice, however, none of the organizations that have been erected to date meet the requirements of ideal collective security. The League of Nations and the United Nations came closest, but both fell far short.

The League, formally established in 1920 when the Versailles Treaty came into force, was meant to include all countries and to resist aggression in all parts of the globe.[14] While all members participated in the General Assembly,

---

14. Thirty-two Allied and Associated powers attended the meeting convened to set up the

the League Council—an inner body that was to consist of five permanent members (the United States, Britain, France, Japan, and Italy) and four smaller powers serving on a rotating basis—was established to guide the operation of the organization.[15] Article 16 of the League Covenant stipulated that a state engaging in aggression "shall *ipso facto* be deemed to have committed an act of war against all other Members of the League."[16] Members would then automatically impose collective economic and diplomatic sanctions. The League Covenant was far more ambiguous on the question of joint military action. Article 10 did not bind members to respond automatically to aggression with military force.[17] Rather, the Council was to decide when the use of force was warranted and to recommend how much military capability each member should contribute to uphold the Covenant (Article 16 [2]). The Covenant also stipulated that the Council's recommendations would be authoritative only when reached unanimously.[18] This provision effectively gave each member of the Council—whether permanent or rotating—the power to exercise a veto.[19]

The United Nations, like the League, emerged in the wake of a devastating war.[20] The UN was also to be global in terms of both its membership and its geographic scope. And the UN Charter, similarly to the League Covenant, established a General Assembly while giving the major powers—the United

League and became its original members. Thirteen neutral states were also invited to join. By 1938, the League had grown to fifty-seven members. See Northedge, *The League of Nations*, pp. 46–47, Appendix B.

15. During the 1920s, the composition of the Council was changed. Germany was given a permanent seat and the number of rotating members was increased. See Webster, *The League of Nations*, pp. 82, 87.

16. The complete text of the League Covenant, embodying amendments in force as of February 1, 1938, can be found in Northedge, *The League of Nations*, Appendix A, pp. 317–327.

17. Article 10 of the Covenant committed members to "undertake to respect and preserve as against external aggression the territorial integrity and existing political independence of all Members of the League," but left open "the means by which this obligation shall be fulfilled."

18. The unanimity rule did not apply to members who were party to the dispute that the Council was seeking to address. See Article 15 (7). Decisions within the General Assembly, for the most part, also required unanimity, though certain issues such as membership and procedure required only a simple or a two-thirds majority. See Northedge, *The League of Nations*, p. 53.

19. Despite the fact that all Council members had this veto power, there was an implicit understanding—at least in the United States—that participation in the League involved a tacit, moral commitment to meet aggression with collective force. This view was fostered by President Wilson's own interpretation of the Covenant. See Stromberg, *Collective Security and American Foreign Policy*, p. 28; and Claude, *Power and International Relations*, pp. 173–174. The League suffered an early setback when the United States Congress refused to approve U.S. participation in the organization, in large part because of concern about entering into an obligation to engage in collective action.

20. The UN was founded in 1945 with fifty-one original members.

States, Great Britain, France, the Soviet Union, and China—considerable control over the body by making them permanent members of the Security Council, the inner body which was to guide the operation of the UN. Unlike the League Covenant, the UN Charter did not provide for automatic economic and diplomatic sanctions in response to aggression. The Charter did, however, go further than the League Covenant in establishing a mechanism through which collective military action would take place. Article 42 granted the Security Council the power to decide if and when a military response to aggressive action was warranted. Article 43 obligated member states "to make available to the Security Council, on its call and in accordance with a special agreement or agreements, armed forces, assistance, and facilities . . . necessary for the purpose of maintaining international peace and security."[21] At the same time, the Charter also granted veto power to the permanent members of the Security Council. The veto ensured that the UN's provisions for collective action could not be directed against any of the major powers, and they prevented the UN from being able to address the most serious threats to peace, disputes between the great powers.[22]

Like the League and the UN, the Concert of Europe emerged from the midst of a postwar settlement.[23] The Concert was established by Great Brit-

---

21. Efforts to negotiate agreements as to the size and nature of the contingent that each member was to keep ready and to contribute to collective action failed to produce concrete results. In this sense, Article 43 did not constitute a legally binding commitment on behalf of members to engage in collective action when requested to do so by the Security Council. See Mumullah Venkat Rao Naidu, *Collective Security and the United Nations: A Definition of the UN Security System* (New York: St. Martin's Press, 1974), p. 36. For a text of the UN Charter see Claude, *Swords into Plowshares,* pp. 463–489.

22. The UN veto provision is even more constraining than the League's unanimity rule in that all permanent members of the Security Council retain veto power regardless of whether they are party to the dispute under consideration. See Claude, *Power and International Relations,* pp. 159–165; and Naidu, *Collective Security and the United Nations,* pp. 36–41.

23. Historians differ as to the period during which the Concert operated. The Concert is commonly dated from the Congress of Vienna (1815) to the Crimean War (1854), though the Concert did exist in name until 1914. Historians also differ as to whether the 1815–54 period should be characterized as a concert or as an example of balancing under anarchy. Edward Gulick, for example, views this period as a classic example of power balancing under multipolarity. See Edward Gulick, *Europe's Classic Balance of Power* (Ithaca: Cornell University Press, 1955). Many historians and almost all political scientists, however, view the years from 1815–54 as one during which a concert clearly operated. See, for example, Paul Schroeder, "The 19th-Century International System: Changes in the Structure," *World Politics,* Vol. 39, No. 1 (October 1986), pp. 1–26; Richard Elrod, "The Concert of Europe: A Fresh Look at an International System," *World Politics,* Vol. 28, No. 2 (January 1976), pp. 159–174; Robert Jervis, "Security Regimes," *International Organization,* Vol. 36, No. 2 (Spring 1982), pp. 173–194; Robert Jervis, "From Balance to Concert"; Paul Gordon Lauren, "Crisis Prevention in Nineteenth-Century Diplomacy," in Alexander George, ed., *Managing U.S.-Soviet Rivalry: Problems of Crisis Prevention*

ain, Prussia, Russia, and Austria at the close of the Napoleonic Wars (1815). France was admitted in 1818. In contrast to the League and the UN, membership in the Concert of Europe was restricted to Europe's major powers. Nor was the Concert intended to be global in its geographic scope. Members focused on regulating relations among each other and preserving peace in Europe; they dealt with disputes in other areas only when colonial conflicts threatened to spill over into Europe. The Concert was predicated upon an understanding that each of the five powers would honor the territorial settlement reached at the Congress of Vienna in 1815. Members agreed to defend the territorial status quo, or to allow change only when they reached a consensus to do so. Collective action emerged through informal negotiations, not through formal mechanisms of the type spelled out in the League Covenant or UN Charter. Decisions were reached through consensus; there was no unanimity rule or veto. Furthermore, mechanisms for implementing collective action were left unstipulated. A British memo of 1818 captured the informality and flexibility of the understanding reached by the powers:

There is no doubt that a breach of the covenant [of the territorial system of Europe] by any one State is an injury which all the other States may, if they shall think fit, either separately or collectively resent, but the treaties do not impose, by express stipulation, the doing so as matter of positive obligation. . . . The execution of this duty [of enforcement] seems to have been deliberately left to arise out of the circumstances of the time and of the case, and the offending State to be brought to reason by such of the injured States as might at the moment think fit to charge themselves with the task of defending their own rights thus invaded.[24]

Despite or, as we will argue, *because* of its informality, the Concert of Europe was able to preserve peace in Europe for almost four decades. The Concert's impressive record is one reason why we base our model for a new collective security organization in Europe on the notion of a concert. But our preference for a concert-based organization also rests on the similarities between the

(Boulder: Westview Press, 1983), pp. 31–64; Stephen Garrett, "Nixonian Foreign Policy: A New Balance of Power—or a Revived Concert?" *Polity*, Vol. 8, No. 3 (Spring 1976), pp. 389–421. For diplomatic histories of the period see Carsten Holbraad, *The Concert of Europe: A Study in German and British International Theory, 1815–1914* (New York: Barnes and Noble, 1970), pp. 2–4; W.N. Medlicott, *Bismarck, Gladstone, and the Concert of Europe* (New York: Greenwood Press, 1969); Charles Webster, *The Foreign Policy of Castlereagh, 1812–1822* (London: G. Bell, 1963); Paul Schroeder, *Metternich's Diplomacy at Its Zenith* (New York: Greenwood Press, 1968); Alan Sked, ed., *Europe's Balance of Power, 1815–1848* (London: Macmillan, 1979).
24. British Memorandum submitted at the Conference of Aix-la-Chapelle, October 1818, cited in René Albrecht-Carrié, *The Concert of Europe* (New York: Walker, 1968), p. 37.

international conditions that gave rise to the nineteenth-century Concert and today's international setting, and on several deductive arguments about how concerts capture the peace-causing effects of collective security. Before making our case for a concert, then, we first examine the conditions that allow collective security to function, and analyze why collective security is preferable to balancing under anarchy.

THE PRECONDITIONS OF COLLECTIVE SECURITY

Three conditions must be present if a collective security organization is to take shape and function effectively.[25] One of these is a structural condition; it has to do with the international distribution of power. The other two are ideational; they have to do with the content of elite beliefs about the international environment. The first condition is that no single state can be so powerful that even the most robust opposing coalition would be unable to marshal preponderant force against it. Put differently, all states in the system must be vulnerable to collective sanctions.[26]

The second condition is that the major powers of the day must have fundamentally compatible views of what constitutes a stable and acceptable international order. There can be no revisionist power, no state intent on overturning the international order for either ideological or power-related reasons. Whether they refer to "a status quo . . . on which the nations with predominant strength agree," or to "a firm nucleus of great power agreement," virtually all students of collective security recognize that it can work only when the major powers share similar visions of international order.[27]

The third condition is that the major powers must "enjoy a minimum of political solidarity and moral community."[28] More specifically, elites must share an awareness of an international community, the preservation of which furthers long-term national interests. It is not sufficient for the major powers simply to share compatible views of a desirable international order; they must also believe that efforts to protect and promote political solidarity are needed to bring this vision of order to fruition. In this sense, national self-

---

25. These conditions are concisely enumerated by Kenneth Thompson in "Collective Security Reexamined," pp. 758–762. Although other studies of collective security often point to other preconditions, they are generally reducible to these three.
26. See Claude, *Power and International Relations*, p. 195.
27. Thompson, "Collective Security Reexamined," p. 758; Marina Finkelstein and Lawrence Finkelstein, "The Future of Collective Security," in Finkelstein and Finkelstein, *Collective Security*, p. 255.
28. Thompson, "Collective Security Reexamined," p. 761.

interest becomes equated with, but not subjugated to, the welfare and stability of that international community. In addition, elites in one state must
believe that elites in other states share appreciation of this community. As
Robert Jervis puts it, "the actors must also believe that the others share the
value they place on mutual security and cooperation."[29] It is this minimum
level of trust that allows states to pass up opportunities for short-term gain
and to exercise restraint under the assumption that others will do the same.
In the words of Hans Morgenthau, "collective security expects the policies
of individual nations to be inspired by the ideal of mutual assistance and a
spirit of self-sacrifice."[30] Before examining whether these conditions are now
present in Europe—that is, whether collective security is feasible—we first
examine whether it is desirable.

The Advantages of Collective Security

In this section, we present three reasons why collective security provides a
more stable—that is, less war-prone—international environment than balancing under anarchy. First, collective security more effectively deters and
resists aggressor states. It does so by making more likely the formation of
an opposing coalition and by confronting aggressors with preponderant, as
opposed to roughly equal, force. Second, collective security organizations
institutionalize, and therefore promote, cooperative relations among states.[31]
Third, collective security ameliorates the security dilemma and therefore
reduces the likelihood that unintended spirals will lead to hostility and
conflict.

MORE EFFECTIVE BALANCING AGAINST AGGRESSORS
In terms of providing for effective balancing against aggressors, collective
security has two main advantages over balancing under anarchy. First, it
strengthens deterrence by reducing the uncertainties of coalition formation
associated with balancing under anarchy. Under anarchy, a state contemplating aggression would be uncertain about whether a balancing coalition

---

29. Jervis, "Security Regimes," pp. 176–178.
30. Morgenthau, *Politics Among Nations*, excerpted in Finkelstein and Finkelstein, *Collective Security*, pp. 222–223.
31. We use the terms collective security and collective security organization interchangeably. The notion of collective security becomes operational only when embodied in formal agreements, conferences, or other institutional mechanisms.

will take shape and about the military strength of that coalition. Collective security both increases the likelihood that a balancing coalition will form and confronts aggressors with the prospect of preponderant, rather than roughly equal, opposing force. Preponderance provides a more robust deterrent than equality and eliminates the possibility that war might result from an aggressor's misperception of the strength of the opposing coalition. Collective security by no means guarantees that a robust opposing coalition will take shape. But it does make it more likely that states will join a balancing coalition by establishing pre-existing commitments to do so. *Ceteris paribus*, a state is more likely to join an opposing coalition if it has made a commitment to do so than if no such commitment exists; states have at least some incentives to fulfill international obligations.[32] Even if the currency of international obligation fails to elicit participation, collective security would still produce a more robust opposing coalition than balancing under anarchy. Under anarchy, only those states directly threatened by the aggressor and states with vital interests in the threatened areas will band together to resist aggression. Under collective security, because states have clear interests in protecting an international order that they see as beneficial to their individual security, they will contribute to the coalition even if they have no vital interests at stake in the actual theater of aggression. As we discuss below, collective security also leads to the formation of a preponderant coalition by providing mechanisms which facilitate and reduce the transaction costs involved in collective action. By increasing both the likelihood that a balancing coalition will emerge and the likelihood that this coalition will possess preponderant military strength, collective security more effectively deters and resists aggression than balancing under anarchy.

Second, collective security facilitates identification of aggressor states. As we argue below, collective security organizations enhance transparency and encourage states to maintain relatively low levels of military—especially offensive—capability. Because of these features, it would be very difficult for a state to develop robust offensive capability without being detected.[33] Fur-

---

32. These incentives stem from two sources. First, a state may face direct economic or diplomatic sanctions for failing to fulfill its commitment to collective security. Second, a state's reputation for cooperation could be damaged, impairing its future relations with other states on a wide range of issues. For further discussion of reputational considerations, see Robert Keohane, *After Hegemony: Cooperation and Discord in the World Political Economy* (Princeton, N.J.: Princeton University Press, 1984), p. 105.

33. This discussion focuses on major aggressor states—powers with sufficient military capability

thermore, a significant military buildup would automatically be interpreted as a sign of aggressive intent, triggering a response. Identification of an aggressor would be more difficult in an anarchic setting: a military buildup undertaken to prepare for war might be interpreted by other powers as an unexceptional manifestation of arms racing and rivalry.[34] An inadequate response could result.[35] Easier identification of aggressor states makes for more timely and effective deterrence.

Critics offer two main rebuttals to the claim that collective security can provide effective deterrence against aggressors. First, they assert that nuclear weapons undermine collective security's deterrent effect because they make it impossible to marshal preponderant force against a nuclear-capable aggressor.[36] Indeed, nuclear weapons would alter the calculus of both the coalition powers defending the status quo and the aggressor state; both would be more reluctant to use force. But deterrence under collective security in a nuclear world would operate much more strongly than in a non-nuclear world. The logic of all against one would mean that an aggressor would face an opposing coalition not only of preponderant conventional force but also of preponderant nuclear capability. Nuclear weapons could embolden an aggressor in its efforts to play a game of brinkmanship; its bargaining stance would be stronger than if it did not have nuclear weapons. But an aggressor

---

to engage in significant and sustained offensive operations. We are not concerned with narrower questions, e.g., identifying which party is responsible for firing the first shot.

34. Britain's reaction to Germany's burgeoning naval program at the turn of the century is a case in point. With the First Naval Law of 1898, Germany embarked on an ambitious program to build a battleship fleet. Although the British Admiralty indeed took note of these developments in calculating naval requirements, it was not until 1904–05 that British war plans began to be reoriented to focus on the possibility of a conflict with Germany. In a collective security setting, a naval program of the size embarked upon by Germany might well have triggered far earlier a reorientation of British war plans. See Paul Kennedy, *The Rise of the Anglo-German Antagonism, 1860–1914* (London: Allen and Unwin, 1982), pp. 251–288; and Paul Kennedy, *The Rise and Fall of British Naval Mastery* (London: Macmillan, 1983), pp. 205–237.

35. Although identification of an aggressor would be easier under collective security, the initial response might be slower than under balancing under anarchy. As argued below, one of the ways in which collective security ameliorates the security dilemma is by encouraging states to tolerate initial acts of defection. In the presence of an emerging aggressor, such tolerance could prove costly: it might lead to a time lag between initial identification of aggressive behavior and an effective response. The wariness associated with balancing under anarchy would, *ceteris paribus*, reduce this lag. However, given high levels of transparency and low initial levels of offensive capability, the lag associated with collective security is not likely to be consequential. Aggressors would enjoy only a quite limited head-start. On the question of time lags and identification of aggressors, see Wolfers, "Collective Defense versus Collective Security," pp. 184, 188 (reprinted in Finkelstein and Finkelstein, *Collective Security*, pp. 128–140).

36. See, for example, Herz, *International Politics in the Atomic Age*, excerpted in Finkelstein and Finkelstein, *Collective Security*, p. 251.

in a nuclear world would be less likely to follow through with military attack than in a non-nuclear world because it would face not only conventional defeat, but also nuclear devastation. Far from undermining deterrence based on preponderant force, nuclear weapons, by raising the potential costs of aggression, should enhance the stabilizing effects of collective security.

The second argument that critics use to challenge collective security's ability to provide robust deterrence stems from the tarnished histories of the League of Nations and the United Nations. The League's failure to respond to successive bouts of aggression during the 1930s, and the UN's marginal significance during the postwar era, it is argued, provide adequate proof that collective security organizations are unable to prevent or even to respond adequately to aggression.[37]

This line of argument is unfounded; the League and the UN might have failed to preserve peace, but the historical record suggests that military, economic, and political conditions at the national level, not collective security itself, were the root of the problem. Without question, the League of Nations failed to organize an effective response to repeated Japanese and German violations of international treaty commitments. It is unjustified, however, to blame the absence of a more timely response on the League or on collective security more generally. The core of the problem was the unwillingness of the major powers to act decisively, not the existence of the League itself.[38] Particular, historically-contingent circumstances—American isolationism, economic and military weakness in Britain and France, British revulsion against involvement in another continental war—were key in delaying a more timely and activist response.[39] It is hard to imagine that had the League not existed, these powers would have been any more inclined to take preemptive

---

37. See, for example, Raymond Aron's comments on the experiences of the United Nations in "Limits to the Powers of the United Nations," *Annals of the American Academy of Political and Social Sciences*, Vol. 296 (November 1954), pp. 20–26 (reprinted in Finkelstein and Finkelstein, *Collective Security*, pp. 239–241).

38. We do admit that the League may have fostered free riding. The mere existence of the League, by enabling the British and French to delude themselves into believing that others would provide for their security, may have contributed to the absence of a more timely and effective response to German and Japanese aggression. This dynamic, however, certainly played a minor role in inhibiting a more appropriate response to rising threats.

39. On the causes of the failure of Britain and France to respond in a more timely fashion see R.P. Shay, *British Rearmament in the 1930s* (Princeton, N.J.: Princeton University Press, 1977); Michael Howard, *The Continental Commitment* (London: Temple Smith, 1972); and Jean Doise and Maurice Vaïsse, *Diplomatie et Outil Militaire, 1871–1969* (Paris: Imprimerie Nationale, 1987).

action against either Japan or Germany. As Roland Stromberg has argued, the failure of the status quo powers to preserve peace during the 1930s "can be explained wholly without reference to the League. . . . The lamentable weakness of the powers opposed to Germany and Japan is of course the key to the period, but it has nothing to do with an abstraction called collective security."[40]

As far as the United Nations is concerned, the core of the problem was that U.S.-Soviet wartime cooperation almost immediately gave way to peacetime discord. The United Nations was formed under the assumption that the two countries emerging from World War II with predominant military capabilities could cooperate in forging a postwar order.[41] But even as the UN was coming into being, the United States and the Soviet Union were pursuing conflicting goals, making collective security untenable. The Cold War era does not represent a legitimate test of collective security because one of the key preconditions was missing: American and Soviet visions of an acceptable international order were simply incompatible.[42] Commitments to collective security were repeatedly challenged—and superseded—by the rivalry and hostility associated with the Cold War.[43] The histories of the League and the UN demonstrate only that collective security does not always work, not that it cannot work.

In addition, the history of the Concert of Europe demonstrates that timely and adequate balancing can in fact occur under collective security. As we illustrate below, Concert members repeatedly resorted to joint diplomatic initiatives, military threats and military action to preserve peace in Europe. The historical record thus tells us that it would be unwarranted to dismiss collective security on the claim that it cannot provide adequate balancing against aggression. We have no reason to doubt the deductive case for the claim that balancing under collective security more effectively deters and stops aggression than balancing under anarchy.

---

40. Stromberg, "The Idea of Collective Security," excerpted in Finkelstein and Finkelstein, *Collective Security*, pp. 233–234.
41. On the views of the Roosevelt administration toward the UN and cooperation with the Soviet Union, see Daniel Yergin, *Shattered Peace: The Origins of the Cold War and the National Security State* (Boston: Houghton Mifflin, 1977), pp. 47–48; and John Lewis Gaddis, *The United States and the Origins of the Cold War, 1941–1947* (New York: Columbia University Press, 1972), pp. 28–31.
42. Inis Claude, "The UN and the Use of Force," *International Conciliation*, No. 532 (March 1961), pp. 325–384 (reprinted in Finkelstein and Finkelstein, *Collective Security*, p. 100).
43. See Wolfers, "Collective Defense versus Collective Security."

INSTITUTIONALIZING AND PROMOTING COOPERATION

A popular criticism of collective security is that it works only when it is not needed. If the conditions for collective security—great power compatibility, a shared sense of international community—are present, critics charge, then a security structure is not needed to preserve peace.[44] Our second argument about the advantages of collective security directly challenges this criticism. We claim that a collective security organization can strengthen and deepen the foundation of cooperative behavior that makes collective security feasible to begin with. We base this claim on the neo-liberal assertion that regimes promote cooperation. Regimes are "sets of implicit or explicit principles, norms, rules, and decision-making procedures around which actors' expectations converge in a given area of international relations."[45] Institutions and organizations are formalized regimes, usually embodied in more explicit and rigorous rules and decision-making procedures. If the neo-liberal argument holds, then a collective security organization, by building on and promoting the political compatibility that makes such an institution possible, may perpetuate and make more durable a peaceful and desirable international setting. As Robert Keohane notes, regimes arise from, but also produce, cooperation: "Although regimes themselves depend on conditions that are conducive to interstate agreements, they may also facilitate further efforts to coordinate policies."[46]

Realists challenge the notion that institutions markedly increase the likelihood of inter-state cooperation. Under anarchy, they claim, "international institutions affect the prospects for cooperation only marginally."[47] The difficulties involved in obtaining security in a self-help environment tend to override the potential cooperation-inducing effects of international institutions. As Joseph Grieco has convincingly argued, because states are fearful that others will exploit their cooperative behavior, and because they are concerned primarily with relative as opposed to absolute gains, cooperation under anarchy is difficult to achieve even in the presence of robust institutions.[48]

---

44. See, for example, Stromberg, "The Riddle of Collective Security," pp. 165–167.
45. See Stephen Krasner, *International Regimes* (Ithaca, N.Y.: Cornell University Press, 1983), p. 2.
46. Keohane, *After Hegemony*, p. 57.
47. Grieco, "Anarchy and the Limits of Cooperation," p. 488.
48. Ibid., pp. 485–507.

While the Realist critique of regime theory indeed has some validity, its claims weaken markedly as anarchy is mitigated. We contend that the ability of institutions to promote cooperation increases substantially as consensual beliefs among the major powers dampen the rivalries and insecurities of a Hobbesian setting. When inter-state cooperation has already begun to emerge because of shifts in elite beliefs, and the Realist assumptions of a competitive, self-help world are thus relaxed, a fertile ground exists for institutions to play a much more prominent role in shaping state behavior. States are less concerned about being exploited. They are more free to pursue absolute as opposed to relative gains.[49] Under these conditions, neo-liberal arguments about the cooperation-inducing effects of institutions become all the more compelling.

In general terms, institutions promote cooperation by clarifying and operationalizing a set of norms, rules, principles, and procedures that guide state behavior and allow for increased coordination of policy. Rules and procedures create a road-map; they define a range of behavior associated with the notion of cooperation and provide states with a set of instructions for preserving a cooperative setting. Institutions also alter a state's expectations about how other states will behave in the future and about how its own behavior will affect the future behavior of other states. States become more willing to cooperate because they assume others will do the same.[50]

In more specific terms, institutions can promote and deepen cooperation through several discrete mechanisms. First, they increase the level of information available to all parties. Even if states have compatible interests, peace may not be stable under anarchy because of the difficulties and costs involved in gathering complete information.[51] Incomplete and asymmetrical information increases uncertainty about the intentions and capabilities of other states, thus heightening fear of exploitation. A collective security organization could disseminate information on force levels and force postures to reassure mem-

---

49. We admit that uncertainty about the future will always make states somewhat concerned about gaps in payoffs that affect their relative position in the international system. But, as Grieco notes, sensitivity to these gaps declines as inter-state relations become more cooperative. See ibid., p. 501.
50. Robert Axelrod and Robert Keohane, "Achieving Cooperation Under Anarchy: Strategies and Institutions," *World Politics*, Vol. 38, No. 1 (October 1985), p. 234; and Krasner, *International Regimes*.
51. For discussion of how uncertainty and incomplete information affect cooperation, see Keohane, *After Hegemony*, pp. 92–97, 100–103.

bers that no party is preparing to engage in aggressive action. Similarly, institutions increase the effectiveness and lower the costs of monitoring and verifying inter-state agreements. In short, institutionalization increases transparency—the sharing of information—and in so doing promotes cooperation.

Second, institutions increase the costs of defection—and help define what constitutes defection—by formalizing punishment regimes and making them more effective.[52] By creating mechanisms for punishing defectors, institutions increase the likelihood that states will incur considerable costs if they pursue non-cooperative behavior. As a result, states contemplating defection will be more likely to be dissuaded from doing so, and states defending the status quo will be less fearful of exploitation and thus more willing to pursue cooperative strategies.[53] An institution would thus enhance collective security's deterrent effect and reinforce its ability to encourage states to practice restraint and self-sacrifice.

Third, institutions can promote cooperation by increasing the likelihood that issue-linkage will lead to international agreements. Institutions bring many different issues into one negotiating forum. Even if states disagree on a specific issue, they may be able to resolve the dispute through reciprocal concessions: one side gives ground on the issue under consideration in return for concessions on some other issue. Institutions also facilitate such arrangements by reducing the transaction costs associated with the negotiation of international agreements. As Robert Keohane puts it, "insofar as their [regimes'] principles and rules can be applied to a wide variety of particular issues, they are efficient: establishing the rules and principles at the outset makes it unnecessary to renegotiate them each time a specific question arises."[54]

Fourth, institutions hold the potential to promote inter-state socialization, to transform a "minimum of political solidarity" into an international community in which states share similar values and normative orientations.[55] Regular meetings and conferences allow ideas and values to cross national boundaries and circulate among different communities of elites. Similarity of

---

52. Defection can take two forms under collective security. First, states might engage in acts of aggression. Second, states might renege on their commitment to resist aggression through collective action. A formalized punishment regime increases the costs of both types of defection.
53. In Keohane's words, "regimes make it more sensible to cooperate by lowering the likelihood of being double-crossed"; *After Hegemony*, p. 97.
54. See Keohane, *After Hegemony*, pp. 90–91; see also pp. 89–92.
55. See G. John Ikenberry and Charles Kupchan, "Socialization and Hegemonic Power," *International Organization*, Vol. 44, No. 3 (Summer 1990), pp. 283–316.

values is conducive to compatible policy preferences.[56] In the early post–World War II years, the network of institutions erected to coordinate policies within the Western alliance played an important role in spreading among the allies the norms associated with liberal multilateralism. The spread of these norms in turn facilitated coordination of national policies.[57] Institutions operating under conditions of mitigated anarchy can thus promote cooperation by deepening the normative and ideational basis of an international community of nations.

These four mechanisms through which institutions promote cooperation counter the charge that a collective security organization is not needed if the conditions that make it possible are present. On the contrary, a peaceful international setting only increases the role that institutions can play in shaping state behavior. Taking concrete steps to perpetuate a peaceful international environment makes far more sense than simply hoping that such an environment will persist of its own accord.

AMELIORATING THE SECURITY DILEMMA

The third major advantage of collective security over balancing under anarchy is its ability to ameliorate the security dilemma. The security dilemma refers to the notion that a state's efforts to increase its security, by threatening another state which then responds with steps to increase its own security, paradoxically erodes the first state's security.[58] The two states, without intending to do so, thus find themselves in a spiral of mounting hostility and arms buildup. The intensity with which the security dilemma operates depends upon a number of conditions: the degree of trust between states, the extent to which uncertainty and incomplete information produce misperception of intentions, whether offensive or defensive forces would have the advantage, and whether states can distinguish between others' offensive and

---

56. There are two related arguments within the literature as to how the dissemination of ideas and beliefs promotes international cooperation. One tradition holds that institutions spread certain beliefs and normative ideals that guide states toward the pursuit of common goals. See, for example, John Ruggie, "International Regimes, Transaction, and Change: Embedded Liberalism in the Postwar Economic Order," in Krasner, *International Regimes*, pp. 193–231. The other tradition suggests that institutions spread "consensual knowledge," which facilitates cooperation. See, for example, Ernst Haas, "Why Collaborate? Issue-Linkage and International Regimes," *World Politics*, Vol. 32, No. 3 (April 1980), pp. 357–405.
57. Ikenberry and Kupchan, "Socialization and Hegemonic Power," pp. 299–303.
58. See Robert Jervis, "Cooperation Under the Security Dilemma," *World Politics*, Vol. 30, No. 2 (January 1978), pp. 167–214.

defensive armaments.[59] The operation of the security dilemma is one of the key reasons that peace under anarchy may not be stable. Even if no states have explicitly aggressive intentions, anarchy fuels the security dilemma and can produce spirals that lead to growing hostility and, ultimately, to conflict.

As Jervis notes, it is impossible to eliminate the security dilemma, but it can be ameliorated: "The ideal solution for a status quo power would be to escape from the state of nature. But escape is impossible. The security dilemma cannot be abolished, it can only be ameliorated. Bonds of shared values and interests can be developed. If actors care about what happens to others and believe that others care about them, they will develop trust and can cooperate for mutual benefit."[60] The conditions that make collective security possible indeed ameliorate the security dilemma to a certain extent. When the major powers hold compatible views of an acceptable international order and share a minimum sense of political community, ideational change has already mitigated the suspicion and competitiveness that fuel the security dilemma. But capitalizing on the presence of these conditions to create a collective security organization is to take further important steps to dampen the sources of unintended spirals.

Collective security ameliorates the security dilemma in four important ways. First, a collective security organization, through the mechanisms outlined in the previous section, promotes and deepens cooperation. Over time, repeated acts of cooperation alter expectations and foster trust and confidence. As states come to expect each other to reciprocate concessions, rather than to exploit them, the wariness that fuels the security dilemma gradually subsides. Fear of exploitation gives way to increasing willingness to practice self-restraint and mutual assistance. Furthermore, an institution promotes the dissemination of values and normative orientations. Collective security thus helps as Jervis writes, to build the "bonds of shared values and interests" that play a key role in ameliorating the security dilemma.

Second, collective security ameliorates the security dilemma by dampening concern about demonstrating resolve. One of the sources of instability associated with balancing under anarchy stems from the tendency of states to seek to strengthen deterrence by engaging in actions intended primarily to bolster a reputation for resolve. Deterrence under anarchy is weakened by a

---

59. Jervis, "Cooperation Under the Security Dilemma"; and Jervis, *Perception and Misperception in International Politics*, pp. 58–113.
60. Jervis, *Perception and Misperception*, pp. 82–83.

potential aggressor's uncertainty about the likelihood of coalition formation. States, even if not faced with imminent threats, therefore have incentives to strengthen deterrence by behaving in ways that demonstrate to potential adversaries that adequate balancing will take place.[61] Such behavior fuels the security dilemma. Actions which one side takes to demonstrate resolve are interpreted by the other side as aggressive acts challenging its own resolve and therefore potentially threatening its core security interests. Collective security, by reducing the uncertainties associated with balancing under anarchy, dampens the need to bolster resolve to make deterrence more credible.[62] Moreover, deterrence under collective security will be most credible when a potential aggressor believes that other states will honor the commitment to collective action and participate in the formation of a cohesive and robust opposing coalition. Given that reassurance and mutual assistance are the key instruments that foster cohesion under collective security, states worried about strengthening deterrence will seek to develop a reputation for cooperation and self-sacrifice, not intransigence.[63]

This logic suggests that, under collective security, states will less frequently engage in actions intended to bolster a reputation for resolve. In addition, even when states do engage in such actions, they are less likely to elicit a response in kind. Because status quo powers are not preoccupied with protecting their own reputations for resolve, relatively minor shifts in the military balance, in the tenor of diplomatic relations, and even in territorial boundaries are less likely to be seen as threats to core security.[64] Collective security allows states to develop a certain degree of immunity toward isolated devel-

---

61. American involvement in Third World conflicts during the Cold War was in large part motivated by a perceived need to demonstrate resolve in the periphery, lest the Soviets be encouraged by U.S. inaction to challenge core American interests. See Robert Johnson, "Exaggerating America's Stakes in Third World Conflicts," *International Security*, Vol. 10, No. 1 (Winter 1984/85), pp. 32–68; and John Lewis Gaddis, *Strategies of Containment: A Critical Appraisal of Postwar American National Security Policy* (Oxford: Oxford University Press, 1982), esp. pp. 198–273.
62. This assumes, of course, that no aggression has taken place. Collective security organizations as a unit must indeed be concerned about their own reputation for action. Failure to respond to major acts of aggression would weaken deterrence by indicating that future acts of aggression might also go unanswered.
63. As Keohane notes, states wanting to promote collective activity want to develop a reputation for keeping their commitments: "Governments will decide whom to make agreements with, and on what terms, largely on the basis of their expectations about their partners' willingness and ability to keep their commitments. A good reputation makes it easier for a government to enter into advantageous international agreements; tarnishing that reputation imposes costs by making agreements more difficult to reach." Keohane, *After Hegemony*, pp. 105–106.
64. On this point, see Jervis, *Perception and Misperception*, pp. 102–107.

opments and changes in the strategic setting that would, under anarchy, have far greater reverberations. Collective security thus ameliorates the security dilemma by making demonstrations of resolve less likely and by decreasing the chances that such demonstrations, when they occur, snowball into major confrontations.

Third, collective security, by increasing transparency and thereby reducing uncertainty and the chances of misperception, decreases the likelihood of unintended spirals. Uncertainty is one of the key factors fueling the security dilemma. When faced with incomplete information about the intentions and capabilities of others, states are forced to remain on guard, to prepare for the worst case. The difficulties involved in interpreting the behavior of others leaves much room for misperception. Uncertainty and incomplete information thus provide fertile ground for unintended spirals.[65] Collective security increases transparency and therefore reduces the likelihood of misperception. Provided with more complete information, states would also have higher confidence in their assessment of others' intentions and capabilities. Accidents and garbled communication would therefore be less likely to trigger an escalation of hostility.[66]

Fourth, collective security ameliorates the security dilemma by enabling states to adopt predominantly defensive military postures. Under collective security, states would need to maintain some level of offensive capability to make credible the threat to counter aggression through collective action. But they would not need offensive capabilities robust enough to carry out major acts of aggression.[67] States do not need robust offense because deterrence is easier under collective security. States are less worried about demonstrating resolve through projecting force to protect third parties, nor do they need to deter through the threat of offensive retaliation. Anarchy, on the other hand, tends to produce robust offensive capabilities.[68] In an anarchic setting, states believe that they need offense to deter potential adversaries through the

---

65. See Jervis, *Perception and Misperception*, pp. 67–82.
66. See Jervis, "From Balance to Concert," pp. 73–76.
67. See Chalmers, "Beyond the Alliance System," p. 240. As Chalmers notes, the offensive capability that the major powers would maintain as a matter of course would be sufficient to invade smaller states. But they would not need sufficient capability to invade each other.
68. In an anarchic setting, all states could conceivably adopt exclusively defensive military postures. If they believed that they could build impenetrable defenses, states might simply barricade themselves in to cope with a threatening and unpredictable international setting. But the competitive environment associated with an anarchic setting is, in reality, likely to produce far more robust offensive capabilities than the more cooperative setting associated with collective security.

prospect of retaliation and to bolster reputations for resolve. Settings in which forces are more offensive in nature are more war-prone than those in which forces are predominantly defensive in nature.[69] States that acquire offensive capability, even if for defensive purposes, threaten their neighbors and thereby induce spirals. The existence of offensively postured forces also creates incentives for preemption; each side wants to take advantage of its offensive orientation. Offensive doctrinal and tactical considerations serve to shorten the fuse.[70] It follows that collective security would ameliorate the security dilemma and enhance stability by reducing the level of offensive capability that states find it prudent to sustain.[71]

To summarize, the advantages of collective security over balancing under anarchy are three-fold. First, collective security more effectively deters and resists aggressor states by making more likely the formation of a balancing coalition and by confronting aggressors with the prospect of preponderant, as opposed to roughly equal, force. Second, collective security institutional-izes, and therefore promotes, cooperation. Third, collective security amelior-ates the security dilemma, thereby enhancing stability and reducing the likelihood of unintended spirals of hostility.

The Case for Concert-Based Collective Security

The preceding section showed why collective security can provide a more stable international environment than balancing under anarchy. The analysis was not meant to suggest, however, that collective security has no shortcom-ings that could jeopardize its ability to foster a peaceful international order. On the contrary, collective security, when operationalized, can fall prey to several types of problems that could impair its ability to preserve peace. We begin this section by considering some of the critical weaknesses associated with ideal collective security. We then argue that a concert-based structure

---

69. See Snyder, *The Ideology of the Offensive;* and Stephen Van Evera, "The Cult of the Offensive and the Origins of the First World War," *International Security,* Vol. 9, No. 1 (Summer 1984), pp. 58–107.
70. For a succinct review of the reasons why offense-dominance makes more war likely, see Van Evera, "Primed for Peace," pp. 11–12.
71. A collective security organization, by increasing transparency, would also make it easier to distinguish between the offensive and defensive capabilities sustained by other states. While it is sometimes impossible to determine whether a given weapon is offensive or defensive (or both) in nature, transparency can provide information on force postures, logistics, bridging equipment, and other indicators of offensive capability. Assurances that others have only mod-erate offensive capability allows states to limit their own offensive capability.

offers many of the advantages outlined above without falling prey to these weaknesses. Finally, we argue that a concert can function successfully in today's international conditions because the features of the nineteenth-century international setting that gave rise to the Concert of Europe are again present. We also show why a contemporary concert is likely to be even more durable and effective in preserving peace than the nineteenth-century Concert.

WEAKNESSES OF IDEAL COLLECTIVE SECURITY

Ideal collective security organizations are distinguished by two features: their inclusivity and the automatic, codified, and binding nature of the commitment their members make to resist collectively acts of aggression. Both features impair the successful functioning of collective security. Inclusivity is problematic because it leads to a large membership and therefore makes political cohesion more difficult to sustain. The greater the number of states in a collective security organization, the greater the probability that disagreements will emerge over what constitutes aggression and when to engage in collective action. Political cohesion would be especially difficult to maintain if the body included states that occupy radically different positions within the international hierarchy of power. Minor powers and major powers may well have differing views of what constitutes an acceptable, just status quo. Even when members reach agreement on these matters, the logistical problems involved in coordinating policies among states can hamper timely, effective action. Large organizations are also more likely to fall prey to what Mancur Olson has called the collective action problem.[72] In large groups that form to provide a collective good, each member has incentives to free-ride rather than contribute to the provision of the good in question. A collective security organization provides a public good, stopping aggression. Each state benefits from deterring or defeating an aggressor regardless of the amount of resources that it commits to the opposing coalition. Because of free-riding, an organization with many members is likely to under-produce the public good in question. The sheer size of ideal collective security organizations

---

72. See Mancur Olson, *The Logic of Collective Action* (Cambridge: Harvard University Press, 1965); Mancur Olson and Richard Zeckhauser, "An Economic Theory of Alliances," *Review of Economics and Statistics*, Vol. 48, No. 3 (August 1966), pp. 266–279; Keohane, *After Hegemony*, pp. 75–79; and Charles Kupchan, "NATO and the Persian Gulf: Examining Intra-Alliance Behavior," *International Organization*, Vol. 42, No. 2 (Spring 1988), pp. 317–346.

thus militates against political cohesion and exacerbates the collective action problem.

Automatic and binding commitments to collective action have several problematic implications. First, fear of being dragged into a war whenever and wherever aggression occurs makes it less likely that states will be willing to participate in a collective security organization. A commitment viewed as automatic and legally binding constitutes too severe a loss of national autonomy. Second, codified stipulations that bind members automatically to undertake collective action potentially open the organization to obsolescence when conflicts of members' interests emerge. If acts of aggression go unanswered or if some members opt out of collective action, the credibility of the organization is jeopardized.[73] Third, codified and binding commitments to stop aggression explicitly stipulate when collective action can and should take place, but also implicitly stipulate when it should not. Ideal collective security would delay balancing against a rising aggressor state by effectively allowing collective action to take place only after a legally defined act of aggression has occurred.[74] While an ideal collective security organization could authorize diplomatic steps to warn a potential aggressor to desist from making war preparations, preemptive military action would not be allowed. This attribute prevents states from taking timely action to stop aggression before it occurs, a serious shortcoming given that it is often less costly to prevent aggression than it is to undo it.

Codified stipulations that delay directed balancing have one final important implication. One of the drawbacks associated with all forms of collective security is that member states, because they rely on *collective* action to resist aggression, individually risk being unprepared to meet an aggressor should a balancing coalition fail to form. States maintain a lower level of preparedness than they would in a self-help environment. Ideal collective security, because it delays directed balancing, means that member states find out only after aggression has already occurred how robust the opposing coalition will

---

73. Deterrence may be undermined as potential aggressors begin to doubt the efficacy of collective security arrangements. Status quo powers may begin to defect from the organization, fearful that it will not meet their security needs. The League of Nations, for example, suffered a serious setback when it failed to block Japanese aggression in Northeast Asia in the early 1930s. According to Northedge, "the League's failure to halt Japan's annexation of Manchuria in 1931–33 and to restore to China what was hers by right was by every test a grave, almost fatal blow . . . to the League." Northedge, *The League of Nations*, p. 161.
74. In Naidu's words, "aggression has to be determined first before releasing the mechanism of sanctions." Naidu, *Collective Security and the United Nations*, p. 20.

actually be. At that point, it may be too late for threatened states to marshal the resources necessary to protect themselves. The later the test of commitments to collective action, the greater the risk that states will find themselves dangerously exposed if a collective security organization unravels.

ADVANTAGES OF A CONCERT

The design of a concert circumvents the flaws of ideal collective security. A concert's small membership facilitates timely joint decision making. A concert is open only to major powers; disagreements are less likely when fewer states interact.[75] A concert's small membership also ameliorates the collective action problem. In small groups, a few powers jointly provide the good in question because it is in their interests to do so. They behave as an oligopoly: they provide the public good while monitoring and reacting strategically to each other's behavior. As Keohane puts it, regimes "are often most useful when relatively few like-minded countries are responsible for both making the essential rules and maintaining them."[76]

Though predicated on the notion of all against one, a concert does not entail codified and automatic commitments to collective action. In addition, a concert functions through an informal decision-making process in which collective action emerges from consensus. A concert's informal decision structure and lack of codification enhance the body's flexibility and resilience. Members do not expect that all instances of aggression will necessarily elicit a collective response. In instances in which one or more states prefer not to engage in collective action, they may be able to justify their abstention and refrain from participation without alienating other members or undermining the foundation of the concert.[77] Acts of aggression can go unanswered with-

---

75. While disagreements can certainly occur in small groups, they are likely to occur less frequently than in large groups.

76. Keohane, *After Hegemony*, pp. 246, 76. For further discussion of why small groups can overcome the collective action problem, see Duncan Snidal, "The Limits of Hegemonic Stability Theory," *International Organization*, Vol. 39, No. 1 (Autumn 1985), pp. 579–614; and Kenneth Oye, "Explaining Cooperation Under Anarchy: Hypotheses and Strategies," *World Politics*, Vol. 38, No. 1 (October 1985), pp. 18–20.

77. Consider the following example from the nineteenth-century Concert. In 1820, rebels calling for political liberalization staged an uprising in Naples. King Ferdinand I responded by granting a constitution. Austria, Prussia, and Russia saw these developments as a threat to conservative regimes in Europe and called a series of conferences. Metternich urged the British to participate in suppressing the revolt, but Castlereagh declined. But, although he initially stood in Metternich's way, Castlereagh eventually came to recognize that Austria had special interests in the area and he pledged to support the actions of Austria, Prussia, and Russia "provided only that they were ready to give every reasonable assurance that their views were not directed to

out eroding the credibility of the organization. In fact, concerts play as important a role in orchestrating inaction as in coordinating collective initiatives. By serving as a forum in which the major powers can make mutual pledges of self-restraint, the body can moderate competition for influence in strategic areas and defuse or, in some cases, prevent great power intervention and conflict.[78]

A concert also retains a subtle undercurrent of competitive balancing and jockeying among its members. This attribute means that divergences of opinion and conflicts of interest not resolved through negotiation will trigger a set of balancing mechanisms, rather than paralyzing and undermining the body, as they would if a veto or unanimity rule existed. Sometimes such balancing occurs simply through applying diplomatic pressure. Other times, temporary coalitions may form. In more extreme circumstances, an offending power may even be temporarily excluded from the concert until its behavior conforms to what is considered acceptable by the other members.[79] The

---

purposes of aggrandisement subversive of the Territorial System of Europe." Circular Despatch to British Missions at Foreign Courts, January 19, 1821, cited in Albrecht-Carrié, *The Concert of Europe*, p. 50. See also Jervis, "Security Regimes," pp. 180–181. Austria, with the authorization of Russia and Prussia, proceeded to send troops to Naples, where they promptly put down the uprising. See Lauren, "Crisis Prevention," p. 47.

78. During the nineteenth-century Concert, members established special intermediary bodies to avoid conflict in contested areas. Buffer zones were used to separate rival powers physically. Neutral zones were established in areas of particular strategic importance in order to preempt competition for their control. Demilitarized zones were used to reduce the likelihood of armed conflict in other potentially contested areas. See Lauren, "Crisis Prevention," pp. 37, 39; and Schroeder, "The 19th-Century International System," pp. 18–20.

79. In 1833–34, for example, an informal alliance of Britain and France lined up against Russia, Prussia, and Austria over the question of Unkiar-Skelessi and Russian predominance at Constantinople. See Paul Schroeder, "Alliances, 1815–1945: Weapons of Power and Tools of Management," in Klaus Knorr, ed., *Historical Dimensions of National Security Problems* (Lawrence: University of Kansas Press, 1976), p. 234. The Concert's handling of the Egyptian Crisis of 1839–41 is another case in point. The crisis revolved around a struggle between Mehemet Ali, the Viceroy of Egypt, and the Sultan, ruler of the Ottoman Empire, for control over Egypt. France, hoping to enhance its position in the Middle East, stood behind Mehemet Ali. The four other Concert members, fearful that the disintegration of the Ottoman Empire would have destabilizing consequences in Europe, backed the Sultan. The four powers banded together against France, excluded the French from the meeting convened in London to deal with the crisis, and authorized the dispatch of British troops to the Middle East. The revolt was soon suppressed. France had little choice but to accept the outcome. Soon after the defeat of Mehemet Ali, Louis Philippe sent a note to the four powers declaring that "the spontaneous actions of several of the signatory Powers [of the Concert] . . . are evidence to us that we should not find them in disagreement with our view. . . . France wishes to maintain the European equilibrium, the care of which is the responsibility of all the Great Powers. Its preservation must be their glory and their main ambition." Cited in Albrecht-Carrié, *The Concert of Europe*, p. 142. For a summary of the crisis see ibid., pp. 129–151.

cooperative framework of a concert and members' interests in preserving peace ensure that subtle balancing does not turn into deliberate exploitation or unintended spirals.[80]

This undercurrent of balancing also combats three other shortcomings of ideal collective security. First, it allows, and in fact encourages, pre-aggression deterrence. Subtle jockeying among members, in combination with the absence of codified agreements stipulating aggression as a necessary condition for collective action, allow a balancing coalition to form as soon as aggressive intent becomes manifest, not only after aggression has already occurred. A concert thus enables members to deter potential aggressors not only through the prospect of countervailing force, but also by taking concrete steps—emergency meetings, sanctions, mobilization of forces, even preemptive action—to deter and resist aggression. Second, this undercurrent of competitive balancing ameliorates the problems of buck-passing and free-riding. Subtle and ongoing balancing among concert members induces them to sustain a prudent degree of watchfulness and readiness. Concerts by no means eliminate free-riding. But by edging a step closer to a self-help environment, they make it less attractive than under ideal collective security for states to depend heavily on others to meet their defense needs. Third, this same watchfulness means that states are less likely to find themselves dangerously exposed if others forgo their commitment to collective security. Because pre-aggression measures are likely to be implemented, the fracture of an opposing coalition, if it is to occur, is likely to happen earlier, not only after aggression has occurred. Individual states will have a better sense of who their ultimate allies will be and how much they will contribute to collective action. This attribute decreases the likelihood that states, when they eventually confront imminent threats, will find themselves unprepared with few allies to come to their aid.[81]

---

80. During the nineteenth-century Concert, members developed several mechanisms to dampen spirals. They sought to fence off regional conflict. Members undertook efforts to resolve colonial disputes and to ensure that heated disputes in the periphery, when unavoidable, not be allowed to spill over into Europe. See Schroeder, "The 19th-Century International System," pp. 14–15. Concert members also established spheres of influence, recognizing that each of the major powers, for historic and geographic reasons, had special prerogatives in certain areas. See Garrett, "Nixonian Foreign Policy," p. 415; and Lauren, "Crisis Prevention," pp. 43–44.

81. The outbreak of the Crimean War in 1854 raises questions about the Concert's ability to prevent conflict among its members. On the surface, it appears that the threat of collective action was insufficient to deter Russia from demanding a degree of influence over the Ottoman Empire that was unacceptable to the other Concert members. France and Britain thus had to intervene to protect the Sultan. A closer historical reading, however, suggests that the series of

A concert indeed has its own set of drawbacks. Because concerts are an attenuated form of collective security—one which retains an undercurrent of ongoing balancing—some of the advantages associated with ideal collective security are less pronounced. The absence of a binding commitment to collective action may weaken deterrence. Potential aggressors may be more uncertain about the likelihood that a balancing coalition will emerge.[82] But a concert would still pose a considerably stronger deterrent than balancing under anarchy; a commitment to collective action—albeit an informal one—would be in place. A concert would also be less effective than ideal collective security in ameliorating the security dilemma. Because a concert retains subtle balancing and an undercurrent of competitive behavior, member states may be more concerned with preserving reputations of resolve. States might maintain more robust offensive capabilities. Unintended spirals might be more likely than under ideal collective security. But concerts still substantially moderate the security dilemma when compared to balancing under anarchy. In these respects, a concert is thus a compromise, but one well worth making, given that it provides an attractive alternative to balancing under anarchy without falling prey to the shortcomings of ideal collective security.

---

revolutions that swept Europe in 1848 effectively brought the Concert to an end and played a key role in precipitating the outbreak of the Crimean War. These revolutions had a devastating effect upon the Concert system for three main reasons. First, they installed a new generation of leaders, many of whom had not been socialized into the norms upon which the Concert was predicated. Second, upheaval politicized the public and fostered a domestic political milieu in which elites increasingly resorted to external success as a means of securing internal cohesion and order. Third, revolution jolted the international status quo in Europe and precipitated a revival of the nationalistic competition and power politics that characterized the pre-1815 era. For a concise review of these events see Anthony Wood, *Europe, 1815–1960* (Harlow: Longman, 1984), pp. 118–152. From this perspective, the cause of the Crimean War was not Russian aggression. On the contrary, the core of the problem was that, despite Austria's earnest efforts to arbitrate the dispute and Russia's willingness to make concessions, Britain and France were predisposed toward going to war, largely for domestic reasons. See Paul Schroeder, *Austria, Great Britain, and the Crimean War: The Destruction of the European Concert* (Ithaca, N.Y.: Cornell University Press, 1972), pp. xii, 136; Norman Rich, *Why the Crimean War? A Cautionary Tale* (Hanover, N.H.: University Press of New England, 1985), pp. 36, 48ff, 57ff, 63–64, 226; John Shelton Curtiss, *Russia's Crimean War* (Durham, N.C.: Duke University Press, 1979), pp. 50, 236. In essence, then, the Crimean War confirmed, rather than caused, the end of the Concert. Europe's major powers confronted each other on the battlefield for the first time since the Napoleonic Wars because the revolutions of 1848 had effectively undermined the conditions necessary for the Concert to function successfully.

82. Deductive analysis of the impact of ideal collective security and concerts on free riding is indeterminate. Ideal collective security, by creating binding commitments and sanctioning defectors, decreases the likelihood of free-riding. However, the expectations of each state that others will uphold their commitment creates added incentives for free-riding. In a concert, the absence of codified commitments reduces the sanction-related costs associated with free-riding, but the undercurrent of balancing and the concert's small size minimize free-riding.

One final disadvantage of a concert is its exclusivity. As it operated during the nineteenth century, the Concert acted as a great power club, effectively ignoring, and at times violating, the concerns of Europe's smaller powers. In a normative sense, this attribute compromises the collective nature of the enterprise of collective security. While a concert's exclusivity may have been politically acceptable in the nineteenth century, it would not be so today. While major powers still have more influence than minor powers in shaping events, international relations have, at least to some extent, been democratized.

Our solution to this political obstacle is to create a hybrid structure that combines the representative breadth of ideal collective security with the effectiveness and practicality of a concert. We call such a structure a concert-based collective security organization. An inner group of Europe's major powers would guide the operation of a region-wide security structure. A concert-based collective security organization would capitalize upon the cooperative potential of today's international setting without violating power realities or entailing undue risks. Such an organization falls far short of ideal collective security, but we believe it represents the highest practicable form of collective security, one that captures its principal advantages without falling prey to its main weaknesses.

WHY A CONCERT IS POSSIBLE TODAY

There is one final and critical reason for basing a new security order on the concept of a concert: a remarkable degree of correspondence exists between the features of the international environment that gave rise to the Concert of Europe in 1815 and the features of today's international environment. Indeed, the post–Cold War era provides an international setting that is even more conducive to the establishment of a concert-based structure than the post–Napoleonic Wars era. Four key features of the nineteenth century setting made possible the formation of a concert and are again present today: (1) common satisfaction with the status quo; (2) common appreciation that war between major powers is of little utility; (3) the practice of reciprocity; (4) a high degree of transparency. It is important to note that these four features encompass two of the three necessary conditions for collective security outlined in the first section: that the major powers share compatible views of an acceptable international order and that a minimum sense of political community exist among them. The third condition—that no state be so powerful that it is immune to collective sanction—we take to be self-evident. Our analysis here shows not only that the general conditions necessary for collective security are present, but also that the same features that gave rise to the Concert of Europe are again present in today's Europe. We now examine these features in more detail, pairing each nineteenth-century feature with its contemporary analogue.

COMMON SATISFACTION WITH THE STATUS QUO. The nineteenth-century Concert was predicated upon the assumption that none of its members desired to alter the international order in a fundamental way, and that the status quo, though subject to peaceful change through consensus, was acceptable. As Paul Lauren notes, "there could be no power so dissatisfied that it questioned the legitimacy of the entire international order."[83] At its core, the Concert revolved around a territorial settlement and the willingness of the major powers to agree to Europe's existing borders. The idea was not that these borders were immutably fixed, but that they could be altered only through the agreement of Concert members. As Richard Elrod put it, the system could thus "accommodate the forces of change and yet preserve peace and stability."[84]

The radical change in Soviet foreign policy orchestrated by Mikhail Gorbachev means that all major powers are again coming to hold a common view of what constitutes an acceptable status quo. Despite recent backsliding, the broad contours of Soviet foreign policy remain compatible with the Western vision of a stable international order. The Soviets have unilaterally withdrawn troops from Eastern Europe, agreed to allow a unified Germany to enter NATO, effectively renounced their support for "liberation movements" in the Third World, and stood firmly behind the international coalition that drove Iraq from Kuwait. They have strongly endorsed international institutions: the Soviets have become firm supporters of the UN, obtained observer status in the General Agreement on Trade and Tariffs, and expressed interest in participating in the World Bank and the International Monetary Fund.[85]

---

83. Lauren, "Crisis Prevention," p. 47.
84. Elrod, "The Concert of Europe," p. 163.
85. This reformulation of policy has been accompanied by a dramatic shift in Soviet thinking about the role that ideology should play in Soviet foreign policy. Prominent analysts are placing increasing focus on national economic interests and have directly attacked ideology as a motive force behind foreign policy. See, for example, Igor Malashenko, "Interesi strani: mnimie i real'nie" (Interests of the Country: Imaginary and Real), *Kommunist*, September 1989, pp. 114–123; and A. Bogaturov, M. Nocov, and K. Pleshakov, "Kto oni, nashi soyuzniki" (Who Are They, Our Allies?), *Kommunist*, January 1990, pp. 105–114.

Change in Soviet thinking about an acceptable international order is not only profound, but also unlikely to be reversed. Market reform and stabilization of the economy require a peaceful international environment: the Soviet economic crisis is so dire that the commitment to lowering defense spending and attracting foreign capital is unlikely to change regardless of the fate of Gorbachev.[86] The range of policy options before the Soviet leadership makes highly unlikely, at least in the near term, a return to an aggressive and ideologically driven foreign policy.[87] While the Soviets and the Western powers still need to resolve outstanding issues, profound change in the Soviet Union suggests that the major powers now agree on the essential features of a desirable international order.

COMMON APPRECIATION THAT WAR BETWEEN MAJOR POWERS IS OF LITTLE UTILITY. At the Congress of Vienna, the victorious powers, just beginning the process of recovering from a series of destructive wars, recognized the need to erect a new system that would reduce the likelihood of armed conflict between major states and allow disputes to be resolved through negotiation. While force would still be effective in dealing with lesser powers, war between major powers was simply too costly.[88] A British official, in negotiations with Russia that paved the way for the Concert, spelled this out: "It seems necessary . . . to form a Treaty to which all principal Powers of Europe should be parties . . . above all, for restraining any projects of aggrandisement and ambition similar to those which have produced all the calamities inflicted on Europe since the disastrous era of the French Revolution."[89] In short, the powers agreed that major war was no longer a useful instrument of policy.

Much stronger beliefs about the dangers of war prevail today. In the nuclear age, the major powers agree that they must avoid war among each other; they believe that force is of declining utility in regulating great power relations. A consensus exists that it would be difficult to contain general war to the conventional level and that even a limited nuclear war would have devastating consequences.[90] Even though there have been no recent conflicts

---

86. Even leading right-wing politicians such as Yegor Ligachev support integration of the Soviet Union into the world economy.
87. See Allen Lynch, "Does Gorbachev Matter Any More?" *Foreign Affairs*, Vol. 69, No. 3 (Summer 1990), pp. 19–29.
88. Garrett, "Nixonian Foreign Policy," p. 395.
89. Official communication to the Russian Ambassador in London, January 19, 1805, cited in Albrecht-Carrié, *The Concert of Europe*, p. 28.
90. The evolution of Soviet thinking about the declining role of military force in international politics has been particularly profound. See, for example, A. Arbatov, "Skol'ko oboroni dostatochno" (How Much Defense Is Enough?), *Mezhdunarodnaya Zhizn'*, No. 3 (March 1989).

between the major powers, World Wars I and II, like the Napoleonic Wars, left vivid memories of the horrors of war. In addition, all the powers are coming to realize that economic capability is an increasingly important determinant of international influence.[91] Some scholars also argue that the experiences of the two World Wars have led to shifts in international standards of what constitutes culturally and morally acceptable behavior. War, according to John Mueller, is becoming obsolete among the major powers.[92]

PRACTICE OF RECIPROCITY. Another feature of the nineteenth century system that facilitated the operation of the Concert was the practice of reciprocity. Reciprocity means that powers makes concessions in the belief that they will be repaid later, either through concessions on the same issue or on some other matter of mutual interest.[93] Concert members frequently entered into mutually self-denying arrangements based on shared appreciation of a broad, long-term understanding of self-interest. For example, in settling the dispute over Greek independence from the Ottoman Empire that broke out in the 1820s, Concert members agreed that they would "not seek, in these arrangements, any augmentation of territory, any exclusive influence, or any commerical advantage for their Subjects, which those of every other Nation may not equally obtain."[94] The practice of reciprocity built up an important degree of trust among the statesmen engaging in Concert diplomacy.

Reciprocity is increasingly coming to characterize relations among the major powers. Mutual concessions have emerged on a broad range of issues. The Soviets have made deep cuts in conventional forces and begun to withdraw troops from Eastern Europe. Although these actions initially occurred on a unilateral basis, the Western powers eventually reciprocated by proposing further mutual cuts in force levels and exercising restraint in reacting to ethnic crises within the Soviet Union. Washington and European capitals have deliberately avoided pressuring Moscow over its treatment of ethnic uprisings in the Baltic republics, Azerbaijan, and Georgia. Soviet approval of NATO membership for a unified Germany was clearly linked to Western offers of economic aid to the Soviet Union. In December 1990, the United States approved a billion dollars in loans to the Soviet Union, explicitly

---

91. See Richard Rosecrance, *The Rise of the Trading State* (New York: Basic Books, 1986).
92. John Mueller, *Retreat from Doomsday: The Obsolescence of Major War* (New York: Basic Books, 1989). See also Carl Kaysen, "Is War Obsolete? A Review Essay," *International Security*, Vol. 14, No. 4 (Spring 1990), pp. 42–64.
93. Jervis, "Security Regimes," p. 180.
94. Cited in Albrecht-Carrié, *The Concert of Europe*, p. 109.

linking U.S. assistance to a relaxation in Moscow's emigration policy.[95] In-creasing reciprocity has indeed furthered the process of ending the Cold War.

HIGH DEGREE OF TRANSPARENCY. The era following the Napoleonic Wars was characterized by a high level of transparency, or sharing of information. France's adversaries had been cooperating and sharing information through the coalition that formed to block Napoleonic ambition. This coalition im-proved the regularized channels of consultation and the highly developed diplomatic system that already existed among the major powers. Shortly after the Congress of Vienna, Castlereagh instructed British diplomats "to adopt an open and direct mode of intercourse in the conduct of business, and to repress on all sides, as much as possible, the spirit of local intrigue in which diplomatic policy is so falsely considered to consist, and which so frequently creates the very evil which it is intended to avert."[96] Frequent and open contact established a level of transparency that eased mutual suspicions and bolstered confidence, thereby facilitating the formation and functioning of the Concert.[97]

An extremely high level of transparency characterizes relations among today's major powers. The NATO allies have for decades been sharing stra-tegic information. Openness between the Western allies and the Soviet Union has also increased in recent years. Summits, confidence building measures, military doctrine seminars, on-site verification, and consultation on the war against Iraq have all served to enhance the flow of information among the major powers. Satellite reconnaissance has also vastly increased the infor-mation available to decision makers.[98] Sharing information is coming to be seen as a way of facilitating cooperation, rather than as a potential risk to national security.

NEW CONDITIONS IN TODAY'S EUROPE

During the past two centuries, so much change has taken place in state structures and inter-state relations that comparisons between the post–Napoleonic Wars era and post–Cold War era must be treated with caution.

95. "Bush Lifting 15-Year-Old Ban," *New York Times*, December 13, 1990. The lifting of the ban also appears to have been linked to Soviet cooperation in dealing with the Persian Gulf crisis.
96. Jervis, "Security Regimes," p. 179.
97. Jervis, "From Balance to Concert," pp. 73–76.
98. John Lewis Gaddis, "The Evolution of a Reconnaissance Satellite Regime," in Alexander George, et al., eds., *U.S.-Soviet Security Cooperation: Achievements, Failures, Lessons* (New York: Oxford University Press, 1988), pp. 353–372.

We have particular confidence in drawing this analogy, however, because four key changes that have occurred since 1815 make the current international setting even more conducive than the nineteenth century to the successful operation of a concert.

THE SPREAD OF DEMOCRACY. Of Europe's major powers, four of the five have enjoyed at least forty years of stable democratic rule. The Soviet Union has also been moving—although haltingly—toward political and economic liberalization. A contemporary concert would not be split ideologically between liberals and monarchists, as was the original Concert.[99] Disputes over how to react to domestic political changes among Europe's smaller states would therefore be less likely to emerge than during the nineteenth century. Furthermore, democracies tend not to go to war against each other. The spread of democracy in Europe should therefore facilitate the formation of a stronger concert.[100]

THE INFORMATION REVOLUTION. The expanding network of telecommunications systems, computers, and copy machines has radically altered the availability of information. The increased flow of ideas and data should strengthen cooperation in Europe through several mechanisms. First, the information revolution furthers the spread of democracy by making impossible the hermetic sealing of society that facilitates totalitarian control. The

---

99. Britain and France were developing parliamentary institutions, while Prussia, Russia, and Austria were staunch defenders of monarchy.

100. Although the historical record offers no cases in which liberal democracies have gone to war against each other, John Mearsheimer justifiably argues that the empirical evidence is too scanty to draw firm conclusions. In Mearsheimer's words, "democracies have been few in number over the past two centuries, and thus there have not been many cases where two democracies were in a position to fight each other." For those cases that do exist, the presence of a common external threat provides at least as compelling an explanation for harmony as does common domestic structure. See Mearsheimer, "Back to the Future," pp. 50–51. The deductive case for the claim that the spread of democracy should lead to a more peaceful international setting is, however, quite compelling. The literature contains six main points. First, leaders that are democratically elected do not need to turn to external ambition as a means of legitimating their rule. Van Evera, "Primed for Peace," p. 27. Second, the common public—the sector which stands to suffer most from war—can use the electoral process to prevent elites from engaging the state in war. Third, citizens in one democratic state will respect the political structure of other democratic states, and therefore be hesitant to engage in hostilities against them. Michael Doyle, "Liberalism and World Politics," *American Political Science Review*, Vol. 80, No. 4 (December 1986), pp. 1160–1161. Fourth, the electoral process tends to produce elites that are risk-averse and policies that are centrist. Both attributes militate against decisions for war. Snyder, "Averting Anarchy in the New Europe," pp. 18–19. Fifth, states willing to submit to the rule of law and civil society at the domestic level are more likely to submit to their analogues at the international level. Flynn and Scheffer, "Limited Collective Security," p. 83. Sixth, democratic debate exposes policy to the marketplace of ideas, thereby allowing unsound ideas to be critically evaluated and challenged. Van Evera, "Primed for Peace," pp. 27.

contagion of political change that altered the face of Eastern Europe in 1989 was unquestionably related to the increasing flow of information and ideas.[101] Second, increased inter-state communication opens societies to the spread of pan-European values and norms. Ideological sources of aggression, such as hyper-nationalism and ethnic hatred, should therefore find less fertile ground in which to take root. Third, the information revolution enhances transparency. Even if states do not enter into arrangements which facilitate the sharing of information, new technologies make data collection and monitoring of arms control agreements far easier.[102] As argued above, enhanced transparency facilitates cooperative behavior.

THE FOUNDATION OF ECONOMIC ACTIVITY. Because of changes in the nature of economic activity and sources of wealth, territorial expansion is today less valued than it was during the nineteenth century. As the orientation of national economies has shifted from agricultural to industrial to post-industrial, territorial conquest has declined in importance as a source of state power.[103] Many of the incentives that drove states to expand during the nineteenth and earlier twentieth centuries are now far less compelling. While Europe's major powers will no doubt compete for influence in Eastern Europe, such competition is likely to focus on economic advantage, as opposed to territorial conquest.

ECONOMIC INTERDEPENDENCE. Europe is now far more economically integrated than it was during the nineteenth century. Interdependence can promote cooperation by creating incentives for states to work together to produce shared gains. Interdependence, however, does not necessarily enhance cooperation. Because states accord higher priority to security than to prosperity, preoccupation with relative, as opposed to absolute, gains means that interdependence promotes cooperation only when gains are shared proportionally. Even if two states both stand to gain from a given economic activity, a state will prevent that gain from being attained if it believes that its partner will obtain a relative advantage that could eventually manifest itself in terms of an increased military threat.[104] Interdependence can also serve as a proximate cause of war. If states believe that their dependence on others is a

---

101. Michael Howard, "The Remaking of Europe," *Survival*, Vol. 32, No. 2 (March/April 1990), pp. 99–106.

102. See, for example, Gaddis, "The Evolution of a Satellite Reconnaissance Regime."

103. Rosecrance, *The Rise of the Trading State*; Kaysen, "Is War Obsolete?" pp. 48–58; Van Evera, "Primed for Peace," pp. 14–16.

104. See Grieco, "Anarchy and the Limits of Cooperation."

source of vulnerability, they may resort to hostility to end such dependence.[105]

But both of these arguments supporting the proposition that interdependence does not promote peace assume a competitive, anarchic international
setting. We maintain that in a European setting characterized by the four
features enumerated above, interdependence is more likely to promote than
to impede cooperative behavior. States are relatively free to pursue prosperity
and absolute gains. A Europe in which security concerns have been minimized should bring out the cooperation-inducing effects of interdependence.
As Mearsheimer himself notes, "cooperation is much easier to achieve if
states worry only about absolute gains, as they are more likely to do when
security is not so scarce. The goal then is simply to insure that the overall
economic pie is expanding and each state is getting at least some part of the
resulting benefits."[106] In today's Europe, economic interdependence should
therefore allow a concert to function even more successfully than during the
nineteenth century.

A New Concert for Europe

Four criteria shape our proposal for a new European collective security organization. First, the structure of the organization should allow effective
leadership and reflect current power realities. Effectively, this means that the
body should be guided by Europe's major powers. Second, the body should
develop mechanisms based on the notion of all against one for deterring and
resisting aggression. It should also develop long-term prophylactic measures
for dampening the domestic sources of expansionist behavior. Militarism,
autocratic rule, and hyper-nationalism have played key roles in leading states
to pursue policies of forceful expansion.[107] Third, the body should avoid

---

105. Japan's decision to advance into Southeast Asia to obtain access to oil is a case in point.
See Michael Barnhart, *Japan Prepares for Total War: The Search for Economic Security, 1919–1941*
(Ithaca, N.Y.: Cornell University Press, 1987). See also Mearsheimer, "Back to the Future,"
pp. 42–48.
106. Mearsheimer, "Back to the Future," pp. 44–45.
107. Military organizations, when they achieve too much political power, may propagate ideas
that persuade the state to pursue aggressive foreign policies. The services support external
ambition in order to further their narrow professional interests. Autocracy gives rise to external
ambition because elites do not face the critical evaluation and the network of moderating checks
and balances associated with democratic systems. In addition, because autocrats lack the legitimacy associated with representative government, they often seek foreign success to sustain
domestic support. Hyper-nationalism refers to belligerent and aggressive ideologies, not those

codified commitments to collective action and allow members the flexibility to tailor their responses to specific challenges as they arise. Fourth, the body should include all European states and thus serve as a vehicle for building a pan-European consensus and promoting cooperation.

What might a new collective security structure for Europe look like? A framework for this structure already exists: the Conference on Security and Cooperation in Europe (CSCE). Founded in 1975 with all European countries (except Albania, but including the Soviet Union) plus Turkey, the United States, and Canada as members, CSCE has dealt with a host of issues: political-military confidence building measures; human rights; and scientific, cultural, and educational cooperation.[108] CSCE played an important role in moderating repression and expanding civil liberties in the Soviet Union and Eastern Europe during the 1980s. Many European leaders have come to look to CSCE as a vehicle for welcome change. That CSCE enjoys legitimacy and popularity, especially in Eastern Europe and the Soviet Union where a new institution is most needed, makes the Conference the ideal venue for a new security structure.[109] In its present form, however, CSCE is too unwieldy to serve as an effective security structure.[110] Each of its thirty-four members has

---

that focus on autonomy or self-determination for specific ethnic or national groups. Hypernationalism contributes to the emergence of aggressor states by infecting the populace with expansionist ideologies. Public clamor for expansion comes to shape elite decision making, pushing the state to pursue more ambitious external policies. For discussion of these domestic sources of aggression see Van Evera, "Primed for Peace," pp. 18–28; Jack Snyder, *Myths of Empire: Domestic Politics and Strategic Ideology*, (Ithaca, N.Y.: Cornell University Press, forthcoming 1991); and Charles Kupchan, *The Vulnerability of Empire*, unpublished manuscript.

108. The first CSCE conference took place in Helsinki and lasted from 1972 to 1975. The meeting produced the "Final Act," which mandated CSCE to focus on three "baskets" of activity: political-military, economic and scientific, and humanitarian issues. For a definitive account of these negotiations, see John Maresca, *To Helsinki: The Conference on Security and Cooperation in Europe* (Durham, N.C.: Duke University Press, 1985).

109. Many scholars have noted that regimes and institutions are harder to create than they are to maintain. It therefore makes sense to house a new security organization in an existing body. See, for example, Keohane, *After Hegemony*, p. 244; and Snyder, "Averting Anarchy in the New Europe," p. 30. The primary reason for housing a new security structure in CSCE is that the body took shape during the Cold War but nevertheless bridged the East-West gap. Jack Snyder (ibid., p. 32) argues that a pan-European institution should emerge from the European Community (EC). Yet the EC does not and, for the foreseeable future, will not include Eastern Europe or the Soviet Union. The military, political, and economic trajectories of the former Eastern Bloc countries are critical variables shaping the prospects for stability in Europe; despite the EC's proven strength, these countries cannot await the day of its hypothetical expansion.

110. In order to enhance its role in shaping a post–Cold War order, CSCE's members took steps to strengthen the body's institutional structure at the Paris Summit in November 1990. See CSCE, "Charter of Paris for a New Europe," Paris, 1990, available from the U.S. Department of State. The new structure revolves around annual summit meetings at the head-of-state level. In

an equal vote and any action requires unanimity. It is wholly unrealistic to assume that the major powers would devolve to such a body responsibility for managing a new European security order. To adhere to the unanimity rule would ensure CSCE only a marginal role in shaping a new Europe. By recasting CSCE along the lines of a concert, however, the body can be turned into a viable collective security structure.[111]

A new security system must find a way of balancing the need to reflect power realities with the need to foster consensus among the states of Europe. We therefore propose a two-tiered design for CSCE: a security group consisting principally of Europe's major powers, with jurisdiction over core-level security issues; and the full thirty-four member body, with jurisdiction over a host of other security-relevant matters. The security group would deal with issues that have direct and immediate bearing on national security, such as arms control, territorial boundaries, and peacekeeping. The strong, efficient leadership that only a small group can provide is essential in these core areas if the efforts to build a collective security organization for Europe are to come to fruition. In dealing with these core-level issues, the security group would take into consideration, but not be bound by, the interests expressed by each of CSCE's members. The full body, while it would indeed have input into core-level security matters, would have exclusive jurisdiction over the following types of issues: enhancing confidence and security building measures (CSBMs), suppressing hyper-nationalism, promoting democratic institutions, and monitoring human rights. On these matters, CSCE would retain its unanimity rule; CSCE's traditional role as a consensus builder would continue.

THE SECURITY GROUP

The new organization should evolve around a concert of Europe's five major powers: the United States, the Soviet Union, Britain, France, and Germany.

---

addition, a Council of Foreign Ministers is to meet periodically, and a Committee of Senior Officials is to gather on a regular basis to support the work of the Council. A secretariat located in Prague will provide administrative services to these three bodies. The Charter also created two new centers with substantive tasks. The Conflict Prevention Center (CPC) will serve to increase military transparency and develop mechanisms for conflict resolution. The Office of Free Elections (OFE) will work to ensure that national elections are open to foreign observers, disseminate election results, and sponsor seminars on the creation of democratic institutions.
111. Others also argue that CSCE should drop its unanimity rule. See, for example, Flynn and Scheffer, "Limited Collective Security"; Goodby, "A New European Concert"; and Mueller, "A United Nations of Europe and North America."

The big five would serve as a core security group within CSCE, bringing the body more into line with current power realities and facilitating its ability to act in a timely and coordinated fashion. A limited number of other CSCE members should join the security group on a rotating basis to ensure input from Europe's smaller countries. We envisage three such members, selection occurring on a regional basis so that the concerns of countries in northern, eastern, and southern Europe are represented. As in any concert, the security group would have no explicit decision-making rules or binding contracts of collective action to enforce commitments to the notion of all against one. Decisions for action would not require unanimity—as they did in the League Council—nor would members have a paralyzing veto, as they do in the UN Security Council. The powers would pledge to respect Europe's existing boundaries and allow alterations only through joint decision. Members acting against the collective will would face censure, temporary exclusion from the group, and, if need be, sanctions. The absence of more formal security guarantees and decision rules provides a flexibility that would be essential to the efficacy of a collective security organization.[112]

During its initial phase of five to ten years, the security group should coexist with NATO. NATO has certainly served well and should remain in place until a workable alternative exists. The near-term strategy would thus be two-track: relying on NATO while nurturing a new pan-European institution. Should all go well and the Soviet Union maintain non-threatening and cooperative foreign policies, NATO would cede increasing responsibility to the security group. The Warsaw Pact already having disappeared, the security group would become the natural forum to oversee continent-wide security issues. This arrangement presents minimal risk to NATO members because if this new security structure fails to develop, NATO can reassert control over European security; the NATO command structure would remain ready to provide collective defense to its members.[113] Furthermore, because

---

112. The security group should meet regularly at each level of the CSCE structure—summit meetings, gatherings of the Council of Foreign Ministers and Committee of Senior Officials, and the Secretariat. Regular conferences among the governmental elites of Europe's major powers are the *sine qua non* of a durable and effective collective security system. The nineteenth-century Concert's lack of institutionalization left it extremely vulnerable to changes in political leadership in member countries.

113. In this respect, the United States must retain the capability to bring significant force to bear on the European continent. Light and heavy divisions, and the lift needed to transport them to Europe, should be readily available. Leaving a sizable U.S. presence of troops and equipment on the continent even after the devolution of NATO's functions to CSCE is also crucial to the successful operation of a new collective security structure. Members must remain

the security group would operate as a concert, retaining an undercurrent of balancing behavior, NATO members would remain watchful for signs of renewed aggressive intent in the Soviet Union. Weapons procurement and operational planning would remain tied, to an appropriate extent, to Soviet behavior and capabilities; concerts do not breed naivete. The security group should develop the following mechanisms to preserve stability in Europe:

ARMS CONTROL NEGOTIATION AND VERIFICATION. Given the demise of the Warsaw Pact, the security group would serve as a natural body to oversee the process of arms control in Europe. Its concert-like structure would allow the United States and the Soviet Union to remain the central parties in negotiations on both nuclear and conventional reductions, but the process would be more open to other European powers. The security group should also establish a permanent verification center. The Treaty on Conventional Armed Forces in Europe (CFE) agreement provides for the creation of a Joint Consultative Group (JCG) to serve as a forum in which participating nations could file complaints regarding compliance. The JCG could be turned into a permanent verification and monitoring center for Europe, pooling information that would be available to all CSCE members.[114] Devolving responsibility for verification and monitoring of arms control agreements to a multinational body would depoliticize the process and make it far less susceptible to the vicissitudes of domestic political change.

PREVENTION OF NUCLEAR PROLIFERATION. The security group should strengthen mechanisms for preventing nuclear proliferation. The presence of nuclear weapons in Europe, provided they continue to be based in an invulnerable manner, would serve to increase the peaceful effects of a concert. These weapons work with, not against, the underlying logic of a concert: they induce caution, minimize the chance that misperception of military capability will lead to deterrence failures, and reinforce the deterrent effects associated with the notion of all against one. A concert-based structure would not, however, rely on nuclear weapons to preserve peace in Europe. It would preserve stability primarily through the stabilizing effects of collective security. Furthermore, a collective security structure, by dampening the insecurity

---

willing and able to uphold their commitment to resist aggression. Britain, as well, should maintain a firm continental commitment, in terms of both capability and resolve, and not allow itself to slip into the illusory belief of the 1930s that its security can best be preserved by avoiding the engagement of its troops on the European continent.

114. For a related idea, see Stanley Sloan, "Conflict to Cooperation: On Building a New Berlin," *International Herald Tribune*, December 9–10, 1988.

that many non-nuclear states may feel in the new Europe, would diminish the incentives of these states to acquire nuclear weapons. The reduced demand for nuclear weapons, current political opposition to proliferation, and the extreme dangers inherent in the spread of nuclear capability make the prevention of proliferation an important task for the security group.[115]

PEACEKEEPING AND JOINT ACTION. Under a peacekeeping mandate, the security group would undertake joint diplomatic and military initiatives. Such actions could range from joint declarations of policy, to joint recognition of newly independent states, to coordinated peacekeeping activities.[116] The demand for peacekeeping in Europe is likely to be related to border conflicts arising from national and ethnic rivalries. Forces might be needed to prevent hostilities, to circumscribe fighting, or to enforce a ceasefire.[117] As during the nineteenth-century Concert, one or more powers could be authorized to act on behalf of all. The security group could also consider the establishment of a permanent multinational peacekeeping unit for rapid deployment in the event of crisis.[118]

AREAS OF SPECIAL INTEREST. Despite the waning of the Cold War, the major powers continue to view certain regions, for geopolitical and historical reasons, as of special importance. The security group should recognize that certain powers will retain areas of special interest and it should delineate each state's rights and obligations in contested areas. Such rights and obligations will exist whether explicitly recognized or not; explicit recognition

---

115. The main dangers involved in proliferation are as follows. First, especially in Europe's less well-developed countries, economic, geographic, and technological factors could hamper efforts to build secure, invulnerable nuclear forces. Vulnerable forces undermine crisis stability. Second, proliferation increases the chances that nuclear weapons might be used as a result of accident or terrorist seizure. Third, emerging nuclear powers, who have thus far been bystanders in the nuclear revolution, may face difficulties integrating nuclear weapons into their military doctrines. Fourth, proliferation in Europe is most likely to occur precisely when it would be most dangerous—when international tensions have forced non-nuclear states to seek the protection of nuclear deterrence. On the advantages and disadvantages of proliferation, see Mearsheimer, "Back to the Future," pp. 37–40.
116. The establishment of joint criteria for diplomatic recognition of new states could be crucial given the growing momentum of independence movements in the Soviet Union and Yugoslavia.
117. A peacekeeping force could be very useful if, for example, Slovenia and Croatia decided to secede from Yugoslavia. Bulgaria and Yugoslavia might come into conflict over the status of Macedonia, as might the Soviet Union and Romania over Moldavia.
118. The organization and dispatch of a peacekeeping unit are often hampered by issues of nation participation, burden-sharing, and force sizing. See Brian Urquhart, "Beyond the 'Sheriff's Posse'," *Survival*, Vol. 32, No. 3 (May/June 1990), pp. 196–205. A standing, multinational force under the direction of the security group would minimize these problems and increase the likelihood of timely deployment.

decreases the chances of misunderstanding.[119] Michael Howard, for example, has argued that the Western powers must accept that the Soviet Union has "a certain *droit de regard* in Eastern Europe."[120] The major powers should similarly recognize Germany's prominent interests in Central Europe.

FENCING OFF REGIONAL CONFLICT. The end of the Cold War will by no means lead to the end of conflict in the Third World. The security group should ensure that peripheral conflicts are fenced off or resolved and not allowed to jeopardize cooperative efforts in Europe. The United States and the Soviet Union already have taken steps in this direction. In Nicaragua, the super-powers cooperated to encourage free elections, and similar arrangements may soon be extended to other areas in Central America.[121] The powers could further dampen rivalry in the periphery by agreeing to strict "rules of the game" governing engagement in third areas.

THE FULL BODY

While the security group would be able to act on core-level security issues without the approval of each CSCE member, it would continuously consult with the full body in reaching decisions.[122] Matters other than core-level security issues would fall under the jurisdiction of the full body. CSCE's traditional mandate would remain fully intact. The thirty-four would con-tinue to strengthen CSBMs through the Conflict Prevention Center (CPC)

---

119. Others agree that spheres of influence should be made explicit. See Van Evera, "Primed for Peace," p. 45; and Mearsheimer, "Back to the Future," p. 34.
120. Howard, "The Remaking of Europe," p. 103.
121. See Michael Kramer, "Anger, Bluff—and Cooperation," *Time Magazine,* June 4, 1990, pp. 38–45. In areas where the legacy of the Cold War remains more prominent—such as Angola, Ethiopia, and Afghanistan—tensions are more fenced off than they were during the 1980s.
122. Some may object that a concert-based structure tramples on the rights of Europe's smaller powers. Establishing a CSCE security group that functions as a concert indeed endows the major powers with predominant influence in Europe. Yet these states have such influence *de facto* from their dominant economic and military capability. In effect, concert-like behavior has characterized European diplomacy for much of the postwar era. Germany, France, and Britain dominate the European Community. The United States, Germany, and Britain effectively call the shots in NATO. A concert structure only formalizes these relationships. Furthermore, the creation of a security group would in fact broaden European input into the formation of policy; the two countries that have dominated the shaping of Europe's strategic landscape—the United States and the Soviet Union—would have to make more room for France, Britain, and Germany. Our proposal leaves to the full body jurisdiction over all security-relevant issues covered by CSCE's current mandate. It also gives the thirty-four member countries input into the full range of core-level security issues that now lie outside CSCE's purview. In addition, by transforming CSCE into an effective pan-European security organization, a concert-based structure strength-ens the voices of East European countries, which are currently unattached to any meaningful security organization.

and would protect human rights in member states. In addition, the full body should oversee the task of developing and implementing prophylactic measures to prevent the emergence of aggressor states.[123] In dealing with these matters, CSCE would maintain its current unanimity rule. The full body should fulfill its tasks through the following mechanisms:

CONFLICT MANAGEMENT. CSCE should continue to develop two procedures for conflict management: examination of unusual military activity and arbitration through third parties.[124] Current procedures within the CPC give all CSCE members the right to request explanation of unusual military activities within forty-eight hours of observation. If the party is unsatisfied with the response, it can refer the matter to a meeting of concerned states. Current proposals for third party arbitration call for a group of experts to serve as fact finders and to make recommendations for resolving disputes. Many CSCE members also favor the identification of a typology of disputes, certain classes of which would be subject to mandatory, binding arbitration.[125]

SHARING OF MILITARY INFORMATION. The full body should oversee and expand the CPC's efforts to increase transparency and encourage contact between national military establishments. The widespread and symmetrical provision of military information is crucial to the operation of a collective security organization and underlies many of its advantages. The CPC is

---

123. Some analysts argue that newly emerging problems such as migration and the environment should be placed on CSCE's security agenda. For example, Flynn and Scheffer "Limited Collective Security," suggests that CSCE should establish a council for environmental cooperation. The traditional notion of national security is indeed being challenged by new threats to national well-being. The potential for massive migrations across Europe could pose formidable problems of border control and place severe strains on national economies. Degradation of the environment could threaten the quality of life in all states. While these are indeed matters that warrant considerable attention, they do not obviate the need to address traditional military concerns. While CSCE's security organs would want to monitor the military implications, if any, of population movements and environmental problems, it would be unwise to widen the already broad mandate outlined above. Differences of opinion over how to deal with migration might spill over into negotiations on military matters. The critical focus of CSCE's security organs on avoiding war in Europe should not be diluted by diverting attention to issues only tangentially related to conflict. See Daniel Deudney, "The Case Against Linking Environmental Degradation to National Security," *Millennium*, Vol. 19, No. 3 (Winter 1990), pp. 461–476; Jessica Tuchman Matthews, "Redefining Security," *Foreign Affairs*, Vol. 68, No. 2 (Spring 1989), pp. 162–177; and Norman Myers, "Environmental Security," *Foreign Policy*, No. 74 (Spring 1989), pp. 23–41.
124. The following discussion draws heavily on interviews with U.S. government officials familiar with the CSCE negotiations.
125. For a comprehensive discussion of third party arbitration, see Goodby, "A New European Concert," pp. 3–6. See also "Report of the CSCE Meeting of Experts on Peaceful Settlement of Disputes" (Valletta, Malta, February 8, 1991), available from the U.S. Department of State; and *CSCE Vienna Follow-Up Meeting: A Framework for Europe's Future*, Selected Documents, No. 35 (Washington: D.C.: U.S. Department of State, Bureau of Public Affairs, January 1989), pp. 7–8.

currently working on improving the dissemination of information on forces-in-being, new weapons deployments, and defense budgets. It is also constructing a new communications network, strengthening provisions for foreign observers to be present at national military maneuvers, and developing plans for new exchanges between military establishments.[126]

SUPPRESSION OF HYPER-NATIONALISM AND PROMOTION OF DEMOCRACY. The full body should establish two permanent commissions to oversee the task of developing and implementing prophylactic measures to prevent aggression. The Commission on Political Development (CPD) would focus on the suppression of hyper-nationalism. History provides ample demonstration of the potentially disastrous consequences of unchecked nationalism.[127] The Commission on Democracy (COD) would concentrate on promoting democratic institutions and values. As we have argued, the spread of democracy will contribute to the preservation of peace in Europe. It is no coincidence that the three principal aggressor states of the twentieth century were ruled by essentially autocratic governments.[128]

The Commission on Political Development can contribute to the suppression of hyper-nationalism through three principal mechanisms. First, the CPD can watch carefully to ensure that national elites do not use hyper-nationalist propaganda as a domestic tool. It should expose those caught doing so, single them out for censure, and pressure them to cease by widely circulating a "blacklist" of irresponsible leaders. Second, efforts to protect the rights of foreign journalists would play an important role in making local elites more accountable for their actions and rhetoric.[129] At the same time, the CPD should take steps to ensure that a free domestic press thrives in all

---

126. See Stanley Sloan, "CSCE: A Start on a Structure," *Arms Control Today*, Vol. 20, No. 10 (December 1990), pp. 4–5. A military doctrine seminar has been scheduled for 1991. These military doctrine seminars enhance transparency by promoting extensive military-to-military contacts. The seminars could serve as an important vehicle for promoting defensive force postures and doctrines of defensive defense.

127. See, for example, Boyd Shafer, *Nationalism: Myth and Reality* (New York: Harcourt, Brace, 1955); Louis L. Snyder, *German Nationalism* (Harrisburg, Pa.: Stackpole, 1952); Berghahn, *Germany and the Approach of War in 1914*; Van Evera, "Primed for Peace," pp. 23–25; and Louis L. Snyder, *Encyclopedia of Nationalism* (New York: Paragon House, 1990).

128. The Reichstag did maintain a marginal degree of political power throughout the pre–World War I era. But the government largely succeeded in emasculating the legislature and investing the kaiser and his advisers with enormous autonomy in formulating policy. The system was, in Hans-Ulrich Wehler's words, "a semi-absolutist, pseudo-constitutional military monarchy." Wehler, *The German Empire, 1871–1918*, trans. Kim Traynor (Leamington Spa, U.K.: Berg Publishers, 1985), p. 60.

129. See *CSCE Vienna Follow-Up Meeting*, p. 33.

member states. The CPD should also become involved in local radio and television programming, in terms of both monitoring broadcasts and countering nationalistic propaganda through its own broadcasts. Third, the CPD can monitor the education system in member states. It is critical that the textbooks used in primary and secondary education present accurate accounts of national history.[130] CSCE should also continue to encourage freedom of access to national archives for all scholars, both foreign and national.[131] CSCE should set forth guidelines in each of these three areas, and access to European development funds should be made contingent upon compliance with these guidelines.

The Commission on Democracy, which would incorporate the existing Office of Free Elections (OFE), can take several steps to promote the spread of democracy. In addition to fulfilling the OFE's current tasks, the COD could open branches in all member countries to support representative institutions and democratic values. Based on the notion that the free flow of ideas undermines authoritarian regimes, the COD should fan the spread of the information revolution. It should help to ensure that all political groups have access to photocopiers, fax machines, and computers. The College of Europe in Bruges would be a natural location for COD activities in the education field. Students from leading national universities could come to Bruges to study democratic theory and pan-European political processes.[132]

Conclusions

We have developed four main arguments in this essay to show that collective security can best preserve peace in post–Cold War Europe. First, we have shown that collective security has clear advantages over balancing under anarchy in promoting international stability. Collective security promises to deter and to resist aggressors more effectively should they emerge. At the same time, it offers to deepen and perpetuate a cooperative and peaceful international environment. Second, we have shown that concert-based col-

---

130. See Van Evera, "Primed for Peace," pp. 52–53.
131. See *CSCE Vienna Follow-Up Meeting*, p. 36.
132. An inter-parliamentary body could serve as a forum for political elites to exchange ideas about democratic procedures. See Joseph Biden, "Helsinki II, Road Map for Revolution," *New York Times*, January 28, 1990. This idea is amplified in "The Support for East European Democracy Act of 1990," U.S. Senate, 102nd Cong., 1st sess., bill before the Committee on Foreign Relations, unpublished, 1990.

lective security is the most appropriate and practicable form of collective security for today's Europe. A concert-based structure, by retaining an ongoing undercurrent of subtle balancing, allows the major powers to keep on guard in a Europe that is still in flux. Third, we have shown that the conditions necessary for a concert-based structure to form and function successfully are present today. Finally, we have argued that CSCE should be recast to function as a concert-based collective security organization. We have laid out mechanisms through which this body can preserve peace in Europe.

In order to minimize the risk that our proposal presents to the Western alliance, we recommend that NATO and a recast CSCE coexist until political and economic conditions in the Soviet Union stabilize. Should the Soviet Union again pursue an aggressive foreign policy, collective security would become unfeasible and NATO would reassert control over European security. On the other hand, if Soviet foreign policy continues on its current trajectory, NATO would gradually cede more security functions to CSCE.[133] The eventual endpoint would involve the dismantling of NATO and the transformation of CSCE into an effective and viable collective security structure built around a small and workable concert of the big five.

This proposal is grounded in historical precedent, would succeed in bringing the European order more into line with the changing strategic landscape, and would provide a more stable and peaceful international environment. Because the world is at a unique historical juncture, it is necessary to rely on the past to think creatively about the future, and to take the initiative in forging a new European order.

---

133. The implementation of a collective security system in Europe might even increase the chances that Soviet reform will continue to move forward. CSCE's efforts to promote democracy could further political reform. Soviet participation in the security group and the broader network of all-European institutions that are likely to emerge would facilitate the process through which Soviet elites come to embrace the norms underpinning a new European security order. On the potential effects of the international environment on Soviet domestic change, see Jack Snyder, "International Leverage on Soviet Domestic Change," *World Politics*, Vol. 42, No. 1 (October 1989), pp. 1–30.

Concerts, Collective Security, and the Future of Europe: A Retrospective

Charles A. Kupchan
and
Clifford A. Kupchan

The analysis presented in "Concerts, Collective Security, and the Future of Europe" has fared well over the course of the first post-Cold War decade. The core arguments about the desirability of collective security remain intact and on solid deductive ground. And with the advantage of a decade of hindsight, the European order we envisaged is far closer to reality than that envisaged by scholars predicting a return to a dangerous and unstable multipolarity.[1]

Our central claim was that collective security has clear advantages over balancing under anarchy in terms of promoting international stability. Should an aggressor state emerge, collective security deters and resists aggression more effectively than unfettered balancing; the opposing coalition consists not just of directly threatened states, but also of states that consider it in their broader interest to preserve international order and stability.[2] In the absence of an aggressor, collective security deepens and perpetuates a peaceful international environment far more effectively than balancing under anarchy by ameliorating the security dilemma and promoting cooperative behavior.

These arguments are not only deductively sound, but they also correspond with the empirical record. NATO has sustained its relevance and appeal precisely because it has moved beyond its role as a traditional alliance and is now functioning as a hybrid between a collective defense and a collective security organization.[3] NATO continues to serve as a hedge against a return of Russian

Charles A. Kupchan is Associate Professor of international affairs at Georgetown University and Senior Fellow at the Council on Foreign Relations. Clifford A. Kupchan is Deputy Coordinator of U.S. Assistance to the New Independent States, U.S. Department of State. The views expressed in this article are the authors' own and not necessarily those of the Department of State or the U.S. Government.

1. See, for example, John J. Mearsheimer, "Back to the Future: Instability in Europe after the Cold War," *International Security*, Vol. 15, No. 1 (Summer 1990), pp. 5–56.
2. For elaboration, see Charles A. Kupchan and Clifford A. Kupchan, "The Promise of Collective Security," *International Security*, Vol. 20, No. 1 (Summer 1995), pp. 54–55, which responds to John J. Mearsheimer, "The False Promise of International Institutions," *International Security*, Vol. 19, No. 3 (Winter 1994/95), pp. 5–49.
3. The hybrid nature of NATO is reflected in its own political guidance, known as the "Strategic Concept." The Strategic Concept was last revisited as the NATO Summit in Washington, D.C. in April 1999. The "Washington Declaration," a summary of the revised Strategic Concept and the summit's main conclusions noted that, "Collective defense remains the core purpose of NATO." At the same time, the document stated that, "NATO is an essential pillar of a wider community of shared values and shared responsibility. Working together, Allies and Partners, including Russia and Ukraine, are developing their cooperation and erasing the divisions imposed by the Cold War to build a Europe whole and free, where security and prosperity are shared and indivisible." NATO Press Release, NAC-S (99) 63, April 23, 1999.

ambition by retaining its ability to marshal a countervailing coalition, but member states have focused their primary attention and resources on preventing and stopping war in the Balkans—often in cooperation with Russia. The Alliance initially reacted with reluctance and hesitation to bloodshed in the Balkans. However, NATO eventually rose to the occasion in Bosnia and Kosovo, demonstrating the willingness of its members to take collective military action even when their security is not directly threatened. In a manner consistent with the spirit and norms of collective security, NATO acted not in self-defense, but to preserve European stability and to defend a broader notion of collective interest. NATO, with the help of the United Nations and the European Union (EU), is following through by running, in all but name, protectorates in both Bosnia and Kosovo.

NATO also has expended considerable effort to deepen and enlarge the zone of stable peace in Europe. It has opened its doors to new members from Central Europe, admitting Hungary, Poland, and the Czech Republic in 1999. At the same time, it has expanded its political and military cooperation with Russia and other former Soviet republics, primarily through the NATO-Russia Founding Act and the Partnership for Peace program. These policies are highly consistent with the practice of collective security. The formal process of enlargement as well as the Founding Act and Partnership for Peace are serving as vehicles for turning former adversaries into new partners and for spreading eastward the norms and habits of cooperation. To be sure, NATO enlargement has contradictory impulses and consequences. It is intended to eliminate geopolitical dividing lines from Europe, but risks alienating Russia and drawing new dividing lines in the process. On paper, NATO's primary mission is collective defense, but in practice its attention and resources go primarily to new missions outside alliance territory. These ambiguities are a direct reflection of the current hybrid state of NATO.

We also stand by our claim that concert-based collective security is the most appropriate and practicable form of collective security. Concerts temper norm-governed international orders with power realities by establishing a small directorate comprised only of major powers, by making collective action contingent on an informal consensus rather than on binding and codified rules, and by retaining an undercurrent of prudential balancing. Indeed, precisely for these reasons, NATO created a concert-like structure—the contact group—to guide its involvement in the Balkans.[4] The contact group's small membership

---

4. Participants in the contact group were the United States, Great Britain, France, Germany, Russia, and Italy. Italy was included because of its proximity to Yugoslavia, its special interests in the region, and its importance as a base for NATO aircraft.

and informality enabled it to coordinate diplomacy and military action in the Balkans, while at the same time managing Russia's relationship with NATO. NATO is quite likely to rely on informal groupings, whether ad hoc or permanent, to coordinate its involvement in future crises.

The conditions necessary for collective security to operate—and preserve peace in Europe—are even more present today than they were a decade ago. The Soviet Union has collapsed and Russia, albeit haltingly, is heading toward becoming a benign power. Assuming Russian reform continues, Europe will soon enjoy a strategic landscape in which all its major states are capitalist, democratic, status quo powers.[5] Most of the smaller states of Central Europe are far along the path of political and economic transition and are readying themselves for full membership in NATO and the European Union. In addition, increasing transparency, the information revolution, and growing political and economic integration through the EU ease residual suspicions and promote reciprocity. Trouble spots remain in Europe's east and southeast, but the trend is one in which the features necessary for collective security to function effectively are becoming increasingly widespread and entrenched.

The advantage of hindsight does necessitate that we amend our original analysis in two important respects. First, we initially envisaged that the Conference on Security and Cooperation in Europe (CSCE)—now called the Organization for Security and Cooperation in Europe (OSCE)—would serve as the most appropriate vehicle for creating a pan-European collective security structure. Instead, NATO has clearly emerged as the institution of choice for the foreseeable future. NATO has eclipsed OSCE both because the United States preferred working through an organization in which it was predominant and because the states of Central Europe preferred the guarantee against a resurgent Russia that only NATO could offer. Whether NATO should have embarked on the process of formal enlargement remains an issue of considerable debate.[6] But the logic of our argument suggests that enlargement should now

---

5. Russia is admittedly still in the midst of an uncertain transition. It is a democracy, but not yet a liberal democracy. Capitalism has begun to take root, but it is a statist version and corruption runs rampant. These conditions provide ample reason for NATO to proceed cautiously in embracing Russia. But these same conditions also increase the urgency of efforts to guide Russian reform and the conduct of its foreign policy by anchoring it in the West and in a pan-European collective security structure.

6. For arguments supporting enlargement, see Ronald Asmus, Richard Kugler, and Stephen Larrabee, "Building a New NATO," *Foreign Affairs*, Vol. 72, No. 4 (1993), pp. 28–40; Strobe Talbott, "Why NATO Should Grow," *The New York Review of Books*, August 10, 1995, pp. 29–30; Henry Kissinger, "Expand NATO Now," *The Washington Post*, December 19, 1994; and Zbigniew Brzezinski, "A Plan for Europe," Foreign Affairs, Vol. 74, No. 1 (1995), pp. 26–42. For arguments against enlargement, see Michael E. Brown, "The Flawed Logic of NATO Expansion," *Survival*, Vol. 37, No. 1 (1995), pp. 34–52; Michael Mandelbaum, "Preserving the New Peace: The Case Against

continue, with NATO eventually extending membership to Russia and other former republics of the Soviet Union as they become stable democracies.[7] NATO and OSCE might then merge into a concert-based structure and manage security on a pan-European basis.

Second, we originally failed to appreciate the important role that the European Union is likely to play—and will need to play — in shaping the evolution of a new security order on the continent. The European Union has done far more than outlast the end of the Cold War. Over the course of the decade, it has consolidated a single market, introduced a single currency, and embarked on efforts to develop greater military capabilities and a common defense policy. EU members have succeeded in pooling their sovereignty and locking in a supranational union that sits comfortably alongside the national state. In so doing, the EU has quietly but steadily helped eliminate security competition among its members, enabling them to focus, with the help of the United States, on extending stability eastward.

In the years ahead, the EU will have to do much more than just check intra-European balancing. NATO and its current brand of concert-like cooperation have enjoyed considerable success over the past decade in large part because one of its members—the United States—has been willing to provide the necessary leadership and assume a disproportionate share of the associated costs and risks. But this imbalance is unlikely to last. The United States will not withdraw from Europe, but neither will it indefinitely remain the continent's pacifier and protector—especially if a demanding mission confronts U.S. forces in East Asia or elsewhere. Like Britain during the nineteenth-century Concert of Europe, the United States will pick its fights carefully and at times refrain from future military contingencies in Europe.

As a consequence, EU members need to develop the political will and military capability to act without the United States. Concerts function successfully when ad hoc coalitions of the willing and able come together to preserve peace. Assuming that the United States will not always be among the willing, the EU needs to be sure that it has the ability to fill the gap. In light of the EU's current momentum toward further integration, decisions about security policy are likely to be made at the collective level, even if military assets continue to belong to individual members. And assuming that America's role as Europe's extraregional balancer declines in the years ahead, a common EU defense

---

NATO Expansion," *Foreign Affairs*, Vol. 74, No. 3 (May/June 1995), pp. 9–13; and Charles Kupchan, "Expand NATO — And Split Europe," *New York Times*, November 27, 1994.

7. On the future of NATO enlargement and eventual Russian membership, see Charles Kupchan, "Rethinking Europe," *The National Interest*, Vol. 56 (Summer 1999), pp. 73–79.

policy also represents wise insurance against the potential reemergence of security rivalries within Europe. In this sense, the concert-based structure we envisage would not operate like the original Concert, in which the leaders of sovereign great powers decided the fate of Europe around a conference table. As the EU continues its journey into the post-sovereign era, it too will have a seat at the table, perhaps at the expense of Europe's individual national states, but to the benefit of the European enterprise and European stability.

In sum, with important empirical modifications, the logic and vision of European security we laid out in 1991 remain compelling. Concert-based collective security provides a model for the future of Europe and a goal for policy makers. As other regions overcome traditional political cleavages and enjoy the conditions that make collective security possible, they may want to follow Europe's lead. Indeed, it may well be worth imagining a global concert as a guiding vision, with a directorate of major powers coordinating relations among and within their respective regions.[8]

---

8. See James Chace and Nicholas Rizopoulos, "Toward a New Concert of Nations: An American Perspective," World Policy Journal, Vol. 16 (Fall 1999), pp. 2–10.

Part V:
Primacy

The Stability of a Unipolar World

William C. Wohlforth

The collapse of the Soviet Union produced the greatest change in world power relationships since World War II. With Moscow's headlong fall from superpower status, the bipolar structure that had shaped the security policies of the major powers for nearly half a century vanished, and the United States emerged as the sole surviving superpower. Commentators were quick to recognize that a new "unipolar moment" of unprecedented U.S. power had arrived.[1] In 1992 the Pentagon drafted a new grand strategy designed to preserve unipolarity by preventing the emergence of a global rival.[2] But the draft plan soon ran into controversy, as commentators at home and abroad argued that any effort to preserve unipolarity was quixotic and dangerous.[3] Officials quickly backed away from the idea and now eschew the language of primacy or predominance, speaking instead of the United States as a "leader" or the "indispensable nation."[4]

The rise and sudden demise of an official strategy for preserving primacy lends credence to the widespread belief that unipolarity is dangerous and unstable. While scholars frequently discuss unipolarity, their focus is always on its demise. For neorealists, unipolarity is the least stable of all structures because any great concentration of power threatens other states and causes them to take action to restore a balance.[5] Other scholars grant that a large

William C. Wohlforth is Assistant Professor of International Relations in the Edmund A. Walsh School of Foreign Service at Georgetown University.

I am indebted to Stephen G. Brooks, Charles A. Kupchan, Joseph Lepgold, Robert Lieber, and Kathleen R. McNamara, who read and commented on drafts of this article.

1. Charles Krauthammer, "The Unipolar Moment," *Foreign Affairs*, Vol. 70, No. 1 (Winter 1990/1991), pp. 23–33.
2. Patrick Tyler, "The Lone Superpower Plan: Ammunition for Critics," *New York Times*, March 10, 1992, p. A12.
3. For the most thorough and theoretically grounded criticism of this strategy, see Christopher Layne, "The Unipolar Illusion: Why New Great Powers Will Arise," *International Security*, Vol. 17, No. 4 (Spring 1993), pp. 5–51; and Layne, "From Preponderance to Offshore Balancing: America's Future Grand Strategy," *International Security*, Vol. 22, No. 1 (Summer 1997), pp. 86–124.
4. The phrase—commonly attributed to Secretary of State Madeleine Albright—is also a favorite of President Bill Clinton's. For example, see the account of his speech announcing the expansion of the North Atlantic Treaty Organization in Alison Mitchell, "Clinton Urges NATO Expansion in 1999," *New York Times*, October 23, 1996, p. A20.
5. Kenneth N. Waltz, "Evaluating Theories," *American Political Science Review*, Vol. 91, No. 4 (December 1997), pp. 915–916; Layne, "Unipolar Illusion"; and Michael Mastanduno, "Preserving

International Security, Vol. 24, No. 1 (Summer 1999), pp. 5–41
© 1999 by the President and Fellows of Harvard College and the Massachusetts Institute of Technology.

concentration of power works for peace, but they doubt that U.S. preeminence can endure.[6] Underlying both views is the belief that U.S. preponderance is fragile and easily negated by the actions of other states. As a result, most analysts argue that unipolarity is an "illusion," a "moment" that "will not last long," or is already "giving way to multipolarity."[7] Indeed, some scholars question whether the system is unipolar at all, arguing instead that it is, in Samuel Huntington's phrase, "uni-multipolar."[8]

Although they disagree vigorously on virtually every other aspect of post–Cold War world politics, scholars of international relations increasingly share this conventional wisdom about unipolarity. Whether they think that the current structure is on the verge of shifting away from unipolarity or that it has already done so, scholars believe that it is prone to conflict as other states seek to create a counterpoise to the overweening power of the leading state. The assumption that unipolarity is unstable has framed the wide-ranging debate over the nature of post–Cold War world politics. Since 1991 one of the central questions in dispute has been how to explain continued cooperation and the absence of old-style balance-of-power politics despite major shifts in the distribution of power.[9]

the Unipolar Moment: Realist Theories and U.S. Grand Strategy after the Cold War," *International Security*, Vol. 21, No. 4 (Spring 1997), pp. 44–98. Although I differ with Waltz on the stability of unipolarity, the title of this article and much of its contents reflect intellectual debts to his work on system structure and stability. See Waltz, "The Stability of a Bipolar World," *Daedalus*, Vol. 93, No. 3 (Summer 1964), pp. 881–901.

6. See Charles A. Kupchan, "After Pax Americana: Benign Power, Regional Integration, and the Sources of Stable Multipolarity," *International Security*, Vol. 23, No. 3 (Fall 1998), pp. 40–79. Samuel P. Huntington maintained this position in Huntington, "Why International Primacy Matters," *International Security*, Vol. 17, No. 4 (Spring 1993), pp. 63–83, but he has since abandoned it. A more bullish assessment, although still more pessimistic than the analysis here, is Douglas Lemke, "Continuity of History: Power Transition Theory and the End of the Cold War," *Journal of Peace Research*, Vol. 34, No. 1 (February 1996), pp. 203–236.

7. As Glenn H. Snyder puts it, the international system "appears to be unipolar, though incipiently multipolar." Snyder, *Alliance Politics* (Ithaca, N.Y.: Cornell University Press, 1997), p. 18. The quoted phrases in this sentence appear in Charles A. Kupchan, "Rethinking Europe," *National Interest*, No. 56 (Summer 1999); Kupchan, "After Pax Americana," p. 41; Layne, "Unipolar Illusion"; Mastanduno, "Preserving the Unipolar Moment"; and Waltz, "Evaluating Theories," p. 914. Although Charles Krauthammer coined the term "unipolar moment" in his article under that title, he argued that unipolarity had the potential to last a generation.

8. Samuel P. Huntington, "The Lonely Superpower," *Foreign Affairs*, Vol. 78, No. 2 (March/April 1999), p. 36. For similar views of the post–Cold War structure, see Aaron L. Friedberg, "Ripe for Rivalry: Prospects for Peace in a Multipolar Asia," *International Security*, Vol. 18, No. 3 (Winter 1993/94), pp. 5–33; and Josef Joffe, "'Bismarck' or 'Britain'? Toward an American Grand Strategy after Bipolarity," *International Security*, Vol. 19, No. 4 (Spring 1995), pp. 94–117.

9. The assumption that realism predicts instability after the Cold War pervades the scholarly debate. See, for example, Sean M. Lynn-Jones and Steven E. Miller, eds., *The Cold War and After: Prospects for Peace—An International Security Reader* (Cambridge, Mass.: MIT Press, 1993); and

In this article, I advance three propositions that undermine the emerging conventional wisdom that the distribution of power is unstable and conflict prone. First, the system is unambiguously unipolar. The United States enjoys a much larger margin of superiority over the next most powerful state or, indeed, all other great powers combined than any leading state in the last two centuries. Moreover, the United States is the first leading state in modern international history with decisive preponderance in *all* the underlying components of power: economic, military, technological, and geopolitical.[10] To describe this unprecedented quantitative and qualitative concentration of power as an evanescent "moment" is profoundly mistaken.

Second, the current unipolarity is prone to peace. The raw power advantage of the United States means that an important source of conflict in previous systems is absent: hegemonic rivalry over leadership of the international system. No other major power is in a position to follow any policy that depends for its success on prevailing against the United States in a war or an extended rivalry. None is likely to take any step that might invite the focused enmity of the United States. At the same time, unipolarity minimizes security competition among the other great powers. As the system leader, the United States has

---

David A. Baldwin, ed., *Neorealism and Neoliberalism: The Contemporary Debate* (New York: Columbia University Press, 1993). For more varied perspectives on realism and unipolarity, see Ethan B. Kapstein and Michael Mastanduno, eds., *Unipolar Politics: Realism and State Strategies after the Cold War* (New York: Columbia University Press, 1999). Explanations for stability despite the balance of power fall roughly into three categories: (1) liberal arguments, including democratization, economic interdependence, and international institutions. For examples, see Bruce M. Russett, *Grasping the Democratic Peace* (Princeton, N.J.: Princeton University Press, 1993); John R. Oneal and Bruce M. Russett, "The Classical Liberals Were Right: Democracy, Interdependence, and Conflict, 1950–1985," *International Studies Quarterly*, Vol. 41, No. 2 (June 1997), pp. 267–294; G. John Ikenberry, "Institutions, Strategic Restraint, and the Persistence of the American Postwar Order," *International Security*, Vol. 23, No. 3 (Winter 1998/99), pp. 43–78. (2) Cultural and ideational arguments that highlight social learning. See John Mueller, *Retreat from Doomsday: The Obsolescence of Major War* (Rochester, N.Y.: University of Rochester Press, 1989); and Alexander Wendt, *Social Theory of International Politics* (Cambridge: Cambridge University Press, 1999), chap. 6. (3) Arguments that highlight systemic and material factors other than the balance of power, such as globalization, the offense-defense balance, or nuclear weapons. See Stephen G. Brooks, "The Globalization of Production and the Changing Benefits of Conquest," *Journal of Conflict Resolution*, Vol. 43, No. 5 (October 1999); and Stephen Van Evera, "Primed for Peace: Europe after the Cold War," in Jones and Miller, *Cold War and After*.

10. I focus on material elements of power mainly because current scholarly debates place a premium on making clear distinctions between ideas and material forces. See Wendt, *Social Theory of International Politics;* and Jeffrey Legro and Andrew Moravcsik, "Is Anybody Still a Realist?" *International Security*, Vol. 24, No. 2 (Fall 1999). Many nonmaterial elements of power also favor the United States and strengthen the argument for unipolarity's stability. On "soft power," see Joseph S. Nye, Jr., *Bound to Lead: The Changing Nature of American Power* (New York: Basic Books, 1990).

the means and motive to maintain key security institutions in order to ease local security conflicts and limit expensive competition among the other major powers. For their part, the second-tier states face incentives to bandwagon with the unipolar power as long as the expected costs of balancing remain prohibitive.

Third, the current unipolarity is not only peaceful but durable.[11] It is already a decade old, and if Washington plays its cards right, it may last as long as bipolarity. For many decades, no state is likely to be in a position to take on the United States in any of the underlying elements of power. And, as an offshore power separated by two oceans from all other major states, the United States can retain its advantages without risking a counterbalance. The current candidates for polar status (Japan, China, Germany, and Russia) are not so lucky. Efforts on their part to increase their power or ally with other dissatisfied states are likely to spark local counterbalances well before they can create a global equipoise to U.S. power.

The scholarly conventional wisdom holds that unipolarity is dynamically unstable and that any slight overstep by Washington will spark a dangerous backlash.[12] I find the opposite to be true: unipolarity is durable and peaceful, and the chief threat is U.S. failure to do enough.[13] Possessing an undisputed preponderance of power, the United States is freer than most states to disregard the international system and its incentives. But because the system is built around U.S. power, it creates demands for American engagement. The more efficiently Washington responds to these incentives and provides order, the more long-lived and peaceful the system. To be sure, policy choices are likely to affect the differential growth of power only at the margins. But given that

---

11. I define "stability" as peacefulness and durability. Kenneth Waltz first conflated these two meanings of stability in "The Stability of a Bipolar World." He later eliminated the ambiguity by defining stability exclusively as durability in *Theory of International Politics* (Reading, Mass.: Addison-Wesley, 1979). I avoid ambiguity by treating peacefulness and durability separately. Durability subsumes another common understanding of stability: the idea of a self-reinforcing equilibrium. To say that an international system is durable implies that it can experience significant shifts in power relations without undergoing fundamental change. See Robert Jervis, *Systems Effects: Complexity in Political and Social Life* (Princeton, N.J.: Princeton University Press, 1997), chap. 3.

12. Because overwhelming preponderance favors both peace and durability, stability is less sensitive to how the United States defines its interests than most scholars assume. In contrast, many realists hold that stability is strictly contingent upon Washington's nonthreatening or status quo stance in world affairs. See Mastanduno, "Preserving the Unipolar Moment." Similarly, Kupchan, "After Pax Americana," argues that the United States' "benign" character explains stability.

13. This was Krauthammer's original argument in "The Unipolar Moment." For a comprehensive review of the debate that reflects the standard scholarly skepticism toward the stability of unipolarity, see Barry R. Posen and Andrew L. Ross, "Competing Visions for U.S. Grand Strategy," *International Security*, Vol. 21, No. 2 (Winter 1996/97), pp. 5–54.

unipolarity is safer and cheaper than bipolarity or multipolarity, it pays to invest in its prolongation. In short, the intellectual thrust (if not the details) of the Pentagon's 1992 draft defense guidance plan was right.

I develop these propositions in three sections that establish my central argument: the current system is unipolar; the current unipolarity is peaceful; and it is durable. I then conclude the analysis by discussing its implications for scholarly debates on the stability of the post–Cold War order and U.S. grand strategy.

Lonely at the Top: The System Is Unipolar

Unipolarity is a structure in which one state's capabilities are too great to be counterbalanced.[14] Once capabilities are so concentrated, a structure arises that is fundamentally distinct from either multipolarity (a structure comprising three or more especially powerful states) or bipolarity (a structure produced when two states are substantially more powerful than all others). At the same time, capabilities are not so concentrated as to produce a global empire. Unipolarity should not be confused with a multi- or bipolar system containing one especially strong polar state or with an imperial system containing only one major power.[15]

---

14. This definition flows from the logic of neorealist balance-of-power theory, but it is consistent with classical balance-of-power thinking. See Layne, "Unipolar Illusion," p. 130 n. 2; Snyder, *Alliance Politics,* chap. 1; Morton Kaplan, *System and Process in International Politics* (New York: Wiley, 1957), pp. 22–36; Harrison Wagner, "What Was Bipolarity?" *International Organization,* Vol. 47, No. 1 (Winter 1993), pp. 77–106; and Emerson M.S. Niou, Peter C. Ordeshook, and Gregory F. Rose, *The Balance of Power: Stability in International Systems* (New York: Cambridge University Press, 1989), p. 76.

15. Germany was clearly the strongest state in Europe in 1910, and the United States was generally thought to be the strongest state in the world in 1960, but neither system was unipolar. One of Waltz's most widely accepted insights was that the world was bipolar in the Cold War even though the two poles shared it with other major powers such as France, Britain, West Germany, Japan, and China. In the same vein, a system can be unipolar, with unique properties owing to the extreme concentration of capabilities in one state, and yet also contain other substantial powers. Cf. Huntington, "Lonely Superpower," who defines unipolarity as a system with only one great power. Throughout this article, I hew as closely as possible to the definitions of central terms in Waltz, *Theory of International Politics,* as they have gained the widest currency. Although the distinction between bipolarity and multipolarity is one of the most basic in international relations theory, scholars do debate whether bipolar structures are more durable or peaceful than multipolar ones. For a concise discussion, see Jack S. Levy, "The Causes of War and the Conditions of Peace," *Annual Review of Political Science,* Vol. 1 (1998), pp. 139–165. There are good reasons for analyzing tripolarity as a distinct structure. See Randall L. Schweller, *Deadly Imbalances: Tripolarity and Hitler's Strategy of World Conquest* (New York: Columbia University Press, 1998).

Is the current structure unipolar? The crucial first step in answering this question is to compare the current distribution of power with its structural predecessors. The more the current concentration of power in the United States differs from past distributions, the less we should expect post–Cold War world politics to resemble that of earlier epochs. I select two cases that allow me to compare concentrations of power in both multipolar and bipolar settings: the Pax Britannica and the Cold War.[16] Within these two cases, I highlight two specific periods—1860–70 and 1945–55—because they reflect the greatest concentrations of power in the system leader, and so have the greatest potential to weaken the case for the extraordinary nature of the current unipolarity. I also include a second Cold War period in the mid-1980s to capture the distribution of power just before the dramatic changes of the 1990s.

QUANTITATIVE COMPARISON

To qualify as polar powers, states must score well on *all* the components of power: size of population and territory; resource endowment; economic capabilities; military strength; and "competence," according to Kenneth Waltz.[17] Two states measured up in 1990. One is gone. No new pole has appeared: $2 - 1 = 1$. The system is unipolar.

The reality, however, is much more dramatic than this arithmetic implies. After all, the two superpowers were hardly equal. Writing in the late 1970s, Waltz himself questioned the Soviet Union's ability to keep up with the United States.[18] The last time the scholarly community debated the relative power of the United States was the second half of the 1980s, when the United States was widely viewed as following Great Britain down the path of relative decline. Responding to that intellectual climate, several scholars undertook quantitative analyses of the U.S. position. In 1985 Bruce Russett compared the U.S. position of the early 1980s with that of the British Empire in the mid-nineteenth century. His conclusion: "The United States retains on all indicators a degree of dominance reached by the United Kingdom at no point" in the nineteenth century.[19]

---

16. Another useful comparison pursued by Layne, "Unipolar Illusion," is the Hapsburg ascendancy in sixteenth- and seventeenth-century Europe. I omit it for space reasons (the comparison to pre-Westphalian international politics is especially demanding) and because of limited data.

17. Waltz, *Theory of International Politics*, p. 131.

18. Writing of the United States in the 1960s, Waltz notes, "Never in modern history has a great power enjoyed so wide an economic and technological lead over the only other great power in the race." Ibid., p. 201. Throughout he is more concerned about the United States' *surplus* power and its associated temptations than about the rising power of any other states.

19. Bruce M. Russett, "The Mysterious Case of Vanishing Hegemony. Or, Is Mark Twain Really Dead?" *International Organization*, Vol. 39, No. 2 (Spring 1985), p. 211. See also Samuel P. Hunt-

In 1990 both Joseph Nye and Henry Nau published detailed studies of the U.S. position in world politics and the international political economy. Their conclusions mirrored Russett's: 1980s' America was a uniquely powerful hegemonic actor with a much more complete portfolio of capabilities than Britain ever had.[20]

In the years since those assessments were published, the United States' main geopolitical rival has collapsed into a regional power whose main threat to the international system is its own further disintegration, and its main economic rival has undergone a decade-long slump. The United States has maintained its military supremacy; added to its share of world product, manufactures, and high-technology production; increased its lead in productivity; and regained or strengthened its lead in many strategic industries.[21] Although recent events do remind us that the fortunes of states can change quickly in world politics even without war, the brute fact of the matter is that U.S. preeminence is unprecedented.

Table 1 shows how U.S. relative power in the late 1990s compares with that of Britain near its peak, as well as the United States itself during the Cold War. The United States' economic dominance is surpassed only by its own position at the dawn of the Cold War—when every other major power's economy was either exhausted or physically destroyed by the recent world war—and its military superiority dwarfs that of any leading state in modern international history. Even the Correlates of War (COW) composite index—which favors states with especially large populations and industrial economies—shows an improvement in the United States' relative position since the mid-1980s.[22]

ington, "The U.S.: Decline or Renewal?" *Foreign Affairs*, Vol. 67, No. 2 (Winter 1988/1989), pp. 76–96; and Susan Strange, "The Persistent Myth of Lost Hegemony," *International Organization*, Vol. 41, No. 4 (Autumn 1987), pp. 551–574.

20. Nye, *Bound to Lead*; and Henry R. Nau, *The Myth of America's Decline: Leading the World Economy into the 1990s* (New York: Oxford University Press, 1990).

21. By the 1980s, U.S. productivity growth had fallen to 1 percent a year. Since 1992 the rate of increase has been as high as 3 percent a year. See Nicholas Valéry, "Innovation in Industry," *Economist*, February 20, 1999, p. 27. For comparisons that show the increased productivity gap in favor of the United States among Organization for Economic Cooperation and Development (OECD) countries, see European Bank for Reconstruction and Development, *Transition Report 1997* (London: EBRD, 1997).

22. The COW index combines the following indicators with equal weights: total population, urban population, energy consumption, iron and steel production, military expenditures, and military personnel. As noted in Table 1, 1996 data were compiled by the author from different sources; COW methodology may lead to different results. I include the COW measure not because I think it is a good one but because it has a long history in the field. Quantitative scholars are increasingly critical of all such composite indexes. Gross domestic product (GDP) is becoming the favored indicator, a trend started by A.F.K. Organski in *World Politics*, 2d ed. (New York: Knopf, 1965): pp. 199–200, 211–215, and furthered by Organski and Jacek Kugler in *The War Ledger* (Chicago:

Table 1. Comparing Hegemonies.

a. Gross Domestic Product as Percentage of "Hegemon"

Year	United States	Britain	Russia	Japan	Austria	Germany	France	China
1870	108	100	90	n.a.	29	46	75	n.a.
1950	100	24	35	11	n.a.	15	15	n.a.
1985	100	17	39	38	n.a.	21	18	46
1997(PPP)	100	15	9	38	n.a.	22	16	53
1997 (exchange rate)	100	16	5	50	n.a.	25	17	10

b. Military Expenditures as Percentage of "Hegemon"

Year	United States	Britain	Russia	Japan	Austria	Germany	France	China
1872	68	100	120	n.a.	44	65	113	n.a.
1950	100	16	107	n.a.	n.a.	n.a.	10	n.a.
1985	100	10	109	5	n.a.	8	8	10
1996	100	13	26	17	n.a.	14	17	13

c. Power Capabilities (COW) as Percentage of "Hegemon"

Year	United States	Britain	Russia	Japan	Austria	Germany	France	China
1872	50	100	50	n.a.	27	50	60	n.a.
1950	100	37	103	n.a.	n.a.	3	21	n.a.
1985	100	22	167	56	n.a.	28	22	156
1996	100	14	43	36	n.a.	21	18	118

SOURCES: GDP figures, 1870–1985, from Angus Maddison, *Monitoring the World Economy, 1820–1992* (Paris: Organization for Economic Cooperation and Development, 1995). GDP figures, 1997 (PPP [purchasing power parity]), from Central Intelligence Agency (CIA) *World Factbook, 1998* (http://www.odci.gov/cia/publications/factbook/index.html). GDP figures, 1997 (exchange rate), from Economist Intelligence Unit, *World Outlook* (London: EIU, 1998). Military expenditures and COW, 1872–1985, from J. David Singer (University of Michigan) and Melvin Small (Wayne State University), "National Material Capabilities Data, 1816–1985" (computer file) (Ann Arbor, Mich.: Inter-University Consortium for Political and Social Research). Military Expenditures, 1997: International Institute of Strategic Studies, *The Military Balance 1997/98* (London: IISS, 1998). COW, 1996, compiled from IISS, *Military Balance 1997/98;* American Iron and Steel Institute, *Annual Statistical Report, 1997* (Washington, D.C.: AISI, 1998); World Bank, *World Development Indicators, 1998* (Washington, D.C.: International Bank for Reconstruction and Development, 1998); and United Nations, *UN Demographic Yearbook, 1996* (New York: United Nations, 1998).

NOTES: n.a.: Data not available or country not classed as a major power for given year. Germany = Federal Republic of Germany and Russia = Soviet Union in 1950 and 1985. a. Maddison's estimates are based on states' modern territories, tending to understate Austrian GDP in 1870. I added Maddison's estimates for Austria, Hungary, and Czechoslovakia. (In Russia's case, I added Finland; no data were available for Poland in 1870.) For comparison, see Paul Bairoch, "Europe's Gross National Product, 1800–1975," Journal of Economic History, Vol. 5, No. 2 (Fall 1976), pp. 273–340, whose estimates for 1860 give Austria 62 percent of Britain's GNP, and Russia 92 percent. According to the CIA, the PPP estimate for 1997 may overstate the size of China's economy by 25 percent. b. China's and Russia's military expenditures for 1996 are estimated using PPP ratios. c. 1996 index compiled by author using sources different from Singer and Small; it is representative of what such a composite index would yield but is not directly comparable to other COW figures.

Figure 1 presents the three measures of capabilities as a distribution among the great powers. It highlights the contrast between the extraordinary concentration of capabilities in the United States in the 1990s and the bipolar and multipolar distributions of the Cold War and the Pax Britannica. Never in modern international history has the leading state been so dominant economically and militarily.

In short, the standard measures that political scientists traditionally use as surrogates for capabilities suggest that the current system is unipolar.[23] But it takes only a glance at such measures to see that each is flawed in different ways. Economic output misses the salience for the balance of power of militarized states such as Prussia, pre–World War II Japan, Nazi Germany, or the Soviet Union, and, in any case, is very hard to measure for some states and in some periods. Military expenditures might conceal gross inefficiencies and involve similar measurement problems. Composite indexes capture the conventional wisdom that states must score well on many underlying elements to qualify as great powers. But any composite index that seems to capture the sources of national power in one period tends to produce patently absurd results for others.

Disaggregating the COW index reveals that Britain's high score in 1870 is the result of its early industrialization (high levels of iron production and coal consumption), the Soviet Union's strong showing in the late Cold War is driven by its massive military and heavy-industrial economy, and China's numbers are inflated by its huge population, numerous armed forces, and giant steel industry.[24] A roughly comparable index (Table 2) shows a more complicated

University of Chicago Press, 1980). Given its weighting of energy consumption, steel production, and military personnel, for example, the COW index had the Soviet Union surpassing U.S. power in 1971. Indeed, despite the fact that the Soviet Union produced, at best, one-third of U.S. GDP in the 1980s, it decisively surpassed the United States on *every* composite power indicator. See John R. Oneal, "Measuring the Material Base of the Contemporary East-West Balance of Power," *International Interactions*, Vol. 15, No. 2 (Summer 1989), pp. 177–196.

23. The only major indicator of hegemonic status in which the United States has continued to decline is net foreign indebtedness, which surpassed $1 trillion in 1996. For a strong argument on the importance of this indicator in governing the international political economy, see Robert Gilpin, *The Political Economy of International Relations* (Princeton, N.J.: Princeton University Press, 1987). There are other power indexes—many of which are linked to highly specific theories—that show continued U.S. decline. See George Modelski and William R. Thompson, *Leading Sectors and World Powers: The Coevolution of Global Economics and Politics* (Columbia: University of South Carolina Press, 1996); and Karen A. Rasler and William R. Thompson, *Great Powers and Global Struggle, 1490–1990* (Lexington: University Press of Kentucky, 1994). By most other measures of naval power or industrial competitiveness, however, the U.S. position has improved in the 1990s.

24. According to the COW index, Britain's relative power peaked in 1860, with a 36 percent share. In that year, Britain consumed 50 percent more energy and produced 35 percent more iron than all the other great powers (including the United States) combined; its urban population was twice

**Figure 1.   Comparing Concentrations of Power: Distribution (percentage) of GDP,
Military Outlays, and COW Index among the Major Powers: 1870–72, 1950,
1985, and 1996–97.**

a. Pax Britannica, 1870–72

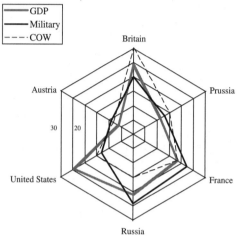

Country	GDP	Military	COW
Britain	24	20	30
Prussia	11	13	15
France	18	22	18
Russia	21	24	15
United States	24	13	15
Austria	6	9	8

b. Early Bipolarity, 1950

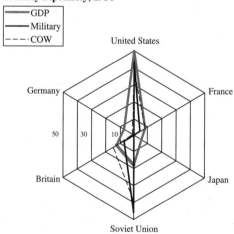

Country	GDP	Military	COW
United States	50	43	38
France	8	4	8
Japan	5	0	0
Soviet Union	18	46	39
Britain	12	7	14
Germany	7	0	1

c. Late Bipolarity, 1985

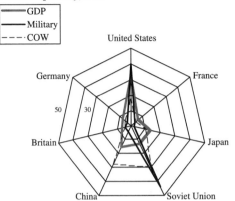

Country	GDP	Military	COW
United States	33	40	18
France	6	3	4
Japan	13	2	10
Soviet Union	13	44	30
China	15	4	28
Britain	6	4	4
Germany	7	3	5

d. Unipolarity, 1996–97

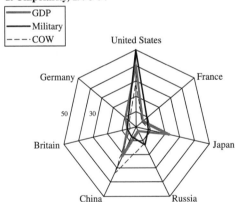

Country	GDP	Military	COW
United States	40	50	28
France	6	9	5
Japan	22	8	10
Russia	3	13	12
China	21	7	33
Britain	6	6	4
Germany	9	7	6

SOURCES: Compiled from data in Table 1.
NOTE: GDP for 1997 is based on PPP exchange rates.

Table 2. Disaggregated COW-Style Indicators for the Major Powers, 1995-97.

	Population (1996, percentage)	Per Capita GDP (1997, PPP)	Manufacturing Production (1995, percentage)	Commercial Energy Use (1996, percentage)	Military Expenditures (1996, percentage)	Military Personnel (1996, percentage)
United States	13	30.2	37	41	52	18
China	62	3.5	8	21	7	36
Japan	6	24.5	27	10	6	3
Germany	4	20.8	14	7	7	5
Russia	7	4.7	n.a.	12	13	30
Britain	3	21.2	6	5	6	3
France	3	22.7	7	5	9	5

SOURCES: Central Intelligence Agency, *World Factbook, 1998* (http://www.odci.gov/cia/publications/factbook/index.html); International Institute of Strategic Studies, *The Military Balance 1997/98* (London: IISS, 1998); World Bank, *World Development Indicators, 1999* (Washington, D.C.: International Bank for Reconstruction and Development, 1999); and National Science Foundation, *Science and Technology Indicators, 1998* (http://www.nsf.gov/sbe/srs/seind98/start.htm).

NOTE: n.a.: Data not available.

picture than that conveyed by simple comparisons of gross economic output or military expenditures. But even this comparison reveals that unlike Britain at its peak, the United States currently leads in every key indicator of power except population and military personnel.[25]

The specific problem with the COW index is its implicit assumption that the wellsprings of national power have not changed since the dawn of the industrial age. Updating such an index to take account of the post–industrial revolution in political economy and military affairs would inevitably be a subjective procedure. By most such "information-age" measures, however, the United States possesses decisive advantages (Table 3). The United States not only has the largest high-technology economy in the world by far, it also has the greatest concentration in high-technology manufacturing among the major powers.[26] Total U.S. expenditures on research and development (R&D) nearly equal the combined total of the rest of the Group of Seven richest countries (and the G-7 accounts for 90 percent of world spending on R&D). Numerous studies of U.S. technological leadership confirm the country's dominant position in all the key "leading sectors" that are most likely to dominate the world economy into the twenty-first century.[27]

The U.S. combination of quantitative and qualitative material advantages is unprecedented, and it translates into a unique geopolitical position. Thanks to a decades-old policy of harnessing technology to the generation of military power, the U.S. comparative advantage in this area mirrors Britain's naval

---

as large as that of the next most urban power (France). This is the indicator Layne, "Unipolar Illusion," uses to make his case for Britain's status as a unipolar power. For more on measuring relative power, polarity, and concentration of capabilities over time, see J. David Singer and Paul F. Diehl, eds., *Measuring the Correlates of War* (Ann Arbor: University of Michigan Press, 1990).

25. Table 2 substitutes per capita gross domestic product for urban population (which was supposed to capture modernization) and manufacturing production for steel production (which was supposed to capture industrial power).

26. OECD, *Science, Technology, and Industry: Scoreboard of Indicators 1997* (Paris: OECD, 1997). By one estimate, the United States accounted for 35.8 percent of total world spending on technology in 1997. Japan accounted for 17.6 percent, Germany 6.6 percent, Britain 5.7 percent, France 5.1 percent, and China 1.6 percent. Mark Landler, "When the Dragon Awakes . . . and Finds That It's Not 1999 Anymore," *New York Times*, May 11, 1999, p. C1.

27. These studies do forecast *future* challenges—as they have since the 1970s. The incentives of nearly all data-gathering agencies are to emphasize U.S. vulnerability, yet as good social scientists, the authors of these studies acknowledge the country's decisive current advantages. See, for example, U.S. Department of Commerce, Office of Technology Policy, *The New Innovators: Global Patenting Trends in Five Sectors* (Washington, D.C.: OTP, 1998). Similarly, according to Valéry, "Innovation in Industry," p. 27, "By 1998, the Council on Competitiveness, an industry think tank in Washington set up to fathom the reasons for the country's decline, concluded that America had not only regained its former strengths, but was now far ahead technologically in the five most crucial sectors of its economy."

preeminence in the nineteenth century. At the same time, Washington's current brute share of great power capabilities—its aggregate potential compared with that of the next largest power or all other great powers combined—dwarfs Britain's share in its day. The United States is the only state with global power projection capabilities; it is probably capable, if challenged, of producing defensive land-power dominance in the key theaters; it retains the world's only truly blue-water navy; it dominates the air; it has retained a nuclear posture that may give it first-strike advantages against other nuclear powers; and it has continued to nurture decades-old investments in military logistics and command, control, communications, and intelligence. By devoting only 3 percent of its gross domestic product (GDP) to defense, it outspends all other great powers combined—and most of those great powers are its close allies. Its defense R&D expenditures are probably greater than those of the rest of the world combined (Table 3). None of the major powers is balancing; most have scaled back military expenditures faster than the United States has. One reason may be that democracy and globalization have changed the nature of world politics. Another possibility, however, is that any effort to compete directly with the United States is futile, so no one tries.

QUALITATIVE COMPARISON

Bringing historical detail to bear on the comparison of today's distribution of power to past systems only strengthens the initial conclusions that emerge from quantitative comparisons. Two major concentrations of power over the last two centuries show up on different quantitative measures of capabilities: the COW measure picks Britain in 1860–70 as an especially powerful actor, and the GDP measure singles out the post–World War II United States. These indicators miss two crucial factors that only historical research can reveal: the clarity of the balance as determined by the events that help decisionmakers define and measure power, and the comprehensiveness of the leader's overall power advantage in each period.[28] Together these factors help to produce a U.S. preponderance that is far less ambiguous, and therefore less subject to challenge, than that of previous leading states.

The end of the Cold War and the collapse of the Soviet Union were much more effective tests of material power relationships than any of the systemic

---

28. This is based on the neoclassical realist argument that power is important to decisionmakers but very hard to measure. See, for a general discussion, Gideon Rose, "Neoclassical Realism and Theories of Foreign Policy," *World Politics*, Vol. 51, No. 1 (October 1998), pp. 144–172.

Table 3. Information-Age Indicators for the Major Powers, 1995-97.

	High-Technology Manufacturing (1995, percentage)	Total R&D Expenditures (1995, percentage)	Defense R&D Expenditures (1995-96, percentage)	Utility Invention Patents Granted in the United States (1997, thousands)	PCs per 1,000 People (1997)	Internet Hosts per 10,000 People (July 1998)	Scientists and Engineers in R&D per Million People (1985-95)
United States	41	53	80	61	407	976	3,732
Britain	6	6	7	2	242	201	2,417
Japan	30	22	2	23	202	107	5,677
France	5	8	8	n.a.	174	73	2,537
Germany	10	11	3	6.8	255	141	3,016
China	8	n.a.	n.a.	n.a.	6	.16	537
Russia	n.a.	n.a.	n.a.	n.a.	32	9	4,358

SOURCES: World Bank, *World Development Indicators, 1999* (Washington, D.C.: International Bank for Reconstruction and Development, 1999); National Science Foundation, *Science and Technology Indicators, 1998* (http://www.nsf.gov/sbe/srs/seind98/start.htm); Organization for Economic Cooperation and Development, *Science, Technology, and Industry: Scoreboard of Indicators, 1997* (Paris: OECD, 1997); and Michael B. Albert, Phyllis Genther Yoshida, and Debra van Opstal, *The New Innovators: Global Patenting Trends in Five Sectors* (Washington, D.C.: U.S. Department of Commerce, Office of Technology Policy, September 1998).

NOTES: n.a.: Data not available. Russia's R&D as a percentage of GDP has fallen to below 0.75. According to Albert, Yoshida, and van Opstal, *The New Innovators*, utility invention patents granted in the United States to nationals of a given country is the best measure of national trends in industrial and technological innovation. Nationals of all European Union states combined were granted 16,400 such patents in 1997. Because the domain name and physical location of internet hosts do not always correlate, data on internet hosts should be considered approximate.

wars of the past two centuries.[29] One reason is simple arithmetic. The greater the number of players, the more difficult it is for any single war or event to clarify relations of power throughout the system. Even very large wars in multipolar systems do not provide unambiguous tests of the relative power of the states belonging to the victorious coalition. And wars often end before the complete defeat of major powers. The systemic wars of the past left several great states standing and ready to argue over their relative power. By contrast, bipolarity was built on two states, and one collapsed with more decisiveness than most wars can generate. The gap between the capabilities of the super-powers, on the one hand, and all other major powers, on the other hand, was already greater in the Cold War than any analogous gap in the history of the European states system. Given that the United States and the Soviet Union were so clearly in a class by themselves, the fall of one from superpower status leaves the other much more unambiguously "number one" than at any other time since 1815.

Moreover, the power gap in the United States' favor is wider than any single measure can capture because the unipolar concentration of resources is *symmetrical*. Unlike previous system leaders, the United States has commanding leads in all the elements of material power: economic, military, technological, and geographical. All the naval and commercial powers that most scholars identify as the hegemonic leaders of the past lacked military (especially land-power) capabilities commensurate with their global influence. Asymmetrical power portfolios generate ambiguity. When the leading state excels in the production of economic and naval capabilities but not conventional land power, it may seem simultaneously powerful and vulnerable. Such asymmetrical power portfolios create resentment among second-tier states that are powerful militarily but lack the great prestige the leading state's commercial and naval advantages bring. At the same time, they make the leader seem vulnerable to pressure from the one element of power in which it does not excel: military capabilities. The result is ambiguity about which state is more powerful, which is more secure, which is threatening which, and which might make a bid for hegemony.

Britain's huge empire, globe-girdling navy, and vibrant economy left strong imprints on nineteenth-century world politics, but because its capabilities were

---

29. The relationship between hierarchies of power revealed by systemic wars and the stability of international systems is explored in Robert Gilpin, *War and Change in World Politics* (Cambridge: Cambridge University Press, 1981). On wars as power tests, see Geoffrey Blainey, *The Causes of War* (New York: Free Press, 1973).

always skewed in favor of naval and commercial power, it never had the aggregate advantage implied by its early industrialization. Indeed, it was not even the international system's unambiguous leader until Russia's defeat in Crimea in 1856. The Napoleonic Wars yielded *three* potential hegemons: Britain, the decisive naval and financial power; Russia, the preeminent military power on the continent; and France, the state whose military prowess had called forth coalitions involving all the other great states. From 1815 to 1856, Britain had to share leadership of the system with Russia, while the power gap between these two empires and France remained perilously small.[30] Russia's defeat in Crimea punctured its aura of power and established Britain's uncontested primacy. But even after 1856, the gap between London and continental powerhouses such as France, Russia, and Prussia remained small because Britain never translated its early-industrial potential into continental-scale military capabilities. The Crimean victory that ushered in the era of British preeminence was based mainly on *French* land power.[31] And Britain's industrial advantage peaked before industrial capabilities came to be seen as the sine qua non of military power.[32]

---

30. It goes without saying that the nineteenth-century international system was perceived as multipolar, although Russia and Britain were seen as being in a class by themselves. See R.W. Seton-Watson, *Britain in Europe, 1789–1914: A Survey of Foreign Policy* (Cambridge: Cambridge University Press, 1937). To gain a sense of Russia's power in the period, it is enough to recall Czar Nicholas's dispatch of 400,000 troops to crush the 1848 revolt in Hungary—and his simultaneous offer to send another contingent across Europe to establish order in Paris should it be necessary. On Russia as Europe's hegemon, see M.S. Anderson, *The Rise of Modern Diplomacy, 1450–1919* (London: Longman, 1993); Adam Watson, "Russia in the European States System," in Watson and Hedley Bull, eds., *The Expansion of International Society* (Oxford: Clarendon, 1984). On Russia and Britain as (rivalrous) "cohegemons," see Paul W. Schroeder, *The Transformation of European Politics* (London: Oxford University Press, 1993); and Gordon A. Craig, "The System of Alliances and the Balance of Power," in J.P.T. Bury, ed., *New Cambridge Modern History*, Volume 10: *The Zenith of European Power, 1830–70* (Cambridge: Cambridge University Press 1960). The best, concise discussion of the nature and limitations of British power in this period is Paul Kennedy, *The Rise and Fall of British Naval Mastery* (London: Macmillan, 1983), chap. 6.

31. For an excellent account of the British debate on the lessons of Crimea, see Olive Anderson, *A Liberal State at War: English Politics and Economics during the Crimean War* (New York: St. Martin's, 1967).

32. Thus the COW measure suffers from a hindsight bias that accords importance to industrial capabilities before their military significance was appreciated. Cf. William B. Moul, "Measuring the 'Balance of Power': A Look at Some Numbers," *Review of International Studies*, Vol. 15, No. 2 (April 1989), pp. 101–121. On the conservatism of nineteenth-century military assessments, see B.H. Liddell-Hart, "Armed Forces and the Art of War: Armies," in Bury, *New Cambridge Modern History*. On the slowly growing perceptions of industrialization and its implications for war, see William H. McNeil, *The Pursuit of Power: Technology, Armed Force, and Society since A.D. 1000* (Chicago: University of Chicago Press, 1982); Dennis Showalter, *Railroads and Rifles: Soldiers, Technology, and the Unification of Germany* (Hamden, Conn.: Archer, 1975); Paul Kennedy, *The Rise of the Anglo-German Antagonism, 1860–1914* (London: Allen and Unwin, 1980); and Kennedy, *Rise and Fall of British Naval Mastery*.

The Cold War power gap between the United States and the Soviet Union was much smaller. World War II yielded ambiguous lessons concerning the relative importance of U.S. sea, air, and economic capabilities versus the Soviet Union's proven conventional military superiority in Eurasia.[33] The conflict clearly showed that the United States possessed the greatest military potential in the world—if it could harness its massive economy to the production of military power and deploy that power to the theater in time. Despite its economic weaknesses, however, Stalin's empire retained precisely those advantages that Czar Nicholas I's had had: the ability to take and hold key Eurasian territory with land forces. The fact that Moscow's share of world power was already in Eurasia (and already in the form of an armed fighting force) was decisive in explaining the Cold War. It was chiefly because of its location (and its militarized nature) that the Soviet Union's economy was capable of generating bipolarity. At the dawn of the Cold War, when the United States' economy was as big as those of all other great powers combined, the balance of power was still seen as precarious.[34]

In both the Pax Britannica and the early Cold War, different measures show power to have been concentrated in the leading state to an unusual degree. Yet in both periods, the perceived power gaps were closer than the measures imply. Asymmetrical power portfolios and small power gaps are the norm in modern international history. They are absent from the distribution of power of the late 1990s. Previous postwar hegemonic moments therefore cannot compare with post–Cold War unipolarity. Given the dramatically different power distribution alone, we should expect world politics to work much differently now than in the past.

---

33. I discuss these lessons in Wohlforth, *Elusive Balance: Power and Perceptions during the Cold War* (Ithaca, N.Y.: Cornell University Press, 1993). A much fuller analysis is available in recent historical works. For the U.S. side, see Marc Trachtenberg, *A Constructed Peace: The Making of the European Settlement, 1945–1963* (Princeton, N.J.: Princeton University Press, 1999); and Melvyn P. Leffler, *A Preponderance of Power: National Security, the Truman Administration, and the Cold War* (Stanford, Calif.: Stanford University Press, 1992). And for the view from Moscow, see Vladislav M. Zubok and Constantine Pleshakov, *Inside the Kremlin's Cold War* (Cambridge, Mass.: Harvard University Press, 1996); and Vojtech Mastny, *The Cold War and Soviet Insecurity: The Stalin Years* (New York: Oxford University Press, 1996).

34. As Marc Trachtenberg summarizes the view from Washington in 1948: "The defense of the West rested on a very narrow base. Even with the nuclear monopoly, American power only barely balanced Soviet power in central Europe." See Trachtenberg, *A Constructed Peace*, p. 91. Cf. Leffler, *A Preponderance of Power*, who is more critical of U.S. officials' power assessments. Nevertheless, Leffler's narrative—and the massive documentary evidence it relies on—would not be possible had the Soviet potential to dominate Eurasia not been plausible.

Unipolarity Is Peaceful

Unipolarity favors the absence of war among the great powers and comparatively low levels of competition for prestige or security for two reasons: the leading state's power advantage removes the problem of hegemonic rivalry from world politics, and it reduces the salience and stakes of balance-of-power politics among the major states. This argument is based on two well-known realist theories: hegemonic theory and balance-of-power theory. Each is controversial, and the relationship between the two is complex.[35] For the purposes of this analysis, however, the key point is that both theories predict that a unipolar system will be peaceful.

HOW TO THINK ABOUT UNIPOLARITY

Hegemonic theory has received short shrift in the debate over the nature of the post–Cold War international system.[36] This omission is unwarranted, for the theory has simple and profound implications for the peacefulness of the post–Cold War international order that are backed up by a formidable body of scholarship. The theory stipulates that especially powerful states ("hegemons") foster international orders that are stable until differential growth in power produces a dissatisfied state with the capability to challenge the dominant state for leadership. The clearer and larger the concentration of power in the leading state, the more peaceful the international order associated with it will be.

---

35. For simplicity, I treat only Waltz's neorealist version of balance-of-power theory. By "hegemonic theory," I mean the theory of hegemonic war and change in Gilpin, *War and Change in World Politics*, as well as power transition theory, which is sometimes applied to pairs of states other than hegemon and challenger. In addition to Organski, *World Politics*, and Organski and Kugler, *War Ledger*, see Jacek Kugler and Douglas Lemke, eds., *Parity and War: Evaluation and Extension of the War Ledger* (Ann Arbor: University of Michigan Press, 1996); and the chapters by George Modelski and William R. Thompson, Manus I. Midlarsky, and Jacek Kugler and A.F.K. Organski in Midlarsky, ed., *Handbook of War Studies* (London: Unwin, 1989). Theories of the balance of power and hegemony are often thought to be competing. I maintained this position in *Elusive Balance*, chap. 1. In many instances, however, they are complementary. See Randall L. Schweller and William C. Wohlforth, "Power Test: Updating Realism in Response to the End of the Cold War," *Security Studies* (forthcoming). For an interesting synthesis with some points of contact with the analysis here, see William R. Thompson, "Dehio, Long Cycles, and the Geohistorical Context of Structural Transition," *World Politics*, Vol. 45, No. 1 (October 1992), pp. 127–152; and Rasler and Thompson, *Great Powers and Global Struggle*.
36. Exceptions include Lemke, "Continuity of History"; and Mark S. Sheetz, "Correspondence: Debating the Unipolar Moment," *International Security*, Vol. 22, No. 3 (Winter 1997/1998), pp. 168–174.

The key is that conflict occurs only if the leader and the challenger disagree about their relative power. That is, the leader must think itself capable of defending the status quo at the same time that the number two state believes it has the power to challenge it. The set of perceptions and expectations necessary to produce such conflict is most likely under two circumstances: when the overall gap between the leader and the challenger is small and/or when the challenger overtakes the leader in *some* elements of national power but not others, and the two parties disagree over the relative importance of these elements. Hence both the overall size and the comprehensiveness of the leader's power advantage are crucial to peacefulness. If the system is unipolar, the great power hierarchy should be much more stable than any hierarchy lodged within a system of more than one pole. Because unipolarity is based on a historically unprecedented concentration of power in the United States, a potentially important source of great power conflict—hegemonic rivalry—will be missing.

Balance-of-power theory has been at the center of the debate, but absent so far is a clear distinction between peacefulness and durability. The theory predicts that any system comprised of states in anarchy will evince a tendency toward equilibrium. As Waltz puts it, "Unbalanced power, whoever wields it, is a potential danger to others."[37] This central proposition lies behind the widespread belief that unipolarity will not be durable (a contention I address below). Less often noted is the fact that as long as the system remains unipolar, balance-of-power theory predicts peace. When balance-of-power theorists argue that the post–Cold War world is headed toward conflict, they are not claiming that unipolarity causes conflict. Rather, they are claiming that unipolarity leads quickly to bi- or multipolarity. It is not unipolarity's peacefulness but its durability that is in dispute.

Waltz argued that bipolarity is less war prone than multipolarity because it reduces uncertainty. By the same logic, unpolarity is the least war prone of all structures.[38] For as long as unipolarity obtains, there is little uncertainty re-

---

37. Waltz, "Evaluating Theories," p. 915.
38. The connection between uncertainty, the number of principal players, and war proneness has been questioned. The key to most recent criticisms of neorealist arguments concerning stability is that the distribution of capabilities alone is insufficient to explain the war proneness of international systems. Ancillary assumptions concerning risk attitudes or preferences for the status quo are necessary. See Levy, "The Causes of War"; Bruce Bueno de Mesquita, "Neorealism's Logic and Evidence: When Is a Theory Falsified?" paper prepared for the Fiftieth Annual Conference of the International Studies Association, Washington, D.C., February 1999; and Robert Powell, "Stability and the Distribution of Power," *World Politics*, Vol. 48, No. 2 (January 1996), pp. 239–267, and

garding alliance choices or the calculation of power. The only options available to second-tier states are to bandwagon with the polar power (either explicitly or implicitly) or, at least, to take no action that could incur its focused enmity. As long as their security policies are oriented around the power and preferences of the sole pole, second-tier states are less likely to engage in conflict-prone rivalries for security or prestige. Once the sole pole takes sides, there can be little doubt about which party will prevail. Moreover, the unipolar leader has the capability to be far more interventionist than earlier system leaders. Exploiting the other states' security dependence as well as its unilateral power advantages, the sole pole can maintain a system of alliances that keeps second-tier states out of trouble.[39]

Until the underlying distribution of power changes, second-tier states face structural incentives similar to those of lesser states in a region dominated by one power, such as North America. The low incidence of wars in those systems is consistent with the expectations of standard, balance-of-power thinking. Otto von Bismarck earned a reputation for strategic genius by creating and managing a complex alliance system that staved off war while working disproportionately to his advantage in a multipolar setting. It does not take a Bismarck to run a Bismarckian alliance system under unipolarity. No one credits the United States with strategic genius for managing security dilemmas among American states. Such an alliance system is a structurally favored and hence less remarkable and more durable outcome in a unipolar system.

In sum, both hegemonic theory and balance-of-power theory specify thresholds at which great concentrations of power support a peaceful structure. Balance-of-power theory tells us that smaller is better.[40] Therefore one pole is best, and security competition among the great powers should be minimal. Hegemonic theory tells us that a clear preponderance in favor of a leading state with a comprehensive power portfolio should eliminate rivalry for primacy. Overall, then, unipolarity generates comparatively few incentives for security or prestige competition among the great powers.

---

sources cited therein. These analyses are right that no distribution of power rules out war if some states are great risk takers or have extreme clashes of interest. The greater the preponderance of power, however, the more extreme the values of other variables must be to produce war, because preponderance reduces the uncertainty of assessing the balance of power.

39. The sole pole's power advantages matter only to the degree that it is engaged, and it is most likely to be engaged in politics among the other major powers. The argument applies with less force to potential security competition between regional powers, or between a second-tier state and a lesser power with which the system leader lacks close ties.

40. Three may be worse than four, however. See Waltz, *Theory of International Politics,* chap. 9; and Schweller, *Deadly Imbalances.*

THE MISSING SYSTEMIC SOURCES OF CONFLICT

Unipolarity does not imply the end of all conflict or that Washington can have its way on all issues all the time. It simply means the absence of two big problems that bedeviled the statesmen of past epochs: hegemonic rivalry and balance-of-power politics among the major powers. It is only by forgetting them that scholars and pundits are able to portray the current period as dangerous and threatening.

To appreciate the sources of conflict that unipolarity avoids, consider the two periods already discussed in which leading states scored very highly on aggregate measures of power: the Pax Britannica and the Cold War. Because those concentrations of power were not unipolar, both periods witnessed security competition and hegemonic rivalry. The Crimean War is a case in point. The war unfolded in a system in which two states shared leadership and *three* states were plausibly capable of bidding for hegemony.[41] Partly as a result, neither the statesmen of the time nor historians over the last century and a half have been able to settle the debate over the origins of the conflict. The problem is that even those who agree that the war arose from a threat to the European balance of power cannot agree on whether the threat emanated from France, Russia, or Britain.[42] Determining which state really did threaten the equilibrium—or indeed whether any of them did—is less important than the fact that the power gap among them was small enough to make all three threats seem plausible at the time and in retrospect. No such uncertainty—and hence no such conflict—is remotely possible in a unipolar system.

Even during the height of its influence after 1856, Britain was never a major land power and could not perform the conflict-dampening role that a unipolar state can play. Thus it would be inaccurate to ascribe the two, long nineteenth-century periods of peace to British power. From 1815 to 1853, London exercised influence in the context of the Concert of Europe, which was based on a Russo-British cohegemony. But because each of these competitive "bookend

---

41. See Schroeder, *Transformation of European Politics*, Paul W. Schroeder, *Austria, Britain, and the Crimean War: The Destruction of the European Concert* (Ithaca, N.Y.: Cornell University Press, 1972); Adam Watson, *The Evolution of International Society* (London: Routledge, 1992); and William E. Echard, *Napoleon III and the Concert of Europe* (Baton Rouge: Louisiana State University Press, 1983), chaps. 1–2.
42. Cf. David M. Goldfrank, *The Origins of the Crimean War* (London: Longman, 1994); Norman Rich, *Why the Crimean War? A Cautionary Tale* (London: University Press of America, 1985); Ludwig Dehio, *The Precarious Balance: Four Centuries of the European Struggle* (New York: Knopf, 1962), chap. 4; David Wetzel, *The Crimean War: A Diplomatic History* (New York: Columbia University Press, 1985); and A.J.P. Taylor's account in Taylor, *The Struggle for Mastery in Europe* (Oxford: Oxford University Press, 1954).

empires" was in possession of a different mix of power resources whose ultimate superiority had not been tested, great power cooperation was always vulnerable to hegemonic rivalry—a problem that helped destroy the concert in the Crimean War. With Britain in "splendid isolation" after 1856, Prussia violently refashioned the balance of power in Europe without having to concern itself greatly about London's preferences. After 1871 Bismarck's diplomacy, backed up by Germany's formidable power, played the crucial role in staving off violent competition for power or security on the continent. Owing to differences in the system structure alone, the long periods of peace in the nineteenth century are much more remarkable achievements of statesmanship than a similarly lengthy peace would be under unipolarity.

Similar sources of conflict emerged in the Cold War. The most recent and exhaustively researched accounts of Cold War diplomacy reveal in detail what the numerical indicators only hint at: the complex interplay between U.S. overall economic superiority, on the one hand, and the Soviet Union's massive conventional military capabilities, on the other.[43] This asymmetrical distribution of power meant that the gap between the two top states could be seen as lopsided or perilously close depending on one's vantage. The fact that the United States was preeminent only in nonmilitary elements of power was a critical factor underlying the Cold War competition for power and security. To produce a military balance, Washington set about creating a preponderance of other capabilities, which constituted a latent threat to Moscow's war planners and a major constraint on its diplomatic strategy. Hence both Moscow and Washington could simultaneously see their rivalry as a consequence of the other's drive for hegemony—sustaining a historical debate that shows every sign of being as inconclusive as that over the origins of the Crimean War. Again, no such ambiguity, and no such conflict, is likely in a unipolar system.

Both hegemonic rivalry and security competition among great powers are unlikely under unipolarity. Because the current leading state is by far the world's most formidable military power, the chances of leadership conflict are more remote than at any time over the last two centuries. Unlike past international systems, efforts by any second-tier state to enhance its relative position can be managed in a unipolar system without raising the specter of a power transition and a struggle for primacy. And because the major powers face

---

43. Trachtenberg, *A Constructed Peace*; Leffler, *A Preponderance of Power*; John Lewis Gaddis, *We Now Know: Rethinking Cold War History* (Oxford: Oxford University Press, 1997); Mastny, *The Cold War and Soviet Insecurity*; and Zubok and Pleshakov, *Inside the Kremlin's Cold War.*

incentives to shape their policies with a view toward the power and preferences of the system leader, the likelihood of security competition among them is lower than in previous systems.

Unipolarity Is Durable

Unipolarity rests on two pillars. I have already established the first: the sheer size and comprehensiveness of the power gap separating the United States from other states. This massive power gap implies that any countervailing change must be strong and sustained to produce structural effects. The second pillar—geography—is just as important. In addition to all the other advantages the United States possesses, we must also consider its four truest allies: Canada, Mexico, the Atlantic, and the Pacific. Location matters. The fact that Soviet power happened to be situated in the heart of Eurasia was a key condition of bipolarity. Similarly, the U.S. position as an offshore power determines the nature and likely longevity of unipolarity. Just as the raw numbers could not capture the real dynamics of bipolarity, power indexes alone cannot capture the importance of the fact that the United States is in North America while all the other potential poles are in or around Eurasia. The balance of power between the sole pole and the second-tier states is not the only one that matters, and it may not even be the most important one for many states. Local balances of power may loom larger in the calculations of other states than the background unipolar structure. Efforts to produce a counterbalance globally will generate powerful countervailing action locally. As a result, the threshold concentration of power necessary to sustain unipolarity is lower than most scholars assume.

Because they fail to appreciate the sheer size and comprehensiveness of the power gap and the advantages conveyed by geography, many scholars expect bi- or multipolarity to reappear quickly. They propose three ways in which unipolarity will end: counterbalancing by other states, regional integration, or the differential growth in power. None of these is likely to generate structural change in the policy-relevant future.[44]

---

44. Here I depart from Waltz, *Theory of International Politics*, pp. 161–162, for whom a stable system is one with no "consequential variation" in the number of poles (e.g., changes between multi-, tri-, bi-, or unipolarity). In the European states system, multipolarity obtained for three centuries. While the multipolar structure itself was long lived, however, the identity of its members (the leading states in the system) changed with much greater frequency—a matter of no small consequence for the governments concerned. By this measure (change in the identity, as opposed to the number, of the states that define the structure), bipolarity had a typical life span. See Bueno de Mesquita, "Neorealism's Logic and Evidence." I expect that the unipolar era will be of comparable duration.

ALLIANCES ARE NOT STRUCTURAL

Many scholars portray unipolarity as precarious by ignoring all the impediments to balancing in the real world. If balancing were the frictionless, costless activity assumed in some balance-of-power theories, then the unipolar power would need more than 50 percent of the capabilities in the great power system to stave off a counterpoise. Even though the United States meets this threshold today, in a hypothetical world of frictionless balancing its edge might be eroded quickly.[45] But such expectations miss the fact that alliance politics always impose costs, and that the impediments to balancing are especially great in the unipolar system that emerged in the wake of the Cold War.

Alliances are not structural. Because alliances are far less effective than states in producing and deploying power internationally, most scholars follow Waltz in making a distinction between the distribution of capabilities among states and the alliances states may form.[46] A unipolar system is one in which a counterbalance is impossible. When a counterbalance becomes possible, the system is not unipolar. The point at which this structural shift can happen is determined in part by how efficiently alliances can aggregate the power of individual states. Alliances aggregate power only to the extent that they are reliably binding and permit the merging of armed forces, defense industries, R&D infrastructures, and strategic decisionmaking. A glance at international history shows how difficult it is to coordinate counterhegemonic alliances. States are tempted to free ride, pass the buck, or bandwagon in search of favors from the aspiring hegemon. States have to worry about being abandoned by alliance partners when the chips are down or being dragged into conflicts of others' making.[47] The aspiring hegemon, meanwhile, has only to make sure its domestic house is in order. In short, a single state gets more bang for the buck than several states in an alliance. To the extent that alliances are inefficient at pooling power, the sole pole obtains greater power per unit of aggregate capabilities than any alliance that might take shape against it. Right away, the odds are skewed in favor of the unipolar power.

The key, however, is that the countercoalitions of the past—on which most of our empirical knowledge of alliance politics is based—formed against cen-

45. I do not deny the utility of making simplifying assumptions when speculating about the balance of power. For one such analysis, see Michael W. Doyle, *Ways of War and Peace: Realism, Liberalism, and Socialism* (New York: W.W. Norton, 1997), pp. 456–473.
46. Waltz, *Theory of International Politics*; and Snyder, *Alliance Politics*.
47. See Snyder, *Alliance Politics*; and Thomas J. Christensen and Jack Snyder, "Chain Gangs and Passed Bucks: Predicting Alliance Patterns in Multipolarity," *International Organization*, Vol. 44, No. 1 (Winter 1990), pp. 137–168.

trally located land powers (France, Germany, and the Soviet Union) that constituted relatively unambiguous security threats to their neighbors. Coordinating a counterbalance against an *offshore* state that has *already* achieved unipolar status will be much more difficult.[48] Even a declining offshore unipolar state will have unusually wide opportunities to play divide and rule. Any second-tier state seeking to counterbalance has to contend with the existing pro-U.S. bandwagon. If things go poorly, the aspiring counterbalancer will have to confront not just the capabilities of the unipolar state, but also those of its other great power allies. All of the aspiring poles face a problem the United States does not: great power neighbors that could become crucial U.S. allies the moment an unambiguous challenge to Washington's preeminence emerges. In addition, in each region there are smaller "pivotal states" that make natural U.S. allies against an aspiring regional power.[49] Indeed, the United States' first move in any counterbalancing game of this sort could be to try to promote such pivotal states to great power status, as it did with China against the Soviet Union in the latter days of the Cold War.

NEW REGIONAL UNIPOLARITIES: A GAME NOT WORTH THE CANDLE

To bring an end to unipolarity, it is not enough for regional powers to coordinate policies in traditional alliances. They must translate their aggregate economic potential into the concrete capabilities necessary to be a pole: a defense industry and power projection capabilities that can play in the same league as those of the United States. Thus all scenarios for the rapid return of multipolarity involve regional unification or the emergence of strong regional unipolarities.[50] For the European, Central Eurasian, or East Asian poles to measure up to the United States in the near future, each region's resources need to fall under the de facto control of one state or decisionmaking authority. In the near term, either true unification in Europe and Central Eurasia (the European Union [EU] becomes a de facto state, or Russia recreates an empire) or unipolar dominance in each region by Germany, Russia, and China or Japan, respectively, is a necessary condition of bi- or multipolarity.

---

48. The key here is that from the standpoint of balance-of-power theory, we are dealing with a structural fait accompli. Of the two powers that made up the bipolar order, one collapsed, leaving the other at the center of a unipolar system. A situation has arisen in which the theory's central tendency cannot operate. Many readers will perceive this state of affairs as a testimony to the weakness of balance-of-power theory. I agree. The weaker the theory, the longer our initial expectations of unipolarity's longevity.
49. On "pivotal states," see Robert Chase, Emily Hill, and Paul Kennedy, *The Pivotal States: A New Framework for U.S. Policy in the Developing World* (New York: W.W. Norton, 1999).
50. Kupchan, "Pax Americana," advocates just such a system.

The problem with these scenarios is that regional balancing dynamics are likely to kick in against the local great power much more reliably than the global counterbalance works against the United States. Given the neighborhoods they live in, an aspiring Chinese, Japanese, Russian, or German pole would face more effective counterbalancing than the United States itself.

If the EU were a state, the world would be bipolar. To create a balance of power globally, Europe would have to suspend the balance of power locally. Which balance matters more to Europeans is not a question that will be resolved quickly. A world with a European pole would be one in which the French and the British had merged their conventional and nuclear capabilities and do not mind if the Germans control them. The EU may move in this direction, but in the absence of a major shock the movement will be very slow and ambiguous. Global leadership requires coherent and quick decisionmaking in response to crises. Even on international monetary matters, Europe will lack this capability for some time.[51] Creating the institutional and political requisites for a single European foreign and security policy and defense industry goes to the heart of state sovereignty and thus is a much more challenging task for the much longer term.[52]

The reemergence of a Central Eurasian pole is more remote. There, the problem is not only that the key regional powers are primed to balance against a rising Russia but that Russia continues to decline. States do not rise as fast as Russia fell. For Russia to regain the capability for polar status is a project of a generation, if all goes well. For an Asian pole to emerge quickly, Japan and China would need to merge their capabilities. As in the case of Europe and Central Eurasia, a great deal has to happen in world politics before either Tokyo or Beijing is willing to submit to the unipolar leadership of the other.

Thus the quick routes to multipolarity are blocked. If states value their independence and security, most will prefer the current structure to a multipolarity based on regional unipolarities. Eventually, some great powers will have the capability to counter the United States alone or in traditional great power

---

51. See Kathleen R. McNamara, "European Monetary Union and International Economic Cooperation," a report on a workshop organized by the International Finance Section, Princeton University, April 3, 1998. Cf. Kupchan, "Rethinking Europe," who contends: "Assuming the European Union succeeds in deepening its level of integration and adding new members, it will soon have influence on matters of finance and trade equal to America's. A more balanced strategic relationship is likely to follow." Many Europeans see a contradiction between widening and deepening the EU.
52. This is why many Americans support an EU "security identity." If all goes well, Europe will become a more useful and outward-looking partner while posing virtually no chance of becoming a geopolitical competitor. See, for example, Zbigniew Brzezinski, *The Grand Chessboard: American Strategy and Its Geostrategic Imperatives* (New York: Basic Books, 1997), chap. 3.

alliances that exact a smaller price in security or autonomy than unipolarity does. Even allowing for the differential growth in power to the United States' disadvantage, however, for several decades it is likely to remain more costly for second-tier states to form counterbalancing alliances than it is for the unipolar power to sustain a system of alliances that reinforces its own dominance.

THE DIFFUSION OF POWER

In the final analysis, alliances cannot change the system's structure. Only the uneven growth of power (or, in the case of the EU, the creation of a new state) will bring the unipolar era to an end. Europe will take many decades to become a de facto state—if it ever does. Unless and until that happens, the fate of unipolarity depends on the relative rates of growth and innovation of the main powers.

I have established that the gap in favor of the United States is unprecedented and that the threshold level of capabilities it needs to sustain unipolarity is much less than the 50 percent that analysts often assume. Social science lacks a theory that can predict the rate of the rise and fall of great powers. It is possible that the United States will decline suddenly and dramatically while some other great power rises. If rates of growth tend to converge as economies approach U.S. levels of per capita GDP, then the speed at which other rich states can close the gap will be limited. Germany may be out of the running entirely.[53] Japan may take a decade to regain the relative position it occupied in 1990. After that, if all goes well, sustained higher growth could place it in polar position in another decade or two.[54] This leaves China as the focus of current expectations for the demise of unipolarity. The fact that the two main contenders to polar status are close Asian neighbors and face tight regional constraints further reinforces unipolarity. The threshold at which Japan or

---

53. See Max Otte, *A Rising Middle Power? German Foreign Policy in Transformation, 1988–1998* (New York: St. Martin's, forthcoming), chap. 3.
54. Assessments of Japan's future growth in the late 1990s are probably as overly pessimistic as those of the 1980s were overly optimistic. According to Peter Hartcher, "Can Japan Recover?" *National Interest*, No. 54 (Winter 1998/1999), p. 33, "Japan's Ministry of International Trade and Industry (MITI) estimates that even if the country manages to emerge from recession, its maximum potential growth rate until the year 2010 is a pathetic 1.8 percent, and a miserable 0.8 percent thereafter. And that is one of the more optimistic estimates." If, in contrast to these assumptions, the Japanese economy recovers in 2000 and grows at a robust annual average rate of 5 percent, while the U.S. economy grows at 2 percent, Japan's economy would surpass the United States' around 2025 (2033 using PPP estimates of the size of the two economies in 1997).

China will possess the capabilities to face the other *and* the United States is very high. Until then, they are better off in a unipolar order.

As a poor country, China has a much greater chance of maintaining sustained high growth rates. With its large population making for large gross economic output, projections based on extrapolating 8 percent yearly growth in GDP have China passing the United States early in the twenty-first century.[55] But these numbers must be used with care. After all, China's huge population probably gave it a larger economy than Britain in the nineteenth century.[56] The current belief in a looming power transition between the United States and China resembles pre–World War I beliefs about rising Russian power. It assumes that population and rapid growth compensate for technological backwardness. China's economic and military modernization has a much longer road to travel than its gross economic output suggests.[57] And managing the political and social challenges presented by rapid growth in an overpopulated country governed by an authoritarian regime is a formidable task. By any measure, the political challenges that lie athwart Beijing's path to polar status are much more substantial than those that may block Washington's efforts to maintain its position. Three decades is probably a better bet than one.

Thus far I have kept the analysis focused squarely on the distribution of material capabilities. Widening the view only slightly to consider key legacies of the Cold War strengthens the case for the robustness of unipolarity. The United States was the leading state in the Cold War, so the status quo already reflects its preferences. Washington thus faces only weak incentives to expand, and the preponderance of power in its control buttresses rather than contradicts the status quo. This reduces the incentives of others to counterbalance the United States and reinforces stability.[58] Another important Cold War legacy

---

55. These calculations are naturally heavily dependent on initial conditions. Assuming the Chinese economy grows at 8 percent a year while the U.S. economy grows at a 2 percent rate, China would surpass the United States in about 2013, extrapolating from 1997 PPP exchange-rate estimates of the two economies' relative size; 2020 if the PPP estimate is deflated as suggested by Central Intelligence Agency economists; and 2040 if market exchange rates are used. On measuring China's economic output, see Angus Maddison, *Monitoring the World Economy, 1820–1992* (Paris: OECD, 1995), appendix C.
56. Ibid., Table C-16e.
57. A balanced appraisal is Avery Goldstein, "Great Expectations: Interpreting China's Arrival," *International Security*, Vol. 22, No. 3 (Winter 1997/98), pp. 36–73.
58. A preponderance of power makes other states less likely to oppose the United States, but it could also tempt Washington to demand more of others. Because an overwhelming preponderance of power fosters stability, the clash of interests would have to be extreme to produce a counterbalance. In other words, the United States would have to work very hard to push all the other great powers and many regional ones into an opposing alliance. The point is important in theory

is that two prime contenders for polar status—Japan and Germany (or Europe)—are close U.S. allies with deeply embedded security dependence on the United States. This legacy of dependence reduces the speed with which these states can foster the institutions and capabilities of superpower status. Meanwhile, the United States inherits from the Cold War a global military structure that deeply penetrates many allied and friendly states, and encompasses a massive and complex physical presence around the world. These initial advantages raise the barriers to competition far higher than the raw measures suggest. Finally, the Cold War and its end appear to many observers to be lessons against the possibility of successful balancing via increased internal mobilization for war. The prospect that domestic mobilization efforts can extract U.S.-scale military power from a comparatively small or undeveloped economy seems less plausible now than it did three decades ago.

THE BALANCE OF POWER IS NOT WHAT STATES MAKE OF IT

For some analysts, multipolarity seems just around the corner because intellectuals and politicians in some other states want it to be. Samuel Huntington notes that "political and intellectual leaders in most countries strongly resist the prospect of a unipolar world and favor the emergence of true multipolarity."[59] No article on contemporary world affairs is complete without obligatory citations from diplomats and scholars complaining of U.S. arrogance. The problem is that policymakers (and scholars) cannot always have the balance of power they want. If they could, neither bipolarity nor unipolarity would have occurred in the first place. Washington, Moscow, London, and Paris wanted a swift return to multipolarity after World War II. And policymakers in all four capitals appeared to prefer bipolarity to unipolarity in 1990–91. Like its structural predecessor, unipolarity might persist despite policymakers' wishes.

Other scholars base their pessimism about unipolarity's longevity less on preferences than on behavior. Kenneth Waltz claims that "to all but the myopic,

---

but moot in practice. Because the post–Cold War world is already so much a reflection of U.S. interests, Washington is less tempted than another state might be to make additional claims as its relative power increases. The result is a preponderance of power backing up the status quo, a condition theorists of many stripes view as an augury of peace and stability. For different perspectives, see E.H. Carr, *The Twenty Years' Crisis: 1919–1939: An Introduction to the Study of International Relations* (London: Macmillan, 1951); Organski, *World Politics*; Gilpin, *War and Change in World Politics*; Powell, "Stability and the Distribution of Power"; and Randall L. Schweller, "Neorealism's Status Quo Bias: What Security Dilemma?" *Security Studies*, Vol. 5, No. 3 (Spring 1996), pp. 225–258.
59. Huntington, "Lonely Superpower," p. 42.

[multipolarity] can already be seen on the horizon. . . . Some of the weaker states in the system will . . . act to restore a balance and thus move the system back to bi- or multipolarity. China and Japan are doing so now."[60] This argument is vulnerable to Waltz's own insistence that a system's structure cannot be defined solely by the behavior of its units. Theory of course cannot predict state action. Whether some states try to enhance their power or form a counterbalancing alliance is up to them. But theory is supposed to help predict the outcome of such action. And if the system is unipolar, counterbalancing will fail. As the underlying distribution of power changes, the probability increases that some states will conclude that internal or external counterbalancing is possible. But there is no evidence that this has occurred in the 1990s. On the contrary, the evidence suggests that states are only now coming to terms with unipolarity.

Most of the counterbalancing that has occurred since 1991 has been rhetorical. Notably absent is any willingness on the part of the other great powers to accept any significant political or economic costs in countering U.S. power. Most of the world's powers are busy trying to climb aboard the American bandwagon even as they curtail their military outlays. Military spending by all the other great powers is either declining or holding steady in real terms. While Washington prepares for increased defense outlays, current planning in Europe, Japan, and China does not suggest real increases in the offing, and Russia's spending will inevitably decline further.[61] This response on the part of the other major powers is understandable, because the raw distribution of power leaves them with no realistic hope of counterbalancing the United States, while U.S.-managed security systems in Europe and Asia moderate the demand for more military capabilities.

The advent of unipolarity does not mean the end of all politics among great powers. Elites will not stop resenting overweening U.S. capabilities. Second-tier great powers will not suddenly stop caring about their standing vis-à-vis other states. Rising states presently outside the great power club will seek the prerequisites of membership. We should expect evidence of states' efforts to explore the new structure and determine their place in it. Most of the action since 1991 has concerned membership in the second tier of great powers. Some seek formal entry in the second tier via nuclear tests or a permanent seat on the United Nations Security Council. Existing members fear a devaluation of

---

60. Waltz, "Evaluating Theories," pp. 915–916.
61. International Institute of Strategic Studies, *The Military Balance 1998/99* (London: IISS, 1999).

their status and resist new aspirants. All of this requires careful management. But it affects neither the underlying structure nor the basic great power hierarchy.

The fact that some important states have more room to maneuver now than they did under bipolarity does not mean that unipolarity is already giving way to some new form of multipolarity.[62] The end of the bipolar order has decreased the security interdependence of regions and increased the latitude of some regional powers. But polarity does not refer to the existence of merely regional powers. When the world was bipolar, Washington and Moscow had to think strategically whenever they contemplated taking action anywhere within the system. Today there is no other power whose reaction greatly influences U.S. action across multiple theaters. China's reaction, for example, may matter in East Asia, but not for U.S. policy in the Middle East, Africa, or Europe. However, *all* major regional powers do share one item on their political agenda: how to deal with U.S. power. Until these states are capable of producing a counterpoise to the United States, the system is unipolar.

The key is that regional and second-tier competition should not be confused with balancing to restructure the system toward multipolarity. If the analysis so far is right, any existing second-tier state that tries such balancing should quickly learn the errors of its ways. This is indeed the fate that befell the two powers that tried (hesitantly, to be sure) to counterbalance: Russia and China. Foreign Minister Yevgeny Primakov's restless "multipolar diplomacy" had run out of steam well before Russia's financial collapse. And Russia's catastrophic decline also derailed China's efforts at creating some kind of counterpoise to the United States. As Avery Goldstein shows, the costs of Beijing's "multipolar diplomacy" dramatically outweighed the benefits. Russia was weak and getting weaker, while the United States held the economic and security cards. Even fairly careful Chinese moves produced indications of a strong local counterbalancing reaction before they showed any promise of increased autonomy vis-à-vis Washington. As a result, the Chinese rethought their approach

---

62. The enhanced autonomy of many regions compared to the bipolar order has given rise to an important new research agenda. See Etel Solingen, *Regional Orders at Century's Dawn* (Princeton, N.J.: Princeton University Press, 1998); and David A. Lake and Patrick N. Morgan, eds., *Regional Orders: Building Security in a New World* (University Park: Pennsylvania State University Press, 1997). This evidence of new regional security dynamics leads many to view the current structure as a hybrid of unipolarity and multipolarity. See Huntington, "Lonely Superpower"; and Friedberg, "Ripe for Rivalry."

in 1996 and made a concerted effort to be a "responsible partner" of the Americans.[63]

Neither the Beijing-Moscow "strategic partnership" nor the "European troika" of Russia, Germany, and France entailed any costly commitments or serious risks of confrontation with Washington. For many states, the optimal policy is ambiguity: to work closely with the United States on the issues most important to Washington while talking about creating a counterpoise. Such policies generate a paper trail suggesting strong dissatisfaction with the U.S.-led world order and a legacy of actual behavior that amounts to band-wagoning. These states are seeking the best bargains for themselves given the distribution of power. That process necessitates a degree of politicking that may remind people faintly of the power politics of bygone eras. But until the distribution of power changes substantially, this bargaining will resemble real-politik in form but not content.

Conclusion: Challenges for Scholarship and Strategy

The distribution of material capabilities at the end of the twentieth century is unprecedented. However we view this venerable explanatory variable, the current concentration of power in the United States is something new in the world. Even if world politics works by the old rules—even if democracy, new forms of interdependence, and international institutions do not matter—we should not expect a return of balance-of-power politics à la multipolarity for the simple reason that we are living in the modern world's first unipolar system. And unipolarity is not a "moment." It is a deeply embedded material condition of world politics that has the potential to last for many decades.

If unipolarity is so robust, why do so many writers hasten to declare its demise? The answer may lie in the common human tendency to conflate power *trends* with existing relationships. The rush to proclaim the return of multipo-larity in the 1960s and 1970s, to pronounce the United States' decline in the 1980s, to herald the rise of Japan or China as superpowers in the 1980s and 1990s, and finally to bid unipolarity adieu after the Cold War are all examples. In each case, analysts changed reference points to minimize U.S. power. In the

---

63. Avery Goldstein, "Structural Realism and China's Foreign Policy: A Good Part of the Story," paper prepared for the annual conference of the American Political Science Association, Boston, Massachusetts, September 3–6, 1998.

bipolarity debate, the reference point became the extremely tight alliance of the 1950s, so any disagreement between the United States and Europe was seen as a harbinger of multipolarity. In the 1980s, "hegemony" was defined as "the U.S. position circa 1946," so the recovery of Europe and Japan appeared as fatal threats to the United States' position. Many analysts have come to define unipolarity as an imperial system such as Rome where there is only one great power and all other states are satrapies or dependencies. As a result, each act of defiance of Washington's preferences on any issue comes to be seen as the return of a multipolar world.

One explanation for this tendency to shift reference points is that in each case the extent of U.S. power was inconvenient for the scholarly debate of the day. Scholars schooled in nineteenth-century balance-of-power politics were intellectually primed for their return in the 1960s. In the 1980s, continued cooperation between the United States and its allies was a more interesting puzzle if the era of U.S. hegemony was over. In the 1990s, unipolarity is doubly inconvenient for scholars of international relations. For neorealists, unipolarity contradicts the central tendency of their theory. Its longevity is a testament to the theory's indeterminacy. For liberals and constructivists, the absence of balance-of-power politics among the great powers is a much more interesting and tractable puzzle if the world is multipolar. The debate would be far easier if all realist theories predicted instability and conflict and their competitors predicted the opposite.

Today's distribution of power is unprecedented, however, and power-centric theories naturally expect politics among nations to be different than in past systems. In contrast to the past, the existing distribution of capabilities generates incentives for cooperation. The absence of hegemonic rivalry, security competition, and balancing is not necessarily the result of ideational or institutional change. This is not to assert that realism provides the best explanation for the absence of security and prestige competition. Rather, the conclusion is that it offers an explanation that may compete with or complement those of other theoretical traditions. As a result, evaluating the merits of contending theories for understanding the international politics of unipolarity presents greater empirical challenges than many scholars have acknowledged.

Because the baseline expectations of all power-centric theories are novel, so are their implications for grand strategy. Scholars' main message to policymakers has been to prepare for multipolarity. Certainly, we should think about how to manage the transition to a new structure. Yet time and energy are limited. Constant preparation for the return of multipolarity means not gearing up intellectually and materially for unipolarity. Given that unipolarity is prone to peace and the probability that it will last several more decades at least, we should focus on it and get it right.

The first step is to stop calling this the "post–Cold War world." Unipolarity is nearing its tenth birthday. Our experience with this international system matches what the statesmen and scholars of 1825, 1928, and 1955 had. The key to this system is the centrality of the United States. The nineteenth century was not a "Pax Britannica." From 1815 to 1853, it was a Pax Britannica et Russica; from 1853 to 1871, it was not a pax of any kind; and from 1871 to 1914, it was a Pax Britannica et Germanica. Similarly, the Cold War was not a Pax Americana, but a Pax Americana et Sovietica. Now the ambiguity is gone. One power is lonely at the top. Calling the current period the true Pax Americana may offend some, but it reflects reality and focuses attention on the stakes involved in U.S. grand strategy.

Second, doing too little is a greater danger than doing too much. Critics note that the United States is far more interventionist than any previous system leader. But given the distribution of power, the U.S. impulse toward interventionism is understandable. In many cases, U.S. involvement has been demand driven, as one would expect in a system with one clear leader. Rhetoric aside, U.S. engagement seems to most other elites to be necessary for the proper functioning of the system. In each region, cobbled-together security arrangements that require an American role seem preferable to the available alternatives. The more efficiently the United States performs this role, the more durable the system. If, on the other hand, the United States fails to translate its potential into the capabilities necessary to provide order, then great power struggles for power and security will reappear sooner. Local powers will then face incentives to provide security, sparking local counterbalancing and security competition. As the world becomes more dangerous, more second-tier states will enhance their military capabilities. In time, the result could be an earlier structural shift to bi- or multipolarity and a quicker reemergence of conflict over the leadership of the international system.

Third, we should not exaggerate the costs. The clearer the underlying distribution of power is, the less likely it is that states will need to test it in arms races or crises. Because the current concentration of power in the United States is unprecedentedly clear and comprehensive, states are likely to share the expectation that counterbalancing would be a costly and probably doomed venture. As a result, they face incentives to keep their military budgets under control until they observe fundamental changes in the capability of the United

States to fulfill its role. The whole system can thus be run at comparatively low costs to both the sole pole and the other major powers. Unipolarity can be made to seem expensive and dangerous if it is equated with a global empire demanding U.S. involvement in all issues everywhere. In reality, unipolarity is a distribution of capabilities among the world's great powers. It does not solve all the world's problems. Rather, it minimizes two major problems— security and prestige competition—that confronted the great powers of the past. Maintaining unipolarity does not require limitless commitments. It involves managing the central security regimes in Europe and Asia, and maintaining the expectation on the part of other states that any geopolitical challenge to the United States is futile. As long as that is the expectation, states will likely refrain from trying, and the system can be maintained at little extra cost.

The main criticism of the Pax Americana, however, is not that Washington is too interventionist. A state cannot be blamed for responding to systemic incentives. The problem is U.S. reluctance to *pay up*. Constrained by a domestic welfare role and consumer culture that the weaker British hegemon never faced, Washington tends to shrink from accepting the financial, military, and especially the domestic political burdens of sole pole status. At the same time, it cannot escape the demand for involvement. The result is cruise missile hegemony, the search for polar status on the cheap, and a grand global broker of deals for which others pay. The United States has responded to structural incentives by assuming the role of global security manager and "indispensable nation" in all matters of importance. But too often the solutions Washington engineers are weakened by American reluctance to take any domestic political risks.

The problem is that structural pressures on the United States are weak. Powerful states may not respond to the international environment because their power makes them immune to its threat. The smaller the number of actors, the greater the potential impact of internal processes on international politics. The sole pole is strong and secure enough that paying up-front costs for system maintenance is hard to sell to a parsimonious public. As Kenneth Waltz argued, "Strong states . . . can afford not to learn."[64] If that was true of the great powers in multi- or bipolar systems, it is even truer of today's unipolar power. The implication is that instead of dwelling on the dangers of overinvolvement and the need to prepare for an impending multipolarity,

---

64. Waltz, *Theory of International Politics*, p. 195.

scholars and policymakers should do more to advertise the attractions of unipolarity.

Despite scholars' expectations, it was not the rise of Europe, Japan, and China that ended bipolarity. The monodimensional nature of the Soviet Union's power and the brittleness of its domestic institutions turned out to be the main threats to bipolar stability. Similarly, a uniting Europe or a rising Japan or China may not become the chief engines of structural change in the early twenty-first century. If the analysis here is right, then the live-for-today nature of U.S. domestic institutions may be the chief threat to unipolar stability. In short, the current world order is characterized not by a looming U.S. threat that is driving other powers toward multipolar counterbalancing, but by a material structure that presupposes and demands U.S. preponderance coupled with policies and rhetoric that deny its existence or refuse to face its modest costs.

Preserving the Unipolar Moment

Michael Mastanduno

Realist Theories and U.S. Grand Strategy after the Cold War

$\mathbf{R}$ealism is now both the dominant paradigm in the study of international relations and the most challenged. During the 1970s, critics turned to bureaucratic politics and cognitive process models to question realism's emphasis on the unitary rational state, and to interdependence models to challenge its acceptance of the utility and fungibility of military power.[1] The beginning of the 1990s brought a renewed wave of criticism, as realists were faulted with failing to predict or anticipate the end of the Cold War and the peaceful transition to a new era.[2] In the immediate aftermath of the Cold War, the dark expectation of some realists of renewed security conflict among major powers has not yet been realized, leading critics to the conclusion that realism's days are numbered and that it is more sensible to place bets on domestic politics, international institutions, or constructivism to explain state behavior in the international arena.[3]

Michael Mastanduno is Associate Professor of Government at Dartmouth College. He is the author of Economic Containment: Cocom and the Politics of East-West Trade *(Cornell University Press, 1992), and co-editor of* Beyond Westphalia? State Sovereignty and International Intervention *(Johns Hopkins University Press, 1995), and* Realism and International Relations After the Cold War *(forthcoming).*

This paper was originally prepared for the project on "Realism and International Relations After the Cold War," sponsored by the Olin Institute for Strategic Studies, Harvard University. I would also like to acknowledge the Center for Global Partnership and the Social Science Research Council for financial support in the form of an Abe Fellowship. For comments and suggestions, I am grateful to Robert Art, Mlada Bukovansky, Dan Deudney, John Ikenberry, Iain Johnston, Ethan Kapstein, Jon Kirshner, Michael Loriaux, and Randy Schweller.

1. Graham Allison, *Essence of Decision* (Boston: Little, Brown, 1971); and Robert O. Keohane and Joseph S. Nye, Jr., *Transnational Relations and World Politics* (Cambridge, Mass.: Harvard University Press, 1972).
2. Charles W. Kegley, Jr., "The Neoidealist Moment in International Studies? Realist Myths and the New International Realities," *International Studies Quarterly*, Vol. 37, No. 2 (June 1993), pp. 131–146; and Richard Ned Lebow and Thomas Risse-Kappen, eds., *International Relations Theory and the End of the Cold War* (New York: Columbia University Press, 1995).
3. Prominent realists have responded by pointing out the conceptual and empirical flaws in competing theoretical frameworks. See John Mearsheimer, "The False Promise of International Institutions," *International Security*, Vol. 19, No. 3 (Winter 1994/95), pp. 5–49; and Joseph M. Grieco, "Anarchy and the Limits of Cooperation: A Realist Critique of the Newest Liberal Institutionalism," *International Organization*, Vol. 42, No. 3 (Summer 1988), pp. 485–507. The "paradigm war" between realists and their critics has been played out in David Baldwin, ed., *Neorealism and Neoliberalism: The Contemporary Debate* (New York: Columbia University Press, 1993); Charles W. Kegley, Jr., ed.,

International Security, Vol. 21, No. 4 (Spring 1997), pp. 49–88
© 1997 by the President and Fellows of Harvard College and the Massachusetts Institute of Technology.

Is that conclusion warranted? This article takes seriously the challenge of the critics and assesses whether realism is useful in explaining U.S. foreign policy after the Cold War. The Cold War's passing provides an ideal opportunity to examine the impact of international structural change—a variable of central importance to realism—on state behavior. I focus on the United States because realism's traditional emphasis has been on the great powers, and after the Cold War the United States has been the dominant power in the international system.

It is critical to stress at the outset that there is no single "theory of realism" and that realism *per se* cannot be tested, confirmed, or refuted. Realism is a research program that contains a core set of assumptions from which a variety of theories and explanations can be developed.[4] Progress within the research program requires the elaboration and testing of specific realist theories, not only against non-realist alternatives but also, in the case of competing realist theories, against each other.[5]

Below I focus on two prominent realist theories that offer competing predictions for U.S. behavior after the Cold War. The first is balance-of-power theory, developed most explicitly by Kenneth Waltz.[6] The second is a modified version

Controversies in International Relations Theory: Realism and the Neoliberal Challenge (New York: St. Martin's, 1995); and Robert O. Keohane, ed., *Neorealism and its Critics* (New York: Columbia University Press, 1986).

4. The assumptions of the realist research program are that 1) states, or more broadly, territorially organized groups, are the central actors on the world stage; 2) state behavior can be explained rationally; 3) states seek power and calculate their interests in terms of power and the international situation they face; and 4) anarchy is the defining characteristic of the international system, which implies that states ultimately must rely on themselves in an inherently competitive environment. For discussion, see Robert O. Keohane, "Theory of World Politics: Structural Realism and Beyond," in Keohane, ed., *Neorealism and Its Critics*, pp. 158–203; Patrick James, "Neorealism as a Research Enterprise: Toward Elaborated Structural Realism," *International Political Science Review*, Vol. 14, No. 2 (1993), pp. 123–148; Mearsheimer, "The False Promise of International Institutions," pp. 10–11; and Steven Forde, "International Realism and the Science of Politics: Thucydides, Machiavelli, and Neorealism," *International Studies Quarterly*, Vol. 39, No. 2 (June 1995), pp. 141–160. Forde points out (pp. 143–145) that classical realists such as Thucydides and Machiavelli, who ground their arguments in human nature as well as in international structure, might not embrace all of the above assumptions as fully as would contemporary structural realists.

5. Daniel Deudney follows this logic in a recent analysis on U.S. nuclear proliferation policy, arguing that realism is not one theory but a "family of related and competing theories." See Deudney, "Dividing Realism: Structural Realism versus Security Materialism on Nuclear Security and Proliferation," *Security Studies*, Vol. 2, Nos. 3/4 (Spring/Summer 1993), pp. 7–36, quote at p. 8. A recent attempt to test "realism" as opposed to particular realist theories found, not surprisingly, that the "scientific study of realism is difficult because it is often not specific enough to be falsifiable." See Frank W. Wayman and Paul F. Diehl, eds., *Reconstructing Realpolitik* (Ann Arbor: University of Michigan Press, 1994), p. 26.

6. Kenneth N. Waltz, *Theory of International Politics* (Reading, Mass.: Addison-Wesley, 1979). Important applications and extensions include Waltz, "The Emerging Structure of International Politics," *International Security*, Vol. 18, No. 2 (Fall 1993), pp. 45–73; Christopher Layne, "The Unipolar Illusion: Why New Great Powers Will Rise," *International Security*, Vol. 17, No. 4 (Spring

of the balance-of-threat theory developed by Stephen Walt.[7] I elaborate the logic of each theory and from each I extrapolate specific sets of predictions for U.S. security policy and for U.S. foreign economic policy.[8] I then test these predictions against the (necessarily preliminary) evidence of the post–Cold War era.[9]

The evidence neither fully supports nor fully contradicts either theory. It does reveal a striking pattern: U.S. post–Cold War security and economic strategies are each explained effectively, but by different realist theories. Balance-of-threat theory accounts for the dominant tendency in U.S. security policy: an effort to preserve America's position at the top of the international hierarchy by engaging and reassuring other major powers. Balance-of-power theory explains the dominant tendency in U.S. foreign economic policy: an effort to mobilize for national economic competition against other major powers. Since each theory provides a plausible explanation for a central aspect of post–Cold War U.S. foreign policy, it would be imprudent to follow the advice of realism's harshest critics and abandon the core paradigm. Yet, realists are hardly in a position to declare victory and go home. The evidence from this single case suggests a need for the further refinement and testing of competing realist theories and for the testing of the stronger realist theories against non-realist alternatives.

In substantive terms, the realist framework illuminates two key developments in contemporary U.S. foreign policy. First, contrary to those who see U.S. security policy after the Cold War as incoherent or directionless, I argue that U.S. officials have in fact followed a consistent strategy in pursuit of a clear objective—the preservation of the United States' preeminent global position.[10] This grand strategy of preserving primacy has spanned the Bush and Clinton

---

1993), pp. 5–51; and John Mearsheimer, "Back to the Future: Instability in Europe After the Cold War," *International Security*, Vol. 15, No. 1 (Summer 1990), pp. 5–56.

7. Stephen M. Walt, *The Origins of Alliances* (Ithaca, N.Y.: Cornell University Press, 1987). In extending Walt's theory I draw on the classical realist distinction between status quo and revisionist states. See, for example, Hans J. Morgenthau, *Politics Among Nations: The Struggle for Power and Peace*, fifth ed. (New York: Knopf, 1978), chaps. 4 and 5.

8. Extrapolation is necessary because balance-of-power and balance-of-threat theory were developed to explain systemic outcomes. Instead, I use them to infer predictions and explanations for the foreign policy of a particular state. And, both theories are usually applied to national security issues. I extend their logic and apply them to U.S. foreign economic policy as well as to U.S. national security policy.

9. Obviously, there are plausible non-realist explanations of post–Cold War U.S. foreign policy. In this article I confine myself to developing and testing competing realist explanations.

10. In a recent article, Barry Posen and Andrew Ross lay out five possible grand strategies for the United States after the Cold War: neo-isolationism, selective engagement, collective security, containment, and primacy. I argue that the United States has in fact chosen to pursue primacy. See Posen and Ross, "Competing Grand Strategies," in Robert J. Lieber, ed., *Eagle Adrift: American Foreign Policy at the End of the Century* (New York: Longman, 1997), pp. 100–134.

administrations, notwithstanding differences in their foreign policy rhetoric. It has decisively shaped U.S. relations with Japan, Germany, Russia, and China. Second, U.S. foreign economic policy has worked at cross-purposes with U.S. national security strategy. In relations with other major powers, the United States, in effect, has been trying simultaneously to play "economic hardball" and "security softball." U.S. officials have been forced to manage the resulting contradiction in order to prevent the friction generated by its foreign economic policy from spilling over and frustrating the attainment of its primary national security objective.

The next two sections of this article examine U.S. security strategy after the Cold War. I lay out balance-of-power theory, generate predictions, and assess them in light of the available evidence. I then do the same for balance-of-threat theory. The following two sections take up U.S. economic strategy after the Cold War. I apply each theory in the area of foreign economic policy, generate predictions, and compare the predictions to the available evidence. A final section discusses theoretical and policy implications.

Balance-of-Power Theory and Post–Cold War U.S. Security Strategy

Waltz's balance-of-power theory remains the most prominent neorealist theory of international relations.[11] From the premises that the international system is anarchic and that states are "like units," Waltz derives the behavioral expectation that balances of power will form and recur. Variations in the distribution of capabilities across states produce different configurations of the balance of power. Multipolar balances are likely to be more war-prone than bipolar balances, and in the latter configuration great powers will rely more on internal than external balancing to assure their survival and protect their interests.

Waltz is careful to emphasize that the purpose of his theory is to explain international outcomes, not the foreign policies of particular states. He claims that "the behavior of states and statesmen is indeterminate."[12] This is not entirely convincing, however, because the international structure provides opportunities and constraints that shape state behavior significantly, even if they do not determine it entirely. In a recent article, Waltz himself argues that "neorealist, or structural, theory leads one to believe that the placement of states in the international system accounts for a good deal of their behavior."[13]

---

11. Waltz, *Theory of International Politics.*
12. Ibid., p. 68.
13. Waltz, "The Emerging Structure of International Politics," p. 45.

He suggests, for example, that the similar structural placement of the United States and the Soviet Union in bipolarity should have led to "striking similarities" in their behavior. As evidence, he points to convergence in their armaments policies, military doctrines, and intervention habits.[14] International structural theory, then, should be useful in explaining the foreign policies of particular states.[15]

States respond to the particular features of their international structural environment.[16] The end of the Cold War and the collapse of the Soviet Union as one pole in a bipolar system clearly represent significant changes in the international environment. What expectations follow with regard to the national security strategy of the United States?

BALANCE-OF-POWER LOGIC AND PREDICTIONS

The first task is to characterize the new structure. This is not straightforward, due to the imprecision of measurement that is characteristic of much of the realist literature on polarity.[17] Waltz complicates the issue by suggesting that after the collapse of the Soviet Union, "bipolarity endures, but in an altered state" because "militarily Russia can take care of itself."[18] This is hard to square with the more common assessment of realists, shared explicitly by Waltz, that to be a great power a state needs to excel not in one area but across a range of capability attributes. For Hans Morgenthau, the list includes geography, industrial capacity, military preparedness, and more elusive categories such as national character, morale, and the quality of government.[19] Waltz tells us that great power rank depends on how states score on a combination of attributes—

---

14. Ibid., pp. 46–49.

15. It is also worth noting that the systemic outcomes of primary interest to structural realists are themselves the results of the foreign policy choices of states, especially the most powerful ones. "Free trade" as a systemic outcome does not occur if the powerful states in the system choose protectionism. "Balancing" does not occur if the major states choose not to balance. For an argument that Waltz's balance-of-power theory should be considered a theory of foreign policy, see Colin Elman, "Neorealist Theories of Foreign Policy: Meaning, Objections, and Implications," paper presented at the annual meeting of the International Studies Association, February 1995.

16. An explicit effort to use international structure to explain foreign economic policy is David A. Lake, *Power, Protection, and Free Trade* (Ithaca, N.Y.: Cornell University Press, 1987). For an argument that international structure decisively shaped the military policies of Latin American states, see João Resende-Santos, "Anarchy and the Emulation of Military Systems: Military Organization and Technology in South America, 1870–1930," *Security Studies*, Vol. 5, No. 3 (Spring 1995), pp. 190–247.

17. See Richard Ned Lebow, "The Long Peace, the End of the Cold War, and the Failure of Realism," in Lebow and Risse-Kappen, eds., *International Relations Theory and the End of the Cold War*, pp. 26–33.

18. Waltz, "The Emerging Structure of International Politics," p. 52.

19. Morgenthau, *Politics Among Nations*, chap. 9.

size of population, resource endowment, economic capability, military strength, and political stability and competence—although he does not propose anything to serve as a scorecard.[20]

Even without precise measurement, to focus on a range of power attributes leads to the conclusion that the United States is now in a category by itself. Only the United States currently excels in military power and preparedness, economic and technological capacity, size of population and territory, resource endowment, political stability, and "soft power" attributes such as ideology.[21] All other would-be great powers are limited or lopsided in one critical way or another. Thus many commentators and theorists have concluded that the current structure is unipolar. In an article extending Waltz's theory to the post–Cold War era, Christopher Layne opens with the assertion that "the Soviet Union's collapse transformed the international system from bipolarity to unipolarity."[22]

Balance-of-power theory is very clear about the behavioral implications of unipolarity. States seek to balance power, and thus the preponderance of power in the hands of a single state will stimulate the rise of new great powers, and possibly coalitions of powers, determined to balance the dominant state. Layne writes that "in unipolar systems, states do indeed balance against the hegemon's unchecked power."[23] The question is not *whether* new powers will rise and balance, but when, and to Layne the answer is similarly clear—"fairly quickly." Waltz and Layne both anticipate a rapid transition, and each suggests that unipolarity will be transformed into multipolarity early in the next century, or within 10–20 years of the end of the Cold War.[24] Since neorealists expect a multipolar world to be more conflictual than a bipolar world, it is not surprising that they tend to be pessimistic regarding the prospects for peace and cooperation among great powers.[25]

---

20. Waltz, "The Emerging Structure of International Politics," p. 50. Earlier, Waltz noted that power is "difficult to measure and compare." Waltz, *Theory of International Politics*, p. 131.
21. See Joseph Nye, *Bound to Lead: The Changing Nature of American Power* (New York: Basic Books, 1992).
22. Layne, "The Unipolar Illusion," p. 5. See also Nye, *Bound to Lead*, and Charles Krauthammer, "The Unipolar Moment," *Foreign Affairs*, Vol. 70, No. 1 (1990/1991).
23. Layne, "The Unipolar Illusion," p. 13.
24. Waltz, "The Emerging Structure of International Politics," p. 50, and Layne, "The Unipolar Illusion," p. 7.
25. See Mearsheimer, "Back to the Future." Layne argues that "neorealist theory leads one to the expectation that the world beyond unipolarity will be one of great power rivalry in a multipolar setting." Layne, "The Unipolar Illusion," p. 40. Waltz does argue, however, that nuclear deterrence reduces the probability of war, even in multipolar settings.

The overall logic of this argument directs neorealists to focus attention on the calculations and capabilities of those states most likely to rise up and balance the power of the preponderant state. Waltz concentrates on Japan, which he views as "ready to receive the mantle [of great power status] if only it will reach for it," and on the prospects for Germany, China, the European Union, and Russian revival.[26] John Mearsheimer, playing out the implications of balance-of-power logic in the regional context, analyzes the incentives for Germany to acquire nuclear capabilities.[27] Layne looks backward as well as forward in seeking to establish that unipolar systems existed in the past and stimulated the rise of new challengers. Like Waltz, he considers Japan to be America's most likely future geopolitical rival and does not count out the possibility of a future hegemonic war between the two.[28]

But what does a unipolar structure imply for the behavior of the state situated at the top of the international hierarchy? The answer suggested by balance-of-power theory is somewhat ironic. On the one hand, the preponderant state in a unipolar system is in an enviable position. It is significantly unconstrained and enjoys wide discretion in its statecraft. The contrast with a bipolar structure, within which that same state is compelled to react to events and tailor policies according to their impact on the bipolar competition, is striking. Yet on the other hand, the preponderant state is helpless to perpetuate this attractive state of affairs. The mere fact of its preponderant power guarantees the rapid rise of competing powers. In short, we should expect the dominant state to savor the unipolar moment, but recognize that it will not last.

Balance-of-power theory suggests further that efforts to preserve unipolarity are bound to be futile and likely to be counterproductive. Instead, the rational strategy for the dominant state is to accept the inevitability of multipolarity and maneuver to take advantage of it. Layne develops the logic most explicitly, and explains the futility of any U.S. effort to preserve its preponderance: "A policy of attempting to smother Germany's and Japan's great power emergence would be unavailing because structural pressures will impel them to become great powers regardless of what the United States does or does not do."[29] Waltz

---

26. Waltz, "Emerging Structure of International Politics." This phrase is quoted at p. 55.

27. Mearsheimer, "Back to the Future," pp. 173–176, 190.

28. Layne, "The Unipolar Illusion," p. 49, 51. In more recent work, Layne concentrates on the hegemonic challenge from China. See Christopher Layne and Bradley Thayer, "The Revolution in Military Affairs and the Future of Stability in Asia," paper presented at the annual meeting of the American Political Science Association, August 1996.

29. Layne, "The Unipolar Illusion," pp. 46–47.

takes a similar position, reflected in his often-quoted statement that "NATO's days are not numbered, but its years are," because potential great powers such as Germany will not tolerate the constraints of a U.S.-dominated institution.[30] Instead of seeking to preserve its preponderance, Layne argues that it is rational for the United States to adopt a posture of "strategic independence," taking on the role of "offshore balancer."[31] Specifically, the United States should extricate itself from its security commitments and forward deployments in Europe and Northeast Asia. It should depend on the dynamics of global and regional balances, and should commit itself militarily as a "last minute" balancer if and only if the balancing efforts of other states fail to prevent the emergence of a new global hegemon.

To summarize, the logic of balance-of-power theory leads plausibly to three predictions of relevance to U.S. security policy in the post–Cold War era. First, we should see the United States, liberated from the confines of the bipolar structure, behaving as an "unconstrained" great power with considerable discretion in its statecraft. Second, we should find evidence that other major powers are, in Waltz's words, "edging away" from the United States and balancing or preparing to balance against it. Third, we should see evidence that the United States accepts the inevitability of multipolarity, which would lead it rationally to disentangle itself from its Cold War commitments and move toward a posture of strategic independence. The evidence at this stage can only be preliminary, but the general tendencies should be clear.

BALANCE-OF-POWER EVIDENCE

There is support for the first prediction, and the evidence is clearest in U.S. intervention policy. Although balance-of-power theory may not be able to predict where and when the United States will intervene, we should see significant differences in the *pattern* of intervention as the international structure changes from bipolarity to unipolarity. More precisely, in the bipolar structure we actually should be able to find a pattern, because the United States was responding to strong constraints and a consistent set of signals from the international system. There was indeed a pattern: the United States intervened fairly consistently to support anti-Soviet or anticommunist regimes around the world.[32]

---

30. Waltz, "The Emerging Structure of International Politics," p. 76.
31. Layne, "The Unipolar Illusion," pp. 45–51.
32. See Stephen D. Krasner, *Defending the National Interest* (Princeton, N.J.: Princeton University Press, 1978).

In the unipolar structure the international constraints have been lifted, and, in the absence of clear signals from the international structure, intervention policy should become more haphazard and episodic. The U.S. response to the breakup of Yugoslavia is instructive. If that breakup had occurred during the Cold War, managing the ensuing conflict would have been an immediate and overwhelming priority for U.S. foreign policy. The prestige and resolve of the United States and the Soviet Union would have been engaged, and there would have been a strong temptation to line up support for opposing sides and engage in a proxy war. In contrast, the collapse of Yugoslavia after the Cold War left the United States with considerably more room to maneuver. As the single dominant power, the United States was free to redefine the problem over a five-year period as one not of vital interest, as one of vital interest, as a European problem, as a humanitarian problem, as a war of aggression and genocide, and as a civil war requiring an honest broker to make peace.

The lack of significant constraint is evident in other ways as well. In the bipolar system U.S. officials worried greatly, some would say obsessively, about the costs to U.S. credibility and prestige of failed or aborted interventions. After the Cold War, U.S. officials seem far less concerned about such less-than-successful interventions. In Somalia, the United States moved quickly from a humanitarian mission to a more ambitious nation-building exercise, but abruptly ended its efforts after taking relatively light casualties in a firefight. In Haiti, a U.S.-led intervention attempt was initially turned back by a rock-throwing mob. Subsequently, the United States engaged its prestige publicly with a clear ultimatum to Haiti's rebellious military, only to scramble at the deadline it set itself for a face-saving compromise with the same rebellious leaders in order to avoid a military encounter.

Commentators have searched in vain for a pattern to U.S. intervention policy since the end of the Cold War. After the Persian Gulf intervention, some anticipated that the United States would take on the role of "global policeman" to enforce order in the international system. But U.S. intervention in Iraq was followed by a clear reluctance to intervene in Bosnia, leaving many to speculate that the presence or absence of oil may have been the determining factor. There was no oil in Somalia, but there was U.S. intervention, clearly driven by humanitarian concerns. Yet similar concerns, even more prominently on display in Rwanda, were met by U.S. resistance to intervention.[33]

---

33. See Alain Destexhe, "The Third Genocide," *Foreign Policy*, No. 97 (Winter 1994–95), pp. 3–17.

There is much less evidence in support of the second and third predictions of balance-of-power theory. Since balance-of-power theorists expect the transition to multipolarity to be rapid, by now we should observe other major powers edging away from and balancing the United States, and we should see the United States disentangling itself from its Cold War commitments, or at least hedging its bets.

Layne and Waltz each provide suggestive evidence of other powers distancing themselves from the United States. Both cite isolated examples of remarks by public officials and academics in the relevant countries suggesting that unipolarity is not a desirable state of affairs. They also point to the desire of Japan and Germany for seats on the UN Security Council, their initial participation in UN peacekeeping efforts, and the role of Germany in forcing European Community recognition of Croatia's and Slovenia's break from the former Yugoslavia.[34]

The bulk of the evidence to this point, however, does not support balance-of-power theory and suggests that a stronger case might be made for the opposite of the theory's predictions. Rather than edging away from the United States, much less balancing it, Germany and Japan have been determined to maintain the pattern of engagement that characterized the Cold War. German officials continue to view the persistence of NATO and forward deployment of U.S. forces within NATO as the cornerstone of their national security strategy. Japan's official strategy continues to be oriented around maintaining and strengthening, for a new era, the U.S.-Japan security treaty. Neither China nor Russia, despite having some differences with the United States, has sought to organize a balancing coalition against it. Indeed, a main security concern for many countries in Europe and Asia is not how to distance from an all-too-powerful United States, but how to prevent the United States from drifting away.

For its part, the United States has been determined to remain engaged. Rather than prepare for multipolarity by disentangling itself from Cold War commitments, the central thrust of post–Cold War U.S. strategy in Europe, Northeast Asia, and the Middle East has been to reinforce and even deepen those commitments. The United States is seeking to preserve the status quo in security relations with its Cold War allies, and is seeking to engage and integrate its Cold War adversaries, Russia and China, into an order that con-

---

34. Waltz, "The Emerging Structure of International Politics," pp. 61–65; and Layne, "The Unipolar Illusion," pp. 35–39.

tinues to reflect the design and preserves the dominant position of the United States.

Balance-of-Threat Theory and Post–Cold War U.S. Security Strategy

The inability of balance-of-power theory thus far to predict effectively U.S. behavior (or that of other major powers) should not lead to the conclusion that "realism" is a useless framework for analyzing international relations after the Cold War. Other theories from within the realist research program may provide more effective explanations. In this section I elaborate the logic and extrapolate predictions for balance-of-threat theory, and apply those predictions to U.S. security strategy.

BALANCE OF THREAT LOGIC AND PREDICTIONS

Stephen Walt expects balancing behavior to be the general tendency in international relations, but he departs from Waltz and his followers on the motivation underlying balancing behavior. Walt argues that balancing behavior is most usefully understood as a response to *threat*.[35] The extent to which states appear as threatening to others depends on a variety of factors, including, but not limited to, the aggregate power resources of the state. Power and threat overlap, but are not identical.[36] Geographic proximity, offensive capability, and aggressive intentions are also relevant considerations.[37] For Walt, "states that are viewed as aggressive are likely to provoke others to balance against them."[38]

The implications of Walt's revision of balance-of-power theory are significant. In a world in which balancing behavior is the norm *and* balancing is a response to threat, it is often rational for states to pursue policies that signal restraint and reassurance. Walt argues that "foreign and defense policies that minimize the threat one poses to others make the most sense in such a

---

35. Walt, *The Origins of Alliances*, p. 21.
36. Layne disagrees, and seeks to disarm Walt's argument and its implications by asserting that "in unipolar systems there is no clearcut distinction between balance of threat and balance of power . . . in a unipolar world, others must worry about the hegemon's capabilities, not its intentions." Layne, "Unipolar Illusion," p. 13.
37. The fact that Walt includes intentions as one aspect of threat moves balance-of-threat theory away from the purely systemic level. Balance-of-power theory is purely systemic; balance-of threat theory includes both systemic factors and the kind of unit-level variables that were present in classical realism.
38. Walt, *The Origins of Alliances*, p. 25.

world."[39] Jack Snyder similarly contends that aggression that threatens other great powers diminishes a state's security in a balance-of-power system.[40]

The logic of balance-of-threat theory suggests that whether or not states balance a dominant state will depend at least in part on the foreign policy *behavior* of the dominant state. In the current unipolar context, the rapid rise of new powers to balance the United States is not a foregone conclusion. U.S. behavior can affect the calculations of other major states and may help to convince them that it is unnecessary to engage in balancing behavior.[41] By this logic, a rapid transition from unipolarity to "great power rivalry in a multipolar setting" is not inevitable. Unipolarity will not be preserved forever, but balance-of-threat theory implies that it may be sustainable for a meaningfully longer period than balance-of-power theorists anticipate.[42]

This implication is important because unipolarity is a preferred world for the United States. In a unipolar world, security threats to the United States are minimized and foreign policy autonomy is maximized. According to realist logic, any great power should prefer to be a unipolar power, regardless of whether or not it possesses expansionist ambitions. For the state at the top, unipolarity is preferable to being a great power facing either the concentrated hostility and threat of a bipolar world or the uncertainty and risk of miscalculation inherent in a multipolar world.

If balance-of-threat theory is correct in positing that states weigh intentions, and not just capabilities, in deciding whether to balance, what predictions follow with regard to post–Cold War U.S. foreign policy? The most important prediction one can infer from the theory is that, as an overall security strategy, the United States will attempt to prolong the "unipolar moment." If unipolarity is the preferred world for the United States, and if the rapid collapse of unipolarity is not inevitable because balancing is a response to threat, then we should anticipate that U.S. officials will pursue policies aimed at dissuading other states from rising to great power status and, singly or in combination, balancing against the United States.

---

39. Ibid., p. 27.
40. Snyder, *Myths of Empire*, pp. 6–9.
41. Waltz concedes something to this argument by suggesting that the "forebearance of the strong [might] reduce the worries of the weak and permit them to relax." Waltz, "The Changing Structure of International Politics," p. 79. Robert Gilpin reminds us that "an international system is stable if no state believes it is profitable to attempt to change the system." Robert Gilpin, *War and Change in World Politics* (Cambridge: Cambridge University Press, 1981), p. 50.
42. For a policy argument that implicitly accepts this logic, see Josef Joffe, "Bismarck or Britain? Toward an American Grand Strategy After Bipolarity," *International Security*, Vol. 19, No. 4 (Spring 1995), pp. 94–117.

It is difficult to pin down the specific policies the United States would pursue in the effort to preserve its preeminent position. It is possible, however, to infer general policy predictions from the logic of the theory. For example, it is reasonable to expect that the dominant state in a unipolar setting will rely on multilateralism in its international undertakings.[43] Multilateral decision-making procedures may be less efficient, and powerful states are often tempted to act unilaterally. But multilateral procedures are more reassuring to other states and may help to convince them that their preferences matter, and that they are not simply being coerced or directed to follow the dictates of the dominant state.[44]

We must also infer from balance-of-threat theory a set of predictions regarding how the dominant state will deal with potential challengers. Again, intentions matter. Just as the behavior of potential challengers will be affected by how they view the intentions of the dominant state, so, too, the behavior of the dominant state will be influenced by its understanding of the foreign policy intentions of potential challengers. The distinction made in classical realism between status quo and revisionist states is useful here. Morgenthau contrasts the status quo nation, whose foreign policy is oriented toward not challenging the existing distribution of power at a particular time, with the imperialist nation, whose foreign policy seeks a reversal of existing power relations.[45] Imperialist or revisionist states tend to be unhappy with the rules governing the international system and the distribution of benefits within that system. Many other realists have built upon this distinction, including Jack Snyder in his analysis of empire, Randall Schweller in his explanation for World War II, Robert Gilpin in his account of hegemonic war and change, and William Wohlforth in his explanation for the end of the Cold War.[46]

---

43. This is counterintuitive in that realists generally play down the significance of international institutions. See, for example, Mearsheimer, "The False Promise of International Institutions." Balance-of-threat theory may lend some insight into why dominant states rely on international institutions even though, as Mearsheimer argues, such institutions do not seem to matter in determining war and peace outcomes.

44. David Fromkin wrote recently that "a recurring theme of international politics throughout 6000 years of recorded history is that when a country becomes far more powerful than its neighbors, its greatness is resented and its neighbors band together against it. We ought to anticipate that reaction by acting whenever possible through multilateral groupings, especially the United Nations, because this assures almost every country a sense of participation in making decisions." Fromkin, "We Can Go It Alone. We Shouldn't," *New York Times*, September 29, 1995, p. A31.

45. Morgenthau, *Politics Among Nations*, pp. 42–51.

46. Snyder, *Myths of Empire*; Randall L. Schweller, "Tripolarity and the Second World War," *International Studies Quarterly*, Vol. 37, No. 1 (March 1993), pp. 73–104; Gilpin, *War and Change in World Politics*; and William C. Wohlforth, "Realism and the End of the Cold War," *International Security*, Vol. 19, No. 3 (Winter 1994/95), pp. 91–129.

We can infer that the response of the dominant state will be shaped by whether other states are revisionist or status quo–oriented in their foreign policy orientation. Balance-of-threat theory should predict policies of accommodation and reassurance from the dominant state in its dealings with status quo states. The purpose of these policies is to reinforce in status quo states the conviction that they are secure and do not need to expand military capabilities significantly and challenge the existing order. Specifically, we should expect the dominant state to avoid, in its own foreign policy, behavior that would be perceived as threatening by status quo states; to help to deter or deflect other threats to the security of status quo states; and to help to provide "outlets" or opportunities for status quo states to demonstrate power or enhance prestige without challenging the existing order.[47]

In dealings with revisionist states, we should anticipate that the dominant state will adopt policies of containment and confrontation. Revisionist states are committed to upsetting the existing international order, and in that sense threaten the primary foreign policy objective of the dominant state. We should expect from the dominant state an effort to organize diplomatic and military coalitions, and at the extreme military action, against revisionist states.[48]

Some potential challengers may be neither status quo nor revisionist. They may be "on the fence," uncertain which way their foreign policy will eventually fall. Balance-of-threat theory leads us to anticipate that the dominant state will approach these challengers with policies of accommodation in the hope of nudging them to support the status quo, rather than with policies of confrontation that would drive them unambiguously into the revisionist camp. We should expect the dominant power to adopt the same set of policies predicted for status quo states, and additionally to take steps to integrate these "undecided" states more fully into the existing order so that, by sharing the benefits of that order, they will have less incentive to destabilize or transform it.

The dominant state in a unipolar structure is in a relatively good position to accept the risks inherent in a foreign policy orientation that errs on the side of reassurance. As the sole dominant power it is best able to afford, at least in the short run, accommodating a state masking revisionist intentions. What would

---

47. Joffe frames a similar set in the form of policy prescriptions for the United States after the cold war. See Joffe, "Bismarck or Britain?" p. 117.

48. As a practical matter, it is critical for state officials to detect a potential challenger's intentions effectively and respond appropriately to them. This classic problem of the security dilemma is a difficult one, given uncertainty and the potential for deception. Morgenthau considered it the "fundamental question" of statecraft, and suggested that the answer determines the "fate of nations." Morgenthau, *Politics Among Nations*, pp. 67–68.

be a "fatal" mistake for a state facing a challenger of equal or greater power is more likely to be a costly but recoverable mistake for the preponderant power in a unipolar setting.

To summarize, the logic of balance-of-threat theory leads to three predictions for U.S. security policy after the Cold War. First, we should expect, as the centerpiece of U.S. grand strategy, an effort to prolong the unipolar moment. Second, we should anticipate that the United States will adopt policies of reassurance toward status quo states, policies of confrontation toward revisionist states, and policies of engagement or integration toward undecided states. Third, we should see the United States emphasizing multilateral processes in its foreign policy undertakings. Before examining the evidence, it is necessary as a preliminary step to discuss the foreign policy orientations of America's potential challengers.

THE STATUS OF POTENTIAL CHALLENGERS

In the current international system, the United States is in the enviable position of not facing any state, or coalition of states, that combines great power capability with clear intent to destabilize the existing order. Instead, the United States faces two potential great powers whose international situation and foreign policy behavior suggest a preference for the status quo, and two others who sit on the fence, with foreign policy intentions and aspirations more uncertain.

Japan and Germany are part of the victorious coalition that prevailed over the Soviet Union in the just-concluded hegemonic struggle. Rather than challenge U.S. hegemony, they are currently status quo powers, content to play a subordinate role within a U.S.-dominated system. The cornerstone of German security policy is the perpetuation of NATO, including the maintenance of U.S. forces in Europe and the U.S. nuclear guarantee. In 1994 German Chancellor Helmut Kohl described the U.S. presence as an "irreplaceable basis for keeping Europe on a stable footing," and that sentiment is echoed routinely by high German officials.[49] German participation in the Western European Union and the Eurocorps has been based on the presumption that European military

---

49. Kohl is quoted in W.R. Smyser, "Germany's New Vision," *Foreign Policy*, No. 97 (Winter 1994-95), p. 154. Defense Minister Volker Ruhe, in a 1995 assessment of German security policy, asserted that "without America, stability has never been, and will never be available." Quoted in Rafael Estrella, "Structure and Functions: European Security and Defense Identity (ESDI) and Combined Joint Task Forces (CJTF)," Draft General Report, North Atlantic Assembly, May 1995, para. 44.

forces must be integrated into NATO rather than standing as autonomous units.[50]

Japan continues to reaffirm the centrality of the U.S.-Japan Security Treaty, which obliges the United States to defend Japan, if necessary with nuclear weapons, and which leaves Japan a partial military power. A comprehensive report on Japan's post–Cold War security strategy put forth in late 1994 by the Defense Issues Council, a prominent advisory body to the prime minister, called for the two countries to "perfect" their bilateral security relationship, which continued to be "indispensable both for the purpose of making Japan's own safety still more certain and for the purpose of making multilateral security cooperation effective."[51] Despite the fact that its neighbors have been increasing their military spending, Japan's official long-term planning document, released in 1995, called for a *reduction* in military forces and equipment, strongly suggesting a preference for continued reliance on the United States to address regional security threats.[52]

For both Japan and Germany, continuities in foreign policy strategy after the Cold War outweigh major differences. Each state was a major beneficiary of the previous international order, and Germany also shared significantly in the "spoils" of the Cold War settlement by recovering the former East Germany. Future intentions are uncertain, but in the absence of unforeseen threats to their security, Japan and Germany are more likely to support the existing order than to challenge or undermine it.[53]

Russia's predicament and behavior suggest a different assessment. Since 1993 Russia has pursued a more assertive foreign policy, most evident in its coercive and interventionist behavior in the "near abroad" and in its desire to influence events in territorially proximate regions such as the Balkans and the Persian Gulf. None of this should come as a shock: the decline in Soviet/Russian prestige and influence was so sharp over such a short period of time

---

50. See Robert J. Art, "Why Western Europe Needs the United States and NATO," *Political Science Quarterly*, Vol. 111, No. 1 (Spring 1996), pp. 1–39.
51. Defense Issues Council, *Recommendations for Japan's Security and Defense Capability*, August 12, 1994, reprinted in *FBIS* (East Asia), October 28, 1994, pp. 1–18, quote at p. 6.
52. See Eric Heginbotham and Richard J. Samuels, "Mercantile Realism and Japanese Foreign Policy," in Ethan Kapstein and Michael Mastanduno, eds., *Realism and International Relations After the Cold War*, unpublished manuscript.
53. On Japan, see Peter Katzenstein and Nobuo Okawara, "Japan's National Security: Structures, Norms, and Policies," and Thomas Berger, "From Sword to Chrysanthemum: Japan's Culture of Anti-Militarism," in *International Security*, Vol. 17, No. 4 (Spring 1993), pp. 84–150. On Germany, see Timothy Garten Ash, "Germany's Choice," *Foreign Affairs*, Vol. 73, No. 4 (July/August 1994), pp. 65–81, and Smyser, "Germany's New Vision."

that one would expect Russia to seek, in the wake of the collapse, to restore some elements of its former great power status and exercise influence as a regional power. Yet, whether that effort will lead ultimately to a renewed strategy of global revisionism is certainly not a foregone conclusion. Russia does not currently possess an expansionist ideology. It has an ongoing need to attend to pressing economic problems at home, and requires international assistance in that effort. And, after decades of being perceived as a destabilizing force, Russia's leaders have a desire to be treated and respected as responsible players in the international system, and to share the benefits, especially economic, of that system. Although tensions between Russia and the West have increased since the "honeymoon period" of 1990–91, Russia's overall approach to the West has remained a cooperative one, and Russia has shown little inclination to enlist others to balance the preponderant power of the United States.[54]

China's combination of rapid growth, international ambition, and a history of discontent with what it perceives as humiliation at the hands of great powers makes it a more likely candidate to launch a global revisionist challenge. China's per capita GDP has almost quadrupled since 1978; it continues to develop and modernize its military capability; and it seems increasingly willing to threaten the use of force to achieve its foreign policy objectives, particularly with regard to Taiwan and the South China Sea.[55] China has the potential for a destabilizing combination of capabilities and intentions. Yet even in this case, a revisionist challenge is not inevitable. China's power position depends on sustaining rapid economic growth over many years, which, in turn, depends on maintaining political stability. Neither are guaranteed. While China, like Russia, seems determined to throw its weight around regionally, it has also exhibited a desire to be respected as a responsible great power and to share the benefits of the existing international order. And, although U.S.-Chinese relations have been strained by the 1989 Tiananmen Square incident, China's post–Cold War military acquisition pattern does not reflect a strategy of balancing the United States, it has not tried to organize an anti-American united front, and its economic dependence on the United States has increased.[56]

---

54. See S. Neil MacFarlane, "Realism and Russian Strategy After the Collapse of the USSR," in Kapstein and Mastanduno, *Realism and International Relations After the Cold War*. He argues Russia's cooperation with the West actually has been strongest in the area of security policy.
55. Kenneth Lieberthal, "A New China Strategy," *Foreign Affairs*, Vol. 74, No. 6 (November/December 1995), pp. 35–49.
56. Iain Johnston, "Realism and Chinese Security Policy in the Post-Cold War Period," in Kapstein and Mastanduno, *Realism and International Relations After the Cold War*.

BALANCE-OF-THREAT EVIDENCE

U.S. security policy since the end of the Cold War has conformed, although not completely, to the predictions of balance-of-threat theory. U.S. officials have sought to preserve the United States' dominant position through efforts to convince the status quo states of Japan and Germany to remain partial great powers, and to integrate the undecided states of Russia and China into a U.S.-centered international order.[57] U.S. officials have emphasized multilateral coalitions and decision-making processes, particularly in cases of military intervention.

To be sure, neither the Bush nor the Clinton administration has advertised, in foreign policy pronouncements, the goal of preventing other states from challenging the preeminent position of the United States.[58] The grand strategy of preserving unipolarity, however, was laid out clearly in the much-discussed Defense Planning Guidance leaked to the press in 1992.[59] The paper concluded that, following the defeat of the Soviet Union, "our strategy must now refocus on precluding the emergence of any future global competitor." The United States "must establish and protect a new order that holds the promise of convincing potential competitors that they need not aspire to a greater role." It must "retain the pre-eminent responsibility for addressing those wrongs which threaten not only our interests, but those of our allies or friends, or which could seriously unsettle international relations." Although U.S. officials publicly distanced themselves from the Guidance at the time it was leaked, its logic and arguments have in fact shaped U.S. security policy.

---

57. As balance-of-threat theory would expect, U.S. officials have responded to regional powers that have revisionist agendas with confrontation rather than engagement. The war against Iraq, the Clinton administration's subsequent "dual containment" strategy towards Iran and Iraq, and the administration's determination to gain collective support for a confrontational approach toward "rogue" or "backlash" states demonstrate this point. See Anthony Lake, "Confronting Backlash States," *Foreign Affairs*, Vol. 73, No. 2 (March/April 1994), pp. 45–55.

58. The public rhetoric of the Clinton administration has emphasized the need to shift from containment to "enlargement,"a somewhat vague doctrine focusing on the strengthening and promotion of democracy, human rights, and free markets worldwide. See *A National Security Strategy of Engagement and Enlargement* (Washington, D.C.: The White House, 1995). After aborted interventions in Somalia and Haiti in 1993, the administration became more pragmatic in practice even though its public statements continued to stress idealist goals. For a critique of Clinton's early foreign policy initiatives, see Michael Mandelbaum, "Foreign Policy as Social Work," *Foreign Affairs*, Vol. 75, No. 1 (January/February 1996), pp. 16–32.

59. "Excerpts from Pentagon's Plan: Prevent the Re-emergence of a New Rival," *New York Times*, March 8, 1992, p. A14. For discussion, see Robert Jervis, "International Primacy: Is the Game Worth the Candle?," *International Security*, Vol. 17, No. 4 (Spring 1993), pp. 53–54, 64; Benjamin Schwarz, "Why America Thinks It Has to Run the World," *Atlantic Monthly*, Vol. 277, No. 12 (June 1996), pp. 92–102; and Posen and Ross, "Competing Grand Strategies," pp. 120–121.

For example, U.S. policy has been dedicated to dissuading Japan from becoming a "normal" great power by deflecting threats to Japanese security, providing avenues for Japan to exhibit international responsibility despite lacking great power status, and assuring that U.S. behavior does not exacerbate Japanese insecurity. The bilateral security treaty remains the key to the relationship for the United States. Shortly after the collapse of the Soviet Union, U.S. officials had announced plans for a continual reduction in troop levels in Asia, but in 1994, the Pentagon called for a halt in the process in order to allay anxieties among Japanese and Asian officials that the United States might be contemplating a phased withdrawal. On the contrary, U.S. officials have termed their strategy for Asia "deep engagement." It calls for the maintenance of the forward deployment of U.S. forces and a commitment to a stabilizing regional role over the indefinite future. In the words of Joseph Nye, then Assistant Secretary of Defense, "For the security and prosperity of today to be maintained for the next twenty years, the United States must remain engaged in Asia, committed to peace in the region, and dedicated to strengthening alliances and friendships. That is what we propose to do."[60] The U.S. strategy is designed to convince Japan that the United States will deter possible threats from Russia or China, and that although Japan should contribute to that effort, there is no need for Japan to replicate the U.S. effort by becoming a full great power. The U.S. presence is intended to reassure Japan's neighbors as well, and to dampen incentives for regional arms races generated by insecurity.

U.S. officials have responded to threats that might, if left unattended, create incentives for Japan to develop independent military capabilities. The U.S.-led war in Iraq served multiple purposes, one of which was to maintain predictable access to Persian Gulf oil, on which Japan depends far more for its economic prosperity than does the United States. The U.S. effort to thwart North Korea's nuclear ambitions was consistent with U.S. nonproliferation strategy in general, and also with the regional strategy of reassuring Japan and discouraging it from having to acquire nuclear capabilities itself. U.S. officials have also been eager to encourage Japan to take on greater international responsibilities that do not require the full attributes of a great power. They have urged Japan to play a greater role in the management of international economic and environmental problems, and have encouraged Japan to take on international peacekeeping obligations, particularly in Southeast Asia but in Africa as well.

---

60. Joseph S. Nye, Jr., "The Case for Deep Engagement," *Foreign Affairs*, Vol. 74, No. 4 (July/August 1995), p. 102.

"Deep engagement" is similarly an apt characterization of the post–Cold War U.S. security strategy in Europe. During the Cold War, the unstated assumption was that NATO's purpose was threefold: to keep the Americans in, the Russians out, and the Germans down. NATO and the European Community were the critical mechanisms to bind Germany and France together and to anchor Germany in a transatlantic political and security community. Following the Cold War and German unification, the United States has continued to pursue a strategy designed to harness the great power potential of Germany while providing for German security in Europe.[61] For U.S. officials, support for German unification and the preservation of NATO, with Germany as a full partner within it, went hand in hand as crucial elements in the post–Cold War settlement.[62] Rather than "edging away" from NATO and the security obligations it imposes, U.S. officials have made clear their intention to transform the alliance and maintain it indefinitely.

The United States has also continued to support European integration, even as members of the European Union contemplate deeper commitments such as monetary and political union and the coordination of foreign and defense policies. Deeper integration has raised the potential for conflict between NATO and emerging European defense cooperation in the Western European Union and Eurocorps. The United States has been willing to support intra-European defense initiatives as long as they remain subordinated to NATO commitments.[63] U.S. officials engineered an arrangement with their European counterparts in 1994 to assure that the Western European Union would utilize rather than replicate NATO's military structure, and that the Eurocorps would come under NATO command during crisis or wartime.[64]

Balance-of-threat theory would anticipate U.S. intervention in conflicts that threaten regional stability and carry the potential for other major powers to develop and project independent military capabilities. America's reluctant and

---

61. Michael Mandelbaum, for example, argues that NATO is still needed "to reassure Germany that it need not arm itself more heavily to remain secure, something that would make Germany's neighbors feel less secure." Mandelbaum, "Preserving the New Peace," *Foreign Affairs*, Vol. 74, No. 3 (May/June 1995), p. 13.
62. See Philip Zelikow and Condoleezza Rice, *Germany United and Europe Transformed* (Cambridge, Mass.: Harvard University Press, 1995), and Art, "Why Western Europe Needs the United States and NATO."
63. As then-Assistant Secretary of State Richard Holbrooke argued, "It would be self-defeating for the WEU to create military structures to duplicate the successful European integration already achieved in NATO. . . . a stronger European pillar of the alliance can be an important contribution to European stability and trans-atlantic burden sharing, *provided it does not dilute NATO.*" Holbrooke, "America, A European Power," *Foreign Affairs*, Vol. 74, No. 2 (March/April 1995), p. 47, emphasis added.
64. Art, "Why Western Europe Needs the United States and NATO."

vacillating policy toward the Bosnian conflict between 1991 and 1994 does not square with this expectaton. By 1995, however, U.S. strategy coalesced and U.S. officials placed the cohesiveness of NATO at the top of their Bosnian policy agenda. In a critical National Security Council meeting late in 1994, the Clinton adminstration decided, in the words of one official, that "NATO is more important than Bosnia," and, in deference to its allies, backed away from its commitment to use air power to protect the safe area of Bihać.[65] Subsequently, in an effort to unite NATO and assure that German and Russian involvement was closely coordinated with the United States, U.S. officials hosted and orchestrated a peace settlement among the warring parties and backed their diplomacy with a commitment of 20,000 ground troops.[66]

Turning to the undecided powers, balance-of-threat theory would predict a U.S. attempt to steer Russian foreign policy away from a possible revisionist challenge and toward support for the status quo. We should expect U.S. efforts to avoid threatening Russian security, to provide opportunities for Russia to recover lost prestige, and to integrate Russia into the existing international order. Indeed, the United States was careful not to provoke or humiliate Russian leaders as the Soviet Union collapsed: recall President Bush's concern that the West not be perceived as dancing triumphantly on the ruins of the Berlin Wall.[67] U.S. officials have also reacted cautiously to Russia's internal security problems and have resisted any temptation to encourage or exploit political instability. They essentially condoned Yeltsin's 1993 assault on the Russian Parliament, and their response to Russian aggression in Chechnya has been critical although restrained. Statements of disapproval have been accompanied by the notable absence of sanctions, despite obvious human rights concerns, and by public acknowledgments that Chechnya is part of the Russian federation.[68]

---

65. This quote is from Michael Kelly, "Surrender and Blame," *New Yorker,* December 19, 1994, p. 51. See also Ruth Marcus and John Harris, "Behind U.S. Policy Shift on Bosnia: Strains in NATO," *Washington Post,* December 5, 1994, p. A26.
66. See Roger Cohen, "Why the Yanks are Going. Yet Again," *New York Times,* November 26, 1995, sec. 4, p. 1. Reflecting on the administration's Bosnia policy, Assistant Secretary Holbrooke conceded that "it took some time to realize that we are still part of the balance of power in Europe. We are needed now to bring stability to the vast land mass from the eastern German border to the western Russian border."
67. Zelikow and Rice, *Germany United and Europe Transformed,* p. 105
68. Holbrooke states that "the Chechnya conflict, terrible though it is, has not changed the nature of U.S. interests." See "America, A European Power," p. 49. Secretary of State Warren Christopher, seemingly struggling to find something positive to say, wrote in 1995 that public debate in Russia over Chechnya and independent media coverage were "reflections of Russia's emerging democracy and civil society." See Warren Christopher, "America's Leadership, America's Opportunity," *Foreign Policy,* No. 98 (Spring 1995), p. 11.

U.S. officials have also tried to bolster Russia's prestige through initiatives intended to highlight Russia's stature as an international actor. Invitations to Russian leaders to attend G-7 summits is one example, and the decision to grant Russia status as the "co-chair" of the U.S.-led Madrid peace conference on the Middle East is another. The Clinton administration worked out a delicate compromise to allow Russian forces to participate in the Bosnian peacekeeping effort under U.S. command when it became evident that Russia desired participation but was unwilling to do so under NATO command.[69] The United States also undertook a major diplomatic effort to ensure Russia's role as a "founding member" and major partner in the construction of a new export control regime, the successor to CoCom, designed to stem the flow of technology and weapons to dangerous states in the developing world. In the interest of furthering Russian economic reform, U.S. officials have facilitated Russia's access to the resources of the International Monetary Fund (IMF), to the point of raising questions as to whether Russia has been treated more generously than other recipients.[70] And they have sought to deepen cooperation with Russia in a revitalized United Nations and in the ongoing nuclear and conventional arms control processes.

One apparent anomaly for balance-of-threat theory is the U.S. commitment to NATO expansion. Russian leaders view NATO expansion as a political affront and a threat to Russian security. In the absence of an imminent threat from Russia, balance-of-threat theory would predict that the United States would resist rather than promote the expansion of NATO to Russia's doorstep.[71] Nevertheless, U.S. officials have encouraged NATO expansion and called for extending full membership to an initial group of East European countries in 1999.

The rationale for NATO expansion is multifaceted and complex, and on reflection the initiative is not wholly inconsistent with the U.S. grand strategy of preserving preponderance. NATO expansion extends and institutionalizes

---

69. Craig Whitney, "Russia Agrees to Put Troops Under U.S., Not NATO," *New York Times,* November 9, 1995, p. A14.

70. See Richard Stevenson, "Did Yeltsin Get a Sweetheart Deal on I.M.F. Loans?" *New York Times,* March 11, 1996, p. A11. During 1996 IMF negotiations with Russia over a $9 billion loan, President Clinton stated publicly that he wanted the deal to go through. IMF officials denied any U.S. influence or that Russia's treatment or conditions were any less stringent that was the usual practice.

71. Michael Mandelbaum accepts this logic in arguing that Russia is "not destined" to disturb the balance of power in Europe and that NATO expansion is "at best premature, at worst counterproductive." See Mandelbaum, "Preserving the New Peace," pp. 9–12.

the U.S. presence in the historically turbulent zone of instability between Russia and Germany. Rather than as the harbinger of a new containment strategy, it is a hedge not only against future Russian expansion, but also against an independent German *Ostpolitik* and possible German-Russian conflict.[72] The U.S. desire to stabilize Eastern Europe yet not offend Russia has forced U.S. officials into a delicate balancing act. They have stressed publicly that Russia does not hold a veto over NATO expansion, but have clearly been influenced by Russia's concerns. U.S. officials have sought to make NATO "Russia-friendly" through Russian participation in the Partnership for Peace, and they have searched with Russian leaders for a formula that would make NATO expansion politically acceptable to Russia.[73]

For China, as for Russia, balance-of-threat theory would predict a U.S. policy that stressed engagement and integration rather than containment. The overall U.S. approach to China is consistent with this prediction. Assistant Defense Secretary Nye argued in 1995 that "it is wrong to portray China as an enemy. Nor is there reason to believe China must be an enemy in the future. . . . A containment strategy would be difficult to reverse. Enmity would become a self-fulfilling prophecy."[74] The Clinton adminstration has termed its alternative strategy "comprehensive engagement," and its primary objective, as Kenneth Lieberthal has noted, is to facilitate China's integration into the existing international order on the condition that China accept the rules of that order and not seek to undermine it.[75] In short, the strategy seeks what to many seems improbable: to turn China into a status quo power.

---

72. Barry Posen and Andrew Ross reach a similar conclusion. They argue NATO expansion is being driven less by the need to respond to an imminent Russian threat, and more to "preserve and widen [U.S.] involvement in European affairs," and "to forestall even a hint of an independent German foreign policy in the east." NATO expansion is essentially "the adaptation of a politically familiar vehicle to the task of preserving U.S. primacy." Posen and Ross, "Competing U.S. Grand Strategies," p. 117.
73. See Andrei Kortunov, "NATO Enlargement and Russia: In Search of an Adequate Response," in David G. Haglund, ed., *Will NATO Go East? The Debate Over Enlarging the Atlantic Alliance* (Kingston, Ontario: Queens University Centre for International Relations, 1996), pp. 69–92; "The Bear Tamer's Next Problem," *The Economist*, February 3, 1996, pp. 19–20; and Jim Mann, "Yeltsin NATO Plan Attracts Interest from Clinton Aides, Central Europe," *Los Angeles Times*, April 22, 1996, p. A10.
74. Nye, "The Case for Deep Engagement," p. 94.
75. Lieberthal, "A New China Strategy," p. 43. Warren Christopher writes that it is up to China to decide whether it will be a destabilizing force, but that "American engagement can help encourage it to enjoy the benefits—and accept the obligations—that come with membership in international institutons and adherence to international norms." Christopher, "America's Leadership, America's Opportunity," p. 12.

A key element of the U.S. approach is closer defense and security cooperation with China. U.S. officials helped to convince China to join the nuclear nonproliferation regime and have engaged Chinese leaders in high-level dialogues on regional security and defense conversion. In the interest of a broader cooperative relationship, the Clinton administration in May 1994 backed away from the priority it had granted to human rights concerns in China policy and explicitly severed the connection between human rights and the granting of most-favored-nation (MFN) status for China.

Although U.S. officials believe that Chinese "misbehavior" continues to strain the bilateral relationship, their response has been muted. Early in 1996, the Clinton administration determined that Chinese sales of nuclear technology to Iran and Pakistan violated nonproliferaton rules, but worked to soften the sanctions it was required by law to impose on China.[76] In March 1996, as China threatened military action against Taiwan, the administration responded with "strategic ambiguity," a display of naval force it hoped would be sufficient to deter China and reassure others in the region without provoking a confrontation with China. In a strong signal of the administration's preference for business as usual, National Security Adviser Anthony Lake stated publicly in the midst of the crisis that the administration planned to renew MFN status for China, even though the State Department's annual human rights report was strongly critical of China.[77]

This review of U.S. relations with potential challengers suggests that balance-of-threat theory provides a strong explanation for U.S. security policy after the Cold War, and one that is more persuasive than that offered by balance-of-power theory. Balance-of-threat theory also anticipates the emphasis in U.S. security policy on multilateral decision-making procedures. To be sure, "multilateralism," and especially the United Nations, became targets of opprobrium in the U.S. Congress and in U.S. public opinion after the aborted intervention in Somalia. Nevertheless, as the Persian Gulf and Bosnian crises illustrate, the preferred strategy of the U.S. executive after the Cold War has been to rely on the UN Security Council to authorize the use of force or strong diplomatic initiatives, and then to proceed with U.S.-orchestrated military or diplomatic coalitions.[78] Multilateral decision-making processes help the United States to

---

76. See Steven Erlanger, "U.S. Set to Impose Limited Trade Sanctions on China," *New York Times*, February 21, 1996, p. A9.
77. Robert S. Greenberger, "U.S. Sends Naval Force Closer to Taiwan," *Wall Street Journal*, March 11, 1996, p. A10.
78. See Bruce W. Jentleson, "Who, Why, What, and How: Debates Over Post–Cold War Military Intervention," in Lieber, *Eagle Adrift*, pp. 61–65.

exercise its dominant power with legitimacy. They are key instruments of statecraft—indeed, of *realpolitik*—for a dominant state that is seeking, in a unipolar setting, to convince other states to cooperate with it rather than to balance against it.

Balance-of-Power Theory and Post–Cold War U.S. Economic Strategy

All realists assume that economic relations are a function of and subordinate to political relations; that the state is a distinct actor with its own goals; and that states, in their economic relationships, must remain sensitive to the possibility of military conflict.[79] Both balance-of-power and balance-of-threat theory build on these assumptions but, as with security strategy, each generates different predictions for U.S. economic strategy after the Cold War. Balance-of-power theory predicts that the primary focus of U.S. foreign economic policy will be to improve America's relative position in economic competition with other major powers. Balance-of-threat theory predicts that the United States will use its economic relationships and power as instruments of statecraft to reinforce its security strategy toward other major powers. In *security* strategy, post–Cold War U.S. behavior has been more consistent with the predictions of balance-of-threat theory. In *economic* strategy, however, U.S. behavior has been more consistent with the predictions of balance-of-power theory.

BALANCE-OF-POWER LOGIC AND PREDICTIONS
Realists emphasize that international economic interactions among states are inherently competitive, most importantly because of the close connection between economic and military power. Throughout history, the military capabilities of a state have depended on the size and level of development of its economy; great economic powers have become great military powers. If economic power is the basis for military strength, then states that are competitive in the military arena will naturally compete, with a sensitivity to relative position, in the economic arena.

In the contemporary era, however, the connection between economic and military capability is not as tight. Nuclear weapons make it possible to develop formidable military power without having great economic capability.[80] Further-

---

79. See Robert Gilpin, *The Political Economy of International Relations* (Princeton, N.J.: Princeton University Press, 1987), and Jonathan Kirshner, "The Political Economy of Realism," in Kapstein and Mastanduno, *Realism and International Relations After the Cold War.*
80. The point is made strongly in Waltz, "The Emerging Structure of International Politics."

more, in a nuclear era the prospects for hegemonic war among great powers may be remote, which further diminishes the strategic importance of relative economic position.[81] Do these considerations, for balance-of-power theorists, imply that international economic competition no longer matters?

The answer is clearly no. Waltz, for example, argues that "economic competition is often as keen as military competition, and since nuclear weapons limit the use of force among great powers at the strategic level, we may expect economic and technological competition among them to become more intense."[82] Balance-of-power theorists point to four reasons.[83] First, the prospects for war among major powers may be remote, but they never disappear completely. Today's benign security environment is tomorrow's threatening one, and today's stalemate in military technology is tomorrow's unforeseen breakthrough in military technology. Economic growth rates and technological advantages cumulate, so that small gaps in the present may become large gaps in the future. Second, even in the absence of threats to military security, states worry about foreign policy autonomy. Increases in relative economic capability expand foreign policy autonomy, because economic resources can be used to influence other states and to minimize vulnerability to the influence attempts of others.[84] Third, states compete to enhance national economic welfare. Prosperity, like security, can be shared, and the pursuit of it is not necessarily a zero-sum game. When scarcities exist, however, international economic relations necessarily become more competitive, and states may struggle over access to capital, natural resources, markets, jobs, or advanced technologies. Finally, success in economic competition brings to a state intangible but potentially important benefits in international status and prestige. Governments, like individuals, are probably more concerned with relative rankings than they are inclined to admit. Not every state is obsessed with being "number one," but most states are likely to derive some benefit from a higher ranking in economic competition (or in education, or sports) relative to states they consider to be their peers.[85]

---

81. See Gilpin, *War and Change in World Politics,* pp. 213–219.
82. Waltz, "The Emerging Structure of International Politics," p. 59.
83. See ibid, and also Layne, "The Unipolar Illusion," pp. 42–45; Samuel P. Huntington, "Why International Primacy Matters," *International Security,* Vol. 17, No. 4 (Spring 1993), pp. 68–83; Mearsheimer, "The False Promise of International Institutions," pp. 20–21; and Joseph Grieco, *Cooperation Among Nations* (Ithaca, N.Y.: Cornell University Press, 1990).
84. See David Baldwin, *Economic Statecraft* (Princeton: Princeton University Press, 1985).
85. See Jonathan Mercer, "Anarchy and Identity," *International Organization,* Vol. 49, No. 2 (Spring 1995), pp. 229–252.

For balance-of-power theory, international economic relations remain an integral part of the ongoing struggle for power and influence among nation-states. But to infer specific predictions for a state's foreign economic policy requires us to recognize again that states respond to the opportunities and constraints of the international structural environment they face. Foreign economic policy depends on the position of the state in the international economic structure[86] and the international security structure.[87]

During the Cold War, U.S. foreign economic policy responded to the incentives of both structures. The emergence of the United States as the dominant economic power led U.S. officials to abandon their traditional policies of economic nationalism in favor of a commitment to construct and maintain a liberal international economy. Bipolarity reinforced this approach in America's economic relations with its principal allies in Western Europe and East Asia. In the interest of strengthening the coalition balancing the Soviet Union, U.S. officials even permitted their allies to maintain trade (and in the case of Japan, investment) policies that discriminated against the United States.[88]

What should balance-of-power theory predict for U.S. foreign economic policy in the post–Cold War era? The key point is that the U.S. position in both the international economic and security structures has changed. The bipolar structure has given way to unipolarity and the U.S. position in the international economic structure has been in *relative* decline. The United States remains very powerful in absolute terms, but its economic position relative to Japan, Germany, and the European Union is less advantageous now than it was from 1945 to 1970.

---

86. According to hegemonic stability theory, large, relatively productive states prefer openness and seek to organize a liberal world economy, while less efficient states, absent intervention by the hegemonic state, prefer protection or to "free ride" on the open markets of others. As the hegemonic state declines, so does its commitment to the liberal world economy. See Lake, *Power, Protection, and Free Trade*; and Stephen Krasner, "American Policy and Global Economic Stability," in William P. Avery and David P. Rapkin, eds., *America in a Changing World Political Economy* (New York: Longman, 1982), pp. 29–48.

87. Joanne Gowa argues that trade among allies, especially in bipolar systems, will be greater than trade between allies and adversaries. Gowa, "Bipolarity, Multipolarity, and Free Trade," *American Political Science Review*, Vol. 79, No. 4 (December 1989), pp. 1245–1266, and *Allies, Adversaries, and International Trade* (Princeton, N.J.: Princeton University Press, 1994).

88. Robert Gilpin, *U.S. Power and the Multinational Corporation* (New York: Basic Books, 1975), pp. 99–112. Bipolarity also shaped the U.S. approach to its primary adversaries, as economic relations with the Soviet Union, Eastern Europe, and China were carefully restricted so as to avoid contributing to those states' military capabilities. See Michael Mastanduno, *Economic Containment: CoCom and the Politics of East-West Trade* (Ithaca, N.Y.: Cornell University Press, 1992).

We can infer from the combination of unipolarity and declining hegemony that the United States will become more sensitive to relative position in economic competition with other major powers. The Cold War situation was anomalous in two ways. First, when the United States was far ahead, it could afford not to worry too much about how to play—and how others were playing—the game of international economic competition. As others catch up, however, the United States should become more concerned with defending and advancing its relative economic position. Second, the need to meet the Soviet threat prompted the United States to subordinate its relative position in international economic competition to the greater good of fostering the overall economic strength of the Western coalition. In the absence of the Soviet threat, the United States should be less inclined to emphasize overall coalition strength and more inclined to treat other major powers as economic, and potentially geopolitical, competitors.

The logic of balance-of-power theory suggests that in the new structural environment, the position of the United States in international economic competition should become a central foreign policy priority. Specifically, we can infer three types of response. First, we should anticipate an effort by U.S. officials to cut down the economic costs of foreign policy commitments. At a minimum, expect burden-sharing to become a priority in foreign policy commitments; at a maximum, expect the United States to alter and diminish the commitments themselves.[89] Second, we should expect the United States to become more like other advanced industrial states in terms of assistance to national firms in international competition, with increased emphasis on export promotion policies, industrial policies, and government-industry collaboration. Third, we should expect U.S. officials to try to reverse or at least adjust the "generous" foreign economic policies characteristic of hegemony and bipolarity. They should be less tolerant of asymmetrical trade, technology, and exchange rate policies that gave advantages to principal economic competitors. And, we should expect their commitment to the multilateral free trade system, which was a critical element in the U.S. Cold War strategy, to diminish.

BALANCE-OF-POWER EVIDENCE

There is sufficient evidence to support each of these predictions as well as the more general expectation of balance-of-power theorists that changes in the

---

89. Robert Gilpin derives this policy implication from his declining hegemony argument. See Gilpin, *War and Change in World Politics*, pp. 232–234.

international economic and security structures will prompt the United States to become more sensitive to relative position in economic competition with other major powers.

First, burden-sharing—the effort to convince other states to pick up a greater share of the costs of U.S. foreign policy commitments—has become increasingly prominent in U.S. statecraft since the end of the Cold War. U.S. officials have pushed Japan to pay all the yen-based costs and roughly 70 percent of the total costs of maintaining U.S. forces in Japan.[90] During the Gulf War, the Bush administration extracted contributions from other coalition members with a zeal and effectiveness that led some observers to calculate that the United States made a net profit on the intervention, and others to characterize U.S. forces as mercenaries.[91] The 1994 deal on nonproliferation struck between the United States and North Korea obliges Japan and South Korea to accept a significant part of the cost of providing alternative energy sources to North Korea. U.S. officials have made clear that they expect the members of the European Union to bear the burden of Bosnian reconstruction.[92] No post–Cold War "Marshall Plan" was devised for Russia and Eastern Europe: burden-sharing disputes characterized the Western aid effort for Russia, and for the most part the United States deferred the economic initiative on Eastern Europe to Germany and its European partners.

Second, U.S. officials have taken a series of aggressive steps to assist U.S. firms in international competition. The Clinton administration has elevated export promotion to the very top of the U.S. foreign policy agenda, including the routine use of diplomatic leverage at the highest levels to create opportunities for U.S. firms.[93] The Commerce Department has emulated the Pentagon in dedicating a "war room" to track international competition for major export contracts around the world.[94] A high priority has been placed upon improving the U.S. position in competition for emerging markets across the developing world, and in 1994 President Clinton himself was instrumental in helping U.S. aircraft suppliers outcompete their European rivals for a $6 billion order from Saudi Arabia. U.S. officials have made the relaxation of national security export

---

90. Nye, "The Case for Deep Engagement," p. 98.
91. U.S. Congress, House, Committee on Ways and Means, *Foreign Contributions to the Costs of the Gulf War*, 102nd Congress, 1st sess., July 31, 1995.
92. Christopher Wren, "The G.I.s Don't Carry a Marshall Plan," *New York Times*, December 17, 1995, p. 14.
93. John Stremlau, "Clinton's Dollar Diplomacy," *Foreign Policy*, No. 97 (Winter 1994–95), pp. 18–35.
94. "Ron Brown, Salesman," *The Economist*, February 25, 1995, p. 32.

controls—which traditionally disadvantaged U.S. firms more than firms in other industrial states—a high priority, especially in areas of U.S. competitive advantage such as computers and electronics. Commercial motivations have also led the Clinton team to weaken restraints on conventional arms sales.

Compared to the governments of other advanced industrial states, the U.S. government still lags in its enthusiasm for civilian industrial policies. Yet an evolution over time is apparent. "Atari Democrats" pushed the idea during the early 1980s without political success. By the late 1980s it became legitimate in the U.S. policy context to promote industrial policy, as long as the primary purpose was defense applications. The Reagan and Bush administrations devoted resources to SEMATECH and encouraged the Defense Advanced Research Projects Agency (DARPA) to fund defense-related civilian technologies such as flat computer-display panels and high-definition television.[95] By the middle of the 1990s, executive officials embraced explicitly the idea of industrial policy directly for commercial applications. DARPA's name dropped "Defense" to become ARPA, and the Clinton administration launched of series of initiatives involving government-business partnerships in industry and advanced technology.[96] The president's often-quoted depiction of economic relations among the United States and other advanced industrial nations as analogous to "big corporations competing in the global marketplace" captures the sentiment underlying these and similar initiatives.

Third, accelerating a pattern that began during the 1970s and 1980s, U.S. officials have become far less tolerant of trade, technology, and exchange rate asymmetries that lend advantage to its primary competitors. Aggressive demands for market access have become the centerpiece of U.S. trade strategy.[97] Struggles with the European Union over aircraft subsidies, broadcasting quotas, and agricultural restrictions reflect this priority, and the concern drove former U.S. Commerce Secretary Robert Mosbacher to demand a "seat at the table" for the United States in order to influence the design of the single European market. Japan, to this point the United States' most intense industrial and technological competitor, has been an even more prominent target. In trade

---

95. "Uncle Sam's Helping Hand," *The Economist*, April 2, 1994, pp. 77–79.
96. Edmund Andrews, "Washington Growing as a Financial Angel to Industry," *New York Times*, May 1, 1994, sec. F, p. 3.
97. See Laura D'Andrea Tyson, *Who's Bashing Whom? Trade Conflict in High Technology Industries* (Washington, D.C.: Institute for International Economics, 1992); and Jagdish Bhagwati and Hugh Patrick, eds., *Aggressive Unilateralism: America's 301 Trade Policy and the World Trading System* (Ann Arbor: University of Michigan Press, 1990).

disputes over satellites, supercomputers, and semiconductors, U.S. officials have sought to disrupt Japan's home market "sanctuary" by countering Japanese infant industry protection and collusive arrangements among Japanese firms and between Japanese government and industry. U.S. behavior in the highly public automotive sector dispute in 1995 was driven in part by similar concerns, as U.S. officials sought to break open the long-term supplier and distributor relationships that shut U.S. firms out of the Japanese market.

U.S. officials have resorted increasingly to the use of exchange rates as a trade weapon in competition with Japan. Since the Plaza Accord of 1985, and in a reversal of the Cold War pattern, the United States has forced Japan to accept a dollar-yen exchange rate that enhances the attractiveness of U.S. exports to Japan and discourages Japanese sales to the United States. The FSX fighter dispute demonstrated dramatically that U.S. officials are no longer willing to encourage, as they did during the Cold War, the transfer to Japan of sensitive U.S. technologies that have commercial significance. The United States wants to stem the flow of critical commercial technologies to Japan and to encourage the "flowback" of Japanese technologies to the United States.[98]

The United States has also begun to counter and emulate the industrial espionage practices that have long been an element of its competitors' national economic strategies.[99] Early in 1995 the French government asked the CIA station chief and his assistants to leave the country in light of accusations that the CIA had been recruiting French officials with responsibilities for General Agreement on Tariffs and Trade (GATT) negotiations and telecommunications policy. U.S. officials criticized the very public French response as unprecedented in relations among allies—but did not deny the allegations.[100] Subsequently, a similar diplomatic controversy broke out with Japan over suspicions that CIA officials had eavesdropped on Japanese officials in an effort to gain advantage for the United States during the auto negotiations. Japan, too, was indignant and demanded explanations. For Japan and France to protest too vigorously is somewhat ironic, but does reflect their discomfort with the idea that the United States might reorient some of its formidable intelligence assets from military collaboration to international economic competition.

---

98. Michael Mastanduno, "Do Relative Gains Matter? America's Response to Japanese Industrial Policy," *International Security*, Vol. 16, No. 1 (Summer 1991), pp. 73–113.
99. See Peter Schweizer, "The Growth of Economic Espionage," *Foreign Affairs*, Vol. 75, No. 1 (January/February 1996), pp. 9–15.
100. Thomas Kamm and Robert Greenberger, "France, in Apparent Espionage Spat, Asks Five Americans to Leave Country," *Wall Street Journal*, February 25, 1995, p. A10.

Finally, there have been changes in the nature of the U.S. commitment to multilateral free trade. To be sure, U.S. officials continue to support the multilateral system. The successful completion of the Uruguay Round and the replacement of the GATT with the more ambitious World Trade Organization (WTO) were high priorities for both the Bush and Clinton administrations. Nevertheless, the strength and durability of the U.S. commitment to the multilateral system have been questioned by its trading partners, and with good reason. The Bush administration was willing to risk the collapse of the Uruguay Round at its 1990 deadline, and pinned the blame on its European competitors for refusing to accede to U.S. demands for radical liberalization in the agricultural sector. An uneasy compromise was reached and the round was finally completed in 1993. Subsequently, the United States dealt serious blows to the nascent WTO by refusing to meet deadlines set under the Uruguay Round for new agreements to liberalize trade in telecommunications, financial services, and maritime transport because the proposed accords did not provide sufficient advantages to U.S. firms in overseas markets. U.S. Trade Representative Charlene Barshefsky defended this stand in 1996 by arguing that "with the Cold War over, trade agreements must stand or fall on their merits. They no longer have a security component. If we do not get reciprocity, we will not get freer trade."[101]

The United States' multilateral commitment has also coexisted uneasily since the mid-1980s with the clear determination of U.S. officials to rely on "aggressive unilateralism" in trade policy, notwithstanding the fact that U.S. tactics have been widely perceived abroad as damaging to the credibility of U.S. diplomacy and the multilateral system.[102] Aggressive unilateralism exploits the advantages of U.S. economic power and produces quicker results than the more consensual multilateral process. U.S. officials have also devoted considerable diplomatic effort to regional liberalization efforts such as the expansion of the North American Free Trade Agreement (NAFTA), while at the same time questioning the need for another comprehensive round of multilateral trade negotiations.[103]

---

101. See Paul Lewis, "Is the U.S. Souring on Free Trade?," *New York Times*, June 25, 1996, p. D1; and Paul Lewis, "U.S. Rejects Accord to Free Trade in Financial Services," *New York Times*, June 30, 1995, p. D1. In financial services, U.S. officials announced they would grant access to foreign firms selectively, depending on the extent of reciprocal access provided to U.S. firms abroad. The European Union and Japan went forward with the agreement absent the participation of the multilateral system's traditional champion.

102. See Bhagwati and Patrick, *Aggressive Unilateralism*.

103. In the words of Deputy U.S. Trade Representative Jeffrey Lang, "I'm not sure the WTO needs glamorous, big negotiating rounds; we should aim for steady, small steps every year." See Lewis, "Is the U.S. Souring on Free Trade?"

Balance-of-Threat Theory and Post–Cold War U.S. Economic Strategy

Earlier I inferred, from the logic of balance-of-threat theory, the prediction that U.S. security strategy after the Cold War would center on the effort to preserve primacy through policies of reassurance and engagement. To develop predictions for U.S. economic strategy requires a bolder extrapolation, because thus far balance-of-threat advocates have devoted relatively little systematic attention to international economic relationships.[104]

BALANCE-OF-THREAT LOGIC AND PREDICTIONS

Balance-of-power theorists expect intensified economic competition after the Cold War to be a logical counterpart to the renewal of security rivalry among great powers in a multipolar setting. From the perspective of balance-of-threat theory, however, neither the rapid transition to multipolarity nor security conflict among rival great powers is inevitable, because states respond not only to capabilities but also to perceptions of threat and foreign policy intention. Balance-of-threat realists foresee the potential for great power cooperation; they worry that preparation for great power rivalry and possible war might lead to a self-fulfilling prophecy according to the logic of the security dilemma.[105]

Two implications follow for international economic relations. First, if great power rivalry can be held in abeyance and the prospects for war are remote, states can afford to be less concerned about relative gains and relative position in international economic competition. There are other reasons for states to be concerned about relative position, but for balance-of-threat theorists these are less pressing than the likelihood of war.[106] Second, attempts to pursue relative economic advantage might actually prove counterproductive, because states respond to perceptions of threat. The pursuit of relative advantage might appear provocative or threatening to other states, triggering the spiral of political tension and rivalry that balance-of-threat theorists hope states will avoid.

We can infer from this logic the general prediction that states will tailor their foreign economic policies to complement and reinforce their national security strategies. Realists generally believe that economic relations are subordinate to

---

104. An important exception is Jervis, "International Primacy: Is the Game Worth the Candle?"
105. Ibid., pp. 56–57, and Stephen Van Evera, "Primed for Peace: Europe After the Cold War," in Sean M. Lynn-Jones and Steven E. Miller, eds., *The Cold War and After: Prospects for Peace*, rev. ed. (Cambridge, Mass.: MIT Press, 1993), pp. 193–243. Van Evera writes (p. 218): "If all states accept the status quo and none wish to change it, wars are far fewer. Indeed, if no aggressor state is on the scene, war can only occur by accident or misunderstanding."
106. Jervis, "International Primacy: Is the Game Worth the Candle?" pp. 67–68.

political relations; if balance-of-threat theory is correct, we should anticipate that states will use economic relationships as instruments to serve broader political goals.[107] We should expect a state that pursues political confrontation in relations with a revisionist state also to pursue economic confrontation. Since the intentions of a revisionist state are already presumed to be hostile, the purpose of economic confrontation would be to isolate the revisionist state and weaken its capabilities. We should expect a state that pursues a political strategy of reassurance in relations with status quo or undecided states to reinforce that strategy by relying on cooperative economic policies. Economic cooperation might increase the capabilities of an undecided state, but might also shape its foreign policy intentions in a manner desired by the initiating state.[108]

These guidelines suggest the following predictions for U.S. economic strategy after the Cold War. In relations with the status quo states of Japan and the European Union, we should expect the strategy of security reassurance to be reinforced by economic engagement. We should see U.S. officials seeking to minimize bilateral conflicts and to emphasize cooperative initiatives such as the launching of free trade agreements. In relations with Russia and China, states with uncertain foreign policy intentions, we should expect the U.S. political strategy of integration to be complemented by economic strategies of integration and cooperation, as part of the broader effort to steer these states to support the U.S.-centered status quo. For revisionist states, such as Iran and Iraq, we should expect economic containment to reinforce political containment.

BALANCE-OF-THREAT EVIDENCE

To what extent have U.S. officials used economic statecraft to reinforce and promote their preferred post–Cold War security strategy? Although the evidence is mixed, the emphasis is clear. U.S. economic strategy thus far has reflected, consistent with balance-of-power theory, a greater concern for the pursuit of relative economic advantage than for using economic relations to

---

107. As Robert Gilpin points out, "in all historical epochs, realist thinkers have focused on the economic dimensions of statecraft." Gilpin, "Richness of the Tradition of Political Realism," p. 308. A prominent contribution in this tradition is Albert Hirschman's classic, *National Power and the Structure of Foreign Trade*, rev. ed. (Berkeley: University of California Press, 1980).
108. For a discussion of the use of economic statecraft to shape a target state's capabilities and intentions, see Mastanduno, *Economic Containment*, chap. 2.

support the preferred national security strategies of reassuring and engaging potential challengers.

The tension between security and economic strategy is strongest in U.S. relations with Japan. As Japanese officials sometimes comment, dealing with the United States in economics and security is like dealing with two different countries. The relationship among U.S. and Japanese security officials has been characterized by a sense of shared objectives, while relations on the economic side have been marked by mistrust and frustration. Disputes have been virtually continuous for a decade: the Toshiba and semiconductor disputes in 1987; the FSX, Super 301, and SII disputes in 1989–90; the Persian Gulf dispute in 1991; President Bush's ill-fated auto sales trip in 1992; conflict over semiconductors again in 1992–93; the collapse of the Framework talks in 1994; and the automotive and economic spying disputes in 1995.[109] Attempts to resolve these disputes call to mind the U.S.-Soviet arms control experience during the Cold War in the sense that each side approaches the other with suspicion and resentment, and fears its partner will exploit the smallest loopholes or ambiguities as an excuse to renege on commitments. Instead of the de-escalation of economic tensions that would complement the security strategy of reassurance, U.S. officials have applied almost relentless economic pressure on Japan.

U.S. economic strategy toward China and the U.S.-China economic relationship have begun to resemble the Japan situation. Concern over China's mounting trade surplus and frustration over obstacles to market access have led to political acrimony and threats of economic sanctions and trade wars. U.S. trade officials speak openly of China as the "next Japan." They view China as adopting Japan's adversarial economic practices as part of its development strategy, and they are determined not to make the "same mistake" of subordinating economic interests to security concerns. Then-U.S. Trade Representative Mickey Kantor expressed the view explicitly in 1995 that the United States must practice economic confrontation against China earlier and more aggressively than it did against Japan. He and other trade officials convinced the White House in early 1996, over the objections of the State Department, that the United States should continue to confront China over its intellectual property

---

109. For background and discussion, see Tyson, *Who's Bashing Whom;* C. Fred Bergsten and Marcus Noland, *Reconcilable Differences? United States-Japan Economic Conflict* (Washington, D.C.: Institute for International Economics, 1993); and Benjamin J. Cohen, "Return to Normalcy? Global Economic Policy at the End of the Century," in Lieber, ed., *Eagle Adrift,* pp. 79–86.

practices even though confrontation might jeopardize the ability of U.S. officials to moderate China's behavior in its conflict with Taiwan.[110]

U.S. economic relations with members of the European Union also have been more a source of tension than of reassurance, with sustained disputes over agriculture, broadcasting, aircraft, telecommunications, government procurement, and other issues played out bilaterally and multilaterally. Even U.S. pressure on Japan has tended to have negative repercussions, as European officials have objected that Japanese accommodation to U.S. market access demands will only force European firms to bear the adjustment costs. By the mid-1990s these festering economic conflicts, compounded by the United States' apparent turn away from Europe in favor of Latin America and Asia, led to concerns on both sides of the transatlantic relationship regarding its long-term stability. In May 1995 the United States responded, as balance-of-threat theory would predict, with economic statecraft, in the form of a proposal for a transatlantic free trade agreement. In proposing the agreement, U.S. officials cautioned that in the absence of "new economic architecture" across the Atlantic, "natural economic juices may force us much further apart than anyone conceives of right now."[111] As of the beginning of 1996, however, plans for a "trans-Atlantic NAFTA" were downgraded to a more modest dialogue on non-tariff barriers, as both U.S. and EU officials conceded that they were not quite prepared for the arduous negotiations that would be required to launch a free trade agreement.[112]

U.S. economic strategy toward Russia has come closest to meeting the predictions of balance-of-threat theory. As part of the larger effort to encourage Russia to sustain political and economic reforms and a pro-Western foreign policy, U.S. officials have facilitated Russia's dealings with the IMF and the G-7, and have provided funds and technical support to assist Russia in dismantling nuclear weapons and in making the transition to a market economy.[113] The fact that Russia is not a serious economic competitor (or, like China, an emerging

---

110. David Sanger, "In a Trade Pact with China, the Ghost of Japan," *New York Times*, February 27, 1995, p. D1, and David Sanger and Steven Erlanger, "U.S. Warns China over Violations of Trade Accord," *New York Times*, February 4, 1996, p. A1.
111. Steven Greenhouse, "U.S. to Seek Stronger Trade and Political Ties with Europe," *New York Times*, May 29, 1995, p. A3.
112. Nathaniel Nash, "Showing Europe That U.S. Still Cares," *New York Times*, December 3, 1995, p. 20.
113. According to one estimate, the United States provided roughly $9 billion in assistance to the former Soviet region between 1990 and 1994. See Charles Weiss, Jr., "The Marshall Plan: Lessons for U.S. Assistance to Central and Eastern Europe and the Former Soviet Union," Occasional Paper (Washington, D.C.: The Atlantic Council, December 1995), p. 23.

competitor) has made it easier for U.S. officials to avoid the kinds of economic conflicts that have characterized U.S. relations with other major powers. Yet, even in this case, U.S. economic statecraft offers only a partial complement to the political engagment strategy. U.S. officials have not offered Russia anything resembling the preferential trade arrangements provided to Western Europe and Japan in their postwar recovery phases, and the U.S. aid program for Russia has caused considerable resentment, with Russian officials complaining that the effort is being driven by U.S. export interests and that the main beneficiaries have not been Russians but U.S. corporations and consulting firms.[114]

Conclusion: Realism and the Future of U.S. Grand Strategy

Realists might be tempted to conclude from this analysis that "realism explains everything," while critics might counter that, by generating contradictory expectations, realism actually explains nothing. Both comments miss the point. Realism *per se* is not an explanation, but a research program from which particular realist explanations can be derived and tested. I assessed two realist theories in this article, and the evidence neither fully supports nor fully refutes either one. However, each theory does provide strong insight into a central aspect of post–Cold War U.S. foreign policy and, taken together, they point to an important tension within overall U.S. strategy.

As both realist theories would predict, U.S. strategy has been responsive to the constraints and opportunities of the international structure and to the U.S. position within it. Bipolarity concentrated U.S. attention on the Soviet challenge and drove economic and security strategy in complementary directions. Unipolarity imposes less of a constraint and affords the United States more room to maneuver. After the Cold War, U.S. security and economic strategy have diverged. Security strategy has been more consistent with the predictions of balance-of-threat theory, while economic strategy has followed more closely the expectations of balance-of-power theory.

Further refinement and testing of each theory is needed. Balance-of-power theory confronts a central puzzle in international relations after the Cold War—the absence of balancing at the core of the international system. Unipo-

---

114. See Charles Flickner, "The Russian Aid Mess," *The National Interest*, No. 38 (Winter 1994-95), pp. 13–18, and David Kramer, "Russian Aid (II)," *The National Interest*, No. 39 (Spring 1995), pp. 78–81.

larity may indeed prove to be a transition, but for balance-of-power theory, the longer unipolarity persists, the more imperative it will become to reconsider the logic of balancing behavior and to reassess the historical evidence that presumably supports the theory.[115] Balance-of-threat theory can explain the persistence of unipolarity, but to do so it must focus on both on the distribution of capabilities and, at the unit level, on foreign policy intentions and behavior. Further advances in balance-of-threat theory require sustained attention to the conceptual and empirical challenges of studying images, intentions, and perceptions of threat in relations among states.[116]

For U.S. officials, the appeal of the security strategy predicted by balance-of-threat theory is not surprising. The temptation to prolong the unipolar moment and the luxuries it affords is a powerful one. That temptation is reinforced by the typical American belief that U.S. power does not threaten anyone, and that the U.S.-led international order provides sufficient benefits so that it is unnecessary for other states to seek to undermine it. The appeal of preserving primacy is also reinforced by inertia—it is easier for U.S. officials to maintain and adjust the practices and institutions of a U.S.-centered international system than to shift to the uncertainty of "strategic independence" in preparation for a multipolar world.

If balance-of-threat theory is correct, then the duration of the unipolar moment will depend not only on the relative distribution of capabilities but also on the effectiveness of U.S. diplomacy. Through policies of engagement and reassurance, U.S. officials can dissuade or at least delay other states from challenging U.S. hegemony and balancing against the United States. The effectiveness of engagement and reassurance, however, will depend on the ability of U.S. officials to meet the following three challenges.

First, U.S. officials must continue to manage the tension between their international economic and security strategies so that economic conflicts do not erode security relationships and eventually trigger a balancing response.[117]

---

115. A recent, critical examination is Paul Schroeder, "Historical Reality vs. Neorealist Theory," *International Security*, Vol. 19, No. 1 (Summer 1994), pp. 108–148.
116. An important recent contribution is Richard K. Herrmann and Michael P. Fisherkeller, "Beyond the Enemy Image and Spiral Model: Cognitive-Strategic Research After the Cold War," *International Organization*, Vol. 49, No. 3 (Summer 1995), pp. 415–450.
117. A forceful argument on the need to bring current U.S. foreign economic policy in line with foreign and security policy is Henry R. Nau, *Trade and Security: U.S. Policies at Cross-Purposes* (Washington, D.C.: AEI Press, 1995). Nau argues (pp. 1–2) that "trade policy has been increasingly isolated from other U.S. foreign policy interests in a single-minded pursuit to capture exports and high-wage jobs for the American economy." Economic nationalists argue the opposite: U.S. economic interests are being compromised in the interest of maintaining a questionable security strategy, and security strategy should line up behind the more aggressive international economic

Thus far, U.S. officials have tried to square the conflicting demands of their two strategies by resorting to economic brinksmanship, especially in relations with Japan. Their tactic is to extract economic benefits by threatening sanctions, only to search for face-saving compromises under the pressure of deadlines to avoid actually having to initiate or escalate trade wars. Brinksmanship can be effective but it is also risky, especially with trading partners who can muster the resolve to resist.[118]

The next several years should bring a respite in economic tensions with Japan, because U.S. competitiveness has recovered strongly since the late 1980s and at the same time the economic threat from Japan has waned.[119] If China does come to replace Japan as America's principal economic competitor, however, management of the conflicting strategies of economic hardball and security softball will become all the more delicate. More so than Japan has been, China is likely to resist U.S. pressure as a matter of national pride. And, from the perspective of U.S. grand strategy, the security stakes are higher because China is an undecided state rather than a long-standing ally that supports the status quo.

Second, U.S. officials must maintain support at home for the preferred policies of engagement and reassurance. This will not be easy because, as Robert Tucker recently observed, the "great issue" of contemporary U.S. foreign policy is "the contradiction between the persisting desire to remain the premier global power and an ever deepening aversion to bear[ing] the costs of this position."[120] The U.S public indeed has displayed an increasing reluctance to bear the costs of a global engagement strategy, especially when it involves the need to risk American lives in faraway places for the purpose not of meeting an identifiable threat but of maintaining "stability." But that risk is difficult to avoid, because the pursuit of primacy induces the United States to be the stabilizer of last resort in regional crises. In a two-week period early in 1996,

strategy even if that means disengaging the United States militarily from Asia. See Chalmers Johnson and E.B. Keehn, "The Pentagon's Ossified Strategy," *Foreign Affairs*, Vol. 74, No. 4 (July/August 1995), pp. 104–105.
118. A recent task force report on U.S.-Japan relations prepared for the U.S. government by the National Research Council addressed this problem, and warned that "it is unrealistic to believe that a 'firewall' can be maintained long-term to protect one aspect of the relationship from significant erosion of goodwill in others." The task force recommended a comprehensive dialogue between the two governments to integrate the economic and security aspects of their relationship. See National Research Council, Report of the Defense Task Force, *Maximizing U.S. Interests in Science and Technology Relations with Japan* (Washington, D.C.: National Academy Press, 1995), p. 81.
119. See Cohen, "Return to Normalcy?" pp. 73–99.
120. Robert W. Tucker, "The Future of a Contradiction," *The National Interest*, No. 43 (Spring 1996), p. 20.

U.S. officials found themselves managing the insertion of 20,000 U.S. troops in Bosnia, prepositioning equipment for a possible renewed Iraqi attack against Kuwait, mediating a crisis on the brink of war between Greece and Turkey, and responding to China's military intimidation of Taiwan.[121]

U.S. officials have responded to the domestic constraint by emphasizing "pragmatism" in military interventions—the attempt to avoid excessive commitments, minimize casualties, and emphasize "exit strategies" even at the risk of leaving unfinished business. But the current intervention in Bosnia can still turn sour, and future interventions are inevitable if the United States continues to pursue the engagement and reassurance of other major powers. It is hard to imagine that the domestically acceptable Persian Gulf formula—clear threat, low casualties, quick settlement, ample external support and financing—can be replicated across a series of regional crises.

Third, U.S. officials must manage what might be called the arrogance of power. The dominant state in any international order faces strong temptations to go it alone, to dictate rather than to consult, to preach its virtues, and to impose its values. In the case of the United States, these temptations are compounded by a democratic political tradition that tends to imbue foreign policy with the values of society and to assure that moral considerations are never far from the surface in discussions of foreign policy.

The United States does succumb to the arrogance of power, as demonstrated by recent conflicts with China over human rights and with America's closest trading partners over the unilateral extension of U.S. sanctions to foreign firms doing business in Cuba, Iran, and Libya.[122] The risks to U.S. grand strategy should be evident. Efforts to impose values or to preach to other states create resentment and over time can prompt the balancing behavior U.S. officials hope to forestall. It is ironic that in a unipolar setting the dominant state, less constrained by other great powers, must constrain itself.

No realist can sensibly expect the current international system to remain in place indefinitely. Eventually, power will check power. But whether or not the transition to a new international order will be prolonged will depend, at least in part, on the skill and resourcefulness of U.S. foreign policy officials. Balance-of-threat theory reminds us to appreciate the classical realist insight that statecraft matters.

121. As Posen and Ross note, "Primacy is notoriously open-ended." Posen and Ross, "Competing Grand Strategies," p. 124.
122. Brian Coleman, "U.S. Envoy to EU Aims to Defuse Anger Over Sanctions on Business with Cuba," *Wall Street Journal*, October 18, 1996, p. A13A.

A NATIONAL SECURITY STRATEGY FOR A NEW CENTURY

THE WHITE HOUSE
OCTOBER 1998

Contents

Preface

As we approach the beginning of the 21st century, the United States remains the world's most powerful force for peace, prosperity and the universal values of democracy and freedom. Our nation's challenge—and our responsibility—is to sustain that role by harnessing the forces of global integration for the benefit of our own people and people around the world.

These forces of integration offer us an unprecedented opportunity to build new bonds among individuals and nations, to tap the world's vast human potential in support of shared aspirations, and to create a brighter future for our children. But they also present new, complex challenges. The same forces that bring us closer increase our interdependence, and make us more vulnerable to forces like extreme nationalism, terrorism, crime, environmental damage and the complex flows of trade and investment that know no borders.

To seize these opportunities, and move against the threats of this new global era, we are pursuing a forward-looking national security strategy attuned to the realities of our new era. This report, submitted in accordance with Section 603 of the Goldwater-Nichols Defense Department Reorganization Act of 1986, sets forth that strategy. Its three core objectives are:

- To enhance our security.

- To bolster America's economic prosperity.

- To promote democracy abroad.

Over the past five years, we have been putting this strategy in place through a network of institutions and arrangements with distinct missions, but a common purpose—to secure and strengthen the gains of democracy and free markets while turning back their enemies. Through this web of institutions and arrangements, the United States and its partners in the international community are laying a foundation for security and prosperity in the 21st century.

This strategy encompasses a wide range of initiatives: expanded military alliances like NATO, its Partnership for Peace, and its partnerships with Russia and Ukraine; promoting free trade through the World Trade Organization and the move toward free trade areas by nations in the Americas and elsewhere around the world; strong arms control regimes like the Chemical Weapons Convention and the Comprehensive Nuclear Test Ban Treaty; multinational coalitions combating terrorism, corruption, crime and drug trafficking; and binding international commitments to protect the environment and safeguard human rights.

The United States must have the tools necessary to carry out this strategy. We have worked diligently within the parameters of the Balanced Budget Agreement to preserve and provide for the readiness of our armed forces while meeting priority military challenges identified in the 1997 Quadrennial Defense Review (QDR). The QDR struck a careful balance between near-term readiness, long-term modernization and quality of life improvements for our men and women in uniform. It ensured that the high readiness levels of our forward-deployed and "first-to-fight" forces would be maintained. The priority we attach to maintaining a high-quality force is reflected in our budget actions. This fiscal year, with Congress' support for the Bosnia and Southwest Asia non-offset emergency supplemental funds, we were able to protect our high payoff readiness accounts. Next year's Defense Budget increases funding for readiness and preserves quality of life for military personnel.

Although we have accomplished much on the readiness front, much more needs to be done. Our military leadership and I are constantly reevaluating the readiness of our forces and addressing problems in individual readiness areas as they arise. I have instructed the Office of Management and Budget and the National Security Council to work with the Department of Defense to formulate a multi-year plan with the necessary resources to preserve military readiness, support our troops, and modernize the equipment needed for the next century. I am confident that our military is—and will continue to be—capable of carrying out our national strategy and meeting America's defense commitments around the world.

We must also renew our commitment to America's diplomacy—to ensure that we have the superb diplomatic representation that our people deserve and our interests demand. Every dollar we devote to preventing conflicts, promoting democracy, and stopping the spread of disease and starvation brings a sure return in security and savings. Yet international affairs spending today totals just one percent of the federal budget—a small fraction of what America invested at the start of the Cold War when we chose engagement over isolation. If America is to continue to lead the world by its own example, we must demonstrate our own commitment to these priority tasks. This is also why we must pay our dues to the United Nations.

Protecting our citizens and critical infrastructures at home is an essential element of our strategy. Potential adversaries—whether nations, terrorist groups or criminal organizations—will be tempted to disrupt our critical infrastructures, impede government operations, use weapons of mass destruction against civilians, and prey on our citizens overseas. These challenges demand close cooperation across all levels of government—federal, state and local—and across a wide range of agencies, including the Departments of Defense and State, the Intelligence Community, law enforcement, emergency services, medical care providers and others. Protecting our critical infrastructure requires new partnerships between government and industry. Forging these new structures will be challenging, but

must be done if we are to ensure our safety at home and avoid vulnerabilities that those wishing us ill might try to exploit in order to erode our resolve to protect our interests abroad.

The United States has profound interests at stake in the health of the global economy. Our future prosperity depends upon a stable international financial system and robust global growth. Economic stability and growth are essential for the spread of free markets and their integration into the global economy. The forces necessary for a healthy global economy are also those that deepen democratic liberties: the free flow of ideas and information, open borders and easy travel, the rule of law, fair and even-handed enforcement, protection for consumers, a skilled and educated work force. If citizens tire of waiting for democracy and free markets to deliver a better life for them, there is a real risk that they will lose confidence in democracy and free markets. This would pose great risks not only for our economic interests but for our national security.

We are taking a number of steps to help contain the current financial turmoil in Asia and other parts of the world. We are working with other industrialized nations, the International Monetary Fund and the World Bank to spur growth, stop the financial crisis from spreading, and help the victims of financial turmoil. We have also intensified our efforts to reform international trade and financial institutions: building a stronger and more accountable global trading system, pressing forward with market-opening initiatives, advancing the protection of labor and the environment and doing more to ensure that trade helps the lives of ordinary citizens across the globe.

At this moment in history, the United States is called upon to lead—to organize the forces of freedom and progress; to channel the unruly energies of the global economy into positive avenues; and to advance our prosperity, reinforce our democratic ideals and values, and enhance our security.

I. Introduction

We must judge our national security strategy by its success in meeting the fundamental purposes set out in the preamble to the Constitution:

> *...provide for the common defence, promote the general Welfare, and secure the Blessings of Liberty to ourselves and our Posterity,...*

Since the founding of the nation, certain requirements have remained constant. We must protect the lives and personal safety of Americans, both at home and abroad. We must maintain the sovereignty, political freedom and independence of the United States, with its values, institutions and territory intact. And, we must promote for the well being and prosperity of the nation and its people.

Challenges and Opportunities

The security environment in which we live is dynamic and uncertain, replete with a host of threats and challenges that have the potential to grow more deadly, but also offering unprecedented opportunities to avert those threats and advance our interests.

Globalization—the process of accelerating economic, technological, cultural and political integration—means that more and more we as a nation are affected by events beyond our borders. Outlaw states and ethnic conflicts threaten regional stability and economic progress in many important areas of the world. Weapons of mass destruction (WMD), terrorism, drug trafficking and organized crime are global concerns that transcend national borders. Other problems that once seemed quite distant—such as resource depletion, rapid population growth, environmental damage, new infectious diseases and uncontrolled refugee migration—have important implications for American security. Our workers and businesses will suffer if foreign markets collapse or lock us out, and the highest domestic environmental standards will not protect us if we cannot get others to achieve similar standards. In short, our citizens have a direct stake in the prosperity and stability of other nations, in their support for international norms and human rights, in their ability to combat international crime, in their open markets, and in their efforts to protect the environment.

Yet, this is also a period of great promise. Globalization is bringing citizens from all continents closer together, allowing them to share ideas, goods and information at the tap of a keyboard. Many nations around the world have embraced America's core values of representative governance, free market economics and respect for fundamental human rights and the rule of law, creating new opportunities to promote peace, prosperity and greater cooperation among nations. Former adversaries now cooperate with us. The dynamism of the global economy is transforming commerce, culture, communications and global relations, creating new jobs and economic opportunity for millions of Americans.

The Imperative of Engagement

Our strategic approach recognizes that we must lead abroad if we are to be secure at home, but we cannot lead abroad unless we are strong at home. We must be prepared and willing to use all appropriate instruments of national power to influence the actions of other states and non-state actors. Today's complex security environment demands that all our instruments of national power be effectively integrated to achieve our security objectives. We must have the demonstrated will and capabilities to continue to exert global leadership and remain the preferred security partner for the community of states that share our interests. We have seen in the past that the international community is often reluctant to act forcefully without American leadership. In many instances, the United States is the only nation capable of providing the necessary leadership and capabilities for an international response to shared challenges. American leadership and engagement

1

in the world are vital for our security, and our nation and the world are safer and more prosperous as a result.

The alternative to engagement is not withdrawal from the world; it is passive submission to powerful forces of change—all the more ironic at a time when our capacity to shape them is as great as it has ever been. Three-quarters of a century ago, the United States helped to squander Allied victory in World War I by embracing isolationism. After World War II, and in the face of a new totalitarian threat, America accepted the challenge to lead. We remained engaged overseas and worked with our allies to create international structures—from the Marshall Plan, the United Nations, NATO and other defense arrangements, to the International Monetary Fund and the World Bank—that enabled us to strengthen our security and prosperity and win the Cold War. By exerting our leadership abroad we have deterred aggression, fostered the resolution of conflicts, strengthened democracies, opened foreign markets and tackled global problems such as protecting the environment. U.S. leadership has been crucial to the success of negotiations that produced a wide range of treaties that have made the world safer and more secure by limiting, reducing, preventing the spread of, or eliminating weapons of mass destruction and other dangerous weapons. Without our leadership and engagement, threats would multiply and our opportunities would narrow.

Underpinning our international leadership is the power of our democratic ideals and values. In designing our strategy, we recognize that the spread of democracy supports American values and enhances both our security and prosperity. Democratic governments are more likely to cooperate with each other against common threats, encourage free trade, and promote sustainable economic development. They are less likely to wage war or abuse the rights of their people. Hence, the trend toward democracy and free markets throughout the world advances American interests. The United States will support this trend by remaining actively engaged in the world. This is the strategy to take us into the next century.

Implementing the Strategy

Our global leadership efforts will continue to be guided by President Clinton's strategic priorities: to

foster regional efforts led by the community of democratic nations to promote peace and prosperity in key regions of the world, to increase cooperation in confronting new security threats that defy borders and unilateral solutions, to strengthen the military, diplomatic and law enforcement tools necessary to meet these challenges and to create more jobs and opportunities for Americans through a more open and competitive economic system that also benefits others around the world. Our strategy is tempered by recognition that there are limits to America's involvement in the world. We must be selective in the use of our capabilities and the choices we make always must be guided by advancing our objectives of a more secure, prosperous and free America.

We must always be prepared to act alone when that is our most advantageous course. But many of our security objectives are best achieved—or can only be achieved—through our alliances and other formal security structures, or as a leader of an ad hoc coalition formed around a specific objective. Durable relationships with allies and friendly nations are vital to our security. A central thrust of our strategy is to strengthen and adapt the security relationships we have with key nations around the world and create new relationships and structures when necessary. Examples include NATO enlargement, the Partnership for Peace, the NATO-Russia Permanent Joint Council, the African Crisis Response Initiative, the regional security dialogue in the ASEAN Regional Forum and the hemispheric security initiatives adopted at the Summit of the Americas. At other times we harness our diplomatic, economic, military and information strengths to shape a favorable international environment outside of formal structures. This approach has borne fruit in areas as diverse as the elimination of nuclear weapons from Ukraine, Kazakhstan and Belarus, our comprehensive assistance package for Russia and other Newly Independent States (NIS), the advancement of peace in Northern Ireland, and support for the transformation of South Africa.

Protecting our citizens and critical infrastructures at home is an intrinsic and essential element of our security strategy. The dividing line between domestic and foreign policy is increasingly blurred. Globalization enables other states, terrorists, criminals, drug traffickers and others to challenge the safety of our citizens and the security of our borders in new ways. The security challenges wrought by globalization demand close cooperation across all levels of government—federal, state and local—and across a wide range of agencies, including the Departments of Defense and State, the Intelligence Community, law enforcement, emergency services, medical care providers and others. Protecting our critical infrastructure requires new partnerships between government and industry. Forging these new structures and relationships will be challenging, but must be done if we are to ensure our safety at home and avoid vulnerabilities that those wishing us ill might try to exploit in order to erode our resolve to protect our interests abroad.

Engagement abroad rightly depends on the willingness of the American people and the Congress to bear the costs of defending U.S. interests—in dollars, energy and, when there is no alternative, the risk of losing American lives. We must, therefore, foster the broad public understanding and bipartisan congressional support necessary to sustain our international engagement, always recognizing that some decisions that face popular opposition must ultimately be judged by whether they advance the interests of the American people in the long run.

II. Advancing U.S. National Interests

The goal of the national security strategy is to ensure the protection of our nation's fundamental and enduring needs: protect the lives and safety of Americans, maintain the sovereignty of the United States with its values, institutions and territory intact, and promote the prosperity and well-being of the nation and its people. In our vision of the world, the United States has close cooperative relations with the world's most influential countries and has the ability to influence the policies and actions of those who can affect our national well-being.

We seek to create a stable, peaceful international security environment in which our nation, citizens and interests are not threatened. The United States will not allow a hostile power to dominate any region of critical importance to our interests. We will work to prevent the spread of nuclear, biological and chemical weapons and the materials for producing them, and to control other potentially destabilizing technologies, such as long-range missiles. We will continue to ensure that we have effective means for countering and responding to the threats we cannot deter or otherwise prevent from arising. This includes protecting our citizens from terrorism, international crime and drug trafficking.

We seek a world in which democratic values and respect for human rights and the rule of law are increasingly accepted. This will be achieved through broadening the community of free-market democracies, promoting an international community that is willing and able to prevent or respond effectively to humanitarian problems, and strengthening international non-governmental movements committed to human rights and democratization. These efforts help prevent humanitarian disasters, promote reconciliation in states experiencing civil conflict and address migration and refugee crises.

We seek continued American prosperity through increasingly open international trade and sustainable growth in the global economy. The health of the international economy directly affects our security, just as stability enhances the prospects for prosperity. Prosperity ensures that we are able to sustain our military forces, foreign initiatives and global influence. In turn, our engagement and influence helps ensure that the world remains stable so the international economic system can flourish.

We seek a cleaner global environment to protect the health and well-being of our citizens. A deteriorating environment not only threatens public health, it impedes economic growth and can generate tensions that threaten international stability. To the extent that other nations believe they must engage in non-sustainable exploitation of natural resources, our long-term prosperity and security are at risk.

Since there are always many demands for U.S. action, our national interests must be clear. These interests fall into three categories. The first includes *vital interests*—those of broad, overriding importance to the survival, safety and vitality of our nation. Among these are the physical security of our territory and that of our allies, the safety of our citizens, our economic well-being and the protection of our critical infrastructures. We will do what we must to defend these interests, including—when necessary—using our military might unilaterally and decisively.

The second category includes situations in which *important national interests* are at stake. These interests do not affect our national survival, but they do affect our national well-being and the character of the world in which we live. In such cases, we will use our resources to advance these interests insofar as the costs and risks are commensurate with the interests at stake. Our efforts to halt the flow of refugees from Haiti and restore democracy in that state, our participation in NATO operations in Bosnia and our efforts to protect the global environment are relevant examples.

The third category is *humanitarian and other interests*. In some circumstances our nation may act because our values demand it. Examples include

5

responding to natural and manmade disasters or violations of human rights, supporting democratization and civil control of the military, assisting humanitarian demining, and promoting sustainable development. Often in such cases, the force of our example bolsters support for our leadership in the world. Whenever possible, we seek to avert humanitarian disasters and conflict through diplomacy and cooperation with a wide range of partners, including other governments, international institutions and non-governmental organizations. This may not only save lives, but also prevent the drain on resources caused by intervention in crises.

Our strategy is based on three national objectives: enhancing our security, bolstering our economic prosperity and promoting democracy abroad.

Enhancing Security at Home and Abroad

Our strategy for enhancing U.S. security recognizes that we face diverse threats requiring integrated approaches to defend the nation, shape the international environment, respond to crises and prepare for an uncertain future.

Threats to U.S. Interests

The current international security environment presents a diverse set of threats to our enduring goals and hence to our security:

- **Regional or State-Centered Threats:** A number of states still have the capabilities and the desire to threaten our vital interests through coercion or aggression. They continue to threaten the sovereignty of their neighbors and international access to resources. In many cases, these states are also actively improving their offensive capabilities, including efforts to obtain or retain nuclear, biological or chemical weapons and, in some cases, long-range delivery systems. In Southwest Asia, both Iraq and Iran have the potential to threaten their neighbors and the free flow of oil from the region. In East Asia, North Korea maintains its forward positioning of offensive military capabilities on its border with South Korea.

- **Transnational threats:** Terrorism, international crime, drug trafficking, illicit arms trafficking, uncontrolled refugee migrations and environmental damage threaten U.S. interests, citizens and the U.S. homeland itself. The possibility of terrorists and other criminals using WMD—nuclear, biological and chemical weapons—is of special concern. Threats to the national information infrastructure, ranging from cyber-crime to a strategic information attack on the United States via the global information network, present a dangerous new threat to our national security. We must also guard against threats to our other critical national infrastructures—such as electrical power and transportation—which increasingly could take the form of a cyber-attack in addition to physical attack or sabotage, and could originate from terrorist or criminal groups as well as hostile states. International drug trafficking organizations have become the most powerful and dangerous organized crime groups the United States has ever confronted due to their sophisticated production, shipment, distribution and financial systems, and the violence and corruption they promote everywhere they operate.

- **Spread of dangerous technologies:** Weapons of mass destruction pose the greatest potential threat to global stability and security. Proliferation of advanced weapons and technologies threatens to provide rogue states, terrorists and international crime organizations the means to inflict terrible damage on the United States, its allies and U.S. citizens and troops abroad. We must continue to deter and be prepared to counter the use or threatened use of WMD, reduce the threat posed by existing arsenals of such weaponry and halt the smuggling of nuclear materials. We must identify the technical information, technologies and materials that cannot be allowed to fall into the hands of those seeking to develop and produce WMD. And we must stop the proliferation of non-safeguarded dual-use technologies that place these destructive capabilities in the hands of parties hostile to U.S. and global security interests.

- **Foreign intelligence collection:** The threat from foreign intelligence services is more diverse, complex and difficult to counter than ever before.

6

This threat is a mix of traditional and non-traditional intelligence adversaries that have targeted American military, diplomatic, technological and commercial secrets. Some foreign intelligence services are rapidly adopting new technologies and innovative methods to obtain such secrets, including attempts to use the global information infrastructure to gain access to sensitive information via penetration of computer systems and networks. These new methods compound the already serious threat posed by traditional human, technical and signals intelligence activities.

- **Failed states:** We can expect that, despite international prevention efforts, some states will be unable to provide basic governance, services and opportunities for their populations, potentially generating internal conflict, humanitarian crises or regional instability. As governments lose their ability to provide for the welfare of their citizens, mass migration, civil unrest, famine, mass killings, environmental disasters and aggression against neighboring states or ethnic groups can threaten U.S. interests and citizens.

The Need for Integrated Approaches

Success in countering these varied threats requires an integrated approach that brings to bear all the capabilities and assets needed to achieve our security objectives—particularly in this era when domestic and foreign policies are increasingly blurred.

To effectively shape the international environment and respond to the full spectrum of potential threats and crises, diplomacy, military force, our other foreign policy tools and our domestic preparedness efforts must be closely coordinated. We must retain a strong foreign assistance program and an effective diplomatic corps if we are to maintain American leadership. We must maintain superior military forces at the level of readiness necessary to effectively deter aggression, conduct a wide range of peacetime activities and smaller-scale contingencies and, preferably in concert with regional friends and allies, win two overlapping major theater wars. The success of all our foreign policy tools is critically dependent on timely and effective intelligence collection and analysis capabilities.

International cooperation will be vital for building security in the next century because many of the threats we face cannot be addressed by a single nation. Globalization of transportation and communications has allowed international terrorists and criminals to operate without geographic constraints, while individual governments and their law enforcement agencies remain limited by national boundaries. Unlike terrorists and criminals, governments must respect the sovereignty of other nations. Accordingly, a central thrust of our strategy is to enhance relationships with key nations around the world to combat transnational threats to common interests. We seek to address these threats by increasing intelligence and law enforcement cooperation, denying terrorists safe havens, preventing arms traders from fueling regional conflicts and subverting international embargoes, and cracking down on drug trafficking, money laundering and international crime.

Building effective coalitions of like-minded nations is not enough. We are continuing to strengthen and integrate our own diplomatic, military, intelligence and law enforcement capabilities so we can act on our own when we must as well as more effectively lead the international community in responding to these threats.

Potential enemies, whether nations, terrorist groups or criminal organizations, are increasingly likely to attack U.S. territory and the American people in unconventional ways. Adversaries will be tempted to disrupt our critical infrastructures, impede continuity of government operations, use weapons of mass destruction against civilians in our cities, attack us when we gather at special events and prey on our citizens overseas. The United States must act to deter or prevent such attacks and, if attacks occurs despite those efforts, must be prepared to limit the damage they cause and respond decisively against the perpetrators. We will spare no effort to bring attackers to justice, ever adhering to our policy toward terrorists that "You can run, but you cannot hide," and where appropriate to defend ourselves by striking at terrorist bases and states that support terrorist acts.

At home, we must have effective capabilities for thwarting and responding to terrorist acts, countering international crime and foreign intelligence collection, and protecting critical national infrastructures. Our efforts to counter these threats cannot be limited exclusively to any one agency within the U.S.

Government. The threats and their consequences cross agency lines, requiring close cooperation among Federal agencies, state and local governments, the industries that own and operate critical national infrastructures, non-governmental organizations and others in the private sector.

Shaping the International Environment

The United States has a range of tools at its disposal with which to shape the international environment in ways favorable to U.S. interests and global security. Shaping activities enhance U.S. security by promoting regional security and preventing or reducing the wide range of diverse threats outlined above. These measures adapt and strengthen alliances and friendships, maintain U.S. influence in key regions and encourage adherence to international norms. When signs of potential conflict emerge, or potential threats appear, we undertake initiatives to prevent or reduce these threats. Our shaping efforts also aim to discourage arms races, halt the proliferation of weapons of mass destruction, reduce tensions in critical regions and combat the spread of international criminal organizations.

Many of our international shaping activities, often undertaken with the cooperation of our allies and friends, also help to prevent threats from arising that place at risk American lives and property at home. Examples include countering terrorism, drug and firearms trafficking, illegal immigration, the spread of WMD and other threats. Increasingly, shaping the security environment involves a wide range of Federal agencies, some of which in the past have not been thought of as having such an international role.

Diplomacy

Diplomacy is a vital tool for countering threats to our national security. The daily business of diplomacy conducted through our missions and representatives around the world is a irreplaceable shaping activity. These efforts are essential to sustaining our alliances, forcefully articulating U.S. interests, resolving regional disputes peacefully, averting humanitarian catastrophe, deterring aggression against the United States and our friends and allies, creating trade and

investment opportunities for U.S. companies, and projecting U.S. influence worldwide.

One of the lessons that has been repeatedly driven home is the importance of preventive diplomacy in dealing with conflict and complex emergencies. Helping prevent nations from failing is far more effective than rebuilding them after an internal crisis. Helping people stay in their homes is far more beneficial than feeding and housing them in refugee camps. Helping relief agencies and international organizations strengthen the institutions of conflict resolution is far less taxing than healing ethnic and social divisions that have already exploded into bloodshed. In short, while crisis management and crisis resolution are necessary tasks for our foreign policy, preventive diplomacy is obviously far preferable.

Credible military force and the demonstrated will to use it are essential to defend our vital interests and keep America safe. But force alone cannot solve all our problems. To be most effective, force, diplomacy and our other policy tools must complement and reinforce each other—for there will be many occasions and many places where we must rely on diplomatic shaping activities to protect and advance our interests.

International Assistance

From the U.S.-led mobilization to rebuild post-war Europe to the more recent creation of export opportunities across Asia, Latin America and Africa, U.S. foreign assistance has assisted emerging democracies, helped expand free markets, slowed the growth of international crime, contained major health threats, improved protection of the environment and natural resources, slowed population growth and defused humanitarian crises. Crises are averted—and U.S. preventive diplomacy actively reinforced—through U.S. sustainable development programs that promote voluntary family planning, basic education, environmental protection, democratic governance and rule of law, and economic empowerment of private citizens.

When combined effectively with other bilateral and multilateral activities, such as through our cooperative scientific and technological programs, U.S. initiatives reduce the need for costly military and humanitarian interventions. Where foreign aid succeeds in consolidating free market policies, substantial growth of American exports has frequently followed. Where crises have occurred, actions such as the Greater Horn of Africa Initiative have helped stanch mass human suffering and created a path out of conflict and dislocation through targeted relief. Other foreign aid programs have worked to help restore elementary security and civic institutions.

Arms Control

Arms control efforts are an essential element of our national security strategy. Effective arms control is really defense by other means. We pursue verifiable arms control agreements that support our efforts to prevent the spread and use of weapons of mass destruction, halt the use of conventional weapons that cause unnecessary suffering, and contribute to regional stability at lower levels of armaments. By increasing transparency in the size, structure and operations of military forces, arms control agreements and confidence-building measures reduce incentives and opportunities to initiate an attack, and reduce the mutual suspicions that arise from and spur on armaments competition. They help provide the assurance of security necessary to strengthen cooperative relationships and direct resources to safer, more productive endeavors. Agreements that preserve our crisis response capability shape the global and regional security environments, and simultaneously reinforce our commitment to allies and partners. Our arms control initiatives are an essential prevention measure for enhancing U.S. and allied security.

Verifiable reductions in strategic offensive arms and the steady shift toward less destabilizing systems remain essential to our strategy. Entry into force of the START I Treaty in December 1994 charted the course for reductions in the deployed strategic nuclear forces of the United States and the Former Soviet Union (FSU). START I has accomplished much to reduce the risk of nuclear war and strengthen international security. On the third anniversary of START I entry into force, the United States and Russia announced that both were two years ahead of schedule in meeting the treaty's mandated reductions.

Once the START II Treaty enters into force, the United States and Russia will each be limited to between 3,000-3,500 total deployed strategic nuclear warheads. START II also will eliminate destabilizing land-based multiple warhead missiles, a truly historic achievement. Russian ratification of START II will open the door to the next round of strategic arms control.

At the Helsinki Summit in March 1997, Presidents Clinton and Yeltsin agreed that once START II enters into force, our two nations would immediately begin negotiations on a START III agreement. They agreed to START III guidelines that, if adopted, will cap the number of strategic nuclear warheads deployed in each country at 2,000-2,500 by the end of 2007— reducing both our arsenals by 80 percent from Cold War heights. They also agreed that START III will, for the first time, require the U.S. and Russia to destroy nuclear warheads, not just the missiles, aircraft and submarines that carry them, and opened the door to possible reductions in non-strategic nuclear weapons. On September 26, 1997, the U.S. and Russia signed a START II Protocol codifying the agreement at Helsinki to extend the end date for reductions to 2007 and exchanged letters on early deactivation by 2003 of those strategic nuclear delivery systems to be eliminated by 2007.

At Helsinki, the two Presidents recognized the Nunn-Lugar Cooperative Threat Reduction (CTR) Program as the vehicle through which the United States would facilitate the deactivation of strategic nuclear delivery systems in the FSU nations. The CTR Program has assisted Ukraine, Kazakhstan and Belarus in becoming non-nuclear weapons states and will continue to assist Russia in meeting its START obligations. The program has effectively supported enhanced safety, security, accounting and centralized control measures for nuclear weapons and fissile materials in the FSU. CTR is also assisting FSU nations in measures to eliminate and prevent the proliferation of chemical weapons and biological weapon-related capabilities. It has supported many ongoing military reductions and reform measures in the FSU, and has contributed to a climate conducive for further progress on non-proliferation.

Also at Helsinki, the Presidents reaffirmed their commitment to the Anti-Ballistic Missile (ABM) Treaty and recognized the need for effective theater missile defenses in an agreement in principle on demarcation between systems to counter strategic ballistic missiles and those to counter theater ballistic missiles. On September 26, 1997, the U.S. Secretary of State and Russian Foreign Minister, along with their counterparts from Belarus, Kazakhstan and Ukraine, signed or initialed five agreements relating to the ABM Treaty. The agreements on demarcation and succession will be provided to the Senate for its advice and consent following Russian ratification of START II.

By banning all nuclear test explosions for all time, the Comprehensive Test Ban Treaty (CTBT) constrains the development of dangerous nuclear weapons, contributes to preventing nuclear proliferation and to the process of nuclear disarmament, and enhances the ability of the United States to monitor suspicious nuclear activities in other countries through a worldwide sensor network and on-site inspections. Nuclear tests in India and Pakistan in May 1998 make it more important than ever to move quickly to bring the CTBT into force and continue establishment of the substantial verification mechanisms called for in the treaty. The President has submitted the treaty, which 150 nations have signed, to the Senate and has urged the Senate to provide its advice and consent this year. Prompt U.S. ratification will encourage other states to ratify, enable the United States to lead the international effort to gain CTBT entry into force and strengthen international norms against nuclear testing. Multilateral and regional arms control efforts also increase U.S. and global security. We seek to strengthen the Biological Weapons Convention (BWC) with a new international regime to ensure compliance. At present, we are negotiating with other BWC member states in an effort to reach consensus on a protocol to the BWC that would implement an inspection system to deter and detect cheating. We are also working hard to implement and enforce the Chemical Weapons Convention (CWC). The United States Senate underscored the importance of these efforts with its April 24, 1997 decision, by a vote of 74-26, to give its advice and consent to ratification of the CWC. The next key step is legislation to implement full compliance with the commercial declarations and inspections that are required by the CWC.

In Europe, we are pursuing the adaptation of the 1990 Conventional Armed Forces in Europe (CFE) Treaty, consistent with the Decision on Certain Basic Elements adopted in Vienna on July 23, 1997 by all 30 CFE states. Success in this negotiation will ensure that this landmark agreement remains a cornerstone of European security into the 21st century and beyond. We continue to seek Russian, Ukrainian and Belarusian ratification of the 1992 Open Skies

Treaty to increase transparency of military forces in Eurasia and North America. We also promote, through international organizations such as the Organization for Security and Cooperation in Europe (OSCE), implementation of confidence and security-building measures, including the 1994 Vienna Document, throughout Europe and in specific regions of tension and instability—even where we are not formal parties to such agreements. The agreements mandated by the Dayton Accords demonstrate how innovative regional efforts can strengthen stability and reduce conflicts that could adversely affect U.S. interests abroad.

President Clinton is committed to ending the tragic damage to innocent civilians due to anti-personnel landmines (APLs). The United States has already taken major steps in the spirit that motivated the Ottawa Convention, while ensuring our ability to meet international obligations and provide for the safety and security of our men and women in uniform. On June 30, 1998, we met—one year ahead of schedule—the President's May 1996 commitment to destroy all of our non-self-destructing APLs by 1999, except those we need for Korea and demining training. To expand and strengthen the Administration policy on APLs that he announced on September 17, 1997, President Clinton signed Presidential Decision Directive 64 in June 1998. It directs the Defense Department to end the use of all APLs, even of self-destructing APLs, outside Korea by 2003 and to pursue aggressively the objective of having APL alternatives ready for Korea by 2006. We will also aggressively pursue alternatives to our mixed anti-tank systems that contain anti-personnel submunitions. We have made clear that the United States will sign the Ottawa Convention by 2006 if we succeed in identifying and fielding suitable alternatives to our self-destructing APLs and mixed anti-tank systems by then. Furthermore, in 1997 the Administration submitted for Senate advice and consent the Amended Landmine Protocol to the Convention on Conventional Weapons, which bans the unmarked, long-duration APLs that caused the worldwide humanitarian problem. We have established a permanent ban on APL exports and are seeking to universalize an export ban through the Conference on Disarmament in Geneva. In 1998 we are spending $80 million on humanitarian demining programs, more than double that of the previous year, and through our "Demining 2010" initiative have challenged the world to increase the effectiveness and efficiency of removing landmines that threaten civilians.

Nonproliferation Initiatives

Nonproliferation initiatives enhance global security by preventing the spread of WMD, materials for producing them and means of delivering them. That is why the Administration is promoting universal adherence to the international treaty regimes that prohibit the acquisition of weapons of mass destruction, including the Nuclear Non-Proliferation Treaty (NPT), the CWC and the BWC. The NPT was an indispensable precondition for the denuclearization of Ukraine, Kazakhstan, Belarus and South Africa. We also seek to strengthen the International Atomic Energy Agency (IAEA) safeguards system and achieve a Fissile Material Cutoff Treaty to cap the nuclear materials available for weapons. A coordinated effort by the intelligence community and law enforcement agencies to detect, prevent and deter illegal trafficking in fissile materials is also essential to our counter-proliferation efforts. The Administration also seeks to prevent destabilizing buildups of conventional arms and limit access to sensitive technical information, equipment and technologies by strengthening multilateral regimes, including the Wassenaar Arrangement on Export Controls for Conventional Arms and Dual-Use Goods and Technologies, the Australia Group (for chemical and biological weapons), the Missile Technology Control Regime (MTCR) and the Nuclear Suppliers Group. We are working to harmonize national export control policies, increase information sharing, refine control lists and expand cooperation against illicit transfers.

Regional nonproliferation efforts are particularly important in three critical proliferation zones. On the Korean Peninsula, we are implementing the 1994 Agreed Framework, which requires full compliance by North Korea with nonproliferation obligations. In the Middle East and Southwest Asia, we encourage regional arms control agreements that address the legitimate security concerns of all parties and continue efforts to thwart and roll back Iran's development of weapons of mass destruction and Iraq's efforts to reconstitute its programs. In South Asia, we seek to persuade India and Pakistan to bring their nuclear and missile programs into conformity with international nonproliferation standards and to sign and ratify the CTBT.

Through programs such as the Nunn-Lugar Cooperative Threat Reduction Program and other initiatives, we aim to strengthen controls over weapons-usable fissile material and prevent the theft or diversion of WMD and related material and technology. We are working to strengthen the Convention on the Physical Protection of Nuclear Material to increase accountability and protection, which complements our effort to enhance IAEA safeguards. We are purchasing tons of highly enriched uranium from dismantled Russian nuclear weapons for conversion into commercial reactor fuel, and working with Russia to redirect former Soviet facilities and scientists from military to peaceful purposes.

To expand and improve U.S. efforts aimed at deterring proliferation of WMD by organized crime groups and individuals in the NIS and Eastern Europe, the Defense Department and FBI are implementing a joint counter proliferation assistance program that provides appropriate training, material and services to law enforcement agencies in these areas. The program's objectives are to assist in establishing a professional cadre of law enforcement personnel in these nations trained to prevent, deter and investigate crimes related to the proliferation and diversion of WMD or their delivery systems; to assist these countries in developing laws and regulations designed to prevent the illicit acquisition or trafficking of WMD, and in establishing appropriate enforcement mechanisms; and to build a solid legal and organization framework that will enable these governments to attack the proliferation problem at home and participate effectively in international efforts.

Military Activities

The U.S. military plays an essential role in building coalitions and shaping the international environment in ways that protect and promote U.S. interests. Through overseas presence and peacetime engagement activities such as defense cooperation, security assistance, and training and exercises with allies and friends, our armed forces help to deter aggression and coercion, promote regional stability, prevent and reduce conflicts and threats, and serve as role models for militaries in emerging democracies. These important efforts engage every component of the Total Force: Active, Reserve, National Guard and civilian.

Deterrence of aggression and coercion on a daily basis is crucial. Our ability to deter potential adversaries in peacetime rests on several factors, particularly on our demonstrated will and ability to uphold our security commitments when they are challenged. We have earned this reputation through both our declaratory policy, which clearly communicates costs to potential adversaries, and our credible warfighting capability. This capability is embodied in ready forces and equipment strategically stationed or deployed forward, in forces in the United States at the appropriate level of readiness to deploy and go into action when needed, in our ability to gain timely access to critical regions and infrastructure overseas, and in our demonstrated ability to form and lead effective military coalitions.

Our nuclear deterrent posture is one of the most visible and important examples of how U.S. military capabilities can be used effectively to deter aggression and coercion, as reaffirmed in a Presidential Decision Directive signed by President Clinton in November 1997. Nuclear weapons serve as a hedge against an uncertain future, a guarantee of our security commitments to allies and a disincentive to those who would contemplate developing or otherwise acquiring their own nuclear weapons. Our military planning for the possible employment of U.S. nuclear weapons is focused on deterring a nuclear war rather than attempting to fight and win a protracted nuclear exchange. We continue to emphasize the survivability of the nuclear systems and infrastructure necessary to endure a preemptive attack and still respond at overwhelming levels. The United States must continue to maintain a robust triad of strategic forces sufficient to deter any hostile foreign leadership with access to nuclear forces and to convince it that seeking a nuclear advantage would be futile. We must also ensure the continued viability of the infrastructure that supports U.S. nuclear forces and weapons. The Stockpile Stewardship Program will guarantee the safety and reliability of our nuclear weapons under the Comprehensive Test Ban Treaty.

While our overall deterrence posture—nuclear and conventional—has been effective against most potential adversaries, a range of terrorist and criminal organizations may not be deterred by traditional deterrent threats. For these actors to be deterred, they must believe that any type of attack against the United States or its citizens will be attributed to them and that we will respond effectively and decisively to protect our national interests and ensure that justice is done.

Our military promotes regional stability in numerous ways. In Europe, East Asia and Southwest Asia, where the U.S. has clear, vital interests, the American military helps assure the security of our allies and friends. The reinforcement of U.S. forces in the Gulf from Fall 1997 to Spring 1998 clearly illustrates the importance of military power in achieving U.S. national security objectives and stabilizing a potentially volatile situation. The U.S. buildup made it clear to Saddam Hussein that he must comply with UN sanctions and cease hindering UNSCOM inspections or face dire consequences. It also denied him the option of moving to threaten his neighbors, as he had done in past confrontations with the international community. Saddam's agreement to open the so-called "presidential sites" to UN inspection was a significant step toward ensuring that Iraq's WMD have been eradicated. It would not have been achieved without American diplomacy backed by force. Our decision maintain a higher continuous force level in the Gulf than we had before this most recent confrontation with Iraq will help deter Saddam from making further provocations and strengthen the resolve of our coalition partners in the Gulf.

We are continuing to adapt and strengthen our alliances and coalitions to meet the challenges of an evolving security environment. U.S. military forces prevent and reduce a wide range of potential conflicts in key regions. An example of such an activity is our deployment to the Former Yugoslav Republic of Macedonia to help prevent the spread of violence to that country. We assist other countries in improving their pertinent military capabilities, including peacekeeping and humanitarian response. With countries that are neither staunch friends nor known foes, military cooperation often serves as a positive means of engagement, building security relationships today that will contribute to improved relations tomorrow.

Our armed forces also serve as a role model for militaries in emerging democracies around the world. Our 200-year history of strong civilian control of the military serves as an example to those countries with histories of non-democratic governments. Through military-to-military activities and increasing links between the U.S. military and the military establishments of Partnership for Peace nations, for instance, we are helping to transform military institutions in Central and Eastern Europe, as well as in the Newly Independent States of the former Soviet Union.

International Law Enforcement Cooperation

As threats to our national security from drug trafficking, terrorism and international crime increase, development of working relations U.S. and foreign law enforcement and judicial agencies will play a vital role in shaping law enforcement priorities in those countries. Law enforcement agencies must continue

to find innovative ways to develop a concerted, global attack on the spread of international crime.

Overseas law enforcement presence leverages resources and fosters the establishment of effective working relationships with foreign law enforcement agencies. U.S. investigators and prosecutors draw upon their experience and background to enlist the cooperation of foreign law enforcement officials, keeping crime away from American shores, enabling the arrest of many U.S. fugitives and solving serious U.S. crimes. This presence develops substantive international links by creating personal networks of law enforcement professionals dedicated to bringing international criminals to justice.

In addition, training foreign law enforcement officers is critical to combating international crime. Such training helps create professional law enforcement organizations and builds citizen confidence in law enforcement officers, who understand and operate under the rule of law. Training also builds a common perspective and understanding of investigative techniques that helps shape international law enforcement priorities. The FBI and other federal law enforcement agencies have provided extensive law enforcement training at the International Law Enforcement Academy in Budapest, Hungary and elsewhere around the world. This training has proved to be enormously effective in developing professional law enforcement and security services in emerging democracies.

Environmental Initiatives

Decisions today regarding the environment and natural resources can affect our security for generations. Environmental threats do not heed national borders and can pose long-term dangers to our security and well-being. Natural resource scarcities can trigger and exacerbate conflict. Environmental threats such as climate change, ozone depletion and the transnational movement of hazardous chemicals and waste directly threaten the health of U.S. citizens.

We have a full diplomatic agenda, working bilaterally and multilaterally to respond aggressively to environmental threats. The Global Environmental Facility (GEF) is an important instrument for this cooperation. With 161 member nations, the GEF is specifically focused on reducing cross-border environmental damage. Our Environmental Security

Initiative joins U.S. agencies with foreign partners to address regional environmental concerns and thereby reduce the risk to U.S. interests abroad. We have also undertaken development of an environmental forecasting system to provide U.S. policymakers advance warning of environmental stress situations which have the potential for significant impact on U.S. interests.

At Kyoto in December 1997, the industrialized nations of the world agreed for the first time to binding limits on greenhouse gases. The agreement is strong and comprehensive, covering the six greenhouse gases whose concentrations are increasing due to human activity. It reflects the commitment of the United States to use the tools of the free market to tackle this problem. It will enhance growth and create new incentives for the rapid development of technologies through a system of joint implementation and emissions trading. The Kyoto agreement was a vital turning point, but we still have a lot of hard work ahead. We must press for meaningful participation by key developing nations. Multilateral negotiations are underway and we will pursue bilateral talks with key developing nations. We will not submit the Kyoto agreement for ratifica-tion until key developing nations have agreed to participate meaningfully in efforts to address global warming.

Additionally, we seek to accomplish the following:

• achieve increased compliance with the Montreal Protocol through domestic and multilateral efforts aimed at curbing illegal trade in ozone depleting substances;

• ratify the Law of the Sea Convention, implement the UN Straddling Stocks Agreement and help to promote sustainable management of fisheries worldwide;

• implement the Program of Action on population growth developed at the 1994 Cairo Conference, lead a renewed global effort to address population problems and promote international consensus for stabilizing world population growth;

• expand bilateral forest assistance programs and promote sustainable management of tropical forests;

• achieve Senate ratification of the Convention to Combat Desertification;

• negotiate an international agreement to ban twelve persistent organic pollutants, including such hazardous chemicals as DDT;

• promote environment-related scientific research in other countries so they can better identify environmental problems and develop indigenous solutions for them;

• increase international cooperation in fighting transboundary environmental crime, including trafficking in protected flora and fauna, hazardous waste and ozone-depleting chemicals;

• ratify the Biodiversity Convention and take steps to prevent biodiversity loss, including support for agricultural research to relieve pressures on forests, working with multilateral development banks and others to prevent biodiversity loss in key regions, and use of the Convention on International Trade in Endangered Species to protect threatened species; and

• continue to work with the Nordic countries and Russia to mitigate nuclear and non-nuclear pollution in the Arctic, and continue to encourage Russia to develop sound management practices for nuclear materials and radioactive waste.

Responding to Threats and Crises

Because our shaping efforts alone cannot guarantee the international security environment we seek, the United States must be able to respond at home and abroad to the full spectrum of threats and crises that may arise. Our resources are finite, so we must be selective in our responses, focusing on challenges that most directly affect our interests and engaging where we can make the most difference. Our response might be diplomatic, economic, law enforcement, or military in nature—or, more likely, some combination of the above. We must use the most appropriate tool or combination of tools—acting in alliance or partnership when our interests are shared by others, but unilaterally when compelling national interests so demand. At home, we must forge an effective partnership of Federal, state and local government agencies, industry and other private sector organizations.

When efforts to deter an adversary—be it a rogue nation, terrorist group or criminal organization—occur in the context of a crisis, they become the leading edge of crisis response. In this sense, deterrence straddles the line between shaping the international environment and responding to crises. Deterrence in crisis generally involves signaling the United States' commitment to a particular country or interest by enhancing our warfighting capability in the theater. Forces in or near the theater may be moved closer to the crisis and other forces rapidly deployed to the area. The U.S. may also choose to make additional statements to communicate the costs of aggression or coercion to an adversary, and in some cases may choose to employ U.S. forces to underline the message and deter further adventurism.

The American people rightfully play a central role in how the United States wields its power abroad. The United States cannot long sustain a commitment without the support of the public, and close consultations with Congress are important in this effort. When it is judged in America's interest to intervene, we must remain clear in purpose and resolute in execution.

Transnational Threats

Today, American diplomats, law enforcement officials, military personnel, members of the intelligence community and others are increasingly called upon to respond to growing transnational threats, particularly terrorism, drug trafficking and international organized crime.

Terrorism

To meet the growing challenge of terrorism, President Clinton signed Presidential Decision Directive 62 in May 1998. This Directive creates a new and more systematic approach to fighting the terrorist threat of the next century. It reinforces the mission of the many U.S. agencies charged with roles in defeating terrorism; it also codifies and clarifies their activities in the wide range of U.S. counter-terrorism programs, including apprehension and prosecution of terrorists, increasing transportation security, and enhancing incident response capabilities. The Directive will help achieve the President's goal of ensuring that we meet the threat of terrorism in the 21st century.

Our policy to counter international terrorists rests on the following principles: (1) make no concessions to terrorists; (2) bring all pressure to bear on all state sponsors of terrorism; (3) fully exploit all available legal mechanisms to punish international terrorists; and (4) help other governments improve their capabilities to combat terrorism. Following these principles, we seek to uncover and eliminate foreign terrorists and their support networks in our country; eliminate terrorist sanctuaries; and counter state-supported terrorism and subversion of moderate regimes through a comprehensive program of diplomatic, law enforcement, economic, military and intelligence activities. We are working to improve aviation security at airports in the United States and worldwide, to ensure better security for all U.S. transportation systems, and to improve protection for our personnel assigned overseas.

Countering terrorism effectively requires day-to-day coordination within the U.S. Government and close cooperation with other governments and international organizations. Foreign terrorists will not be allowed to enter the United States, and the full force of legal authorities will be used to remove foreign terrorists from the United States and prevent fundraising within the United States to support foreign terrorist activity. We have seen positive results from the increasing integration of intelligence, diplomatic, military and law enforcement activities among the Departments of State, Justice, Defense, Treasury, Energy, Transportation, the CIA and other intelligence agencies. The Administration is working with Congress to increase the ability of these agencies to combat terrorism through augmented funding and manpower.

The United States has made concerted efforts to deter and punish terrorists and remains determined to apprehend and bring to justice those who terrorize American citizens. In January 1998, the United States signed the International Convention for the Suppression of Terrorist Bombings. The Convention fills an important gap in international law by expanding the legal framework for international cooperation in the investigation, prosecution and extradition of persons who engage in such bombings. Whenever possible, we use law enforcement and diplomatic tools to wage the fight against terrorism. But there have been, and will be, times when law enforcement and diplomatic tools are simply not enough, when our very national security is challenged, and when we must take extraordinary steps to protect the safety of our citizens. As long as terrorists continue to target American citizens, we reserve the right to act in self defense by striking at their bases and those who sponsor, assist or actively support them. We exercised that right in 1993 with the attack against Iraqi intelligence headquarters in response to Baghdad's assassination attempt against former President Bush. We exercised that right again in August 1998.

On August 7, 1998, 12 Americans and nearly 300 Kenyans and Tanzanians lost their lives, and another 5,000 were wounded when our embassies in Nairobi and Dar es Salaam were bombed. Soon afterward, our intelligence community acquired convincing information from a variety of reliable sources that the network of radical groups affiliated with Osama bin Laden, perhaps the preeminent organizer and financier of international terrorism in the world today, planned, financed and carried out the bombings. The groups associated with bin Laden come from diverse places, but share a hatred for democracy, a fanatical glorification of violence and a horrible distortion of their religion to justify the murder of innocents. They have made the United States their adversary precisely because of what we stand for and what we stand against.

On August 20, 1998, our Armed Forces carried out strikes against terrorist facilities and infrastructure in Afghanistan. Our forces targeted one of the most active terrorist bases in the world. It contained key elements of the bin Laden network's infrastructure and has served as a training camp for literally thousands of terrorists from around the globe. Our forces also attacked a factory in Sudan associated with the bin Laden network that was involved in the production of materials for chemical weapons. The strikes were a necessary and proportionate response to the imminent threat of further terrorist attacks against U.S. personnel and facilities. Afghanistan and Sudan had been warned for years to stop harboring and supporting these terrorist groups. Countries that persistently host terrorists have no right to be safe havens.

Placing terrorism at the top of the diplomatic agenda has increased international information sharing and law enforcement efforts. At the June 1997 Denver Summit of the Eight, the leaders of Canada, France, Germany, Italy, Japan, Russia, the United Kingdom and the United States reaffirmed their determination to combat terrorism in all forms, their opposition to

concessions to terrorist demands and their determination to deny hostage-takers any benefits from their acts. They agreed to intensify diplomatic efforts to ensure that by the year 2000 all States have joined the international counterterrorism conventions specified in the 1996 UN resolution on measures to counter terrorism. The eight leaders also agreed to strengthen the capability of hostage negotiation experts and counterterrorism response units, to exchange information on technologies to detect and deter the use of weapons of mass destruction in terrorist attacks, to develop means to deter terrorist attacks on electronic and computer infrastructure, to strengthen maritime security, to exchange information on security practices for international special events, and to strengthen and expand international cooperation and consultation on terrorism.

International Crime

International crime is a serious and potent threat to the American people at home and abroad. Drug trafficking, illegal trade in firearms, financial crimes—such as money laundering, counterfeiting, advanced fee and credit card fraud, and income tax evasion—illegal alien smuggling, trafficking in women and children, economic espionage, intellectual property theft, computer hacking and public corruption are all linked to international criminal activity and all have a direct impact on the security and prosperity of the American people.

Efforts to combat international crime can have a much broader impact than simply halting individual criminal acts. The efficiency of the market place depends on transparency and effective law enforcement, which limit distorting factors such as extortion and corruption. A free and efficient market implies not only the absence of state control but also limits on unlawful activities that impede rational business decisions and fair competition. Additionally, the integrity and reliability of the international financial system will be improved by standardizing laws and regulations governing financial institutions and improving international law enforcement cooperation in the financial sector.

To address the increasing threat from these diverse criminal activities, we have formulated an International Crime Control Strategy that provides a framework for integrating the federal government response to international crime. The strategy's major goals and initiatives are to:

- Extend our crime control efforts beyond U.S. borders by intensifying activities of law enforcement and diplomatic personnel abroad to prevent criminal acts and prosecute select criminal acts committed abroad.

- Protect U.S. borders by enhancing our inspection, detection, monitoring and interdiction efforts, seeking stiffer criminal penalties for smuggling, and targeting law enforcement resources more effectively against smugglers.

- Deny safe haven to international criminals by negotiating new international agreements for evidence sharing and prompt arrest and extradition of fugitives (including nationals of the requested country), implementing strengthened immigration laws to prevent criminals from entering the United States and provide for their prompt expulsion when appropriate, and promoting increased cooperation with foreign law enforcement authorities.

- Counter international financial crime by combating money laundering and reducing movement of criminal proceeds, seizing the assets of international criminals, enhancing bilateral and multilateral cooperation against financial crime, and targeting offshore sources of international fraud, counterfeiting, electronic access device schemes, income tax evasion and other financial crimes.

- Prevent criminal exploitation of international trade by interdicting illegal technology exports, preventing unfair and predatory trade practices, protecting intellectual property rights, countering industrial theft and economic espionage, and enforcing import restrictions on harmful substances, dangerous organisms and protected species. In fiscal year 1997, the Customs Service seized $59 million in goods and $55 million in currency being taken out of the country illegally.

- Respond to emerging international crime threats by disrupting new activities of international organized crime groups, enhancing intelligence efforts, reducing trafficking in human beings (involuntary servitude, alien smuggling, document fraud and denial of human rights), crimes against children, and increasing enforcement efforts against high technology and computer-related crime.

- Foster international cooperation and the rule of law by establishing international standards, goals and objectives to combat international crime and by actively encouraging compliance, improving bilateral cooperation with foreign governments and law enforcement authorities, expanding U.S. training and assistance programs in law enforcement and administration of justice, and strengthening the rule of law as the foundation for democratic government and free markets.

The growing threat to our security from transnational crime makes international law enforcement cooperation vital. We are negotiating and implementing updated extradition and mutual legal assistance treaties that reflect the changing nature of international crime and prevent terrorists and criminals from exploiting national borders to escape prosecution. Moreover, since the primary motivation of most international criminals is greed, powerful asset seizure, forfeiture and money laundering laws are key tools for taking action against the financial underpinnings of international crime. Increasing our enforcement powers through bilateral and multilateral agreements and efforts makes it harder for criminals to enjoy their ill-gotten gains.

At the Birmingham Summit in May 1998, the leaders of the G-8 adopted a wide range of measures to strengthen the cooperative efforts against international crime that they launched at their summit in Lyon two years ago. They agreed to increase cooperation on transnational high technology crime, money laundering and financial crime, corruption, environmental crimes, and trafficking in drugs, firearms and women and children. They also agreed to fully support negotiations on a UN Convention on Transnational Organized Crime, which will broaden many of the efforts underway among the G-8 to the rest of the international community.

No area of criminal activity has greater international implications than high technology crime because of the global nature of information networks. Computer hackers and other cyber-criminals are not hampered by international boundaries, since information and transactions involving funds or property can be transmitted quickly and covertly via telephone and information systems. Law enforcement faces difficult challenges in this area, many of which are impossible to address without international consensus and cooperation. We seek to develop and implement new agreements with other nations to address high technology crime, particularly cyber-crime.

We are making a concerted effort at home and abroad to shut down the illicit trade in firearms, ammunition and explosives that fuels the violence associated with terrorism, drug trafficking and international crime. The President has signed legislation amending the Arms Export Control Act to expand our authority to monitor and regulate the activities of arms brokers and we have intensified reviews of applications for licenses to export firearms from the United States to ensure that they are not diverted to illicit purposes. The Bureau of Alcohol, Tobacco and Firearms (ATF) has tightened up proof of residency requirements for aliens purchasing firearms from dealers in the United States, and ATF and the Customs Service have intensified their interdiction and investigative efforts at U.S. borders.

In the international arena, the United States is working with its partners in the G-8 and through the UN Crime Commission to expand cooperation in combating illicit arms trafficking. In November 1997, the United States and its partners in the Organization of American States (OAS) signed the Inter-American Convention Against the Illicit Manufacturing of and Trafficking in Firearms—the first international agreement designed to prevent, combat and eradicate illegal trafficking in firearms, ammunition and explosives. We are now negotiating an international agreement that would globalize the OAS convention. Additionally, the ATF and Customs Service have provided training and assistance to other nations on tracing firearms, combating internal smuggling and related law enforcement topics.

Drug Trafficking

We have shown that with determined and relentless efforts, we can make significant progress against the scourge of drug abuse and drug trafficking. In the United States, drug use has dropped 49 percent since 1979. Recent studies show that drug use by our young people is stabilizing, and in some categories, declining. Overall, cocaine use has dropped 70 percent since 1985 and the crack epidemic has begun to recede. Today, Americans spend 37 percent less on drugs than a decade ago.

That means over $34 billion reinvested in our society, rather than squandered on drugs.

The aim of the *U.S. National Drug Control Strategy* is to cut drug availability in the United States by half over the next 10 years—and reduce the consequences of drug use and trafficking by 25 percent over the same period—through expanded prevention efforts, improved treatment programs, strengthened law enforcement and tougher interdiction. Our strategy recognizes that, at home and abroad, prevention, treatment and economic alternatives must be integrated with intelligence collection, law enforcement and interdiction. Its ultimate success will require concerted efforts by the public, all levels of government and the private sector together with other governments, private groups and international organizations.

Domestically, we seek to educate and enable America's youth to reject illegal drugs, increase the safety of America's citizens by substantially reducing drug-related crime and violence, reduce health and social costs to the public of illegal drug use, and shield America's air, land and sea frontiers from the drug threat. Working with Congress and the private sector, the Administration has launched a major antidrug youth media campaign and will seek to extend this program through 2002. With congressional support and matching dollars from the private sector, we will commit to a five-year, $2 billion public-private partnership to educate our children to reject drugs.

In concert with our allies abroad, we seek to stop drug trafficking by reducing cultivation of drug-producing crops, interdicting the flow of drugs at the source and in transit (particularly in Central and South America, the Caribbean, Mexico and Southeast Asia), and stopping drugs from entering our country. The Strategy includes efforts to strengthen democratic institutions and root out corruption in source nations, prosecute major international drug traffickers and destroy trafficking organizations, prevent money laundering and use of commercial air and maritime transportation for drug smuggling, and eradicate illegal drug crops and encourage alternate crop development or alternative employment in source nations. We seek to achieve a counterdrug alliance in this hemisphere, one that could serve as a model for enhanced cooperation in other regions.

The United States is aggressively engaging international organizations, financial institutions and non-governmental organizations in counternarcotics cooperation. At the Birmingham Summit in May 1998, the leaders of the G-8 endorsed the principle of shared responsibility for combating drugs, including cooperative efforts focused on both eradication and demand reduction. They agreed to reinforce cooperation on reducing demand and curbing trafficking in drugs and chemical precursors. They also agreed on the need for a global strategy to eradicate illicit drugs. The United States supports the UN International Drug Control Program's goal of dramatically reducing coca and opium poppy cultivation by 2008 and the program's efforts to combat drug production, trafficking and abuse in some of the most remote regions of the world. At the UN General Assembly Special Session on drug trafficking and abuse in June 1998, President Clinton and other world leaders strengthened existing international counterdrug institutions, reconfirmed the global partnership against drug abuse and stressed the need for a coordinated international approach to combating drug trafficking.

Emerging Threats at Home

Due to our military superiority, potential enemies, whether nations or terrorist groups, may be more likely in the future to resort to terrorist acts or other attacks against vulnerable civilian targets in the United States instead of conventional military operations. At the same time, easier access to sophisticated technology means that the destructive power available to terrorists is greater than ever. Adversaries may thus be tempted to use unconventional tools, such as WMD or information attacks, to threaten our citizens, and critical national infrastructures.

Managing the Consequences of WMD Incidents

Presidential Decision Directive 62, signed in May 1998, established an overarching policy and assignment of responsibilities for responding to terrorist acts involving WMD. The Federal Government will respond rapidly and decisively to any terrorist incident in the United States, working with state and local governments to restore order and deliver emergency assistance. The Department of Justice, acting through the FBI, has the overall lead in operational response to a WMD incident. The

Federal Emergency Management Agency (FEMA) supports the FBI in preparing for and responding to the consequences of a WMD incident.

The Domestic Terrorism Program is integrating the capabilities and assets of a number of Federal agencies to support the FBI, FEMA and state and local governments in consequence management. The program's goal is to build a capability in 120 major U.S. cities for first responders to be able to deal with WMD incidents by 2002. In fiscal year 1997, the Defense Department provided training to nearly 1,500 metropolitan emergency responders—firefighters, law enforcement officials and medical personnel—in four cities. In fiscal year 1998, the program will reach 31 cities. Eventually, this training will reach all cities via the Internet, video and CD ROM.

Under the Domestic Terrorism Program, the Defense Department will maintain military units to serve as augmentation forces for weapons of mass destruction consequence management and to help maintain proficiency of local emergency responders through periodic training and exercises. The National Guard, with its mission and long tradition of responding to national emergencies, has an important role to play in this effort. The President announced in May 1998 that the Defense Department will train Army National Guard and reserve elements to assist state and local authorities to manage the consequences of a WMD attack. This training will be given to units in Massachusetts, New York, Pennsylvania, Georgia, Illinois, Texas, Missouri, Colorado, California and Washington.

The Domestic Terrorism Program enlists the support of other agencies as well. The Department of Energy plans for and provides emergency responder training for nuclear and radiological incidents. The Environmental Protection Agency plans for and provides emergency responder training for hazardous materials and environmental incidents. The Department of Health and Human Services, through the Public Health Service and with the support of the Department of Veterans Affairs and other Federal agencies, plans and prepares for a national response to medical emergencies arising from the terrorist use of weapons of mass destruction.

The threat of biological weapons is particularly troubling. In his May 1998 commencement speech at Annapolis, the President announced a comprehensive strategy to protect our civilian population from the scourge of biological weapons. There are four critical areas of focus:

- First, if a hostile nation or terrorists release bacteria or viruses to harm Americans, we must be able to identify the pathogens with speed and certainty. We will upgrade our public health and medical surveillance systems. These improvements will benefit not only our preparedness for a biological weapons attack—they will enhance our ability to respond quickly and effectively to outbreaks of emerging infectious diseases.

- Second, our emergency response personnel must have the training and equipment to do their jobs right. As described above, we will help ensure that federal, state and local authorities have the resources and knowledge they need to deal with a crisis.

- Third, we must have the medicines and vaccines needed to treat those who fall sick or prevent those at risk from falling ill because of a biological weapons attack. The President will propose the creation of a civilian stockpile of medicines and vaccines to counter the pathogens most likely to be in the hands of terrorists or hostile powers.

- Fourth, the revolution in biotechnology offers enormous possibilities for combating biological weapons. We will coordinate research and development efforts to use the advances in genetic engineering and biotechnology to create the next generation of medicines, vaccines and diagnostic tools for use against these weapons. At the same time, we must continue our efforts to prevent biotechnology innovations from being applied to development of ever more difficult to counter biological weapons.

Protecting Critical Infrastructures

Our military power and national economy are increasingly reliant upon interdependent critical infrastructures—the physical and information systems essential to the operations of the economy and government. They include telecommunications, energy, banking and finance, transportation, water systems and emergency services. It has long been the policy of the United States to assure the continuity

and viability of these critical infrastructures. But advances in information technology and competitive pressure to improve efficiency and productivity have created new vulnerabilities to both physical and information attacks as these infrastructures have become increasingly automated and interlinked. If we do not implement adequate protective measures, attacks on our critical infrastructures and information systems by nations, groups or individuals might be capable of significantly harming our military power and economy.

To enhance our ability to protect these critical infrastructures, the President signed Presidential Decision Directive 63 in May 1998. This directive makes it U.S. policy to take all necessary measures to swiftly eliminate any significant vulnerability to physical or information attacks on our critical infrastructures, especially our information systems. We will achieve and maintain the ability to protect them from intentional acts that would significantly diminish the abilities of the Federal Government to perform essential national security missions and to ensure the general public health and safety. We will protect the ability of state and local governments to maintain order and to deliver minimum essential public services. And we will work with the private sector to ensure the orderly functioning of the economy and the delivery of essential telecommunications, energy, financial and transportation services. Any interruption or manipulation of these critical functions must be brief, infrequent, manageable, isolated and minimally detrimental to the welfare of the United States.

The National Infrastructure Protection Center (NIPC) integrates relevant federal, state, and local government entities as well as the private sector, and provides the national focal point for gathering information on threats to the infrastructures. It serves as a national resource for identifying and assessing threats, warning about vulnerabilities, and conducting criminal investigations. The NIPC will also coordinate the federal government's response to an incident, including mitigation, investigation and monitoring reconstruction efforts.

Smaller-Scale Contingencies

Smaller-scale contingency operations encompass the full range of military operations short of major theater warfare, including humanitarian assistance, peace operations, enforcing embargoes and no-fly zones, evacuating U.S. citizens, reinforcing key allies, and limited strikes and intervention. These operations will likely pose the most frequent challenge for U.S. forces and cumulatively require significant commitments over time. These operations will also put a premium on the ability of the U.S. military to work closely and effectively with other U.S. Government agencies, non-governmental organizations, regional and international security organizations and coalition partners.

Under certain circumstances the U.S. military may provide appropriate and necessary humanitarian assistance. Those circumstances are when a natural or manmade disaster dwarfs the ability of the normal relief agencies to respond or the need for relief is urgent, and the military has a unique ability to respond quickly with minimal risk to American lives. In these cases, the United States may intervene when the costs and risks are commensurate with the stakes involved and when there is reason to believe that our action can make a real difference. Such efforts by the United States and the international community will be limited in duration, have a clearly defined end state and be designed to give the affected country the opportunity to restore its own basic services. This policy recognizes that the U.S. military normally is not the best tool for addressing long-term humanitarian concerns and that, ultimately, responsibility for the fate of a nation rests with its own people.

At times it will be in our national interest to proceed in partnership with others to preserve, maintain and restore peace. American participation in peace operations takes many forms, such as the NATO-led coalition in Bosnia, the American-led UN force in Haiti, the Military Observer Mission Ecuador and Peru (MOMEP), and our participation in the multilateral coalition operation in the Sinai. The question of command and control in multinational contingency operations is particularly critical. Under no circumstances will the President ever relinquish his constitutionally mandated command authority over U.S. forces, but there may be times when it is in our interest to place U.S. forces under the temporary operational control of a competent allied or United Nations commander.

Not only must the U.S. military be prepared to successfully conduct multiple smaller-scale contingencies worldwide, it must be prepared to do so in the face of challenges such as terrorism, information operations and the threat or use of weapons of mass destruction. U.S. forces must also remain prepared to withdraw from contingency operations if needed to deploy to a major theater war. Accordingly, appropriate U.S. forces will be kept at a high level of readiness and will be trained, equipped and organized to be multi-mission capable.

21

Major Theater Warfare

Fighting and winning major theater wars is the ultimate test of our Total Force—a test at which it must always succeed. For the foreseeable future, the United States, preferably in concert with allies, must remain able to deter and defeat large-scale, cross-border aggression in two distant theaters in overlapping time frames. Maintaining such a capability deters opportunism elsewhere while we are heavily committed to deterring or defeating aggression in one theater, or while conducting multiple smaller-scale contingencies and engagement activities in other theaters. It also provides a hedge against the possibility that we might encounter threats larger or more difficult than we expected. A strategy for deterring and defeating aggression in two theaters ensures we maintain the capability and flexibility to meet unknown future threats, while continued global engagement helps preclude such threats from developing.

Fighting and winning major theater wars entails at least three particularly challenging requirements. First, we must maintain the ability to rapidly defeat initial enemy advances short of enemy objectives in two theaters, in close succession. The United States must maintain this ability to ensure that we can seize the initiative, minimize territory lost before an invasion is halted and ensure the integrity of our warfighting coalitions. To meet this challenge, the forces that would be first to respond to an act of aggression are kept at full readiness, and the forces that follow them are kept at a level that supports their being ready to deploy and go into action when called for in the operations plan for the contingency.
Second, the United States must plan and prepare to fight and win under conditions where an adversary may use asymmetric means against us— unconventional approaches that avoid or undermine our strengths while exploiting our vulnerabilities. This is of particular importance and a significant challenge. Because of our dominance in the conventional military arena, adversaries who challenge the United States are likely to use asymmetric means, such as WMD, information operations or terrorism.

The WMD threat to our forces is receiving the special attention it deserves. We are enhancing the preparedness of our Armed Forces to effectively conduct sustained operations despite the presence, threat or use of WMD. Such preparedness requires the capability to deter, detect, protect against and respond to the use of WMD when necessary. The Administration has significantly increased funding to enhance biological and chemical defense capabilities and has begun the vaccination of military personnel against the anthrax bacteria, the most feared biological weapon threat today. These efforts reinforce our deterrent posture and complement our nonproliferation efforts by reducing the political and military value of WMD and their means of delivery.

We are enhancing our ability to defend against hostile information operations, which could in the future take the form of a full-scale, strategic information attack against our critical national infrastructures, government and economy—as well as attacks directed against our military forces. As other countries develop their capability to conduct offensive information operations, we must ensure that our national and defense information infrastructures are well protected and that we can quickly recognize, defend against and respond decisively to an information attack.

Third, our military must also be able to transition to fighting major theater wars from a posture of global engagement—from substantial levels of peacetime engagement overseas as well as multiple concurrent smaller-scale contingencies. Withdrawing from such operations would pose significant political and operational challenges. Ultimately, however, the United States must accept a degree of risk associated with withdrawing from contingency operations and engagement activities in order to reduce the greater risk incurred if we failed to respond adequately to major theater wars.

Our priority is to shape effectively the international environment so as to deter the onset of major theater wars. Should deterrence fail, however, the United States will defend itself, its allies and partners with all means necessary.

Preparing Now for an Uncertain Future

We must prepare for an uncertain future even as we address today's security problems. This requires that we keep our forces ready for shaping and responding requirements in the near term, *while at the same time* evolving our unparalleled capabilities to ensure we can effectively shape and respond in the future.

The 1997 Quadrennial Defense Review (QDR) struck a fine balance between near-term readiness, long-term modernization and quality of life improvements for our men and women in uniform. A key element of this balance was our decision to increase funding for modernization to protect long-term readiness. In this context we decided to make modest reductions in personnel, primarily in support positions, across the force structure. But in all these decisions we ensured that the high readiness levels of our forward-deployed and "first-to-fight" forces were maintained. While preparing for the challenges of the next century, the readiness of today's force remains one of our highest priorities. That is why the Administration, in partnership with the Congress, will continue to assure we maintain the best-trained, best-equipped and best-led military force in the world for the 21st Century.

Government-wide, we will continue to foster innovative approaches, capabilities, technologies and organizational structures to better protect American lives, property and interests at home and abroad. In our defense efforts, we will continue to explore new approaches for integrating the Active and Reserve components into a Total Force optimum for future missions, modernize our forces, ensure the quality of military personnel, and take prudent steps to position ourselves to effectively counter unlikely but significant future threats. We will also continue our rapidly growing efforts to integrate and improve the capability of Federal, state and local agencies—and our private sector partners—to protect against and respond to transnational threats at home.

The military challenges of the 21st century, coupled with the aging of key elements of the U.S. force structure, require a fundamental transformation of our military forces. Although future threats are fluid and unpredictable, U.S. forces are likely to confront a variety of challenges across the spectrum of conflict, including efforts to deny our forces access to critical

regions, urban warfare, information warfare, and attacks from chemical and biological weapons. To meet these challenges, we must transform our forces by exploiting the Revolution in Military Affairs. Improved intelligence collection and assessment coupled with modern information processing, navigation and command and control capabilities are at the heart of the transformation of our warfighting capabilities. Through a carefully planned and focused modernization program, we can maintain our technological superiority and replace Cold War-era equipment with new systems capable of taking full advantage of emerging technologies. With these advanced systems, the U.S. military will be able to respond rapidly to any contingency, dominate the battlespace and conduct day-to-day operations much more efficiently and effectively.

To support this transformation of our military forces, we will work cooperatively with the Congress to enact legislation to implement the Defense Reform Initiative, which will free up resources through a Revolution in Business Affairs. This revolution includes privatization, acquisition reform and elimination of excess infrastructure through two additional base realignment and closure (BRAC) rounds in 2001 and 2005. The Revolution in Military Affairs and the Revolution in Business Affairs are interlocking revolutions: With both, and only with both, we will ensure that U.S. forces continue to have unchallenged superiority in the 21st century.

It is critical that we renew our commitment to America's diplomacy—to ensure we have the diplomatic representation required to support our global interests. This is central to our ability to remain an influential voice on international issues that affect our well-being. We will preserve that influence so long as we retain the diplomatic capabilities, military wherewithal and economic base to underwrite our commitments credibly.

We must continue aggressive efforts to construct appropriate twenty-first century national security programs and structures. The Defense Department, State Department and other international affairs agencies are similarly reorganizing to confront the pressing challenges of tomorrow as well as those we face today. Federal, state and local law enforcement and emergency response agencies are enhancing their ability to deal with terrorist threats. Government and industry are exploring ways to protect critical national infrastructures. We will continue looking across our government to see if during this time of transition we are adequately preparing to meet the national security challenges of the next century.

Without preparing today to face the pressing challenges of tomorrow, our ability to exert global leadership and to create international conditions conducive to achieving our national goals would be in doubt. Thus, we must strive to strike the right balance between the near-term readiness requirements of shaping and responding and the longer-term transformation requirements associated with preparing now for national security challenges in the twenty-first century.

Overarching Capabilities

Certain capabilities and technologies are critical to protecting the United States itself and to the worldwide application of U.S. national power for shaping the international environment and responding to the full spectrum of threats and crises.

Quality People

Quality people—military and civilian—are our most critical asset. The quality of our men and women in uniform will be the deciding factor in all future military operations. In order to fully realize the benefits of the transformation of our military forces, we must ensure that we remain the most fully prepared and best trained fighting force in the world. Our people will continue to remain the linchpin to successfully exploiting our military capabilities across the spectrum of conflict. To ensure the quality of our military personnel, we will continue to place the highest priority on initiatives and programs that support recruiting, quality of life, and the training and education of our men and women in uniform.

We must also have quality civilian personnel in the government agencies that support our national security, from our diplomatic corps, to the intelligence community and law enforcement. Effectively countering transnational threats requires personnel with a variety of highly specialized skills that either are not readily available in the private sector, or are in high demand in the private sector. Persons with advanced training in information technology are a prominent example. Recruiting and retaining quality people with requisite skills is a significant challenge, and we are exploring innovative approaches for ensuring that government personnel needs are met.

Intelligence, Surveillance and Reconnaissance

Our intelligence, surveillance, and reconnaissance (ISR) capabilities are critical instruments for implementing our national security strategy. The U.S. intelligence community provides critical support to the full range of our activities abroad—diplomatic, military, law enforcement, and environmental. Comprehensive collection and analytic capabilities are needed to provide warning of threats to U.S. national security, give analytical support to the policy and military communities, provide near-real time intelligence in times of crisis while retaining global perspective, identify opportunities for advancing our national interests, and maintain our information advantage in the international arena.

ISR operations must cover a wider range of threats and policy needs than ever before. We place the highest priority on preserving and enhancing intelligence capabilities that provide information on states and groups that pose the most serious threats to U.S. security. Current intelligence priorities include states whose policies and actions are hostile to the United States; countries or other entities that possess strategic nuclear forces or control nuclear weapons, other WMD or nuclear fissile materials; transnational threats, including terrorism, international crime and drug trafficking; potential regional conflicts that might affect U.S. national security interests; intensified counterintelligence against foreign intelligence collection inimical to U.S. interests, including economic and industrial espionage; information warfare threats; and threats to U.S. forces and citizens abroad. Intelligence support is also required to develop and implement U.S. policies to promote democracy abroad, identify threats to our information and space systems, monitor arms control agreements. support humanitarian efforts and protect the environment.

Our ISR capabilities include world-wide collection of news and media broadcasts, reporting from informants close to important events abroad, space-based and airborne collection of imagery and signals intelligence, and integrated, in-depth analysis of all these sources by highly skilled analysts. Exploiting our tremendous advantage in continuous, non-intrusive, space-based imaging and information processing, the ISR system provides the ability to monitor treaty compliance, military movements and the development, testing and deployment of weapons of mass destruction. Using ISR products to support diplomatic and military action contributes to global security by demonstrating that the United States is an invaluable ally, or would be a formidable foe.

U.S. intelligence capabilities were reviewed twice by independent panels in 1998. In the wake of the May 1998 Indian nuclear tests, retired Admiral David E. Jeremiah led a panel that examined the Intelligence Community's ability to detect and monitor foreign nuclear weapons programs. In July 1998, the Commission to Assess the Ballistic Missile Threat to the United States issued a report on the challenges we face in attempting to monitor the progress of foreign ballistic missile programs. Both reviews identified specific areas of intelligence collection and analysis that need improvement. The Intelligence Community is taking aggressive action to improve its capabilities in those areas and we will work closely with the Congress to address the recommendations in the two reports.

While our ISR capabilities are increasingly enhanced by and dependent upon advanced technologies, there remains no substitute for informed, subjective human judgment. We must continue to attract and retain enough highly qualified people to provide human intelligence collection, translation and analysis in those many emerging areas where there simply is no technological substitute, and we must forge strong links to the private enterprises and public institutions whose expertise is especially critical. Increased cooperation among the agencies in the Intelligence Community and the fusion of all intelligence disciplines provide the most effective collection and analysis of data on high priority intelligence issues.

We must also be mindful of the continuing need for effective security and counterintelligence programs. To protect sensitive national security information, we must be able to effectively counter the collection efforts of foreign intelligence services through

vigorous counterintelligence efforts, comprehensive security programs and constant evaluation of the intentions and targets of foreign intelligence services. Counterintelligence remains integral to and underlies the entire intelligence mission, whether the threat comes from traditional espionage or the theft of our vital economic information. Countering foreign efforts to gather technological, industrial and commercial information requires close cooperation between government and the private sector. Awareness of the threat and adherence to prescribed personnel, information and physical security standards and procedures, based on risk management principles, are critical.

Space

We are committed to maintaining our leadership in space. Unimpeded access to and use of space is essential for protecting U.S. national security, promoting our prosperity and ensuring our well-being in countless ways.

Space has emerged in this decade as a new global information utility with extensive political, diplomatic, military and economic implications for the United States. We are experiencing an ever-increasing migration of capabilities to space as the world seeks to exploit the explosion in information technology. Telecommunications, telemedicine, international financial transactions and global entertainment, news, education, weather and navigation all contribute directly to the strength of our economy—and all are dependent upon space capabilities. Over 500 US companies are directly involved in the space industry, with 1996 revenues of $77 billion projected to reach $122 billion by 2000.

Our policy is to promote development of the full range of space-based capabilities in a manner that protects our vital security interests. We will deter threats to our interests in space and, if deterrence fails, defeat hostile efforts against U.S. access to and use of space. We will also maintain the ability to counter space systems and services that could be used for hostile purposes against our ground, air and naval forces, our command and control system, or other capabilities critical to our national security. We are carefully regulating U.S. commercial space-based remote sensing to ensure that space imagery is not used to the detriment of U.S. security interests. At the same time, we will continue efforts to prevent the spread of weapons of mass destruction to space, and continue to form global partnerships with other space-faring nations across the spectrum of economic, political, environmental and security issues. These efforts require a balanced approach across all types of U.S. space assets—national security, military, and commercial. We will remain vigilant to ensure that we do not compromise our technological superiority while promoting partnerships in space.

Missile Defense

We have robust missile defense development and deployment programs focused on systems to protect deployed U.S. forces and our friends and allies against theater ballistic missiles armed with conventional weapons or WMD. These systems will complement and strengthen our deterrence and nonproliferation efforts by reducing incentives to develop or use WMD. Significantly, Presidents Clinton and Yeltsin agreed at the Helsinki Summit to maintain the ABM Treaty as a cornerstone of strategic stability, yet adapt it to meet the threat posed by shorter-range missiles—a threat we seek to counter with U.S. theater missile defense (TMD) systems. The ABM-TMD demarcation agreement signed in New York on September 26, 1997 helps clarify the distinction between ABM systems, which the ABM Treaty limits, and TMD systems, which the ABM Treaty does not limit. The demarcation agreement does not limit any current U.S. core TMD programs, all of which have been certified by the United States as compliant with the ABM Treaty.

Although it remains the view of the intelligence community that it is unlikely that countries other than Russia, China and perhaps North Korea will deploy an ICBM capable of reaching any part of the U.S. before 2010, we are developing, consistent with our obligations under the ABM Treaty, a limited national missile defense capability that would position the U.S.

to make a decision as early as the year 2000 to deploy within three years a credible national missile defense system.

National Security Emergency Preparedness

We will do all we can to deter and prevent destructive and threatening forces such as terrorism, WMD use, disruption of our critical infrastructures, natural disasters and regional or state-centered threats from endangering our citizens. But if an emergency occurs, we must also be prepared to respond effectively at home and abroad to protect lives and property, mobilize the personnel, resources and capabilities necessary to effectively handle the emergency, and ensure the survival of our institutions and national infrastructures. National security emergency preparedness is imperative, and comprehensive, all-hazard emergency planning by Federal departments, agencies and the military continues to be a crucial national security requirement.

Overseas Presence and Power Projection

Due to our alliance commitments and other vital interests overseas, we must have a force structure and deployment posture that enable us to success-fully conduct military operations across the spectrum of conflict, often in theaters distant from the United States. Maintaining a substantial overseas presence promotes regional stability by giving form and substance to our bilateral and multilateral security commitments and helps prevent the development of power vacuums and instability. It contributes to deterrence by demonstrating our determination to defend U.S., allied, and friendly interests in critical regions and better positions the United States to respond rapidly to crises. Equally essential is effective and efficient global power projection, which is the key to the flexibility demanded or our forces and ultimately provides our national leaders with more options in responding to potential crises and conflicts. Being able to project power allows us to shape, deter, and respond even when we have no permanent presence or a limited infrastructure in the region.

Extensive transportation, logistics and command, control, communications and intelligence (C3I) capabilities are unique U.S. strengths that enhance our conventional deterrent and helps to shape the international environment. Strategic mobility allows the United States to be first on the scene with assistance in many national or international crises and is a key to successful American leadership and engagement. The deployment of US and multinational forces requires maintaining and ensuring access to sufficient fleets of aircraft, ships, vehicles and trains, as well as bases, ports, prepositioned equipment and other infrastructure. The United States must have a robust Defense Transportation System, including both military assets and U.S. flag commercial sealift and airlift, to remain actively engaged in world affairs.

Our need for strategic mobility to deploy our forces overseas is one of the primary reasons we are committed to gaining Senate advice and consent to ratification of the Law of the Sea Convention. Need for this treaty arose from the breakdown of customary international law as more and more nations unilaterally declared ever larger territorial seas and other claims over the oceans that threatened the global access and freedom of navigation that the United States must have to protect its vital national interests. In addition to lending the certainty of the rule of law to an area critical to our national security, the treaty protects our economic interests and preserves our leadership in global ocean policy. The Law of the Sea Convention thus buttresses the strategic advantages that the United States gains from being a global power.

Promoting Prosperity

The second core objective of our national security strategy is to promote America's prosperity through efforts at home and abroad. Our economic and security interests are inextricably linked. Prosperity at home depends on stability in key regions with which we trade or from which we import critical commodities, such as oil and natural gas. Prosperity also demands our leadership in international development, financial and trade institutions. In turn, the strength of our diplomacy, our ability to maintain an unrivaled military and the attractiveness of our values abroad depend in large part on the strength of our economy.

Strengthening Macroeconomic Coordination

As national economies become more integrated internationally, the United States cannot thrive in isolation from developments abroad. Our economic health is vulnerable to disturbances that originate outside our borders. As such, cooperation with other states and international organizations is vital to protecting the health of the global economic system and responding to financial crises.

The recent financial troubles in Asia have demonstrated that global financial markets dominated by private capital flows provide both immense opportunities and great challenges. Developing ways to strengthen the international financial architecture is an urgent and compelling challenge. At the November 1997 Asia Pacific Economic Cooperation Forum (APEC) meeting, President Clinton and the other APEC leaders agreed to hold a series of meetings of finance ministers and central bank governors to address the Asian financial crisis and international financial reform. The meetings began in February 1998 with representatives from 22 countries and observers from the major international financial institutions. The on-going efforts of this group, commonly referred to as the Willard Group or G-22, has helped to identify measures to prevent and better manage financial crises and reform the international financial system.

The ultimate objective of our reform efforts is a stable, resilient global financial system that promotes strong global economic growth providing benefits broadly to workers and investors in all countries. International financial institutions, particularly the International Monetary Fund (IMF), have a critical role to play in this effort by promoting greater openness and transparency, by building strong national financial systems, and by creating mechanisms so that the private sector shares more fully in the responsibility for preventing and resolving crises.

Openness and Transparency: For capital to flow freely and safely to where it can be used most efficiently to promote growth, high quality information about each economy and investment opportunity must also be freely available. The IMF introduced the Special Data Dissemination Standard (SDDS) in 1996 to improve the information collection and publication practices of countries accessing international capital markets. At present, 45 countries subscribe to the SDDS, but we need to encourage those IMF members who do not subscribe but seek access to international capital markets—particularly emerging market economies—to participate in the SDDS. International financial institutions also have a responsibility to make their activities open and transparent as a means of enhancing their credibility and accountability. The IMF recently has shown leadership in promoting openness and transparency; however, more needs be done in this area.

Financial Sector Reform: The IMF's recent review of the Asian crisis experience highlighted the key role played by the domestic financial sector as the flash point and transmission mechanism for the crisis and contagion. Rapid growth and expanding access to international capital had run ahead of the development in countries in trouble of a genuine credit culture to assess risk and channel investment efficiently and of an effective financial sector regulatory and supervisory mechanism. The situation was further exacerbated by inconsistent macroeconomic policies, generous explicit and implicit government guarantees, significant injections of public funds to provide liquidity support to weak institutions, and to some extent capital controls that distorted the composition of capital flows.

Crisis Resolution: Our efforts to reduce the risks of crises caused by poor policy or investor decisions need to be complemented by measures to equip investors, governments and the international financial system with the means to deal with those crises that do occur. The IMF plays the central role in the system by providing conditional international assistance to give countries the breathing room to stabilize their economies and restore market confidence. Two U.S.-inspired initiatives have enhanced the IMF's role: the Emergency Financing Mechanism, which provides for rapid agreement to extraordinary financing requests in return for more intense regular scrutiny, and the Supplemental Reserve Facility, which enables the IMF to lend at premium rates in short-term liquidity crises and improve borrower incentives. To fulfill its crisis resolution responsibility, the IMF must have adequate resources. We are concerned that IMF liquidity has fallen to dangerously low levels that could impair the Fund's capacity to respond to renewed pressures and meet normal demands. The Administration is making an intensive effort to obtain the necessary

Congressional approval to meet our obligations to the IMF.

Recent crises have brought home that in a global financial market we need to find more effective mechanisms for sharing with the private sector the burden of managing such problems. In a world in which trillions of dollars flow through international markets every day, there is simply not going to be enough official financing to meet the crises that could take place. Moreover, official financing should not absolve private investors from the consequences of excessive risk-taking and thus create the "moral hazard" that could plant the seeds of future crises.

Broadening the Financial Reform Agenda: In recent years, the IMF has broadened its perspective to take account of a wider range of issues necessary for economic growth and financial stability. It is seeking to create a more level playing field in which private sector competition can thrive; reduce unproductive government spending, including excessive military expenditures and subsidies and guarantees to favored sectors and firms; protect the most vulnerable segments of society from bearing the brunt of the burden of adjustment; and encourage more effective participation by labor and the rest of civil society in the formulation and implementation of economic policies, including protection of labor rights.

The United States and the other leading industrialized nations are also promoting a range of World Bank and regional development bank reforms that the United States has been urging for a number of years. Key elements include substantially increasing the share of resources devoted to basic social programs that reduce poverty; safeguarding the environment; supporting development of the private sector and open markets; promotion of good governance, including measures to fight corruption and improve the administration of justice; and internal reforms of the multilateral development banks (MDBs) to make them more efficient. Furthermore, international financial institutions such as the IMF and MDBs have played a strong role in recent years in countries and regions of key interest to the United States, such as Russia, the Middle East, Haiti and Bosnia.

Enhancing American Competitiveness

We seek to ensure a business environment in which the innovative and competitive efforts of the private sector can flourish. To this end, we will continue to encourage the development, commercialization and use of civilian technology. We will invest in a world-class infrastructure for the twenty-first century, including the national information and space infrastructure essential for our knowledge-based economy. We will invest in education and training to develop a workforce capable of participating in our rapidly changing economy. And we will continue our efforts to open foreign markets to U.S. goods and services.

Enhancing Access to Foreign Markets

In a world where over 95 percent of the world's consumers live outside the United States, we must expand our international trade to sustain economic growth at home. Our prosperity as a nation in the twenty-first century will depend upon our ability to compete effectively in international markets. The rapidly expanding global economy presents enormous opportunities for American companies and workers. Over the next decade the global economy is expected to grow at three times the rate of the U.S. economy. Growth will be particularly powerful in many emerging markets. If we do not seize these opportunities, our competitors surely will. We must continue working hard to secure and enforce agreements that protect intellectual property rights and enable Americans to compete fairly in foreign markets.

Trade agreement implementing authority is essential for advancing our nation's economic interests. Congress has consistently recognized that the President must have the authority to break down foreign trade barriers and create good jobs. Accordingly, the Administration will work with Congress to fashion an appropriate grant of fast track authority.

The Administration will continue to press our trading partners—multilaterally, regionally and bilaterally—to expand export opportunities for U.S. workers, farmers and companies. We will position ourselves at the center of a constellation of trade relationships—such as the World Trade Organization, APEC, the Transatlantic Marketplace and the Free Trade Area of the Americas (FTAA). We will seek to negotiate agreements, especially in sectors where the U.S. is most competitive—as we did in the Information

Technology Agreement and the World Trade Organization (WTO) Financial Services and Telecommunications Services Agreements. As we look ahead to the next WTO Ministerial meeting, to be held in the United States in late 1999, we will aggressively pursue an agenda that addresses U.S. trade objectives. We will also remain vigilant in enforcing the trade agreements reached with our trading partners. That is why the U.S. Trade Representative and the Department of Commerce created offices in 1996 dedicated to ensuring foreign governments are fully implementing their commitments under these agreements.

Promoting an Open Trading System

The successful conclusion of the Uruguay Round of negotiations under the General Agreement on Tariffs and Trade significantly strengthened the world trading system. The U.S. economy is expected to gain over $100 billion per year in GDP once the Uruguay Round is fully implemented. The Administration remains committed to carrying forward the success of the Uruguay Round and to the success of the WTO as a forum for openly resolving disputes.

We have completed the Information Technology Agreement (ITA) which goes far toward eliminating tariffs on high technology products and amounts to a global annual tax cut of $5 billion. We look to complete the first agreement expanding products covered by the ITA in 1998. We also concluded a landmark WTO agreement that will dramatically liberalize world trade in telecommunications services. Under this agreement, covering over 99 percent of WTO member telecommunications revenues, a decades old tradition of telecommunications monopolies and closed markets will give way to market opening deregulation and competition— principles championed by the United States.

The WTO agenda includes further negotiations to reform agricultural trade, liberalize service sector markets, and strengthen protection for intellectual property rights. At the May 1998 WTO Ministerial, members agreed to initiate preparations for these negotiations and to consider other possible negotiating topics, including issues not currently covered by WTO rules. These preparatory talks will continue over the course of the next year so that the next round of negotiations can be launched at the 1999 WTO ministerial meeting in the United States.

We also have a full agenda of accession negotiations with countries seeking to join the WTO. As always, the United States is setting high standards for accession in terms of adherence to the rules and market access. Accessions offer an opportunity to help ground new economies in the rules-based trading system and reinforce their own reform programs. This is why we will take an active role in the accession process dealing with the 32 applicants currently seeking WTO membership.

Through Organization for Economic Cooperation and Development (OECD) negotiations of a Multilateral Agreement on Investment, we are seeking to establish clear legal standards on expropriation, access to binding international arbitration for disputes and unrestricted investment-related transfers across borders. Also in the OECD, the United States is taking on issues such as corruption and labor practices that can distort trade and inhibit U.S. competitiveness. We seeking to have OECD members outlaw bribery of foreign officials, eliminate the tax deductibility of foreign bribes, and promote greater transparency in government procurement. To date, our efforts on procurement have been concentrated in the World Bank and the regional development banks, but our initiative to pursue an agreement on transparency in WTO member procurement regimes should make an additional important contribution. We have also made

important strides on labor issues. The WTO has endorsed the importance of core labor standards sought by the United States since the Eisenhower Administration—the right to organize and bargain collectively, and prohibitions against child labor and forced labor. We will continue pressing for better integration of the international core labor standards into the WTO's work, including through closer WTO interaction with the International Labor Organization (ILO).

We continue to ensure that liberalization of trade does not come at the expense of national security or environmental protection. For example, the national security, law enforcement and trade policy communities worked together to make sure that the WTO agreement liberalizing global investment in telecommunications was consistent with U.S. national security interests. Moreover, our leadership in the Uruguay Round negotiations led to the incorporation of environmental provisions into the WTO agreements and creation of the Committee on Trade and Environment, where governments continue to pursue the goal of ensuring that trade and environment policies are mutually supportive. In addition, with U.S. leadership, countries participating in the Summit of the Americas are engaged in sustainable development initiatives to ensure that economic growth does not come at the cost of environmental protection.

In May 1998, President Clinton presented to the WTO a set of proposals to further U.S. international trade objectives:

- First, that the WTO make further efforts to eliminate trade barriers and pursue a more open global trading system in order to spur economic growth, better jobs, higher incomes, and the free flow of ideas, information and people.

- Second, that the WTO provide a forum where business, labor, environmental and consumer groups can provide regular input to help guide further evolution of the WTO. The trading system we build for the 21st century must ensure that economic competition does not threaten the livelihood, health and safety of ordinary families by eroding environmental and consumer protection or labor standards.

- Third, that a high-level meeting of trade and environmental officials be convened to provide direction for WTO environmental efforts, and that the WTO and the International Labor Organization commit to work together to ensure that open trade raises the standard of living for workers and respects core labor standards.

- Fourth, that the WTO open its doors to the scrutiny and participation of the public by taking every feasible step to bring openness and accountability to its operations, such as by opening its dispute settlement hearings to the public and making the briefs for those hearings publicly available.

- Fifth, that the nations of the world join the United States in not imposing any tariffs on electronic commercial transmissions sent across national borders. The revolution in information technology represented by the Internet is the greatest force for prosperity in our lifetimes; we cannot allow discriminatory barriers to stunt the development of this promising new economic opportunity. An electronic commerce work program was agreed to at the May 1998 WTO Ministerial. It will be reviewed at the 1999 ministerial meeting.

- Sixth, that all WTO members make government purchases through open and fair bidding and adopt the OECD antibribery convention. Prosperity depends upon government practices that are based upon the rule of law rather than bureaucratic caprice, cronyism or corruption.

- Seventh, that the WTO explore a faster trade negotiating process and develop an open trading system that can change as fast as the global marketplace. Positive steps include annual tariff and subsidy reductions in agriculture, greater openness and competition in the services sector, further tariff reductions in the industrial sector, and stronger intellectual property protection.

Export Strategy and Advocacy Program

The Administration created America's first national export strategy, reforming the way government works with the private sector to expand exports. The new Trade Promotion Coordination Committee (TPCC) has been instrumental in improving export promotion efforts, coordinating our export financing, implementing a government-wide advocacy initiative and updating

market information systems and product standards education.

The export strategy is working, with the United States regaining its position as the world's largest exporter. While our strong export performance has supported millions of new, export-related jobs, we must export more in the years ahead if we are to further strengthen our trade balance position and raise living standards with high-wage jobs. Our objective remains to expand U.S. exports to over $1.2 trillion by the year 2000, which will mean over 2.5 million new American jobs and a total of over 14.6 million jobs supported by exports.

Enhanced Export Control

The United States is a world leader in high technology exports, including satellites, cellular phones, computers and commercial aircraft. Some of this technology has direct or indirect military applications. For that reason, the United States government carefully controls high technology exports through a licensing process involving the Department of Defense, the Department of State, the Commerce Department and other agencies. Changes to U.S. export controls over the last decade have allowed America's most important growth industries to compete effectively overseas and create good jobs at home while ensuring that proper safeguards are in place to protect important national security interests.

The cornerstone of our export control policy is protection of our national security; but imposing the tightest possible restrictions on high technology exports is not always the best way to protect our security. In an increasingly competitive global economy, the United States retains a monopoly over very few technologies. As a result, rigid export controls increasingly would not protect our national security because the same products can be obtained readily from foreign sources. Rigid controls would make U.S. high technology companies less competitive globally, thus losing market share and becoming less able to produce the innovative, cutting-edge products for the U.S. military and our allies.

Our current policy—developed in the Reagan and Bush Administrations and continued by President Clinton—recognizes that we must balance a variety of factors. In the wake of the Cold War, the Bush Administration accelerated the process of moving the licensing of essentially commercial items from the State Department's Munitions List to the Commerce-administered Commodity Control List in order to promote high technology exports by making license decisions more predictable and timely. In 1995, by Executive Order, President Clinton expanded the right of the Departments of Defense, State and Energy and the Arms Control and Disarmament Agency to fully participate in the decision-making process. Previously, these agencies reviewed only certain dual-use applications; as a result of the Executive Order, they have the right to review every dual-use application. If any of these agencies disagree with a proposed export, it can block the license and put the issue into a dispute resolution process that can ultimately rise to the President. As a result, reviews of dual-use licenses are today more thorough and broadly based than ever before.

While our export controls and the regulations that implement them have become easier for American exporters to follow, we have also enhanced our ability to identify, stop and prosecute those who attempt to evade them. For example, in fiscal year 1997 efforts of the Commerce Department's criminal investigators led to over $1 million in criminal fines and over $16 million in civil penalties. We have significant enforcement weapons to use against those who would evade our export controls, and we are using them vigorously.

Finally, U.S. efforts to stem proliferation cannot be effective without the cooperation of other countries. To that end, we have strengthened multilateral cooperation through the Nuclear Suppliers Group, the Missile Technology Control Regime, the Australia Group (for the control of chemical and biological weapons-related related items), the Chemical Weapons Convention, and the Wassenaar Arrangement, which through U.S. leadership is shaping multilateral export controls for the next century. These multilateral efforts enlist the world community in the battle against the proliferation of weapons of mass destruction, advanced conventional weapons and sensitive technologies, while at the same time producing a level playing field for U.S. business by ensuring that our competitors face corresponding export controls.

Providing for Energy Security

The United States depends on oil for about 40 percent of its primary energy needs and roughly half of our oil needs are met with imports. Although we import less than 10% of Persian Gulf exports, our allies in Europe and Japan account for about 85% of these exports, thus underscoring the continued strategic importance of the region. We are undergoing a fundamental shift away from reliance on Middle East oil. Venezuela is our number one foreign supplier and Africa supplies 15% of our imported oil. Canada, Mexico and Venezuela combined supply more than twice as much oil to the United States as the Arab OPEC countries.

The Caspian Basin, with potential oil reserves of 160 billion barrels, promises to play an increasingly important role in meeting rising world energy demand in coming decades. We have made it a priority to work with the countries of the region to develop multiple pipeline ventures that will ensure access to the oil. We are also working on several fronts to enhance the stability and safeguard the independence of these nations. While these developments are significant, we must remember that the vast majority of proven oil reserves lie in the Middle East and that the global oil market is largely interdependent.

Conservation measures and research leading to great-er energy efficiency and alternative fuels are a critical element of the U.S. strategy for energy security. The U.S. economy has grown roughly 75 percent since the first oil shock in 1973. During that time U.S. oil consumption remained virtually stable, reflecting conservation efforts and increased energy efficiency. Our research must continue to focus on developing highly efficient transportation systems and to shift them to alternative fuels, such as hydrogen, ethanol or methanol from biomass, and others. This research will also help address concerns about climate change by providing new approaches for meeting guidelines on emission of greenhouse gases. Over the longer term, U.S. dependence on access to foreign oil sources may be increasingly important as domestic resources are depleted. Although U.S. oil consumption has been essentially level since 1973, our reliance on imported oil has increased due to a decline in domestic production. Domestic oil production declined during that period because oil prices were not high enough to generate new oil exploration sufficient to sustain production levels from our depleted resource base. Conservation and energy research notwithstand-ing, the United States will continue to have a vital interest in ensuring access to foreign oil sources. We must continue to be mindful of the need for regional stability and security in key producing areas to ensure our access to and the free flow of these resources.

Promoting Sustainable Development Abroad

Environmental and natural resource issues can impede sustainable development efforts and promote regional instability. Many nations are struggling to provide jobs, education and other services to their citizens. The continuing poverty of a quarter of the world's people leads to hunger, malnutrition, economic migration and political unrest. Malaria, AIDS and other epidemics, including some that can spread through environmental damage, threaten to overwhelm the health facilities of developing countries, disrupt societies and stop economic growth.

Sustainable development improves the prospects for democracy in developing countries and expands the demand for U.S. exports. It alleviates pressure on the global environment, reduces the attraction of the illegal drug trade and other illicit commerce, and improves health and economic productivity. U.S. foreign assistance focuses on four key elements of sustainable development: broad-based economic growth, environmental security, population and health, and democracy.

We will continue to advocate environmentally sound private investment and responsible approaches by international lenders. The multilateral development banks are now placing increased emphasis upon sustainable development in their funding decisions, including assisting borrowing countries to better manage their economies. The U.S. Initiative on Joint Implementation, part of the Administration's Climate Change Action Plan, encourages U.S. businesses and non-governmental organizations to apply innovative technologies and practices to reduce greenhouse gas emissions and promote sustainable development abroad. The initiative, which includes 32 projects in 12 countries, has proven effective in transferring technology for environmentally sound, sustainable development. The Global Environmental Facility provides a source of financial assistance to the developing world for climate change, biodiversity and oceans initiatives that will benefit all the world's citizens. Environmental damage in countries of the NIS and Central and Eastern Europe continues to impede their ability to emerge as prosperous, independent countries. We are focusing technical assistance and encouraging non-governmental environmental groups to provide expertise to the NIS and Central and Eastern European nations that have suffered the most acute environmental crises.

Promoting Democracy

The third core objective of our national security strategy is to promote democracy and human rights. The number of states moving away from repressive governance toward democratic and publicly accountable institutions is impressive. Since the success of many of those changes is by no means assured, our strategy must focus on strengthening their commitment and institutional capacity to implement democratic reforms.

Emerging Democracies

We seek international support in helping strengthen democratic and free market institutions and norms in countries making the transition from closed to open societies. This commitment to see freedom and respect for human rights take hold is not only just, but pragmatic, for strengthened democratic institutions benefit the United States and the world.

The United States is helping consolidate democratic and market reforms in Central and Eastern Europe and the NIS. Integrating the Central and Eastern European nations into European security and economic organizations, such as NATO and the EU, will help lock in and preserve the impressive progress these nations have made in instituting democratic and market-economic reforms. Our intensified interaction with Ukraine has helped move that country onto the path of economic reform, which is critical to its long-term stability. In addition, our efforts in Russia, Ukraine and the other NIS facilitate our goal of achieving continued reductions in nuclear arms and compliance with international nonproliferation accords.

Continuing advances in democracy and free markets in our own hemisphere remain a priority, as reflected by the President's 1997 trips to Latin America and the Caribbean and the Summit of the Americas in Santiago this year. In the Asia Pacific region, economic dynamism is increasingly associated with political modernization, democratic evolution and the widening of the rule of law—and it has global impacts. We are particularly attentive to states whose entry into the camp of market democracies may influence the future direction of an entire region; South Africa now holds that potential with regard to sub-Saharan Africa.

The methods for assisting emerging democracies are as varied as the nations involved. We must continue leading efforts to mobilize international economic and political resources, as we have with Russia, Ukraine and the other NIS. We must take firm action to help counter attempts to reverse democracy, as we have in Haiti and Paraguay. We must give democratic nations the fullest benefits of integration into foreign markets, which is part of the reason NAFTA and the Uruguay Round of GATT ranked so high on our agenda and why we are now working to forge the FTAA. We must help these nations strengthen the pillars of civil society, supporting administration of justice and rule of law programs, assisting the development of democratic civil-military relations, and training foreign police and security forces to solve crimes and maintain order without violating the basic rights of their citizens. And we must seek to improve their market institutions and fight corruption and political discontent by encouraging good governance practices.

Adherence to Universal Human Rights and Democratic Principles

We must sustain our efforts to press for political liberalization and respect for basic human rights worldwide, including in countries that continue to defy democratic advances. Working bilaterally and through multilateral institutions, the United States promotes universal adherence to international human rights and democratic principles. Our efforts in the United Nations and other organizations are helping to make these principles the governing standards for acceptable international behavior.

We will also continue to work—bilaterally and with multilateral institutions—to ensure that international human rights principles protect the most vulnerable or traditionally oppressed groups in the world—women, children, workers, refugees and persons persecuted on the basis of their religious beliefs or ethnic descent. To this end, we will seek to strength-en and improve the UN Human Rights Commission and other international mechanisms that promote human rights

and address violations of international humanitarian law, such as the international war crimes tribunals for the former Yugoslavia and Rwanda.

To focus additional attention on the more vulnerable or traditionally oppressed people, we seek to spearhead new international initiatives to combat the sexual exploitation of minors, child labor, homelessness among children, violence against women and children, and female genital mutilation. We will continue to work with individual nations, such as Russia and China, and with international institutions to combat religious persecution. We are encouraging governments to not return people to countries where they face persecution. We ask that they provide asylum or offer temporary protection to persons fleeing situations of conflict or generalized human rights abuses. We seek to ensure that such persons are not returned without due consideration of their need for permanent protection.

Violence against women and trafficking in women and girls is are international problem with national implications. We have seen cases of trafficking in the United States for purposes of forced prostitution, sweatshop labor and domestic servitude. The United States is committed to combating trafficking in women and girls with a focus on the areas of prevention, victim assistance and protection, and enforcement. On March 11, 1998, President Clinton directed a wide range of expanded efforts to combat violence against women in the United States and around the world, including efforts to increase national and international awareness of trafficking in women and girls. The President called for continued efforts to fully implement the 1994 Violence Against Women Act and restore its protection for immigrant victims of domestic violence in the United States so that they will not be forced to choose between deportation and abuse. He also called upon the Senate to give its advice and consent to ratification to the Convention on the Elimination of all Forms of Discrimination Against Women, which will enhance our efforts to combat violence against women, reform unfair inheritance and property rights, and strengthen women's access to fair employment and economic opportunity.

The United States will continue to speak out against human rights abuses and carry on human rights dialogues with countries willing to engage us constructively. Because police and internal security services can be a source of human rights violations, we use training and contacts between U.S. law enforcement and their foreign counterparts to help address these problems. Federal law enforcement agents can serve as role models for investigators in countries where the police have been instruments of oppression and at the same time reduce international crime and terrorism that affects U.S. interests. In appropriate circumstances, we must be prepared to take strong measures against human rights violators. These include economic sanctions, as have been maintained against Nigeria, Iraq, Burma, North Korea and Cuba, visa restrictions and restricting sales of arms and police equipment that may be used to commit human rights abuses.

Humanitarian Activities

Our efforts to promote democracy and human rights are complemented by our humanitarian programs, which are designed to alleviate human suffering, help establish democratic regimes that respect human rights and pursue appropriate strategies for economic development. These efforts also enable the United States to help prevent humanitarian disasters with far more significant resource implications.

We also must seek to promote reconciliation in states experiencing civil conflict and to address migration and refugee crises. To this end, the United States will provide appropriate financial support and work with other nations and international bodies. such as the International Committee of the Red Cross and the UN High Commissioner for Refugees. We also will assist efforts to protect the rights of refugees and displaced persons and to address the economic and social root causes of internal displacement and international flight. Finally, we will cooperate with other states to curb illegal immigration into this country.

Private firms and associations are natural allies in activities and efforts intended to bolster market economies. We have natural partners in labor unions, human rights groups, environmental advocates, chambers of commerce and election monitors in promoting democracy and respect for human rights and in providing international humanitarian assistance; thus, we should promote democratization efforts through private and non-governmental groups as well as foreign governments.

Supporting the global movement toward democracy requires a pragmatic, long-term effort focused on both values and institutions. Our goal is a broadening of the community of free-market democracies and stronger international non-governmental movements committed to human rights and democratization.

III. Integrated Regional Approaches

Our policies toward different regions reflect our overall strategy tailored to unique challenges and opportunities.

Europe and Eurasia

European stability is vital to our own security. The United States has two strategic goals in Europe. The first is to build a Europe that is truly integrated, democratic, prosperous and at peace. This would complete the mission the United States launched 50 years ago with the Marshall Plan and the North Atlantic Treaty Organization (NATO).

Our second goal is to work with our allies and partners across the Atlantic to meet the global challenges no nation can meet alone. This means working together to support peace efforts in troubled regions, to counter global threats such as the spread of weapons of mass destruction and dual-use technology, and to build a more open world economy and without barriers to transatlantic trade and investment. We will continue to strengthen the OSCE's role in conflict prevention and crisis management and seek closer cooperation with our European partners in dealing with non-military security threats through our New Transatlantic Agenda with the European Union (EU).

Enhancing Security

NATO remains the anchor of American engagement in Europe and the linchpin of transatlantic security. As a guarantor of European security and a force for European stability, NATO must play a leading role in promoting a more integrated and secure Europe, prepared to respond to new challenges. We will maintain approximately 100,000 military personnel in Europe to fulfill our commitments to NATO, provide a visible deterrent against aggression and coercion, contribute to regional stability, respond to crises,

sustain our vital transatlantic ties and preserve U.S. leadership in NATO.

NATO enlargement is a crucial element of the U.S. and Allied strategy to build an undivided, peaceful Europe. The end of the Cold War changed the nature of the threats to this region, but not the fact that Europe's stability is vital to our own national security. The addition of well-qualified democracies, which have demonstrated their commitment to the values of freedom and the security of the broader region, will help deter potential threats to Europe, deepen the continent's stability, bolster its democratic advances, erase its artificial divisions, and strengthen an Alliance that has proven its effectiveness both during and since the Cold War.

In December 1997, the NATO foreign ministers signed the three protocols of accession for Poland, Hungary, and the Czech Republic, making them full members of the Alliance subject to ratification by all current and incoming NATO members. On May 21, 1998, the President signed the instruments of ratification for the three protocols following a strong, bipartisan 80-19 vote of approval in the U.S. Senate. Poland, Hungary, and the Czech Republic will make the Alliance stronger while helping to enlarge Europe's zone of democratic stability. They have been leaders in Central Europe's dramatic transformation over the past decade and have helped make Central Europe the continent's most robust zone of economic growth. They will strengthen NATO through the addition of military resources, strategic depth and the prospect of greater stability in Europe's central region. Our Alliance with them will improve our ability to protect and advance our interests in the transatlantic area and contribute to our security in the years to come.

At the same time, we have vigorously pursued efforts to help other countries that aspire to membership become the best possible candidates. Together with our Allies we are enhancing the Partnership for Peace and continuing political contacts with aspiring states. We are also continuing bilateral programs to advance this agenda, such as the President's Warsaw Initiative, which is playing a critical role in helping the militaries of Central and Eastern Europe and Eurasia become more interoperable with NATO. Building on the increasing links between NATO and the Partnership for Peace nations, Partners will increasingly contribute to real-world NATO missions, as many are doing in the NATO-led operation in Bosnia.

Some European nations do not desire NATO membership, but do desire strengthened ties with the Alliance. The Partnership for Peace provides an ideal venue for such relationships. It formalizes relations, provides a mechanism for mutual beneficial interaction and establishes a sound basis for combined action should that be desired. For all these reasons, Partnership for Peace will remain a central and permanent part of the European security architecture.

NATO also is pursuing several other initiatives to enhance its ability to respond to new challenges and deepen ties between the Alliance and Partner countries. NATO has launched the Euro-Atlantic Partnership Council to strengthen political dialogue and practical cooperation with all Partners, and established a NATO-Ukraine Charter, which provides a framework for enhanced relations. As a result of the 1997 NATO-Russia Founding Act, NATO and Russia developed the Permanent Joint Council to enhance political consultation and practical cooperation, while retaining NATO's decision-making authority. Our shared goal remains constructive Russian participation in the European security system.

The North Atlantic Treaty Organization will hold its Fiftieth Anniversary summit meeting in Washington on April 24-25, 1999. This summit will mark NATO's extraordinary record of success over the past fifty years in protecting the security of the United States and our European allies. As agreed at the 1997 Madrid summit, we hope to use the upcoming summit meeting in Washington to welcome the entry of Poland, Hungary, and the Czech Republic as new members of the alliance. Looking to the future, the summit will advance the common work of NATO allies and partners to build an undivided Europe that is peaceful, prosperous, and democratic.

As we help build a comprehensive European security architecture, we must continue to focus on regional security challenges.

Southeastern Europe and the Balkans: There are significant security challenges in Southeastern Europe. Instability in this region could threaten the consolidation of reforms, disrupt commerce and undermine our efforts to bring peace to Bosnia and other parts of the former Yugoslavia.

The United States has an abiding interest in peace and stability in Bosnia because continued war in that region threatens all of Europe's stability. Implementation of the Dayton Accords is the best hope for creating a self-sustaining peace in Bosnia. NATO-led forces are contributing to a secure environment in Bosnia and providing essential support for the broader progress we are making in implementing the Dayton Accords. Further progress is necessary, however, to create conditions that will allow implementation to continue without a large military presence. We are committed to full implementation of the Dayton Accords and success in Bosnia. We support the efforts of the International Criminal Tribunal for the former Yugoslavia and broader efforts to promote justice and reconciliation in Bosnia.

We are deeply concerned about the ongoing bloodshed in Kosovo, which threatens security and stability throughout the Balkan region. We are firmly convinced that the problems in Kosovo can best be resolved through a process of open and unconditional dialogue between authorities in Belgrade and the Kosovar Albanian leadership. We seek a peaceful resolution of the crisis that guarantees restoration of human and political rights which have been systematically denied the Kosovar Albanian population since Belgrade withdrew autonomy in 1989. In support of that objective, NATO is reviewing options for deterring further violence against the civilian population in Kosovo and stabilizing the military situation in the region.

We are redoubling our efforts to advance the integration of several new democracies in Southeastern Europe (Bulgaria, Romania, Slovenia and the Former Yugoslavian Republic of Macedonia) into the European mainstream. More specifically, the President's Action Plan for Southeast Europe seeks to promote further democratic, economic, and military reforms in these countries, to encourage greater regional cooperation, and to advance common interests, such as closer contact with NATO, and increased law enforcement training and exchanges to assist in the fight against organized crime.

Tensions on Cyprus, Greek-Turkish disagreements in the Aegean and Turkey's relationship with the EU have serious implications for regional stability and the evolution of European political and security structures. Our goals are to stabilize the region by reducing long-standing Greek-Turkish tensions and pursuing a comprehensive settlement on Cyprus. A democratic, secular, stable and Western-oriented Turkey is critical to these efforts and has supported broader U.S. efforts to enhance stability in Bosnia, the NIS and the Middle East, as well as to contain Iran and Iraq.

The Baltic States: For over fifty years, the United States has recognized the sovereignty and independence of the republics of Estonia, Latvia and Lithuania. During this period, we never acknowledged their forced incorporation into the Soviet Union. The special nature of our relationship with the Baltic States is recognized in the Charter of Partnership signed on January 16, 1998, which clarifies the principles upon which U.S. relations with the Baltic states are based and provides a framework for strengthening ties and pursuing common goals. These goals include integration of Latvia, Lithuania and Estonia into the transatlantic community and development of close, cooperative relationships among all the states in Northeastern Europe. The Charter also establishes mechanisms for high-level review and adjustment of this cooperation.

Northern Ireland: After a 30-year winter of sectarian violence, Northern Ireland has the promise of a springtime of peace. The agreement that emerged from the Northern Ireland peace talks on April 10, 1998 opened the way to build a society based on enduring peace, justice and equality. On May 22, 1998, the people of Ireland and Northern Ireland seized this opportunity to turn the common tragedy of Northern Ireland's past into a shared triumph for the future by strongly endorsing the peace accord. In so doing, they have written a new chapter in the rich history of their island by creating the best chance for peace in a generation.

The United States actively promoted this peace process and will continue to stand with those who seek to build lasting peace and enduring prosperity in Ireland and Northern Ireland. They can count on the continuing aid, support and encouragement of the United States. The task of making the peace endure will be difficult. Some may seek to undermine this agreement by returning to violence. Anyone who does so, from whatever side and whatever faction, will have no friends in America. We will work closely with British and Irish law enforcement and intelligence officials to prevent outrages before they happen by identifying terrorists and their sources of financial and material support.

We will continue to work with Northern Ireland's leaders as they seek to transform the promise of the Accord into a reality—with new democratic institutions and new economic opportunities for all of Northern Ireland's people. Working through the International Fund for Ireland and the private sector, we will help the people seize the opportunities that peace will bring to attract new investment to create new factories, workplaces and jobs, and establish new centers of learning to prepare for the 21st Century.

Newly Independent States (NIS): The United States is pursuing a wide range of security objectives in the NIS. We seek to bring Russia, Ukraine and the other NIS into a new, cooperative European security order, which includes strengthening their participation in NATO Partnership for Peace activities and building effective NATO-Russia and NATO-Ukraine partnerships. We seek to reduce the threat of nuclear war and the spread of nuclear weapons and materials, as well as other weapons of mass destruction and their delivery systems, especially to outlaw states.

The United States has vital security interests in the evolution of Russia, Ukraine and the other NIS into democratic market economies, peacefully and prosperously integrated into the world community. The governmental and financial sectors in this region appear especially susceptible to penetration by organized criminal groups, who have the ability to subvert and destroy these nascent institutions. Further democratic and economic reforms and integration into the WTO and other international economic institutions will strengthen the rule of law and respect for human rights, foster growth by expanding private sector activity, and encourage open and cooperative policies toward the global community.

Promoting Prosperity

Europe is a key element in America's global commercial engagement. Europe and the United States produce over half of all global goods and services. More than 60% of total U.S. investment abroad is in Europe and fourteen million workers on both sides of the Atlantic earn their livelihoods directly from transatlantic commerce. As part of the New Transatlantic Agenda launched at the 1995 U.S.-EU Summit in Madrid, the United States and the EU agreed to take concrete steps to reduce barriers to trade and investment through the creation of an open New Transatlantic Marketplace. We have concluded Mutual Recognition Agreements eliminating redundant testing and certification requirements covering $50 billion in two-way trade. Our governments are also cooperating closely with the Transatlantic Business Dialogue, a U.S.-European business partnership, to address a wide range of trade barriers.

Building on the New Transatlantic Agenda, the United States and the EU launched the Transatlantic Economic Partnership on May 18, 1998. This is a major new initiative to deepen our economic relations, reinforce our political ties and reduce trade frictions that have plagued our bilateral relationship. The first element of the initiative is reducing barriers that affect manufacturing, agriculture and services. In the manufacturing area we will focus on standards and technical barriers that American businesses have identified as the most significant obstacle to expanding trade. In the agricultural area we will focus on regulatory barriers that have inhibited the expansion of agriculture trade, particularly in the biotechnology area. In the area of services we will seek to open our markets further and to create new opportunities for the number of service industries that are so active in the European market.

The second element of the Transatlantic Economic Partnership is a broader, cooperative approach to addressing a wide range of trade issues. We agreed to maintain current practices, and will continue not imposing duties on electronic transmissions and develop a work program in the WTO for electronic commerce. We will seek to adopt common positions and effective strategies for accelerating compliance with WTO commitments on intellectual property. We will seek to promote government procurement opportunities, including promoting compatibility of electronic procurement information and government contracting systems. We will seek innovative ways to promote our shared labor and environmental values around the world. To promote fair competition, we will seek to enhance the compatibility of our procedures with potentially significant reductions in cost for American companies.

The United States strongly supports the process of European integration embodied in the EU. We are also encouraging bilateral trade and investment in non-EU countries and supporting enlargement of the EU. We recognize that EU nations face significant economic challenges with nearly 20 million people unemployed, and that economic stagnation has eroded public support for funding outward-looking foreign policies and greater integration. We are working closely with our European partners to expand employment, promote long-term growth and support the New Transatlantic Agenda.

By supporting historic market reforms in Central and Eastern Europe and in the NIS, we both strengthen our own economy and help new democracies take root. Poland, economically troubled as recently as 1989, now symbolizes the new dynamism and rapid growth that extensive, free-market reforms make possible. Recent economic turbulence in Russia demonstrates that the transition to a more prosperous, market-based economy will be a long-term process characterized by promise and disappointment. In Ukraine, reinvigorating economic reform remains a key challenge to strengthening national security and independence. Much remains to be done throughout the region to assure sustainable economic recoveries and adequate social protection.

The United States will continue helping the NIS economies integrate into international economic and other institutions and develop healthy business climates. We will continue to mobilize the international community to provide assistance to support reform. The United States is working closely with Russia and Ukraine in priority areas, including defense conversion, the environment, trade and investment, and scientific and technological cooperation. We are also encouraging investment, especially by U.S. companies, in NIS energy resources and their export to world markets, thereby expanding and diversifying world energy supplies and promoting prosperity in the NIS.

Ultimately, the success of economic and financial reforms in the countries recently emerged from communism will depend more on private investment than official aid. One of our priorities, therefore, is to help countries stimulate foreign and domestic investment. At the Helsinki Summit, Presidents Clinton and Yeltsin defined an ambitious reform agenda covering key tax, energy and commercial laws crucial for Russia to realize its potential for attracting foreign investment. Further, the Presidents outlined steps to accelerate Russian membership on commercial terms in key economic organizations such as the WTO. It is in both Russia's interest and ours that we work with Russian leaders on passage of key economic and commercial legislation. We are cooperating with Russia to facilitate oil and gas exports to and through Russia from neighboring Caspian countries. We also support development of new East-West oil and gas export routes across the Caspian Sea and through the Transcaucasus and Turkey.

Ukraine is at an important point in its economic transition—one that will affect its integration with Europe and domestic prosperity. The United States has mobilized the international community's support for Ukrainian economic reform, pushed to improve Ukraine's investment climate, and championed its integration into key European, transatlantic and global economic institutions. Two other challenges stand out: first, to instill respect for the rule of law so that a more transparent, level economic playing field is established and democratic governance prevails; and, second, to gain international support as it seeks to close down Chernobyl and reform its energy sector. The U.S.-Ukraine Binational Commission, chaired by Vice President Gore and President Kuchma, serves as a focal point to coordinate bilateral relations and to invigorate Ukrainian reform efforts.

A stable and prosperous Caucasus and Central Asia will help promote stability and security from the Mediterranean to China and facilitate rapid development and transport to international markets of the large Caspian oil and gas resources, with substantial U.S. commercial participation. While the new states in the region have made progress in their quest for sovereignty and a secure place in the international arena, much remains to be done in democratic and economic reform and in settling regional conflicts, such as Nagorno-Karabakh and Abkhazia.

Promoting Democracy

Thoroughgoing democratic and economic reforms in the NIS and Europe's former communist states are the best measures to avert conditions which could foster aggressive nationalism and ethnic hatreds. Already, the prospect of joining or rejoining the Western democratic family has dampened the forces of nationalism and strengthened the forces of democracy and reform in many countries of the region.

The independence, sovereignty, territorial integrity, and democratic and economic reform of the NIS are important to American interests. To advance these goals, we are utilizing our bilateral relationships, our leadership of international institutions, and billions of dollars in private and multilateral resources. But the circumstances affecting the smaller countries depend in significant measure on the fate of reform in the largest and most powerful—Russia. The United States will continue vigorously to promote Russian reform and international integration, and discourage any reversal in the progress that has been made. Our economic and political support for the Russian government depends on its commitment to internal reform and a responsible foreign policy.

East Asia and the Pacific

President Clinton's vision of a new Pacific community links security interests with economic growth and our commitment to democracy and human rights. We continue to build on that vision, cementing America's role as a stabilizing force in a more integrated Asia Pacific region.

Enhancing Security

Our military presence has been essential to maintaining the stability that has enabled most nations in the Asia Pacific region to build thriving economies for the benefit of all. To deter aggression and secure our own interests, we will maintain approximately 100,000 U.S. military personnel in the region. Our commitment to maintaining an active military presence in the region and our treaty alliances with Japan, South Korea, Australia, Thailand and the Philippines serve as the foundation for America's continuing security role.

We are maintaining healthy relations with the Association of Southeast Asian Nations (ASEAN), which now includes Singapore, Malaysia, Thailand, Indonesia, the Philippines, Brunei, Vietnam, Laos and Burma. We are also supporting regional dialogue—such as in the ASEAN Regional Forum (ARF)—on the full range of common security challenges. By meeting on confidence-building measures such as search and rescue cooperation and peacekeeping, the ARF can help enhance regional security and understanding.

Japan

The United States and Japan reaffirmed our bilateral security relationship in the April 1996 Joint Security Declaration. The alliance continues to be the cornerstone for achieving common security objectives and for maintaining a stable and prosperous environment for the Asia Pacific region as we enter the twenty-first century. In September 1997, both Governments issued the revised Guidelines for U.S.-Japan Defense Cooperation which will result in greater bilateral cooperation in peacekeeping and humanitarian relief operations, in situations in areas surrounding Japan, and in the defense of Japan itself. The revised Guidelines, like the U.S.-Japan security relationship itself, are not directed against any other country.

In April 1998, in order to support the new Guidelines, both governments agreed to a revised Acquisition and Cross-Servicing Agreement (ACSA) which expands the exchange of provision of supplies and services to include reciprocal provision of logistics support during situations surrounding Japan that have an important influence on Japan's peace and security. While the guidelines and its related efforts have specifically focused on regional security, both countries have continued to cooperate in the implementation of the Special Action Committee on Okinawa (SACO) Final report. This effort initiated plans and measures to realign, consolidate, and reduce U.S. facilities and areas in Okinawa in order to ease the impact of U.S. Forces' presence on the people of Okinawa. Implementation of SACO will ultimately aid in ensuring the maintenance of U.S. operational capabilities and force presence in the Asia-Pacific region.

U.S.-Japan security cooperation extends to promoting regional peace and stability, seeking universal adherence to the Nuclear Non-Proliferation Treaty, and addressing the dangers posed by transfers of destabilizing conventional arms and sensitive dual-use goods and technologies. Our continued progress in assisting open trade between our countries and our broad-ranging international cooperation, exemplified by the Common Agenda, provide a sound basis for our relations into the next century.

Korean Peninsula

Tensions on the Korean Peninsula remain the principal threat to peace and stability in East Asia. The Democratic People's Republic of Korea (DPRK) has publicly stated a preference for peaceful reunification, but continues to dedicate a large portion of dwindling resources to enhance the combat capability of its huge military forces. Renewed conflict has been prevented since 1953 by a combination of the Armistice Agreement, which brought an end to open hostilities; the United Nations Command, which has visibly represented the will of the UN Security Council to secure peace; and the physical presence of U.S. and ROK troops in the Combined Forces Command, which has demonstrated the alliance's resolve.

The inauguration of Kim Dae-jung as President of the Republic of Korea on February 25, 1998 marked an important turning point on the Korean Peninsula. It marked the triumph of democracy in South Korea and the first peaceful transition of power from the ruling party to an opposition party. It was also a remarkable triumph for President Kim, who had been denied the Presidency in 1971 by voter intimidation and fraud, kidnapped and almost murdered by government agents, sentenced to death in 1991, imprisoned for six years and in exile or under house arrest for over ten years. President Kim personifies the victory of democracy over dictatorship in South Korea.

President Kim has set a new course toward peace and stability on the Korean Peninsula by opening new channels for dialogue and seeking areas for cooperation between North and South. During their summit meeting in June 1998, President Clinton and President Kim discussed the situation on the Korean Peninsula. reaffirming South Korea's role as lead interlocutor with the North Koreans and the importance of our strong defense alliance. President Clinton expressed strong support for President Kim's vision of engagement and efforts toward reconciliation with the North. The United States is working to create conditions of stability by maintaining solidarity with our South Korean ally, emphasizing America's commitment to shaping a peaceful and prosperous Korean Peninsula and ensuring that an isolated and struggling North Korea does not opt for a military solution to its political and economic problems.

Peaceful resolution of the Korean conflict with a non-nuclear, reunified peninsula will enhance stability in the East Asian region and is clearly in our strategic interest. We are willing to improve bilateral political and economic ties with North Korea—consistent with the objectives of our alliance with the ROK—to draw the North into more normal relations with the region and the rest of the world. Our willingness to improve bilateral relations will continue to be commensurate with the North's cooperation in efforts to reduce tensions on the peninsula. South Korea has set a shining example for nonproliferation by forswearing nuclear weapons, accepting safeguards, and developing a peaceful nuclear program that brings benefits to the region. We are firm that North Korea must freeze and dismantle its graphite-moderated reactors and related facilities and fully comply with its NPT obligations under the Agreed Framework. We also seek to cease North Korea's chemical and biological weapon programs and ballistic missile proliferation activities. The United States, too, must fulfill its obligations under the Agreed Framework and the Administration will work with the Congress to ensure the success of our efforts to address the North Korean nuclear threat. The North must also engage in a productive dialogue with South Korea; continue the recently revived United Nations Command-Korean People's Army General Officer Dialogue talks at Panmunjon; participate constructively in the Four Party Talks among the United States, China, and North and South Korea to reduce tensions and negotiate a peace agreement; and support our efforts to recover the remains of American servicemen missing since the Korean War.

China

A stable, open, prosperous People's Republic of China (PRC) that assumes its responsibilities for building a more peaceful world is clearly and profoundly in our interests. The prospects for peace and prosperity in Asia depend heavily on China's role as a responsible member of the international

community. China's integration into the international system of rules and norms will influence its own political and economic development, as well as its relations with the rest of the world. Our relationship with China will in large measure help to determine whether the 21st century is one of security, peace, and prosperity for the American people. Our success in working with China as a partner in building a stable international order depends on establishing a productive relationship that will build sustained domestic support.

Our policy toward China is both principled and pragmatic: expanding our areas of cooperation while dealing forthrightly with our differences. Seeking to isolate China is clearly unworkable. Even our friends and allies around the world would not support us; we would succeed only in isolating ourselves and our own policy. More importantly, choosing isolation over engagement would not make the world safer. It would make it more dangerous. It would undermine rather than strengthen our efforts to foster stability in Asia and halt the proliferation of weapons of mass destruction. It would hinder the cause of democracy and human rights in China, set back worldwide efforts to protect the environment, and cut off one of the world's most important markets.

President Jiang Zemin's visit to the United States in October 1997—the first state visit by the President of China to the United States in twelve years—marked significant progress in the development of U.S.-PRC relations. President Clinton's reciprocal visit to Beijing in June 1998—the first state visit by an American president to China in this decade—further expanded and strengthened our relations. The two summits were important milestones toward building a constructive U.S.-China strategic partnership.

In their 1997 summit, the two Presidents agreed on a number of steps to strengthen cooperation in international affairs: establishing a Washington-Beijing presidential communications link to facilitate direct contact, regular presidential visits to each other's capitals, and regular exchanges of visits by cabinet and sub-cabinet officials to consult on political, military, security and arms control issues. They agreed to establish a consultation mechanism to strengthen military maritime safety—which will enable their maritime and air forces to avoid accidents, misunderstandings or miscalculations—and to hold discussions on humanitarian assistance and disaster relief. In their June 1998 meeting, they agreed to continue their regular summit meetings and to intensify the bilateral dialogue on security issues.

Arms control and non-proliferation issues were high on the agenda for 1998 summit, which expanded and strengthened the series of agreements that were reached at the 1997 summit. In Beijing, Presidents Clinton and Jiang announced that the United States and China will not target their strategic nuclear weapons at each other. They confirmed their common goal to halt the spread of weapons of mass destruction. We welcomed China's statement that it attaches importance to issues related to the Missile Technology Control Regime (MTCR) and missile nonproliferation and that it has begun to actively study joining the MTCR. Our two nations will continue consultations on MTCR issues in 1998. Both sides agreed to further strengthen controls on the export of dual-use chemicals and related production equipment and technology to assure they are not used for production of chemical weapons, and China announced that it has expanded the list of chemical precursors which it controls. The two Presidents issued a joint statement calling for strengthening of the Biological Weapons Convention and early conclusion of a protocol establishing a practical and effective compliance mechanism and improving transparency. They issued a joint statement affirming their commitment to ending the export and indiscriminate use of anti-personnel landmines and to accelerating global humanitarian demining. We also reached agreement with China on practices for end-use visits on U.S. high technology exports to China, which will establish a framework for such exports to China.

China is working with the United States on important regional security issues. In June 1998, China chaired a meeting of the permanent members of the UN Security Council to forge a common strategy for moving India and Pakistan away from a nuclear arms race. China condemned both countries for conducting nuclear tests and joined us in urging them to conduct no more tests, to sign the Comprehensive Test Ban Treaty, to avoid deploying or testing missiles, and to work to resolve their differences through dialogue. At the 1998 summit, Presidents Clinton and Jiang issued a joint statement on their shared interest in a peaceful and stable South Asia and agreed to continue to coordinate their efforts to strengthen peace and stability in that region. On the Korean Peninsula, China has become a force for peace and stability, helping us to convince North

Korea to freeze its dangerous nuclear program, playing a constructive role in the four-party peace talks.

The United States and China are working to strengthen cooperation in the field of law enforcement and mutual legal assistance, including efforts to combat international organized crime, narcotics trafficking, alien smuggling, illegal immigration, counterfeiting and money laundering. We have established a joint liaison group for law enforcement cooperation and assigned counternarcotics officers to each other's embassies in 1998.

Our key security objectives for the future include:

- sustaining the strategic dialogue begun by the recent summits and other high-level exchanges;

- enhancing stability in the Taiwan Strait through peaceful approaches to cross-Strait issues and encouraging dialogue between Beijing and Taipei;

- strengthening China's adherence to international nonproliferation norms, particularly in its export controls on ballistic missile and dual use technologies;

- achieving greater openness and transparency in China's military;

- encouraging a constructive PRC role in international affairs through active cooperation in ARF, the Asia Pacific Economic Cooperation Forum (APEC) and the Northeast Asia Security Dialogue; and

- improving law enforcement cooperation with PRC officials through increased liaison and training.

Southeast Asia

Our strategic interest in Southeast Asia centers on developing regional and bilateral security and economic relationships that assist in conflict prevention and resolution and expand U.S. participation in the region's economies. U.S. security objectives in the region are to maintain our security alliances with Australia, Thailand and the Philippines, to sustain security access arrangements with Singapore and other ASEAN countries, and to encourage the emergence of a strong, cohesive ASEAN capable of enhancing regional stability and prosperity.

Our policy combines two approaches: First, maintaining our increasingly productive relationship with ASEAN—especially our security dialogue under the ARF. Second, pursuing bilateral initiatives with individual Southeast Asian nations to promote political stability, foster market-oriented economic reforms, and reduce or contain the effects of Asian organized crime, particularly the flow of heroin from Burma and other countries in the region.

Promoting Prosperity

A prosperous and open Asia Pacific is key to the economic health of the United States. On the eve of the recent financial problems in Asia, the 18 members of APEC contributed about one-half of total global gross domestic product and exports. Thirty percent of U.S. exports go to Asia, supporting millions of U.S. jobs, and we export more to Asia than Europe. In states like California, Oregon and Washington, exports to Asia account for more than half of each state's total exports. U.S. direct investments in Asia represent about one-fifth of total U.S. direct foreign investment.

Our economic objectives in East Asia include recovery from the recent financial crisis, continued progress within APEC toward liberalizing trade and investment, increased U.S. exports to Asian countries through market-opening measures and leveling the playing field for U.S. business, and WTO accession for China and Taiwan on satisfactory commercial terms. Opportunities for economic growth abound in Asia and underlie our strong commitment to multilateral economic cooperation, such as via the annual APEC leaders meetings.

Promoting sustainable development, protecting the environment and coping with the global problem of climate change are important for ensuring long-term prosperity in the Asia Pacific region. The Kyoto Agreement was a major step forward in controlling the greenhouse gases that are causing climate change, but its success depends on meaningful participation by key developing nations as well as the

industrialized nations of the world. Rapid economic growth in China and India make their participation essential to the global effort to control greenhouse gases.

The Asian Financial Crisis

Over the last decade, the global economy has entered a new era—an era of interdependence and opportunity. Americans have benefited greatly from the worldwide increase of trade and capital flows. This development has contributed to steady GNP growth, improvements in standards of living, more high paying jobs (particularly in export-oriented industries), and low inflation.

The United States has enormously important economic and national security interests at stake in East Asia. Prolonged economic distress and financial instability will have an adverse effect on U.S. exports to the region, the competitiveness of American companies, and the well being of American workers. There also is a risk that if the current crisis is left unchecked its effects could spread beyond East Asia. Simply put, we cannot afford to stand back in hopes that the crisis will resolve itself. When we act to help resolve the Asian financial crisis, we act to protect the well-being of the American people.

In the face of this challenge, our primary objective is to help stabilize the current financial situation. Our strategy has four key elements: support for economic reforms; working with international financial institutions to provide structural and humanitarian assistance; providing bilateral humanitarian aid and contingency bilateral financial assistance if needed; and urging strong policy actions by Japan and the other major economic powers to promote global growth.

We will continue to support South Korea, Thailand and Indonesia as they implement economic reforms designed to foster financial stability and investor confidence in order to attract the capital flows required to restore economic growth. These reform programs have at their core restructuring the financial sector, promoting greater transparency in trade and investment laws and regulations, and ending policy-directed lending practices. All three nations face a difficult road ahead that will test their political will. The international community can continue to help ameliorate adverse consequences of the crisis, but only resolute action to keep to the agreed policy course will bring a resumption of sustained growth.

Although the Asian financial crisis is having a crippling effect, we believe the underlying fundamentals for economic recovery are good and are confident that full and vigorous implementation of economic reforms combined with the efforts of the international community will lead to the restoration of economic growth to the countries of the region. U.S. initiatives in APEC will open new opportunities for economic cooperation and permit U.S. companies to expand their involvement in substantial infrastructure planning and construction throughout the region. While our progress in APEC has been gratifying, we will explore options to encourage all Asia Pacific nations to pursue open markets.

The United States will continue to work with the IMF, the World Bank, other international financial institutions, the governments in East Asia and the private sector to help stabilize financial markets, restore investor confidence and achieve much-needed reforms in the troubled East Asian economies. Our goal is to help the region recover quickly and to build a solid, resilient foundation for future economic growth in the region.

China

Bringing the PRC more fully into the global trading system is manifestly in our national interest. China is one of the fastest growing markets for our goods and services. As we look into the next century, our exports to China will support hundreds of thousands of jobs across our country. For this reason, we must continue our normal trade treatment for China, as every President has done since 1980, strengthening instead of undermining our economic relationship.

An important part of integrating China into the market-based world economic system is opening China's highly protected market through lower border barriers and removal of distorting restraints on economic activity. We have negotiated landmark agreements to combat piracy of intellectual property and advance the interests of our creative industries. We have also negotiated—and vigorously enforced—agreements on textile trade. At their 1997 and 1998 summits, President Clinton and President Jiang agreed to take a number of positive measures to expand U.S.-China trade and economic ties. We will continue to press

China to open its markets (in goods, services and agriculture) as it engages in sweeping economic reform.

It is in our interest that China become a member of the WTO; however, we have been steadfast in leading the effort to ensure that China's accession to the WTO occurs on a commercial basis. China maintains many barriers that must be eliminated, and we need to ensure that necessary reforms are agreed to before accession occurs. At the 1997 summit, the two leaders agreed that China's full participation in the multilateral trading system is in their mutual interest. They agreed to intensify negotiations on market access, including tariffs, non-tariff measures, services, standards and agriculture, and on implementation of WTO principles so that China can accede to the WTO on a commercial basis at the earliest possible date. They reiterated their commitment to this process in their 1998 summit.

China has been a helpful partner in international efforts to stabilize the Asian financial crisis. In resisting the temptation to devalue its currency, China has seen that its own interests lie in preventing another round of competitive devaluations that would have severely damaged prospects for regional recovery. It has also contributed to the rescue packages for affected economies.

Japan

The Administration continues to make progress on increasing market access in Asia's largest economy. Since the beginning of the first Clinton Administration, the United States and Japan have reached 35 trade agreements designed to open Japanese markets in key sectors, including autos and auto parts, telecommunications, civil aviation, insurance and glass. The Administration also has intensified efforts to monitor and enforce trade agreements with Japan to ensure that they are fully implemented. The United States also uses multilateral venues, such as WTO dispute settlement and negotiation of new multilateral agreements, to further open markets and accomplish our trade objectives with Japan.

During the period from 1993 to 1996, U.S. exports to Japan increased from $47.9 billion to $67.6 billion, and the bilateral trade deficit fell from $59.4 billion to $47.6 billion. The recent economic downturn in Japan, however, has reversed this positive trend with the bilateral trade deficit for the first four months 1998 already at $20.8 billion, up 32 percent from the same period in 1996. Sustained global expansion and recovery in Asia cannot be achieved when the second largest economy in the world, accounting for more than half of Asian output, is in recession and has a weakened financial system.

Japan has a crucial role to play in Asia's economic recovery. Japan must generate substantial growth to help maintain a growing world economy and absorb a growing share of imports from emerging markets. To do this Japan must reform its financial sector, stimulate domestic demand, deregulate its economy, and further open its markets to foreign goods and services. We look forward to substantial and effective actions to achieve a domestic demand-led recovery, to restore health to the financial sector and to make progress on deregulation and opening markets. Strong, immediate, tangible actions by the Japanese Government are vital to make Japan again an engine of growth and to help spur a broader economic recovery in Asia, as well as reinvigorate a critical market for U.S. goods and services.

South Korea

At their summit meeting in June 1998, President Clinton reaffirmed to President Kim that the United States will continue its strong support for his efforts to reform the Korean economy, liberalize trade and investment, strengthen the banking system and implement the IMF program. President Clinton reiterated our commitment to provide bilateral finance if needed under appropriate conditions. The two presidents discussed a number of concrete steps to promote growth in both our countries and explored ways to more fully open our markets and to further integrate the Republic of Korea into the global economy, including new discussions on a bilateral investment treaty. They also signed an Open Skies agreement which permits unrestricted air service between our two countries.

Thailand

Thailand, a key U.S. security partner in the region, also faces serious economic difficulties. The U.S. government continues to work with Thailand to ease

the strain of the financial crisis. We are taking concrete steps to lessen the financial burden of military programs, including decreasing the scope of military contacts such as visits and exercises, and looking for ways to reduce the impact of the crisis on security assistance programs. The Royal Thai armed forces have earned high marks for their stabilizing influence.

Promoting Democracy

Some have argued that democracy is unsuited for Asia or at least for some Asian nations—that human rights are relative and that Western support for international human rights standards simply mask a form of cultural imperialism. The democratic aspirations and achievements of the Asian peoples prove these arguments incorrect. We will continue to support those aspirations and to promote respect for human rights in all nations. Each nation must find its own form of democracy, and we respect the variety of democratic institutions that have emerged in Asia. But there is no cultural justification for tyranny, torture or denial of fundamental freedoms. Our strategy includes efforts to:

• pursue a constructive, goal-oriented approach to achieving progress on human rights and rule of law issues with China;

• foster a meaningful political dialogue between the ruling authorities in Burma and the democratic opposition;

• work with the new government of Indonesia to promote improved respect for human rights, strengthened democratic processes and an internationally acceptable political solution in East Timor;

• work with ASEAN to restore democracy to Cambodia and encourage greater respect for human rights; and

• achieve the fullest possible accounting of missing U.S. service members, promote greater respect for human rights in Vietnam, and press for full Vietnamese implementation of the Resettlement Opportunity for Vietnamese Returnees (ROVR) program.

The Western Hemisphere

Our hemisphere enters the twenty-first century with an unprecedented opportunity to secure a future of stability and prosperity—building on the fact that every nation in the hemisphere except Cuba is democratic and committed to free market economies. The end of armed conflict in Central America and other improvements in regional security have coincided with remarkable political and economic progress throughout the Americas. The people of the Americas are already taking advantage of the vast opportunities being created as emerging markets are connected through electronic commerce and as robust democracies allow individuals to more fully express their preferences. Sub-regional political, economic and security cooperation in North America, the Caribbean, Central America, the Andean region and the Southern Cone have contributed positively to peace and prosperity throughout the hemisphere. Equally important, the people of the Americas have reaffirmed their commitment to combat together the difficult new threats of narcotics and corruption. U.S. strategy is to secure the benefits of the new climate in the hemisphere while safeguarding the United States and our friends against these threats.

The 1994 Summit of the Americas in Miami produced hemispheric agreement to negotiate the Free Trade Area of the Americas (FTAA) and agreements on measures that included continued economic reform and enhanced cooperation on issues such as the environment, counternarcotics, money laundering and corruption. Celebrating the region's embrace of democracy and free markets, that historic meeting committed the United States to a more cooperative relationship with the hemisphere. U.S. agencies have used the Miami Summit Action Plan to establish productive relationships and strengthen cooperation with their Latin American and Caribbean counterparts in a host of areas.

Our engagement with the hemisphere reached unprecedented levels in 1997 and 1998. In May 1997, President Clinton traveled to Mexico for a summit meeting with President Zedillo, then held summits with Central American leaders in Costa Rica and Caribbean leaders in Barbados, highlighting the importance of working with our neighbors to solve problems of great concern to Americans such as drugs, immigration and transnational crime. In October 1997, in Venezuela, Brazil and Argentina, the President underscored opportunities for cooperation with vibrant democracies and their fast growing markets.

This substantial engagement with the hemisphere at the beginning of the President's second term continued at the Second Summit of the Americas in Santiago, Chile in April 1998. At the Summit, the leaders of the hemisphere focused on the areas needed to prepare our citizens for the 21st century: education, democracy, economic integration and poverty relief.

Enhancing Security

The principal security concerns in the hemisphere are transnational in nature, such as drug trafficking, organized crime, money laundering, illegal immigration, and terrorism. In addition, our hemisphere is leading the way in recognizing the dangers to democracy produced by corruption and rule of law issues. These threats, especially narcotics, produce adverse social effects that undermine the sovereignty, democracy and national security of nations in the hemisphere.

We are striving to eliminate the scourge of drug trafficking in our hemisphere. At the Santiago Summit, the assembled leaders launched a Multilateral Counterdrug Alliance to better organize and coordinate efforts in the hemisphere to stem the production and distribution of drugs. The centerpiece of this alliance is leading the way in recognizing the member country's progress in achieving their agreed counternarcotics goals. Summit leaders also agreed to improve cooperation on extraditing and prosecuting individuals charged with narcotics trafficking and related crimes; strengthen efforts against money laundering and forfeiture of assets used in criminal activity; reinforce international and national mechanisms to halt illicit traffic and diversion of chemical precursors; enhance national programs for fostering greater awareness of the dangers of drug abuse, preventing illicit drug consumption and providing treatment, rehabilitation and reintegration; and eliminate illicit crops through national alternative development programs, eradication and interdiction.

We are also pursuing a number of bilateral and regional counternarcotics initiatives. As part of our partnership with Mexico, we are striving to increase counterdrug and law enforcement cooperation, while in the Caribbean we are intensifying a coordinated effort on counternarcotics and law enforcement. The reduction in trade barriers resulting from the North American Free Trade Agreement (NAFTA) allows more inspection resources to be directed to thwarting attempts by organized crime to exploit the expanding volume of trade for increased drug smuggling.

The Santiago Summit addressed other transnational security concerns as well. Summit leaders called for the rapid ratification and entry into force of the 1997 Inter-American Convention to Combat the Illicit Manufacturing of and Trafficking in Firearms, Ammunition Explosives and Related Material. They also agreed to encourage states to accede to the international conventions related to terrorism and convene, under the auspices of the OAS, the Second Specialized Inter-American Conference to evaluate the progress attained and to define future courses of action for the prevention, combat and elimination of terrorism.

We are advancing regional security cooperation through bilateral security dialogues, multilateral efforts in the Organization of American States (OAS) and Summit of the Americas on transparency and regional confidence and security building measures, exercises and exchanges with key militaries (principally focused on peacekeeping), and regular Defense Ministerials. Working with Argentina, Brazil and Chile, the other three guarantor nations of the Peru-Ecuador peace process, the United States has brought the parties closer to a permanent solution to this decades-old border dispute, the resolution of which is important to regional stability. The Military Observer Mission, Ecuador-Peru (MOMEP), composed of the four guarantor nations, successfully separated the warring factions, created the mutual confidence and security among the guarantor nations. The U.S. sponsored multilateral military exercise focused on combating drug trafficking, supporting disaster relief (particularly important because of the El Nino phenomenon) and participation in international peacekeeping. It has spurred unprecedented exercises among neighboring countries in Central America and the Southern Cone. Additionally, the Southern Cone has increasingly shared the burden of international peacekeeping operations. The Santiago Summit tasked the OAS to expand topics relating to confidence and security building measures with the goal of convening a Special Conference on Security by the beginning of the next decade. Several countries in the region have joined our call to promote transparency by

publishing white papers on defense. Our efforts to encourage multilateral cooperation are enhancing confidence and security within the region and will help expand our cooperative efforts to combat the transnational threats to the Western Hemisphere, particularly in Columbia where social, political and criminal violence is spilling across borders. We are also working to ensure successful transfer of stewardship of the Panama Canal to the Panamanian people.

In light of the advances in democratic stability throughout Latin America and mindful of the need for restraint, the Administration has moved to case-by-case consideration of requests for advanced conventional arms transfers, on par with other areas of the world. Such requests will be reviewed in a way that will serve our objectives of promoting defense cooperation, restraint in arms acquisition and military budgets, and an increased focus on peacekeeping, counternarcotics efforts and disaster relief.

Promoting Prosperity

Economic growth and integration in the Americas will profoundly affect the prosperity of the United States in the 21st century. Latin America has become the fastest growing economic region in the world and our fastest growing export market. In 1998, our exports to Latin America and the Caribbean are expected to exceed those to the EU.

Building on the vision articulated at Miami in 1994 and the groundwork laid by trade ministers over the last four years, the Santiago Summit launched formal negotiations to initiate the FTAA by 2005. The negotiations will cover a broad range of important issues, including market access, investment, services, government procurement, dispute settlement, agriculture, intellectual property rights, competition policy, subsidies, anti-dumping and countervailing duties. A Committee on Electronic Commerce will explore the implications of electronic commerce for the design of the FTAA, and a Committee on Civil Society will provide a formal mechanism for labor, business, consumer, environmental and other non-government organizations to make recommendations on the negotiations so that all citizens can benefit from trade. Governments also will cooperate on promoting core labor standards recognized by the International Labor Organization.

We seek to advance the goal of an integrated hemisphere of free market democracies by consolidating NAFTA's gains and obtaining Congressional Fast Track trade agreement implementing authority. Since the creation of NAFTA, our exports to Mexico have risen significantly while the Agreement helped stabilize Mexico through its worst financial crisis in modern history. Considering that Mexico has now become our second-largest export market, it is imperative that its economy remain open to the United States and NAFTA helps to ensure that. We will continue working with Mexico and interested private parties to continue the mutually beneficial trade with our largest trading partner and neighbor to the north, Canada. We are also committed to delivering on the President's promise to negotiate a comprehensive free trade agreement with Chile because of its extraordinary economic performance and its active role in promoting hemispheric economic integration.

While we support the freer flow of goods and investment, there is also reason to be sensitive to the concerns of smaller economies during the period of transition to the global economy of the 21st century. To address this problem, and in light of the increased competition NAFTA presents to Caribbean trade, we will seek Congressional approval to provide enhanced trade benefits under the Caribbean Basin Initiative (CBI) to help prepare that region for participation in the FTAA. With the assistance of institutions such as OPIC, we will encourage the private sector to take the lead in developing small and medium-sized businesses in the Caribbean through the increased flow of investment capital. We must also encourage Caribbean countries and territories to implement programs to attract foreign and domestic investment.

At the Santiago Summit, the hemisphere's leaders reaffirmed that all citizens must participate in the opportunities and prosperity created by free market democracy. They pledged to ensure access to financial services for a significant number of the 50 million micro, small and medium size enterprises in the hemisphere by the year 2000, to work with multilateral institutions and regional organizations to invest about $400-500 million over the next three years, and to streamline and decentralize property registration and titling procedures and assure access to justice for the poor. Governments will enhance participation by promoting core labor standards recognized by the ILO, strengthening gender equity, working to eliminate exploitative child labor,

negotiating a new Declaration of Principles on Fundamental Rights of Workers, and promoting education and training for indigenous populations. To improve quality of life, Summit leaders pledged to pursue elimination of measles by the year 2000 and reduce the incidence of diseases such as pneumonia and mumps by the year 2002, to strengthen regional networks of health information such as through telemedicine, to give highest priority to reducing infant malnutrition, and to strengthen cooperation to implement Santa Cruz Sustainable Development Plan of Action.

Promoting Democracy

Many Latin American nations have made tremendous advances in democracy and economic progress over the last several years. But our ability to sustain the hemispheric agenda depends in part on meeting the challenges posed by weak democratic institutions, persistently high unemployment and crime rates, and serious income disparities. In some Latin American countries, citizens will not fully realize the benefits of political liberalization and economic growth without regulatory, judicial, law enforcement and educational reforms, as well as increased efforts to integrate all members of society into the formal economy.

At the Santiago Summit, the hemisphere's leaders reaffirmed their commitment to strengthening democracy, justice and human rights. They agreed to intensify efforts to promote democratic reforms at the regional and local level, protect the rights of migrant workers and their families, improve the capabilities and competence of civil and criminal justice systems, and encourage a strong and active civil society. They pledged to promptly ratify the Inter-American Convention Against Corruption to strengthen the integrity of governmental institutions. They supported the creation of a Special Rapporteur for Freedom of Expression as part of the Inter-American Commission for Human Rights. The Rapporteur will help resolve human rights cases involving the press and focus international attention on attacks against the hemisphere's emerging Fourth Estate, as their investigative reporting provokes increasing threats from drug traffickers and other criminal elements. Summit leaders also agreed to establish an Inter-American Justice Studies Center to facilitate training of personnel, to exchange of information and other forms of technical cooperation to improve judicial systems, to end impunity, combat corruption and provide protection from rising domestic and international crime, and to create a secure legal environment for trade and investment.

The hemisphere's leaders agreed at the Santiago Summit that education is the centerpiece of reforms aimed at making democracy work for all the people of the Americas. The Summit Action Plan adopted at Santiago will build on the achievements of the 1994 Miami Summit. It will advance numerous cooperative efforts based on the guiding principles of equity, quality, relevance and efficiency. The Santiago Plan's targets are to ensure by the year 2010 primary education for 100% of children and access to quality secondary education for at least 75% of young people. The plan also includes solid commitments to finance schools, textbooks, teacher training, technology for education, to create education partnerships between the public and private sectors, to use technology to link schools across national boundaries and to increase international exchanges of students.

We are also seeking to strengthen norms for defense establishments that are supportive of democracy, transparency, respect for human rights and civilian control in defense matters. Through continued engagement with regional armed forces, facilitated by our own modest military activities and presence in the region, we are helping to transform civil-military relations. Through initiatives such as the Defense Ministerial of the Americas and the Center for Hemispheric Defense Studies, we are increasing civilian expertise in defense affairs and reinforcing the positive trend in civilian control.

Haiti and Cuba are of special concern to the United States. The restoration of democracy in Haiti remains a positive example for the hemisphere. In Haiti we continue to support respect for human rights and economic growth by a Haitian government capable of managing its own security and paving the way for a fair presidential election in 2000. Our efforts to train law enforcement officers in Haiti have transformed the police from a despised and feared instrument of repression to an accountable public safety agency. We are committed to working with our partners in the region and in the international community to meet the challenge of institutionalizing Haiti's economic and political development. Haiti will benefit from a Caribbean-wide acceleration of growth and investment,

stimulated in part by enhancement of CBI benefits. The United States remains committed to promoting a peaceful transition to democracy in Cuba and forestalling a mass exodus that would endanger the lives of migrants and the security of our borders. While maintaining pressure on the regime to make political and economic reforms, we continue to encourage the emergence of a civil society to assist the transition to democracy when the change comes. In March 1998, President Clinton announced a number of measures designed to build on the success of the Pope's January 1998 visit to Cuba, expand the role of the Catholic Church and other elements of civil society, and increase humanitarian assistance. As the Cuban people feel greater incentive to take charge of their own future, they are more likely to stay at home and build the informal and formal structures that will make transition easier. Meanwhile, we remain firmly committed to bilateral migration accords that ensure migration in safe, legal and orderly channels.

The Middle East, Southwest and South Asia

The May 1998 Indian and Pakistani nuclear tests clearly illustrate that a wide range of events in this region can have a significant impact on key U.S. security objectives. Choices made in the Middle East, Southwest and South Asia will determine whether terrorists operating in and from the region are denied the support they need to perpetrate their crimes, whether weapons of mass destruction will imperil the region and the world, whether the oil and gas fields of the Caucasus and Central Asia become reliable energy sources, whether the opium harvest in Afghanistan is eliminated, and whether a just and lasting peace can be established between Israel and the Arab countries.

Enhancing Security

The United States has enduring interests in pursuing a just, lasting and comprehensive Middle East peace, ensuring the security and well-being of Israel, helping our Arab friends provide for their security, and maintaining the free flow of oil at reasonable prices. Our strategy reflects those interests and the unique characteristics of the region as we work to extend the range of peace and stability.

51

The Middle East Peace Process

An historic transformation has taken place in the political landscape of the Middle East: peace agreements are taking hold, requiring concerted implementation efforts. The United States—as an architect and sponsor of the peace process—has a clear national interest in seeing the process deepen and widen to include all Israel's neighbors. We will continue our steady, determined leadership—standing with those who take risks for peace, standing against those who would destroy it, lending our good offices where we can make a difference and helping bring the concrete benefits of peace to people's daily lives. Future progress will require movement in the following areas:

- continued Israeli-Palestinian engagement on remaining issues in the Interim Agreement, and negotiation of permanent status issues;

- resuming Israeli-Syrian and Israeli-Lebanese negotiations with the objective of achieving peace treaties; and

- normalization of relations between Arab states and Israel.

Southwest Asia

In Southwest Asia, the United States remains focused on deterring threats to regional stability, countering threats posed by WMD and protecting the security of our regional partners, particularly from Iraq and Iran. We will continue to encourage members of the Gulf Cooperation Council (GCC) to work closely on collective defense and security arrangements, help individual GCC states meet their appropriate defense requirements and maintain our bilateral defense agreements.

We will maintain an appropriate military presence in Southwest Asia using a combination of ground, air and naval forces. As a result of the confrontation with Iraq in late 1997 and early 1998 over to Iraqi interference with UN inspection teams, we increased our continuous military presence in the Gulf to back our on-going efforts to bring Iraq into compliance with UN Security Council resolutions. Our forces in the Gulf are backed by our ability to rapidly reinforce the region in time of crisis, which we demonstrated convincingly in late 1997 and early 1998. We remain committed to enforcing the no-fly zones over northern and southern Iraq, which are essential for implementing the UN resolutions and preventing Saddam from taking large scale military action against Kuwait or the Kurd and Shia minorities in Iraq.

We would like to see Iraq's reintegration into the international community; however, we have made clear that Iraq must comply with all relevant UN Security Council resolutions. Saddam Hussein must cease the cynical manipulation of UN humanitarian programs and cooperate with Security Council Resolution 1153, which authorizes increased humanitarian assistance to the people of Iraq. Iraq must also move from its posture of deny, delay and obscure to a posture of cooperation and compliance with the UN Security Council resolutions designed to rid Iraq of WMD and their delivery systems. Iraq must also comply with the memorandum of understanding reached with UN Secretary General Kofi Annan in February 1998. Our policy is directed not against the people of Iraq but against the aggressive behavior of the government. Until that behavior changes, our goal is containing the threat Saddam Hussein poses to Iraq's neighbors, the free flow of Gulf oil and broader U.S. interests in the Middle East.

Our policy toward Iran is aimed at changing the behavior of the Iranian government in several key areas, including its efforts to obtain weapons of mass destruction and long-range missiles, its support for terrorism and groups that violently oppose the peace process, its attempts to undermine friendly governments in the region, and its development of offensive military capabilities that threaten our GCC partners and the flow of oil.

There are signs of change in Iranian policies. In December 1997, Iranian officials welcomed Chairman Arafat to the Islamic Summit in Tehran and said that, although they did not agree with the peace process, they would not seek to impose their views and would accept what the Palestinians could accept. In January 1998, President Khatemi publicly denounced terrorism and condemned the killing of innocent Israelis. Iran's record in the war against drugs has greatly improved and it has received high marks from the UN for its treatment of more than two million Iraqi and Afghan refugees. Iran is participating in diplomatic efforts to bring peace and stability to Afghanistan and is making a welcome effort to improve relations with its neighbors in the Gulf.

We view these developments with interest, both with regard to the possibility of Iran assuming its rightful place in the world community and the chance for better bilateral ties. We also welcome statements by President Khatemi that suggest a possibility of dialogue with the United States, and are taking concrete steps in that direction. This month, we implemented a new, more streamlined procedure for issuing visas to Iranians who travel to the United States frequently. We also revised our Consular Travel Warning for Iran so that it better reflects current attitudes in Iran towards American visitors. We have supported cultural and academic exchanges, and facilitated travel to the United States by many Iranians.

However, these positive signs must be balanced against the reality that Iran's support for terrorism has not yet ceased, serious violations of human rights persist, its efforts to develop long range missiles, including the 1,300 kilometer-range Shahab-3 it flight tested in July 1998, and its efforts to acquire WMD continue. The United States will continue to oppose any country selling or transferring to Iran materials and technologies that could be used to develop long-range missiles or weapons of mass destruction. Similarly, we oppose Iranian efforts to sponsor terror.

We are ready to explore further ways to build mutual confidence and avoid misunderstandings with Iran. We will strengthen our cooperation with allies to encourage positive changes in Iranian behavior. If a dialogue can be initiated and sustained in a way that addresses the concerns of both sides, then the United States would be willing to develop with the Islamic Republic a road map leading to normal relations.

South Asia

South Asia has experienced an important expansion of democracy and economic reform. Our strategy is designed to help the peoples of that region enjoy the fruits of democracy and greater stability by helping resolve long-standing conflict and implementing confidence-building measures. Regional stability and improved bilateral ties are also important for U.S. economic interests in a region that contains a fifth of the world's population and one of its most important emerging markets. We seek to establish relationships with India and Pakistan that are defined in terms of their own individual merits and reflect the full weight

and range of U.S. strategic, political and economic interests in each country. In addition, we seek to work closely with regional countries to stem the flow of illegal drugs from South Asia, most notably from Afghanistan.

The United States has long urged India and Pakistan to take steps to reduce the risk of conflict and to bring their nuclear and missile programs into conformity with international standards. The Indian and Pakistani nuclear test explosions were unjustified and threaten to spark a dangerous nuclear arms race in Asia. As a result of those tests and in accordance with our laws the United States imposed sanctions against India and Pakistan. The sanctions include termination of assistance except for humanitarian assistance for food or other agricultural commodities; termination of sales of defense articles or services; termination of foreign military financing; denial of non-agricultural credit, credit guarantees or other financial assistance by any agency of the U.S. Government; prohibiting U.S. banks from making any loan or providing any credit to the governments of India and Pakistan except for the purpose of purchasing food or other agricultural commodities; and prohibiting export of specific goods and technology subject to export licensing by the Commerce Department.

India and Pakistan are contributing to a self-defeating cycle of escalation that does not add to the security of either country. They have put themselves at odds with the international community over these nuclear tests. In concert with the other permanent members of the UN Security Council and the G-8 nations, the United States has called on both nations to renounce further nuclear tests, to sign the Comprehensive Test Ban Treaty immediately and without conditions, and to resume their direct dialogue and take decisive steps to reduce tensions in South Asia. We also strongly urge these states to refrain from any actions, such as testing, deployment or weaponization of ballistic missiles, that would further undermine regional and global stability. And we urge them to join the clear international consensus in support of nonproliferation and to join in negotiations in Geneva for a cut off of fissile material production.

Promoting Prosperity

The United States has two principle economic objectives in the region: to promote regional economic cooperation and development, and to ensure unrestricted flow of oil from the region. We seek to promote regional trade and cooperation on infrastructure through the multilateral track of the peace process, including revitalization of the Middle East and North Africa (MENA) economic summits.

The United States depends on oil for about 40 percent of its primary energy needs and roughly half of our oil needs are met with imports. Although we import less than 10% of Persian Gulf exports, our allies in Europe and Japan account for about 85% of these exports. Previous oil shocks and the Gulf War underscore the strategic importance of the region and show the impact that an interruption of oil supplies can have on the world's economy. Appropriate responses to events such as Iraq's invasion of Kuwait can limit the magnitude of the crisis. Over the longer term, U.S. dependence on access to these and other foreign oil sources will remain important as our reserves are depleted. The United States must remain vigilant to ensure unrestricted access to this critical resource. Thus, we will continue to demonstrate U.S. commitment and resolve in the Persian Gulf.

Promoting Democracy

We encourage the spread of democratic values throughout the Middle East and Southwest and South Asia and will pursue this objective by a constructive dialogue with countries in the region. In Iran, for example, we hope the nation's leaders will carry out the people's mandate for a government that respects and protects the rule of law, both in its internal and external affairs. We will promote responsible indigenous moves toward increasing political participation and enhancing the quality of governance and will continue to vigorously challenge many governments in the region to improve their human rights records. Respect for human rights also requires rejection of terrorism. If the nations in the region are to safeguard their own citizens from the threat of terror, they cannot tolerate acts of indiscriminate violence against civilians, nor can they offer refuge to those who commit such acts.

U.S. policies in the Middle East and Southwest Asia are not anti-Islamic—an allegation made by some opponents of our efforts to help bring lasting peace and stability to the region. Islam is the fastest-growing religious faith in the United States. We respect deeply its moral teachings and its role as a source of inspiration and instruction for hundreds of millions of people around the world. U.S. policy in

the region is directed at the actions of governments and terrorist groups, not peoples or faiths. The standards we would like all the nations in the region to observe are not merely Western, but universal.

Africa

In recent years, the United States has supported significant change in Africa with considerable success: multi-party democracies are more common and elections are more frequent and open, human rights are more widely respected, the press is more free, U.S.-Africa trade is expanding, and a pragmatic consensus on the need for economic reform is emerging. A new, post-colonial generation of leadership is reaching maturity in Africa, with more democratic and pragmatic approaches to solving their countries' problems and developing their human and natural resources.

To further those successes, President Clinton made an unprecedented 12-day trip to Africa in March-April 1998. With President Museveni of Uganda, he co-hosted the Entebbe Summit for Peace and Prosperity to advance cooperation on conflict prevention, human rights and economic integration. The summit was attended by Prime Minister Meles of Ethiopia, Presidents Moi of Kenya, Mkapa of Tanzania, Bizimungu of Rwanda and Kabila of Congo. During the trip, the President unveiled a number of new programs to support democracy, prosperity and opportunity, including initiatives on education, rule of law, food security, trade and investment, aviation, and conflict resolution. President Clinton directly addressed the violent conflicts that have threatened African democracy and prosperity.

Sustaining our success in Africa will require that we identify those issues that most directly affect our interests and where we can make a difference through efficient targeting of our resources. A key challenge is to engage the remaining autocratic regimes to encourage those countries to follow the example of other African countries that are successfully implementing political and economic reforms.

Enhancing Security

Serious transnational security threats emanate from pockets of Africa, including state-sponsored terrorism, narcotics trafficking, international crime, environmental damage and disease. These threats can only be addressed through effective, sustained engagement in Africa. We have already made significant progress in countering some of these threats—investing in efforts to combat environmental damage and disease, leading international efforts to halt the proliferation of land mines and the demining of Angola, Mozambique, Namibia, Rwanda, Ethiopia and Eritrea. We continue efforts to reduce the flow of narcotics through Africa and to curtail international criminal activity based in Africa. We seek to keep Africa free of weapons of mass destruction by supporting South Africa's nuclear disarmament and accession to the NPT as a non-nuclear weapon state, securing the indefinite and unconditional extension of the NPT, and promoting establishment of the African Nuclear Weapons Free Zone.

Libya and Sudan continue to pose a threat to regional stability and the national security and foreign policy interests of the United States. Our policy toward Libya is designed to block its efforts to obtain weapons of mass destruction and development of conventional military capabilities that threaten its neighbors, and to compel Libya to cease its support for terrorism and its attempts to undermine other governments in the region. The government of Libya has continued these activities despite calls by the Security Council that it demonstrate by concrete actions its renunciation of terrorism. Libya also continues to defy the United Nations by refusing to turn over the two defendants in the terrorist bombing of Pan Am 103. We remain determined that the perpetrators of this act and the attack on UTA 772 be brought to justice. We have moved to counter Sudan's support for international terrorism and regional destabilization by imposing comprehensive sanctions on the Khartoum regime, continuing to press for the regime's isolation through the UN Security Council, and enhancing the ability of Sudan's neighbors to resist Khartoum-backed insurgencies in their countries through our Frontline States initiative.

Persistent conflict and continuing political instability in some African countries remain chronic obstacles to Africa's development and to U.S. interests there, including unhampered access to oil and other vital natural resources. Our efforts to resolve conflict include working to fully implement the Lusaka Accords in Angola, sustaining the fragile new government in Liberia, supporting the recently restored democratic government in Sierra Leone and the Economic Community of West African States Monitoring Group (ECOMOG) efforts to ensure security there, and achieving a peaceful, credible transition to democratic government in Nigeria, the Democratic Republic of the Congo and Congo-Brazzaville.

To foster regional efforts to promote prosperity, stability and peace in Africa, the United States in 1996 launched the African Crisis Response Initiative (ACRI) to work with Africans to enhance their capacity to conduct effective peacekeeping and humanitarian operations. We are coordinating with the French, British, other donor countries and African governments in developing a sustainable plan of action. The United States has already trained battalions from Uganda, Senegal, Malawi, Mali and Ghana, and is planning to train troops in Benin and Cote D'Ivoire later this year. We are consulting closely on ACRI activity with the UN Department of Peacekeeping Operations, the Organization of African Unity (OAU) and its Crisis Management Center, and African sub-regional organizations already pursuing similar capacity enhancements. We hope and expect that other African countries will also participate in the effort in the future, building a well-trained, interoperable, local capacity for peacekeeping and humanitarian operations in a region that has been fraught with turbulence and crisis and all too dependent upon outside assistance to deal with these problems.

On April 1, 1998, President Clinton announced that the United States will be establishing the African Center for Security Studies (ACSS). The ACSS will be a regional center modeled after the George C. Marshall Center in Germany, designed in consultation with African nations and intended to promote the exchange of ideas and information tailored specifically for African concerns. The goal is for ACSS to be a source of academic yet practical instruction in promoting the skills necessary to make effective national security decisions in democratic governments, and engage African military and civilian defense leaders in a substantive dialogue about defense policy planning in democracies.

Promoting Prosperity

A stable, democratic, prosperous Africa will be a better economic partner, a better partner for security and peace, and a better partner in the fights against drug trafficking, crime, terrorism, disease and environmental degradation. An economically dynamic Africa will be possible only when Africa is fully integrated into the global economy. Our aim, therefore, is to assist African nations to implement economic reforms, create favorable climates for trade and investment, and achieve sustainable development. A majority of sub-Saharan Africa's 48 countries have adopted market-oriented economic and political reforms in the past seven years.

To support this positive trend, the President has proposed the Partnership for Economic Growth and Opportunity in Africa to support the economic transformation underway in Africa. The Administration is working closely with Congress to implement key elements of this initiative through rapid passage of the African Growth and Opportunity Act. By significantly broadening market access, spurring growth in Africa and helping the poorest nations eliminate or reduce their bilateral debt, this bill will better enable us to help African nations undertake difficult economic reforms and build better lives for their people through sustainable growth and development.

Further integrating Africa into the global economy has obvious political and economic benefits. It will also directly serve U.S. interests by continuing to expand an already important new market for U.S. exports. The more than 700 million people of sub-Saharan Africa represent one of the world's largest largely untapped markets. Although the United States enjoys only a seven percent market share in Africa, already 100,000 American jobs depend on our exports there. Increasing both the U.S. market share and the size of the African market will bring tangible benefits to U.S. workers and increase prosperity and economic opportunity in Africa. To encourage U.S. trade with and investment in Africa, we are pursuing several new initiatives and enhancements to the Partnership for Economic Growth and Opportunity, including greater market access, targeted technical assistance, enhanced bilateral and World Bank debt relief, and increased bilateral trade ties.

To further our trade objectives in Africa, the President inaugurated the Ron Brown Commercial Center in Johannesburg, South Africa on March 28, 1998. The Center, which is operated and funded by the Department of Commerce, provides support for American companies looking to enter or expand into the sub-Saharan African market. It promotes U.S. exports through a range of support programs and facilitates business contacts and partnerships between African and American businesses. The Center also serves as a base for other agencies such as the Export-Import Bank, the Trade Development Agency and USTR to expand their assistance to business.

Because safe air travel and secure airports are necessary for increasing trade, attracting investment, and expanding tourism, the President on April 1, 1998 announced the "Safe Skies for Africa" initiative. The goals of this $1.2 million program—funded by the Departments of State and Transportation—are to work in partnership with Africa to increase the number of sub-Saharan African countries that meet ICAO standards for aviation safety, improve security at 8-12 airports in the region within 3 years, and improve regional air navigation services in Africa by using modern satellite-based navigation aids and communications technology. The initiative focuses on safety assessments and security surveys in selected countries and formulating action plans together with Africa civil aviation authorities to bring aviation safety and security practices in Africa up to accepted world standards.

To support the desire of African nations to invest in a better and healthier future for their children, the President on March 24, 1998 announced three new initiatives to improve educational standards, ensure adequate food and agricultural production, and fight the deadly infectious diseases that claim the lives of too many African children.

- The Education for Development and Democracy Initiative seeks to boost African integration into the global community by improving the quality of, and technology for, education in Africa. The initiative is centered on community resource centers, public-private partnerships, and educating and empowering girls. We plan on spending approximately $120 million over two years in support of this initiative.

- The Africa Food Security Initiative will assist African nations in strengthening agriculture and food security in a number of key areas, including production of healthy and alternative crops, better market efficiency and distribution of existing crops, increased trade and investment in agricultural industries, attacking crop diseases, and increasing access to agricultural technology systems to assist with increased crop production and distribution. Our pilot budget for the first two years of the initiative will be $61 million, which complements USAID's current investments in these efforts.

- The third initiative is combating the infectious diseases that claim many young lives. To help combat malaria, we will provide an additional $1 million grant to provide further assistance to the Multilateral Initiative on Malaria. The grant will focus on continuing educational seminars and will support the Regional Malaria Lab in Mali to reinforce its position as a regional center of excellence in Africa. This effort will complement our ongoing Infectious Disease Initiative for Africa that focuses on surveillance, response, prevention and building local resistance to infectious diseases.

Promoting Democracy

In Africa as elsewhere, democracies have proved more peaceful, stable and reliable partners with which we can work and are more likely to pursue sound economic policies. We will continue to work to sustain the important progress Africans have achieved to date and to broaden the growing circle of African democracies.

Restoration of democracy and respect for human rights in Nigeria has long been one of our major objectives in Africa. In June 1998, President Clinton reaffirmed to Nigeria's new leadership the friendship of the United States for the people of Nigeria and underscored our desire for improved bilateral relations in the context of Nigeria taking swift and significant steps toward a successful transition to a democratically elected civilian government that respects the human rights of its citizens. The release

of some political prisoners by the Nigerian government is an encouraging sign, but much more needs to be done and the United States will continue to press for a credible transition to a democratic, civilian government.

Through President Clinton's $30 million Great Lakes Justice Initiative, the United States will work with both the people and governments of the Democratic Republic of Congo, Rwanda and Burundi to support judicial systems which are impartial, credible, effective and inclusive. This initiative seeks to strengthen judicial bodies, such as relevant Ministries of Justice and Interior; improve the functioning of court systems, prosecutors, police and prison systems; work with national officials on specific problem areas such as creation of civilian police forces and legal assistance programs; support training programs for police and judiciary officials; develop improved court administration systems; provide human rights training for military personnel and support prosecution of abuses perpetrated by military personnel; demobilize irregular elements of standing armies and reintegrate them into society and programs; and demobilize child soldiers.

In addition, we will work with our allies to find an effective formula for promoting stability, democracy and respect for human rights in the Democratic Republic of Congo so that it and a democratic Nigeria can become the regional centers for economic growth, and democratic empowerment that they can and should be. In order to help post-apartheid South Africa achieve its economic, political, democratic and security goals for all its citizens, we will continue to provide substantial bilateral assistance, vigorously promote U.S. trade and investment, and pursue close cooperation and support for our mutual interests and goals through the versatile Binational Commission chaired by the Vice Presidents of each country.

Ultimately, the prosperity and security of Africa depends on extensive political and economic reform, and it is in the U.S. interest to support and promote such reforms.

IV. Conclusions

Today, on the brink of the twenty-first century, we are building new frameworks, partnerships and institutions—and adapting existing ones—to strengthen America's security and prosperity. We are working to construct new cooperative security arrangements, rid the world of weapons that target whole populations, build a truly global economy, and promote democratic values and economic reform. Because diplomatic and military responses alone may not deter threats to our national security from non-state actors such as criminals and terrorist groups, we must promote increased cooperation among law enforcement officials and improved methods for dealing with international crime and terrorism. Ours is a moment of historic opportunity to create a safer, more prosperous tomorrow—to make a difference in the lives of our citizens.

This promising state of affairs did not just happen, and there is no guarantee that it will endure. The contemporary era was forged by steadfast American leadership over the last half century—through efforts such as the Marshall Plan, NATO, the United Nations and the World Bank. The clear dangers of the past made the need for national security commitments and expenditures obvious to the American people. Today, the task of mobilizing public support for national security priorities is more complicated. The complex array of unique dangers, opportunities and responsibilities outlined in this strategy are not always readily apparent as we go about our daily lives focused on immediate concerns. Yet, in a more integrated and interdependent world, we must remain actively engaged in world affairs to successfully advance our national interests. To be secure and prosperous, America must continue to lead.

Our international leadership focuses on President Clinton's strategic priorities: to foster regional efforts led by the community of democratic nations to promote peace and prosperity in key regions of the world, to create more jobs and opportunities for Americans through a more open and competitive trading system that also benefits others around the world, to increase cooperation in confronting new security threats that defy borders and unilateral solutions, and to strengthen the intelligence, military, diplomatic and law enforcement tools necessary to meet these challenges. Our international leadership is ultimately founded upon the power of our democratic ideals and values. The spread of democracy supports American values and enhances our security and prosperity. The United States will continue to support the trend toward democracy and free markets by remaining actively engaged in the world.

Our engagement abroad requires the active, sustained support of the American people and the bipartisan support of the U.S. Congress. This Administration remains committed to explaining our security interests, objectives and priorities to the nation and seeking the broadest possible public and congressional support for our security programs and investments. We will continue to exercise our leadership in the world in a manner that reflects our national values and protects the security of this great nation.

Suggestions for Further Reading

$\mathbf{T}$he literature on U.S. foreign policy and grand strategy is large and growing. Virtually every issue of the leading journals on international issues contains at least one article on the overall course of American foreign policy or the problems confronting the United States in a particular region. Numerous books and articles continue to debate the likely pattern of international politics in the post–Cold War world. In selecting publications for the following list, we have attempted to include many of the most prominent and important books and articles that address the questions raised in this volume. We have limited our suggestions to works that focus on the broad outlines of American strategy. Many additional references can be found in the citations in each chapter included in this book.

Classics on American Grand Strategy and Foreign Policy

Gaddis, John Lewis. *Strategies of Containment: A Critical Appraisal of Postwar American National Security Policy.* New York: Oxford University Press, 1982.
Gilbert, Felix. *To the Farewell Address: Ideas of Early American Foreign Policy.* Princeton, N.J.: Princeton University Press, 1961.
Kennan, George F. *American Diplomacy, 1900–1950.* Chicago: University of Chicago Press, 1951.
Lippmann, Walter. *U.S. Foreign Policy: Shield of the Republic.* Boston: Little, Brown, 1943.
Morgenthau, Hans J. *In Defense of the National Interest: A Critical Examination of American Foreign Policy.* New York: Knopf, 1951.
Spykman, Nicholas J. *America's Strategy in World Politics: The United States and the Balance of Power.* New York: Harcourt, Brace, 1942.

The Changing Security Environment: Contending Visions of the Post–Cold War World

Biddle, Stephen. "Assessing Theories of Future Warfare." *Security Studies,* Vol. 8, No. 1 (Autumn 1998), pp. 1–74.
Brzezinski, Zbigniew. *Out of Control: Global Turmoil on the Eve of the Twenty-First Century.* New York: Scribner, 1993.
Byman, Daniel, and Stephen Van Evera. "Why They Fight: Hypotheses on the Causes of Contemporary Deadly Conflict." *Security Studies,* Vol. 7, No. 3 (Spring 1998), pp. 1–50.
Fukuyama, Francis. "The End of History?" *The National Interest,* No. 16 (Summer 1989), pp. 3–18.
Huntington, Samuel P. *The Clash of Civilizations and the Remaking of World Order.* New York: Simon and Schuster, 1996.

Ikenberry, G. John. "The Myth of Post–Cold War Chaos." *Foreign Affairs*, Vol. 75, No. 3 (May/June 1996), pp. 79–91.
Jervis, Robert. "The Future of World Politics: Will it Resemble the Past?" *International Security*, Vol. 16, No. 3 (Winter 1991/92), pp. 39–73.
Kaplan, Robert. "The Coming Anarchy." *The Atlantic Monthly*, February 1994, pp. 44–76.
Kennedy, Paul M. *Preparing for the Twenty-First Century*. New York: Random House, 1993.
Lynn-Jones, Sean M., and Steven E. Miller, eds. *The Cold War and After: Prospects for Peace*, expanded edition. Cambridge, Mass.: The MIT Press, 1993.
Mandelbaum, Michael. "Is Major War Obsolete?" *Survival*, Vol. 40, No. 4 (Winter 1998–99), pp. 20–38.
Mueller, John. *Retreat from Doomsday: The Obsolescence of Major War*. New York: Basic Books, 1989.
Singer, Max, and Aaron Wildavsky. *The Real World Order: Zones of Peace, Zones of Turmoil*. Chatham, N.J.: Chatham House, 1993.
Waltz, Kenneth N. "The Emerging Structure of International Politics." *International Security*, Vol. 18, No. 2 (Fall 1993), pp. 44–79.

Analyses of Contemporary U.S. Strategy

Allison, Graham T., and Gregory Treverton, eds. *Rethinking American Security: Beyond Cold War to New World Order*. New York: Norton, 1992.
Bergsten, C. Fred. "The Primacy of Economics." *Foreign Policy*, No. 87 (Summer 1992), pp. 3–24.
Brinkley, Douglas. "Democratic Enlargement: The Clinton Doctrine." *Foreign Policy*, No. 106 (Spring 1997), pp. 111–127.
Carter, Ashton B., and William J. Perry. *Preventive Defense: A New Security Strategy for America*. Washington, D.C.: Brookings, 1999.
David, Steven R. "Why the Third World Still Matters." *International Security*, Vol. 17, No. 3 (Winter 1992/93), pp. 127–159.
Deibel, Terry L. "Strategies Before Containment: Patterns for the Future." *International Security*, Vol. 16, No. 4 (Spring 1992), pp. 79–108.
Haass, Richard N. "What to Do With American Primacy." *Foreign Affairs*, Vol. 78, No. 5 (September/October 1999), pp. 37–49.
Huntington, Samuel P. "America's Changing Strategic Interests." *Survival*, Vol. 33, No.1 (January/February 1991), pp. 3–17.
Huntington, Samuel P. "The Lonely Superpower." *Foreign Affairs*, Vol. 78, No. 2 (March/April 1999), pp. 35–49.
Joffe, Josef. "'Bismarck' or 'Britain'? Toward an American Grand Strategy after Bipolarity." *International Security*, Vol. 19, No. 4 (Spring 1995), pp. 94–117.
Kupchan, Charles A. "After Pax Americana: Benign Power, Regional Integration, and the Sources of a Stable Multipolarity." *International Security*, Vol. 23, No. 2 (Fall 1998), pp. 40–79.

Kurth, James. "America's Grand Strategy: A Pattern of History." *The National Interest,* No. 43 (Spring 1996), pp. 3–19.

Lieber, Robert J., ed. *Eagle Adrift: American Foreign Policy at the End of the Century.* New York: Longman, 1997.

Mandelbaum, Michael. "Foreign Policy as Social Work." *Foreign Affairs,* Vol. 75, No. 1 (January/February 1996), pp. 16–32.

The Case for Strategic Restraint

Buchanan, Patrick J. "America First–and Second, and Third." *The National Interest,* No. 19 (Spring 1990), pp. 77–82.

Buchanan, Patrick J. *A Republic, Not an Empire: Reclaiming America's Destiny.* Washington, D.C.: Regnery, 1999.

Layne, Christopher. *The Peace of Illusions: International Relations Theory and American Grand Strategy in the Post–Cold War World,* Ithaca, N.Y.: Cornell University Press, forthcoming.

Nordlinger, Eric A. *Isolationism Reconfigured: American Foreign Policy for a New Century.* Princeton, N.J.: Princeton University Press, 1995.

Ravenal, Earl. "The Case For Adjustment." *Foreign Policy,* No. 81 (Winter 1990–91), pp. 3–19.

Tonelson, Alan. "Superpower Without A Sword." *Foreign Affairs,* Vol. 72, No. 3 (Summer 1993), pp. 166–180.

Tucker, Robert W. *A New Isolationism: Threat or Promise?* New York: Universe Books, 1972.

The Case for Selective Engagement

Art, Robert J. "A U.S. Military Strategy for the 1990s: Reassurance without Dominance." *Survival,* Vol. 34, No. 4 (Winter 1992–93), pp. 3–23.

Art, Robert J. *Selective Engagement: An American Garnd Strategy.* The Century Foundation, forthcoming.

Steel, Ronald. *Temptations of a Superpower.* Cambridge, Mass.: Harvard University Press, 1995.

Van Evera, Stephen. "Why Europe Matters, Why the Third World Doesn't." *Journal of Strategic Studies,* Vol. 13, No. 2 (June 1990), pp. 1–51.

The Case for Cooperative Security and New Approaches to Collective Security

Carter, Ashton B., William J. Perry, and John D. Steinbruner. *A New Concept of Cooperative Security.* Washington, D.C.: Brookings, 1992.

Evans, Gareth. "Cooperative Security and Intrastate Conflict." *Foreign Policy,* No. 96 (Fall 1994), pp. 3–20.

Luck, Edward. "Making Peace." *Foreign Policy,* No. 89 (Winter 1992–93), pp. 137–155.

Nolan, Janne E., ed. *Global Engagement: Cooperation and Security in the 21st Century.* Washington, D.C.: Brookings, 1994.

Ruggie, John Gerard. *Winning the Peace: America and World Order in the New Era.* New York: Columbia University Press, 1996.

Ullman, Richard. *Securing Europe.* Princeton, N.J.: Princeton University Press, 1991.

The Case for Primacy

Kagan, Robert. "The Case for Global Activism." *Commentary,* Vol. 98, No. 3 (September 1994), pp. 40–44.

Khalilzad, Zalmay. *From Containment to Global Leadership? America and the World After the Cold War.* Santa Monica, Calif.: The RAND Corporation, 1995.

Khalilzad, Zalmay. "U.S. Grand Strategies: Implications for the World." In Khalilzad, ed., *Strategic Appraisal, 1996.* Santa Monica, Calif.: The RAND Corporation, 1996.

Khalilzad, Zalmay. "Losing the Moment? The United States and the World After the Cold War." *The Washington Quarterly,* Vol. 18, No. 2 (Spring 1995), pp. 87–107.

Krauthammer, Charles. "The Unipolar Moment." *Foreign Affairs,* Vol. 70, No. 1 (America and the World 1990–91), pp. 23–33.

Kristol, William, and Robert Kagan. "Toward a Neo–Reaganite Foreign Policy." *Foreign Affairs,* Vol. 75, No. 4 (July/August 1996), pp. 18–32.

Muravchik, Joshua. *The Imperative of American Leadership: A Challenge to Neo–Isolationism.* Washington, D.C.: AEI Press, 1996.

International Security

The Robert and Renée Belfer Center for
Science and International Affairs
John F. Kennedy School of Government
Harvard University

Articles in this reader were previously published in
International Security, a quarterly journal sponsored and
edited by The Robert and Renée Belfer Center for Science and
International Affairs at the John F. Kennedy School of
Government at Harvard University, and published by MIT
Press Journals. To receive subscription information about the
journal or find out more about other readers in our series,
please contact MIT Press Journals at Five Cambridge Center,
Fourth Floor, Cambridge, MA, 02142-1493.